Doors of Oaxaca

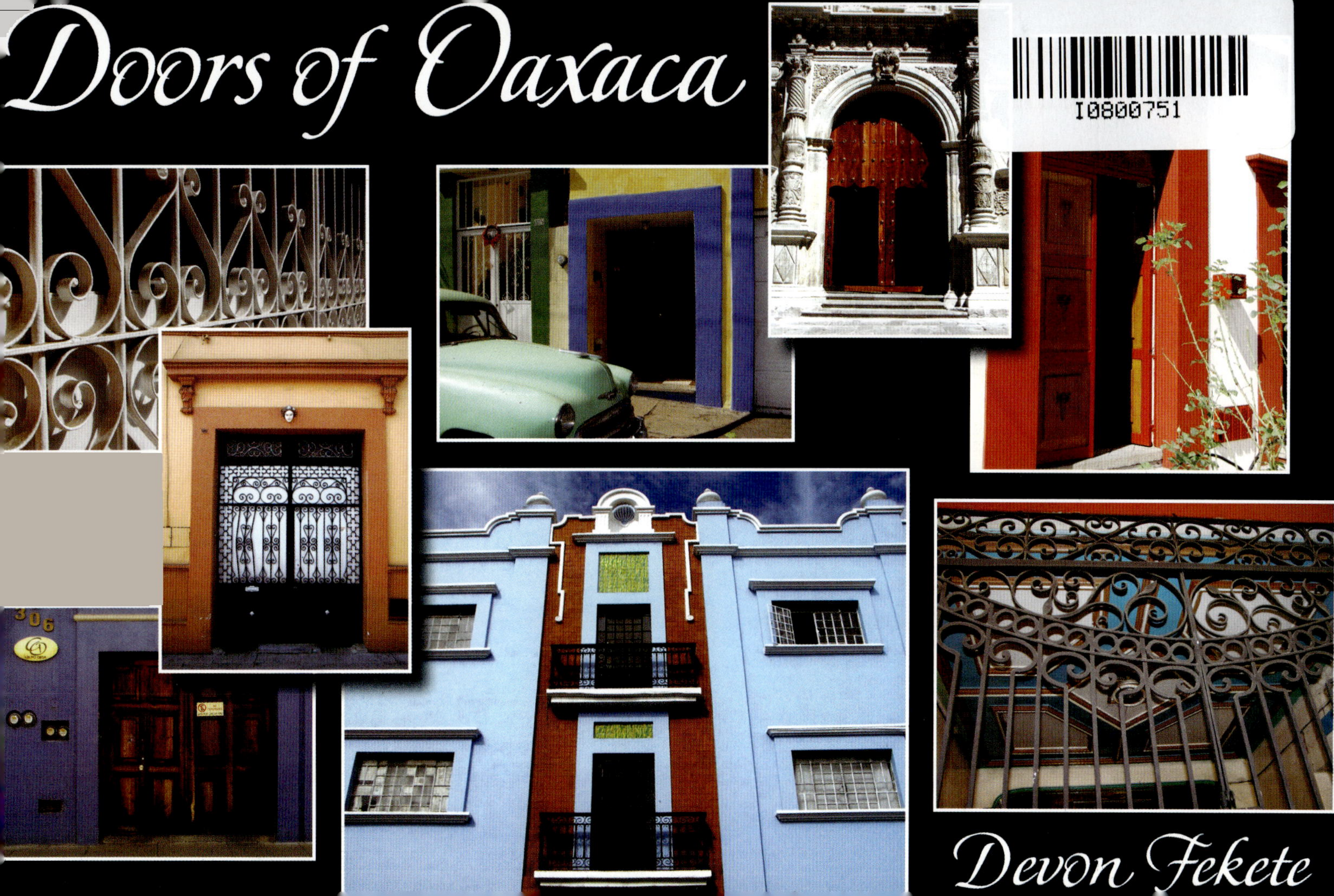

Devon Fekete

Library of Congress Control Number: 2006937489

Designed by John P. Cheek
Cover design by Bruce Waters
Type set in Benguiat Bk BT/Souvenir Lt BT

ISBN: 978-0-7643-2665-3
Printed in China

Published by Schiffer Publishing Ltd.
4880 Lower Valley Road
Atglen, PA 19310
Phone: (610) 593-1777; Fax: (610) 593-2002
E-mail: Info@schifferbooks.com

For the largest selection of fine reference books on this and related subjects, please visit our web site at:
www.schifferbooks.com
We are always looking for people to write books on new and related subjects. If you have an idea for a book please contact us at the above address.

This book may be purchased from the publisher.
Include $3.95 for shipping.
Please try your bookstore first.
You may write for a free catalog.

In Europe, Schiffer books are distributed by
Bushwood Books
6 Marksbury Ave.
Kew Gardens
Surrey TW9 4JF England
Phone: 44 (0) 20 8392-8585; Fax: 44 (0) 20 8392-9876
E-mail: info@bushwoodbooks.co.uk
Website: www.bushwoodbooks.co.uk
Free postage in the U.K., Europe; air mail at cost.

Dedication

I dedicate this book to my wife, Ana, and my daughter, Sofia. I am a very lucky monkey.

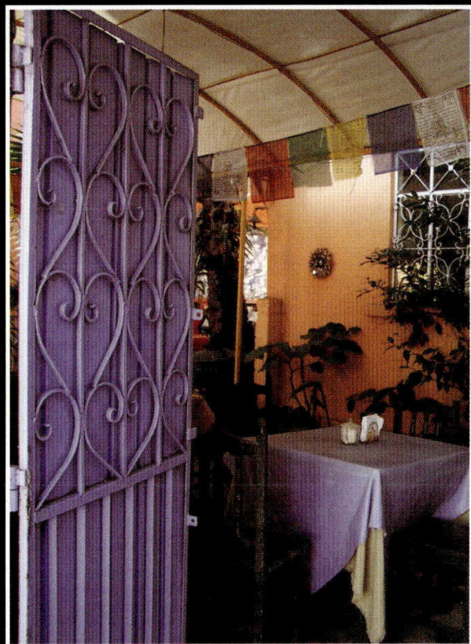

Acknowledgments

The people of Oaxaca have been so good to me. I want to thank them all for welcoming me as one of their own, and helping me to discover and embrace this world of Oaxaca. Special thanks to my wife, Ana, and mother-in-law, Rosario, for helping and supporting me. I also want to thank the people at Schiffer Publishing for working with me and sharing my vision.

A Note from the Author

I first experienced Oaxaca in the spring of 1995, at the age of twenty. I was young, restless, and looking for change. I dropped out of school, quit my job at the coffee house, bought a used truck, and drove across the U.S. and Mexico. I started off from Detroit and eventually arrived in Oaxaca City, a colonial town nestled in a temperate valley in Southeast Mexico. The place immediately took hold of me, and I decided to park the truck and try to settle in. I got a job teaching English, which provided enough money to rent out the corner of someone's kitchen, which I considered a step up from living in my truck. This afforded me some time to explore the beauty and richness of Oaxaca.

I fell in love with Oaxaca; its architecture, the people, the culture, cuisine, art, its plant life, and climate. My stay in Oaxaca was a life-altering journey from which I have never fully returned. I met a wonderful native and we soon married. Eleven years later, we live with our daughter in Michigan, and return to Oaxaca each year for an extended stay. We visit

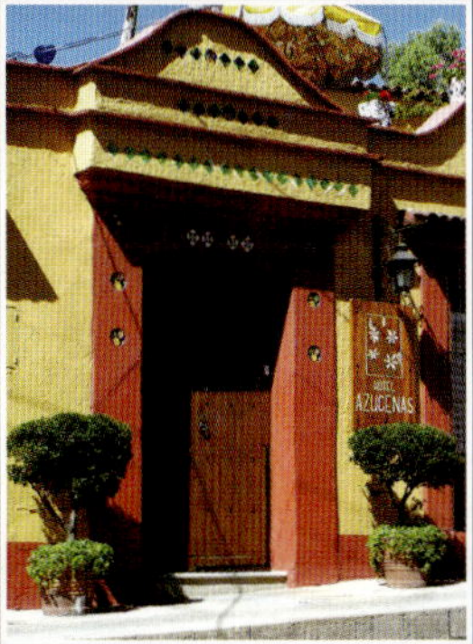 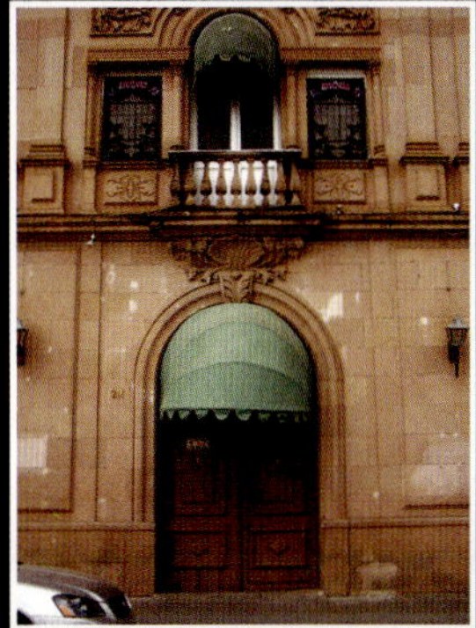 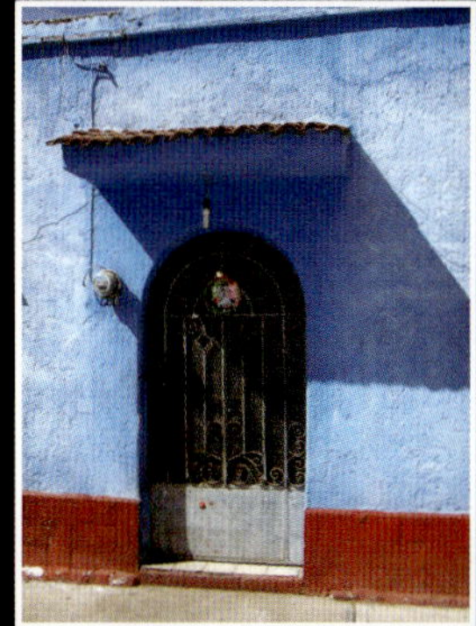 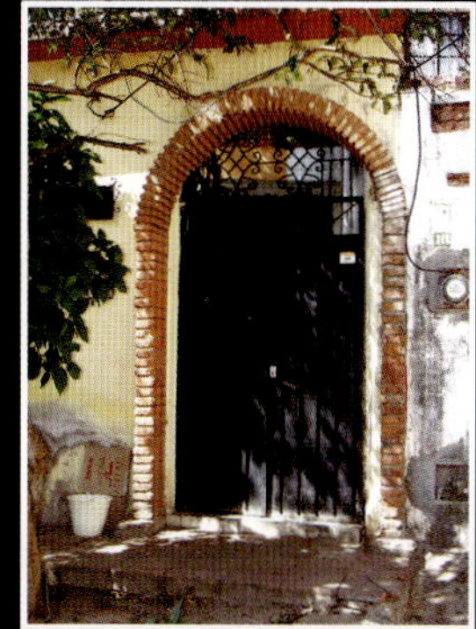 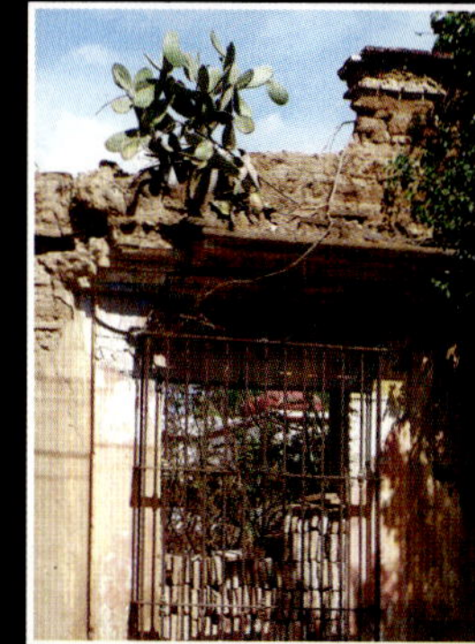

with family and I walk the city to people watch, and absorb the city's mood and architecture.

I became fascinated early on with Oaxaca's doors, and began relying on them over the years as landmarks to navigate the city. I developed an enduring appreciation and sense of familiarity with many of them. We were in Oaxaca visiting family during the 2006 New Year when I decided to take on the task of documenting all my favorite doors of Oaxaca with the family camera. It became a two week obsession, after realizing there were far too many doors to capture leisurely in my free time. I made photo-documenting these doors my mission; I totally focused on creating a robust archive of these striking, Oaxacan artifacts.

I returned to the States with sunburn, badly blistered feet, and a large photo album of my beloved Oaxacan doors. My wife suggested I send the album to Schiffer Publishing curious as to whether others would share my interest. To my surprise, Schiffer saw past my lack of technical skill and amateur equipment, and offered to publish a book on my album of doors. It is an honor to share this special piece of Oaxacan history, architecture, and culture with those who have such appreciations. I would like to consider this book a humble tribute to the city and its people, from whom I have gained a great appreciation for life, the world, and humanity.

For me, the magic of Oaxaca manifests on these pages. I can smell, hear, and feel the spirit of the city as I gaze at these doors. I hope you enjoy my humble "vacation-quality" photos, and that the spirit of Oaxaca speaks to you from these pages. Thank you for taking time to discover *the Doors of Oaxaca*.

Oaxaca

Oaxaca is a place of truth, beauty, and contradiction. Its people are warm and generous, adaptable to change, yet deeply-seated in tradition. The surrounding Sierra Madre mountains provide a natural, inhospitable barrier to the outside world, which has helped preserve Oaxaca's ancient customs, cultures, and dialects. To me, the valley of Oaxaca is like a big bowl of humanity. Here, the earth is somehow personified; traits of mankind are portrayed in a condensed and timeless fashion.

Oaxaca seems to hold a mirror up to the world and the human spirit. It is a place of vibrant life and continuous decay; extreme wealth and poverty; constant motion yet little change; ingenuity and creativity; mysticism and mythology; pride and humility; love and hope; tragedy and despair. It has a rhythm of chaotic harmony, and is the most alien place –and the most familiar place I have ever been. Its people are complex and busy, yet live simply with a strong sense of purpose, family, and community. Love is the primary ingredient on every dinner table. Authenticity is the focus of its architecture and design.

- Oaxaca is known as Mexico's most colonial city, and the cultural and artistic Mecca of Mexico.

- The State of Oaxaca has more than three million residents. It is about the size of Indiana, and is situated at just over 5000 feet in altitude.

- The home and birth place of Benito Juárez, credited with winning the War of Reform (1858-61), and becoming the most beloved president in Mexican history (1861-63, 1867-72). Juarez is the only full blooded Native American to serve as president of Mexico.

- Oaxaca has between 14-18 indigenous tribes, and up to 90 distinct dialects (reports vary).

- The four major archeological sites in Oaxaca are: Monte Alban, Mitla, Dainzú, and Yagul. Each is distinct in architecture and design.

- The city of Oaxaca is the state capitol, and is home to between 300,000 - 500,000 people (reports vary).

- There are dozens of foods and dishes unique to Oaxaca. Oaxaca is best known for its *quesillo*, a fresh cheese rolled up like a ball of yarn. *Chapulines* (toasted grasshoppers) and yellow mole, a thick, smoky, spicy sauce used over a variety of meat dishes.

- *Nicoatole*, a pudding made with corn, milk, and sugar is a favorite local dessert.

- Oaxaca is the home of many famous artists, including Rufino Tamayo (1899-1991), Rodolfo Morales (1925-2001), and Francisco Toledo. Oaxaca has dozens of art museums and galleries within walking distance of one another.

- The streets and homes of Oaxaca are filled with music. Famous musicians from Oaxaca include Alvaro Carrillo (1921-1969), Susana Harp, and Lila Downs.

• Oaxaca is known for its handmade wood carvings and furniture, tapestries, clothing and textiles, leather-works, and its unique black and green pottery.

• The botanical epicenter of Mexico, Oaxaca is known widely for its varieties of corn and agave. Agave is the plant used to make Oaxacan mescal and tequila.

• Oaxaca's Spanish colonial architecture dates back to the early sixteenth century. Many buildings are constructed with a green sandstone called *cantera verde* that seems to change color tones from dawn to dusk.

• Santo Domingo de Guzman church and former monastery is one of the largest and most significant ecclesiastical buildings in Mexico.

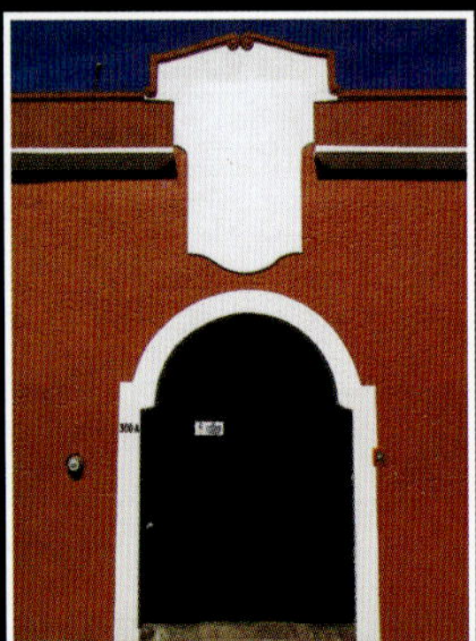

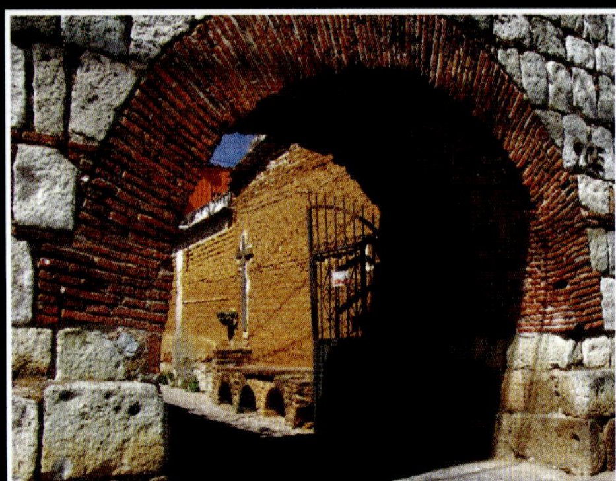

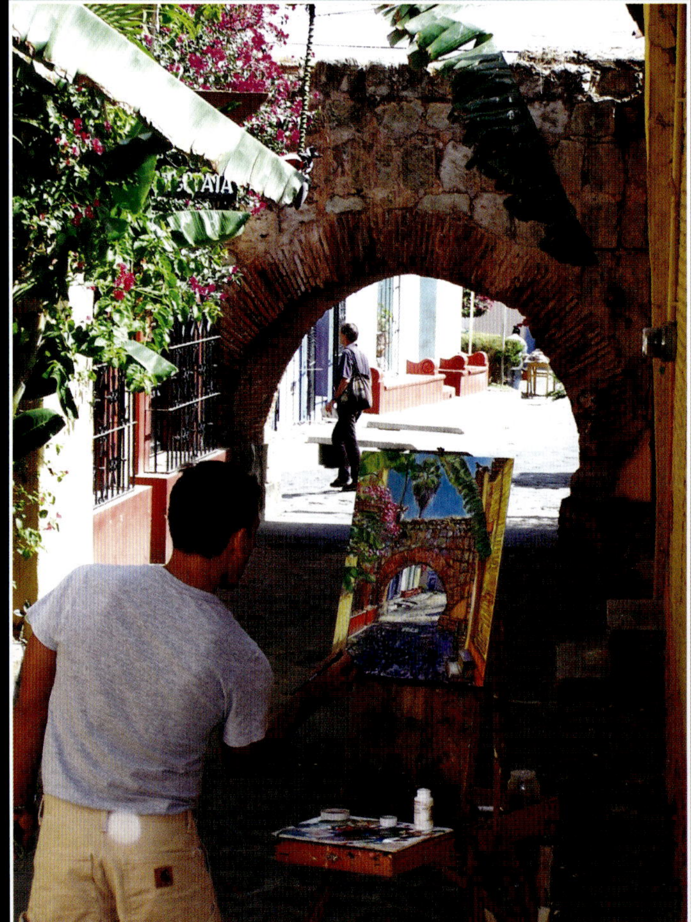

I have admired these doors for so long that they have taken on life for me. No two are the same; each is a face as unique as your own. They are rich in texture and color, and both towering and tiny in stature. Their charm seems only to enhance with age and weathering. These doors are the curtains that separate two stages. They are witnesses to the stories and events that are played out in public streets and within private dwellings. Generations of drama and routine, beginnings and endings, have been acted out in front of these doors. These are the memories of the Doors of Oaxaca.

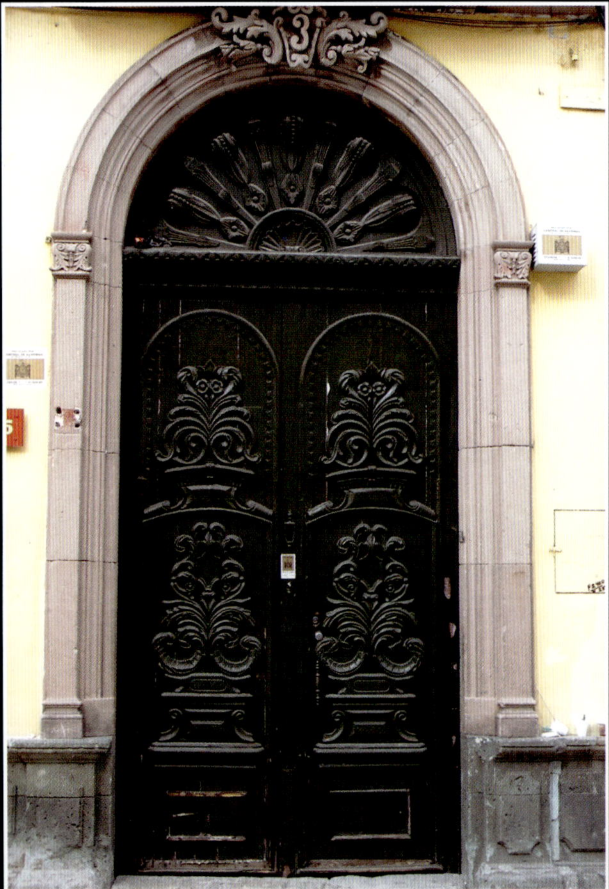

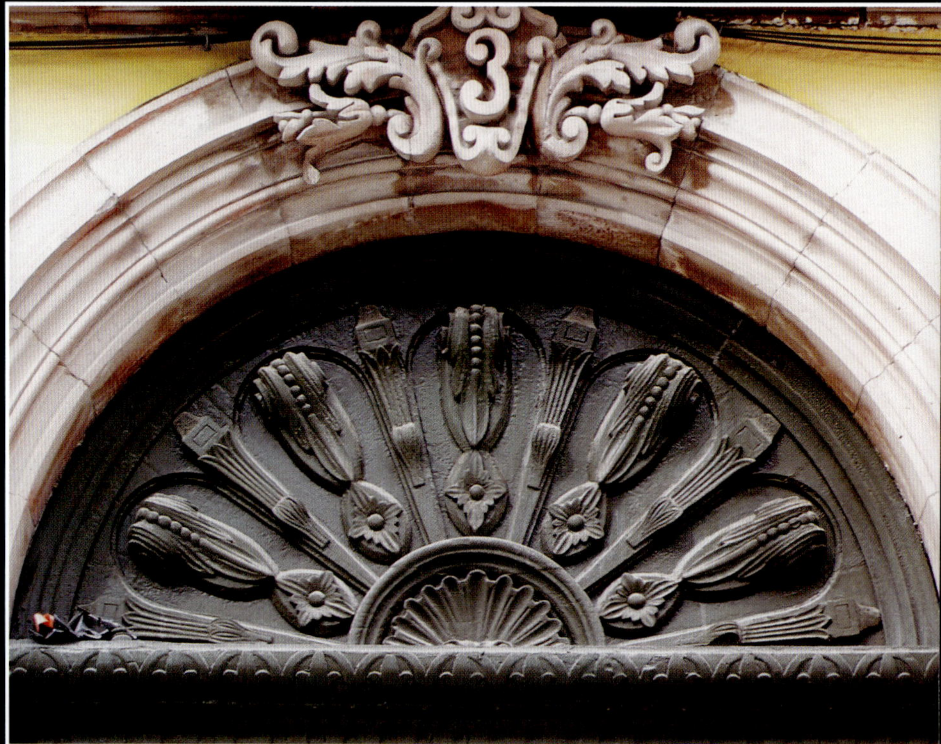

This beautiful door is located on Guerrero Street, on the Southeast corner of the center plaza, el zócalo.

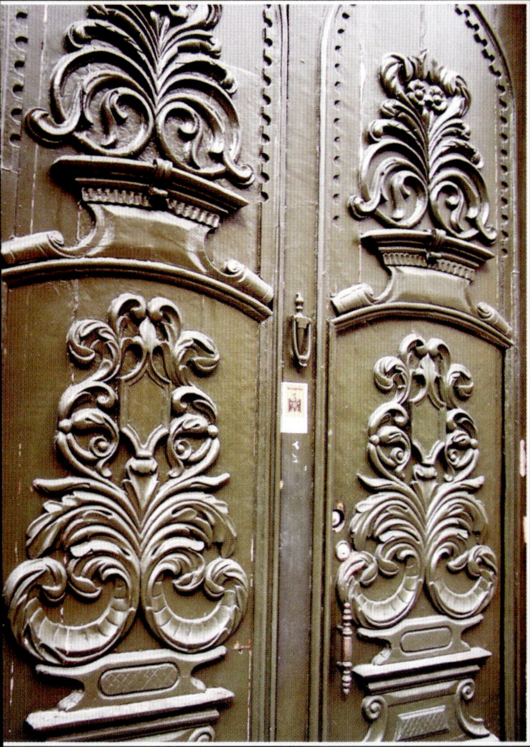

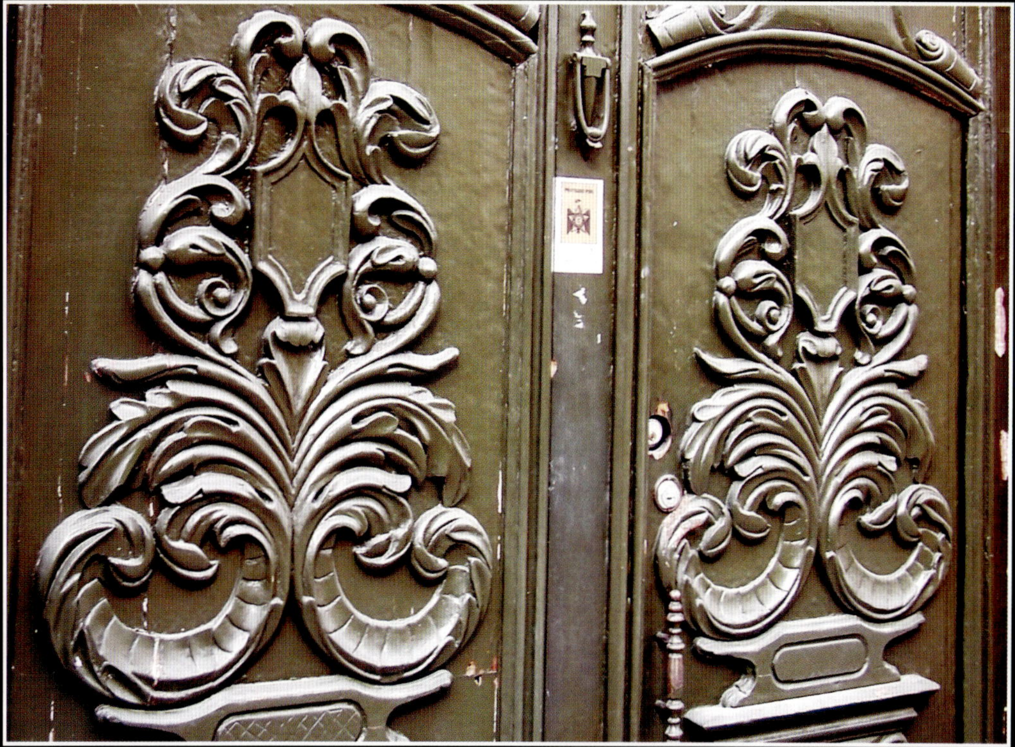

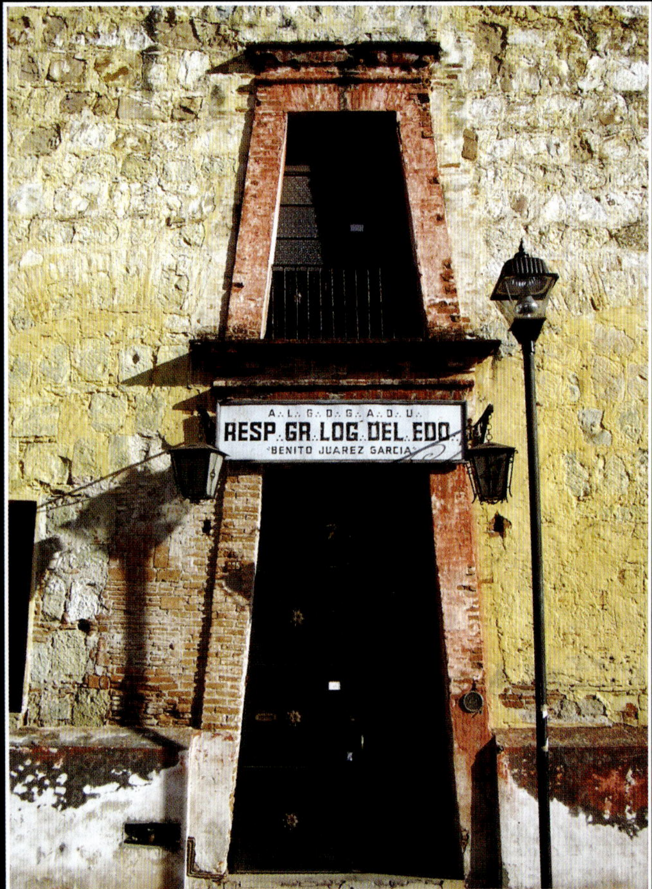
A.·.L.·.G.·.D.·.G.·.A.·.D.·.U.·.
RESP.·.GR.·.LOG.·.DEL.·.EDO.·.
"BENITO JUAREZ GARCIA"

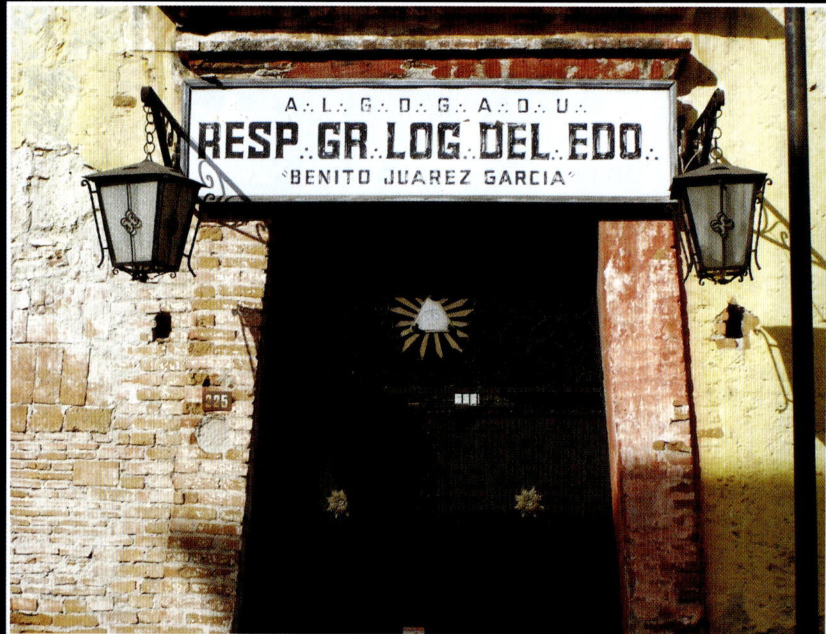
A.·.L.·.G.·.D.·.G.·.A.·.D.·.U.·.
RESP.·.GR.·.LOG.·.DEL.·.EDO.·.
"BENITO JUAREZ GARCIA"

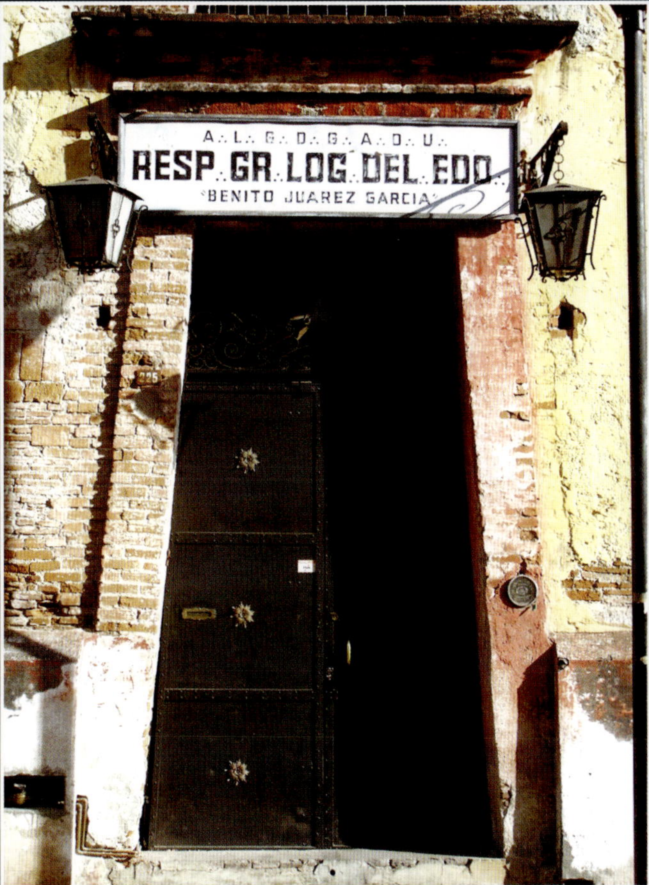

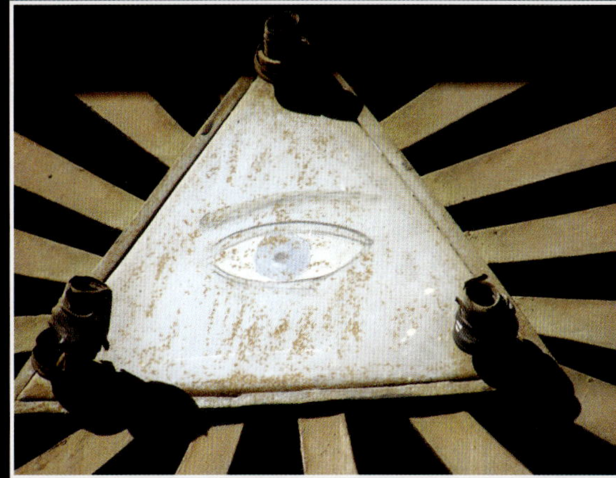

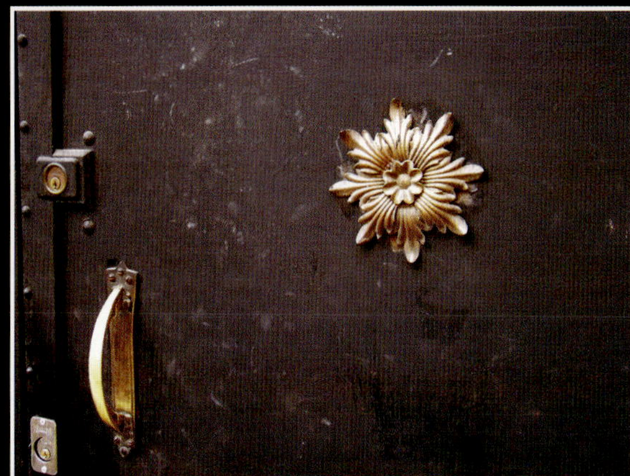

This door is located on Murguía Street, adjacent to the Ex-convent of Santa Catalina, now known as the Camino Real Hotel.

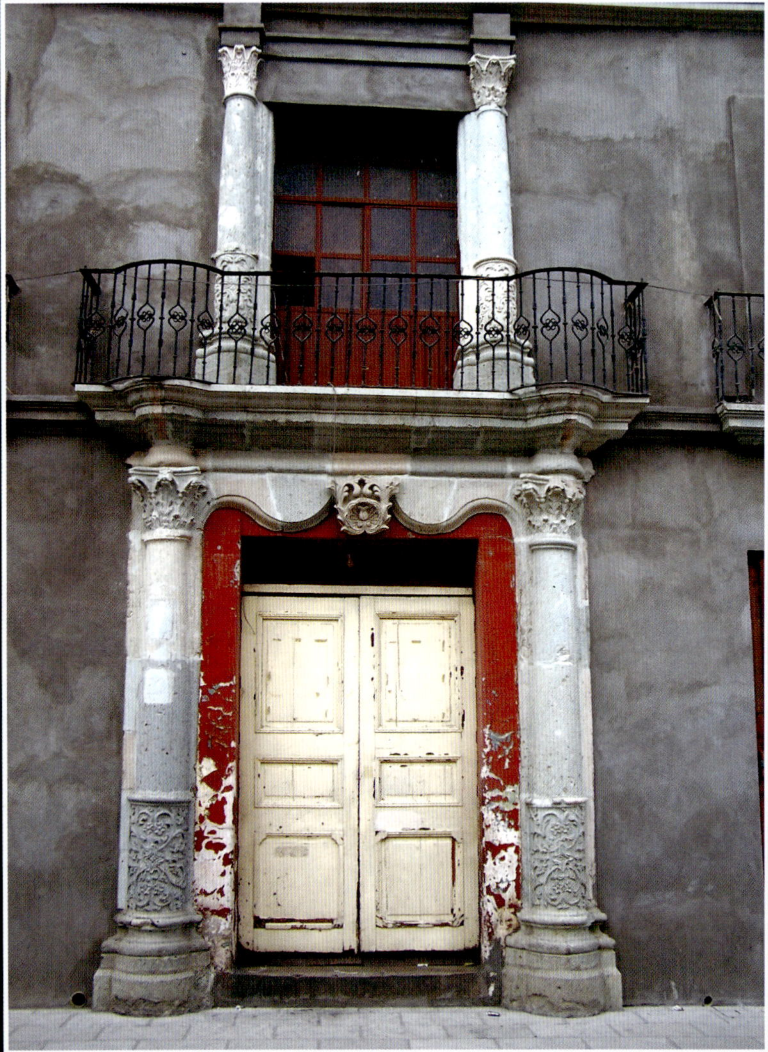

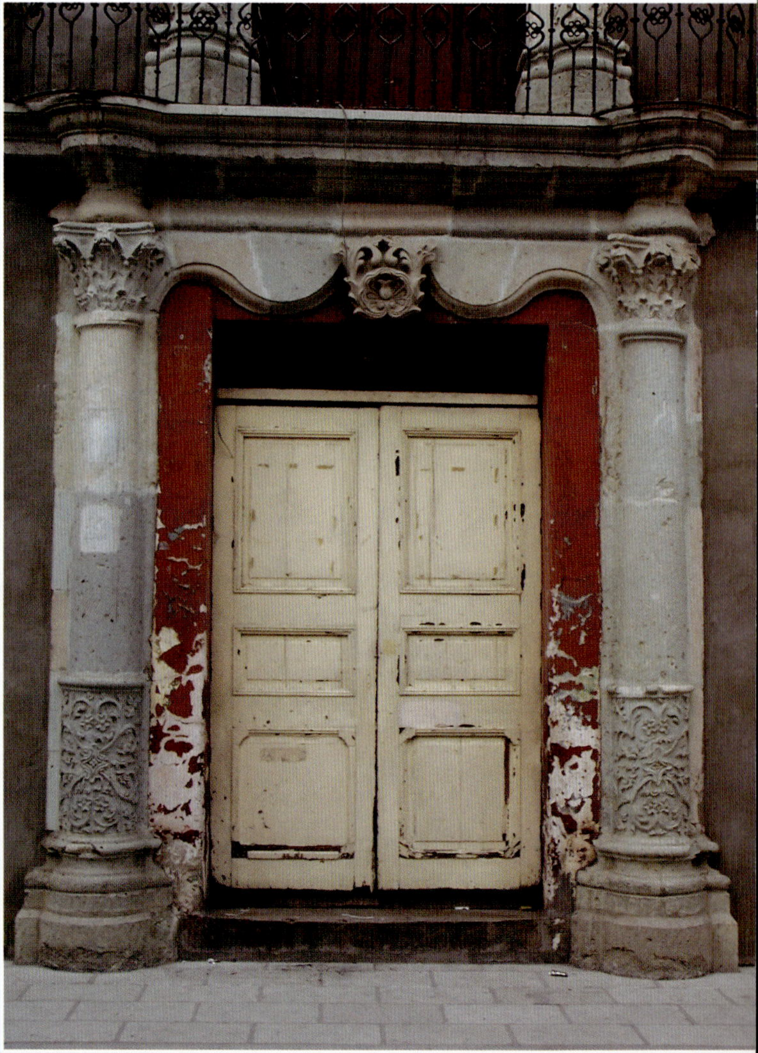

This door, located on the corner of Xicotencatl and Hidalgo Streets, is the front entrance to one of the oldest, largest, and most well known hardware stores in the city called Tubos y Conexiones.

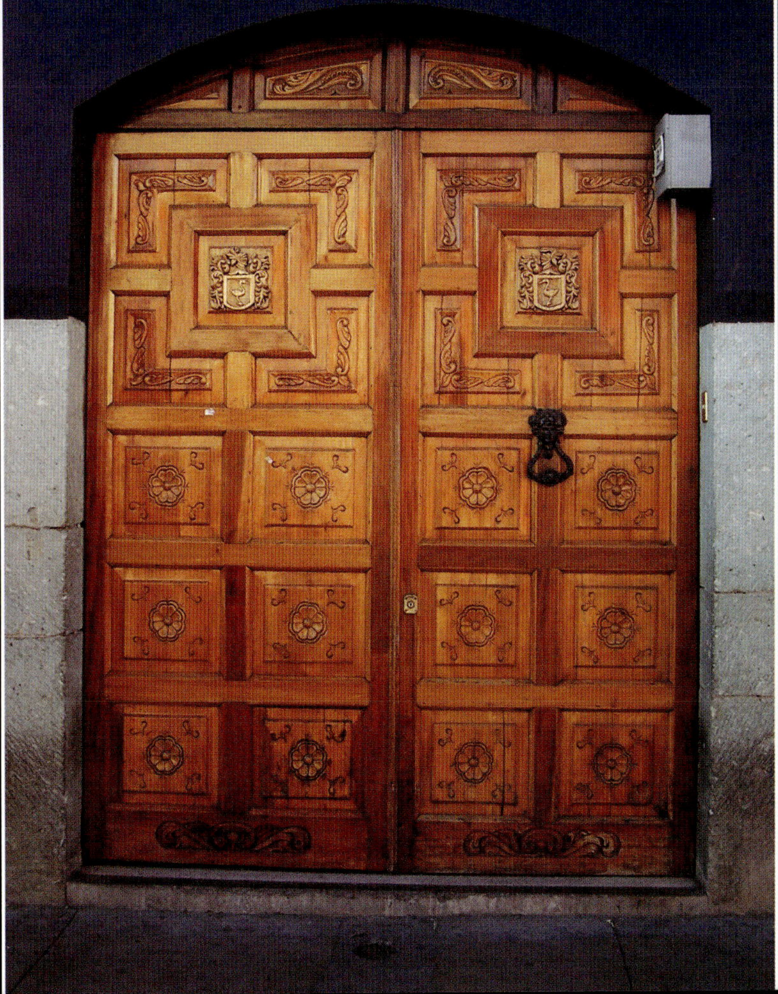

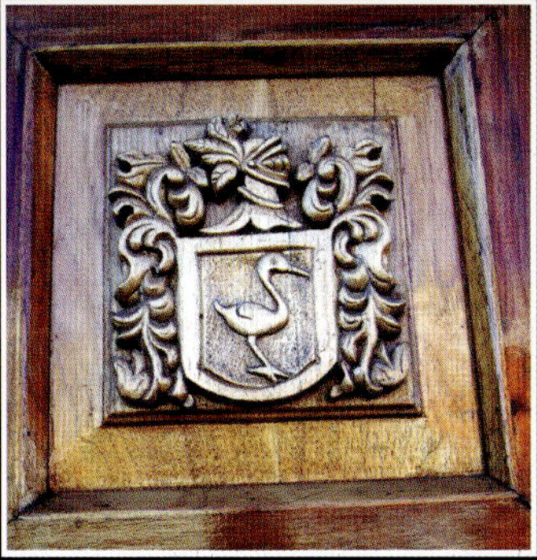

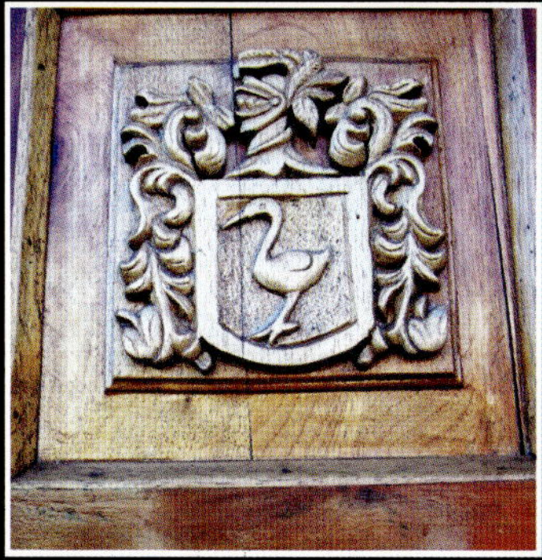

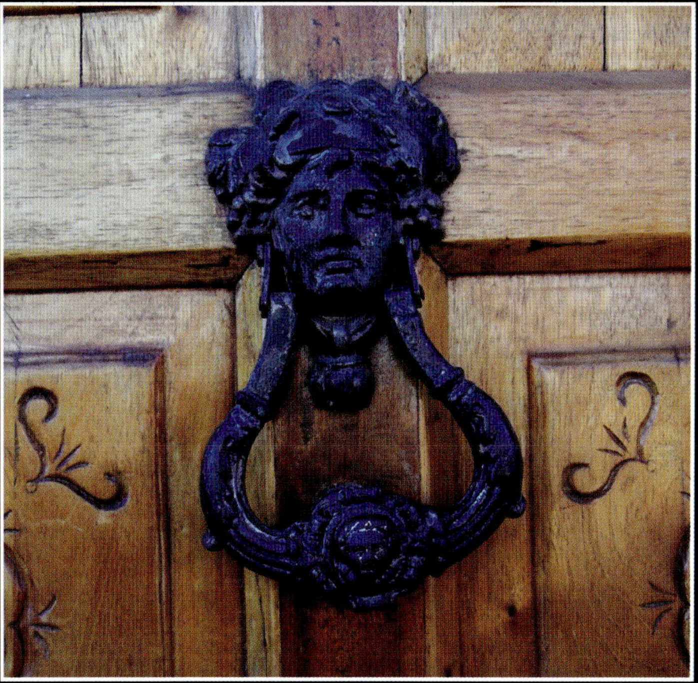

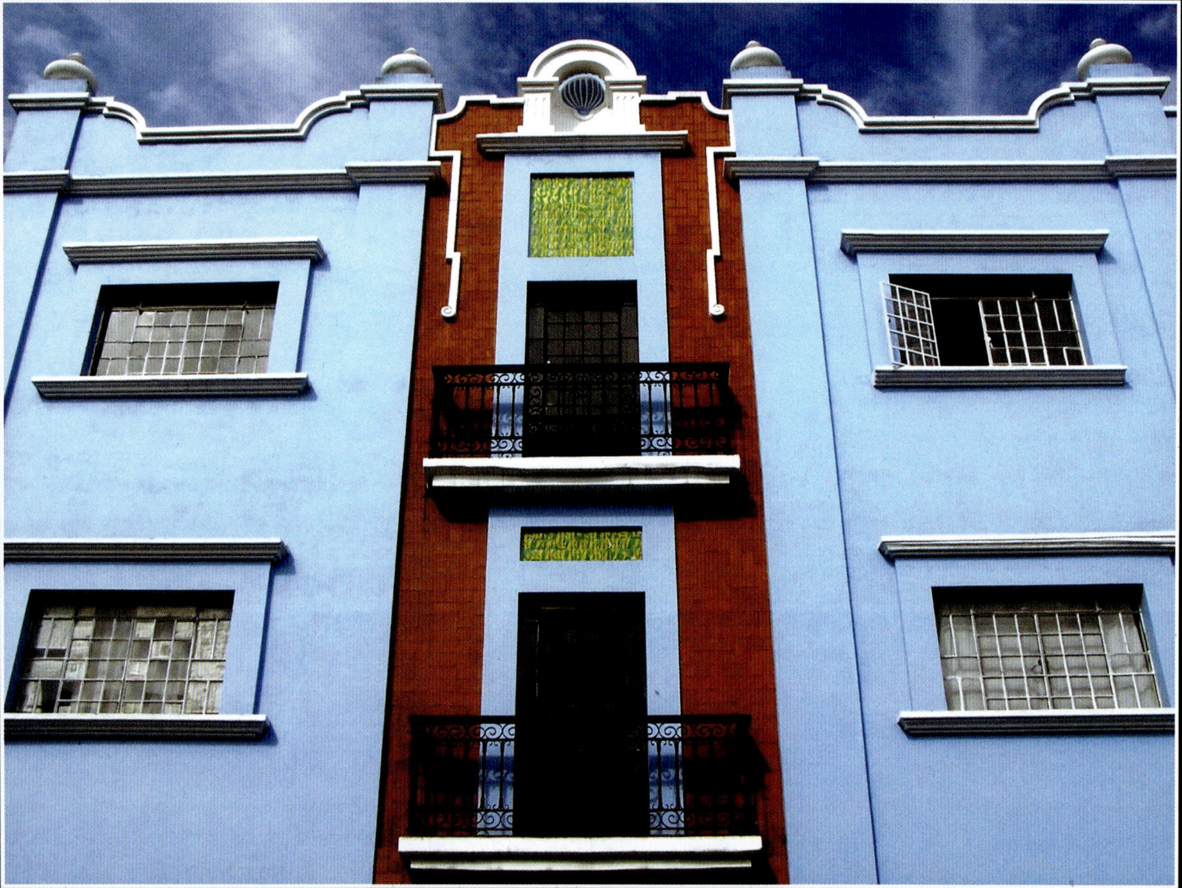

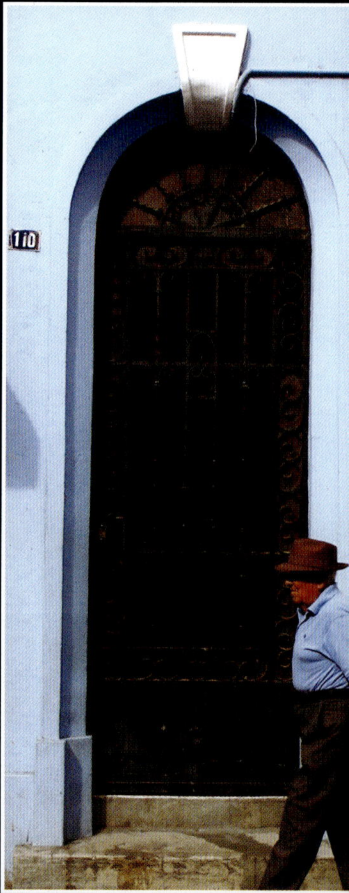
110

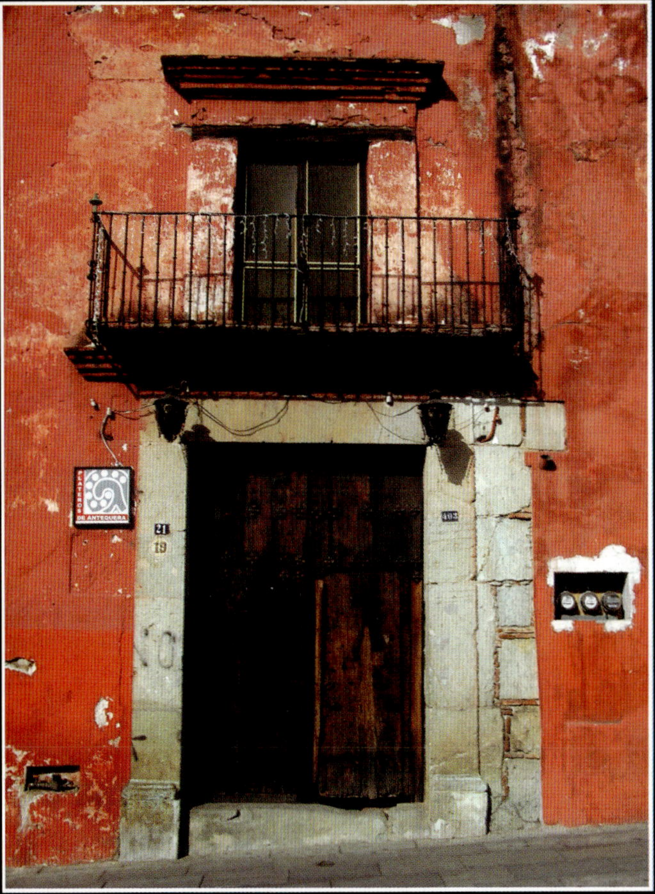
PLATEROS
DE ANTEQUERA
21
19
403

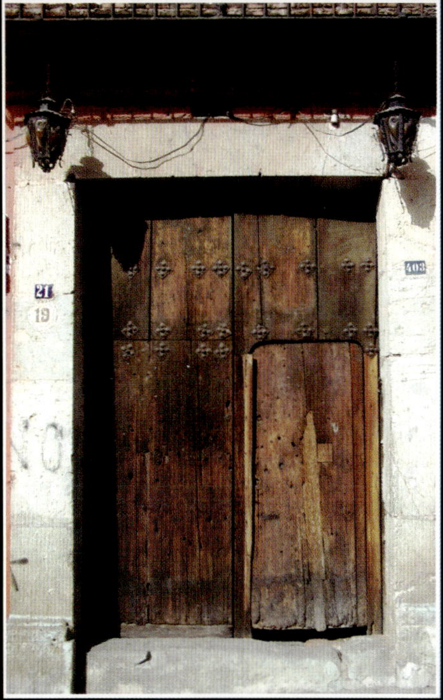
21
19
403

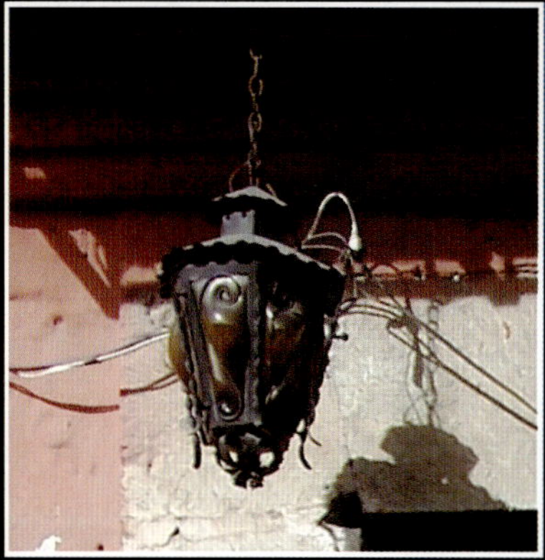

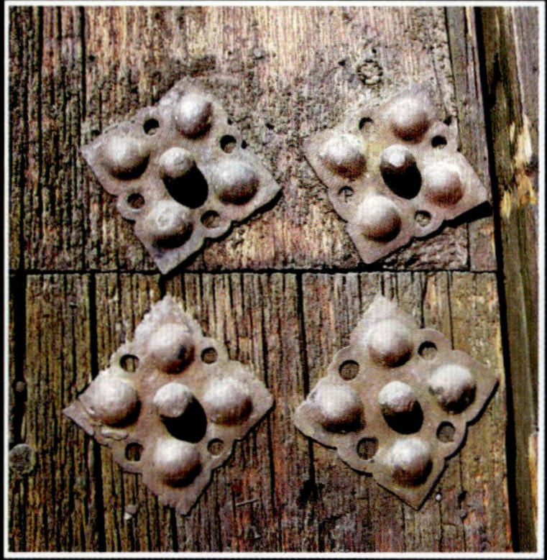

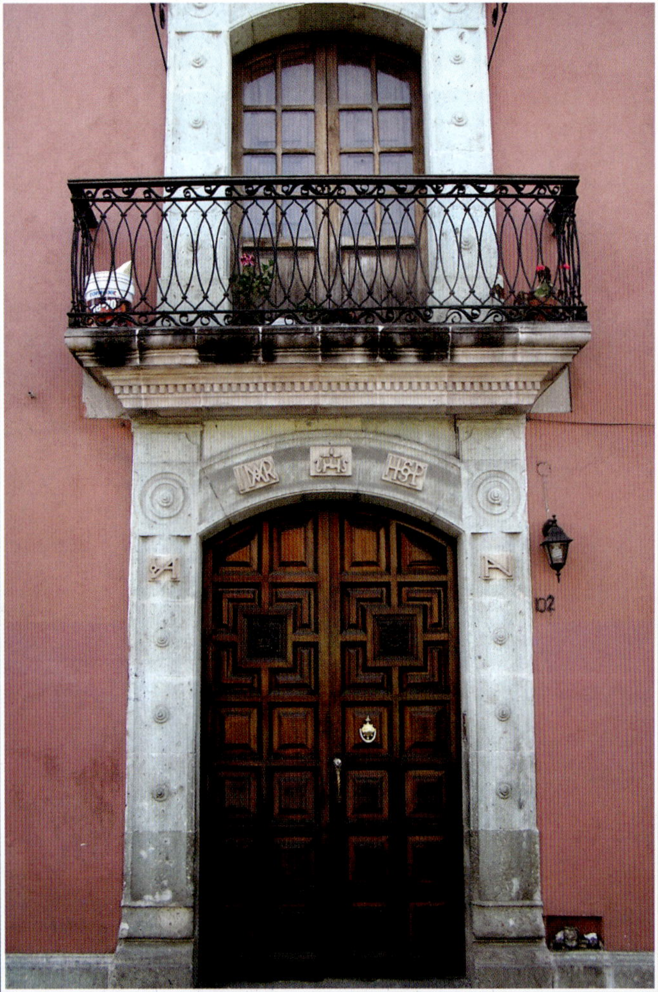
102

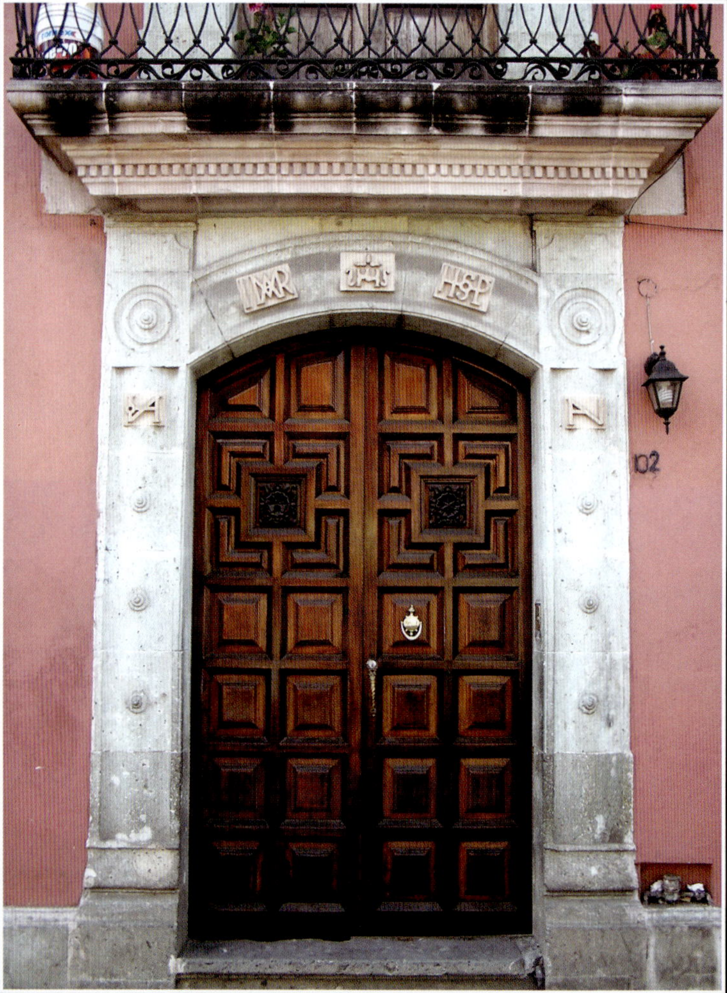
102

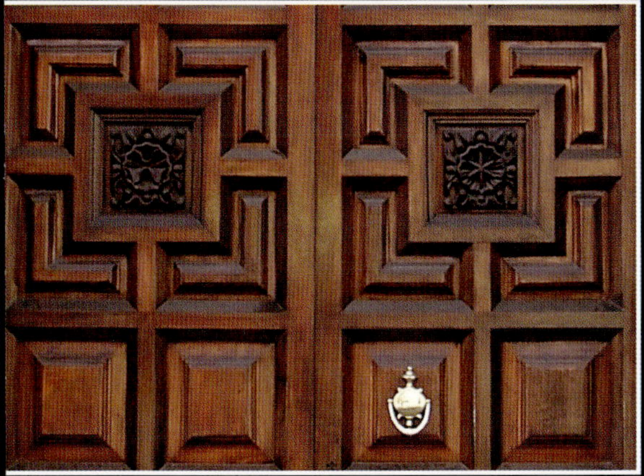
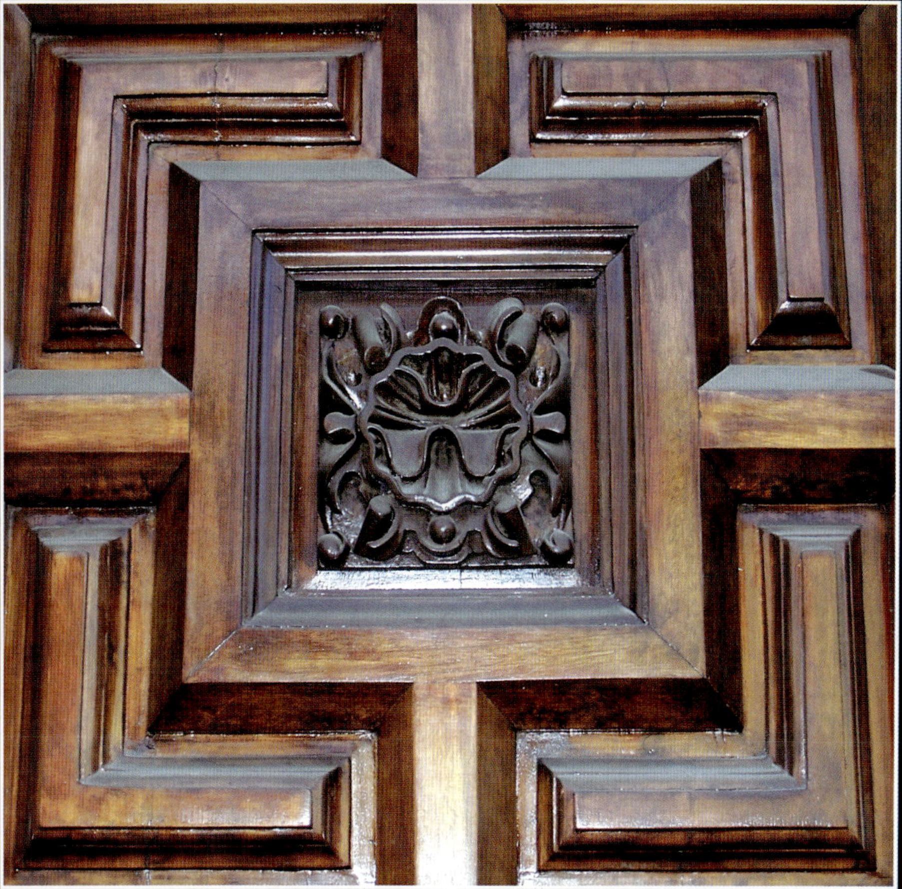

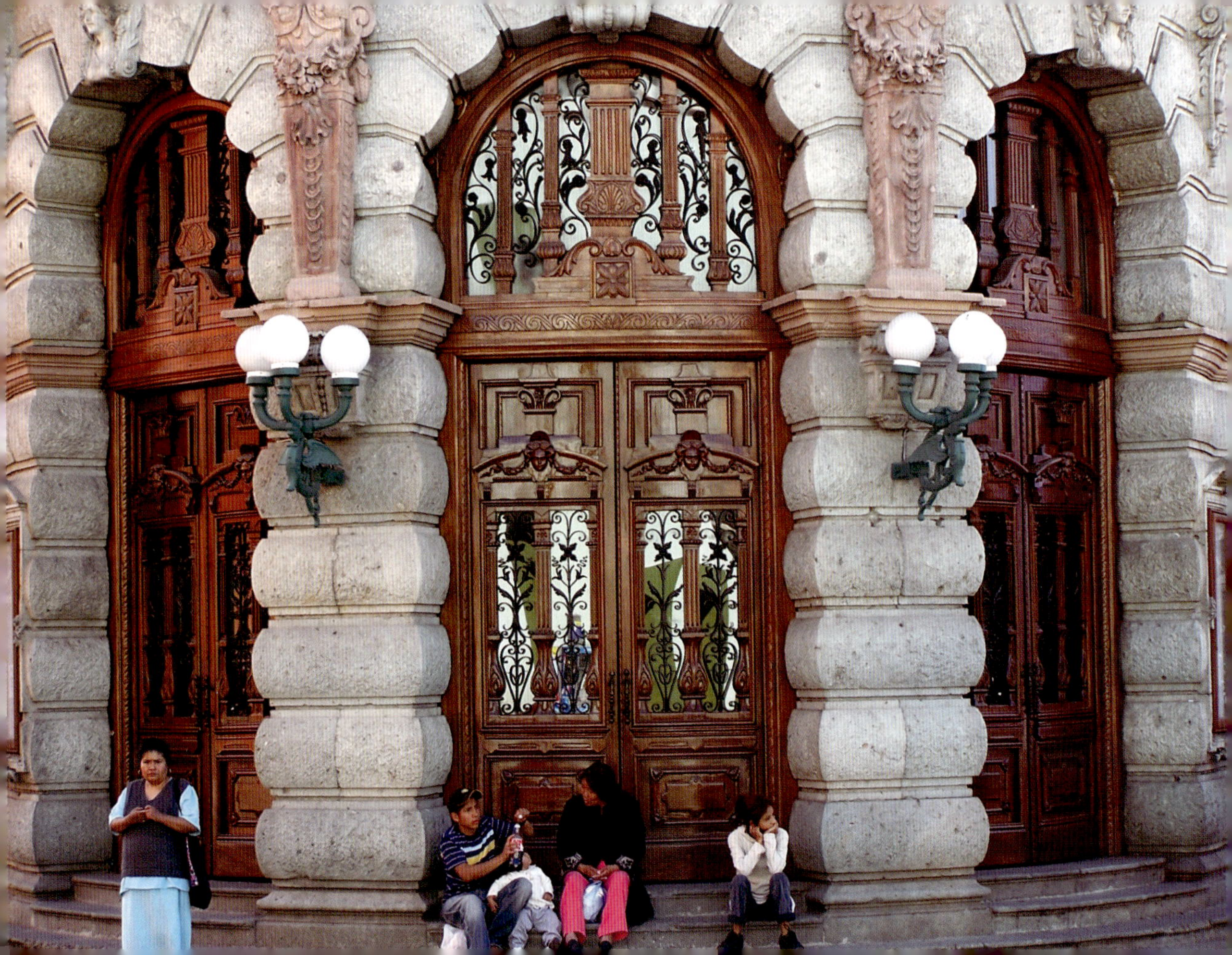

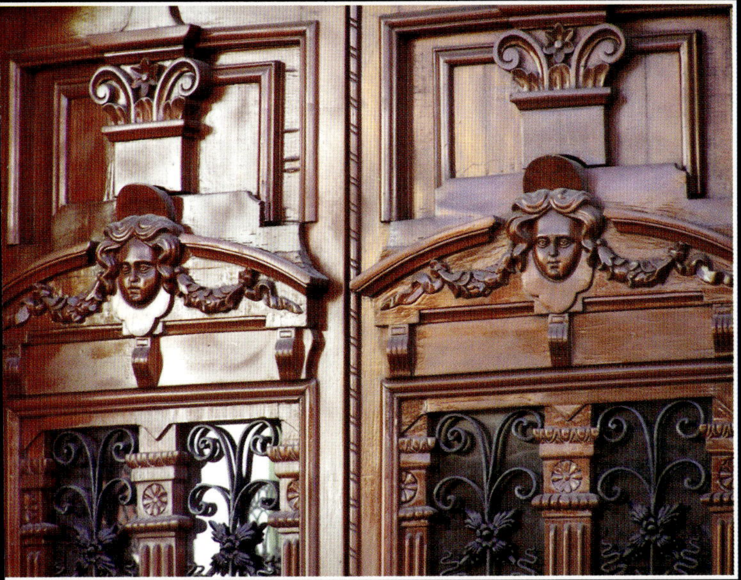

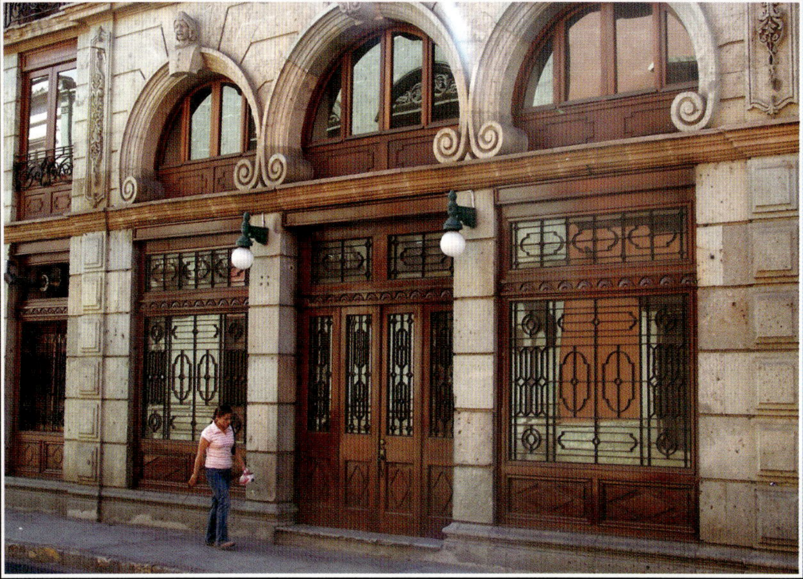

Front entrance of the Macedonio Alcalá Theatre, located on the corner Independencia Street and Armenta y López Street. Construction began in 1903 and was completed in 1909. Over its one hundred years, it has been a boxing and wrestling arena, circus tent, government inauguration hall, and movie theatre,

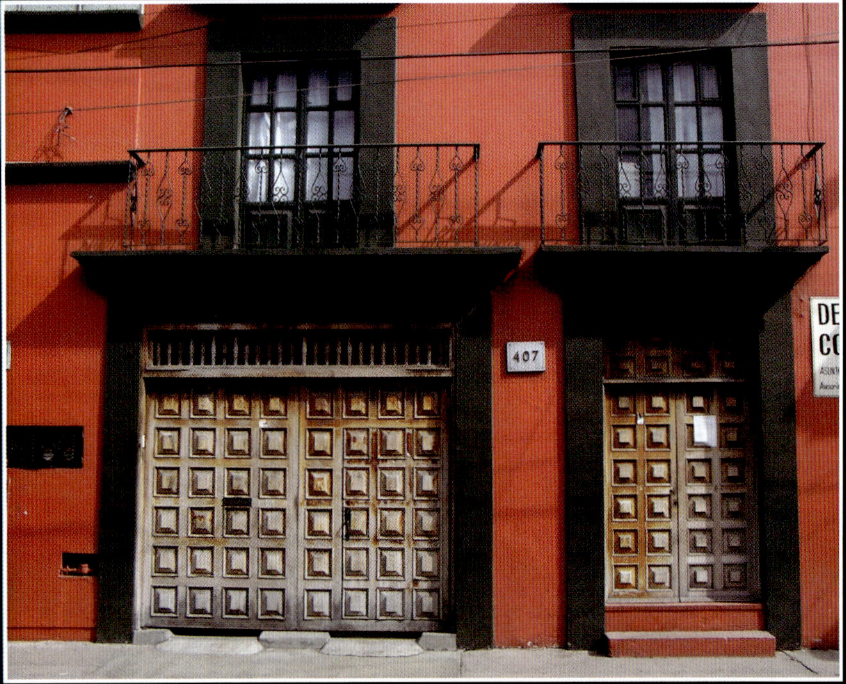
407

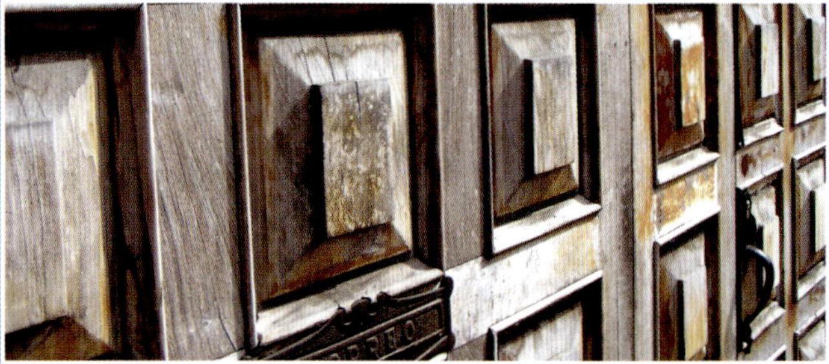

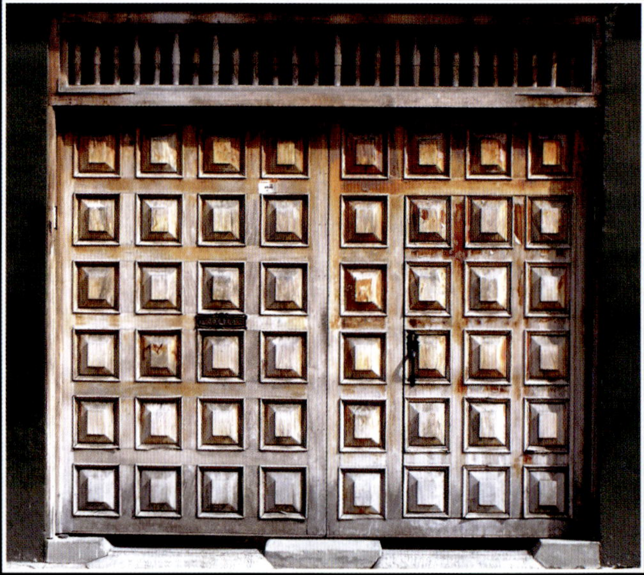

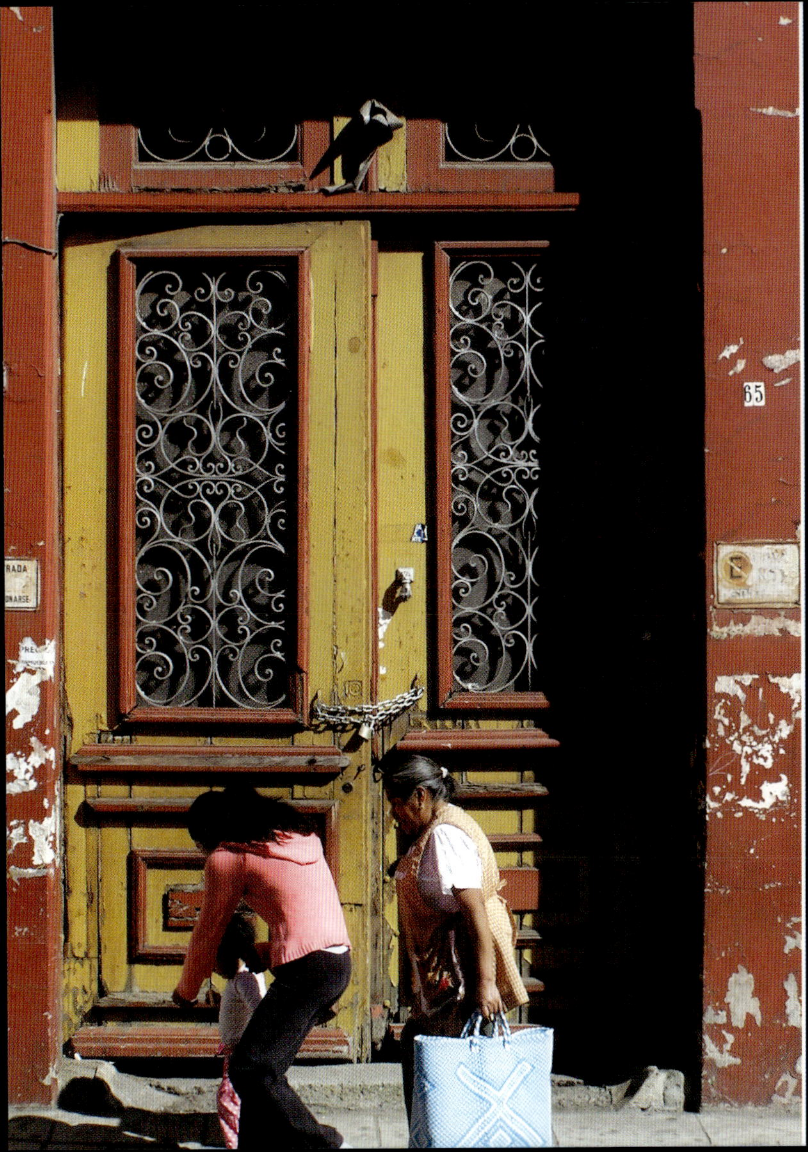

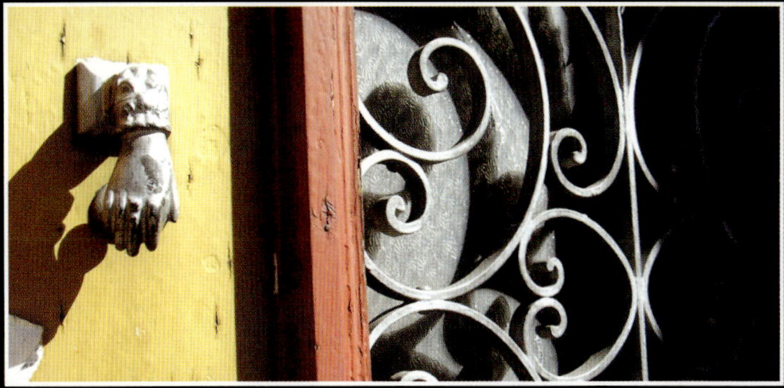

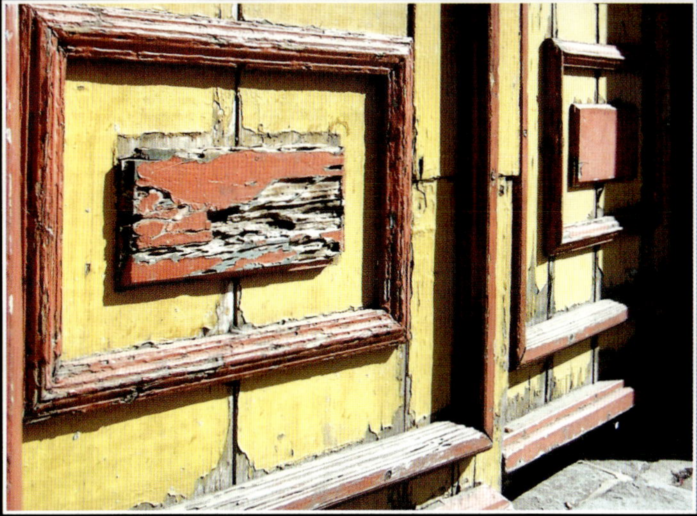

This home is located on Independencia Street, close to where Avenida Juárez intersects. Avenida Juárez Street was named after Benito Juárez, who was from Oaxaca and became the most famous president in Mexican history (1861-63, 1867-72). He is the only full-blooded Native American to serve as President, and was credited with leading victory in the Reform War (1858-61).

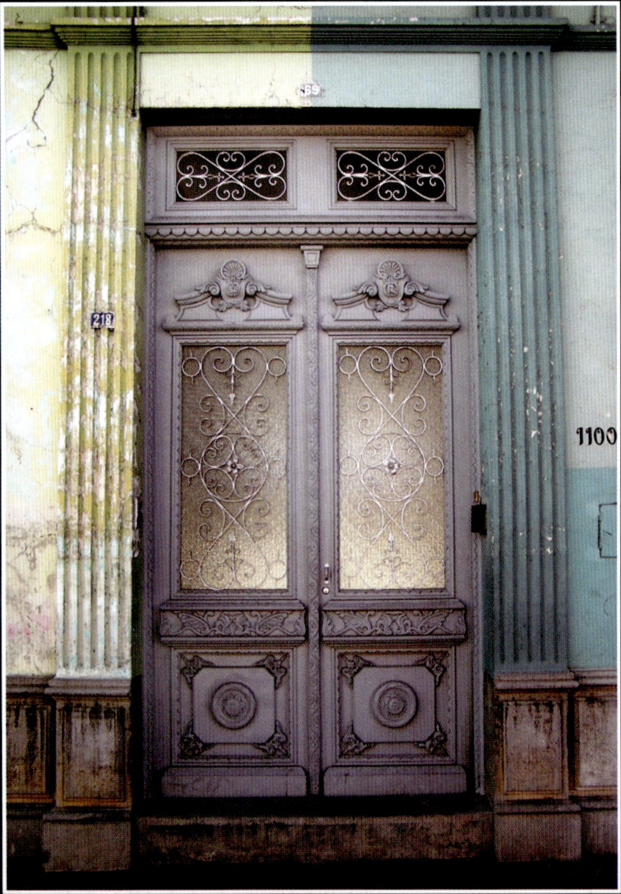

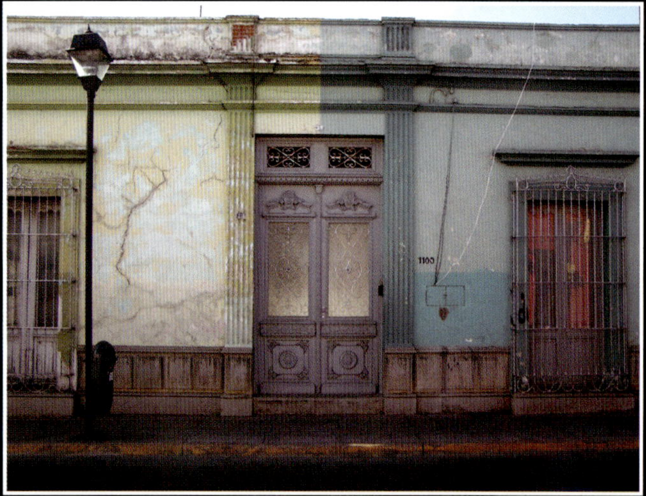

This home is located near the corner of Independencia Street and Melchor Ocampo Street.

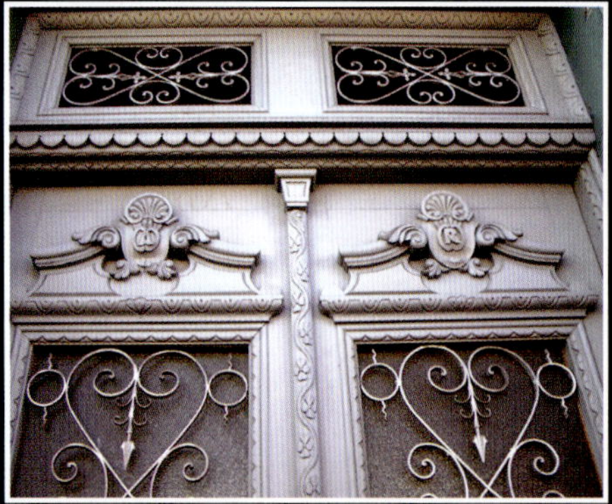

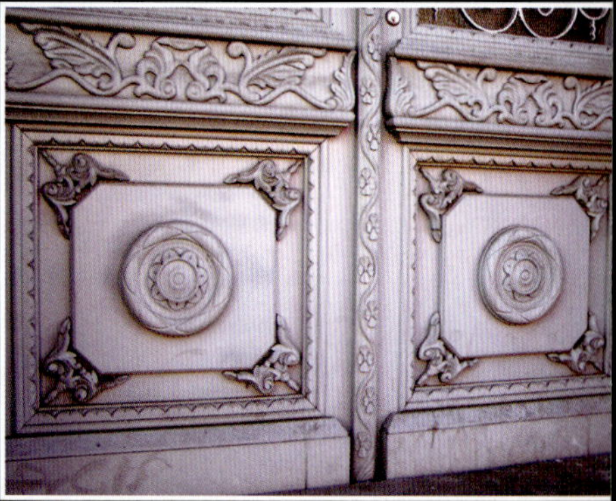

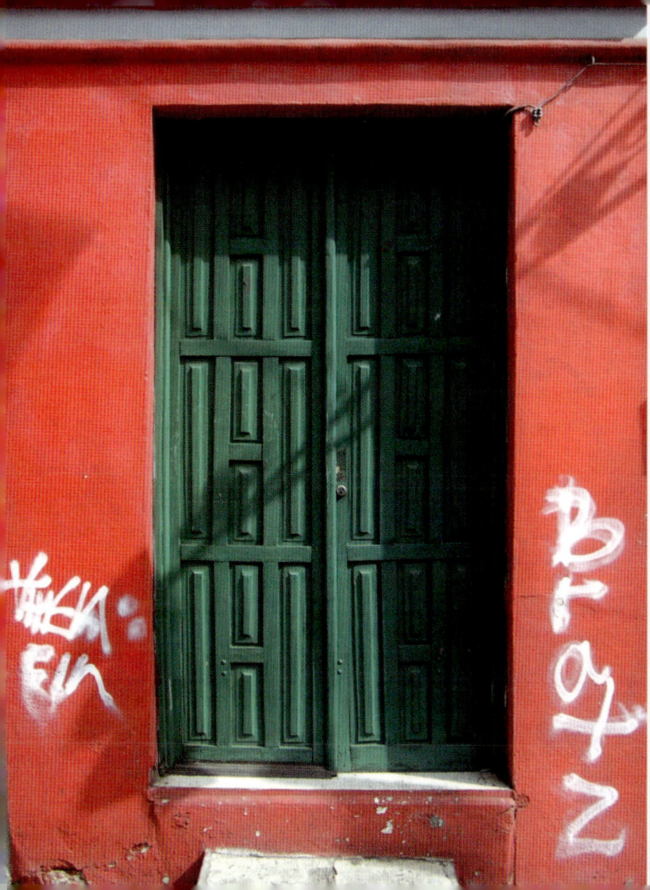

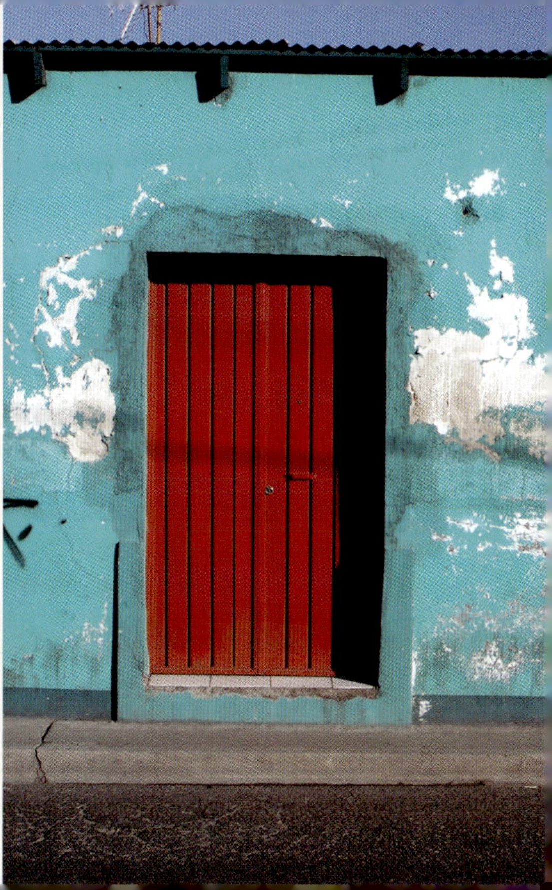

Two adjacent doors to the same house located on the corner of Colón Street and Fiallo Street.

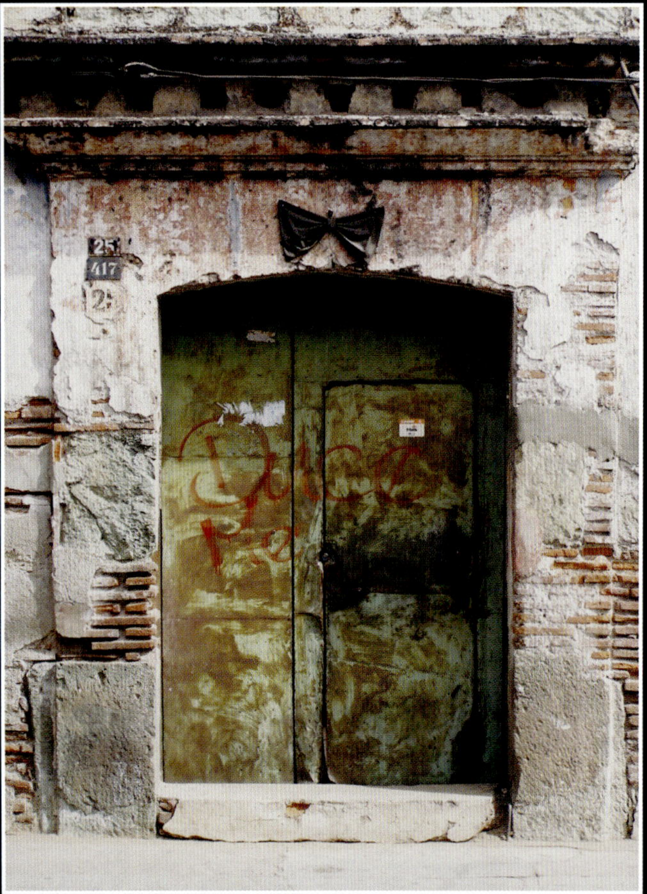

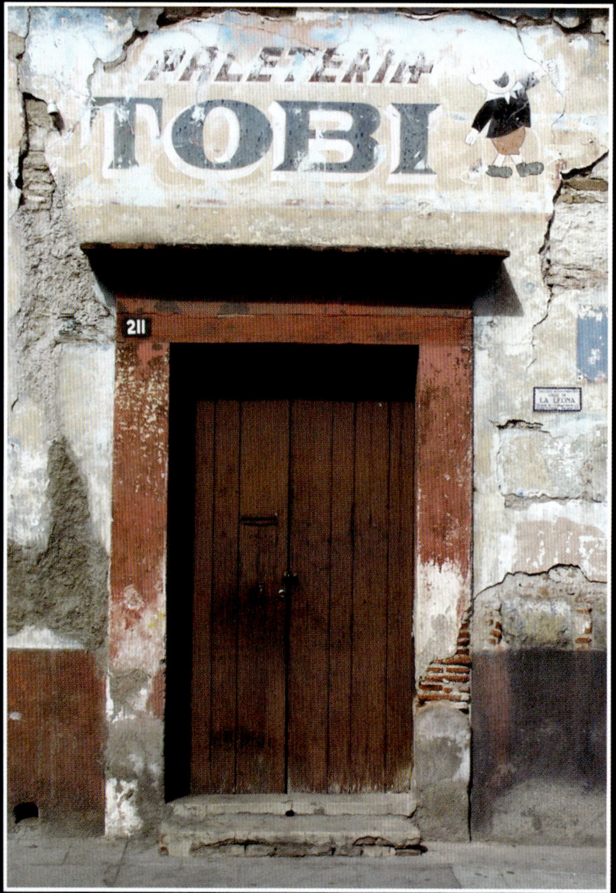

(Left) The black bow is a mourning bow. These dark bows hang over the doors of families who are mourning the death of a loved one. Many of these bows have been hanging for years.

(Right) The door to a one time famous popsicle store called Tobi.

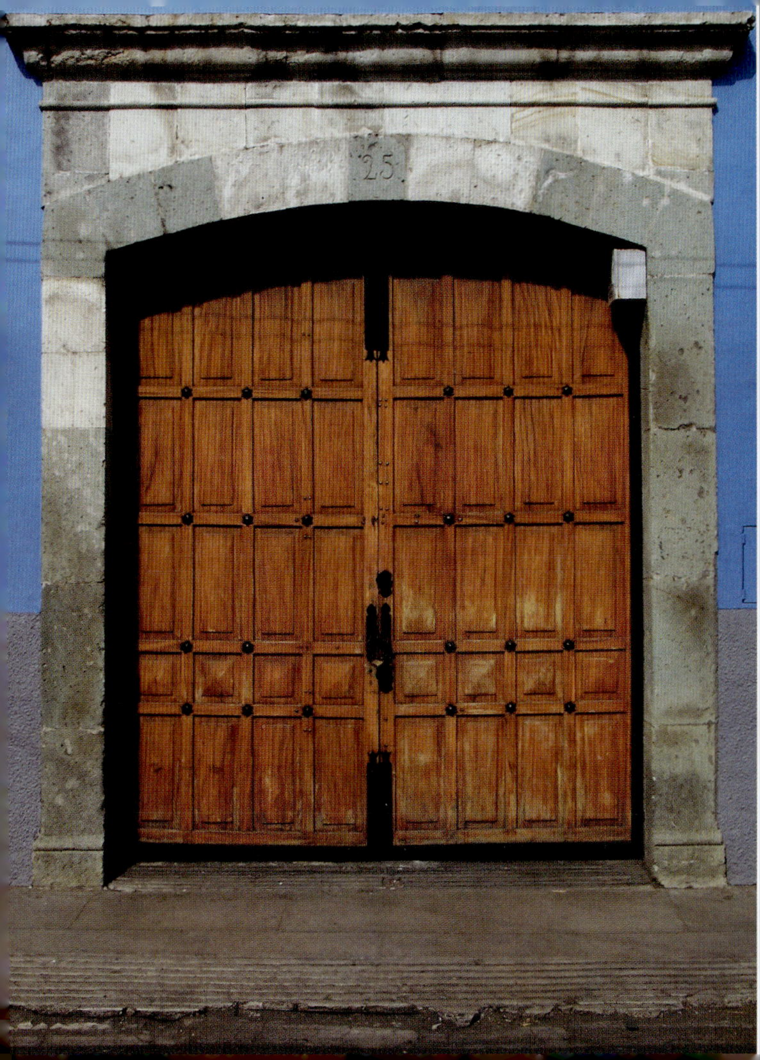
25

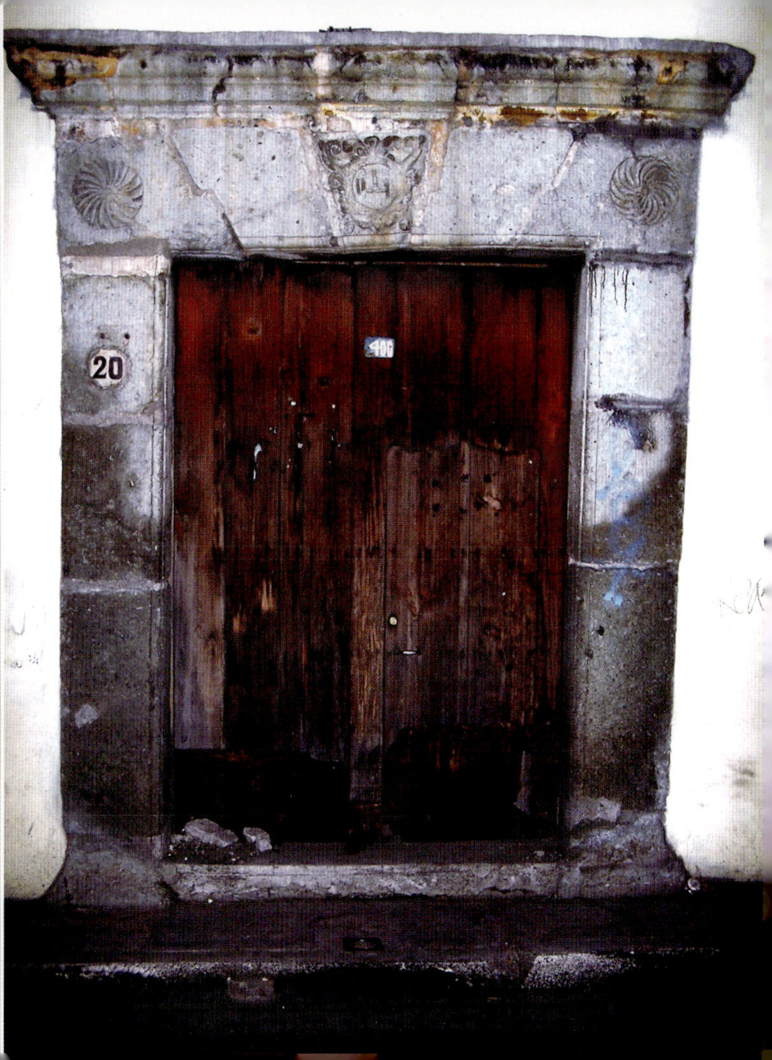
20

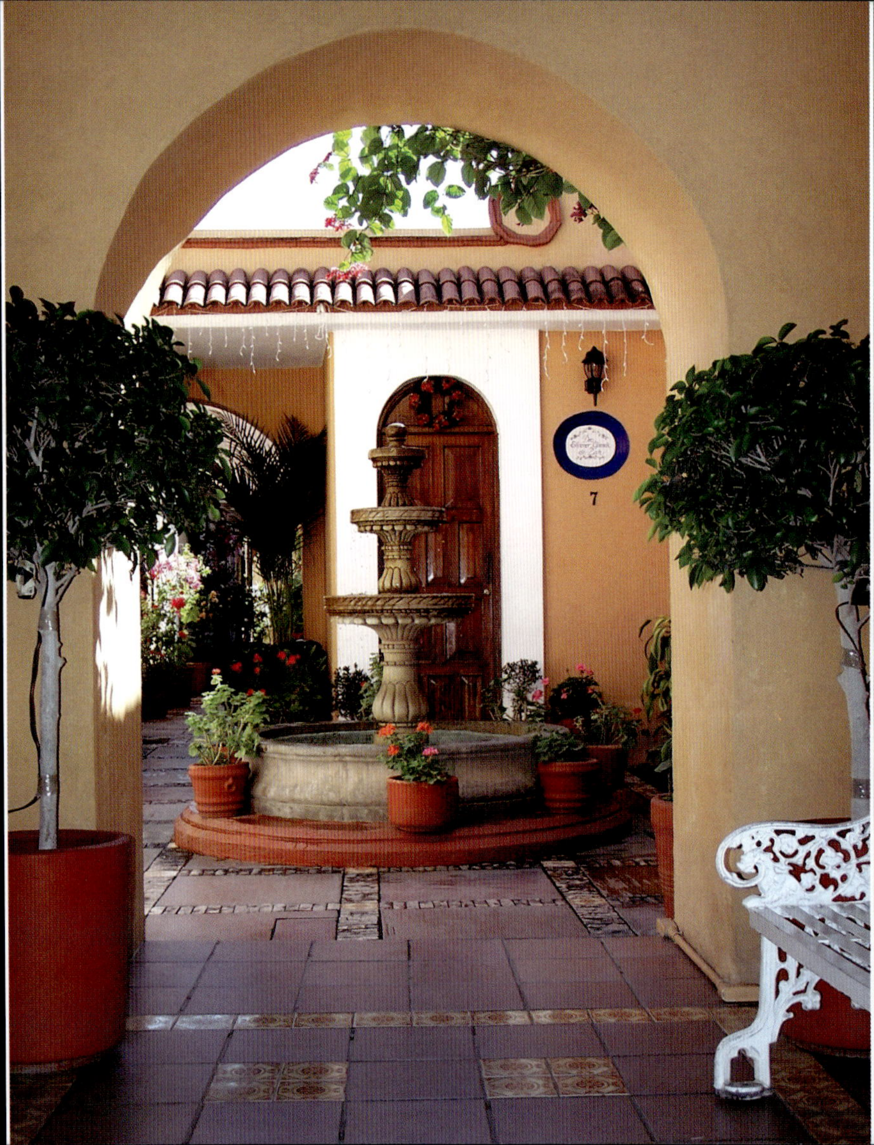
7

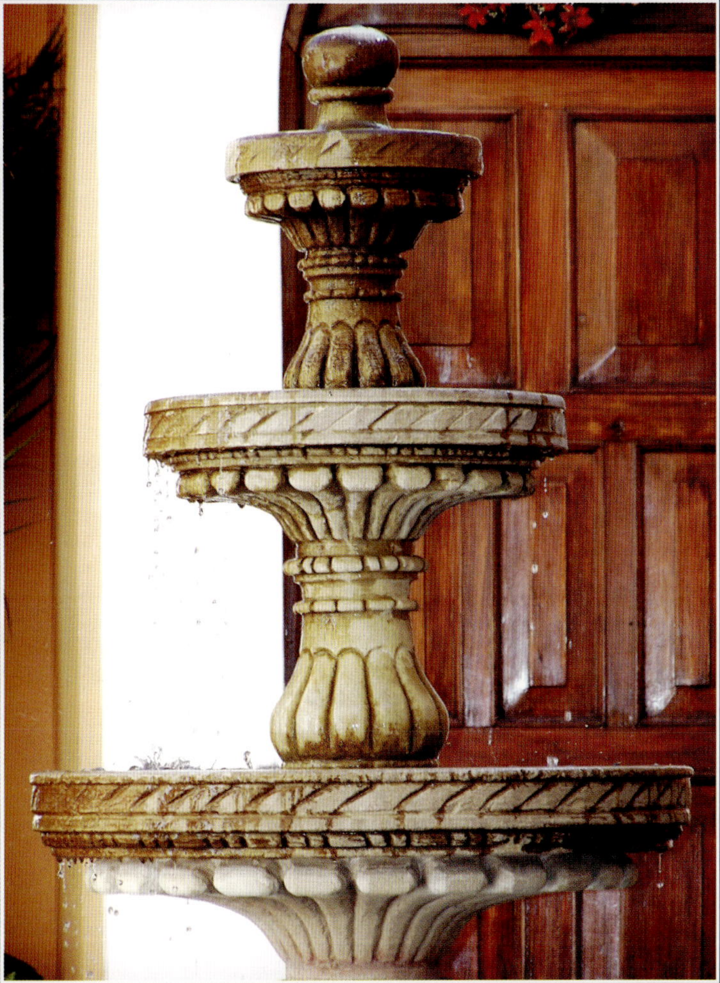

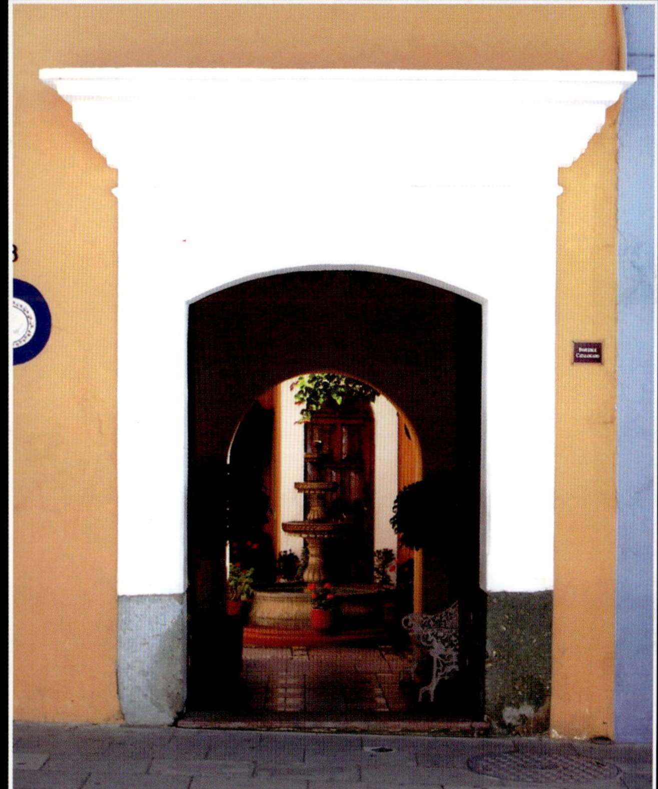

This house, now a medical center, is located on Cinco de Mayo Street a half block south of the most important church in Oaxaca, the Santo Domingo de Guzmán.

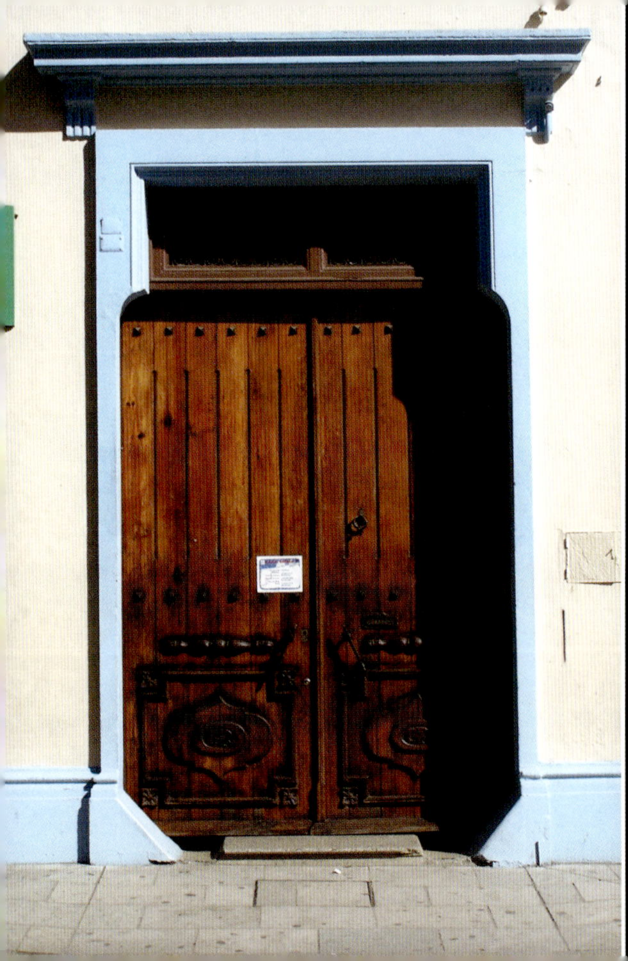

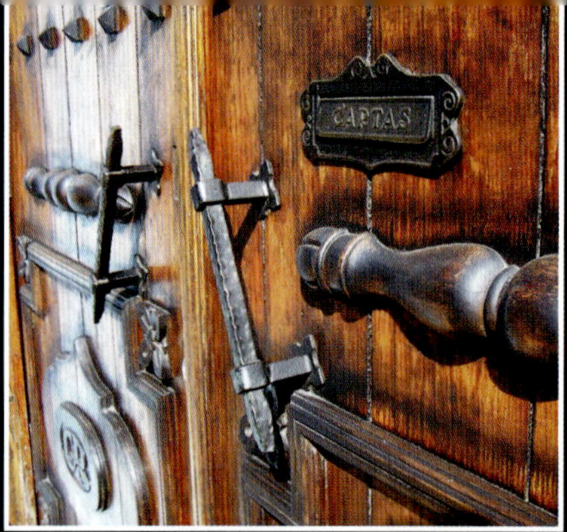
CARTAS

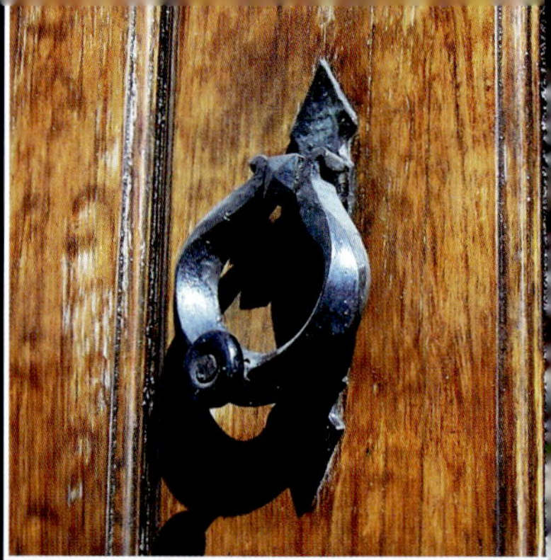

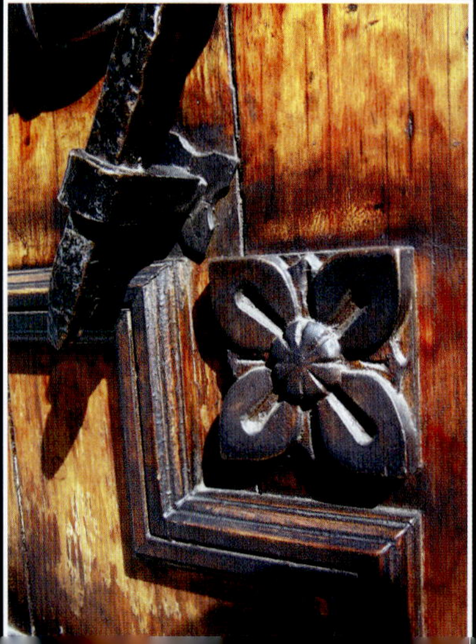

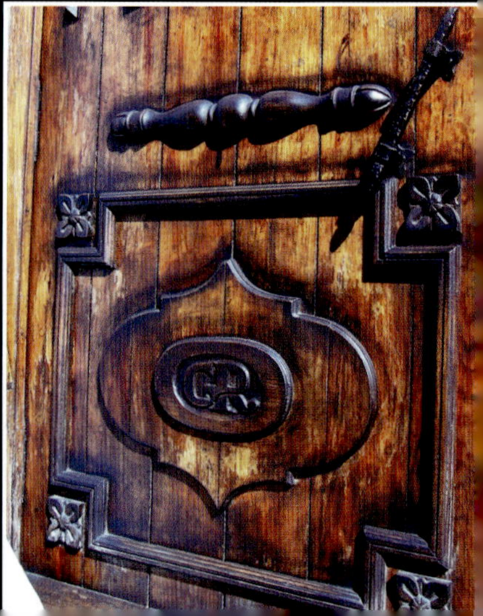

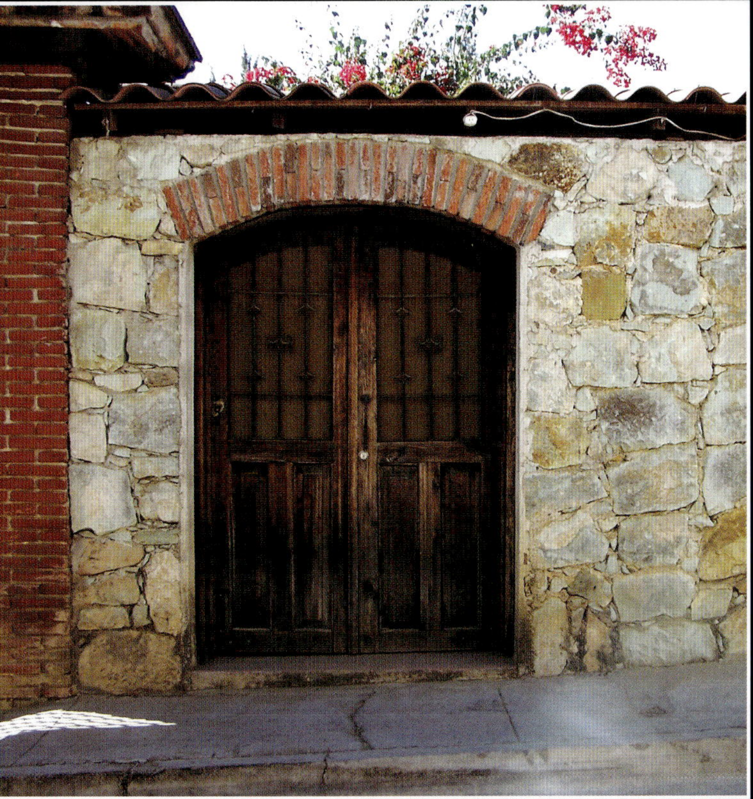

This door is on Hidalgo Street, the main street in San Felipe del Agua, a small, beautiful town located in the foothills just north of Oaxaca City.

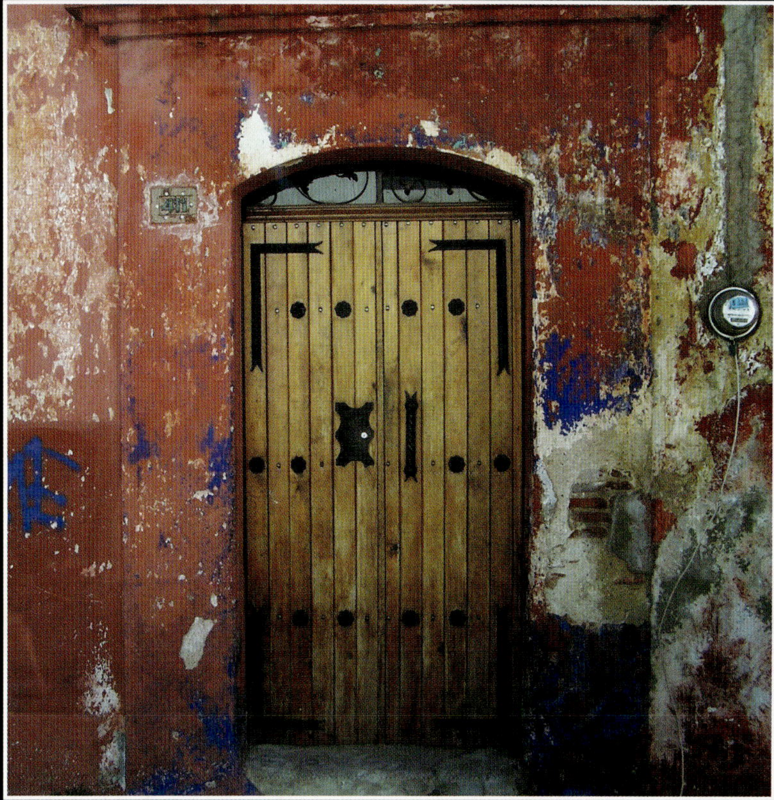

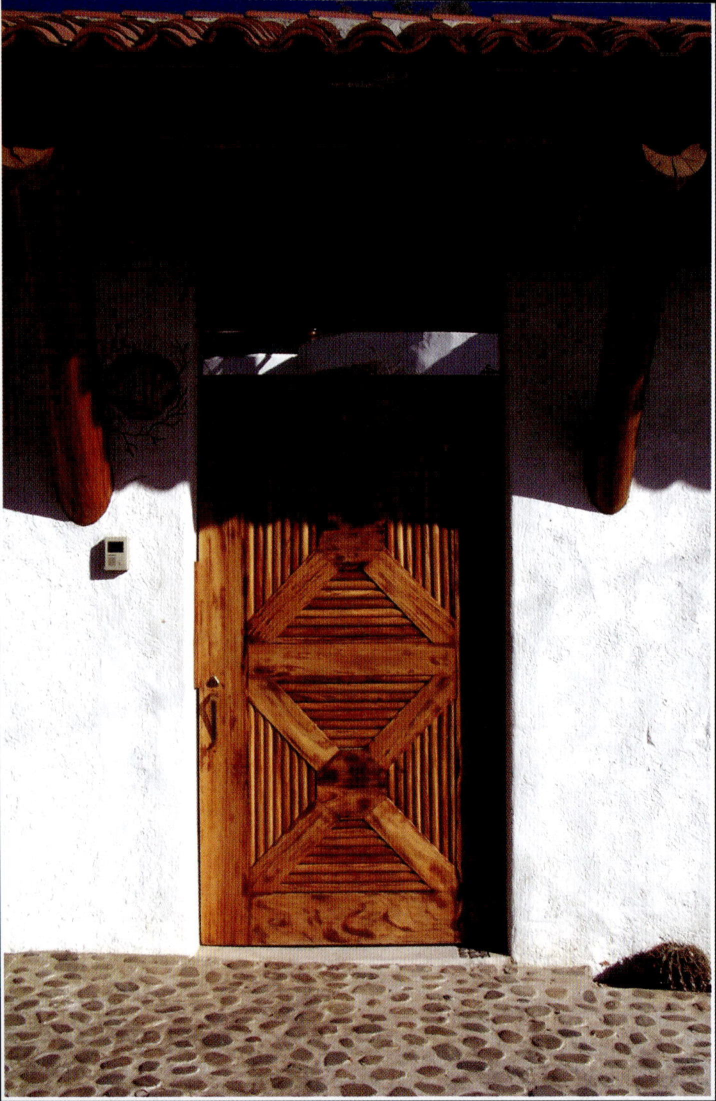
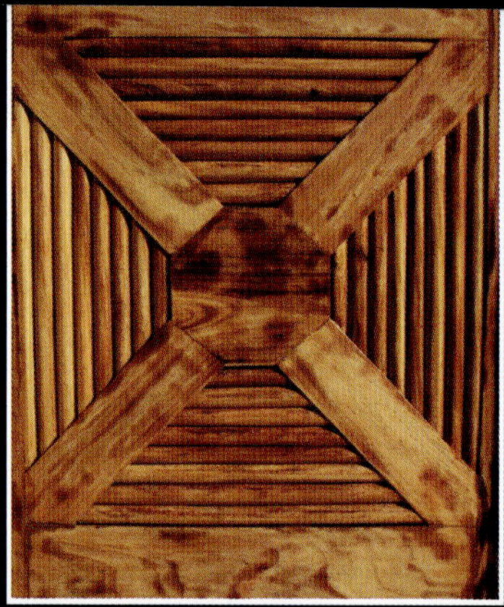
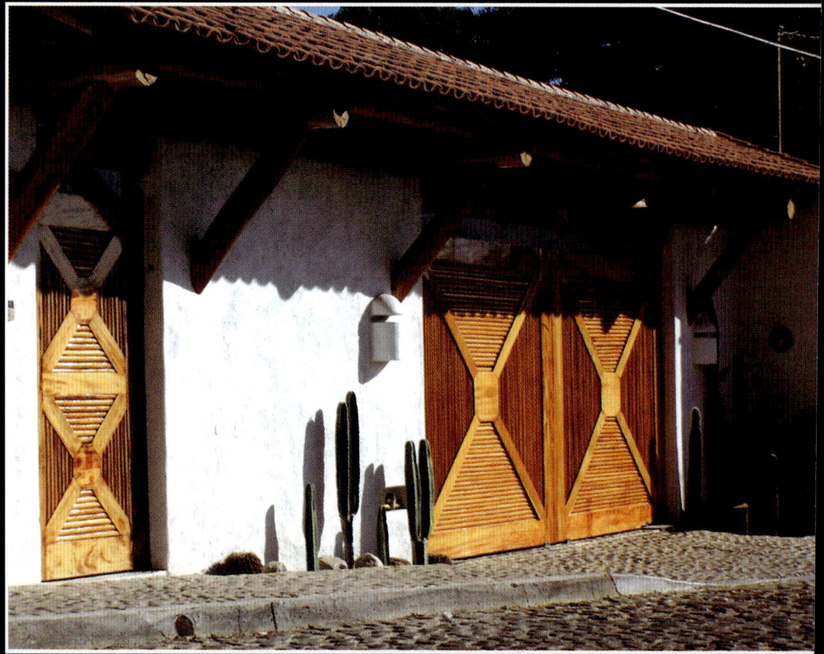

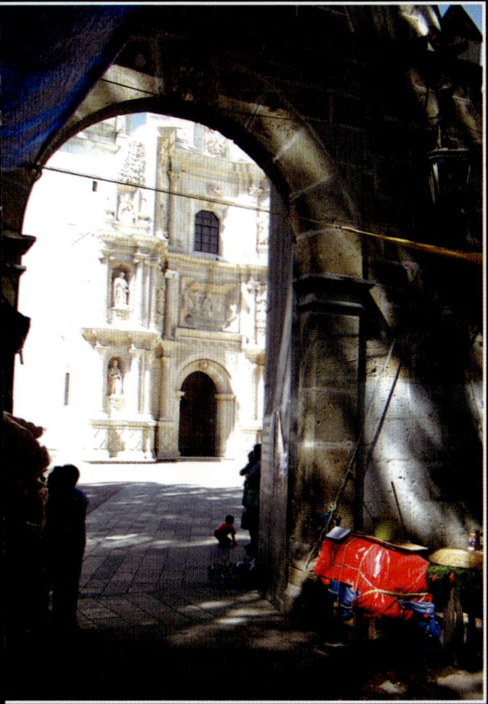

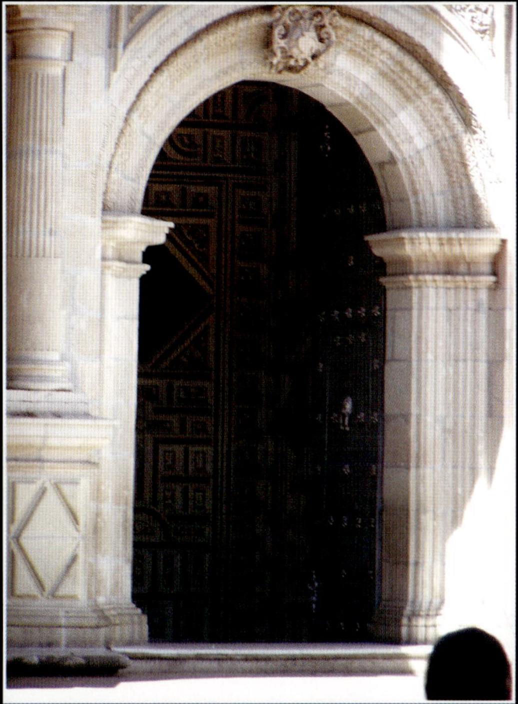

These two photographs of the main door of La Soledad Church were taken from the same viewpoint in the Plaza La Soledad.

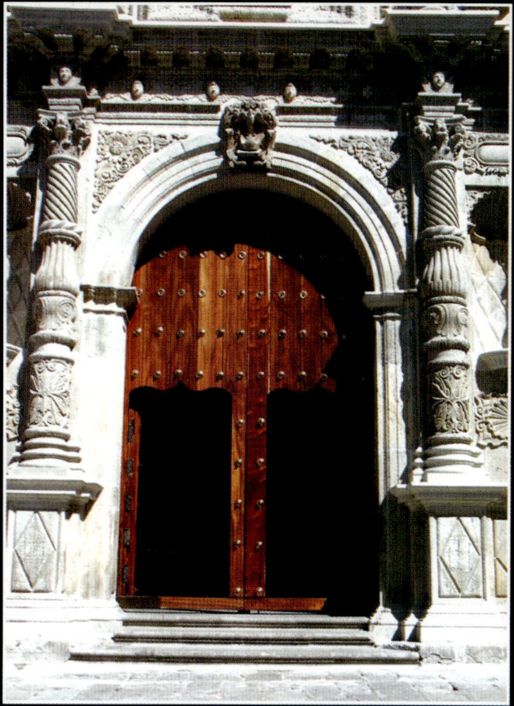

The Southwest entrance to the Iglesia de la Soledad (the Church of loneliness) on Independencia Street.

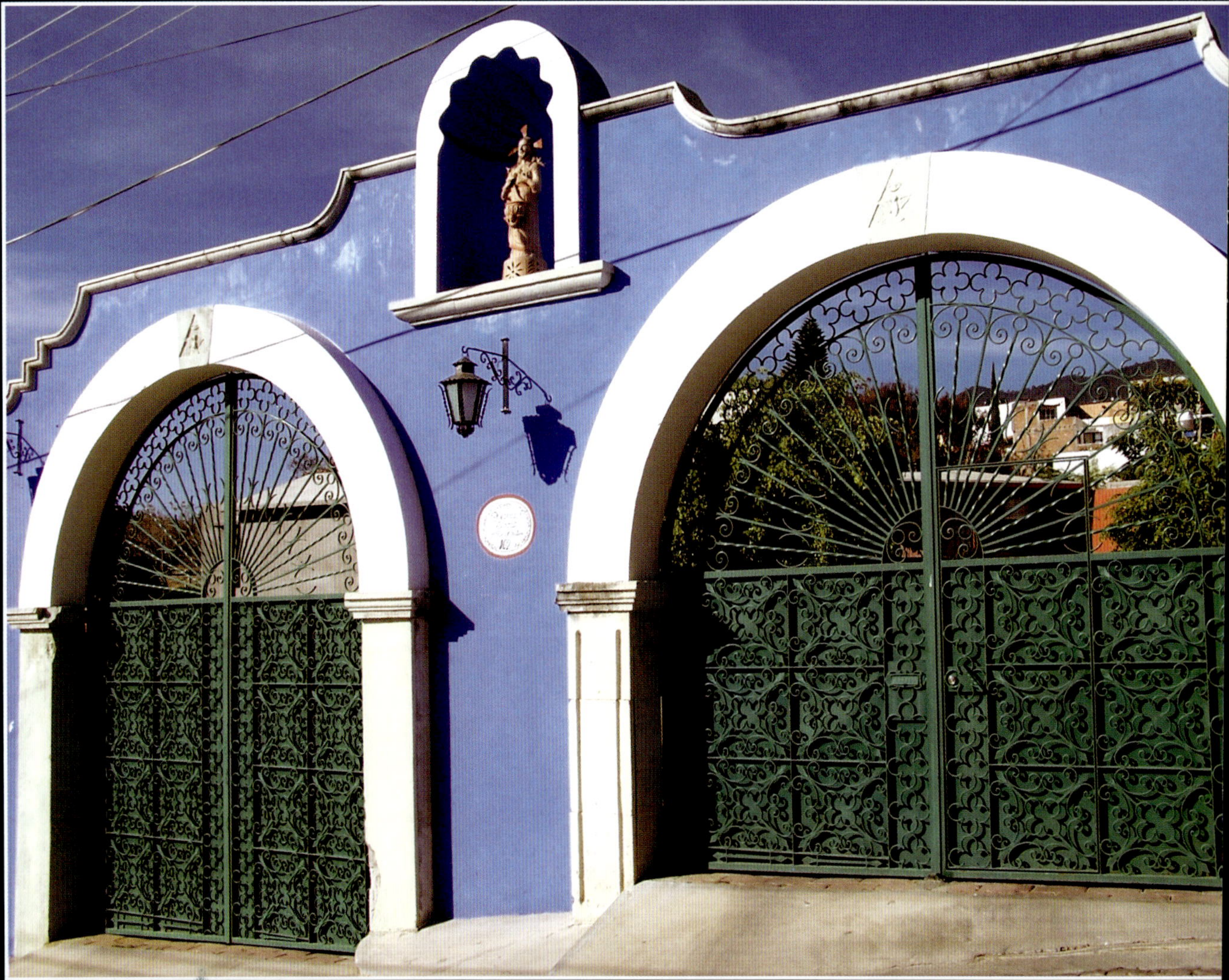

A home in San Felipe del Agua (Saint Philip of Water).

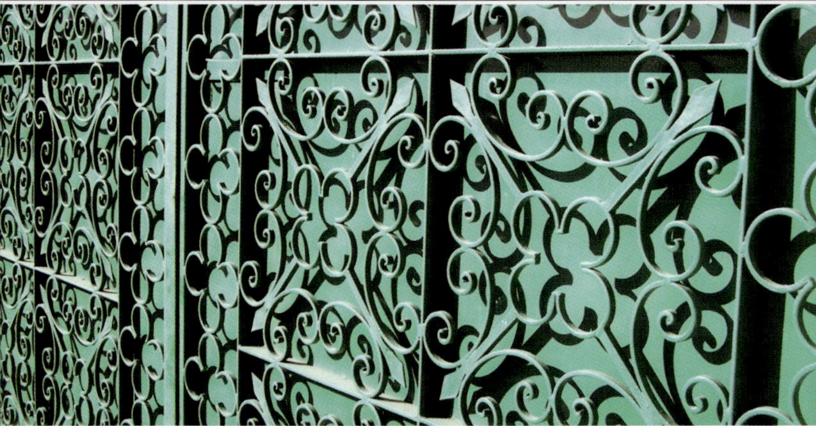
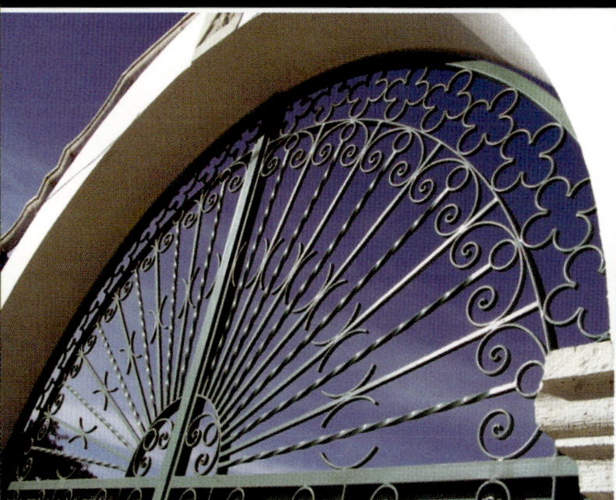
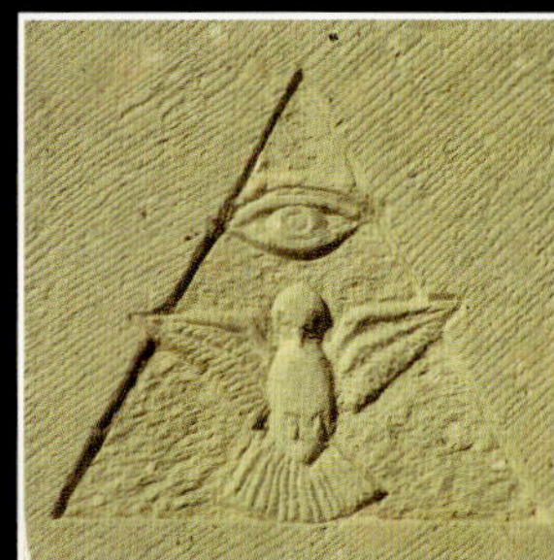
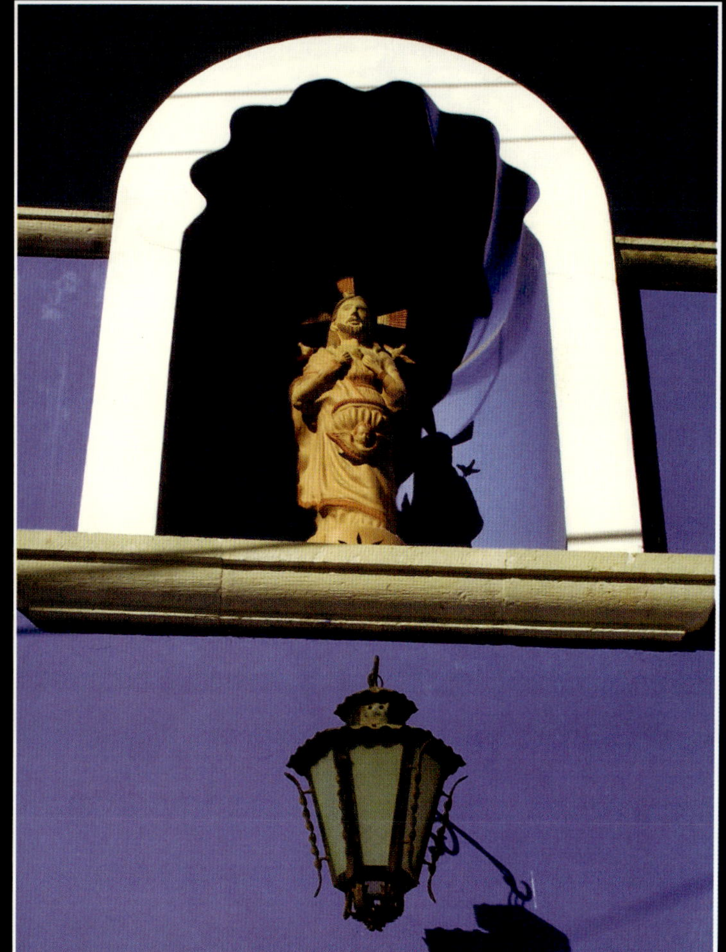

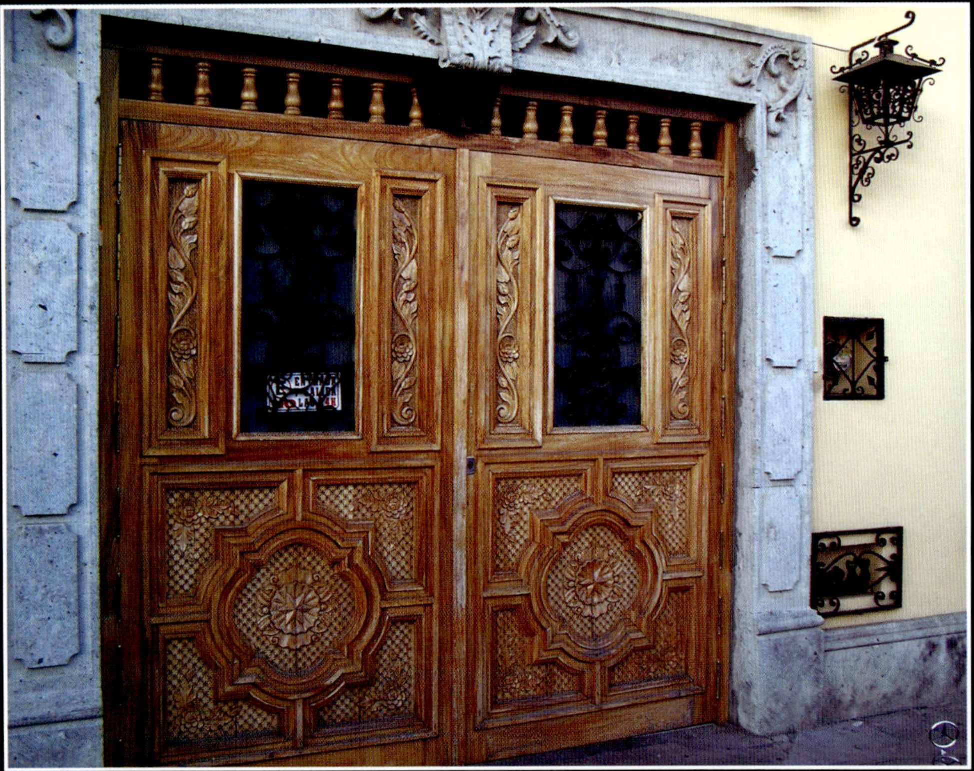

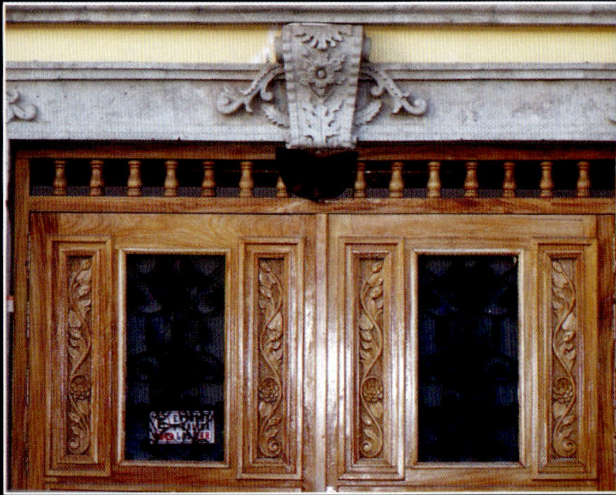

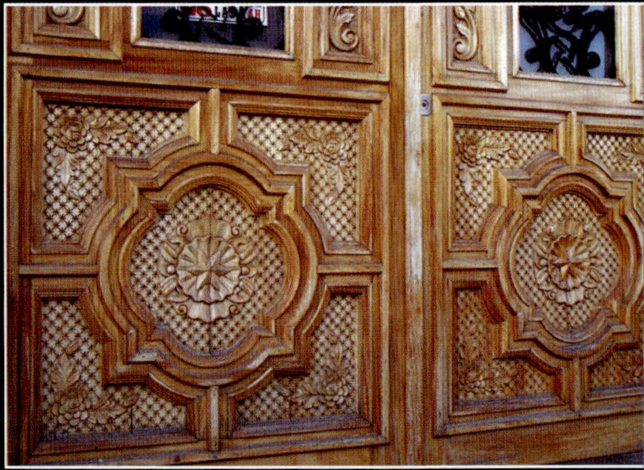

This home is located on Guerrero Street and Manuel Doblado Street, near the Merced Church.

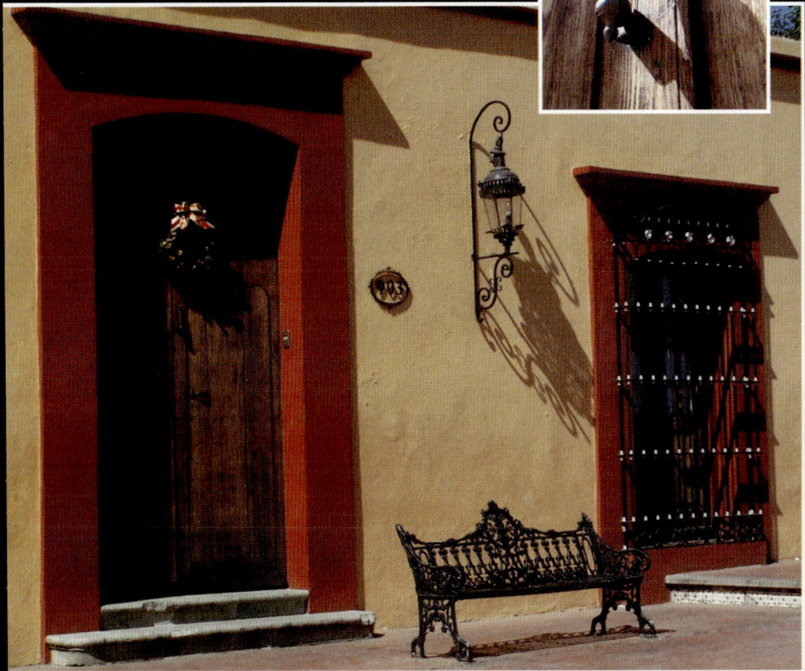

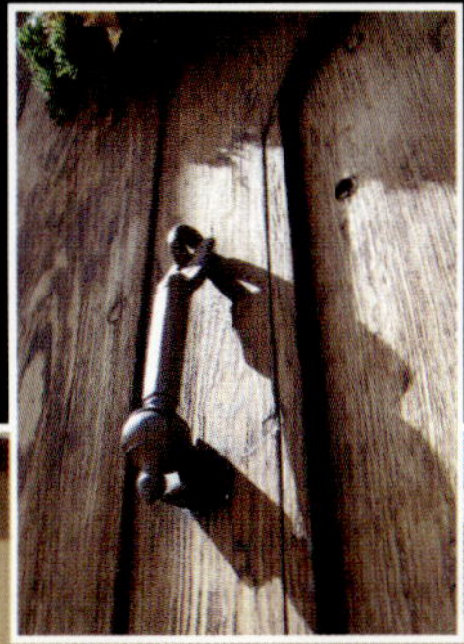

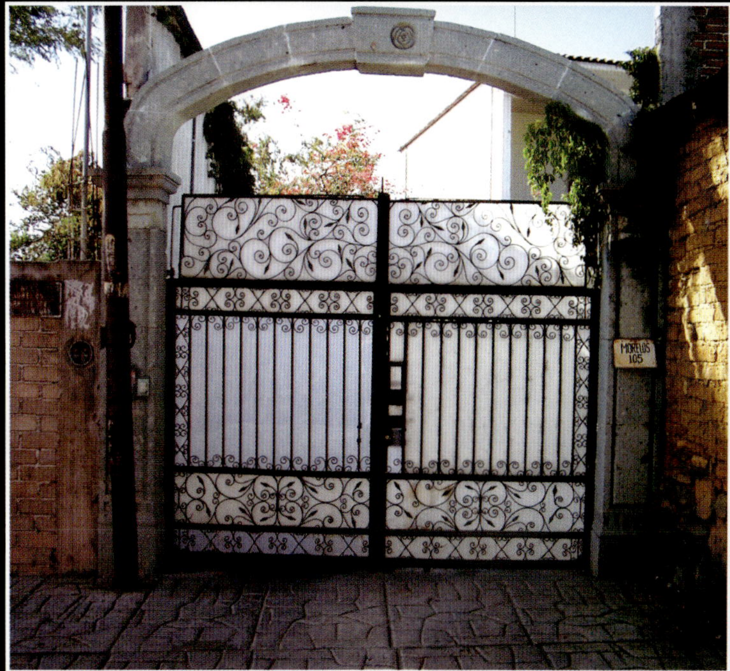
MORELOS
105

Building located on the busy Avenida Juárez.

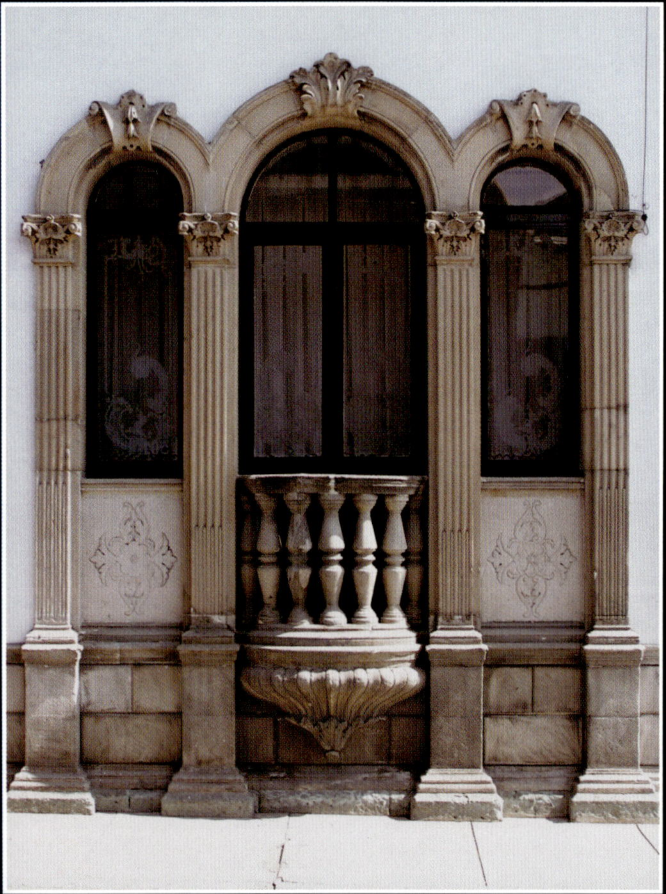

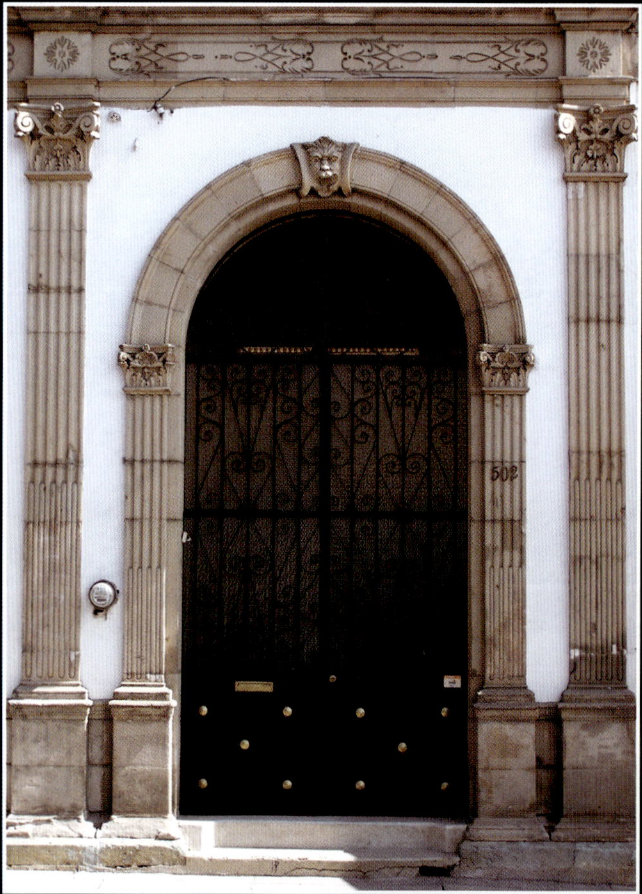

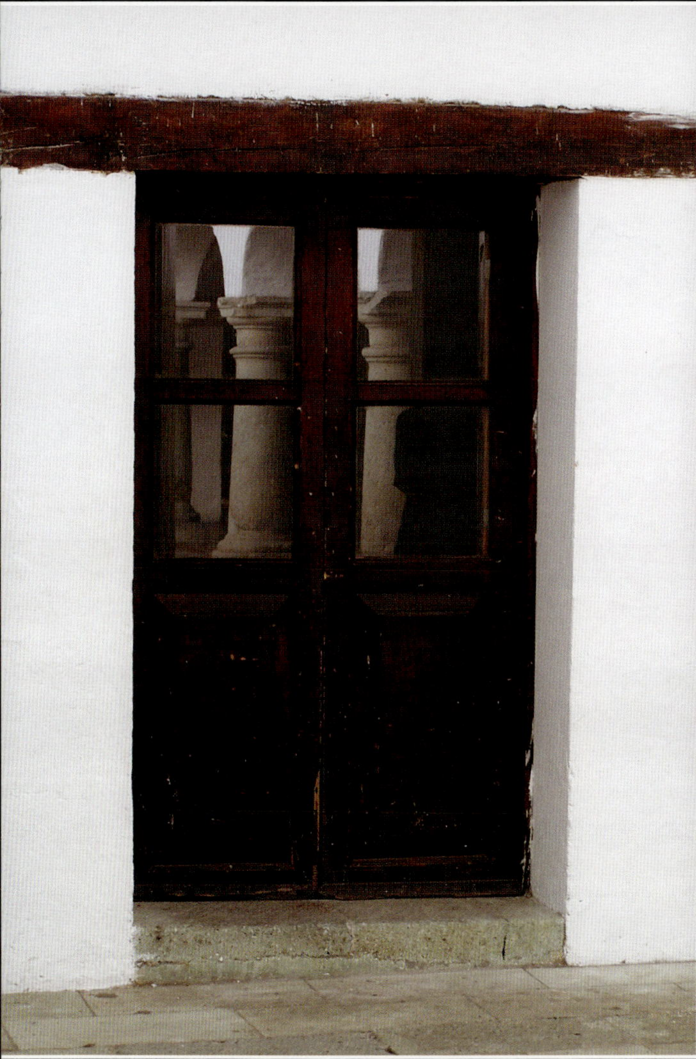

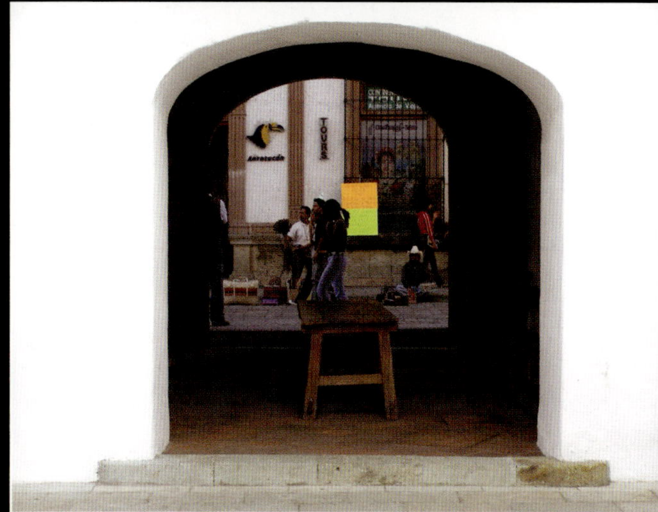

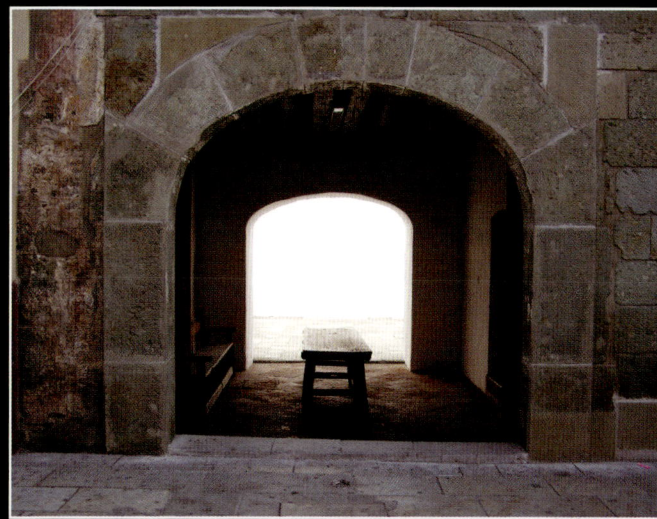

These doors belong to a museum called the Hernán Cortés House, located on the main pedestrian street, Alcalá.

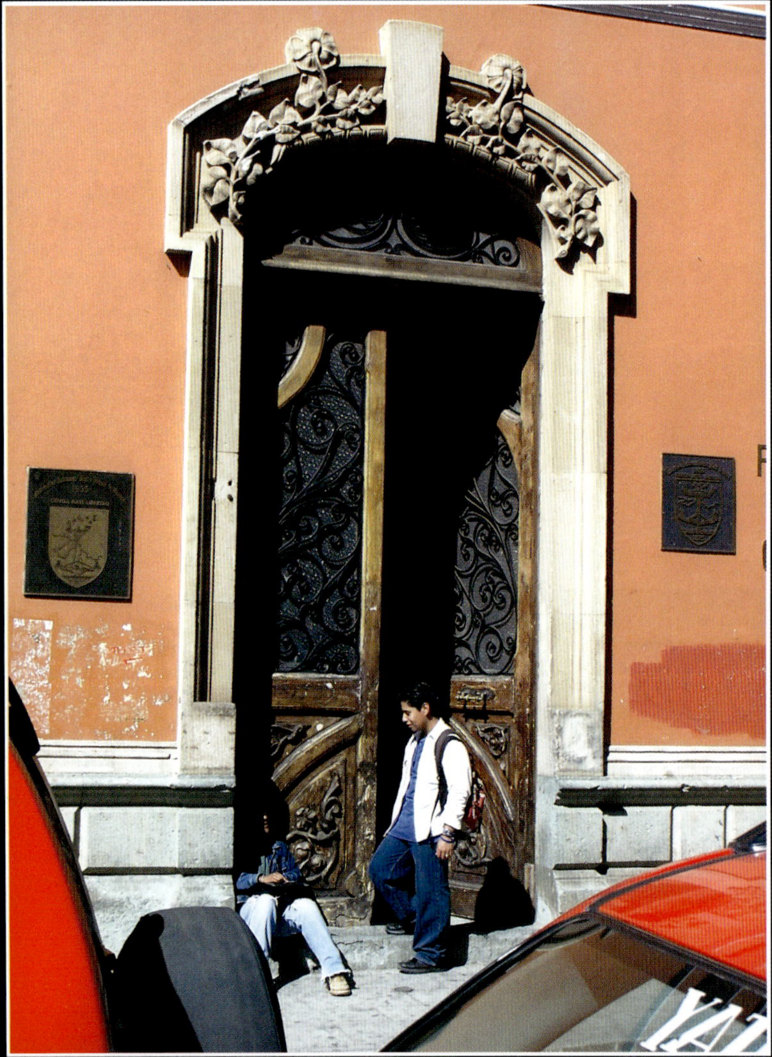

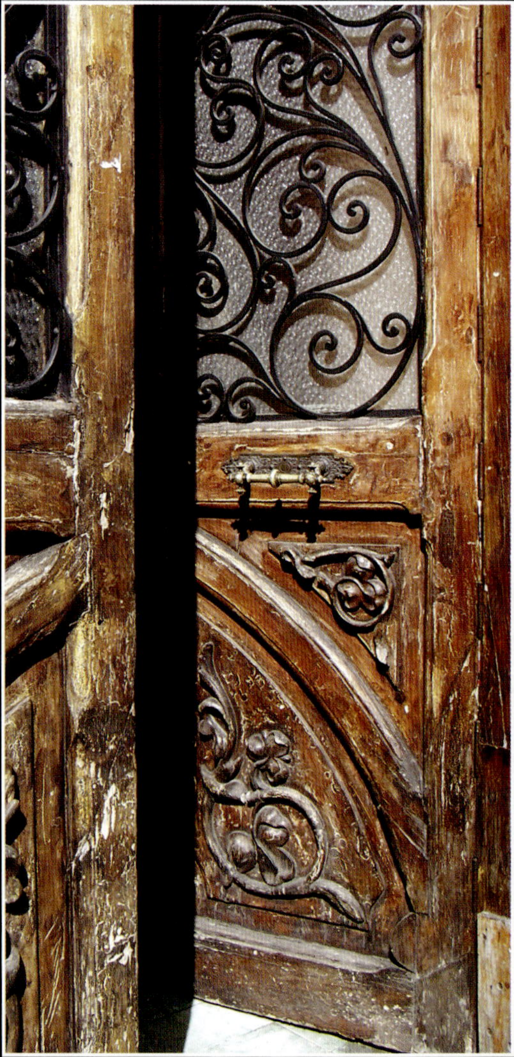

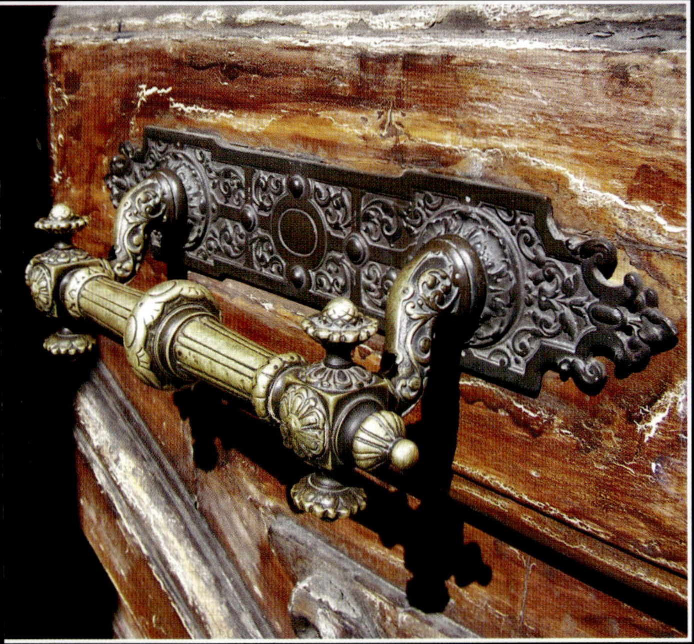

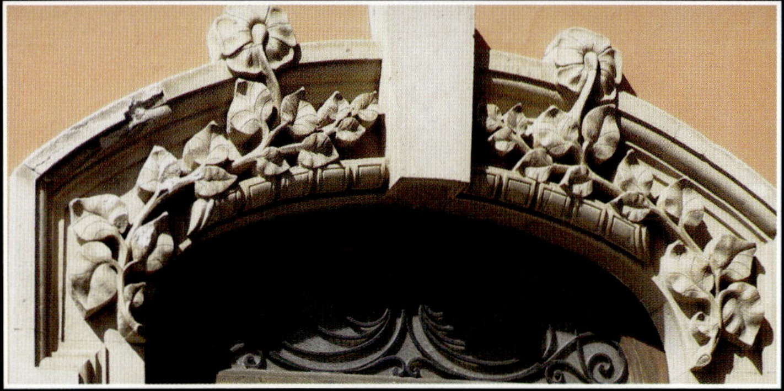

This is a school of fine arts, located on the corner of Cinco de Mayo Street and Morelos Street.

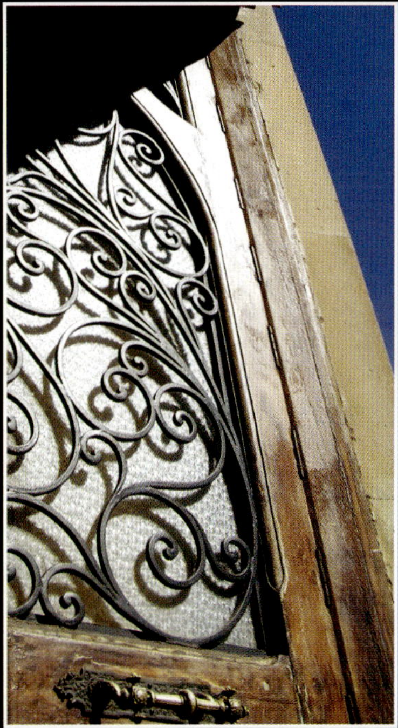

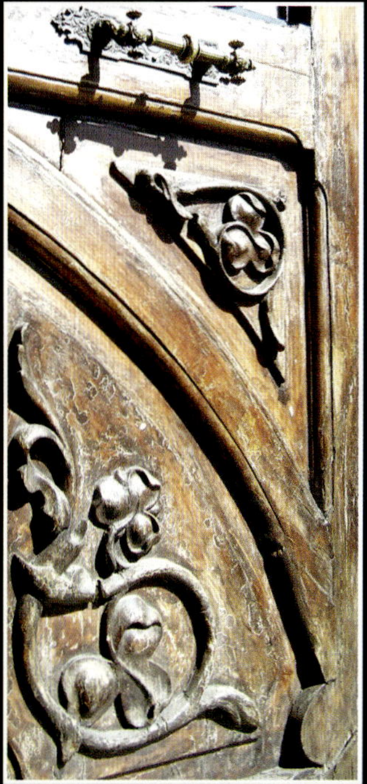

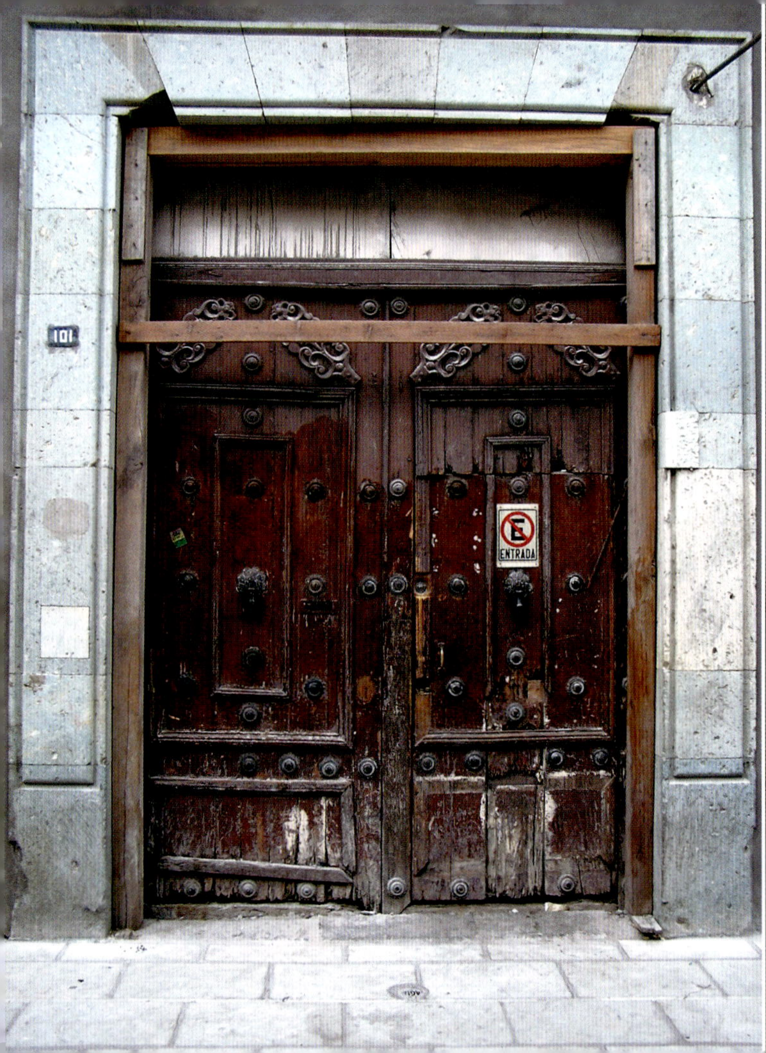
101
E
ENTRADA

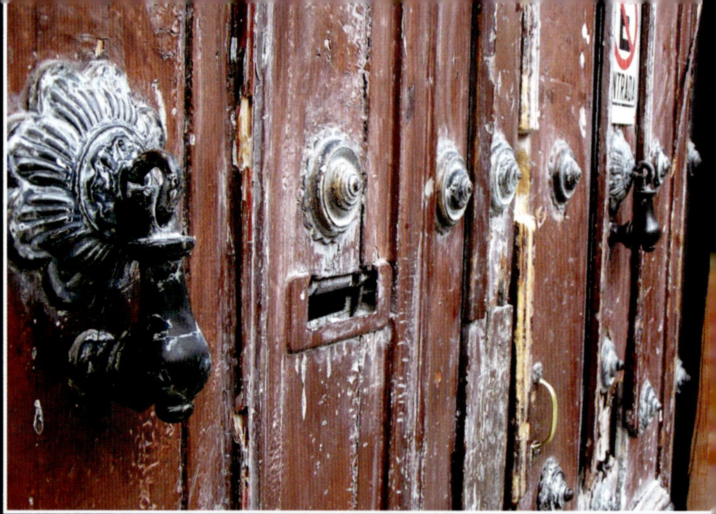

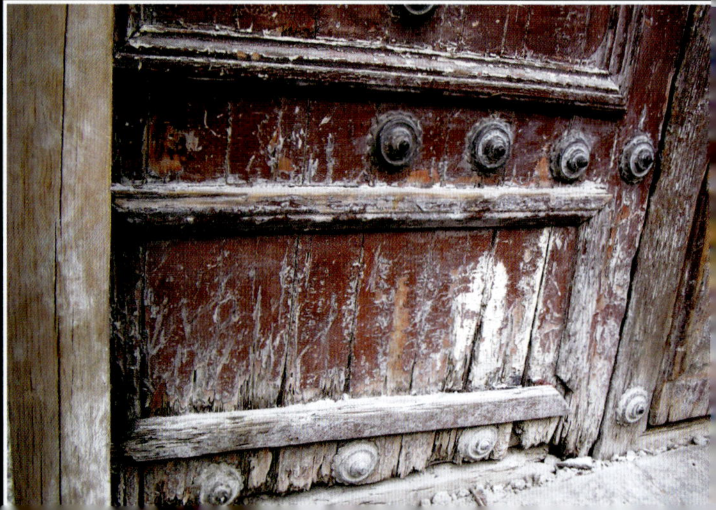

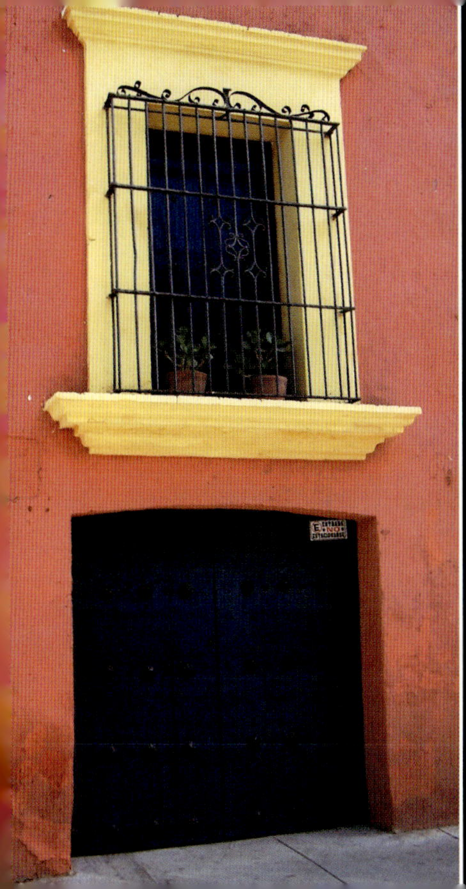

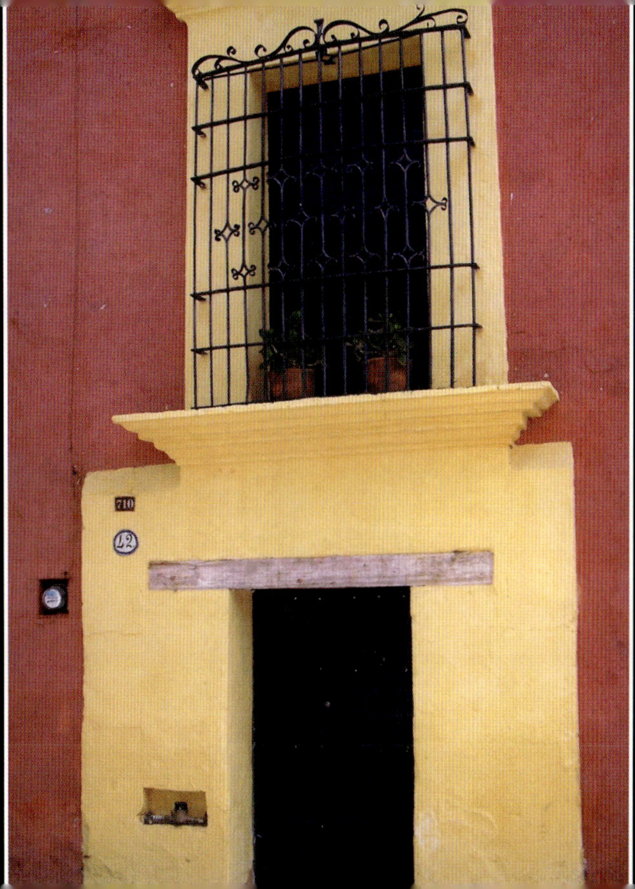
710
12

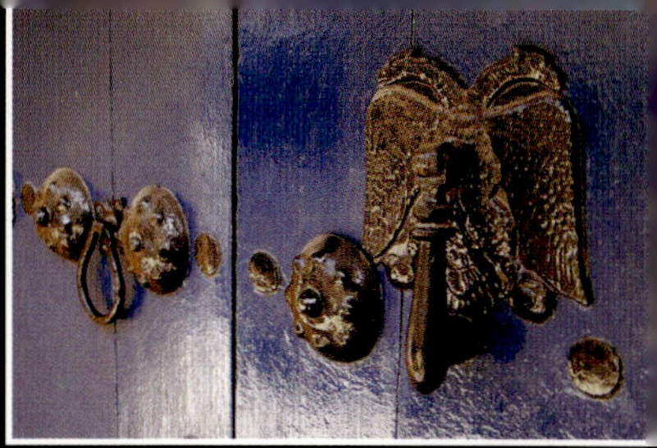

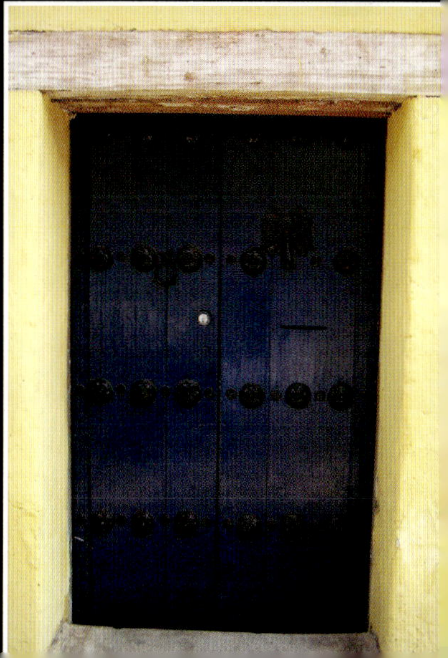

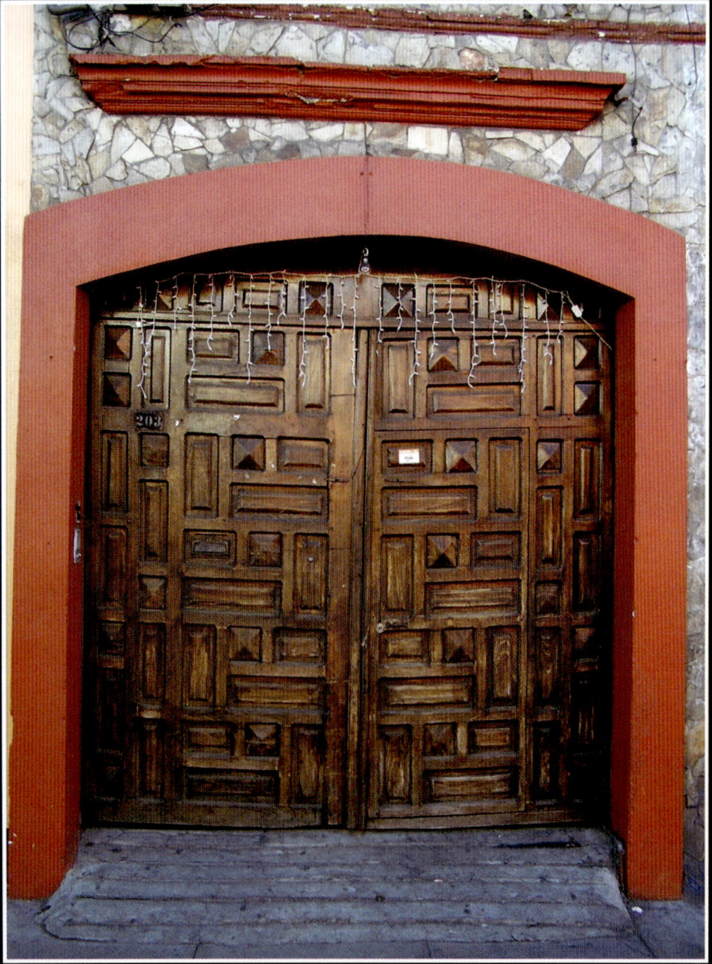

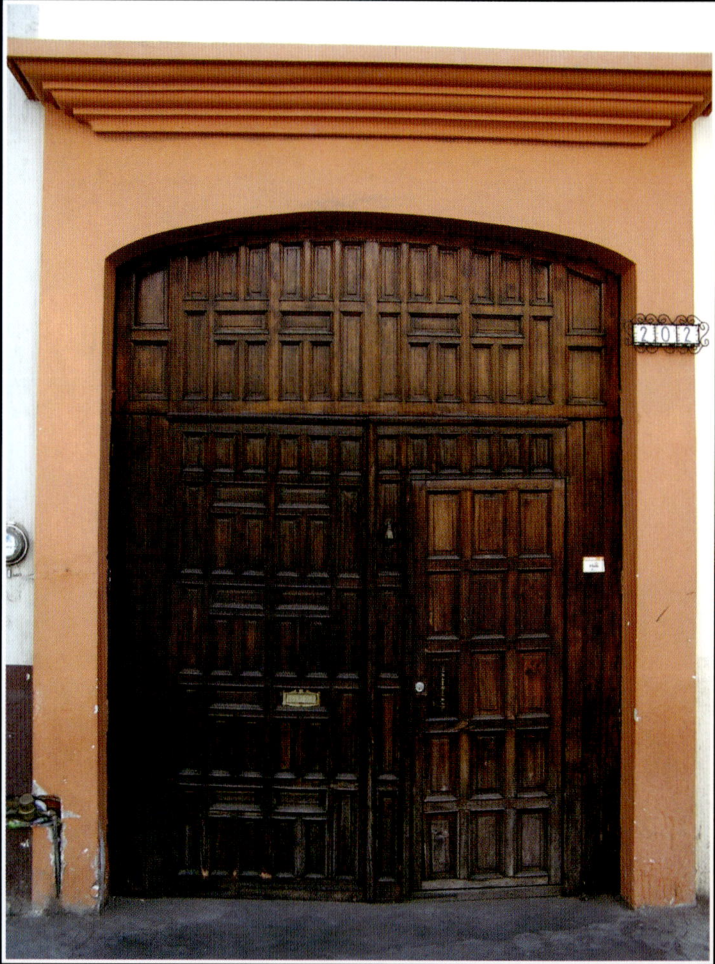

203 Xicotencatl Street.

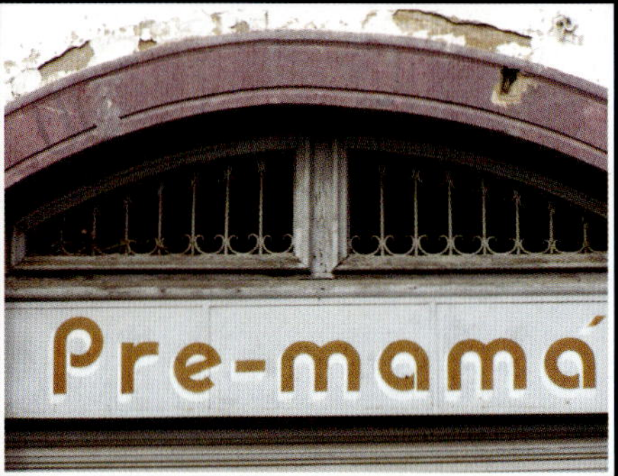

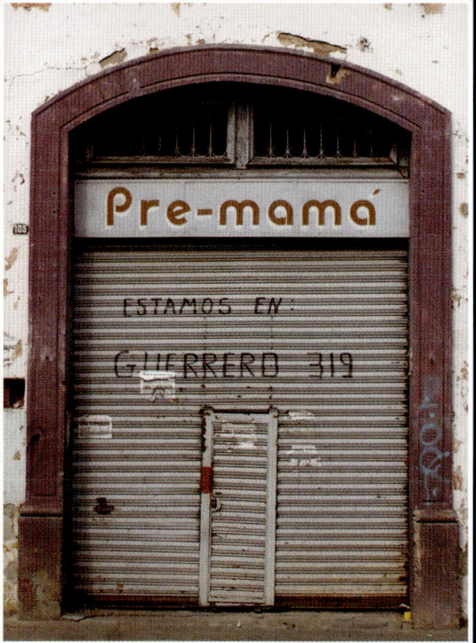

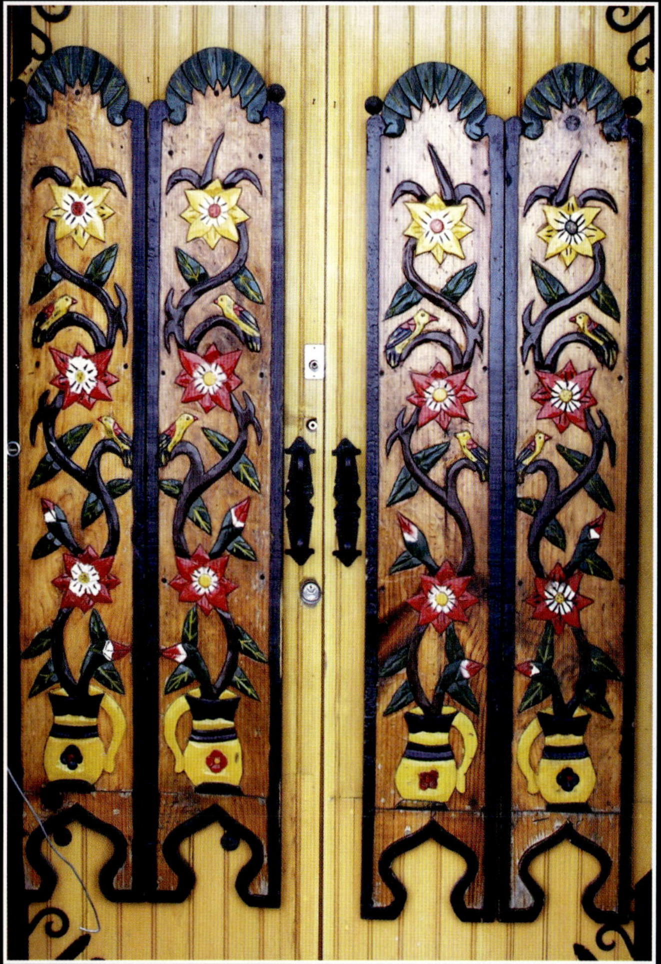

A once maternity shop located on Colón Street.

A jewelry and craft shop located on Cinco de Mayo, just South of the Santo Domingo Church.

Formerly the convent of the San José Church, The Instituto de Bellas Artes (Institute of Beautiful Arts) located on Morelos Street, across from the municipal plaza.

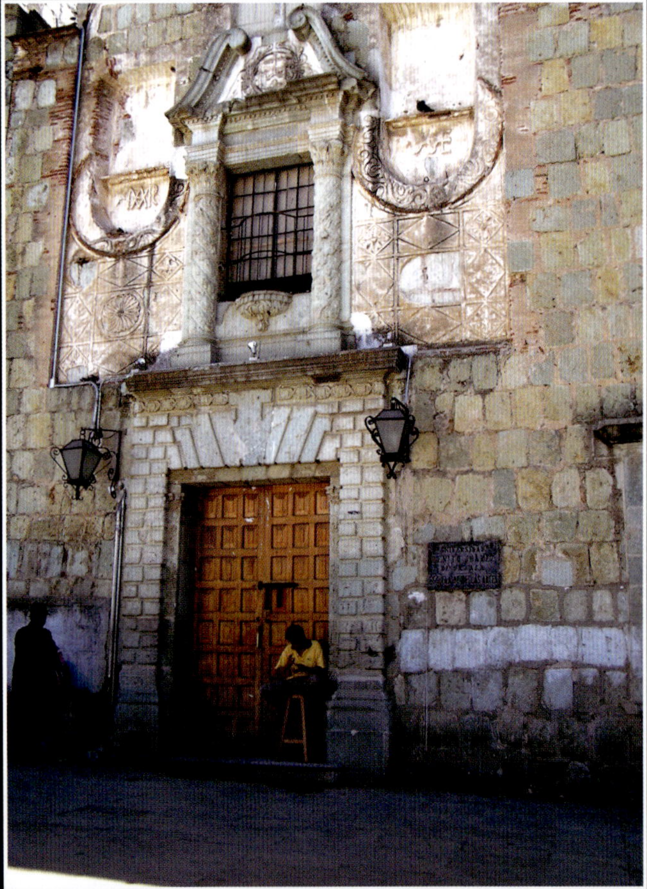

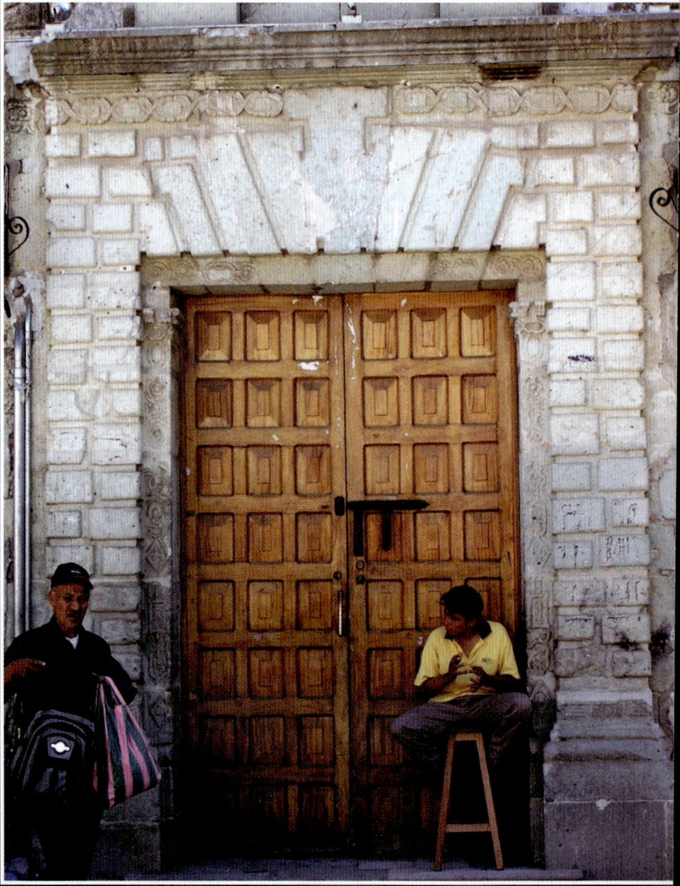

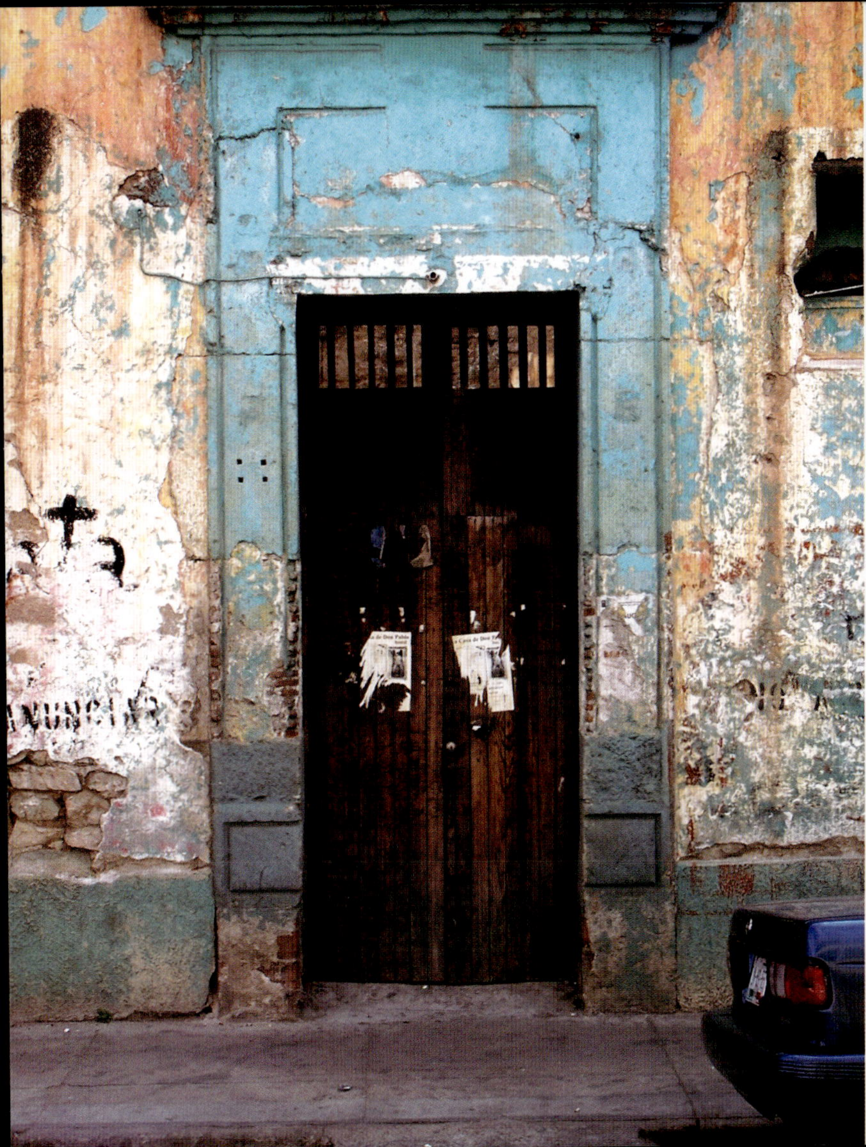

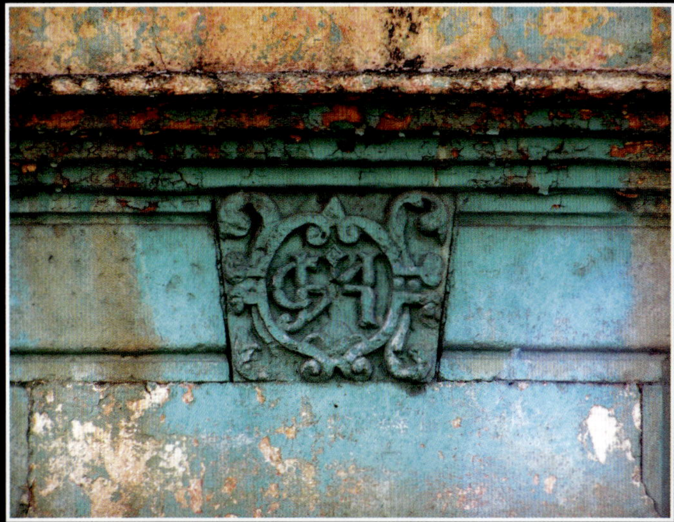

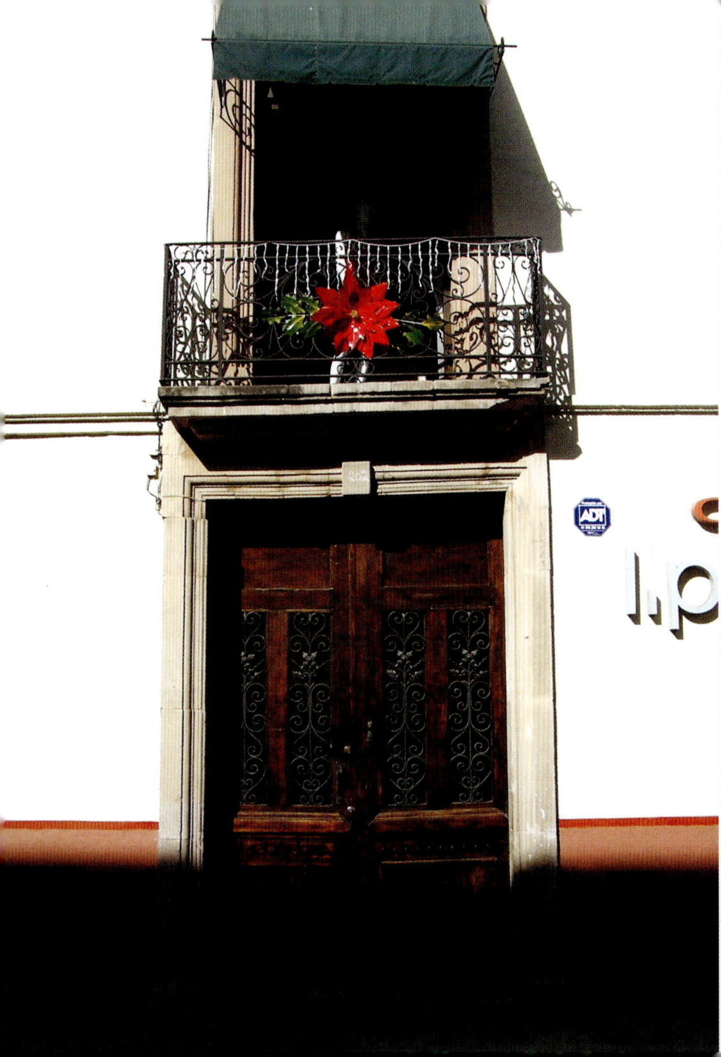

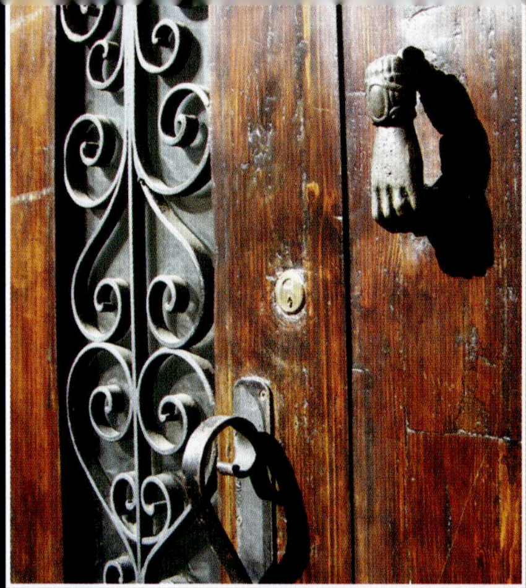

Located on Guerrero Street, across from the San Agustín Church.

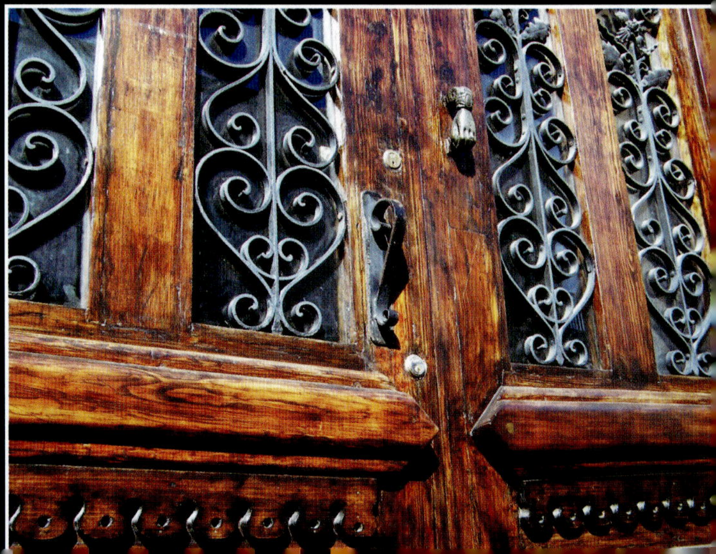

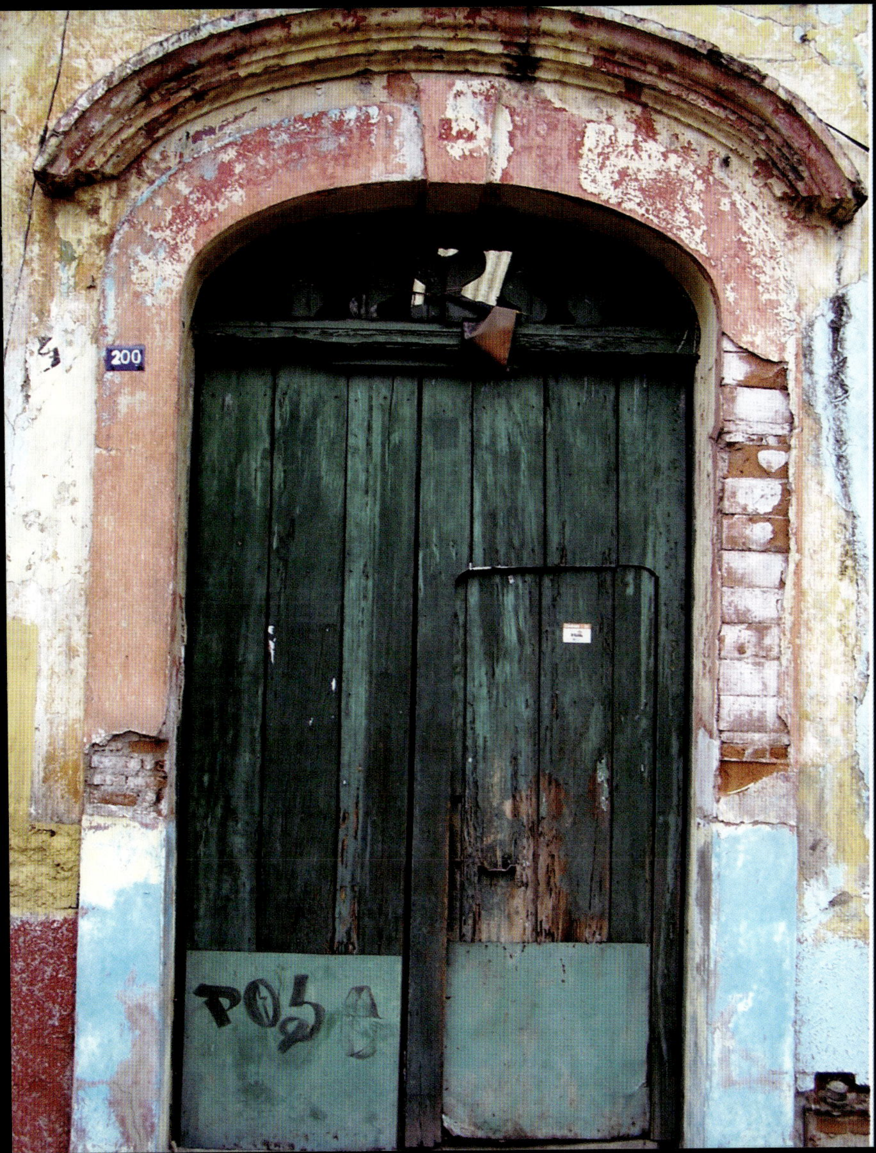

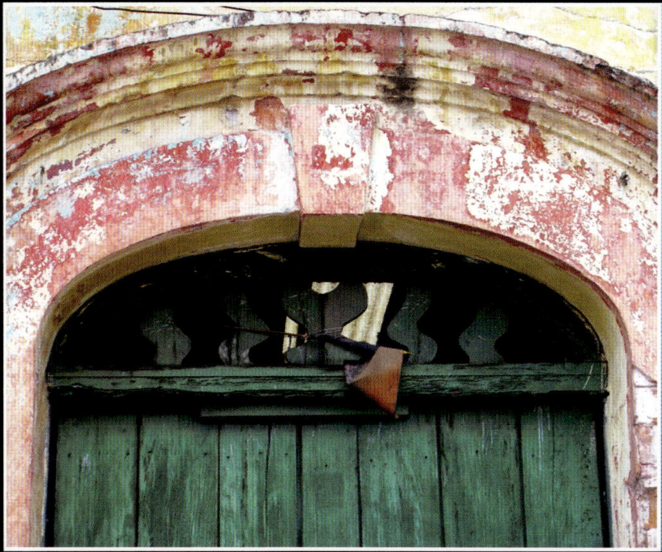

Located on Pino Suárez Street, the dark banner above the door symbolizes a family in mourning.

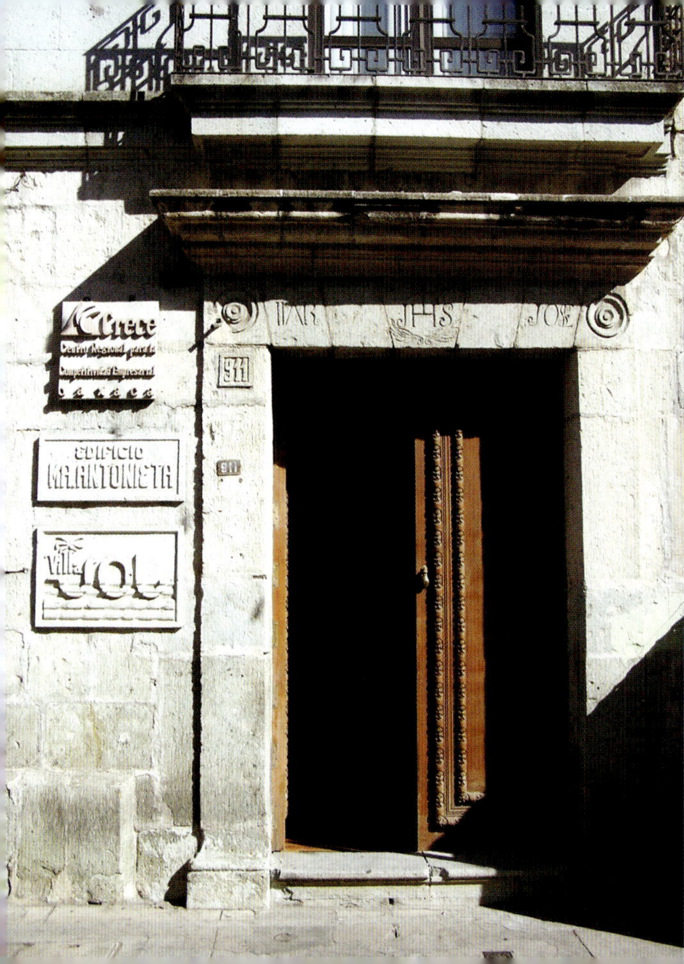

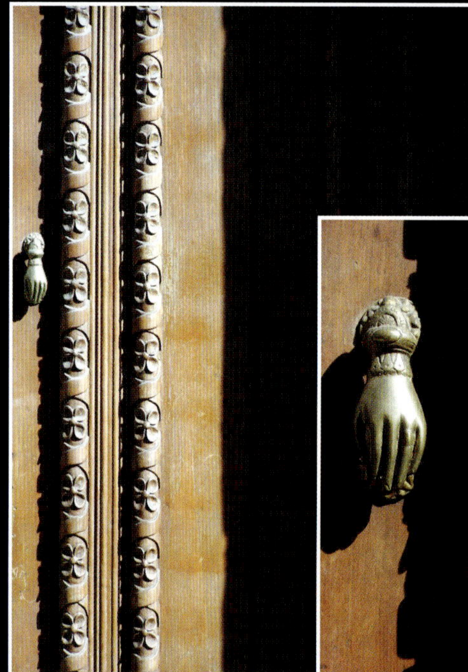

This building is named The María Antonieta.

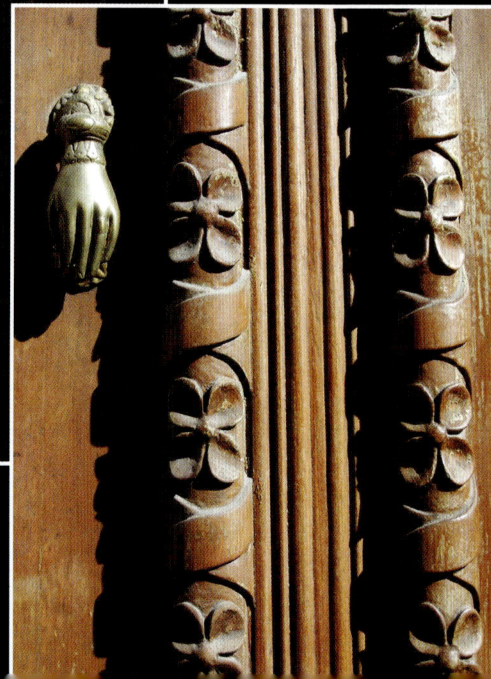

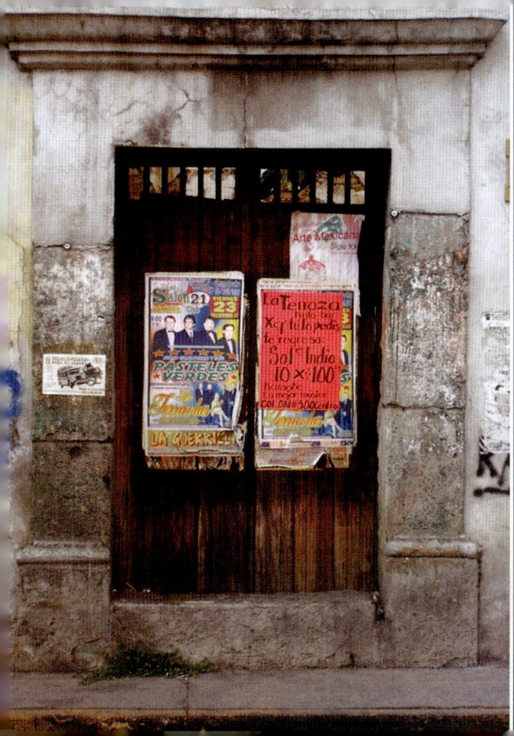

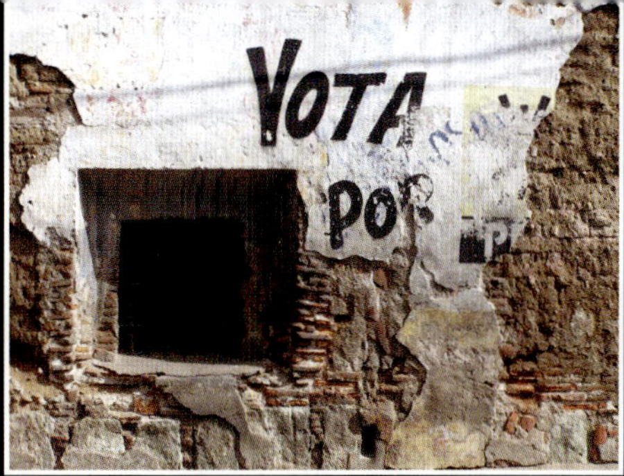

Photograph of the corner of Melchor Ocampo and Rayón Street.

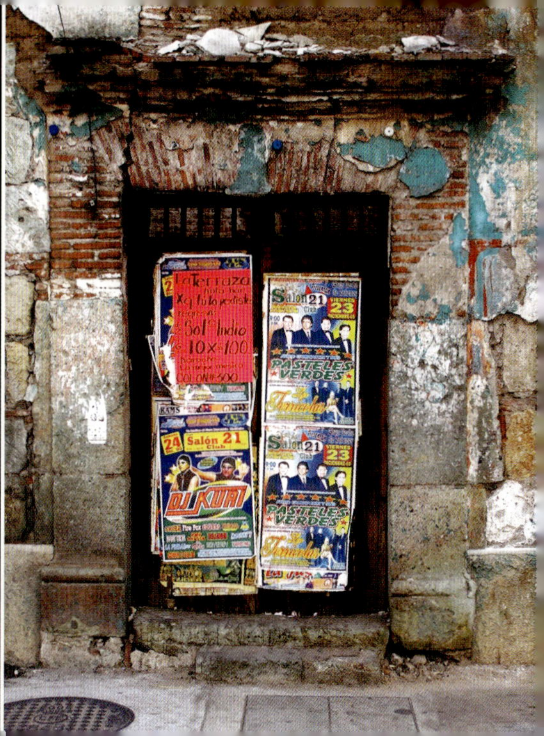

A fabric shop named Modatela, located on the corner of Colón Street and Armenta y López Street.

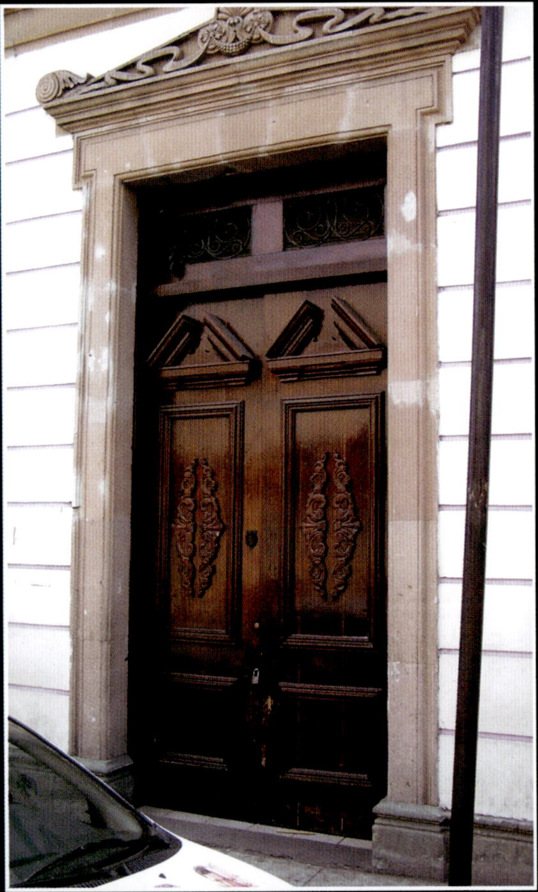

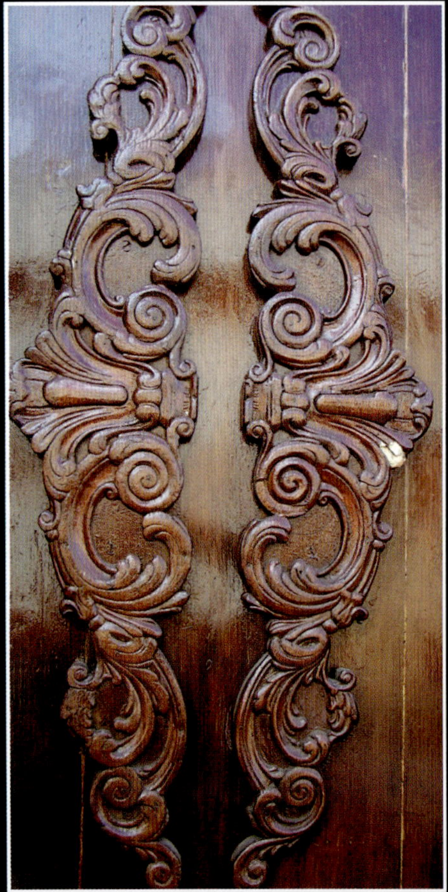

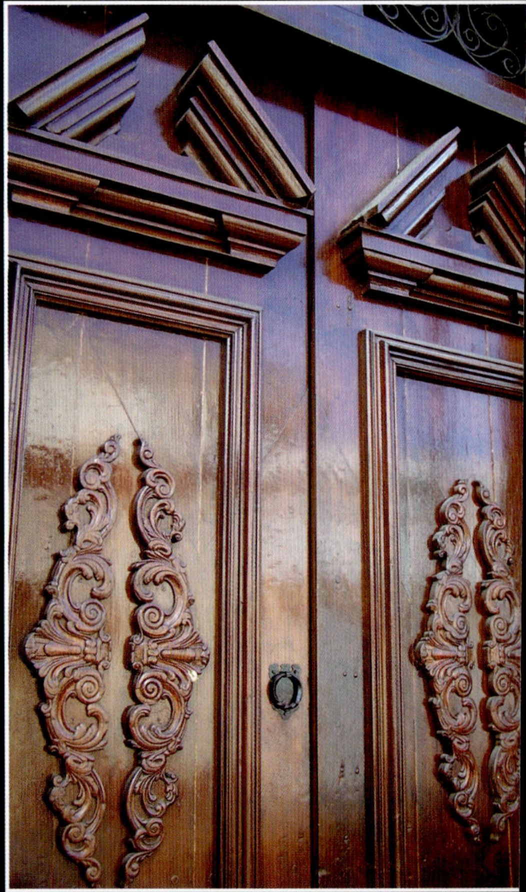

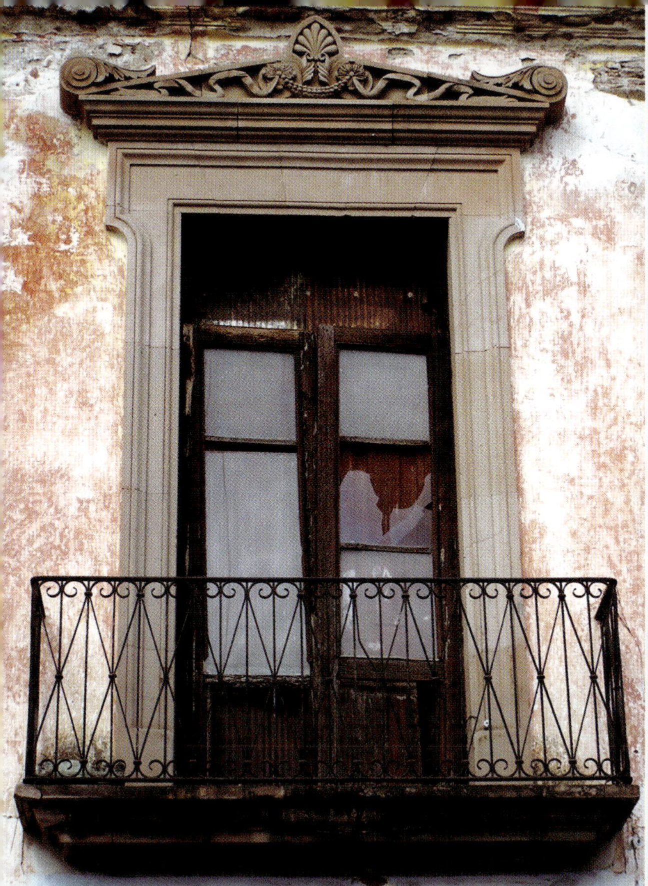

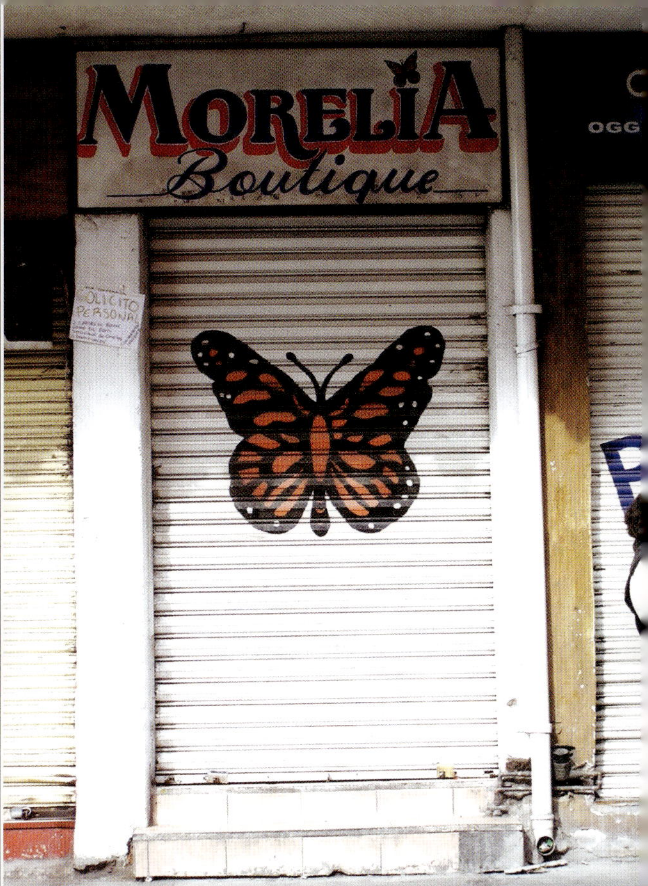
MORELIA
Boutique

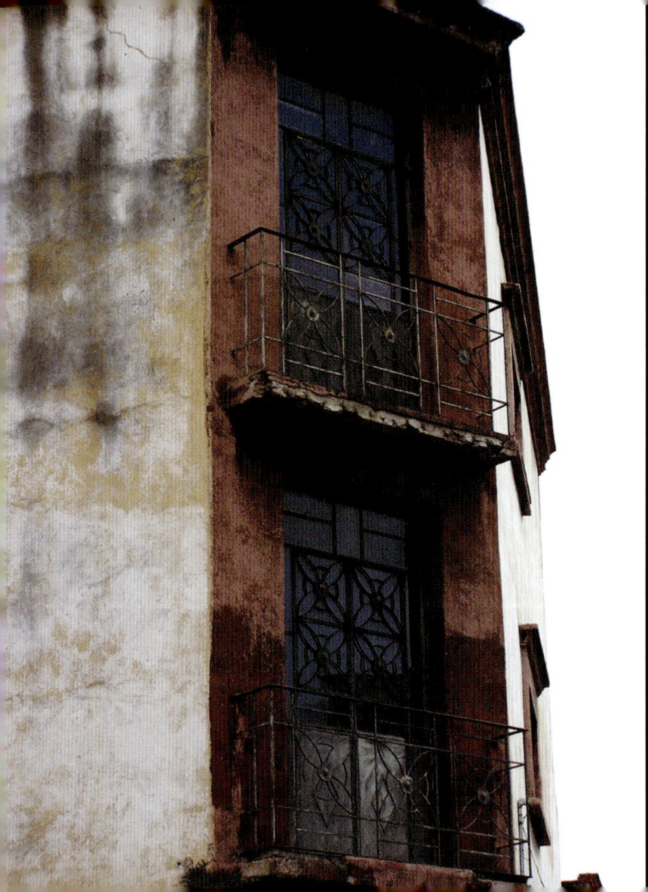

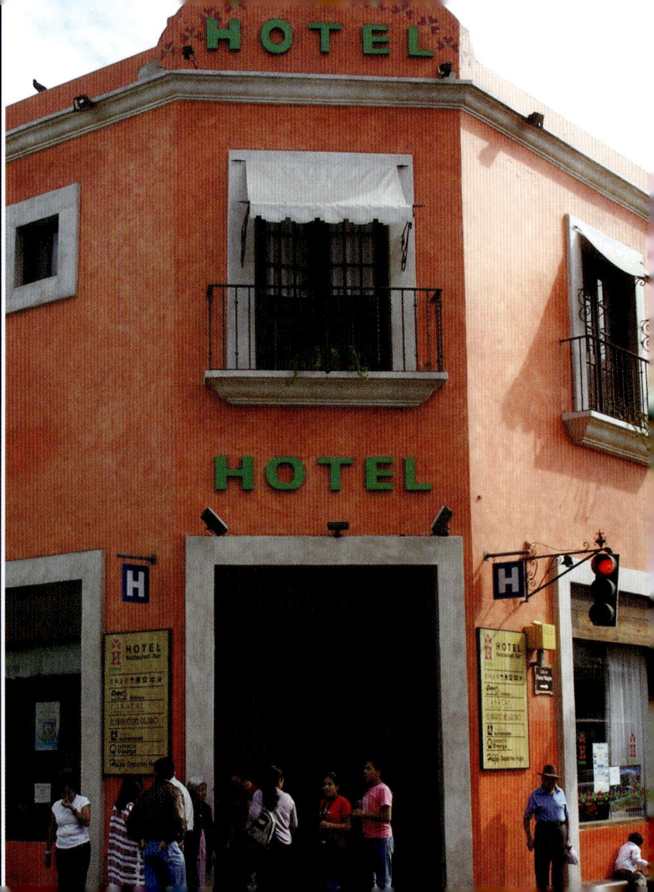
HOTEL
HOTEL
H
H

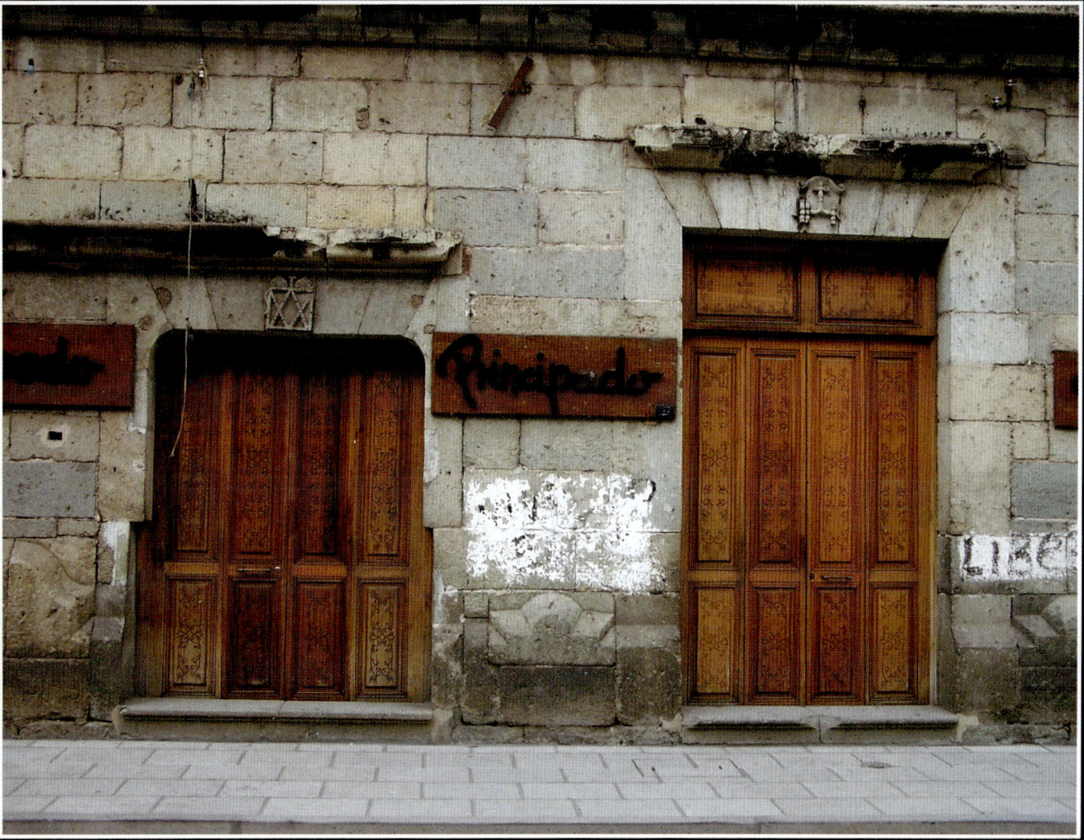

A well-known department store near the center plaza (el zócalo), named the Principado.

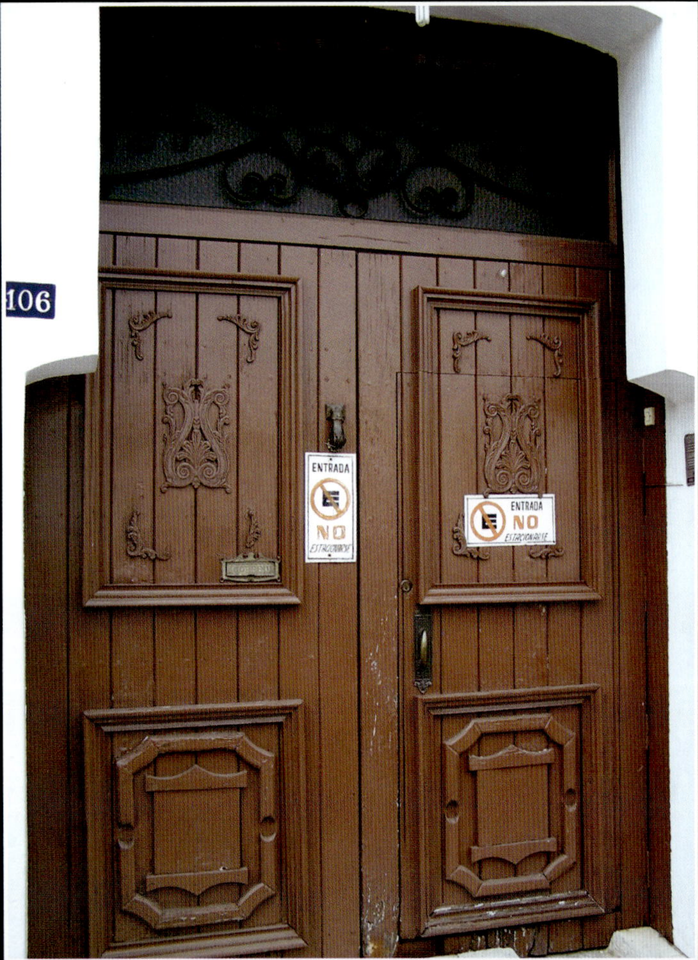
106
ENTRADA
NO
ESTACIONARSE
ENTRADA
NO
ESTACIONARSE

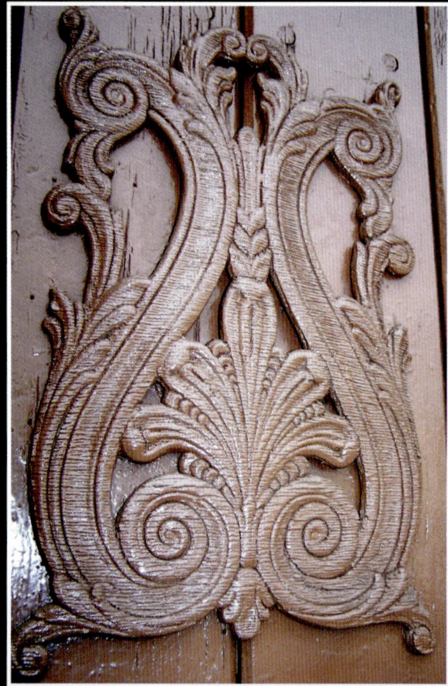

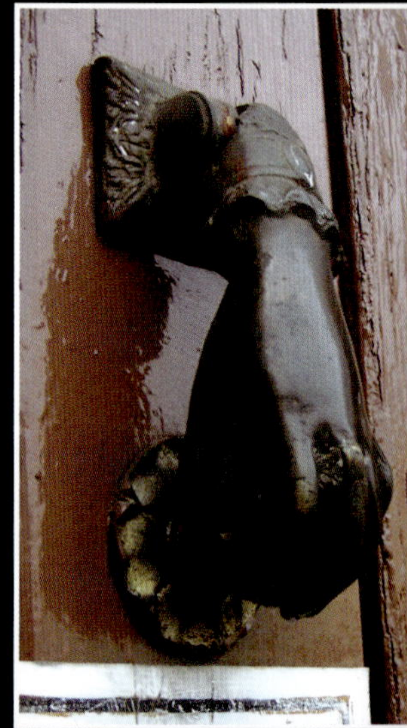

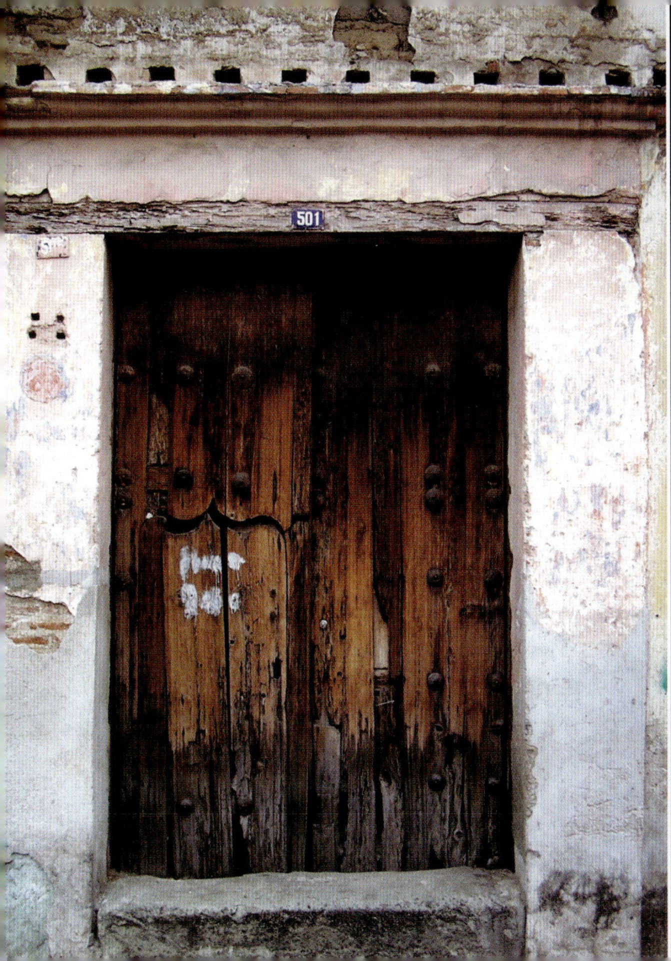
501

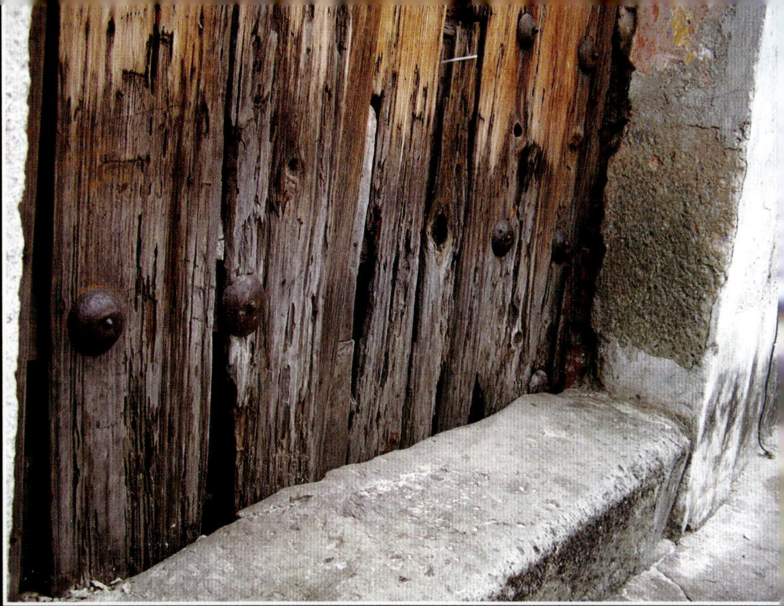

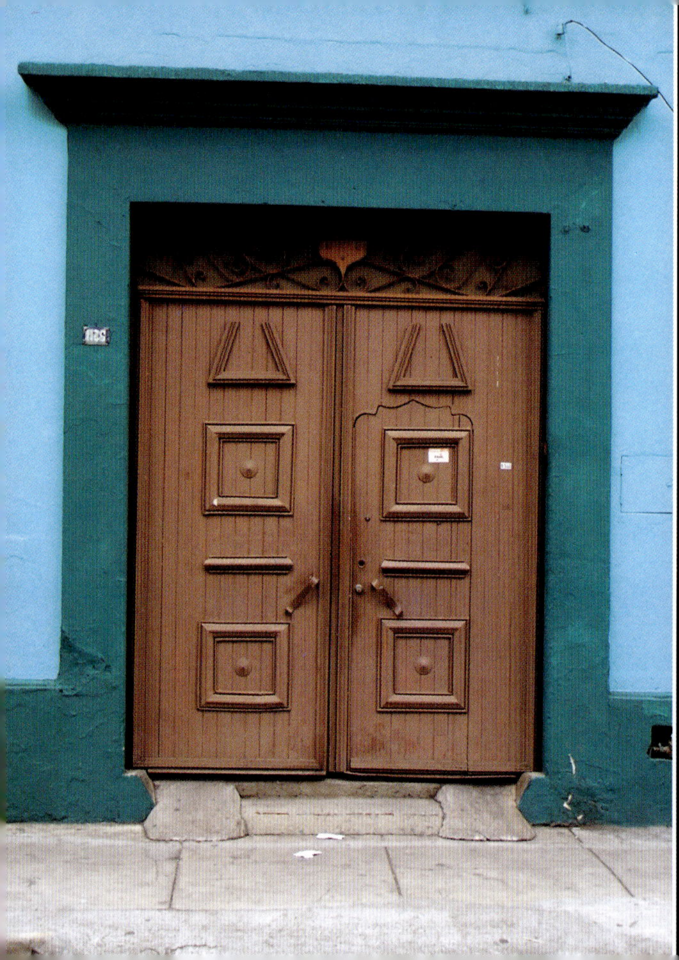

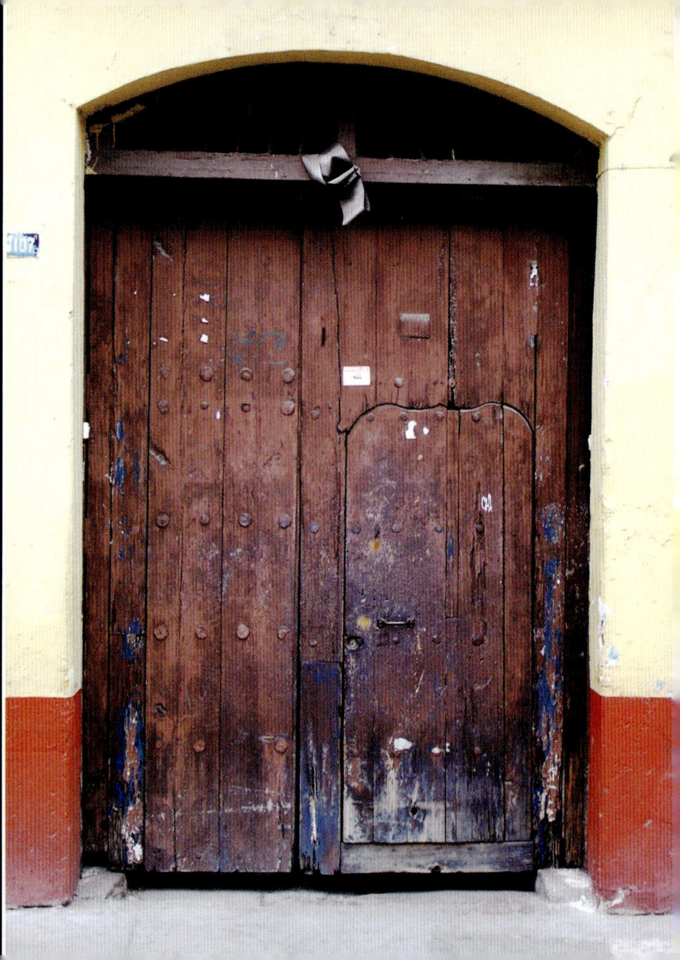

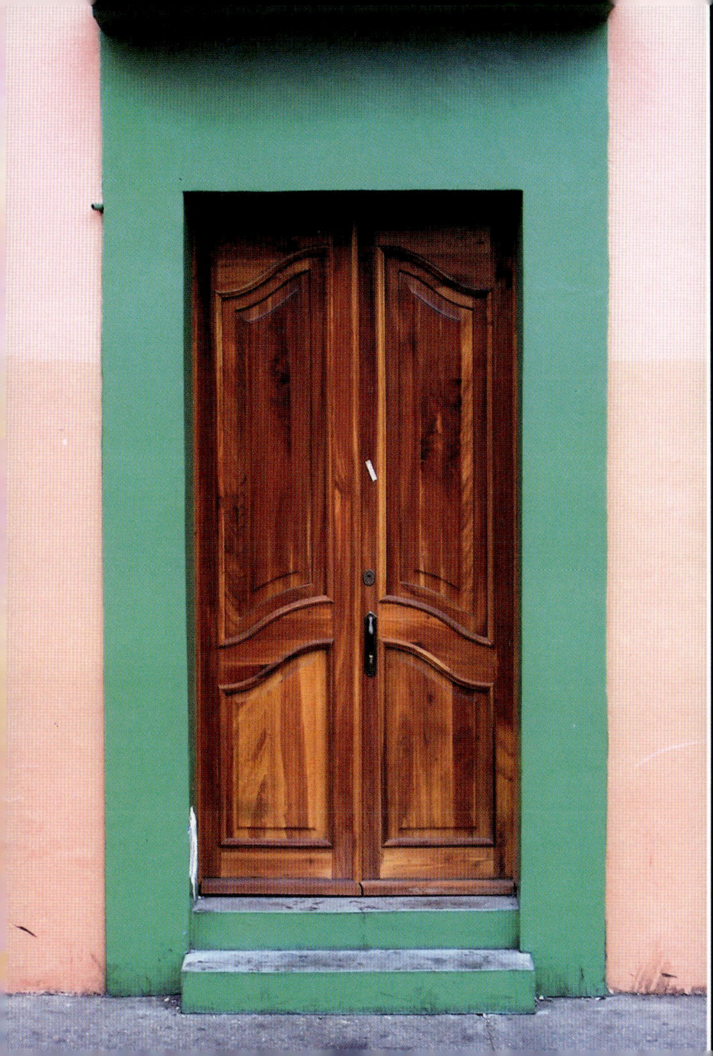
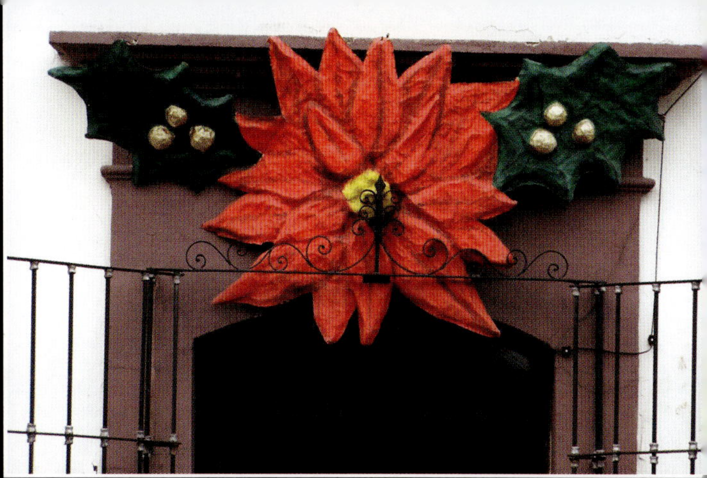
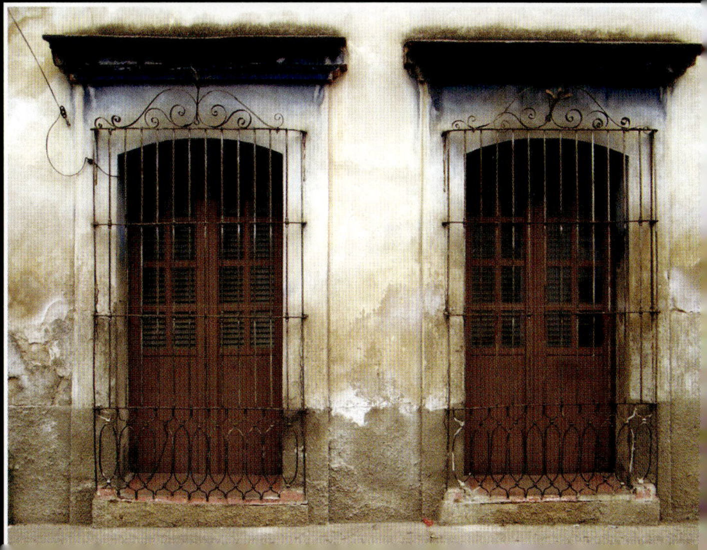

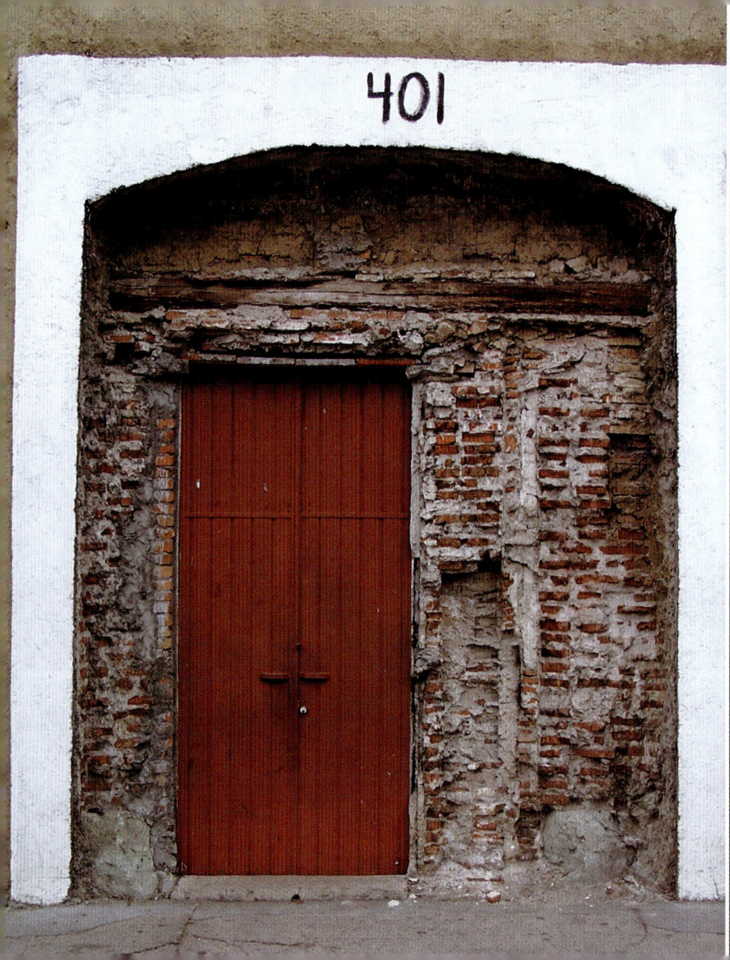
401

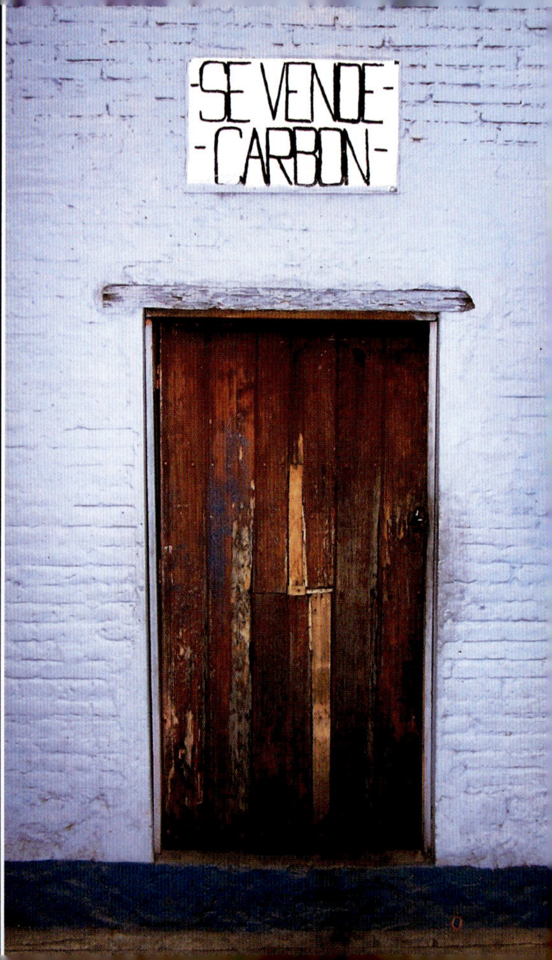
-SE VENDE-
-CARBON-

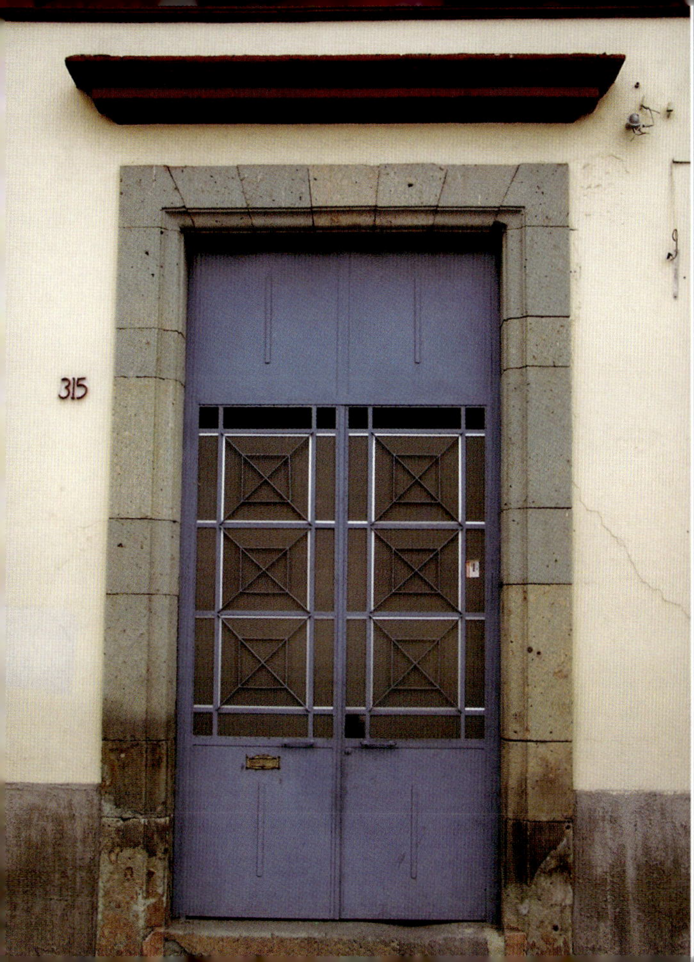
315

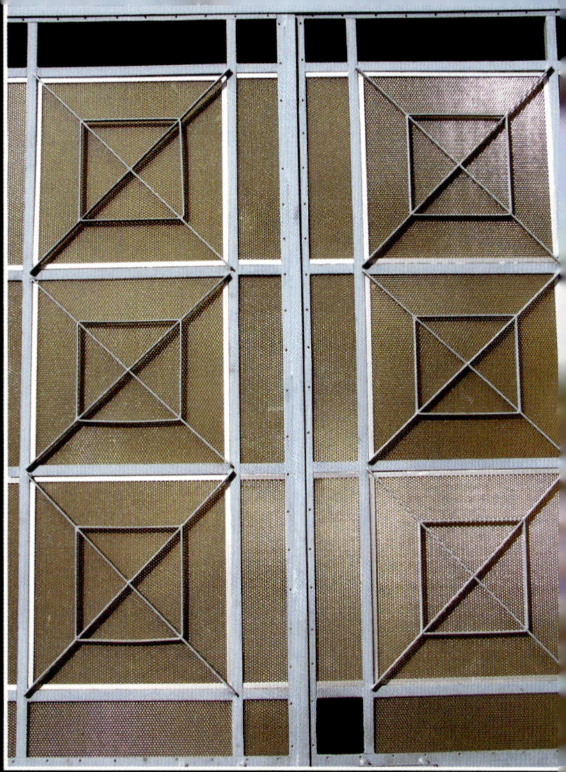

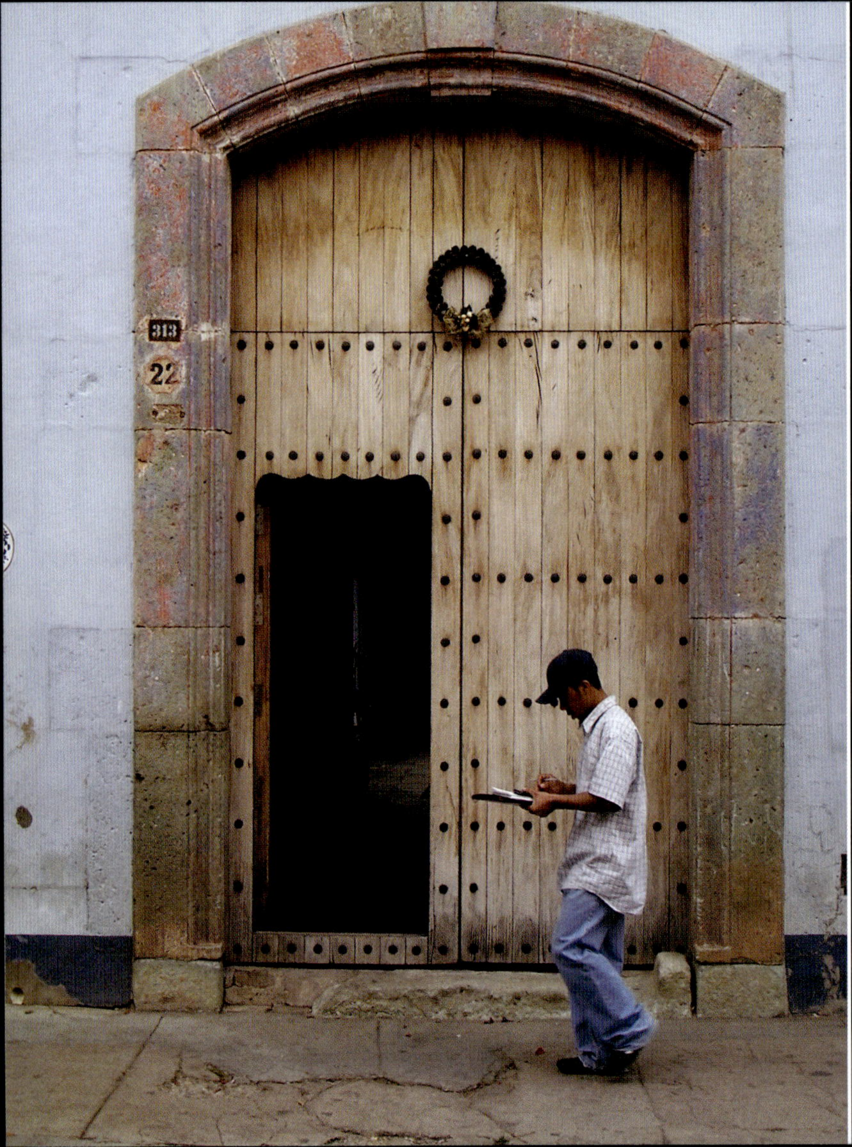
313
22
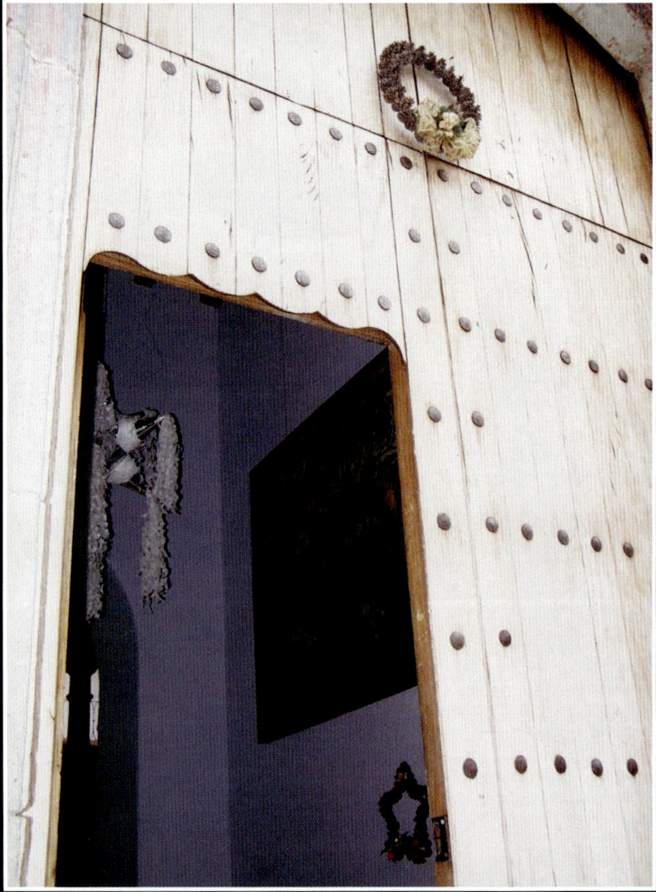

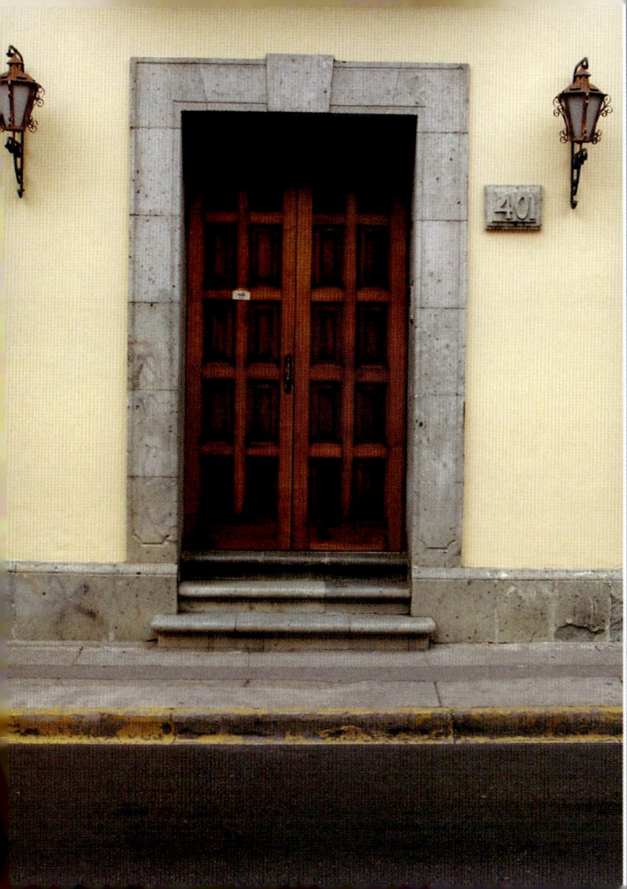
401

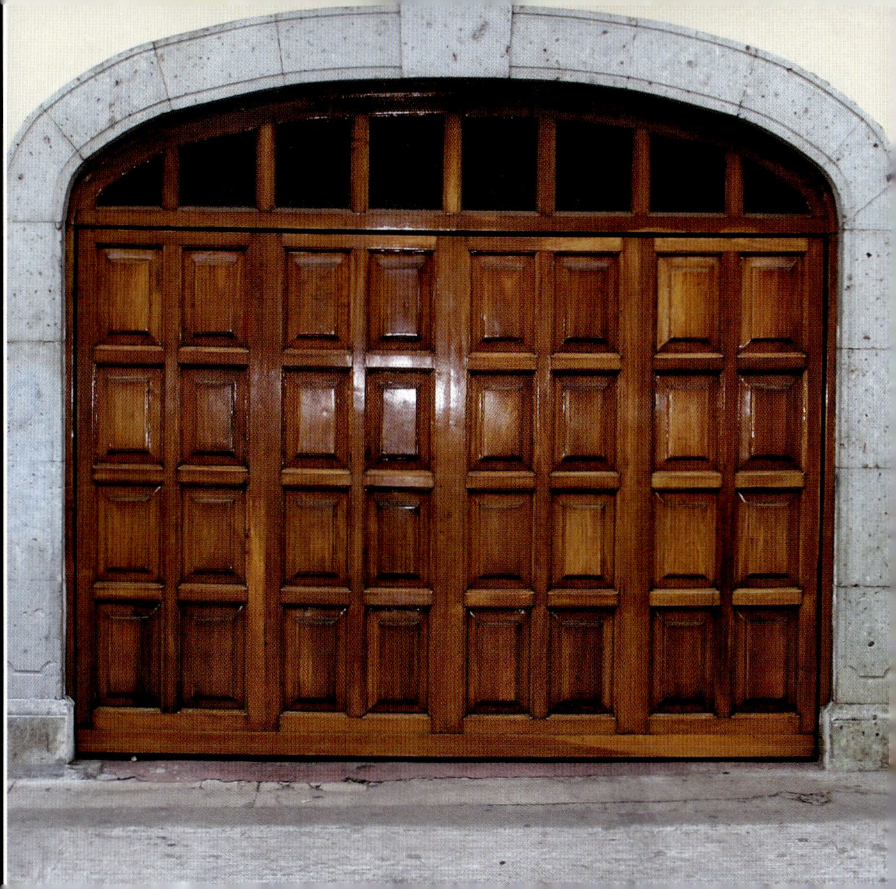

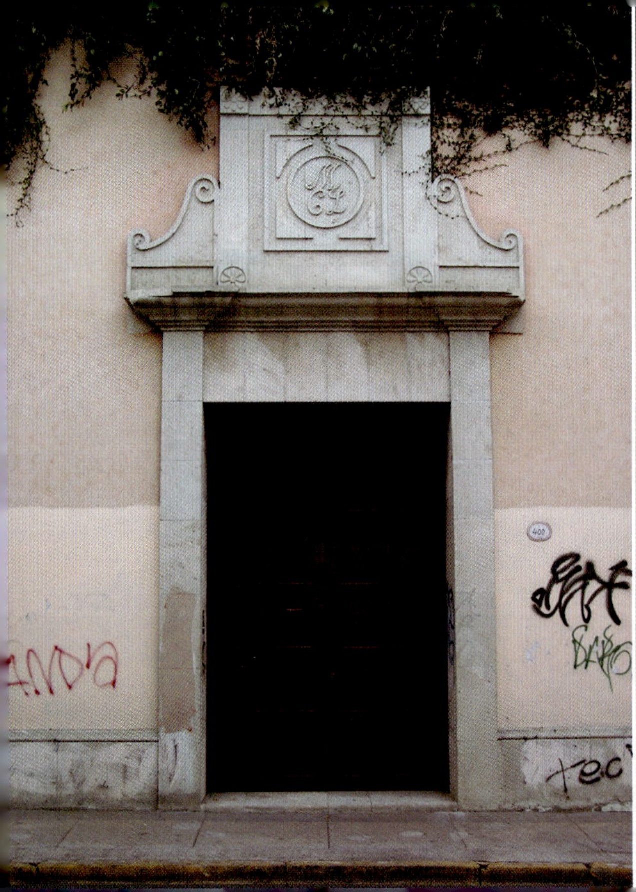

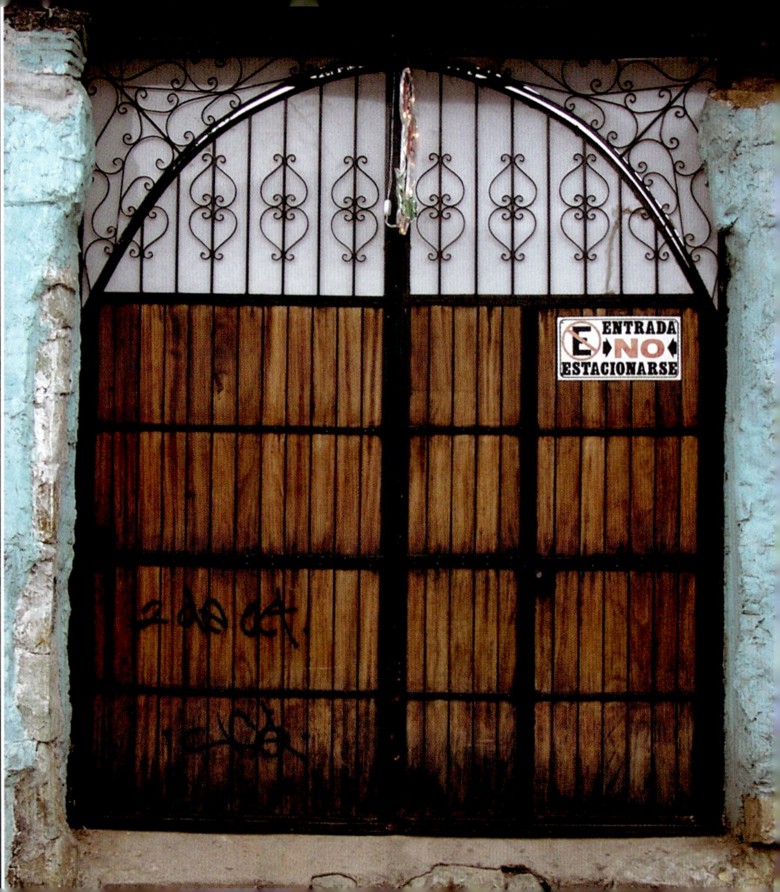
ENTRADA
NO
ESTACIONARSE

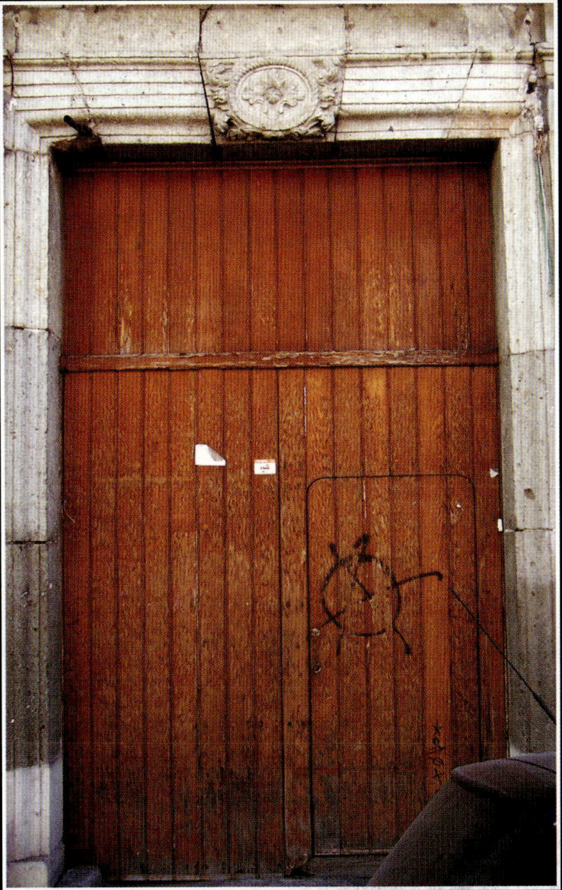

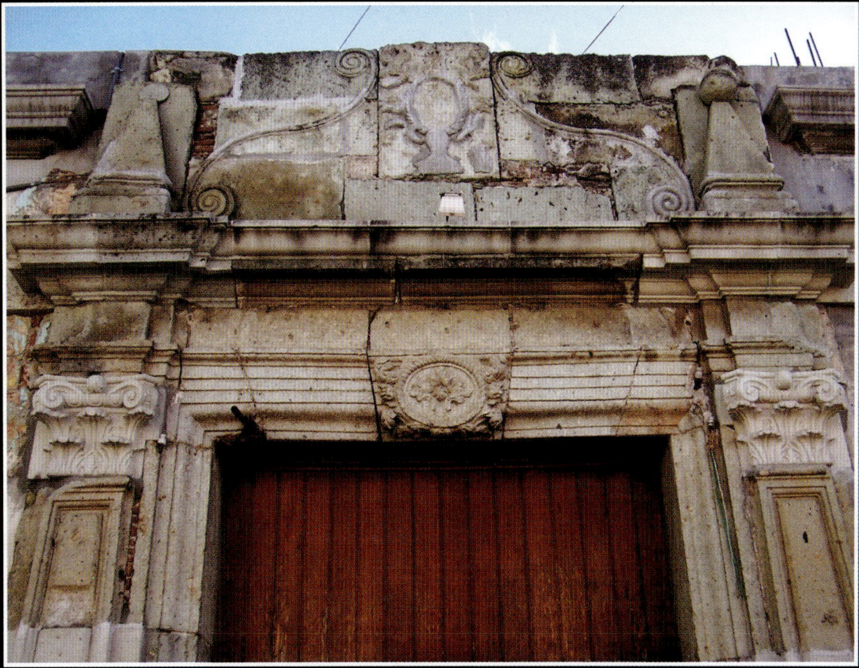

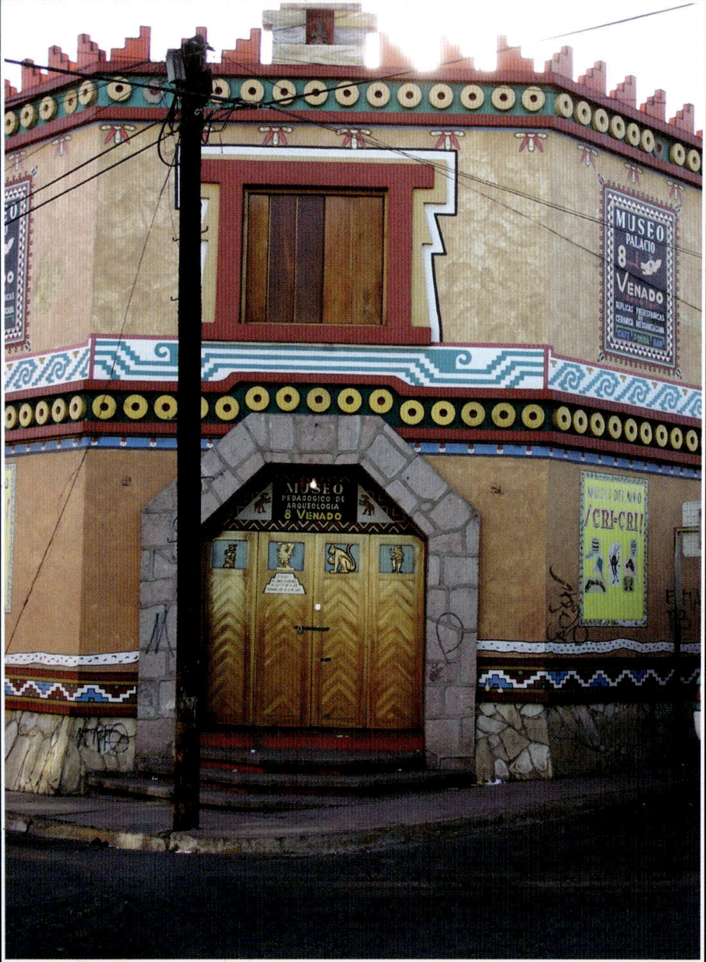

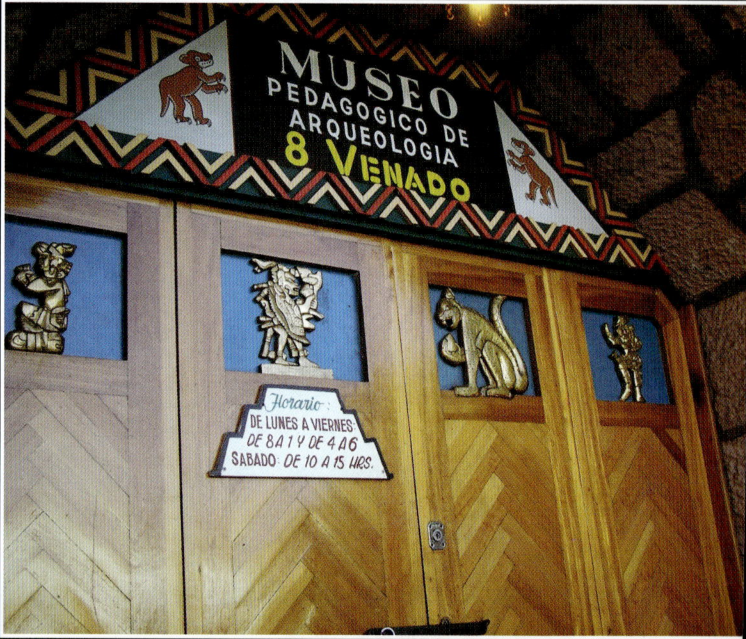

A children's museum, called the Eight Deer Museum, located on the corner of the La Noria Street and Xicotencatl Street.

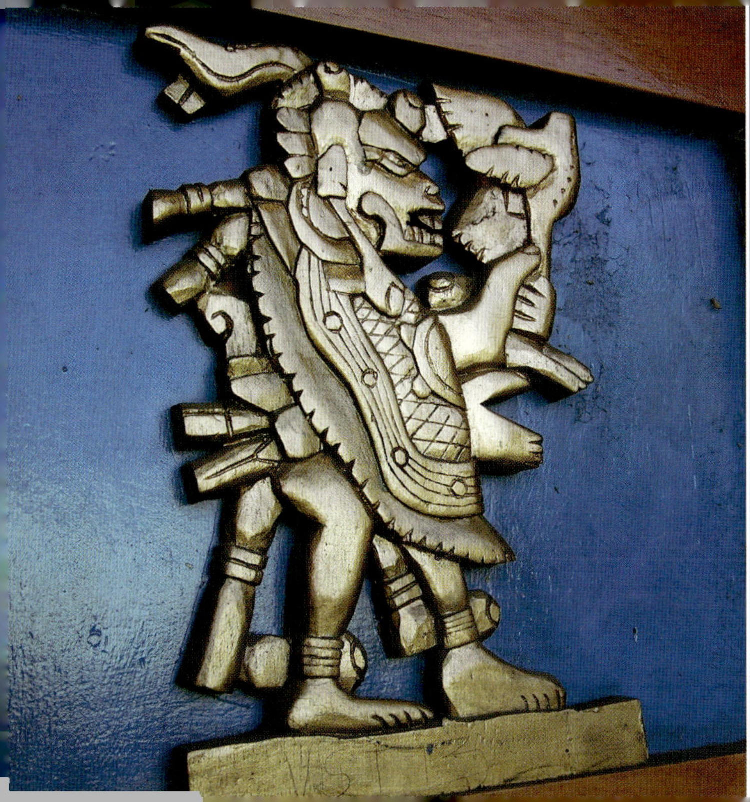

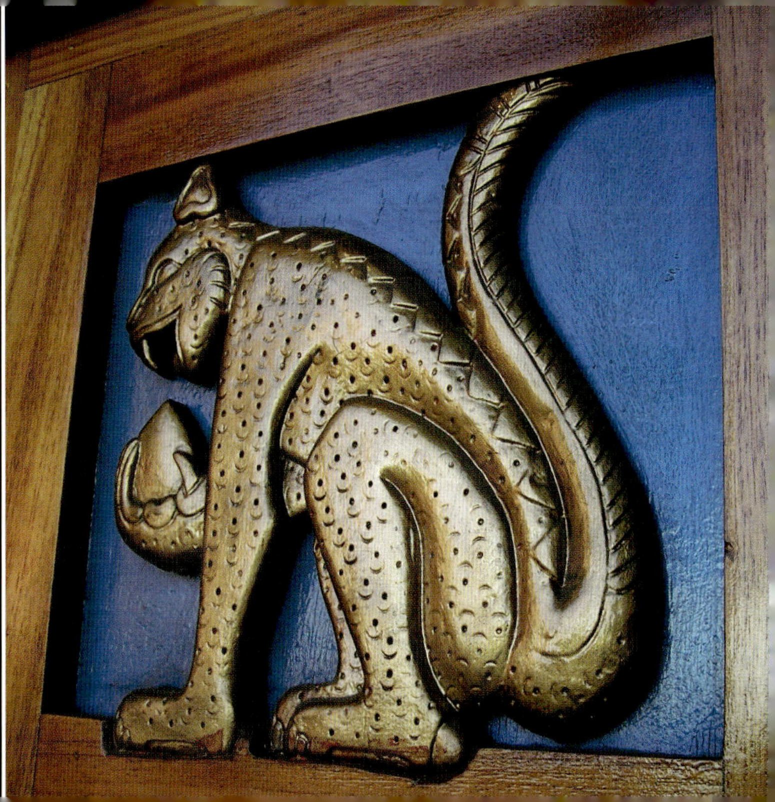

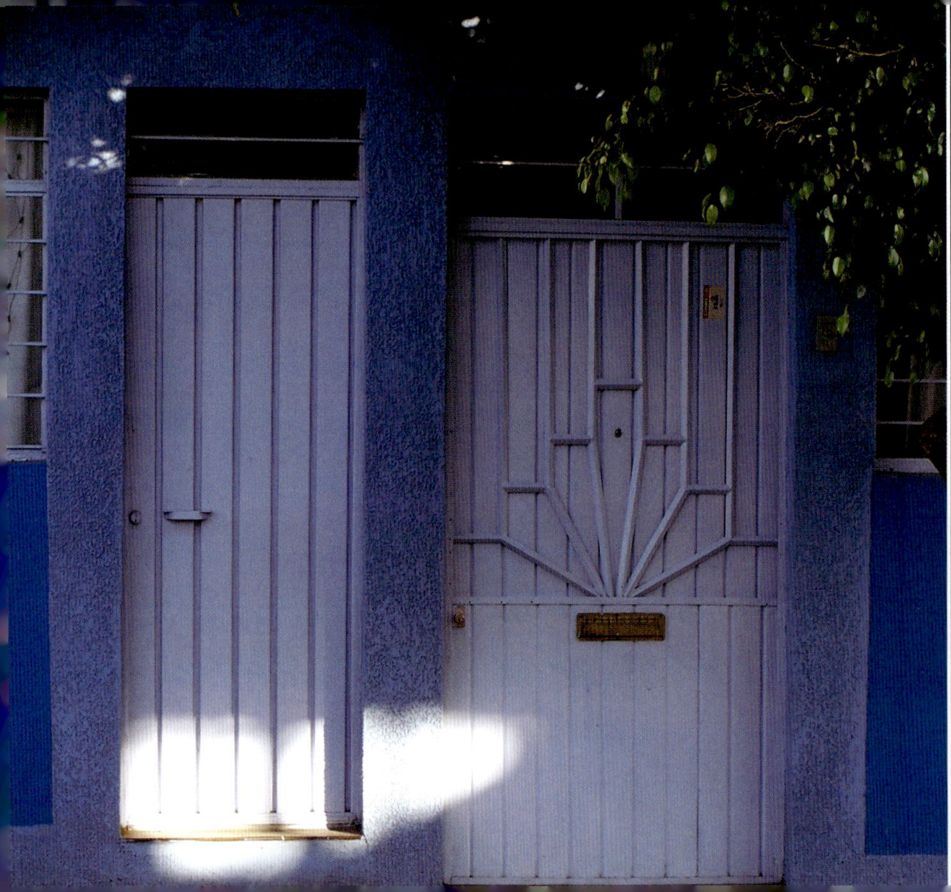

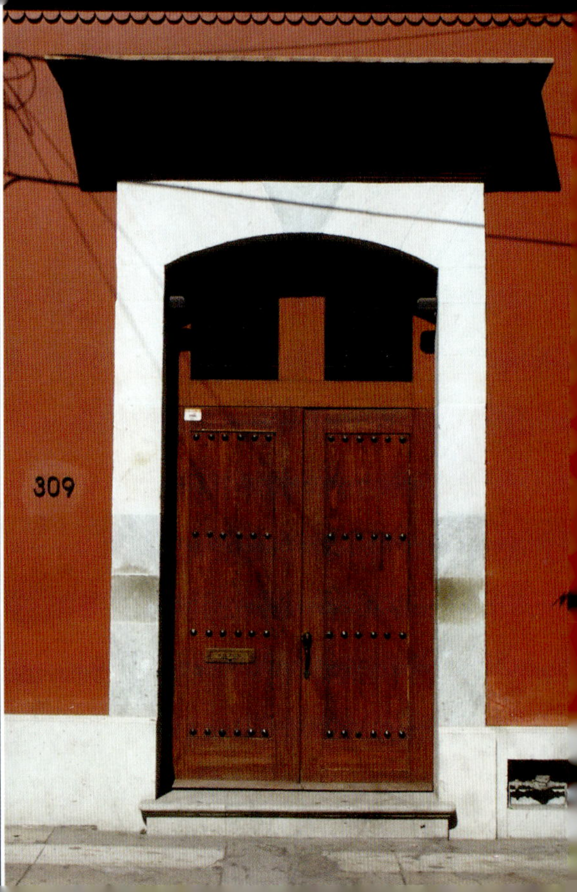
309

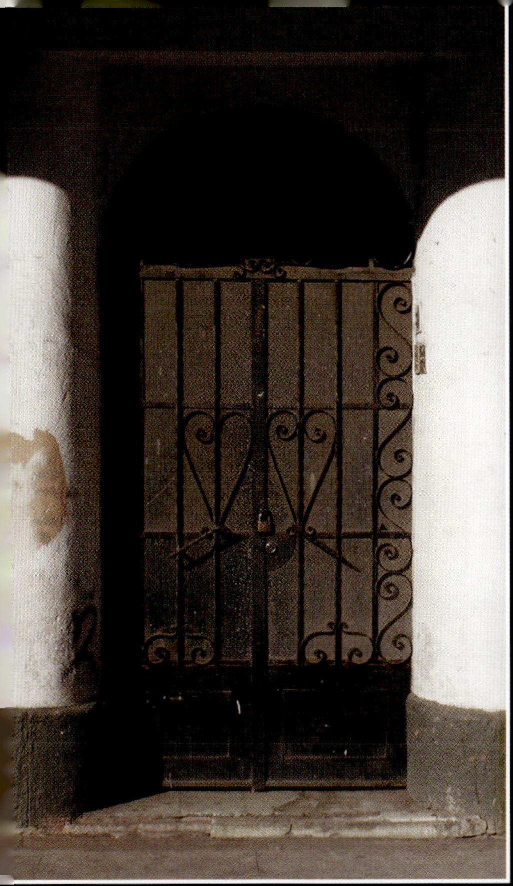

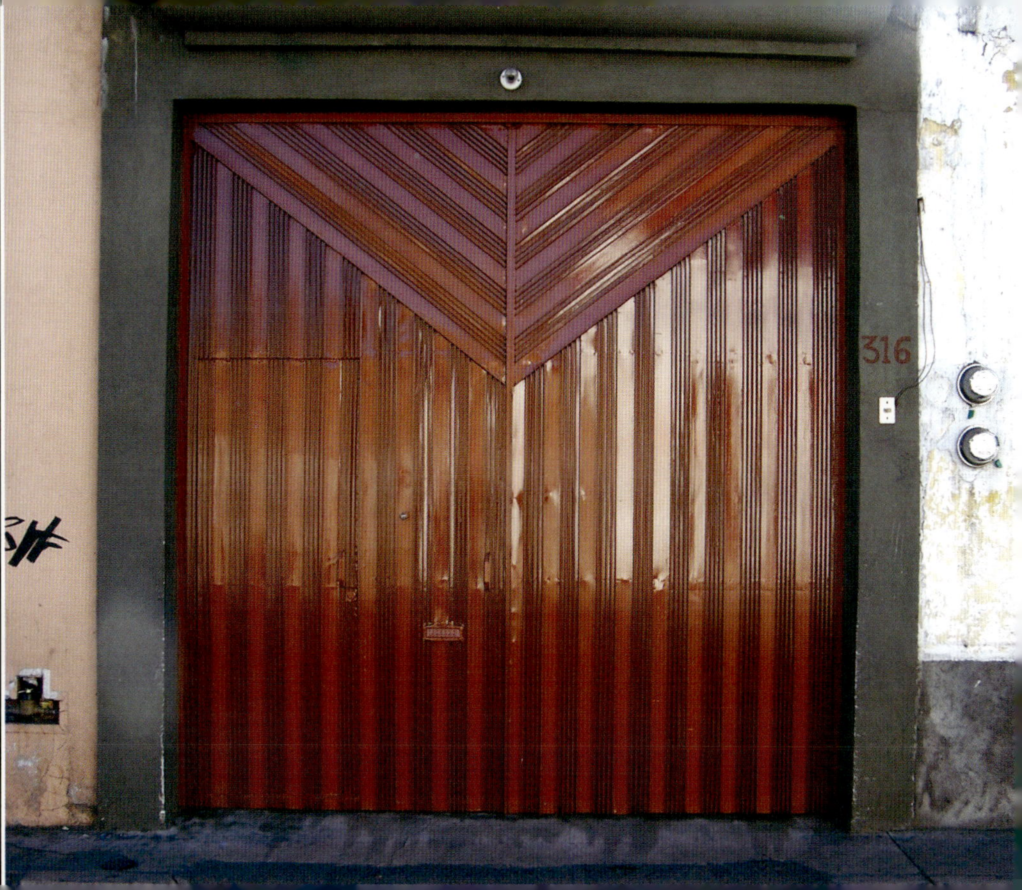
316

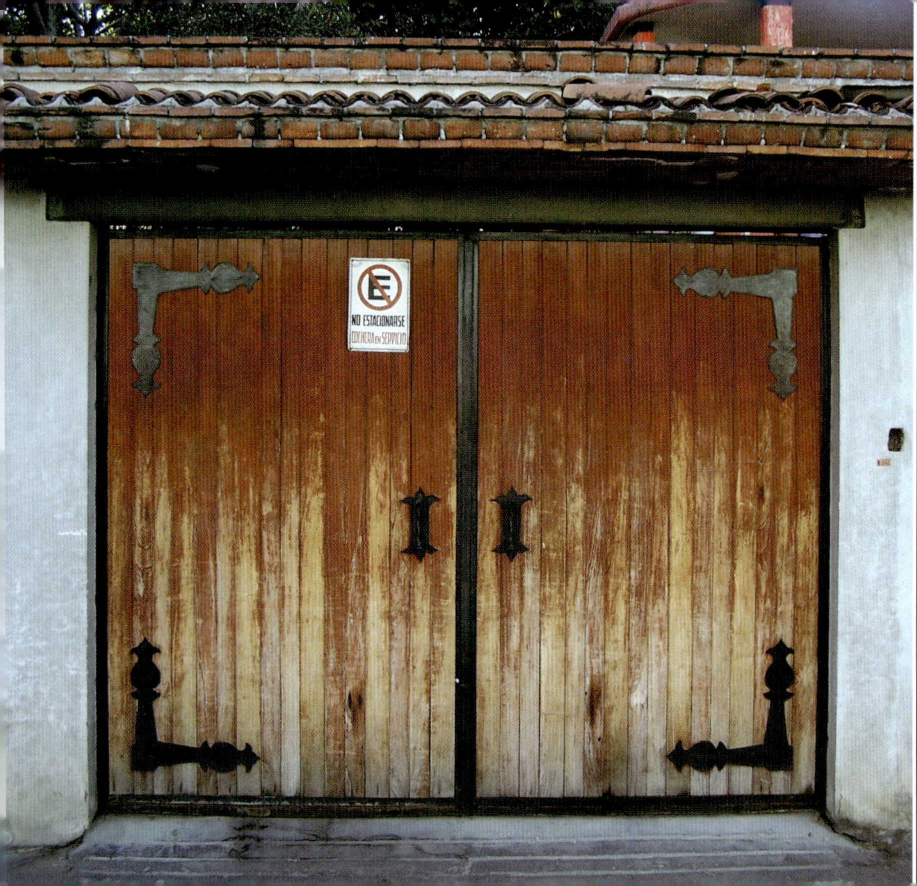
E
NO ESTACIONARSE
COCHERA EN SERVICIO

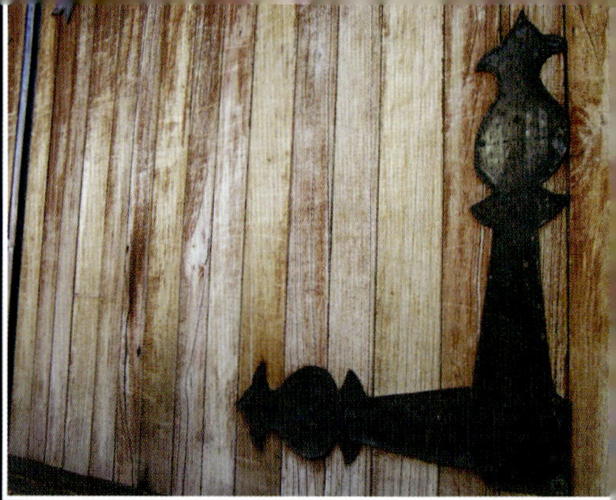

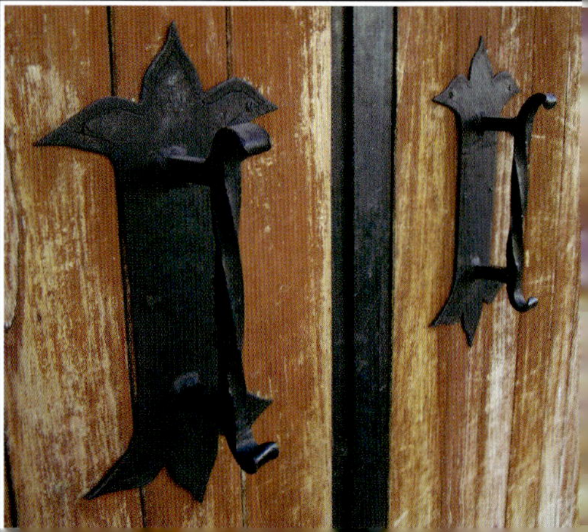

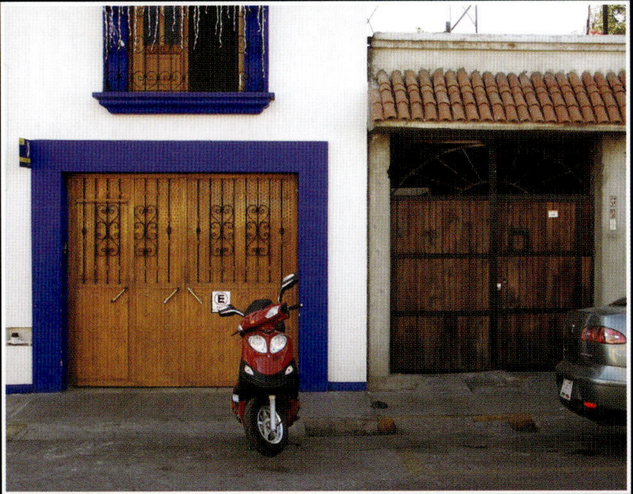

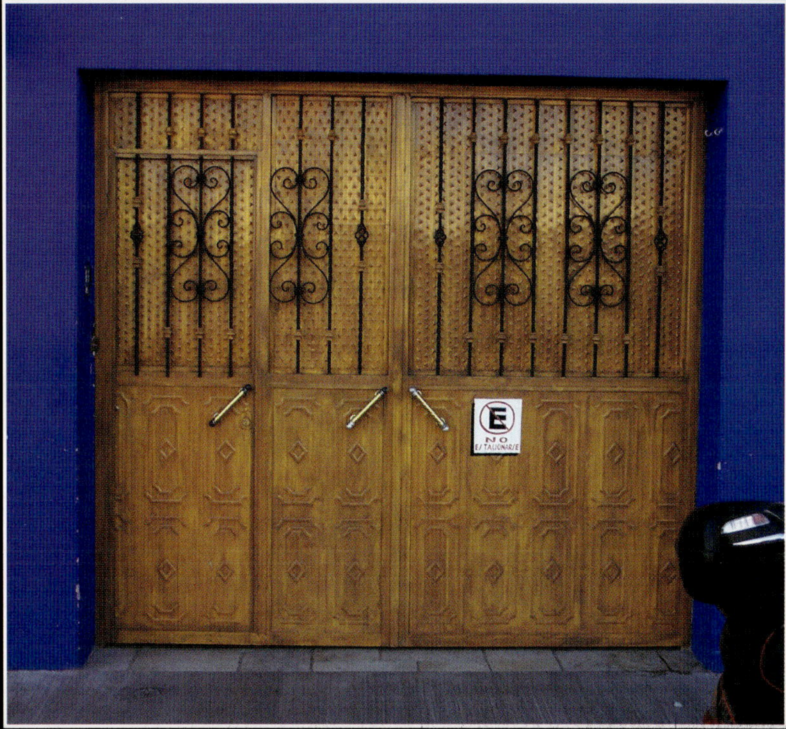

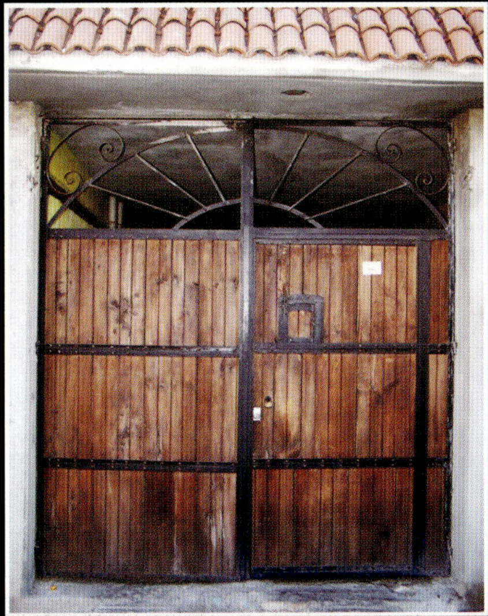

Xicotencatl Street.

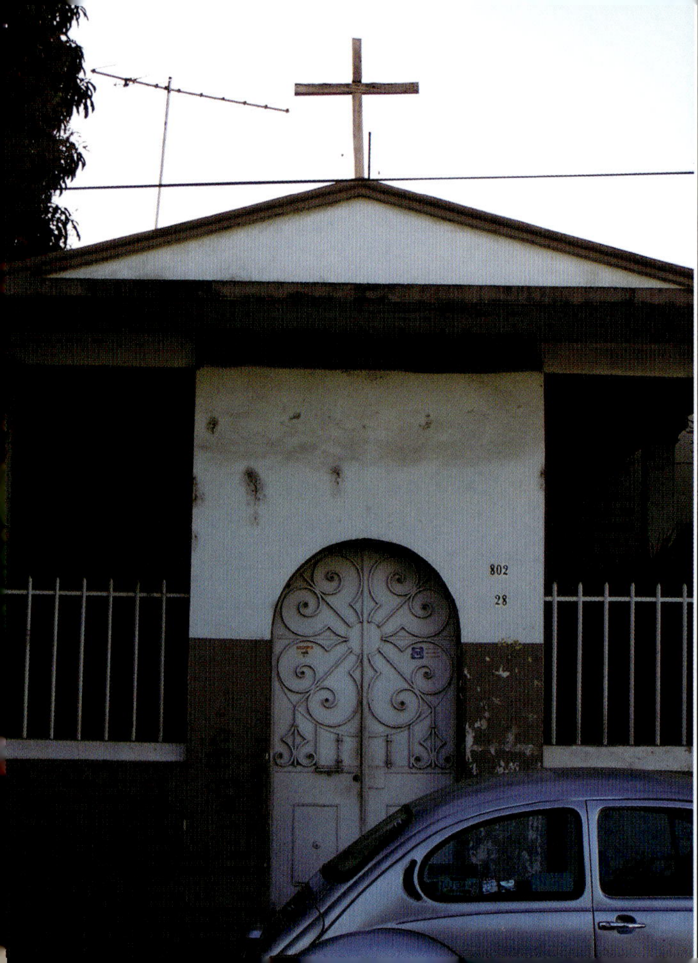
802
28

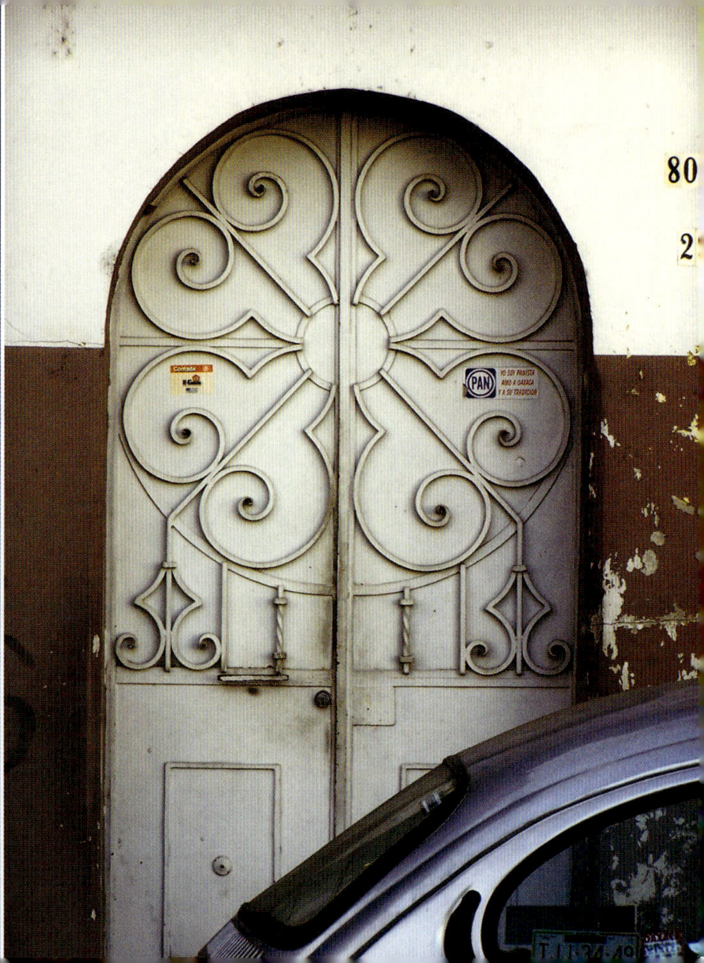
80
2
PAN

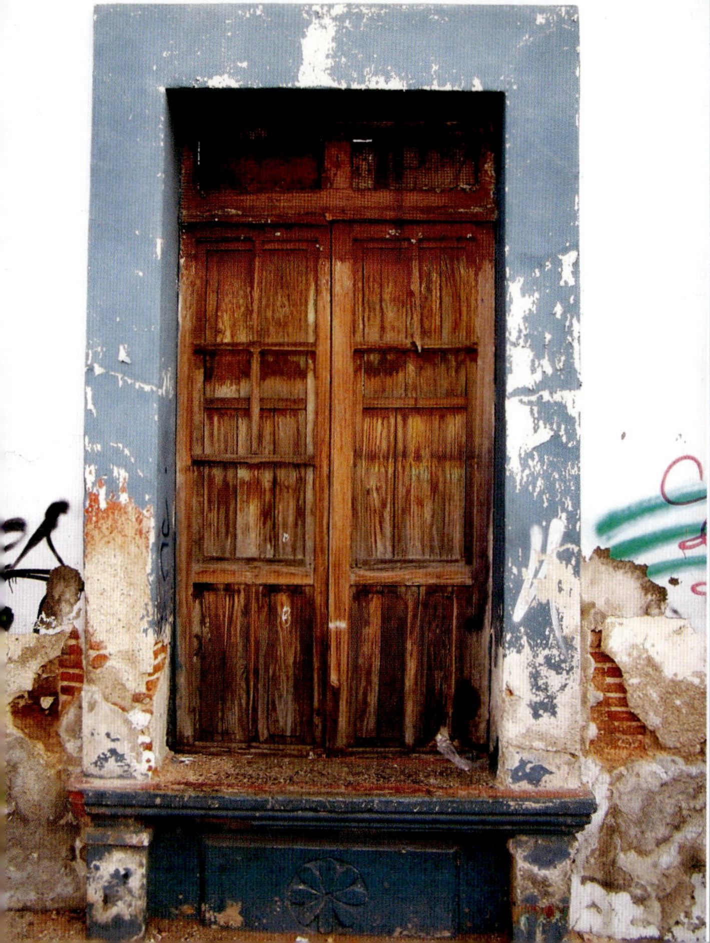

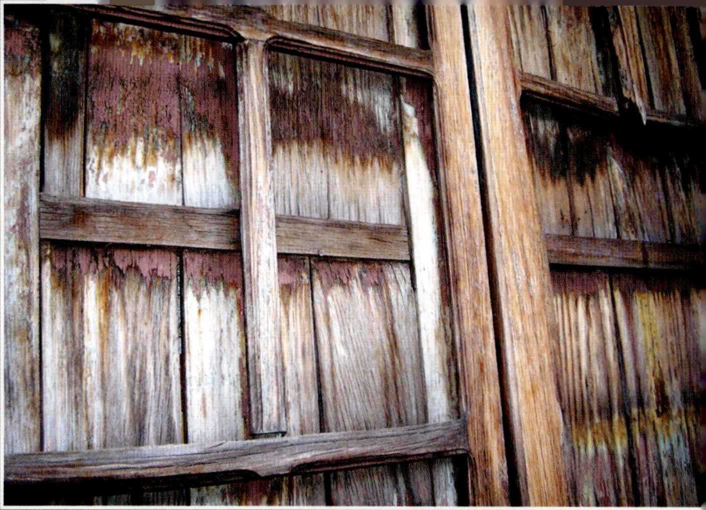

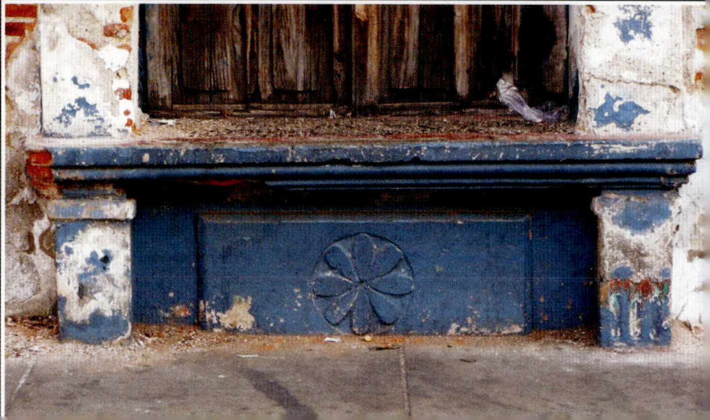

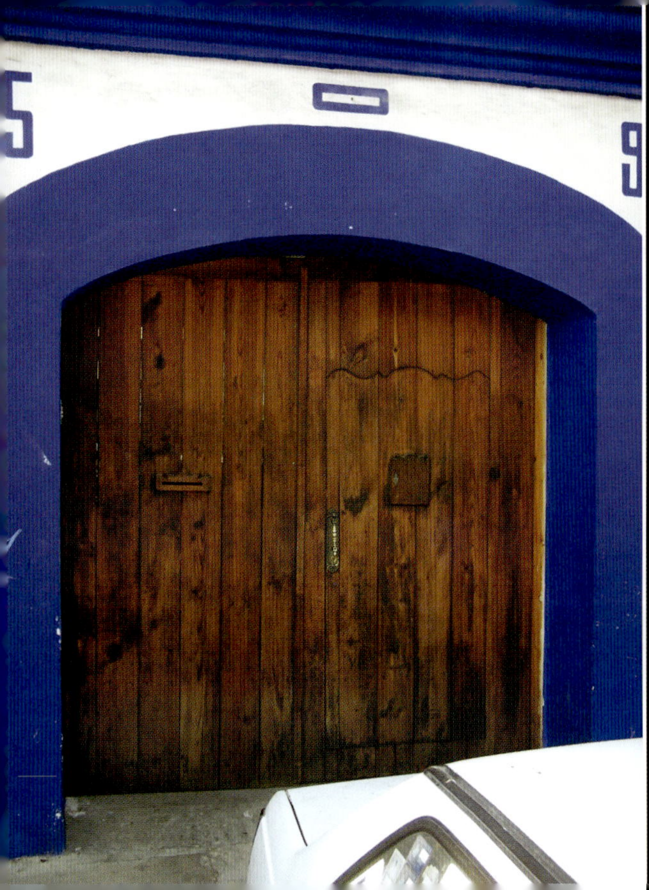
5
9

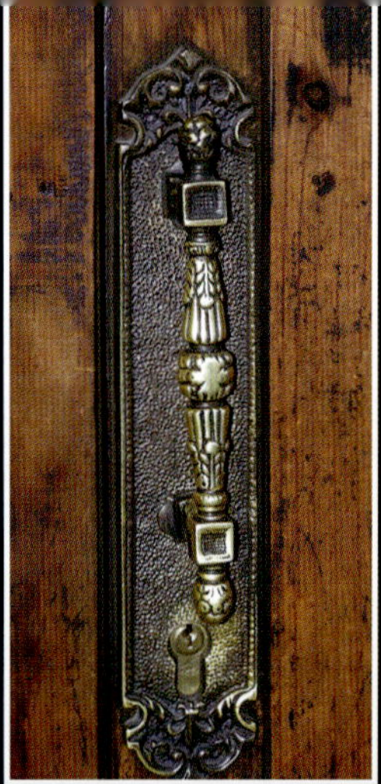

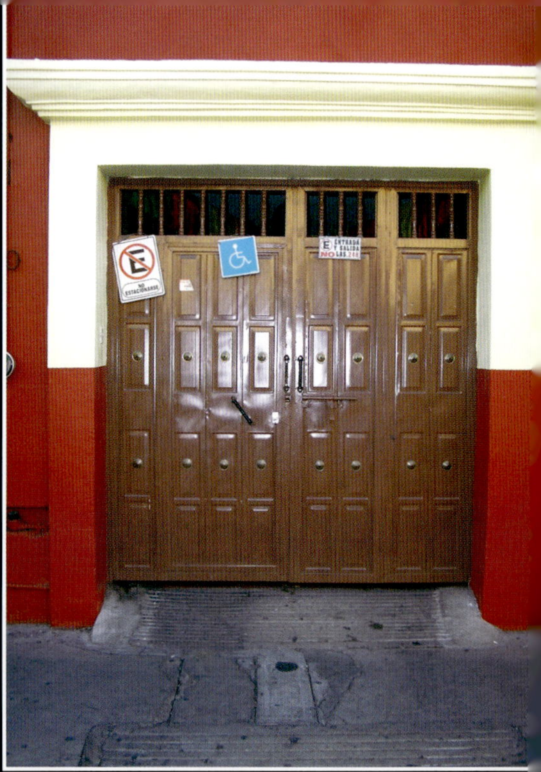
E
NO
ESTACIONARSE
E ENTRADA
Y SALIDA
NO LAS 24H

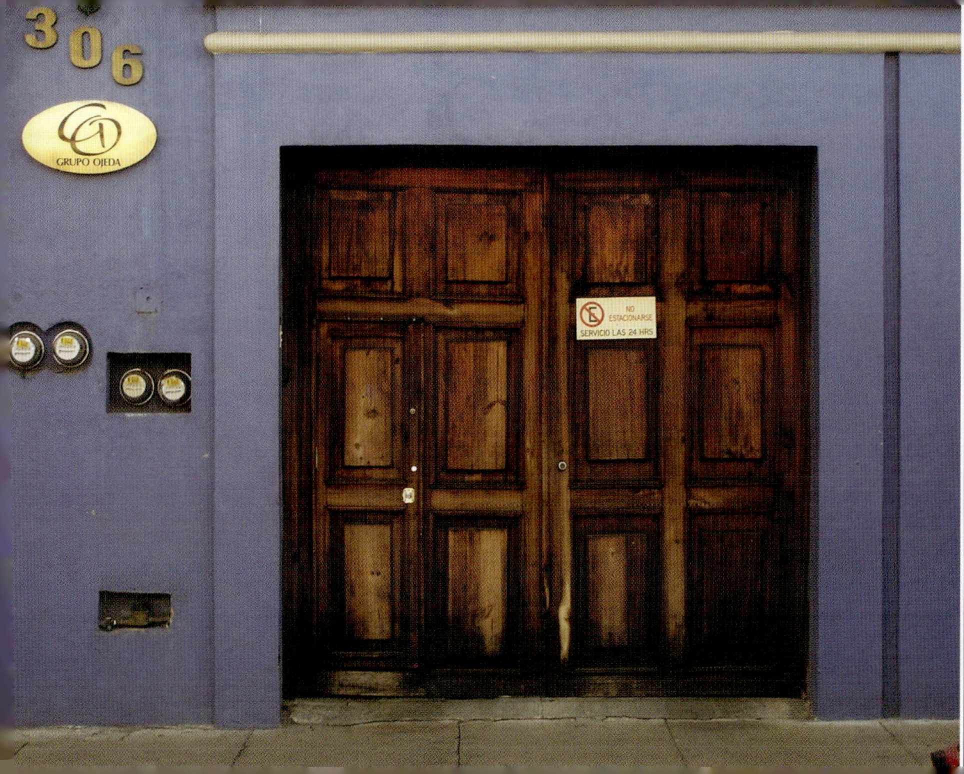
306
GRUPO OJEDA
NO ESTACIONARSE
SERVICIO LAS 24 HRS

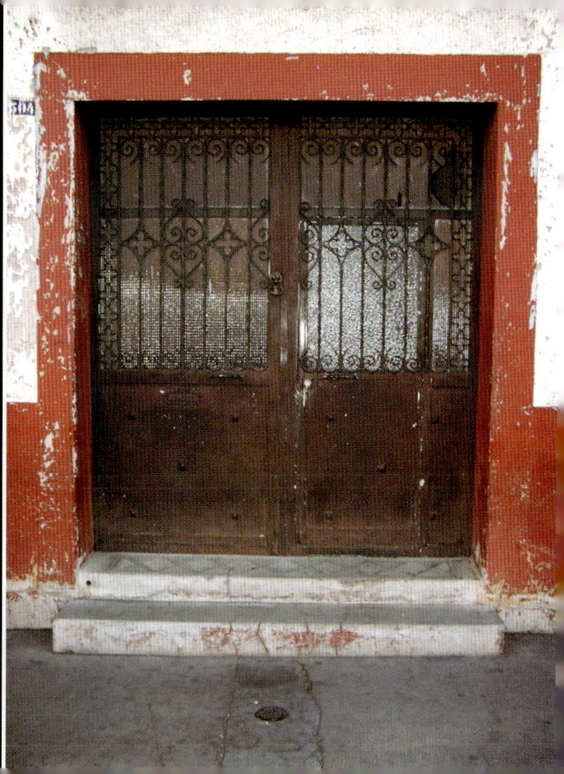

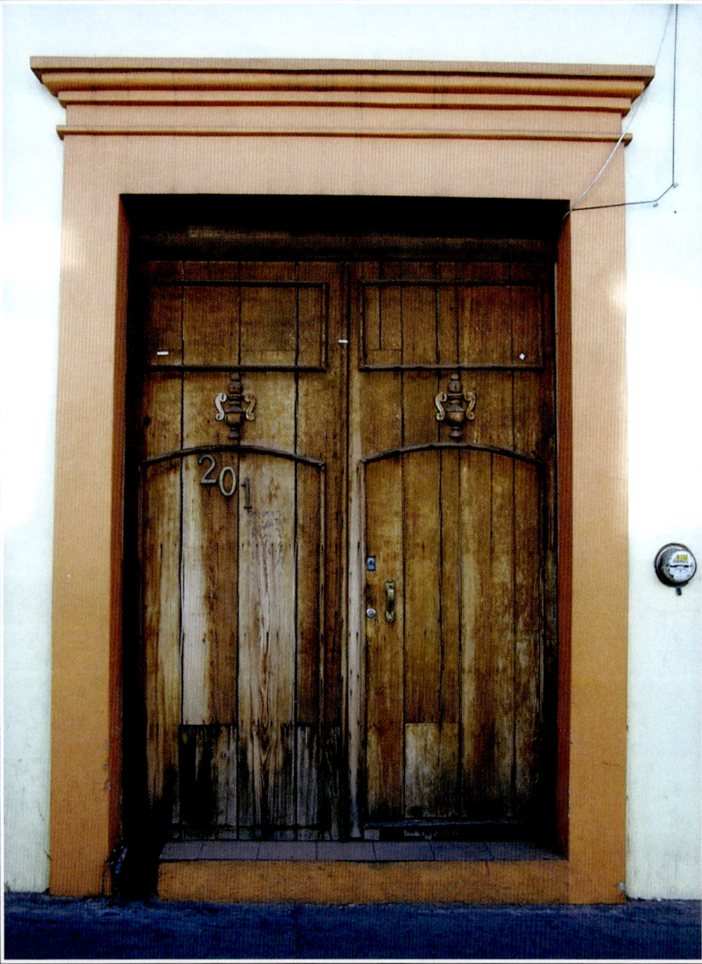
201

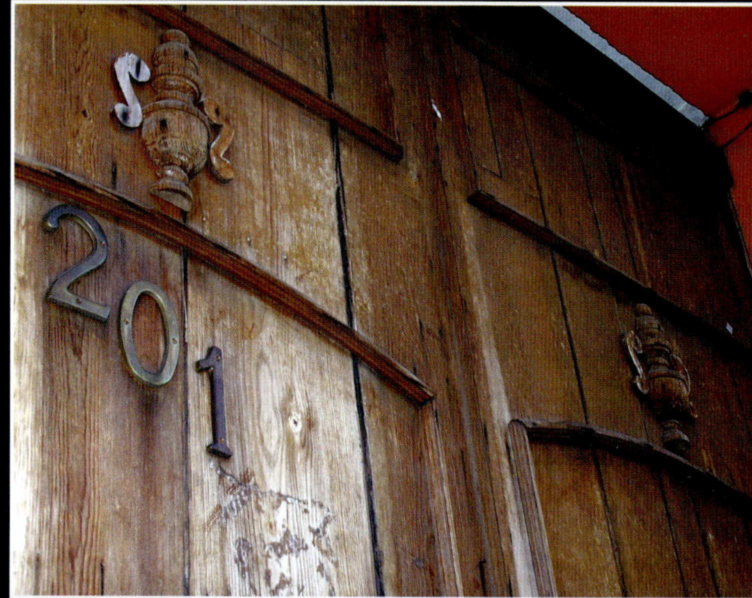
201

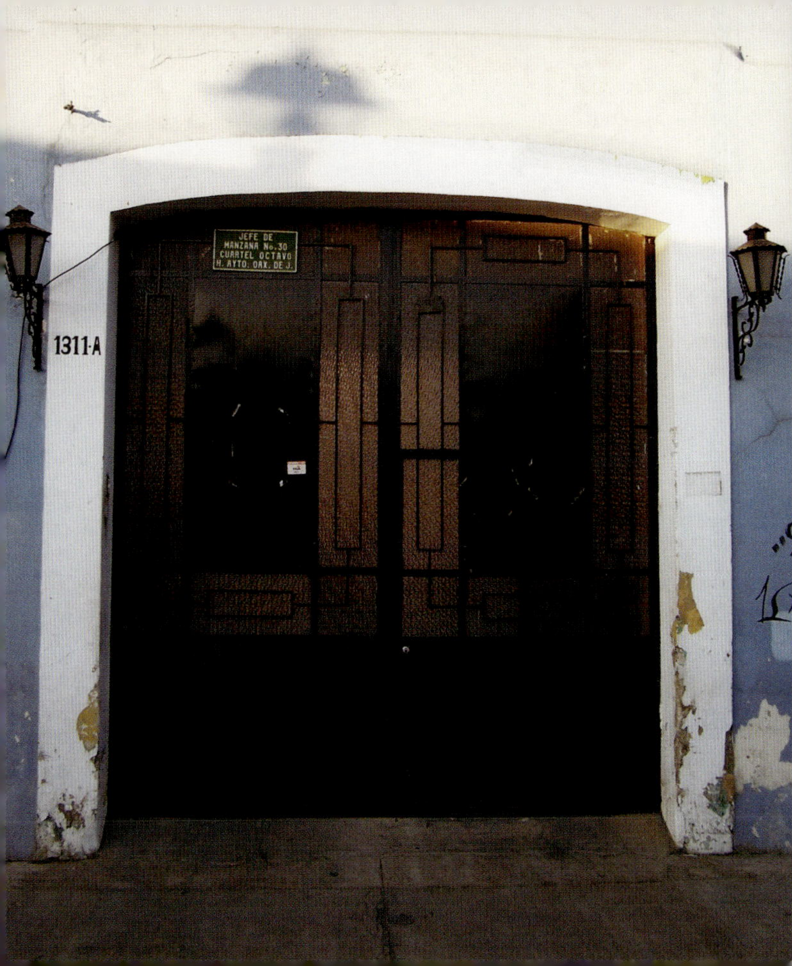

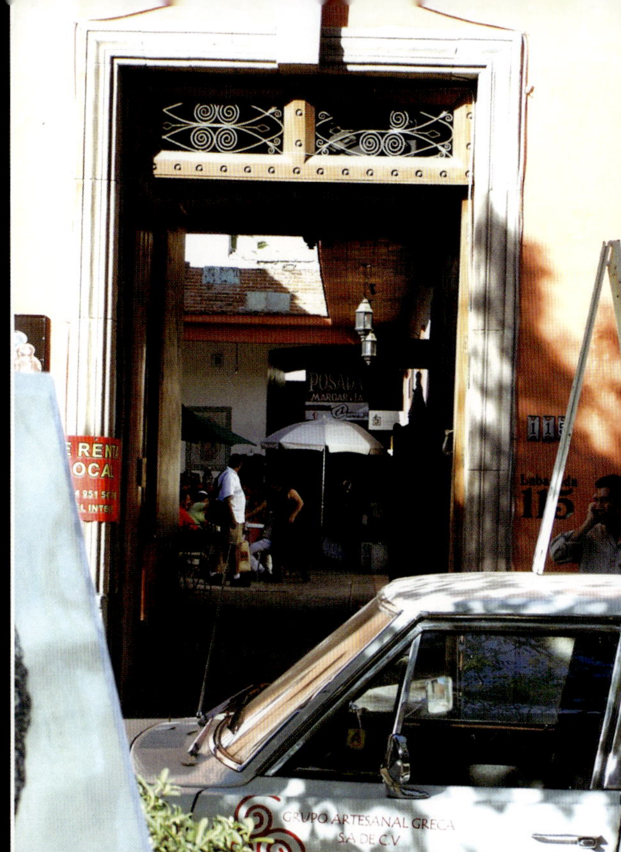

A shop located on the Abasolo Street, in front of the La Bastida Garden.

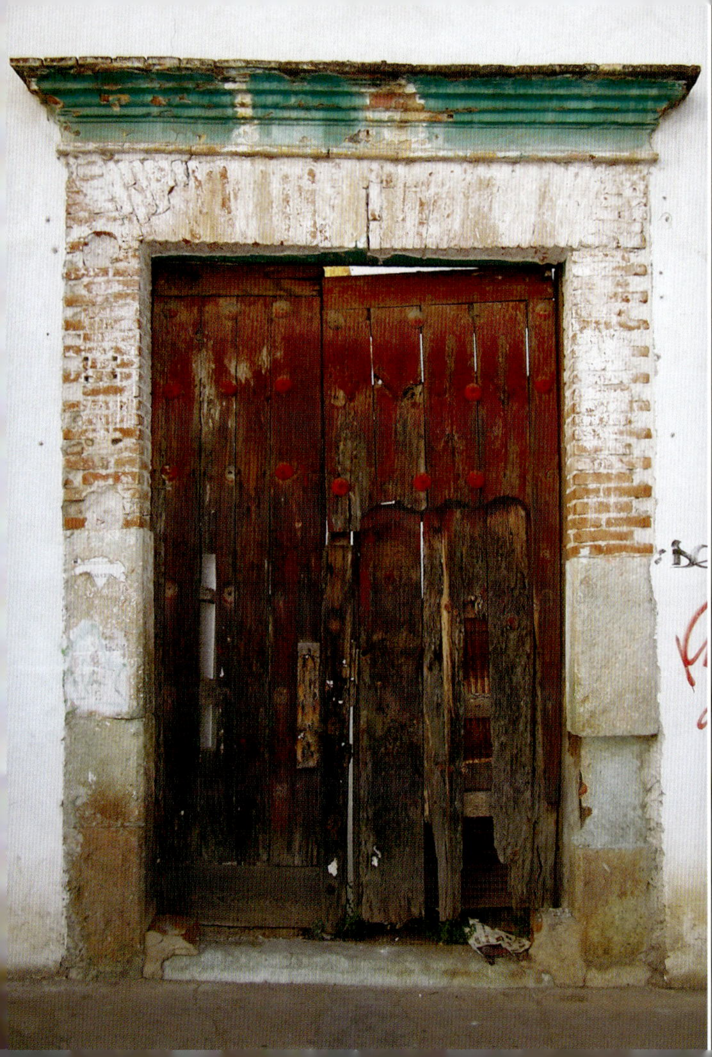

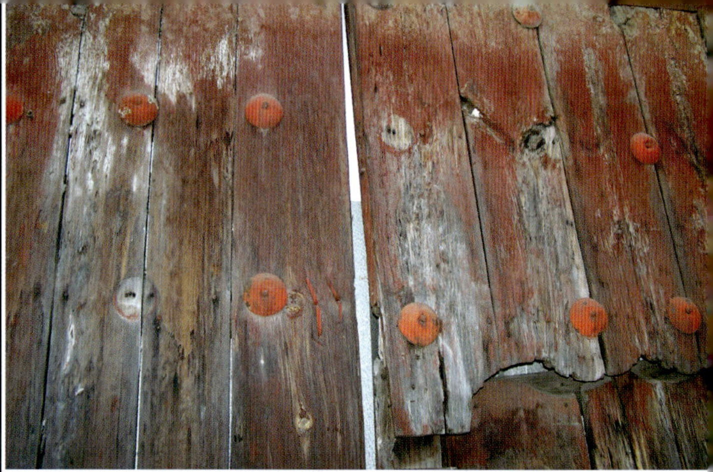

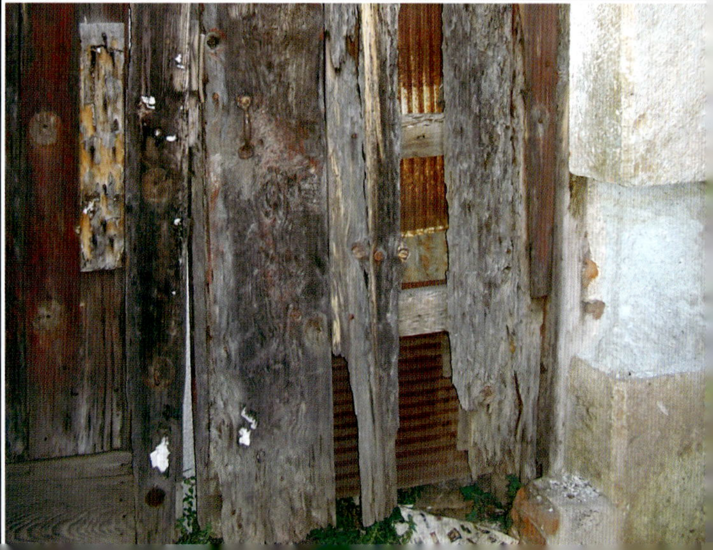

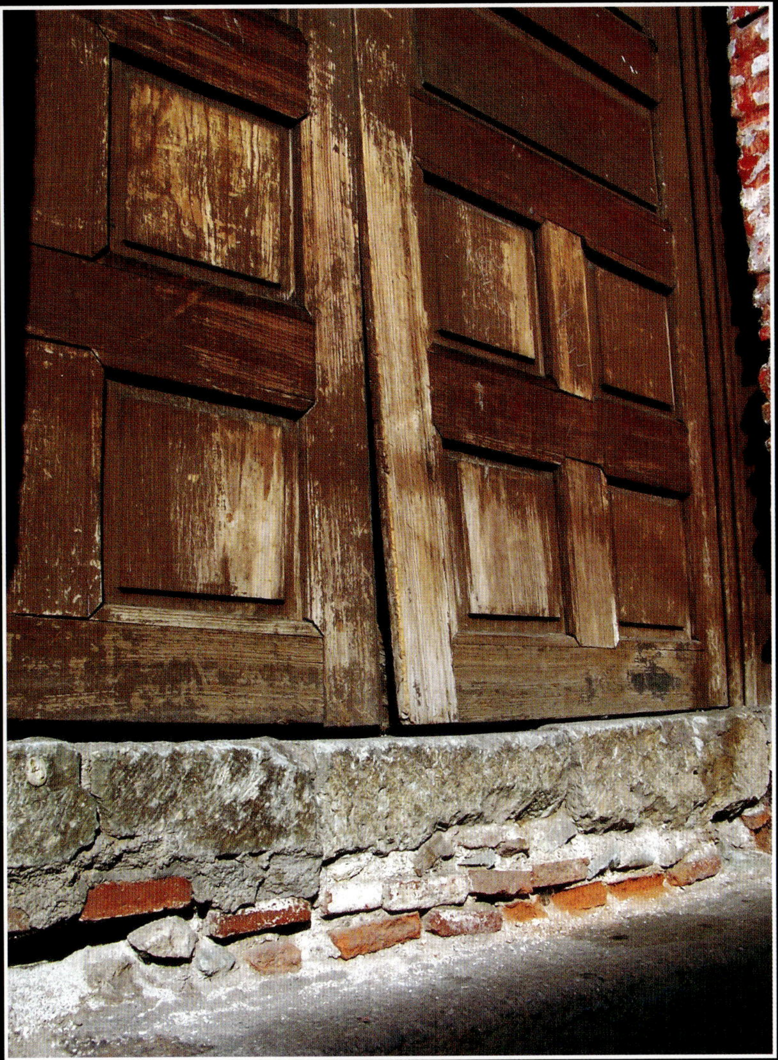

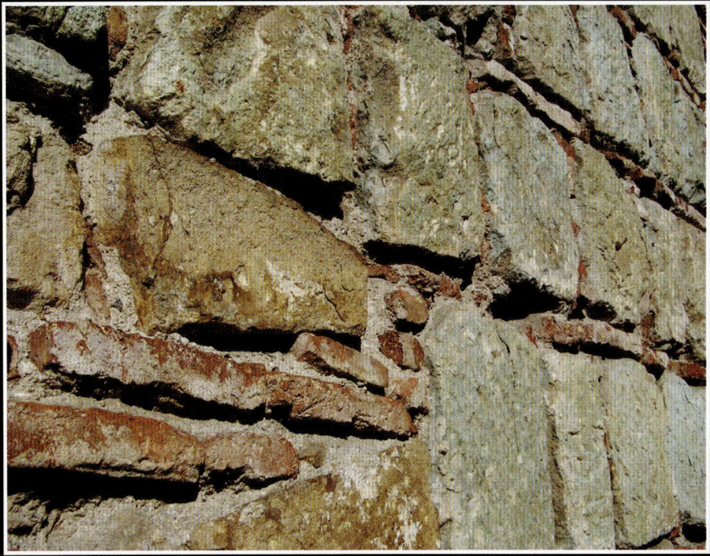

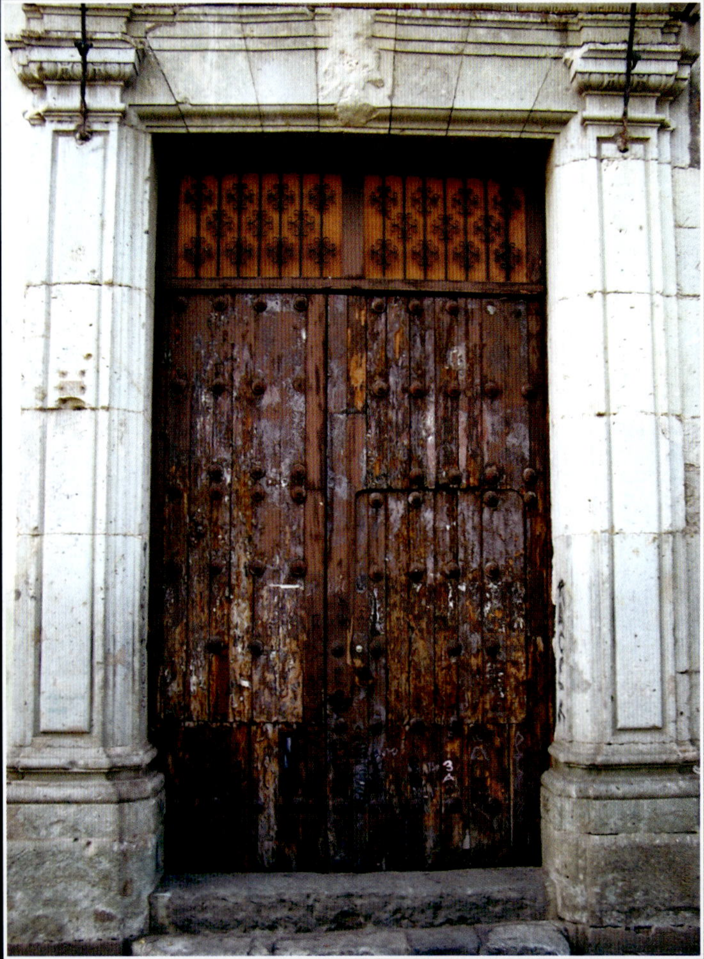

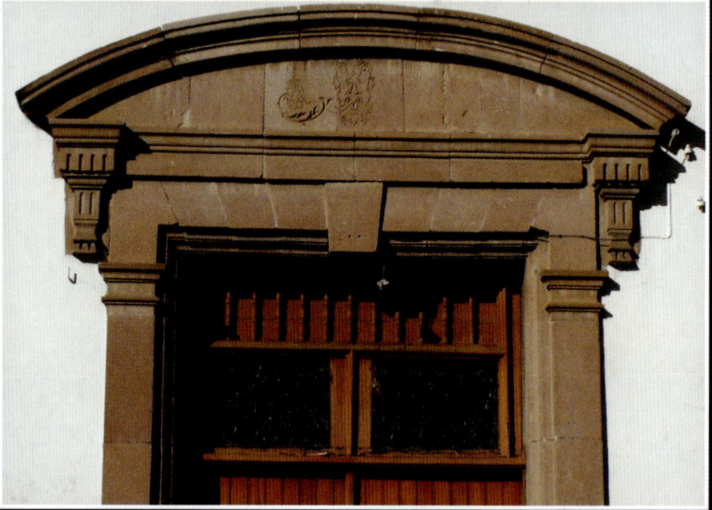

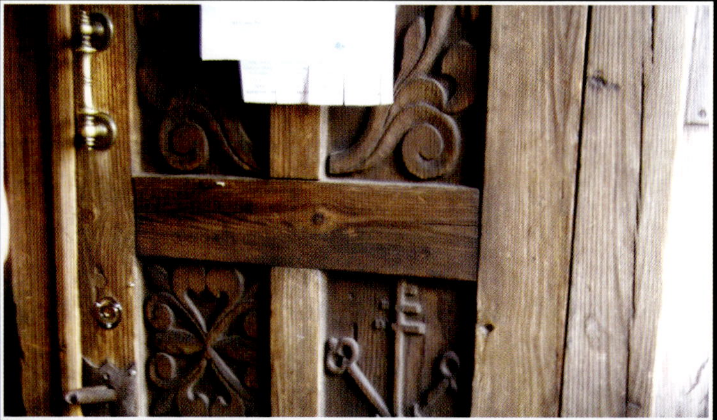

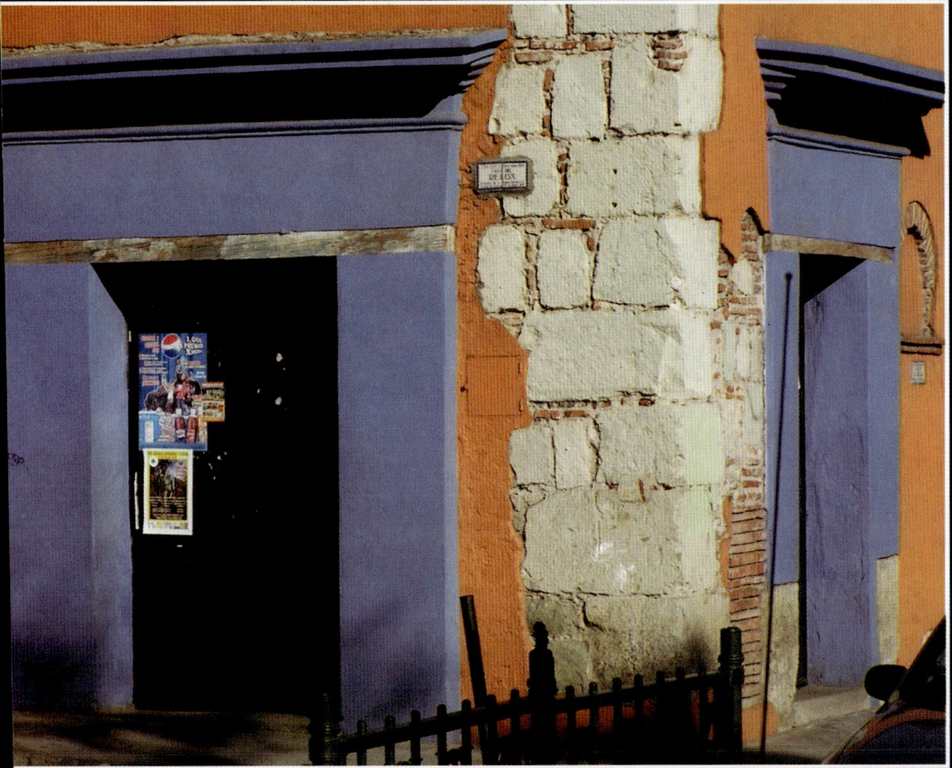

This store is located on the corner of Cinco de Mayo Street and Abasolo Street.

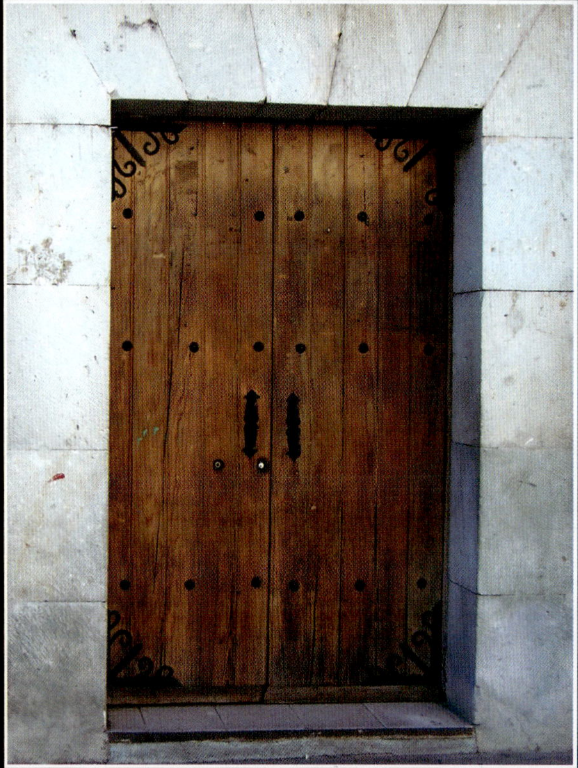

This door hides a crafts shop located on the corner of Murguia and Cinco de Mayo Street.

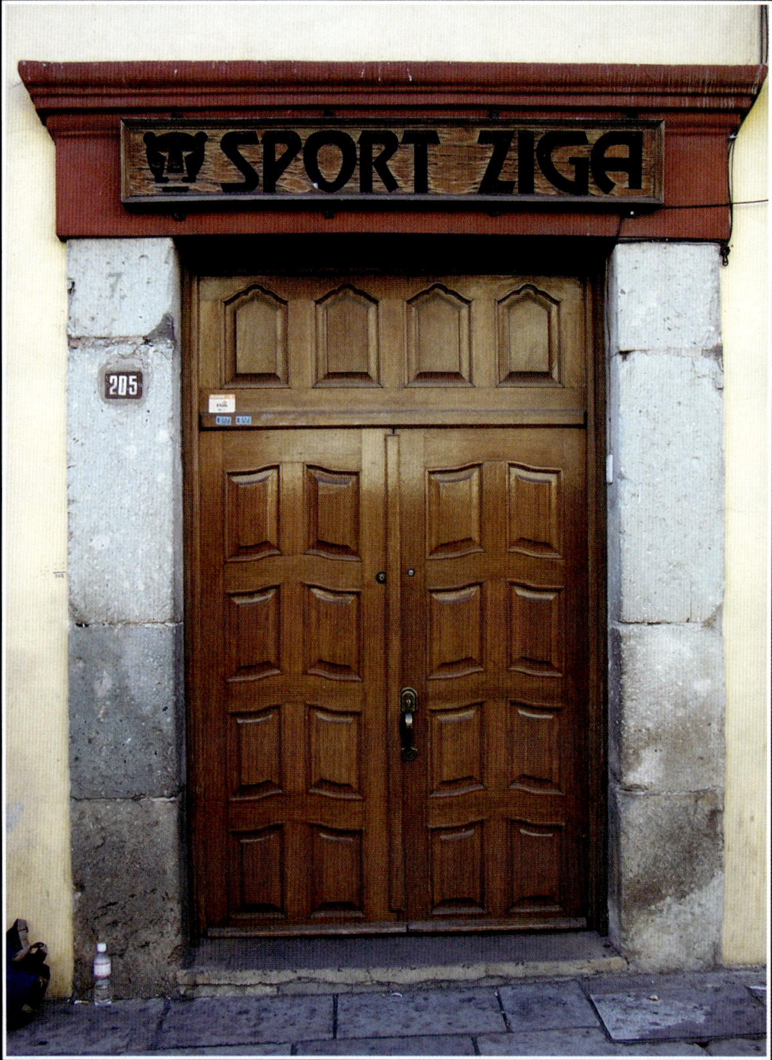

Clothing store on Alcalá Street.

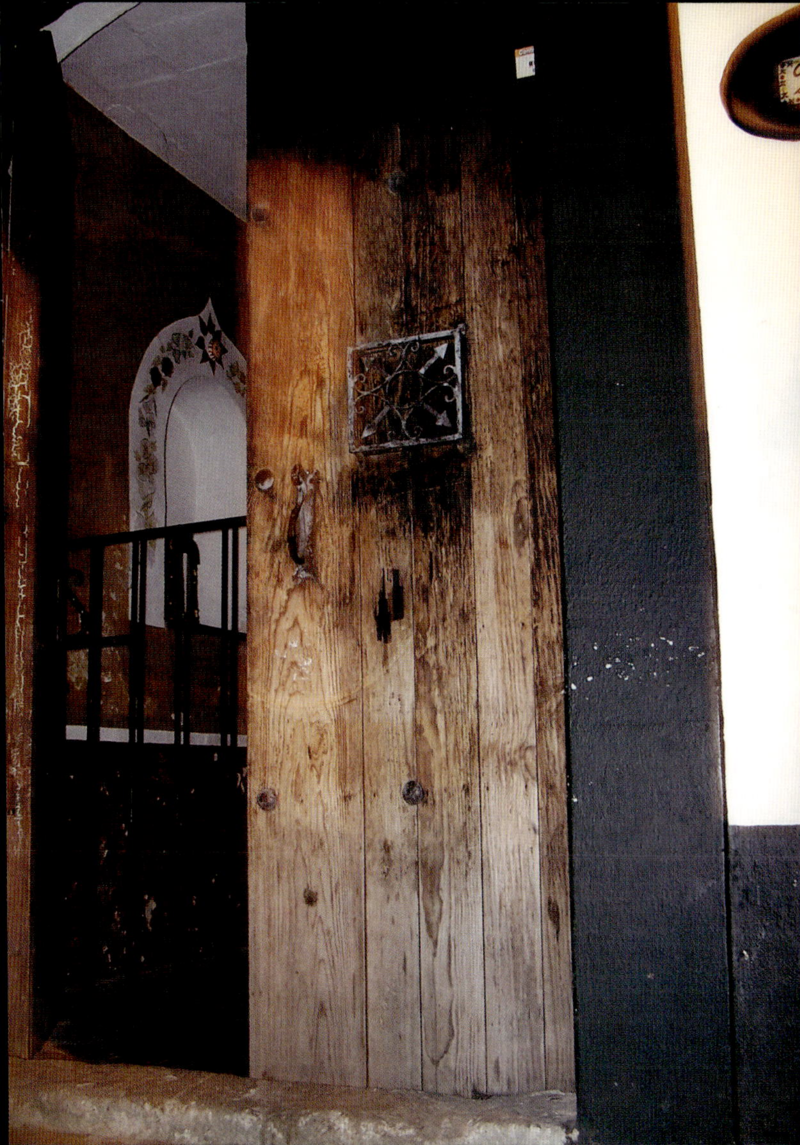

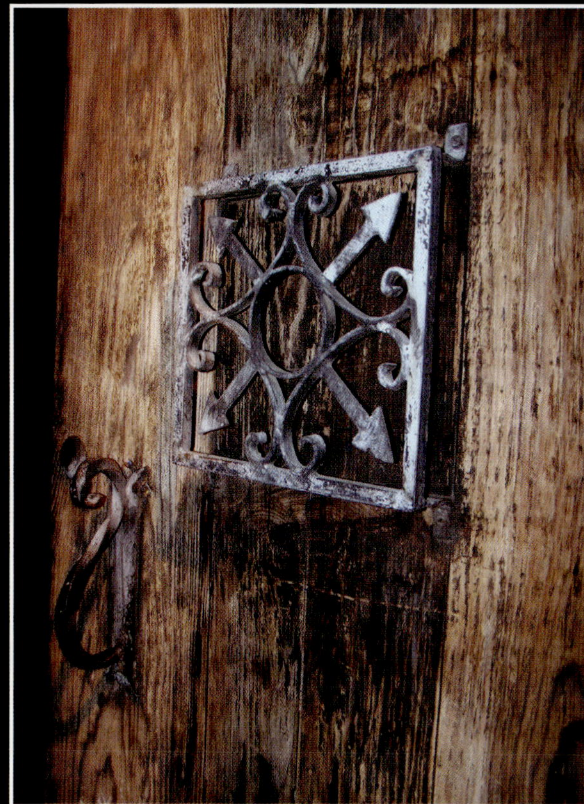

Calle Constitutión

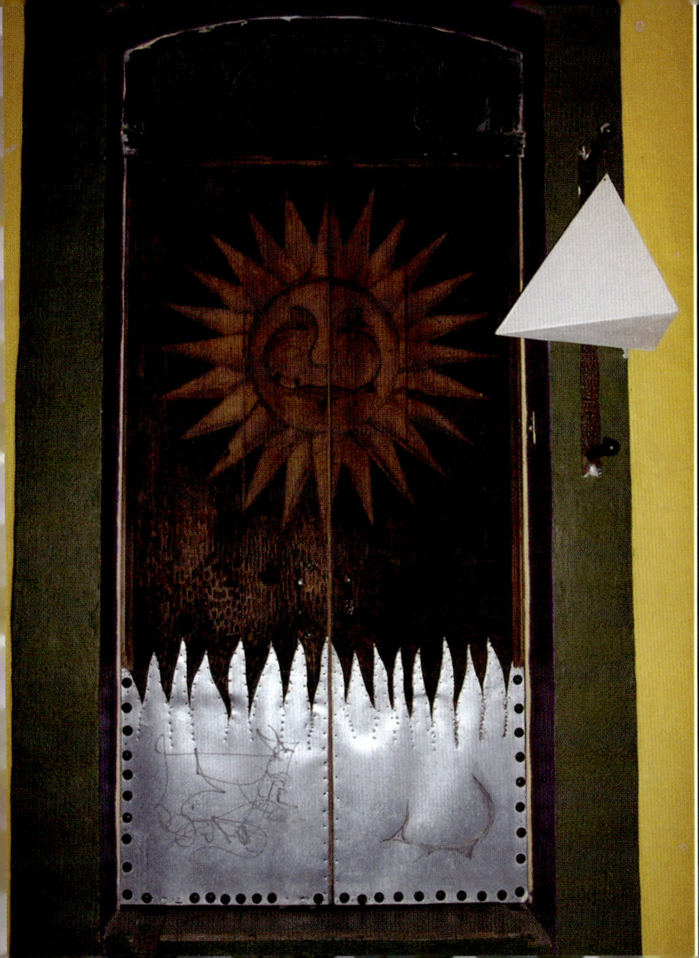

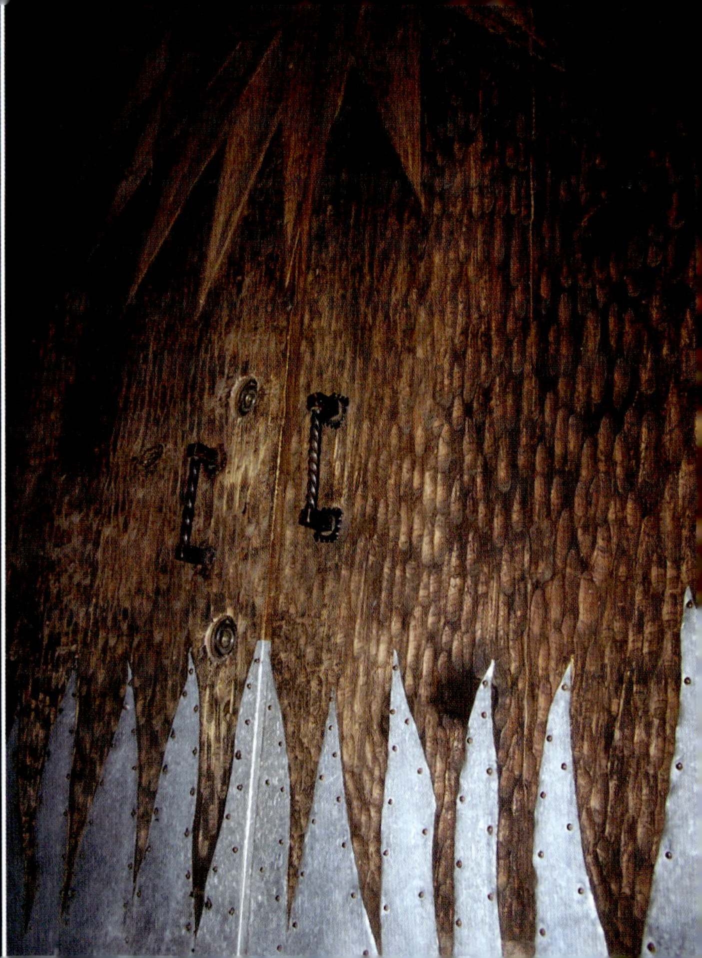

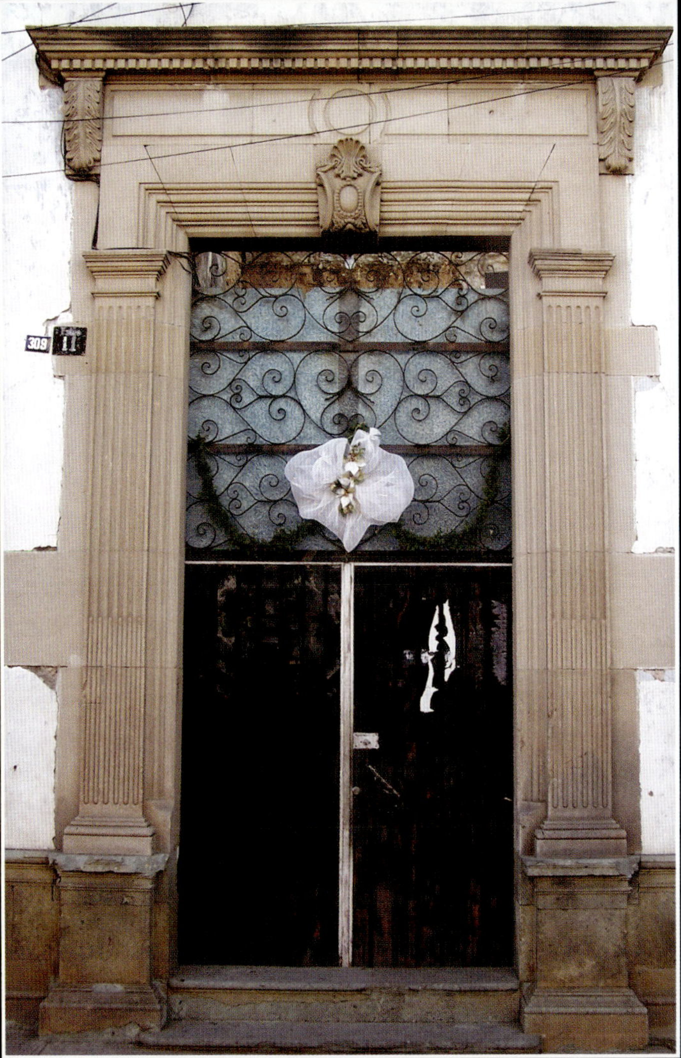

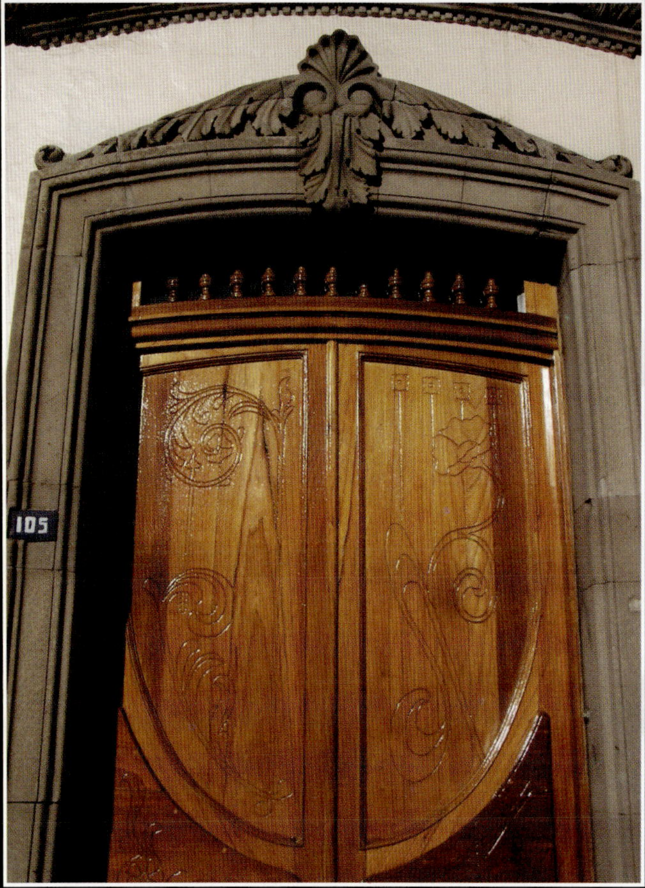

García Vigíl Street.

Some home owners display Christmas crafts on the doors during the season.

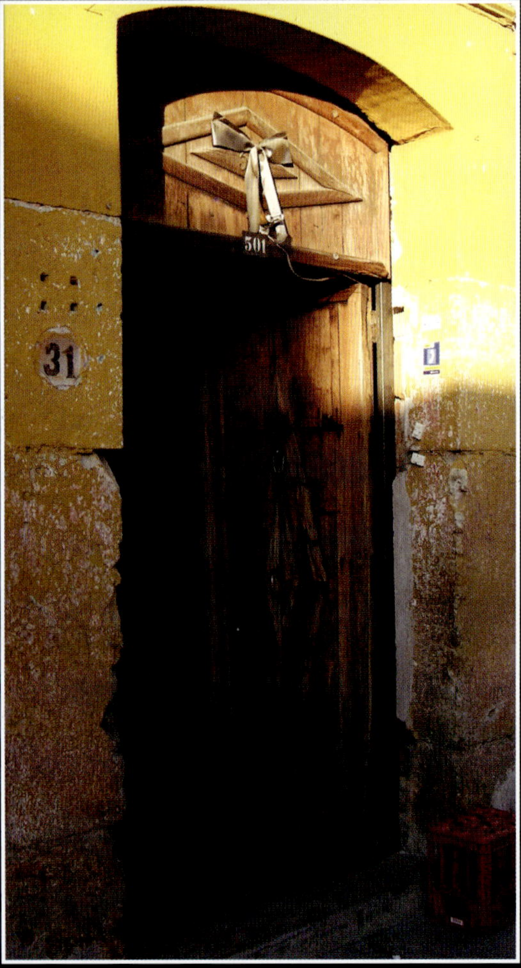

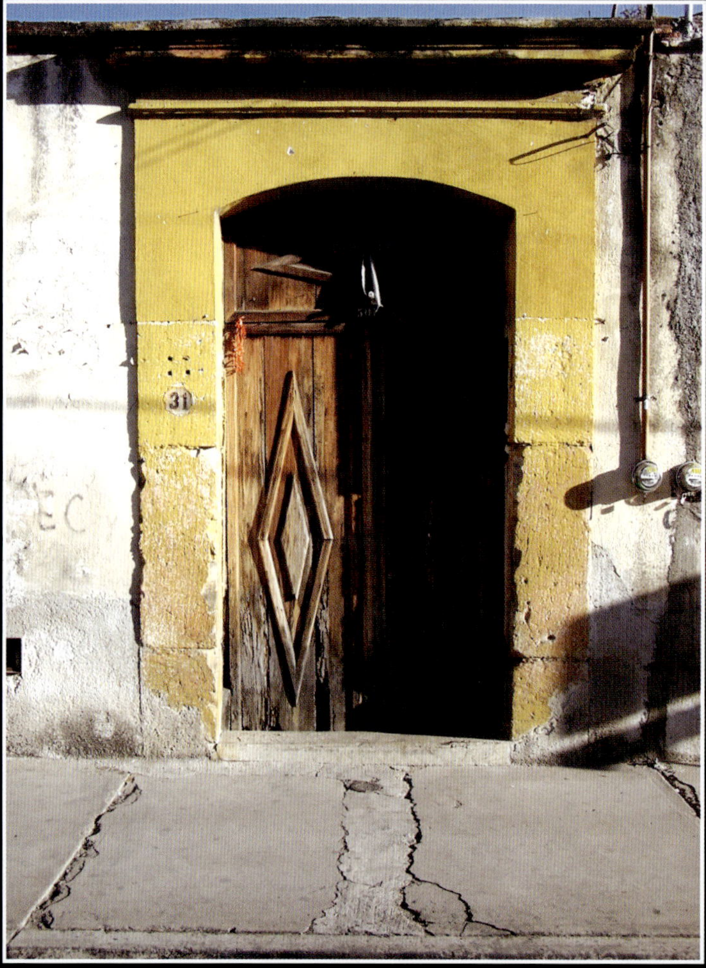

The bow over this door on Guerrero Street symbolizes the family is in mourning.

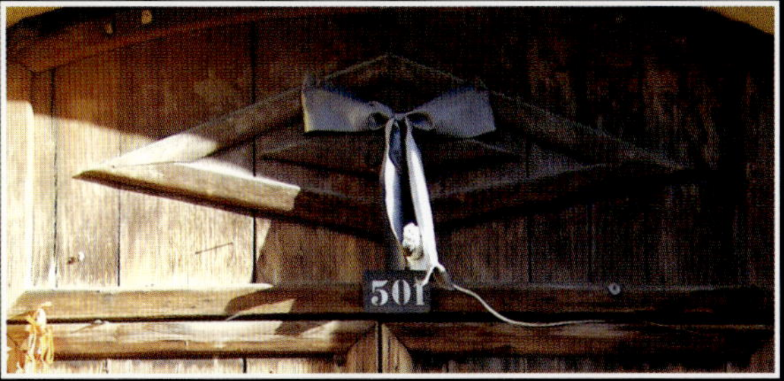

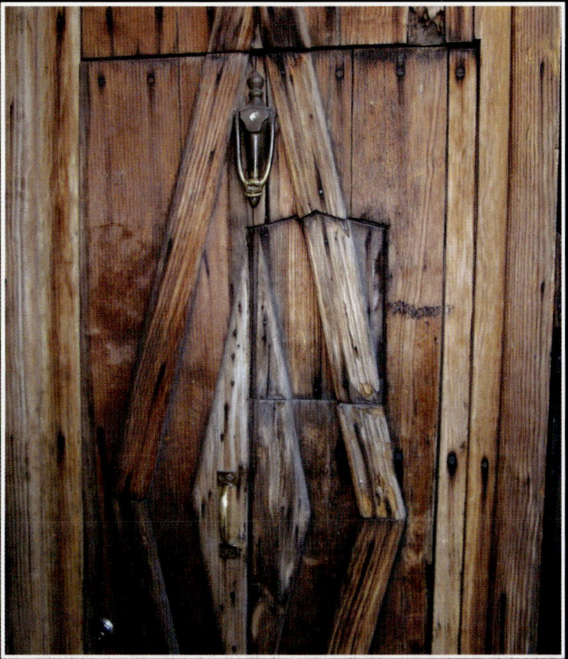

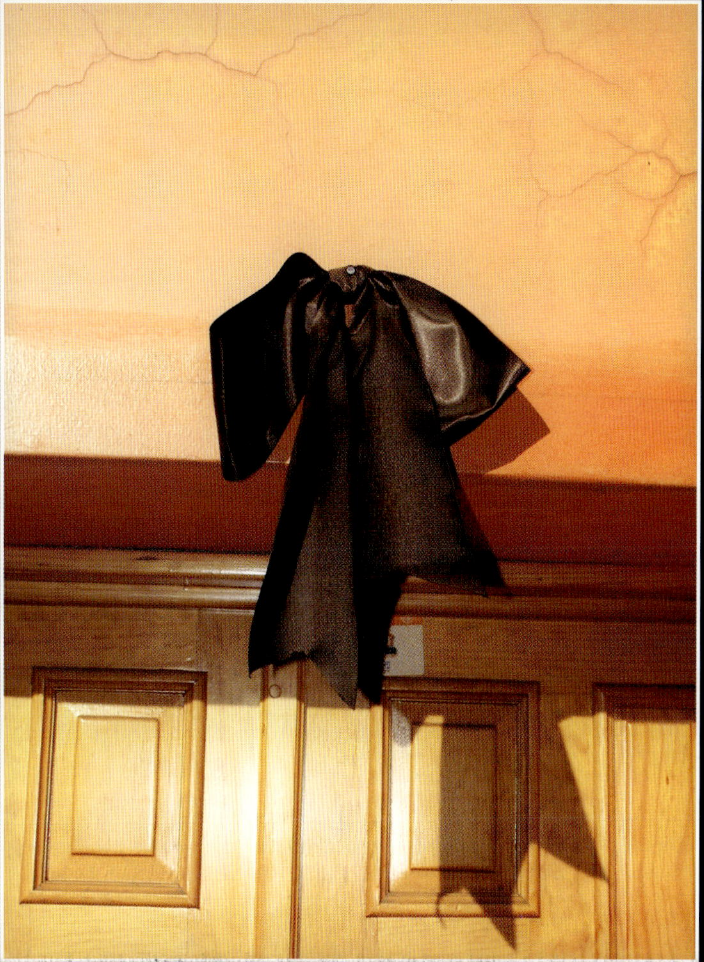

These dark bows hang over the doors of families who are mourning the death of a loved one. Many of these bows have been hanging for years.

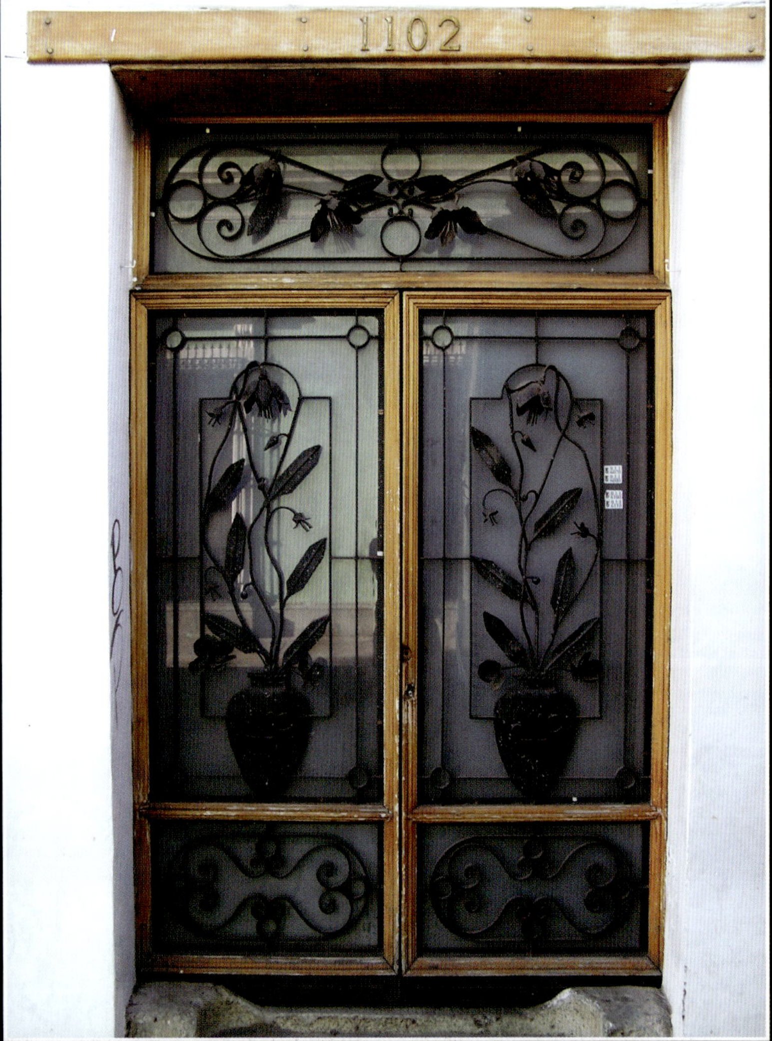

1102 Hidalgo Street.

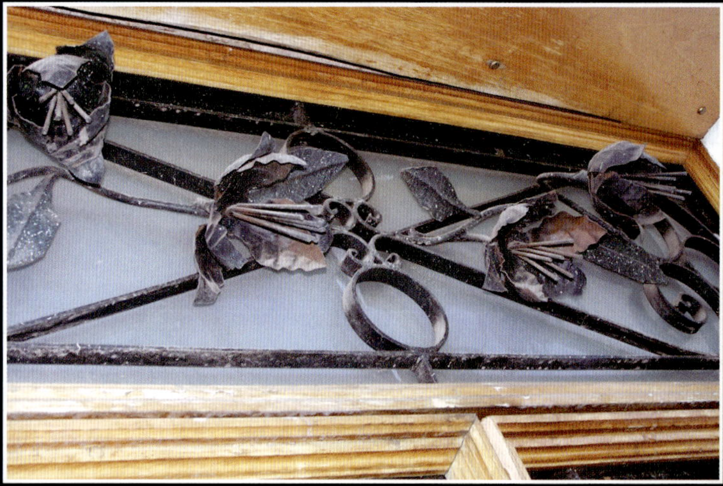

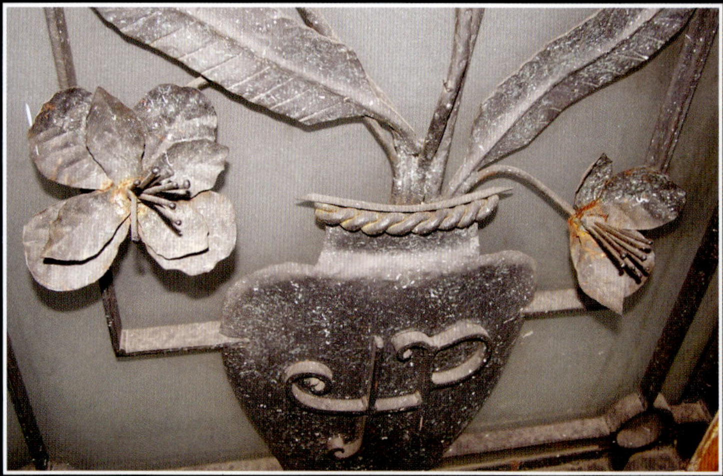

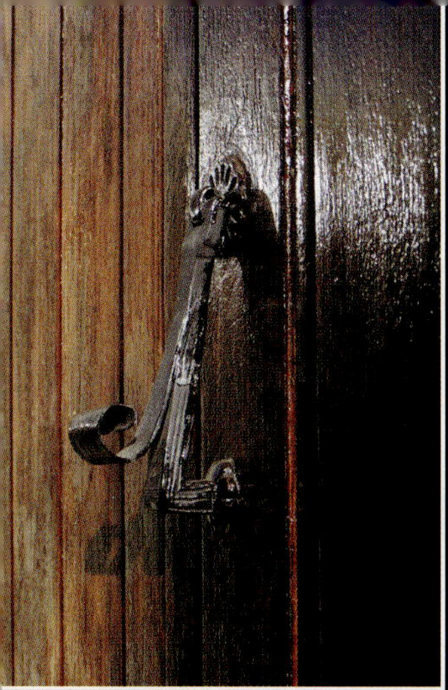
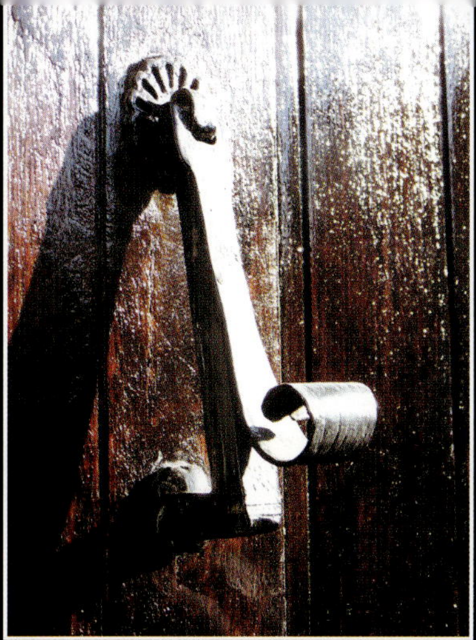
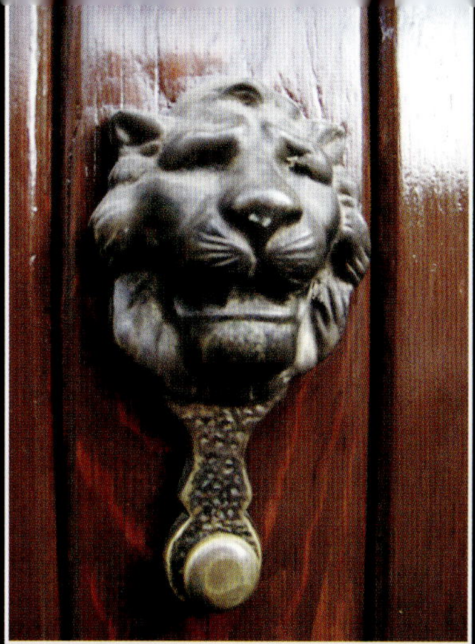
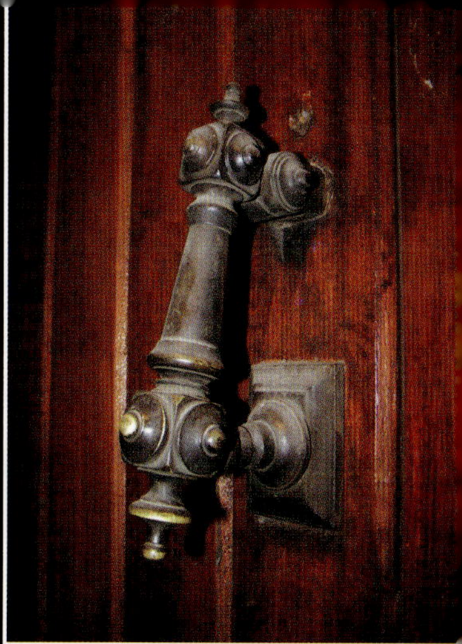
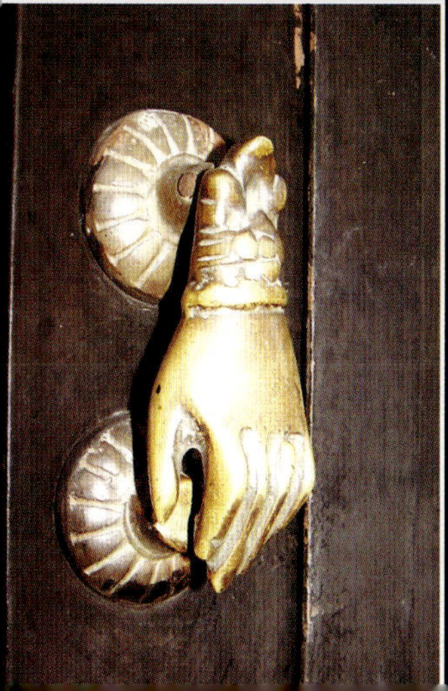
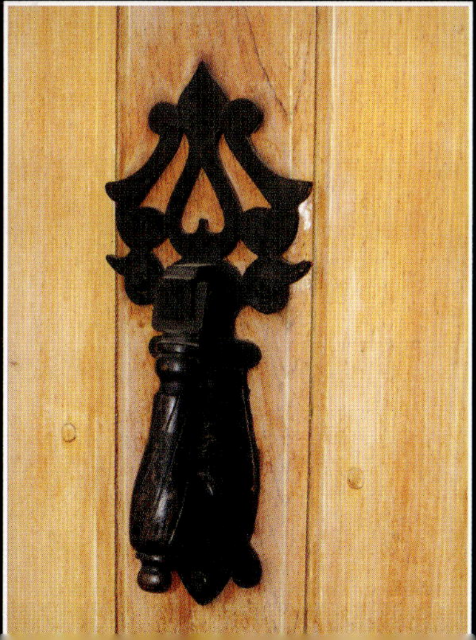
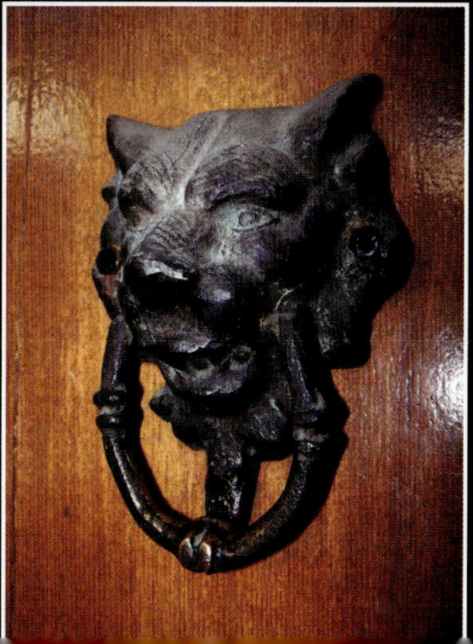
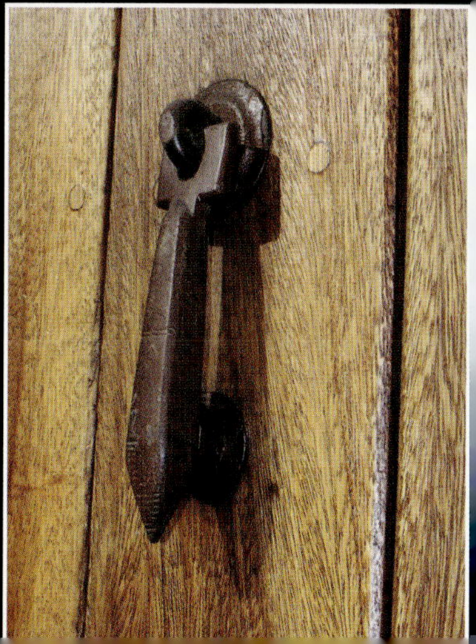

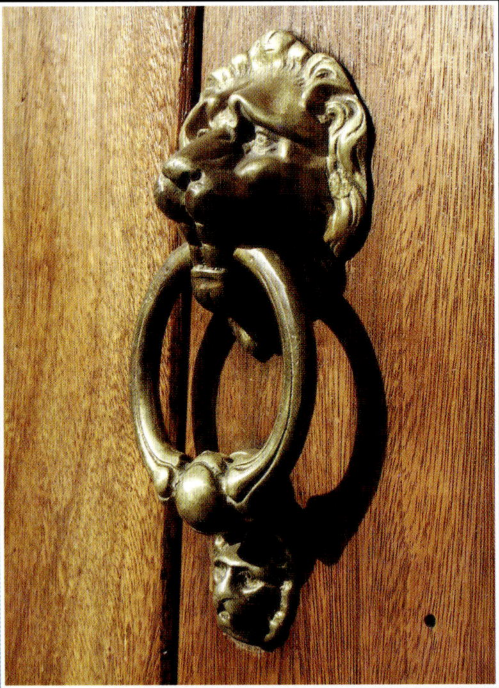

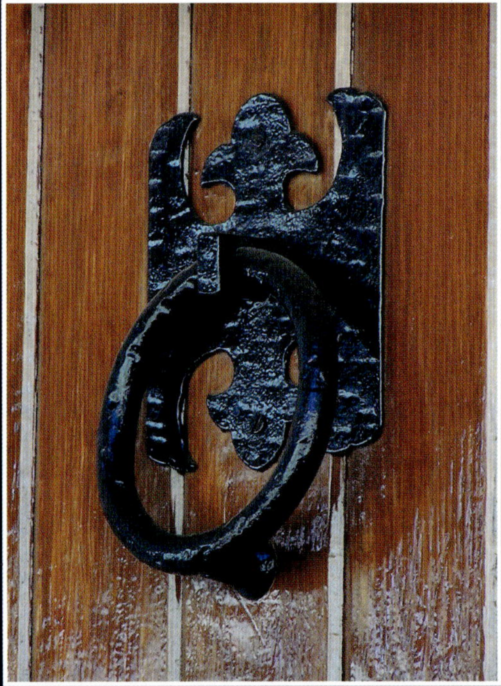

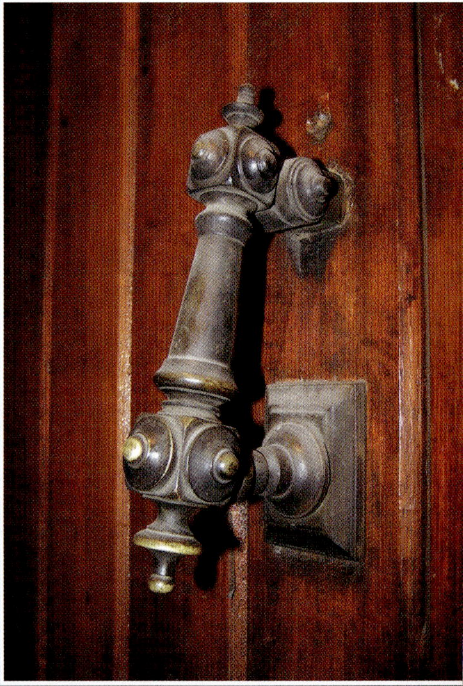

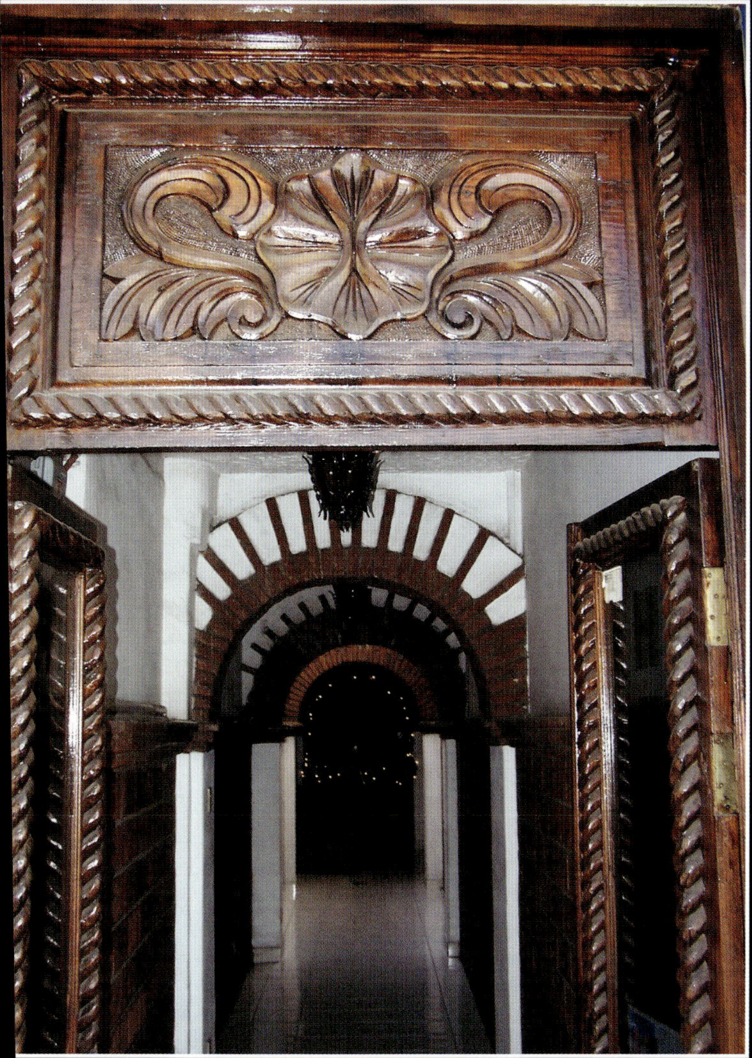

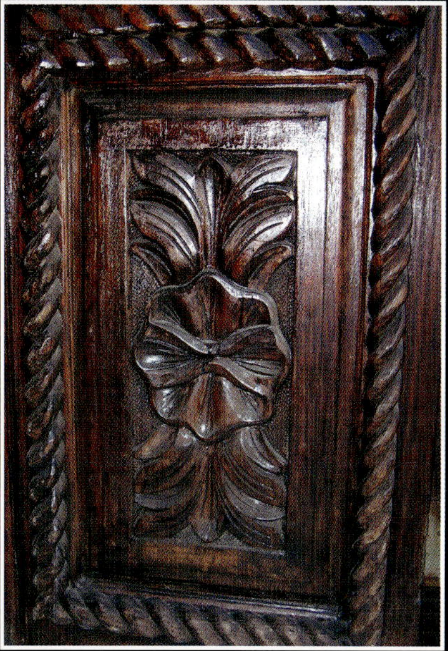

The Santa Clara Hotel on Morelos Street.

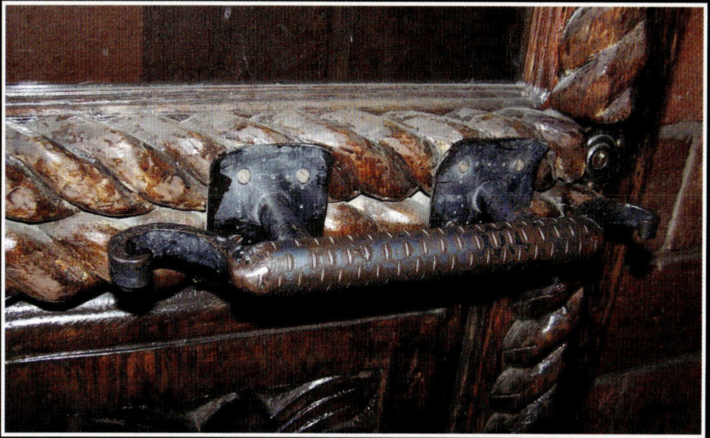

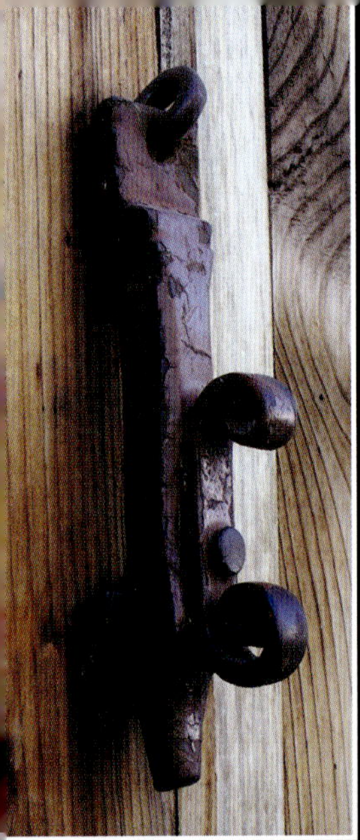

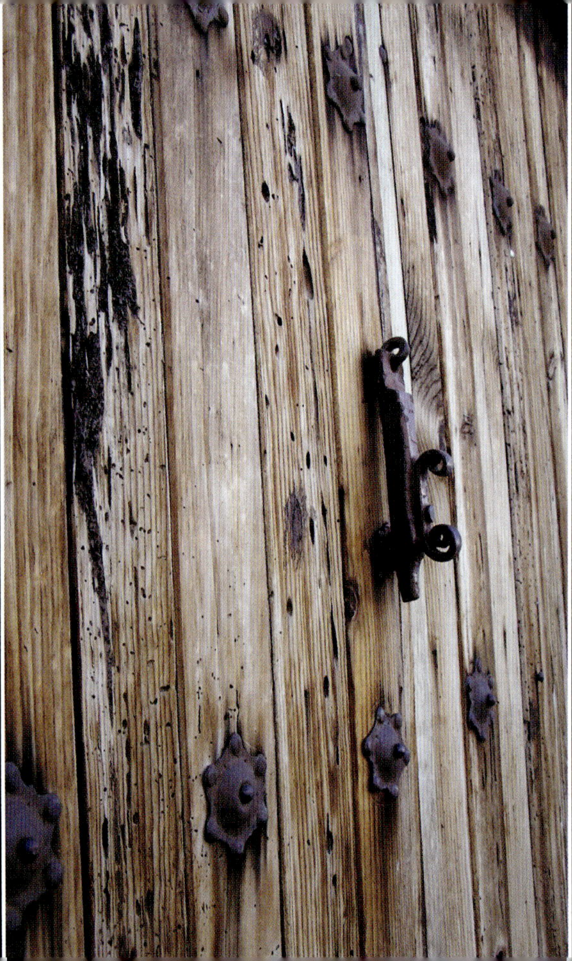

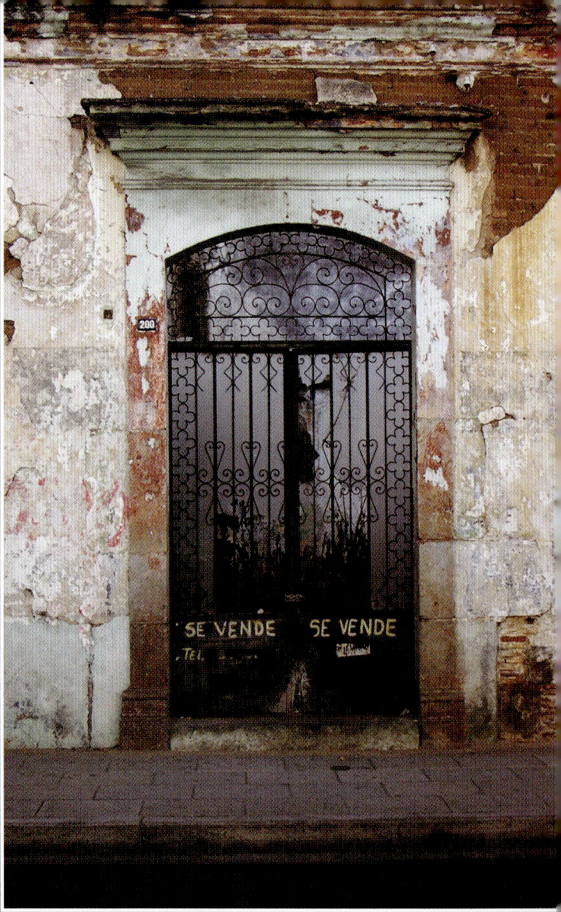

Pino Suárez Street.

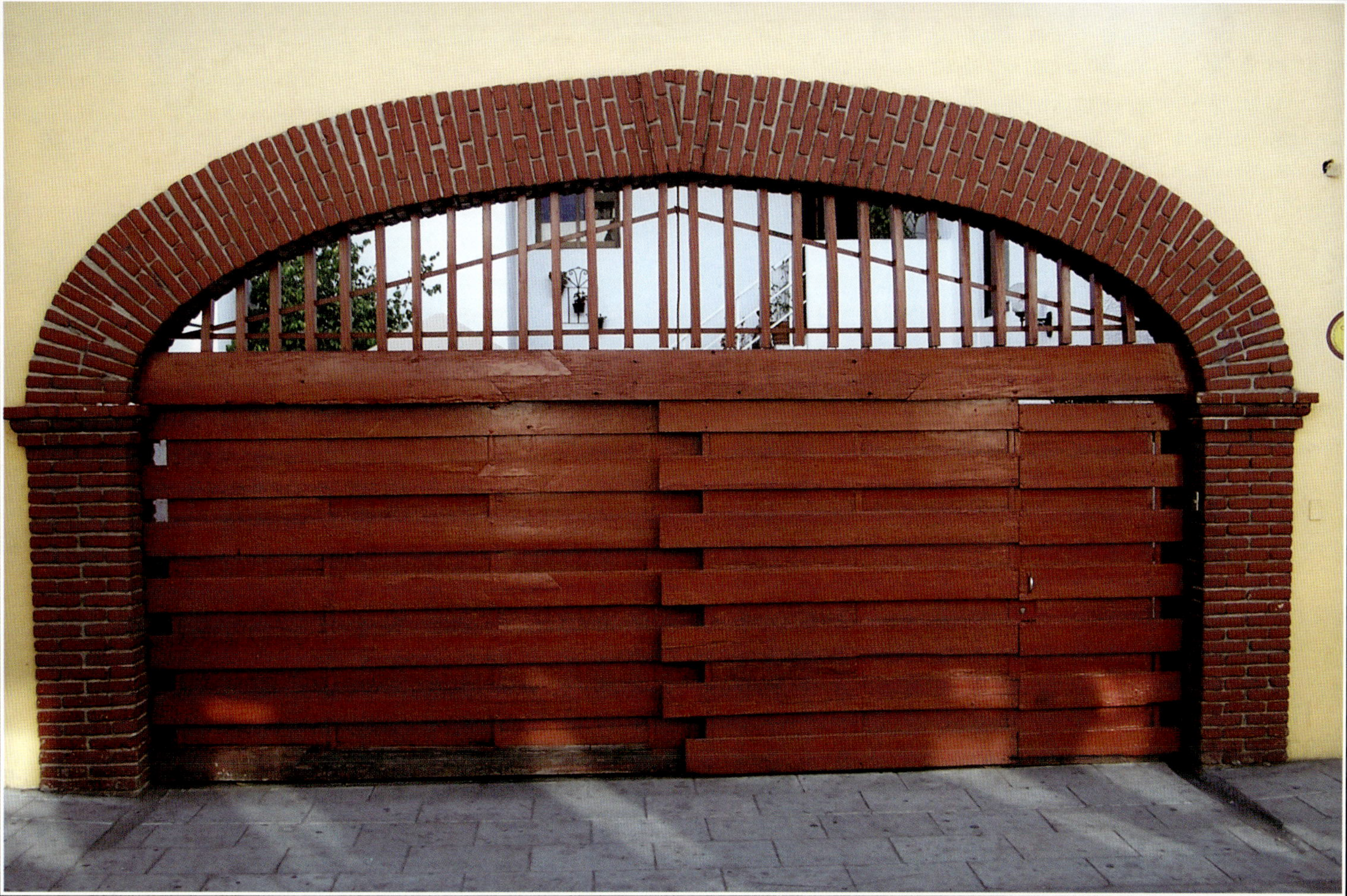

Reforma Street.

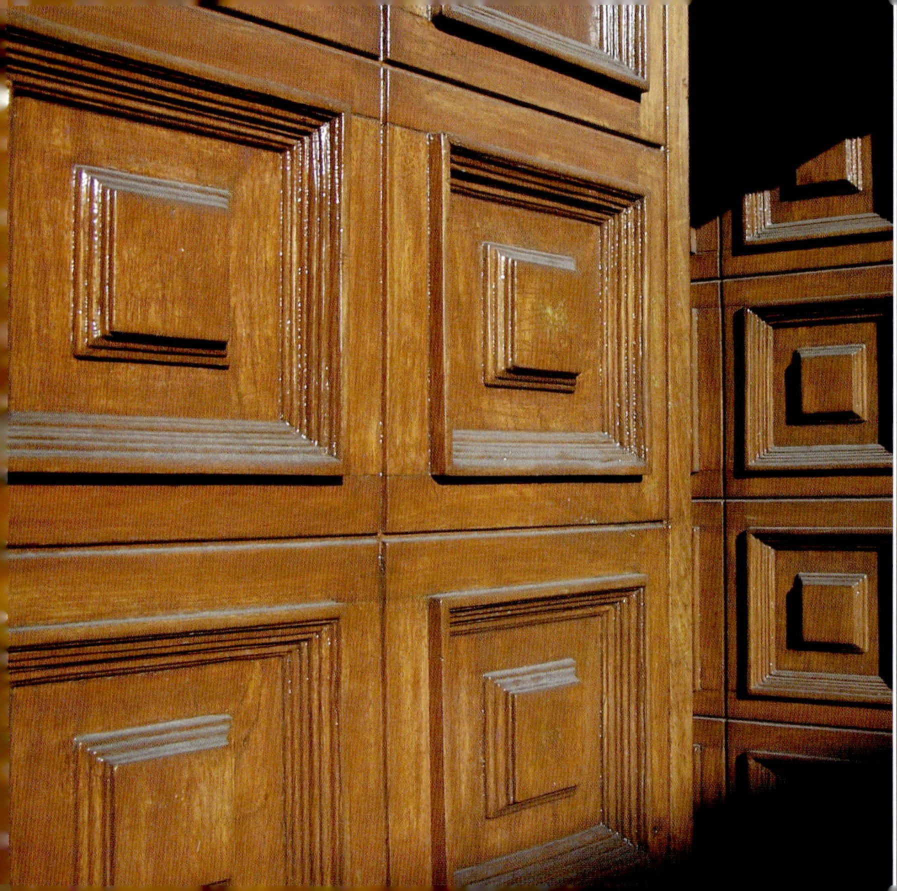

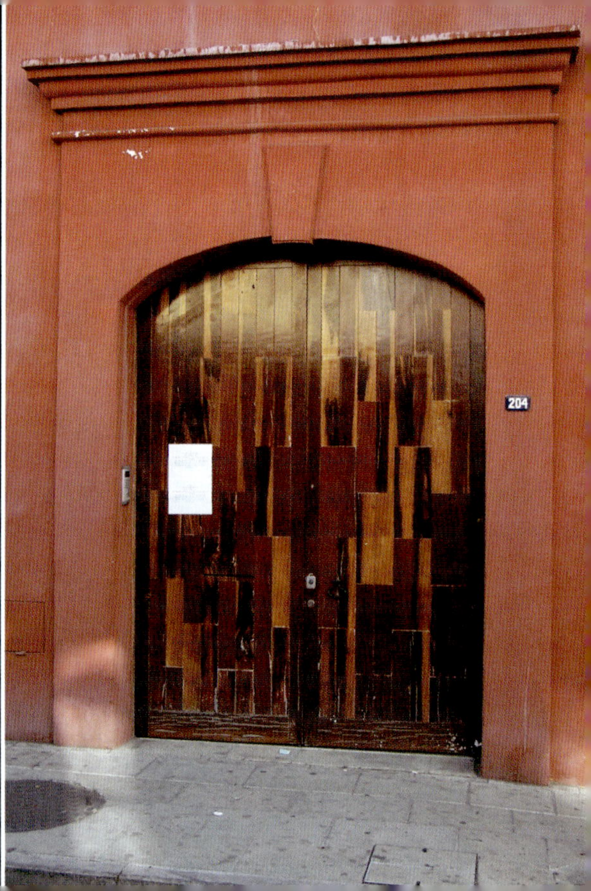
204

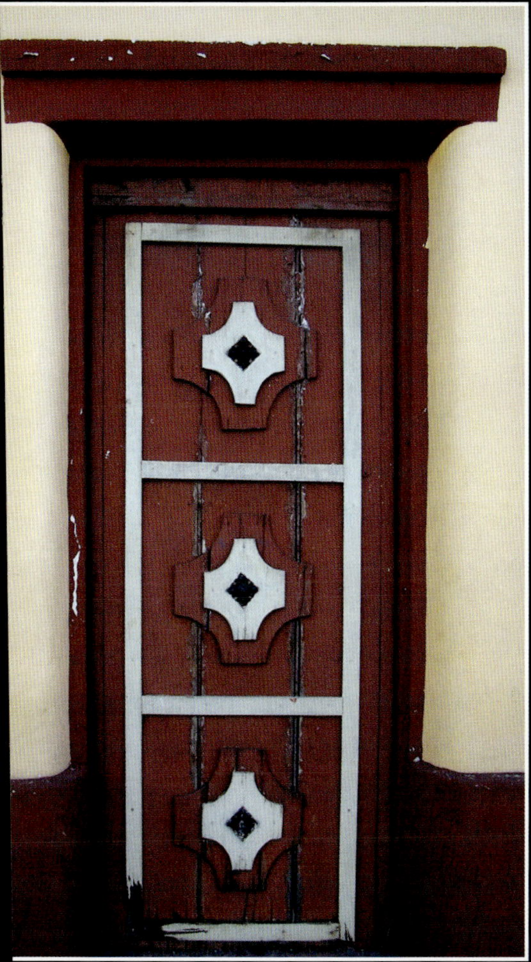
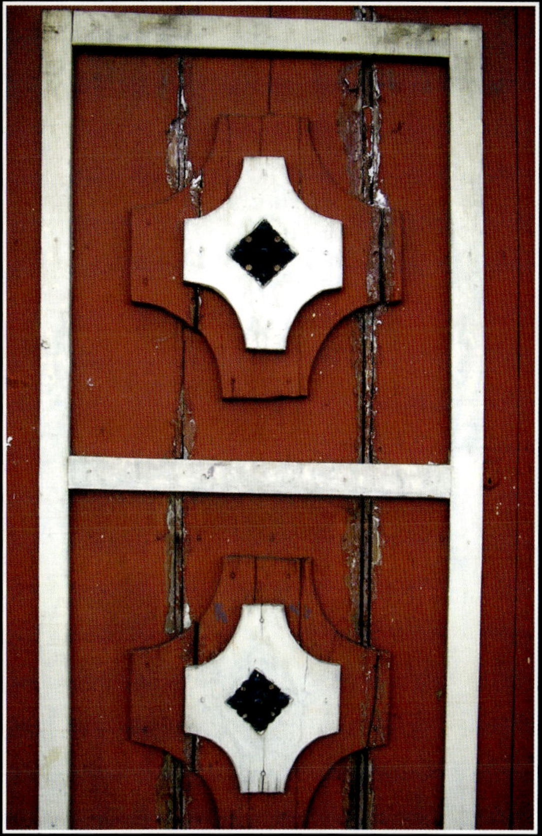
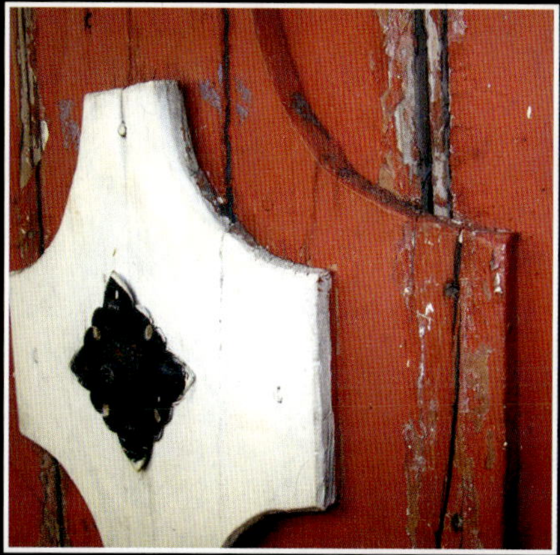

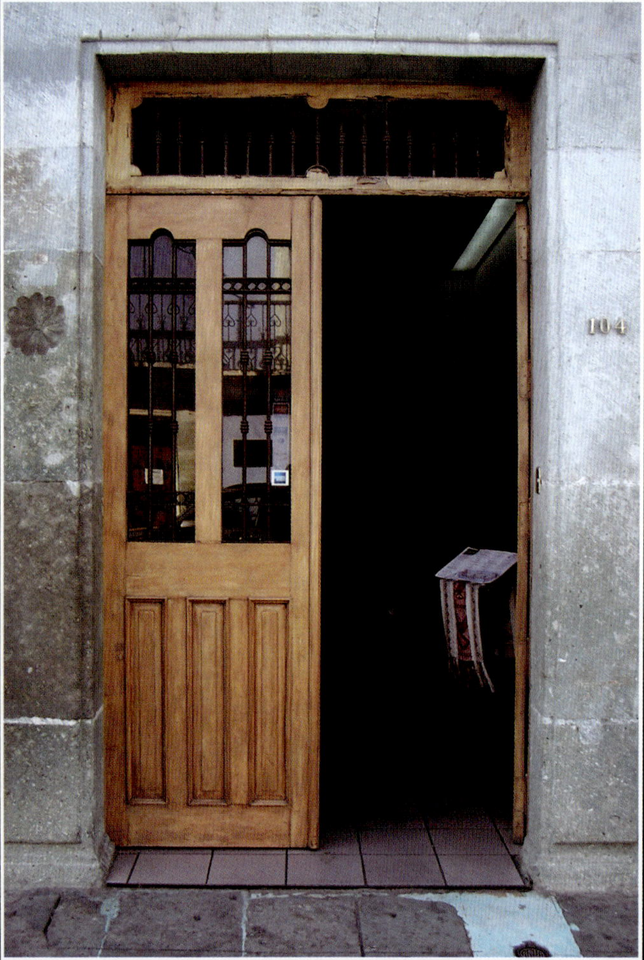

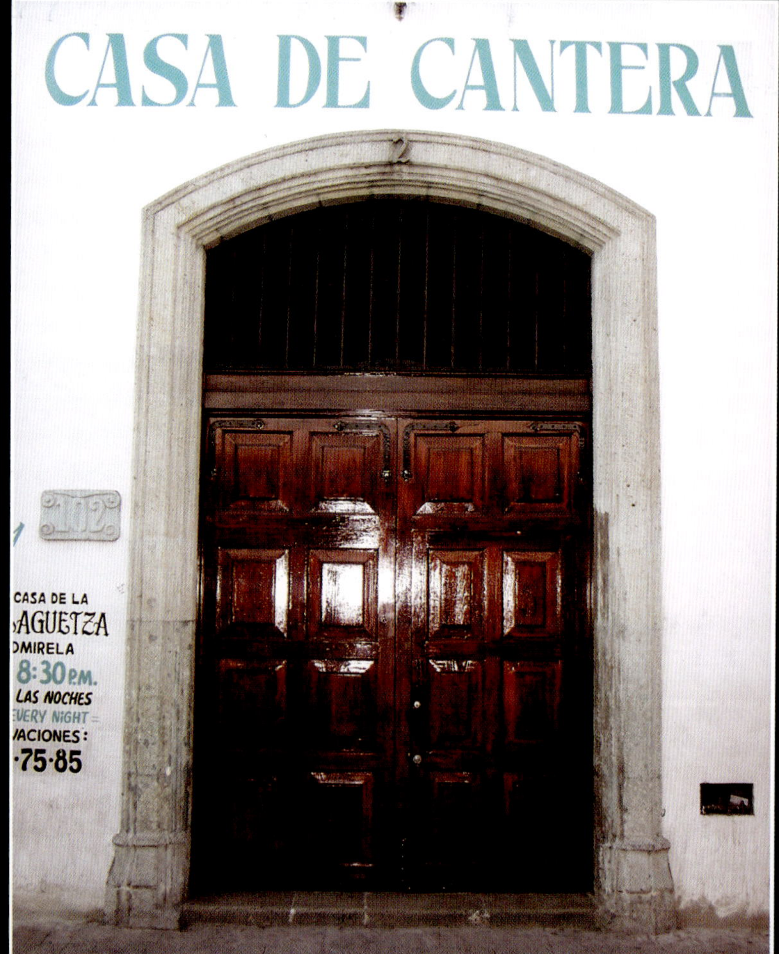

Murguía Street.

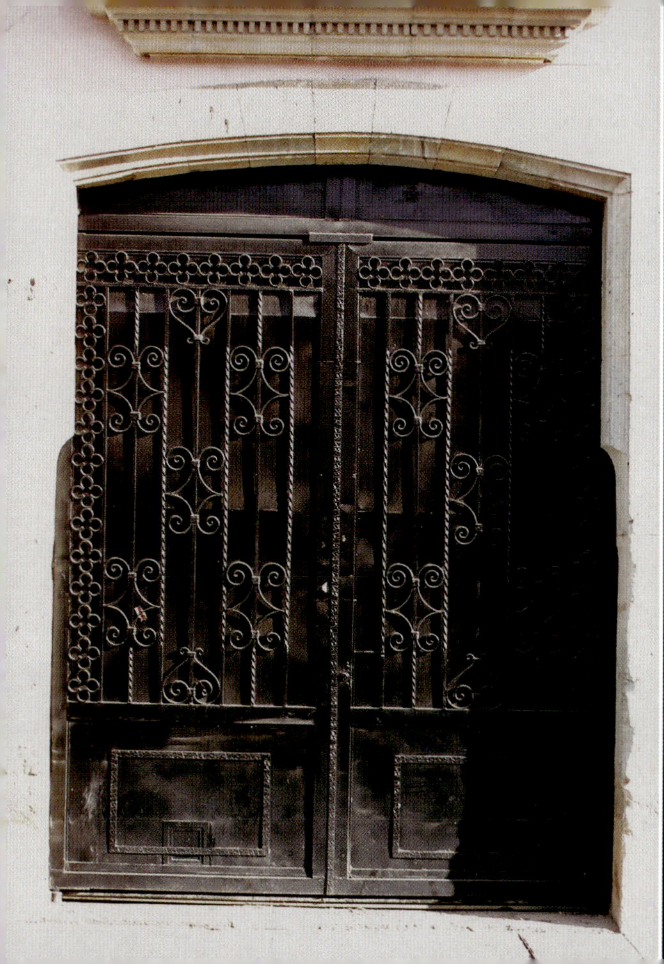

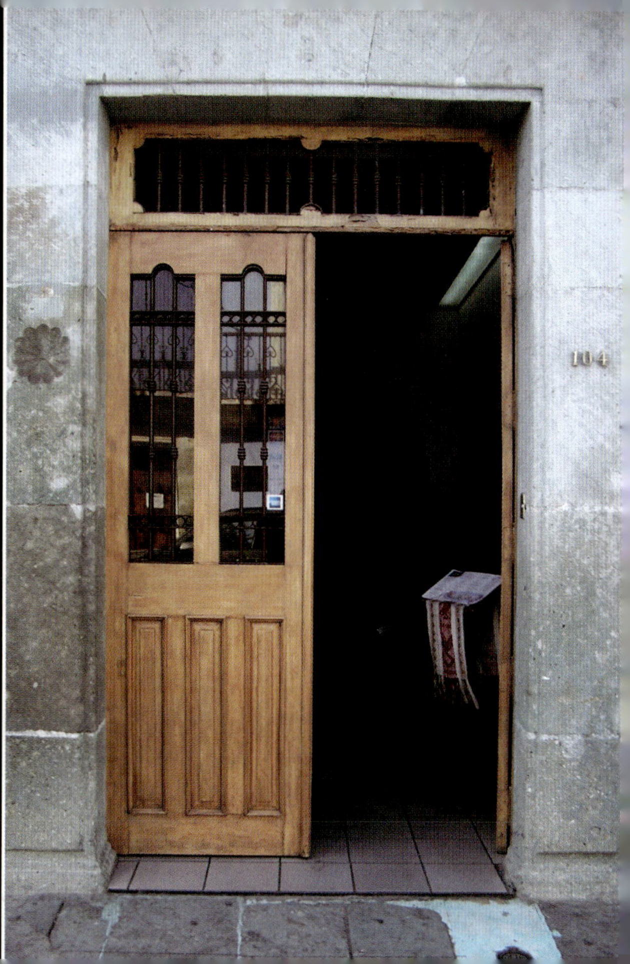

104

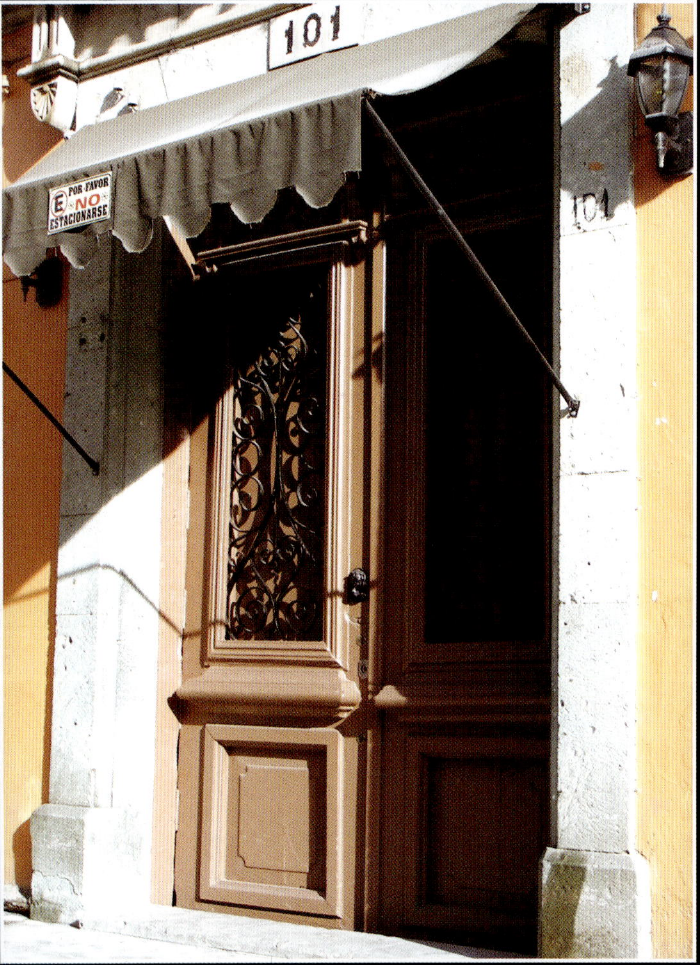

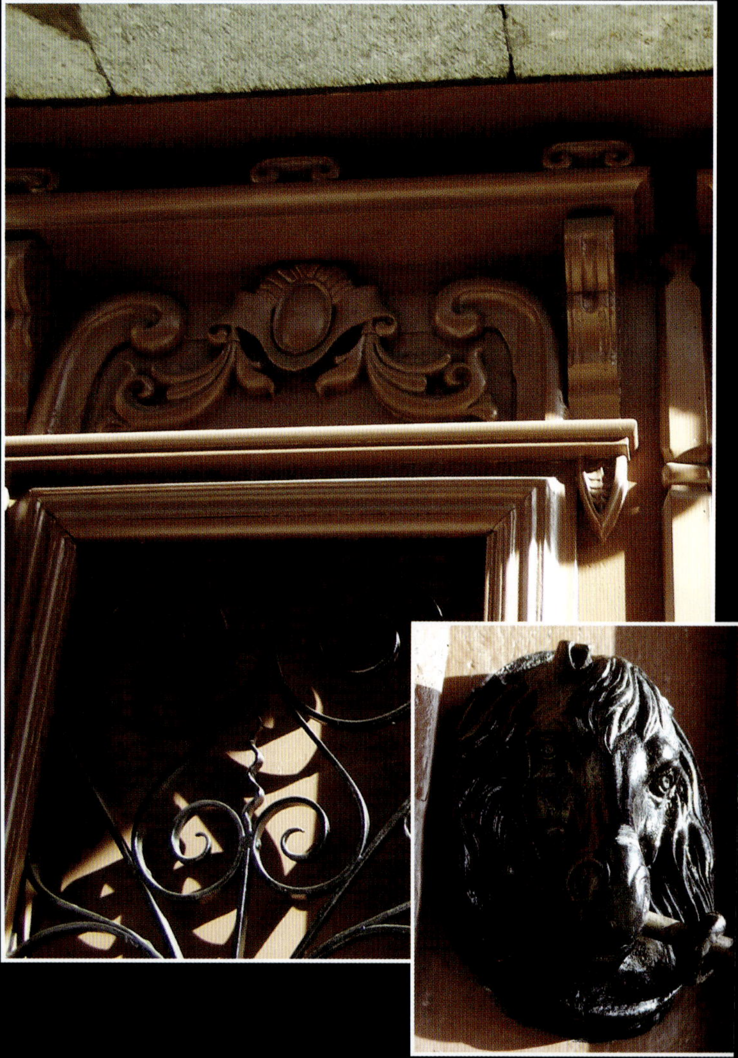

Guerrero Street near the San Agustín Church.

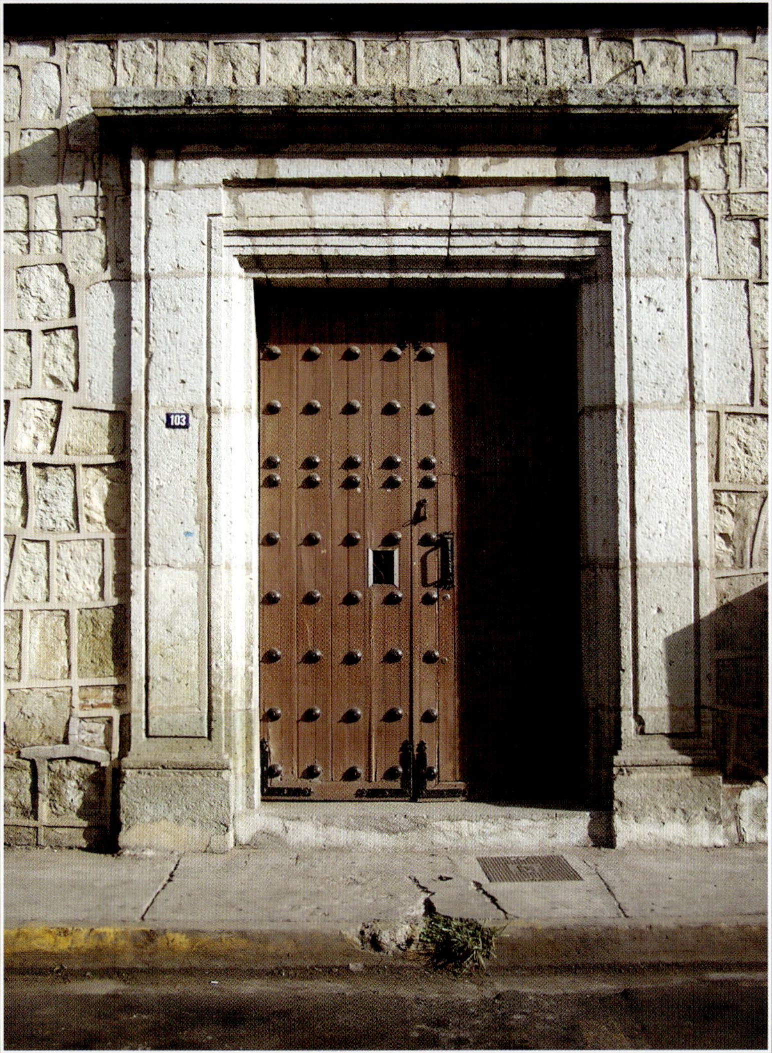
103

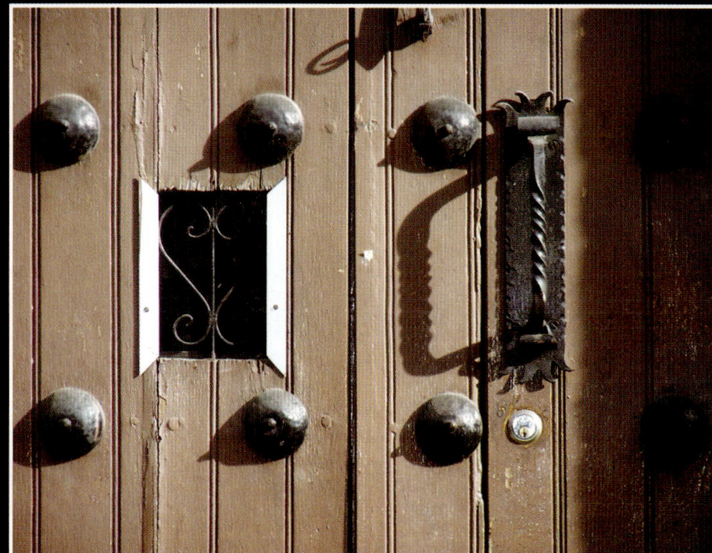

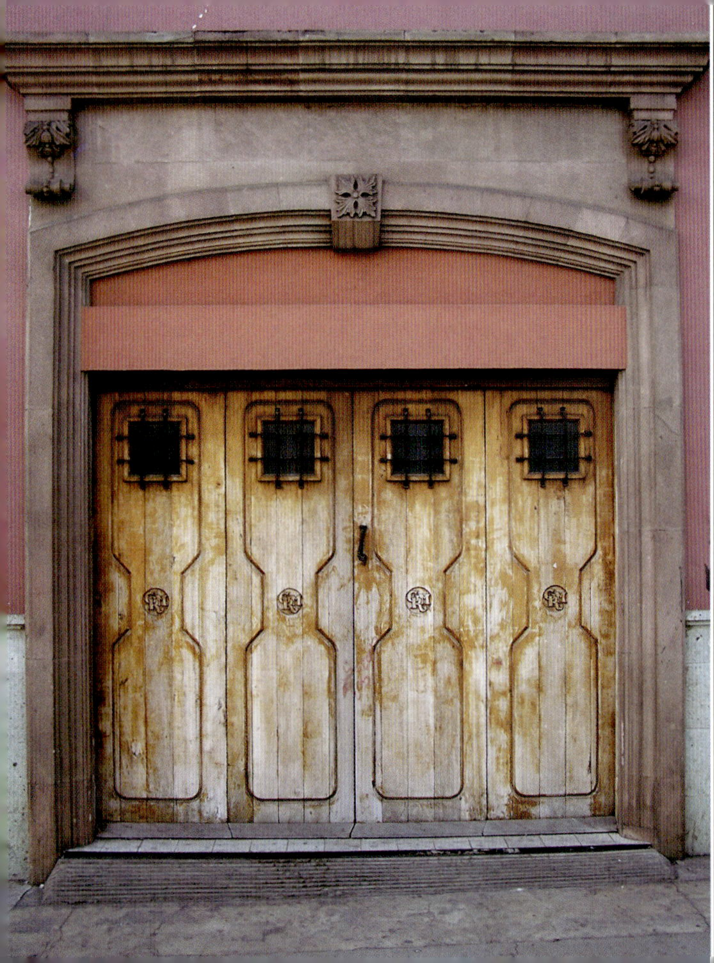

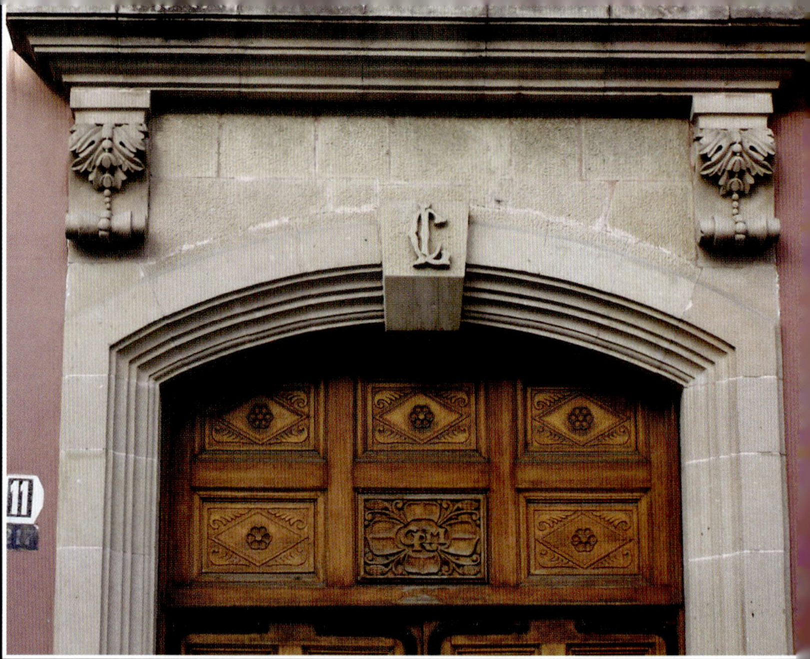

The corner of García Vigil and Matamoros Street.

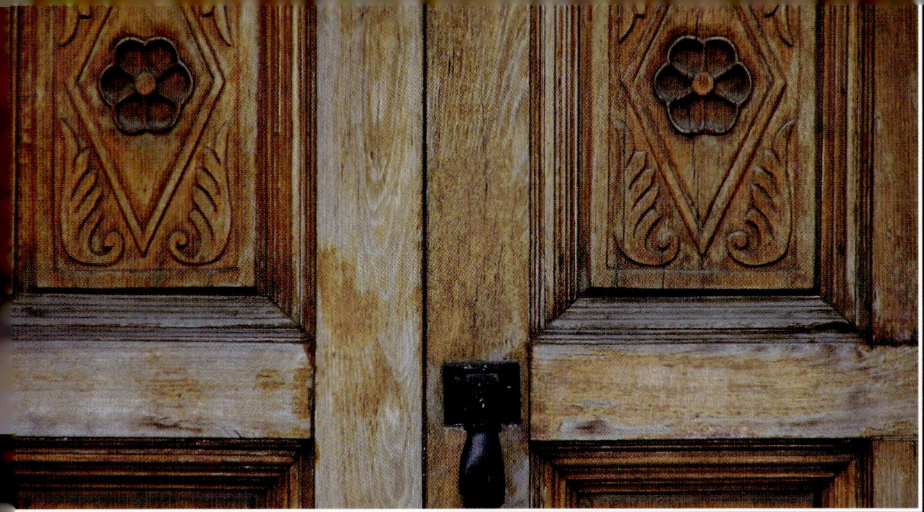
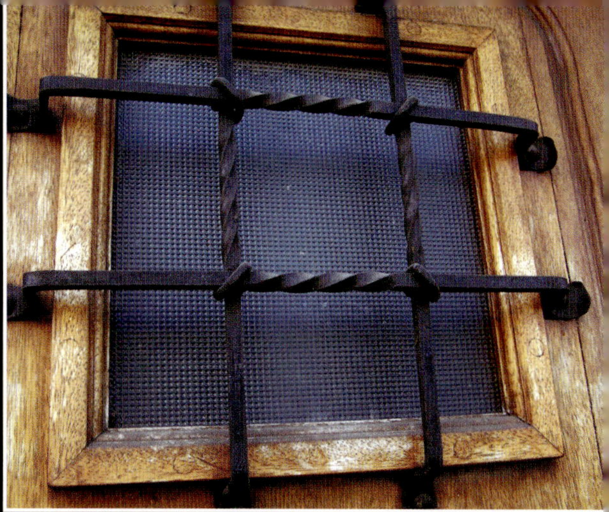
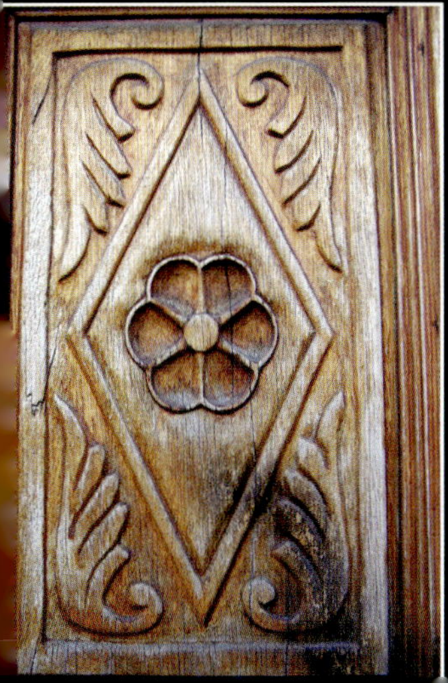
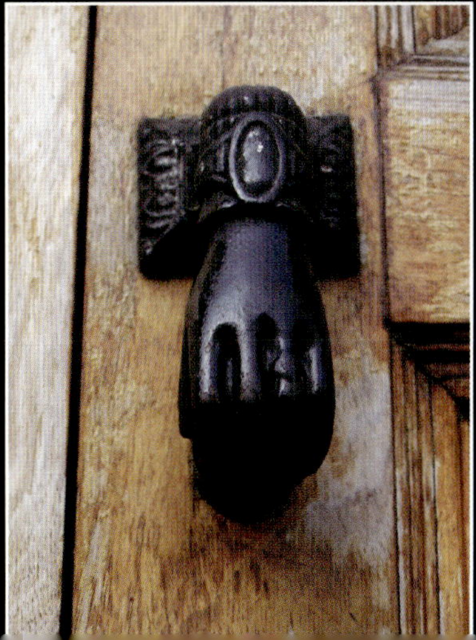
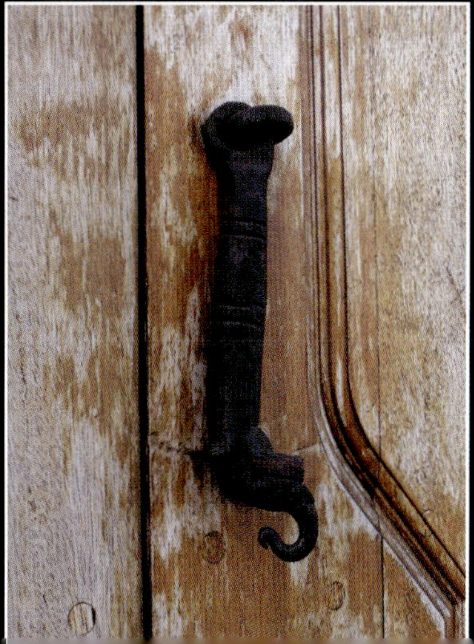
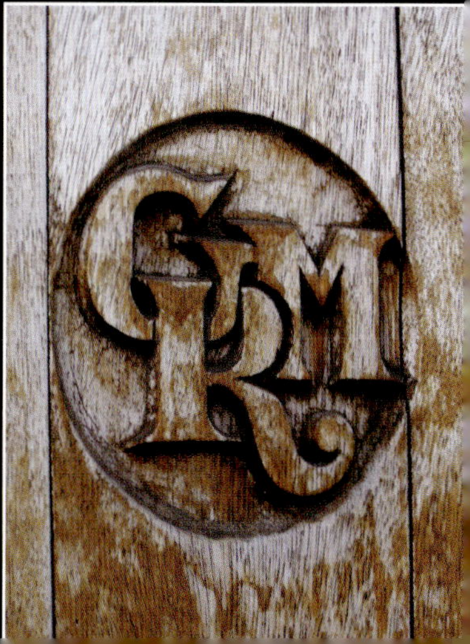

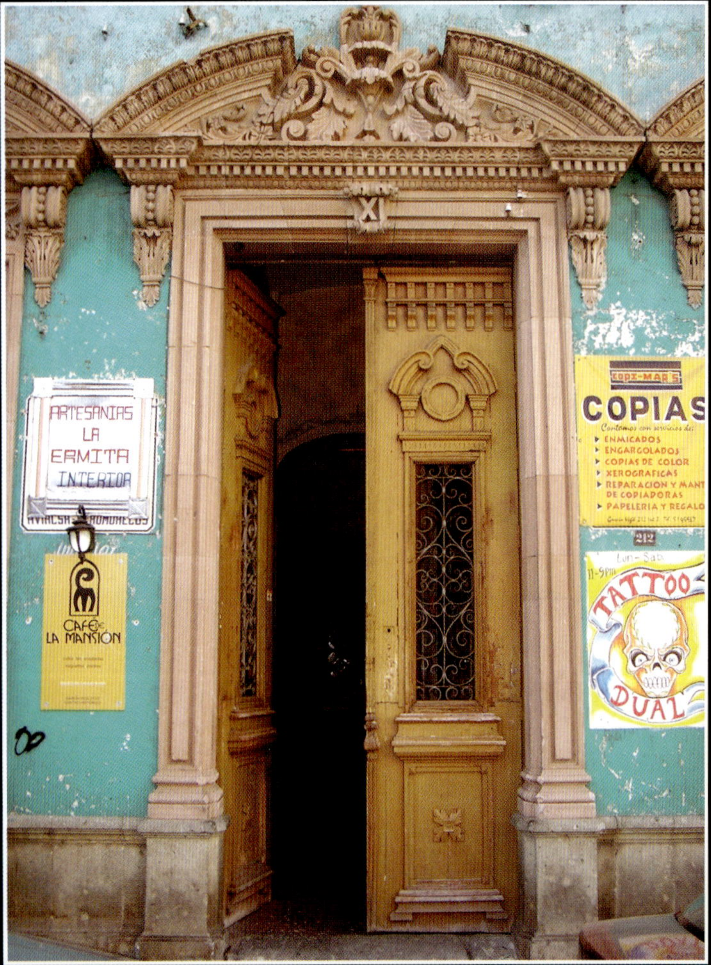

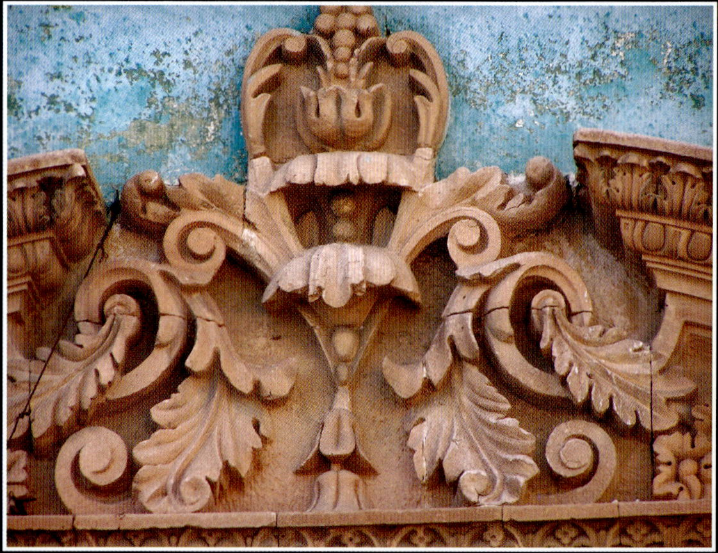

García Vigil Street.

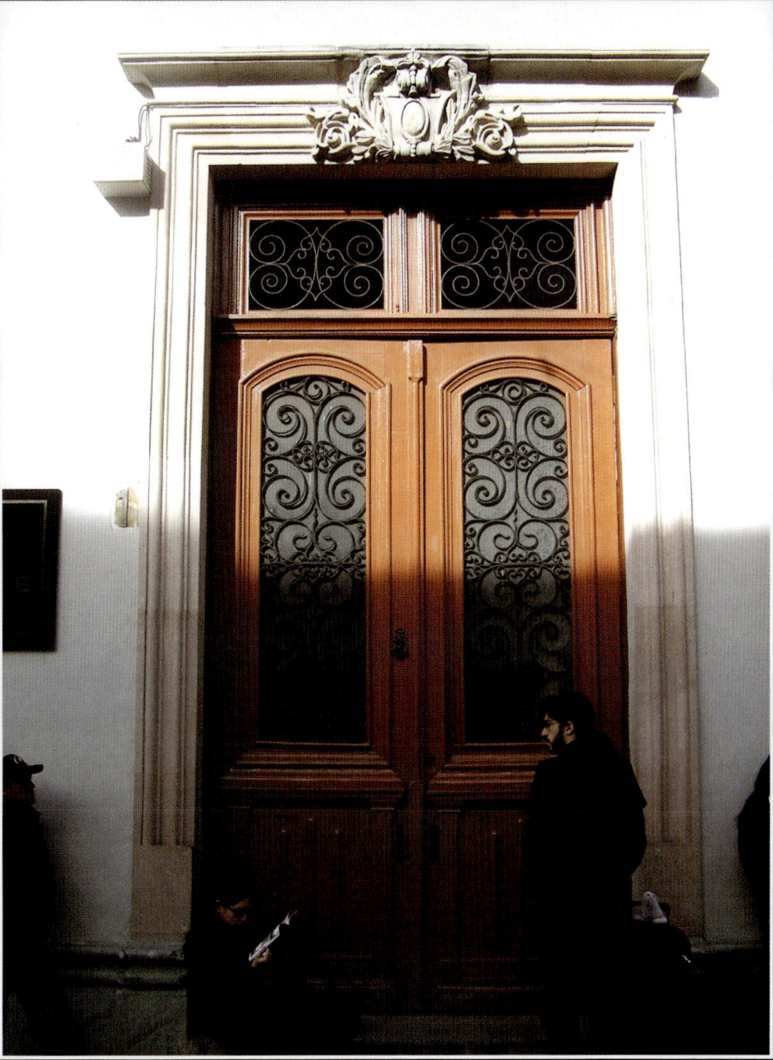

García Vigil Street, a half-block north of the Cathedral Church.

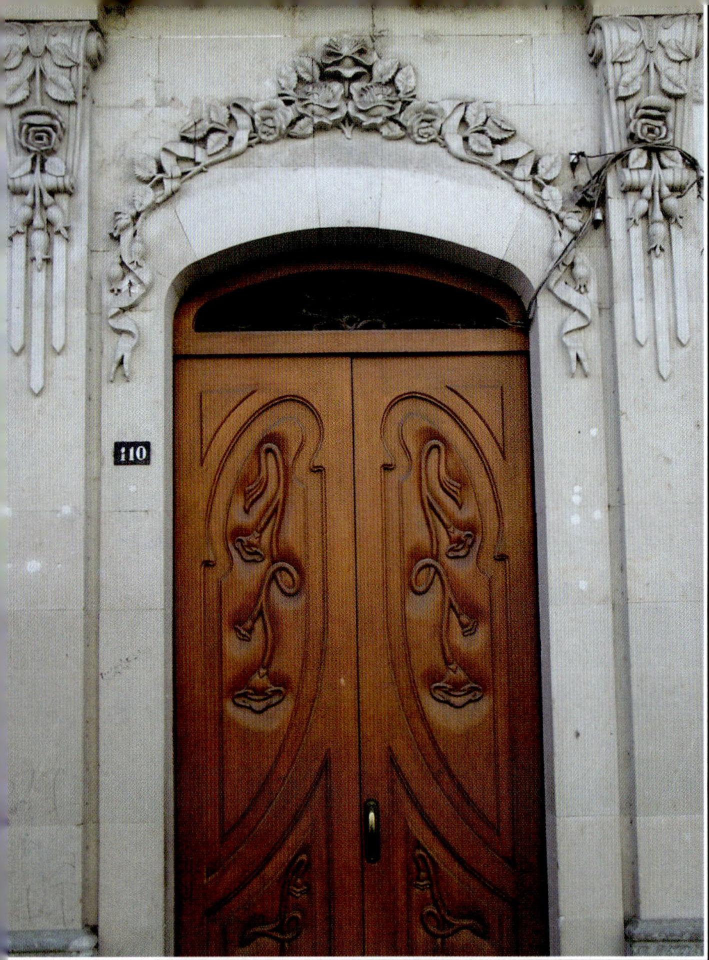

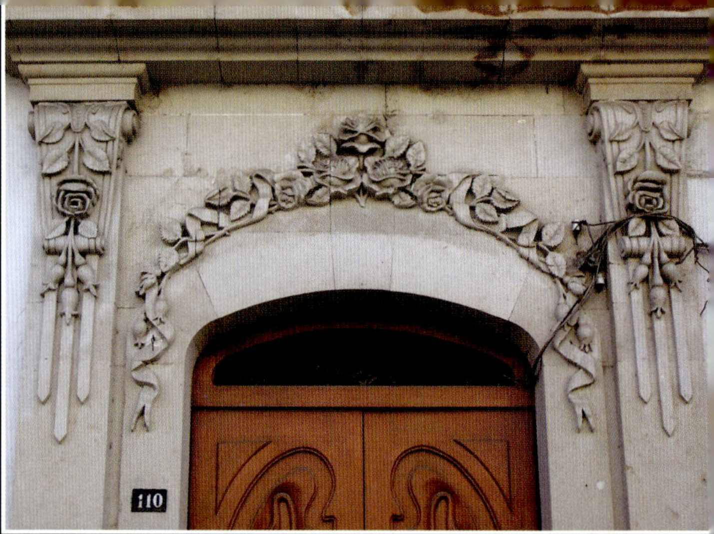

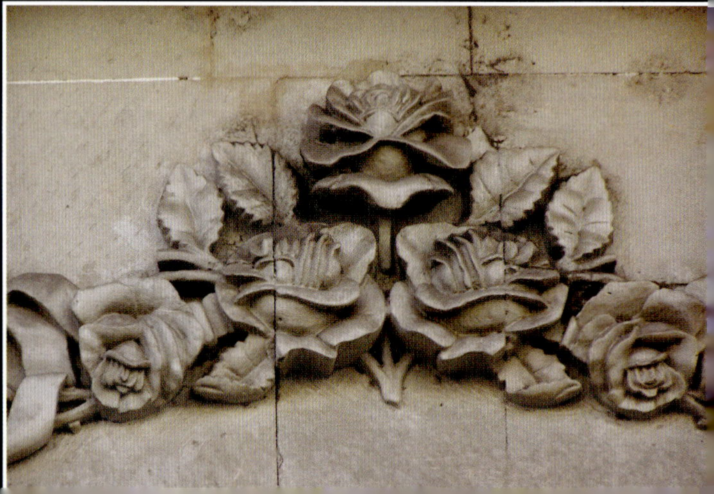

García Vigil Street.

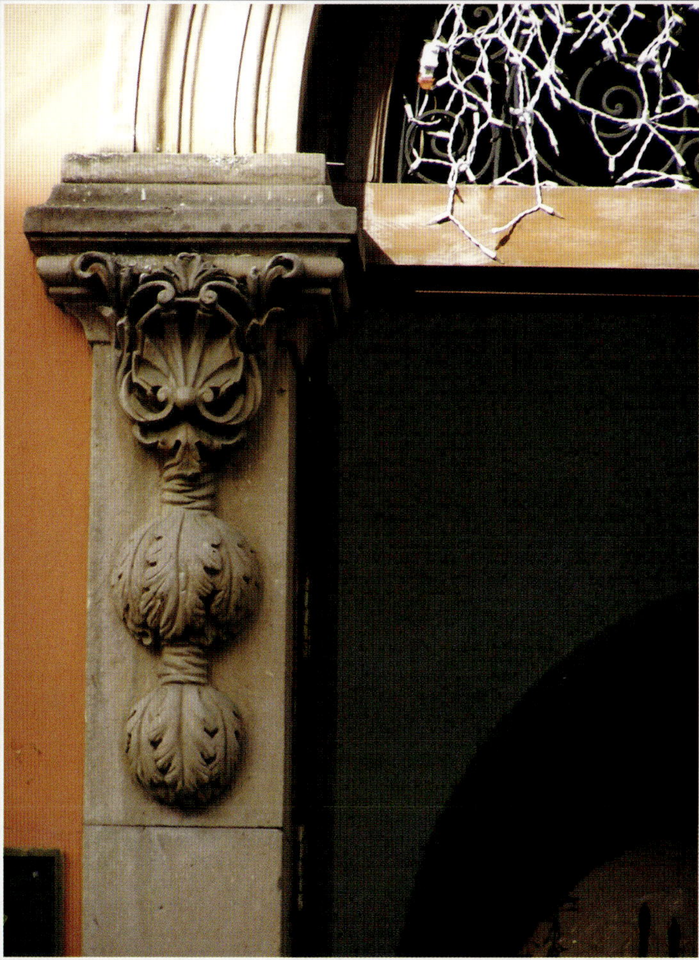

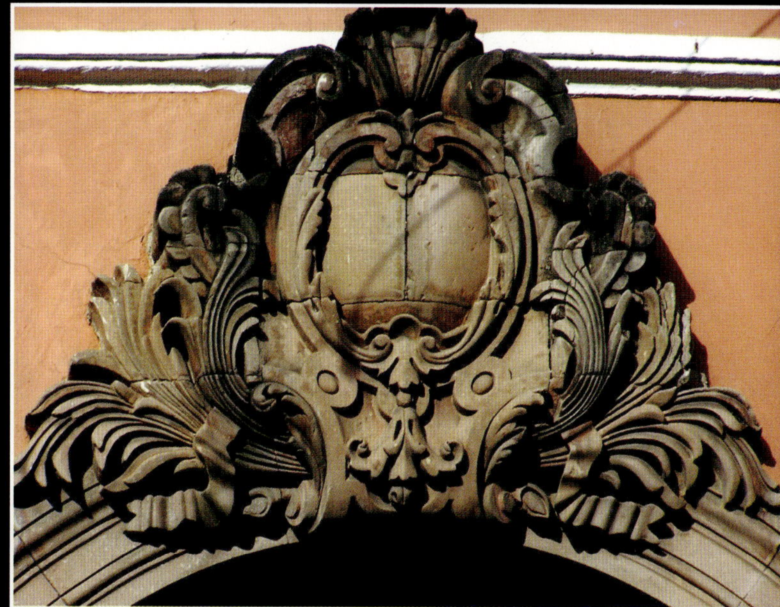

The Cathedral Restaurant.

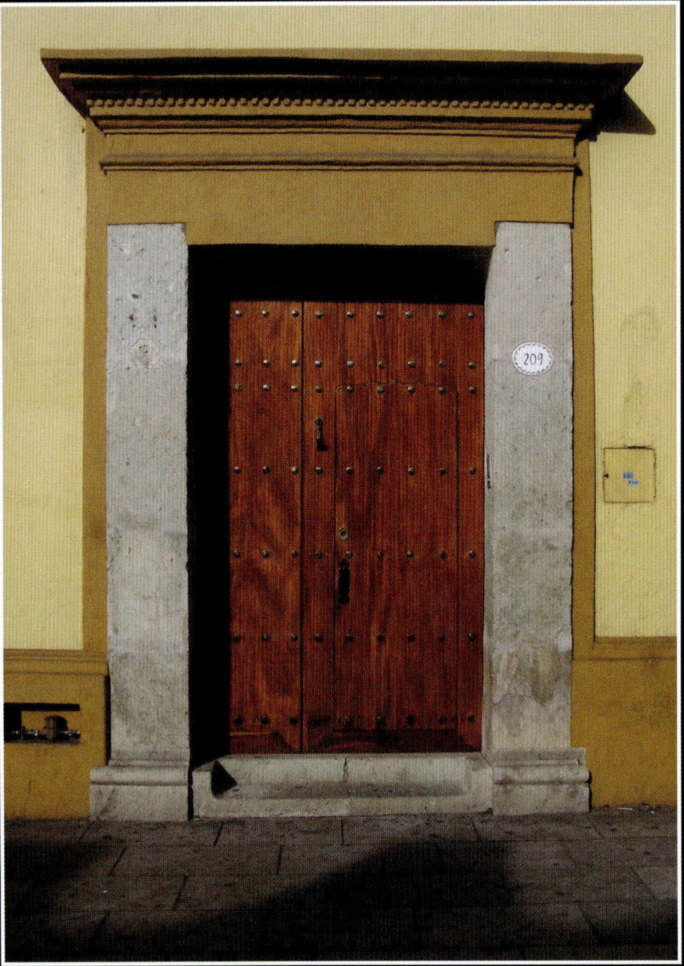
209
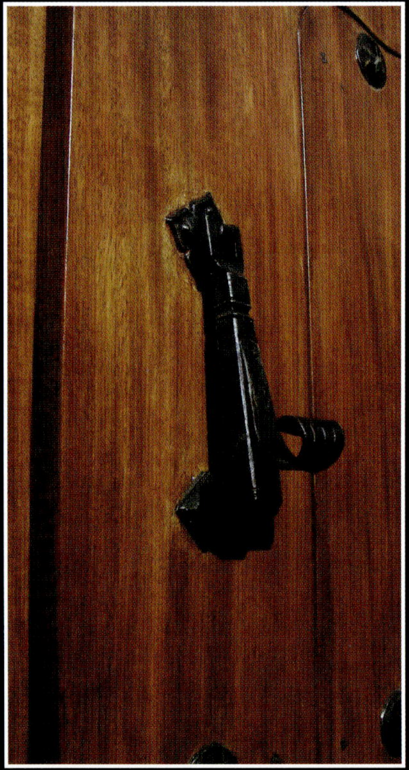
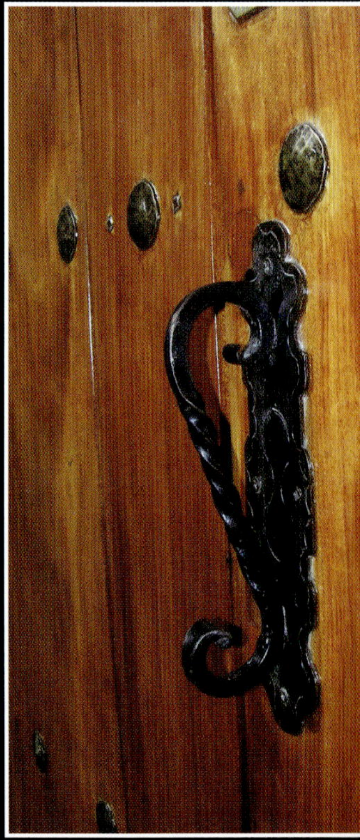

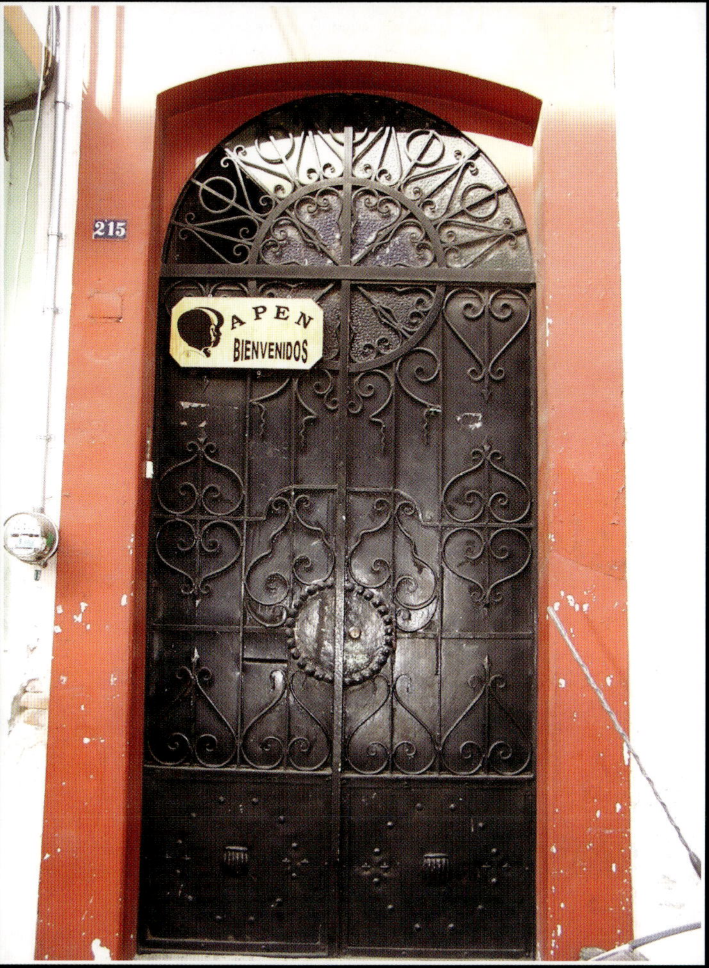
215
APEN
BIENVENIDOS

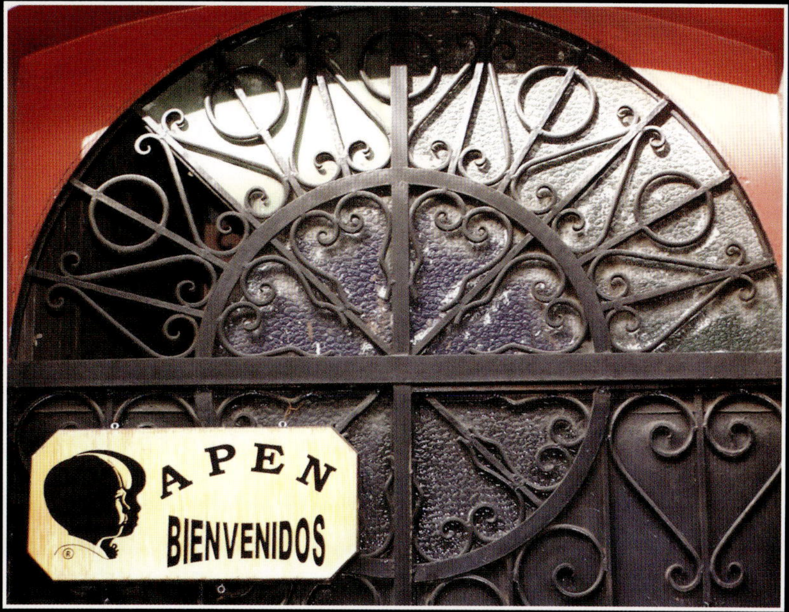
APEN
BIENVENIDOS

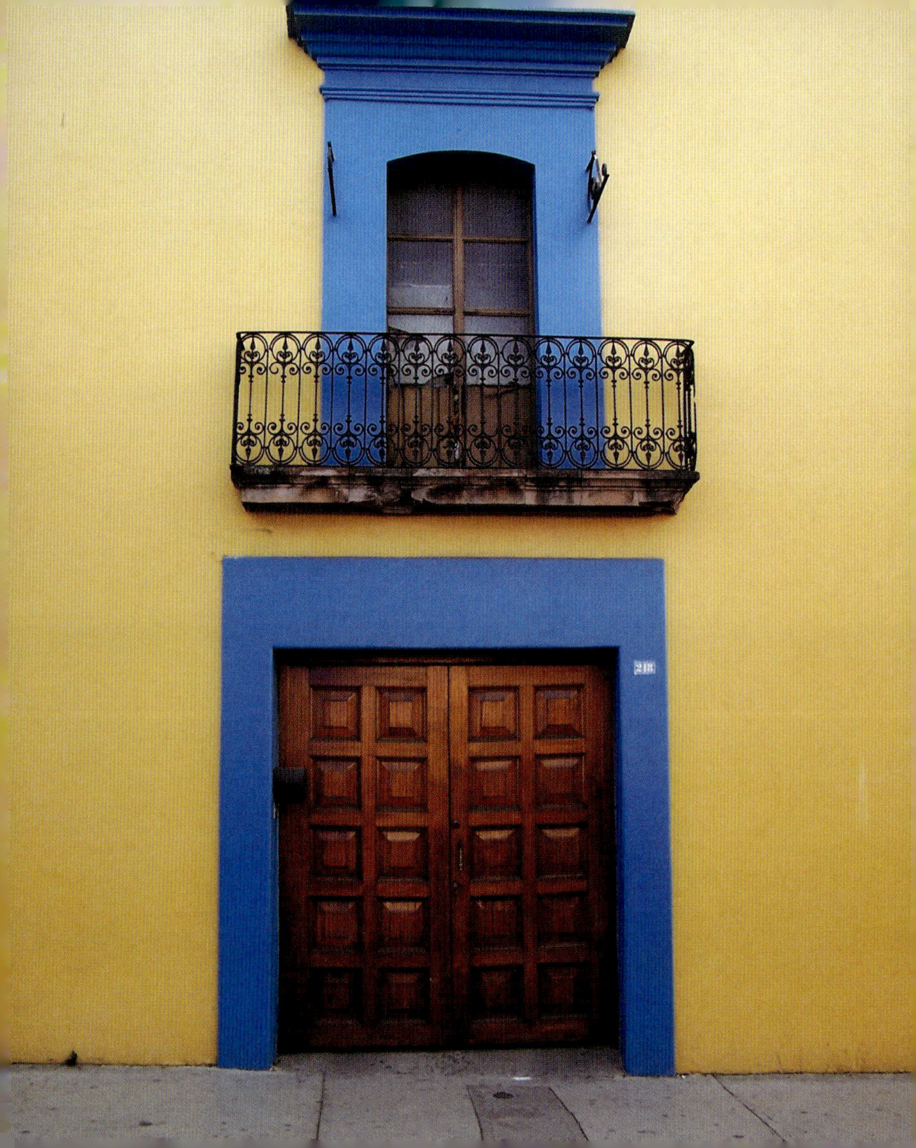

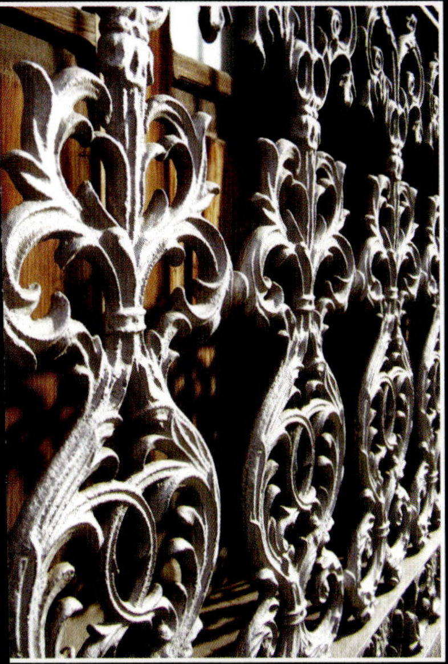
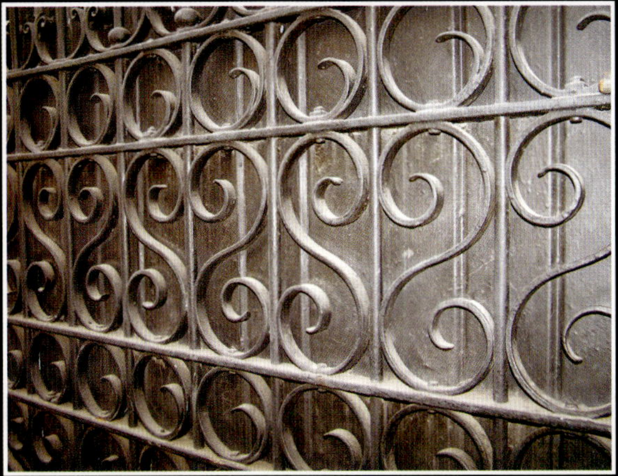

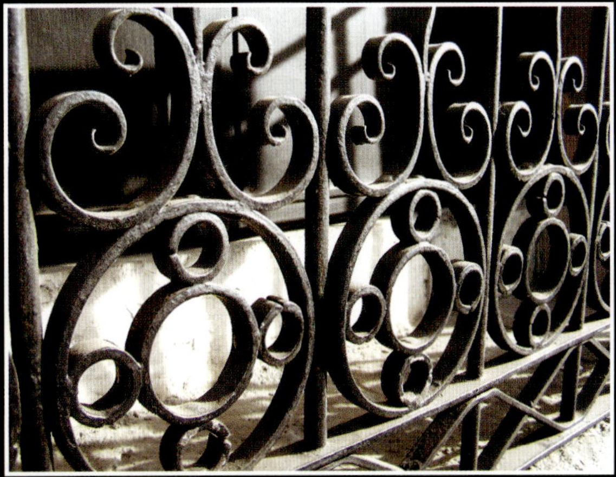
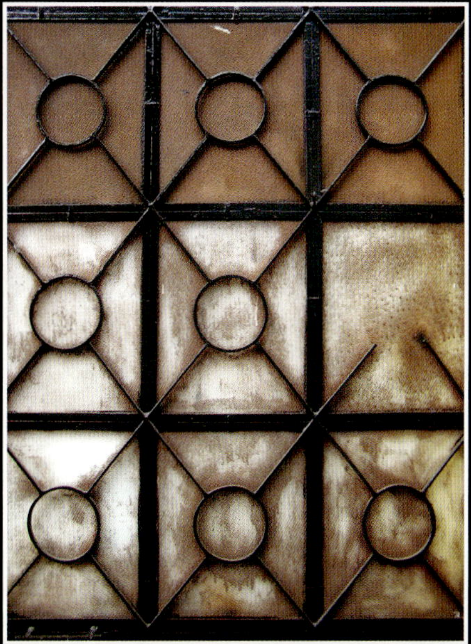

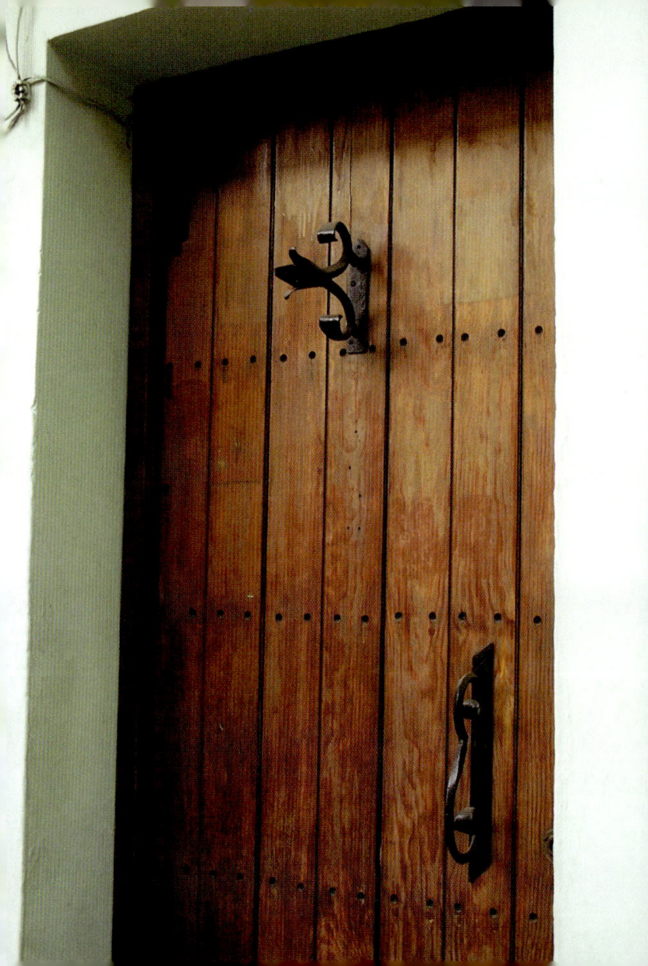
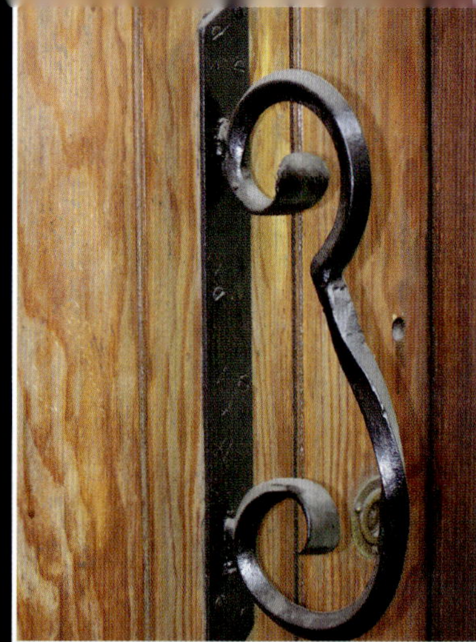
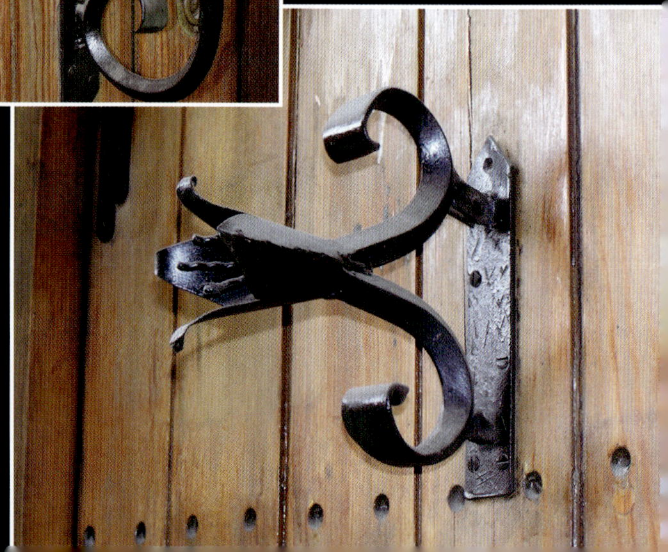

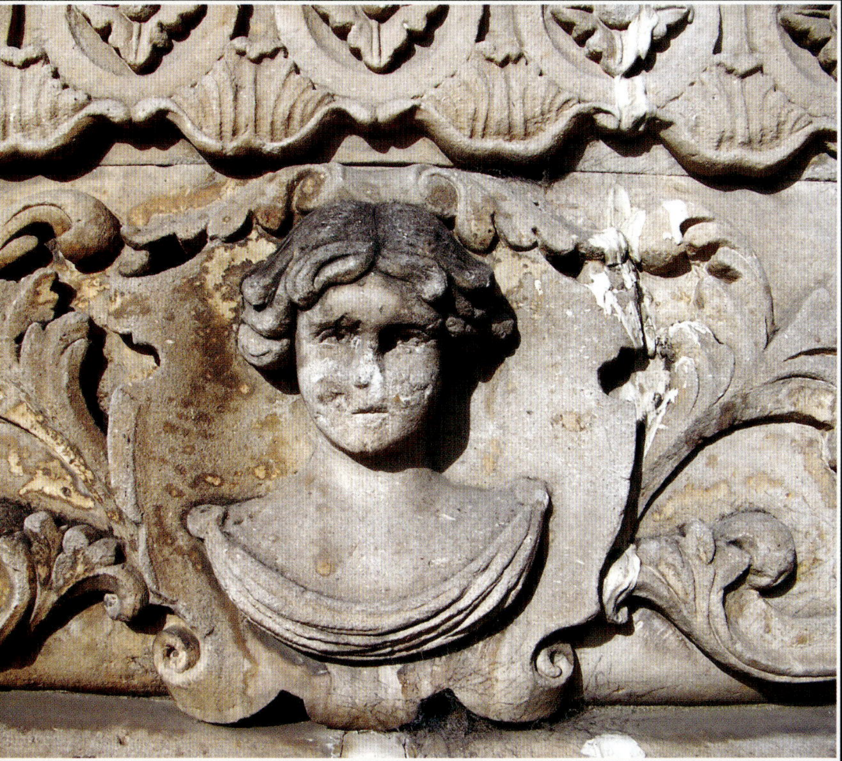

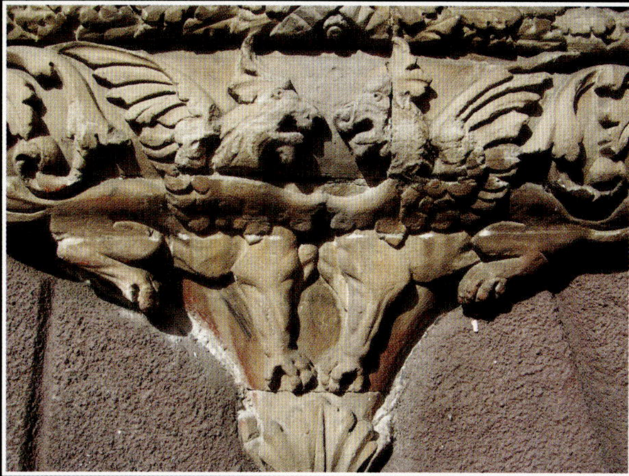

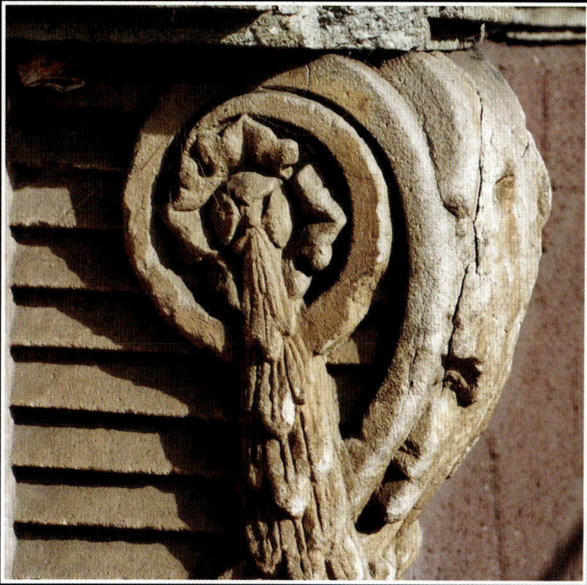

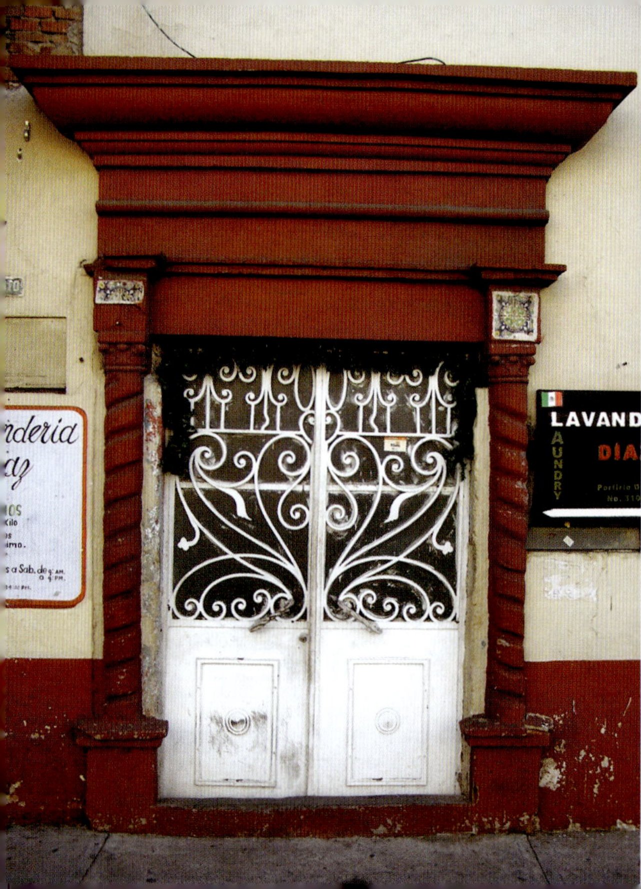

A dry cleaner located on the Porfirio Díaz Street.

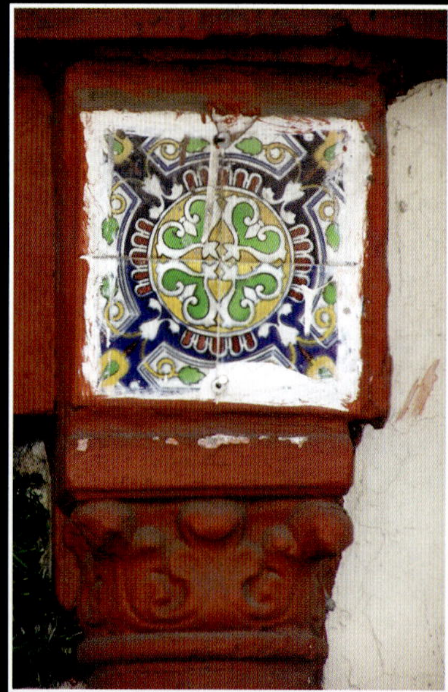

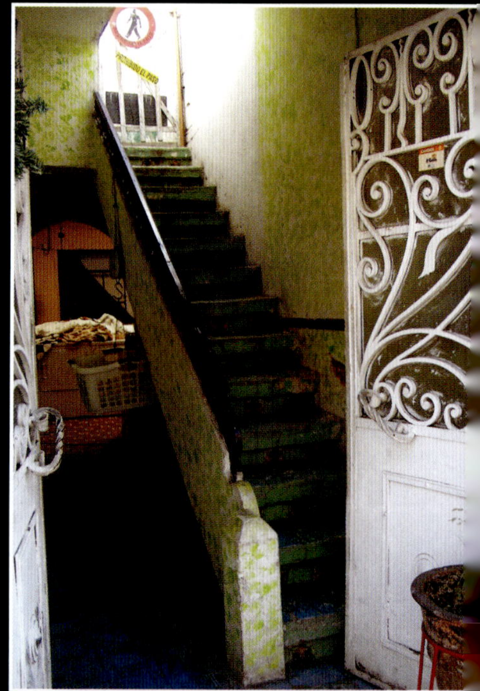

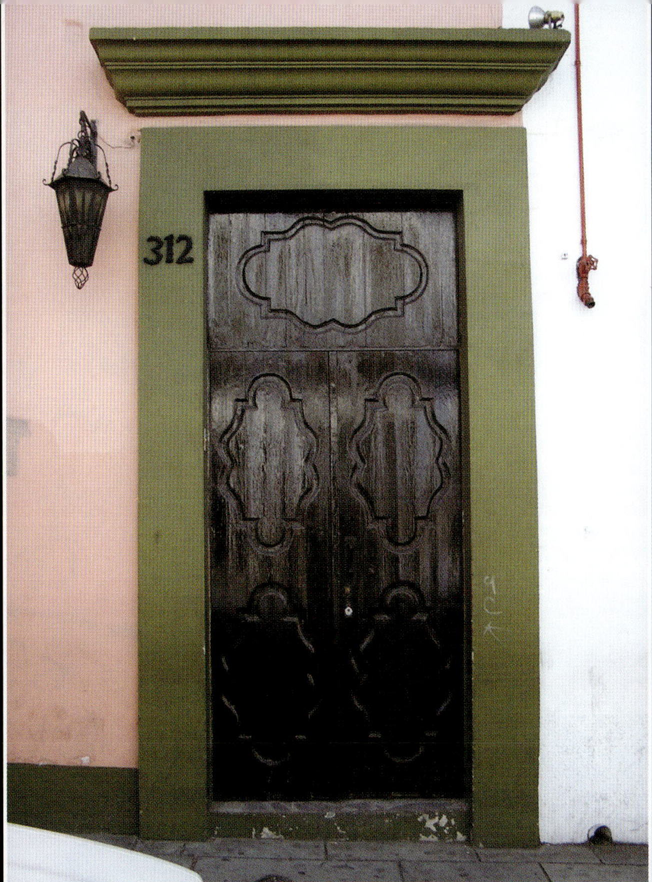
312

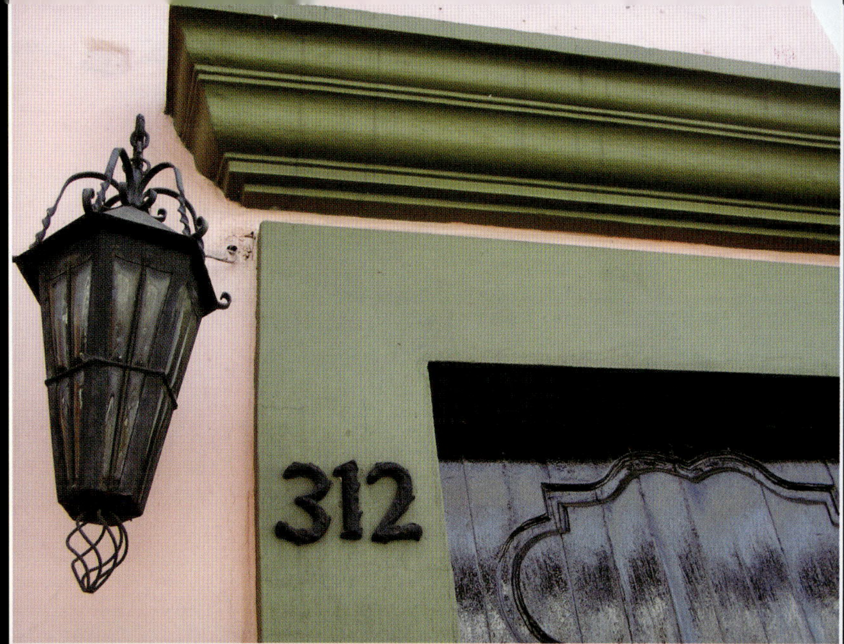
312

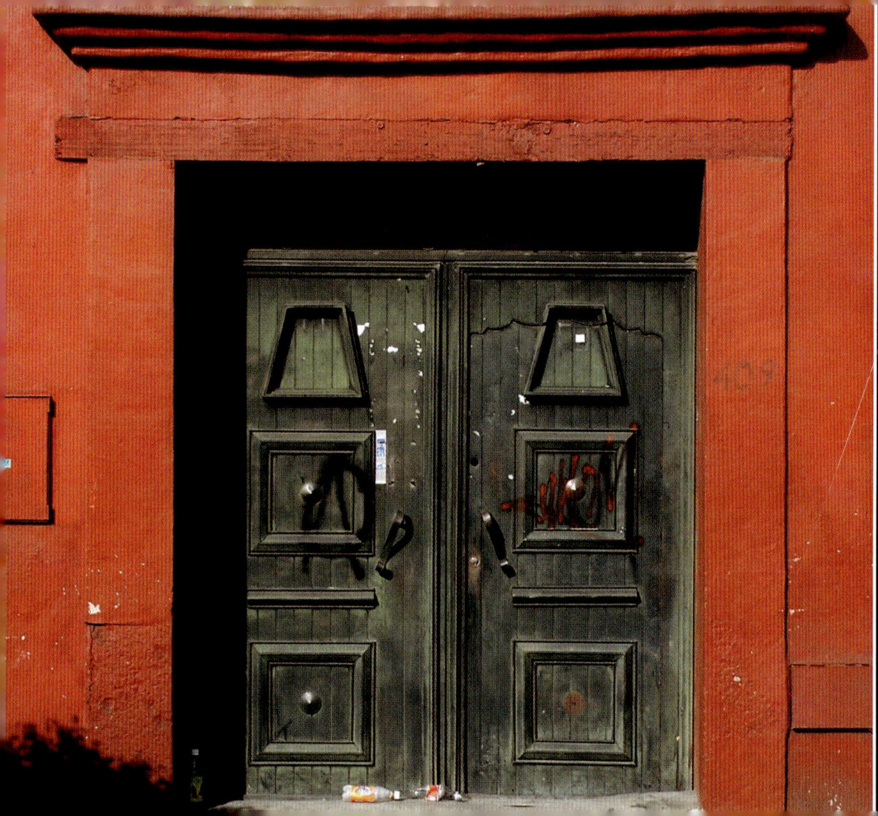

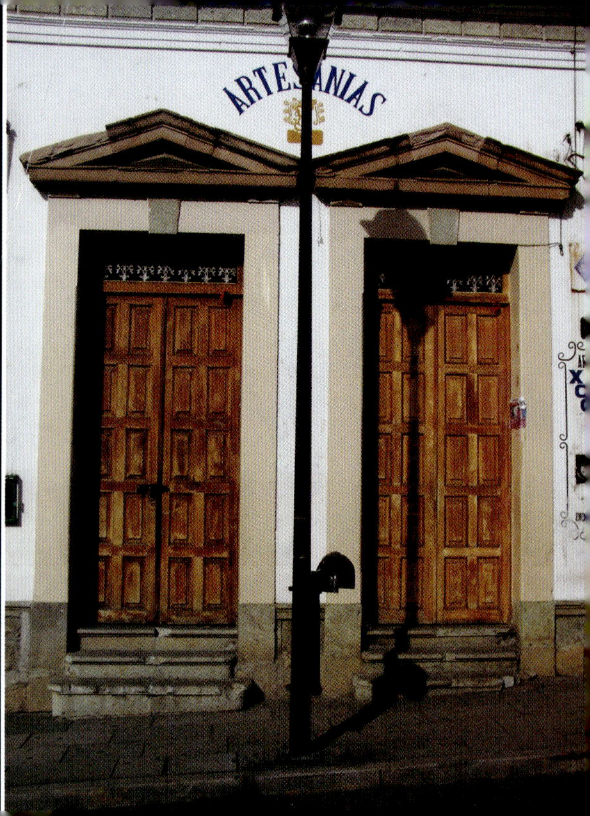
ARTESANIAS

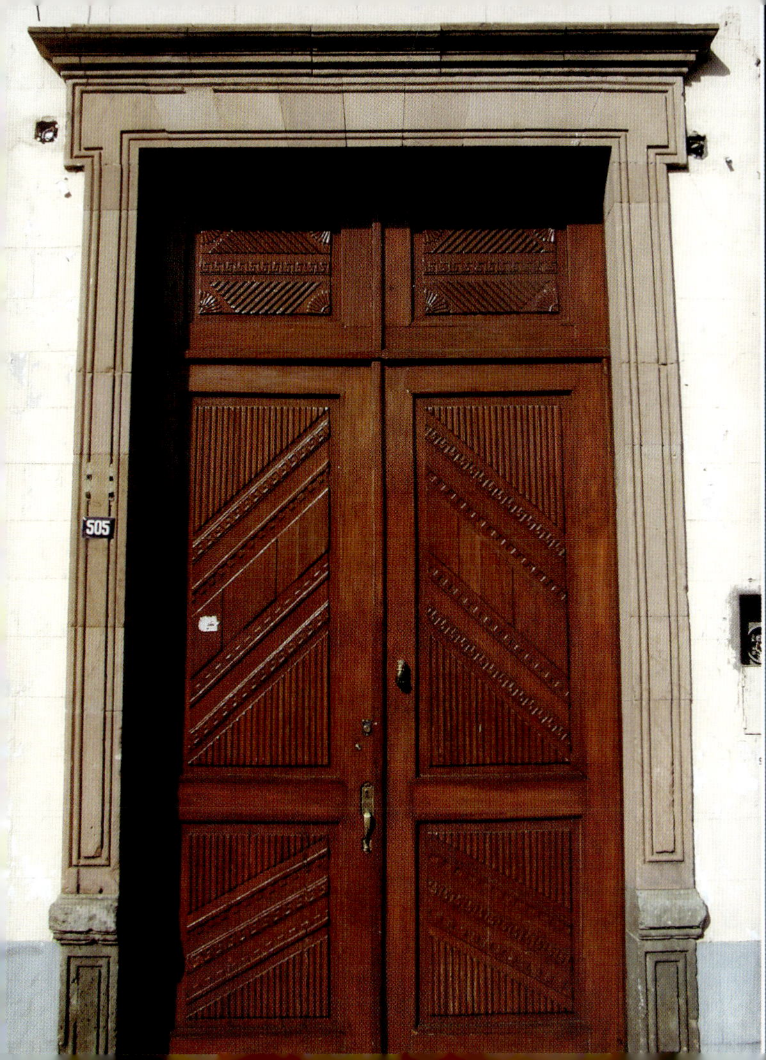

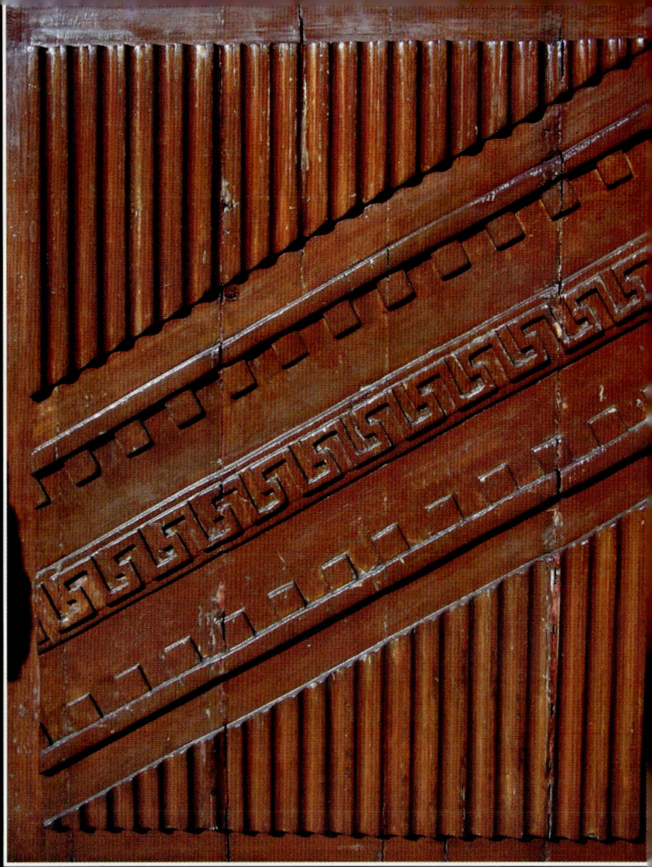

García Vigil Street.

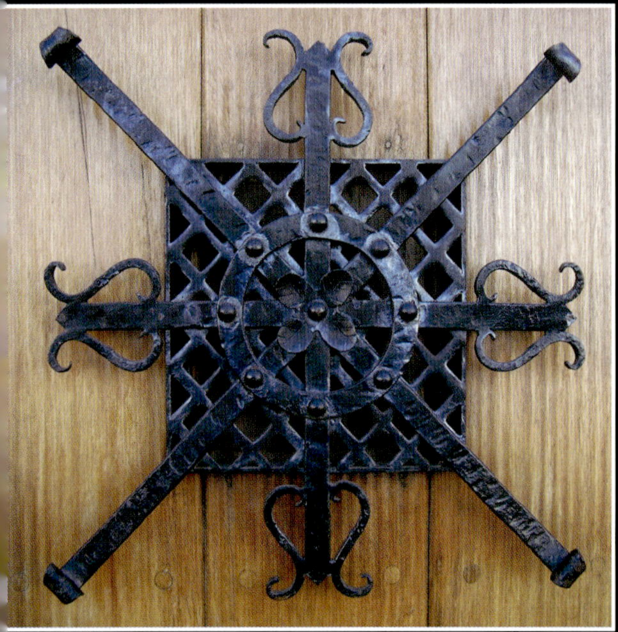

García Vigil Street.

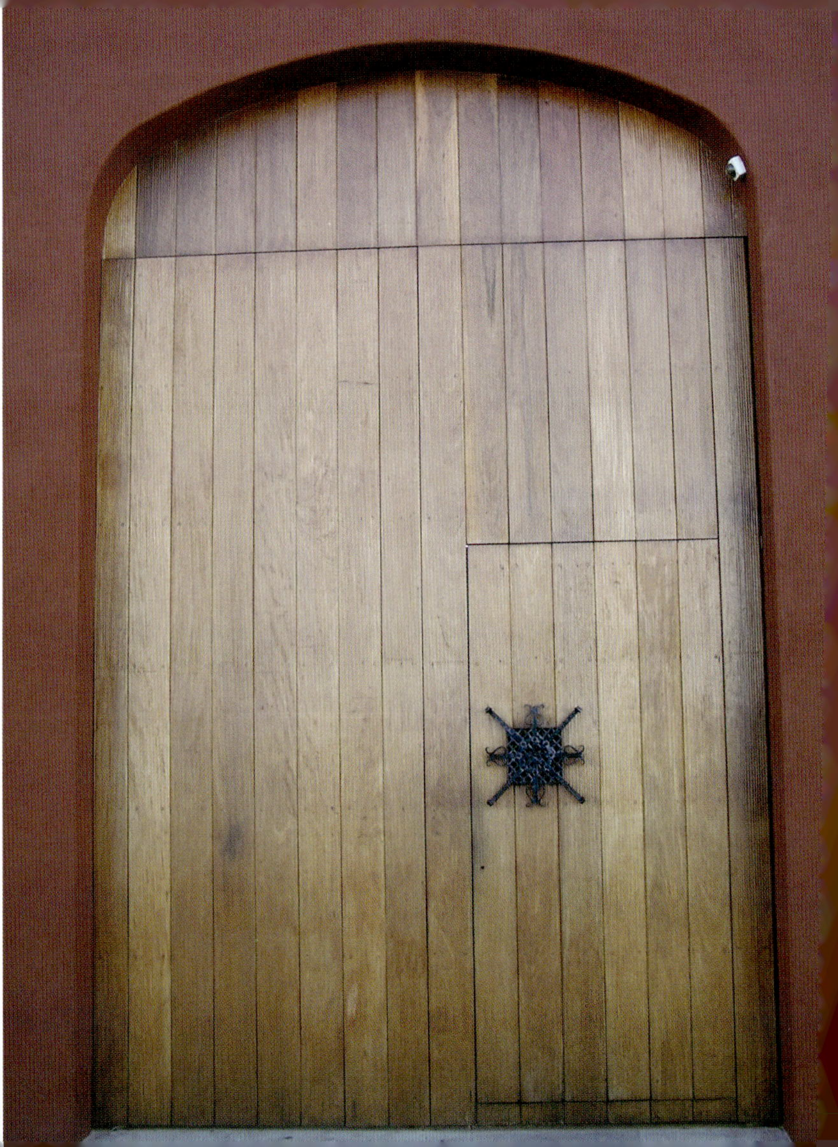

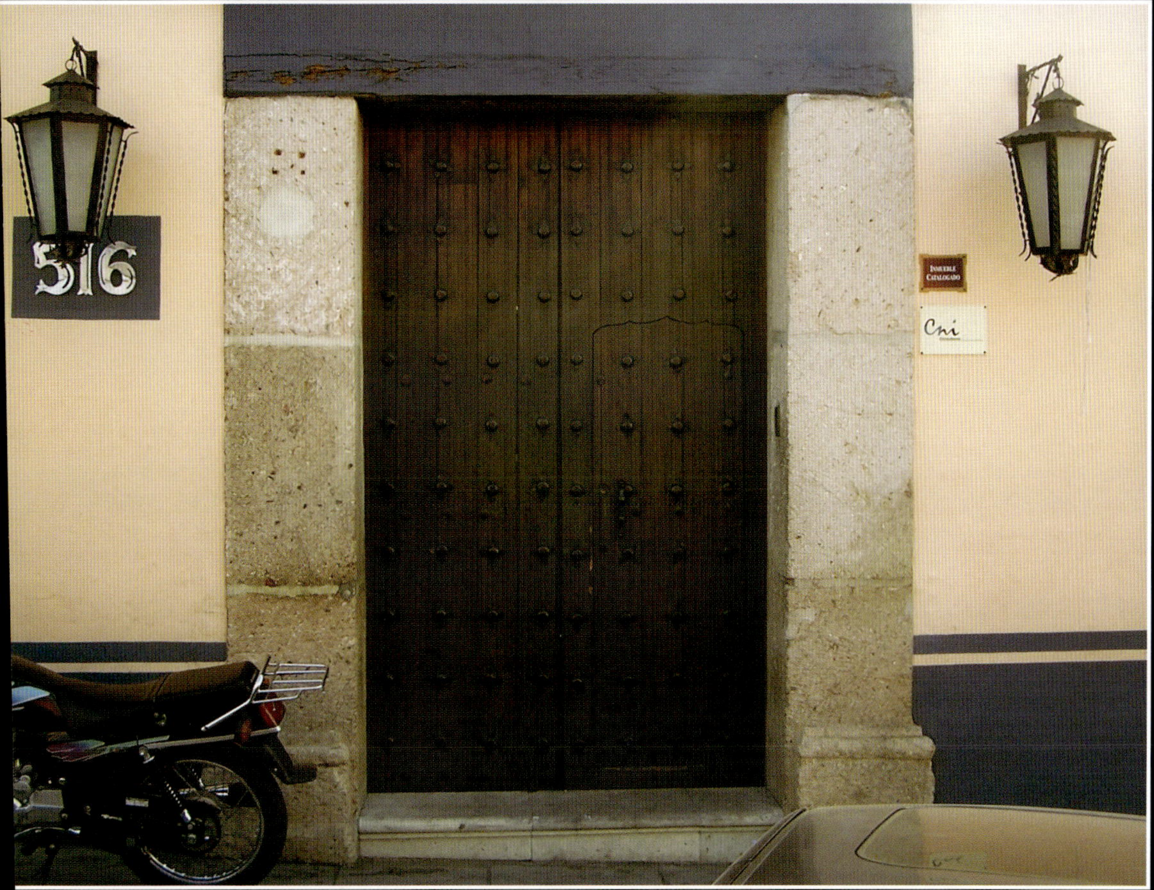

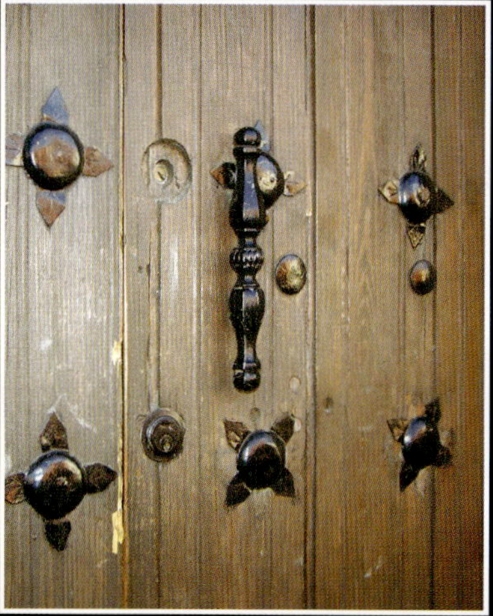

Another building on García Vigil Street.

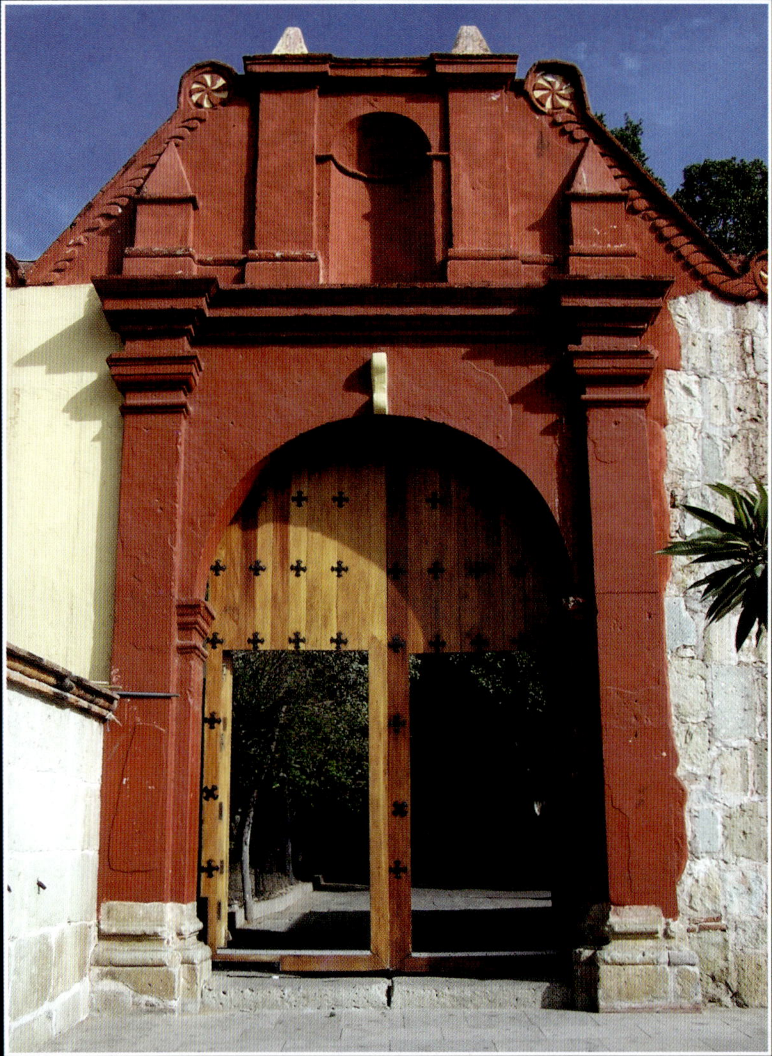

The Carmen Alto Church, built in the seventeenth century.

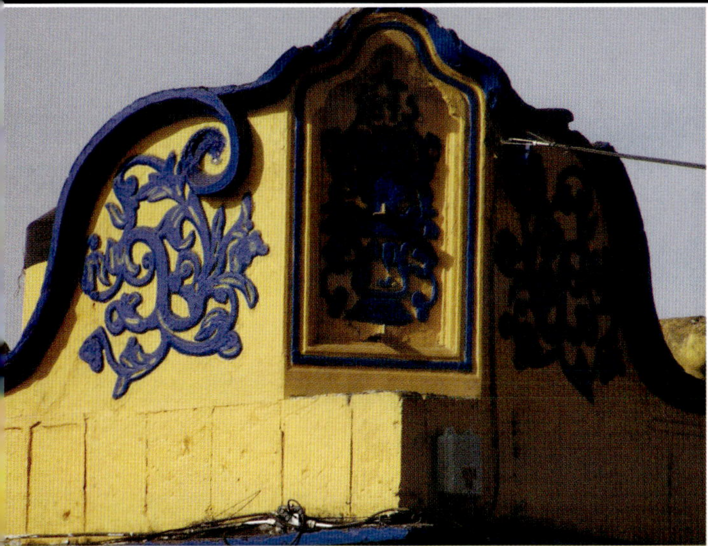

The date above this door reads 1875.

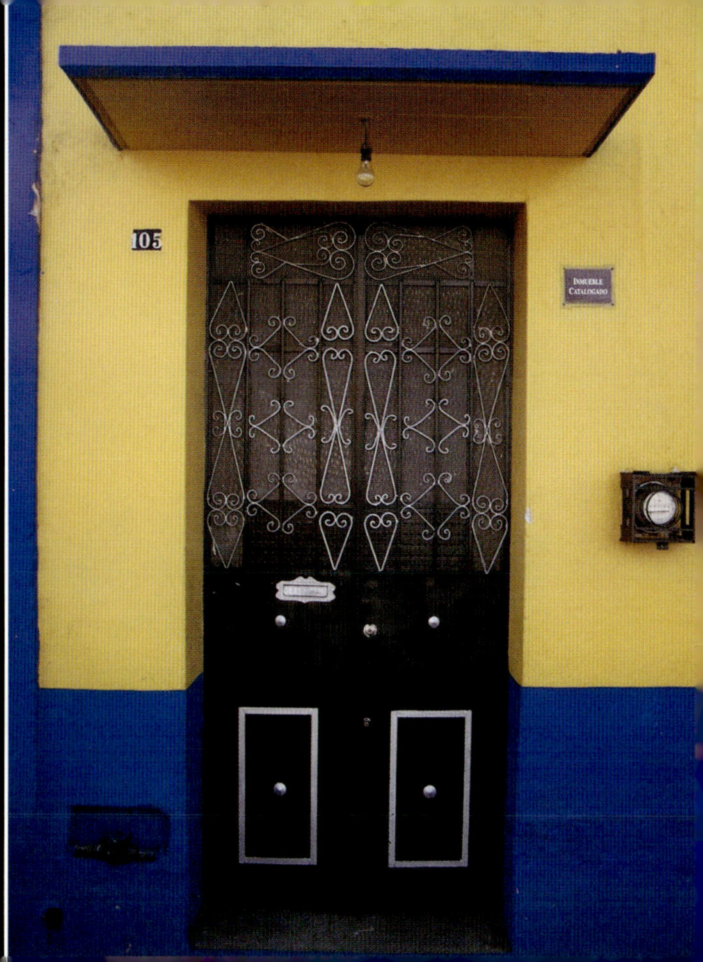

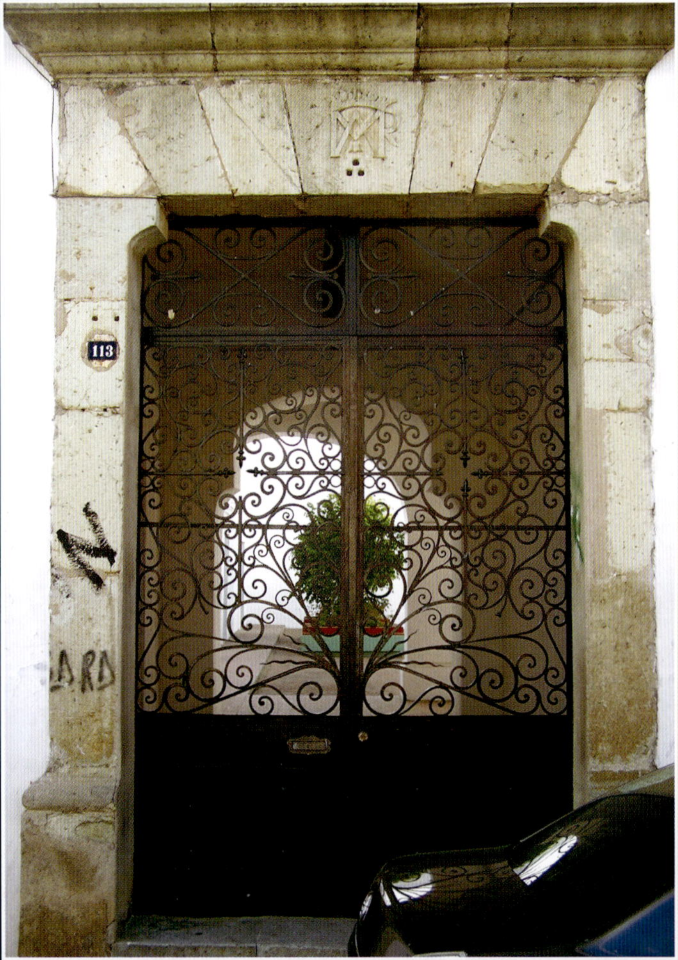
113

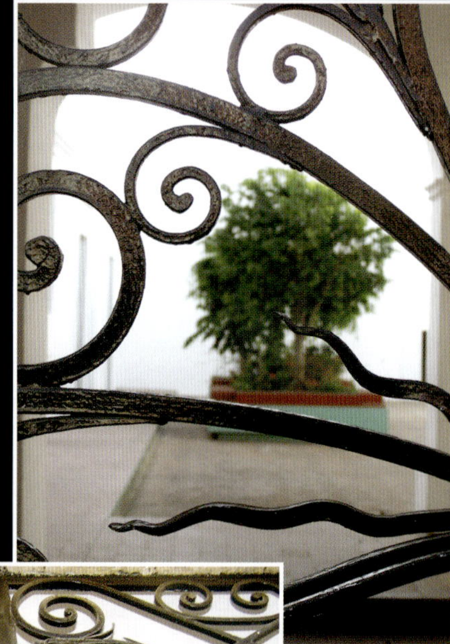

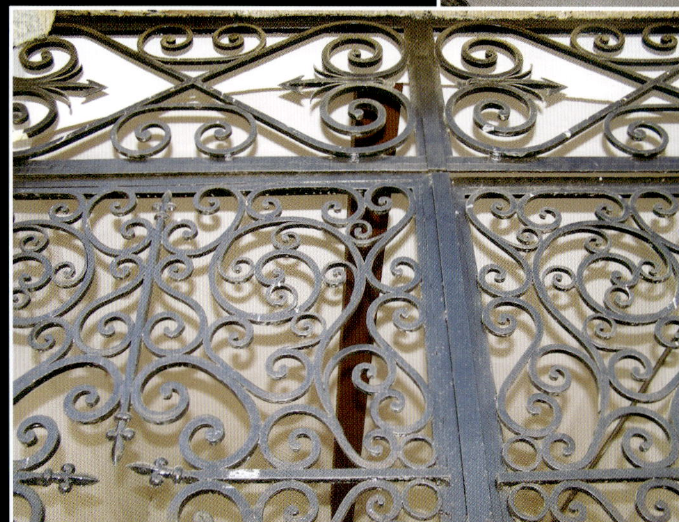

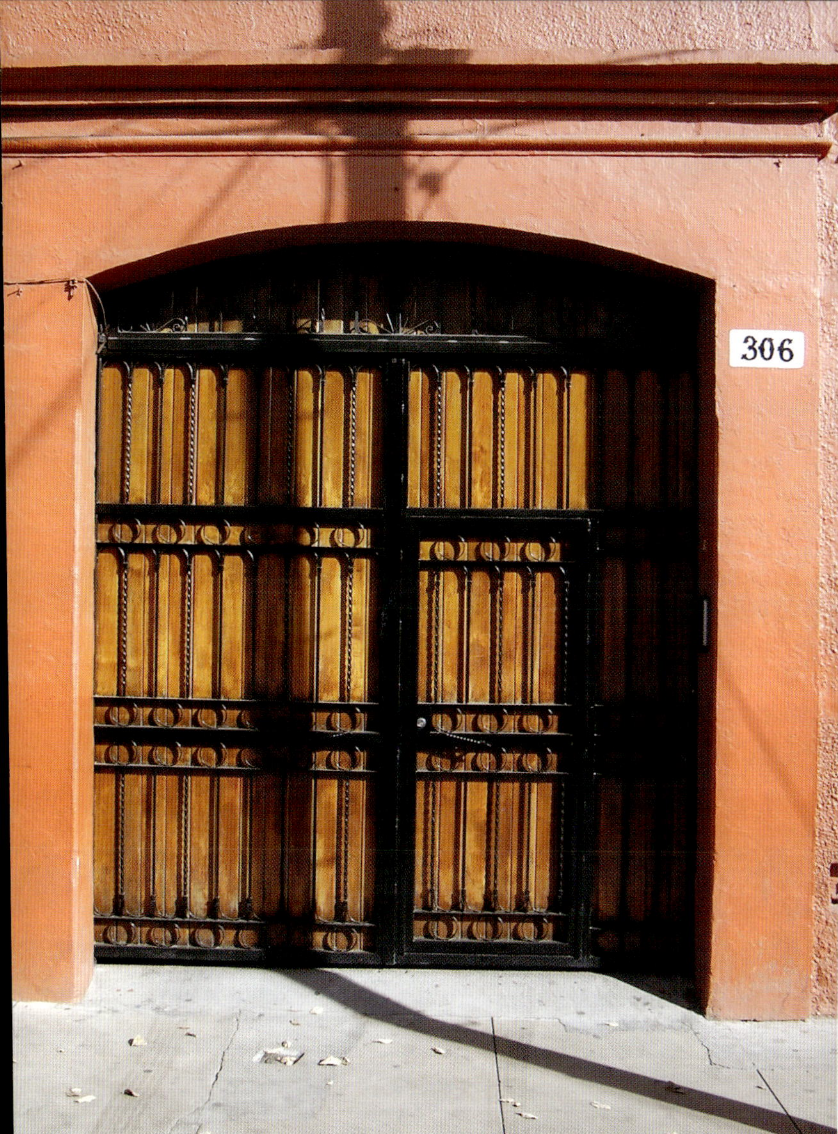
306

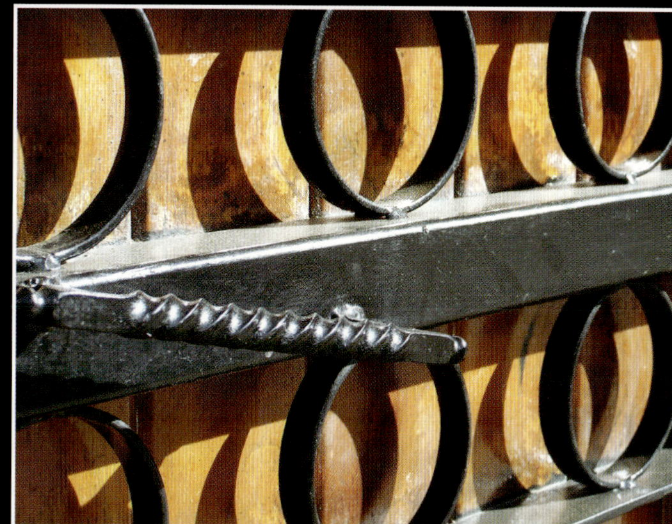

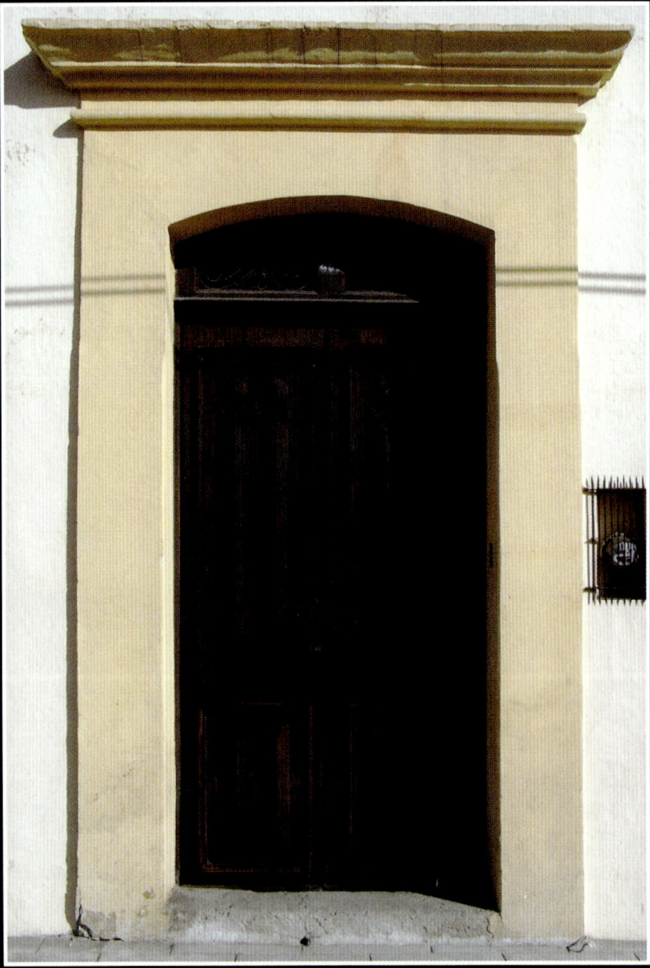

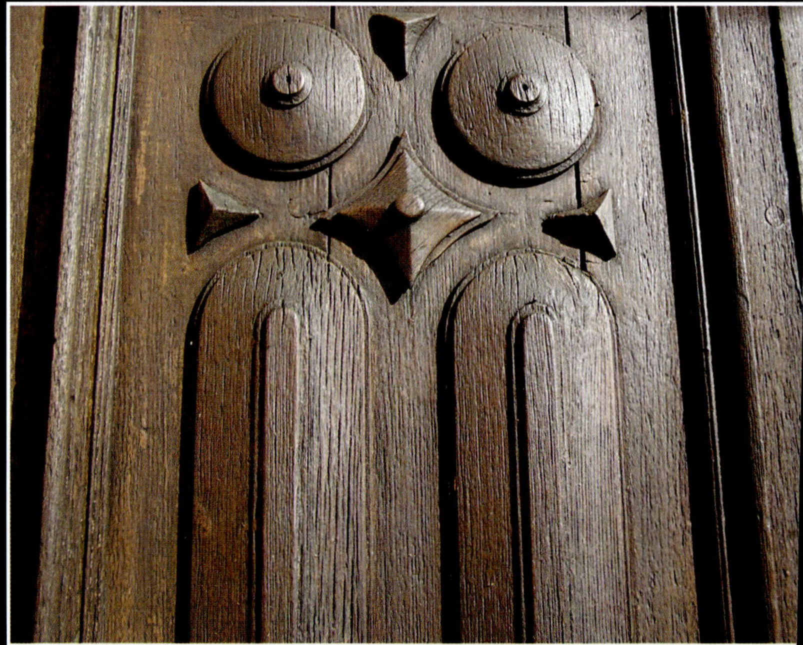

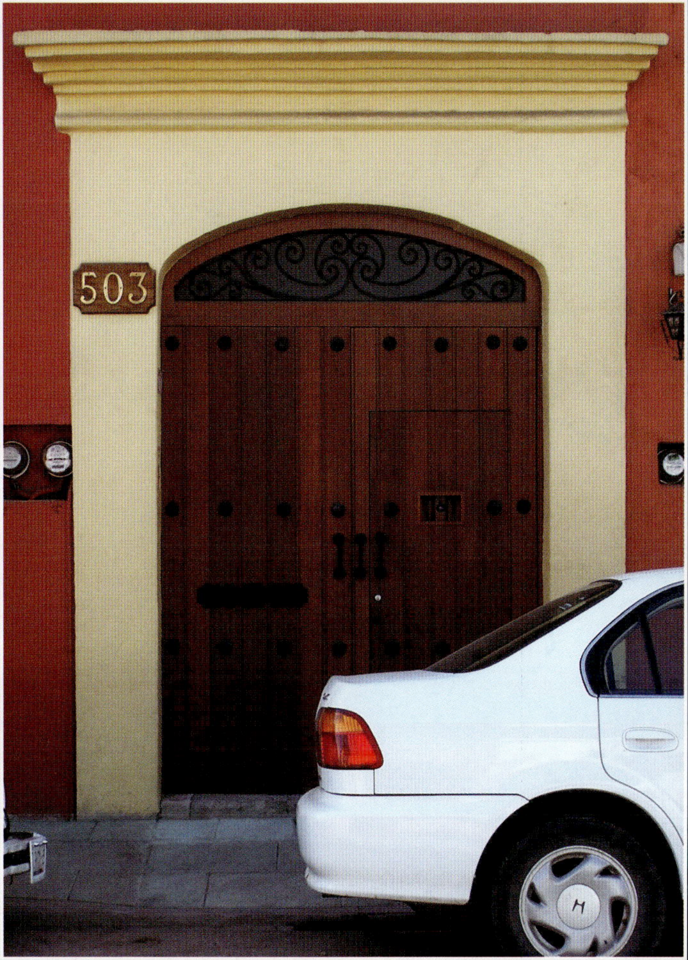
503

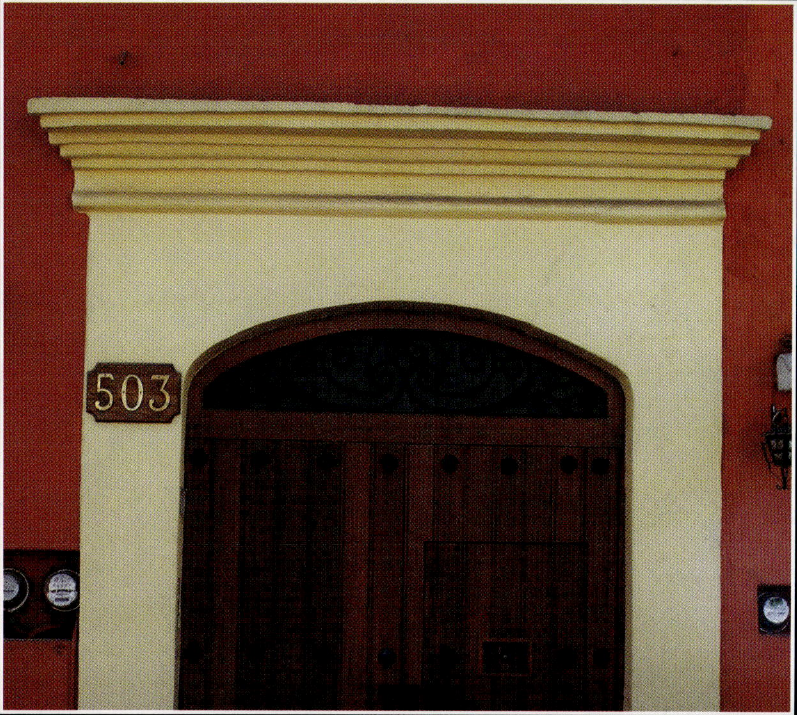
503

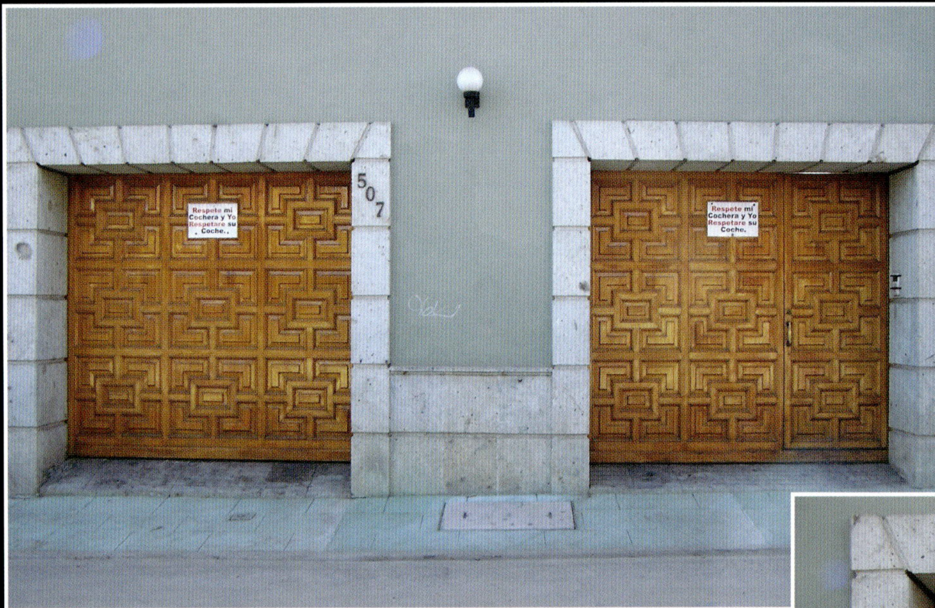

"Respect my garage and I'll respect your car."

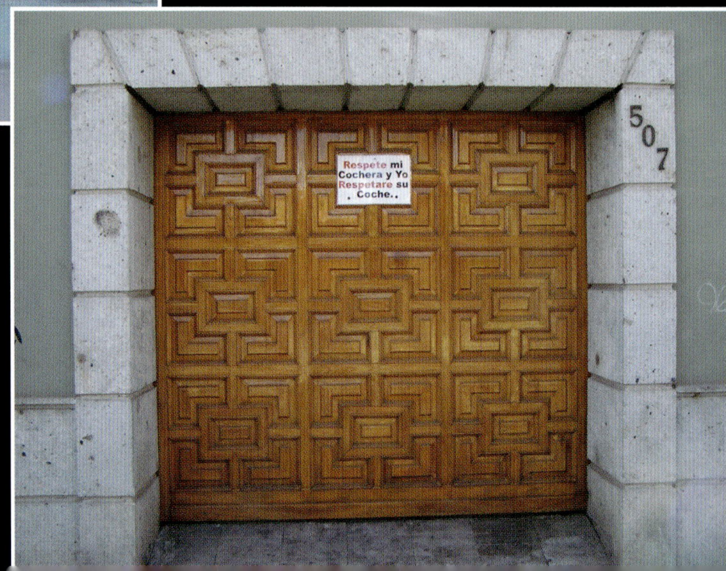

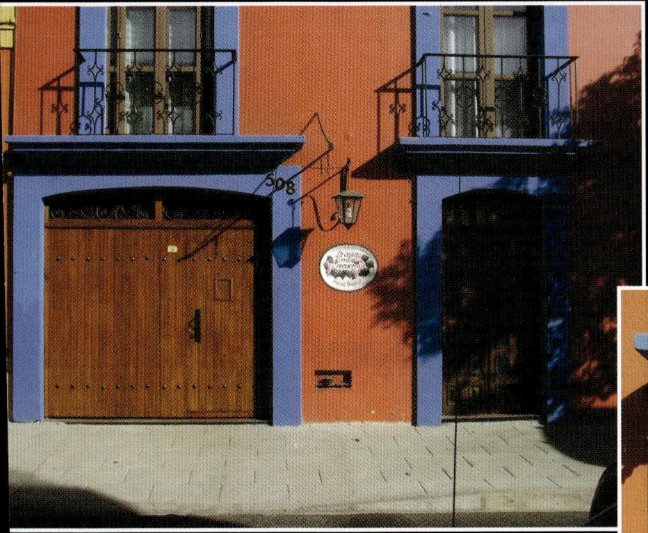

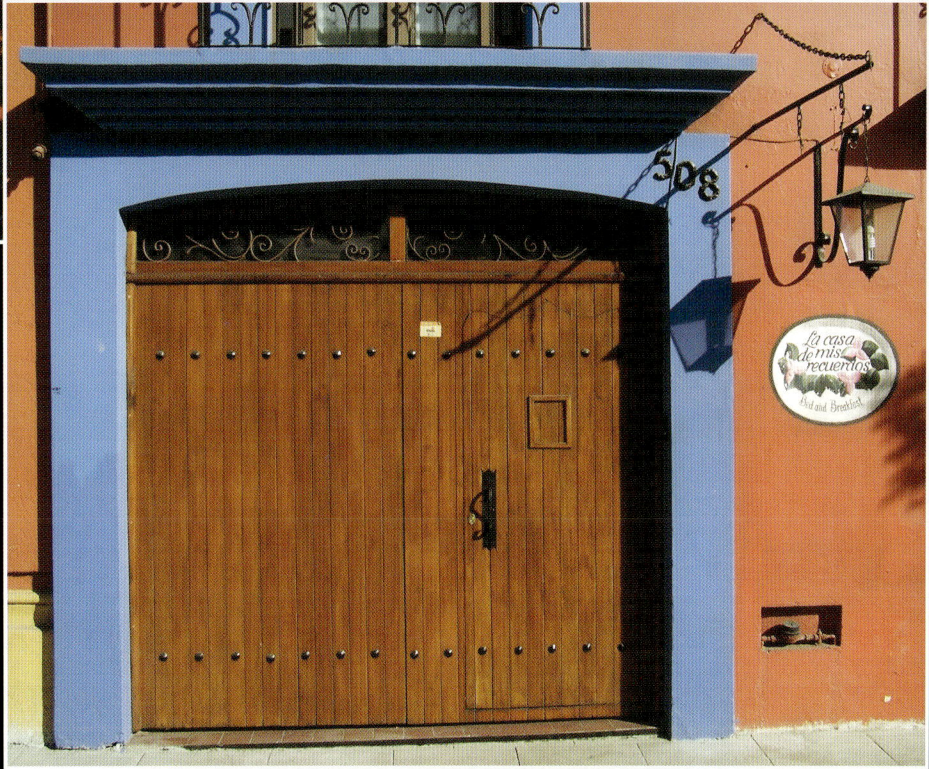

A bed-and-breakfast named La Casa de Mis Recuerdos (The House of My Memories).

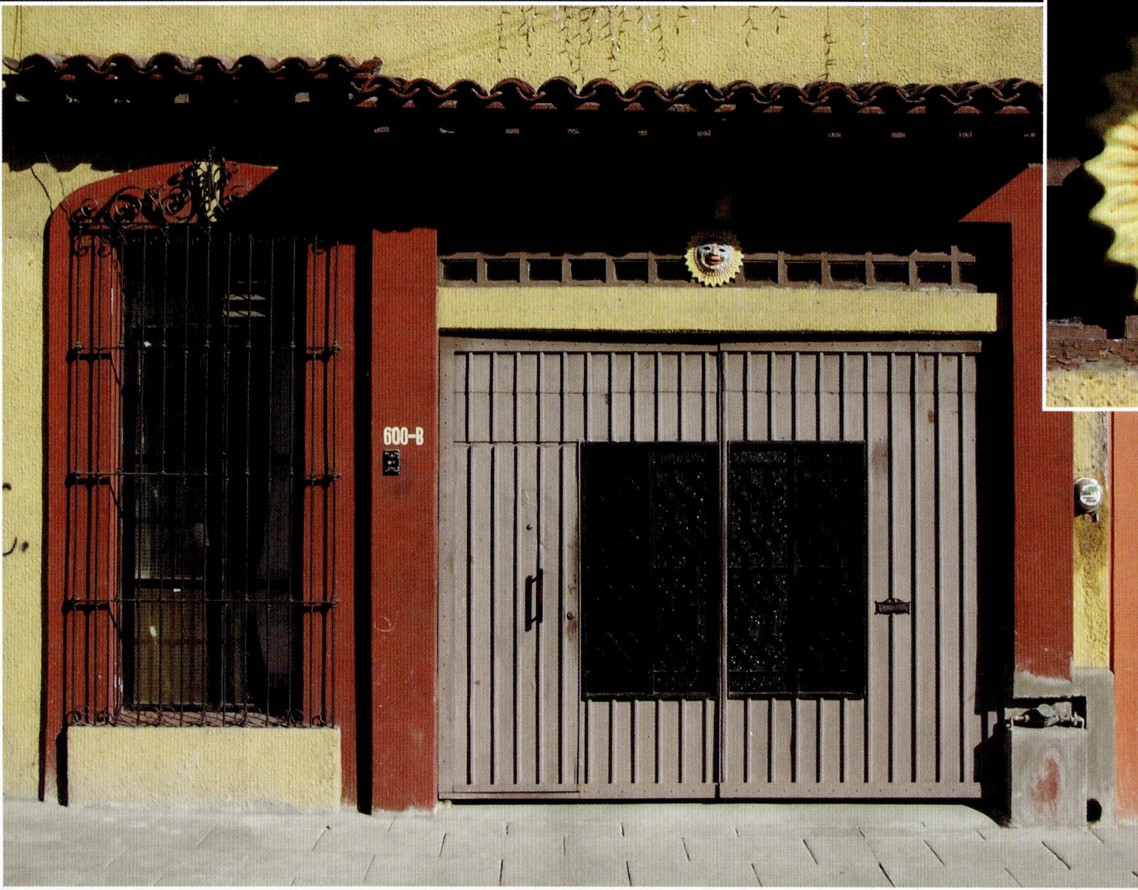

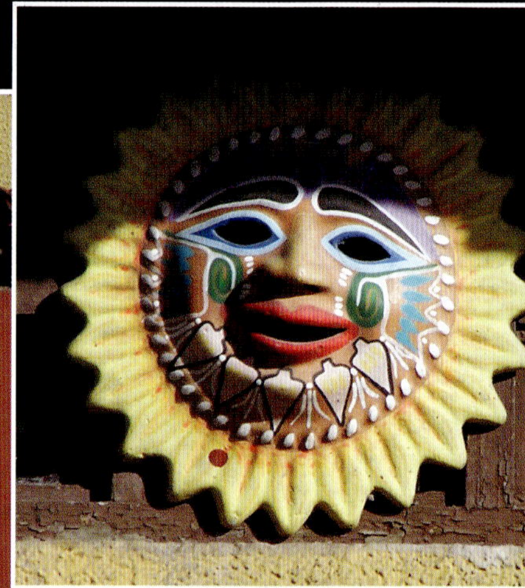

600 Pino Suárez Street near the Llano Garden, once a Zoo in the early 1970's.

This house is located on Hidalgo Street, the main street in San Felipe del Agua, a small suburb in the foothills of the mountains just north of downtown Oaxaca.

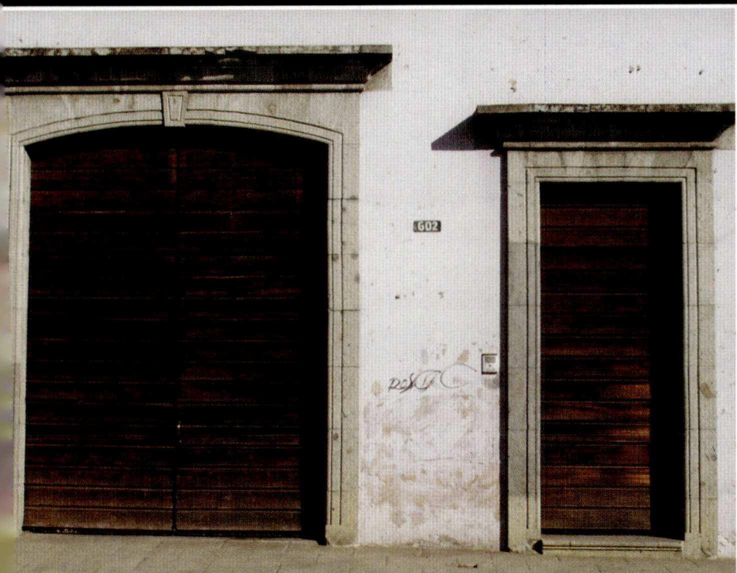

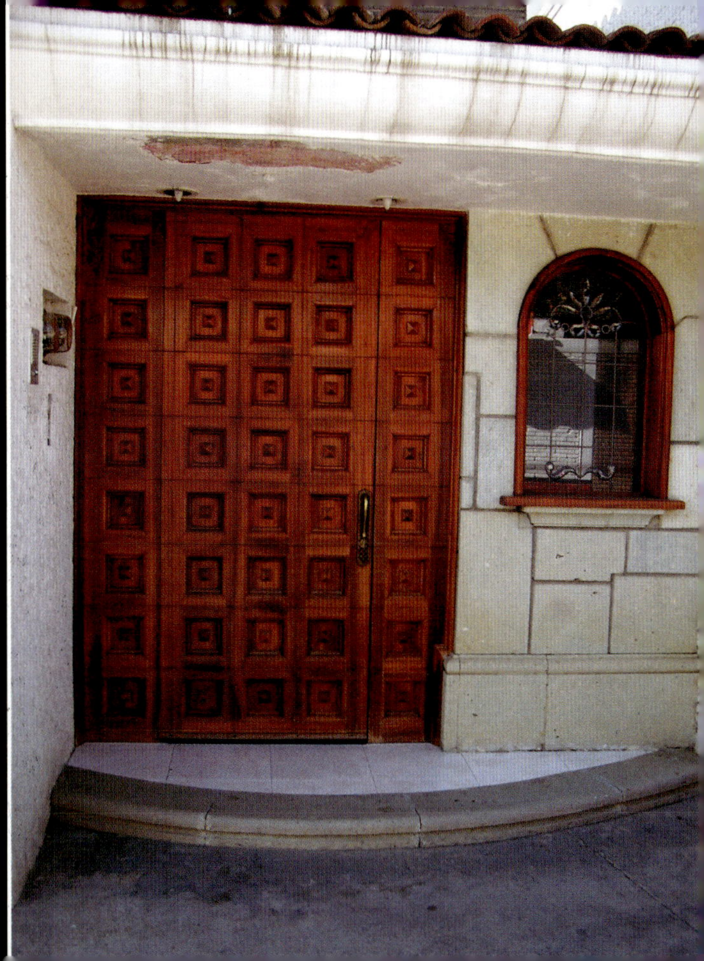

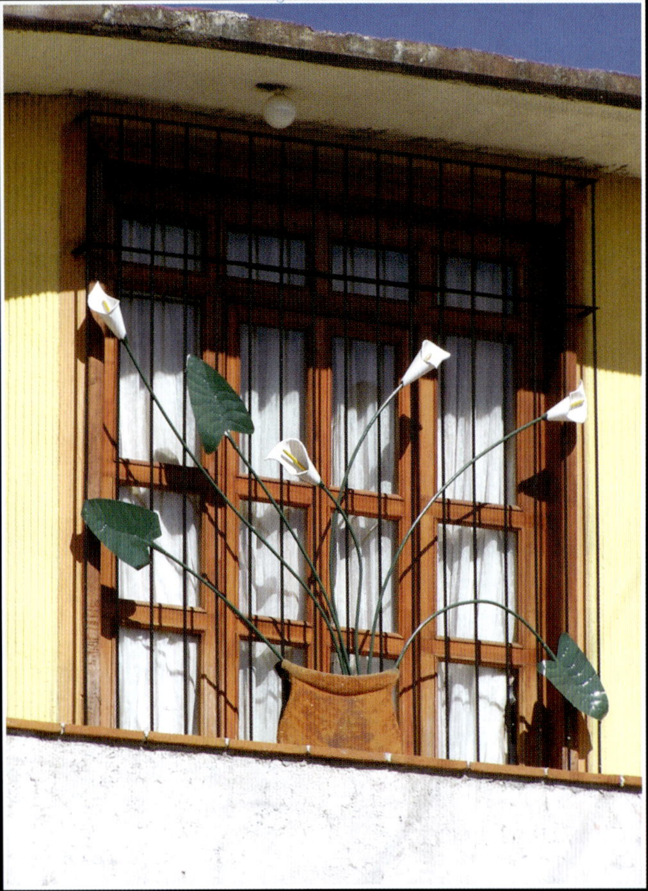

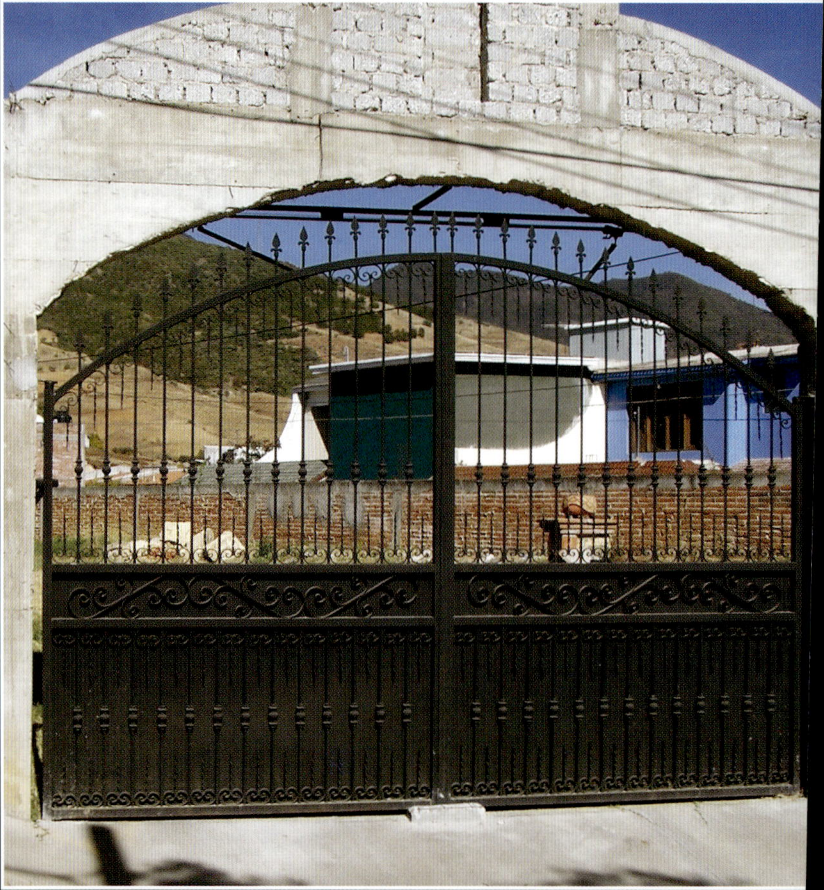

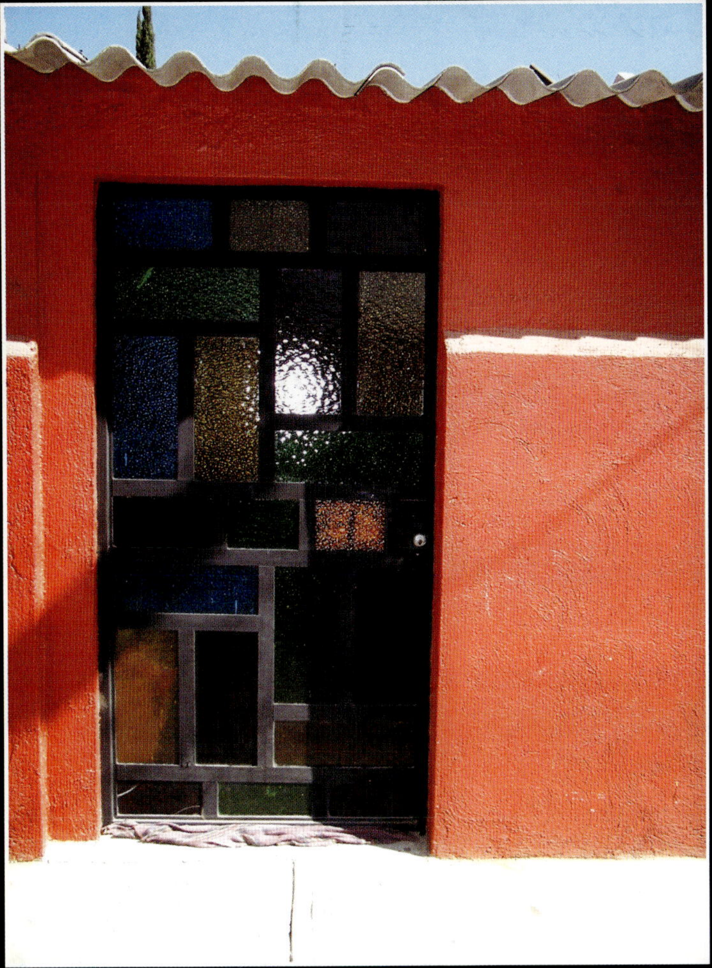

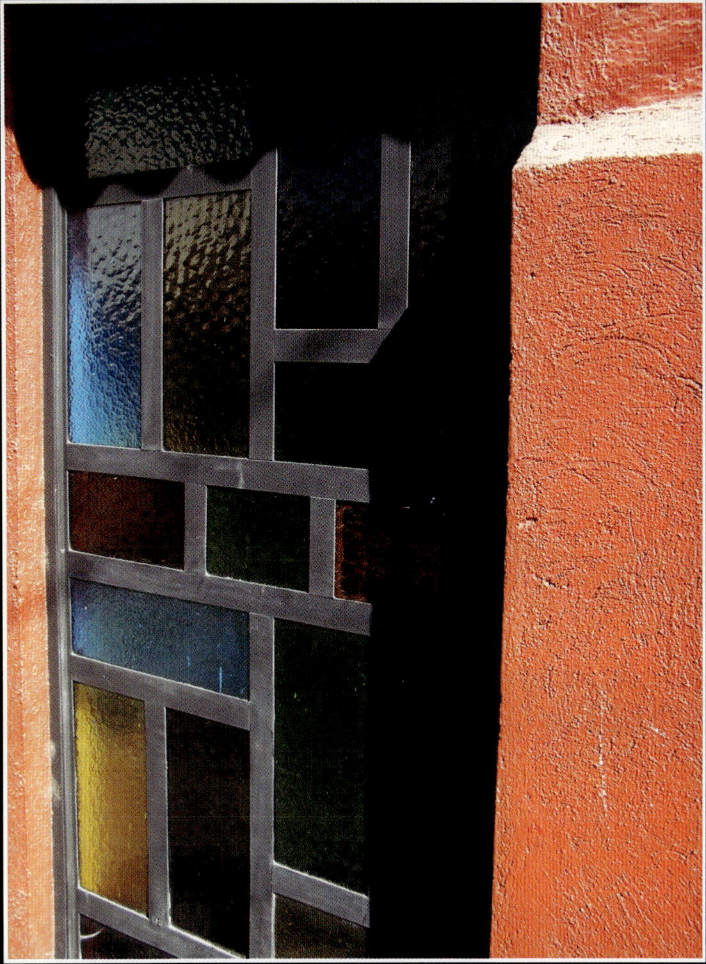

Hidalgo Street in San Felipe del Agua.

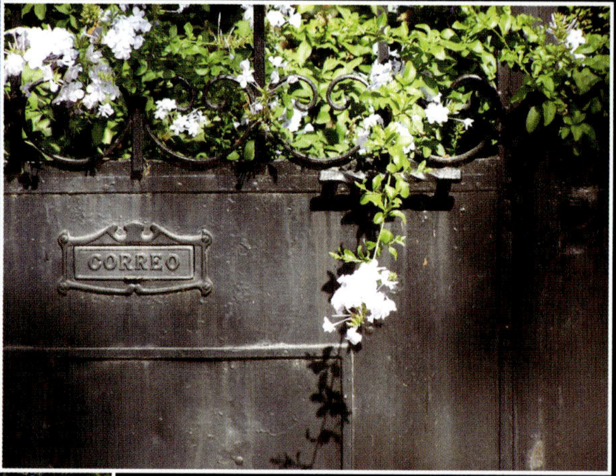

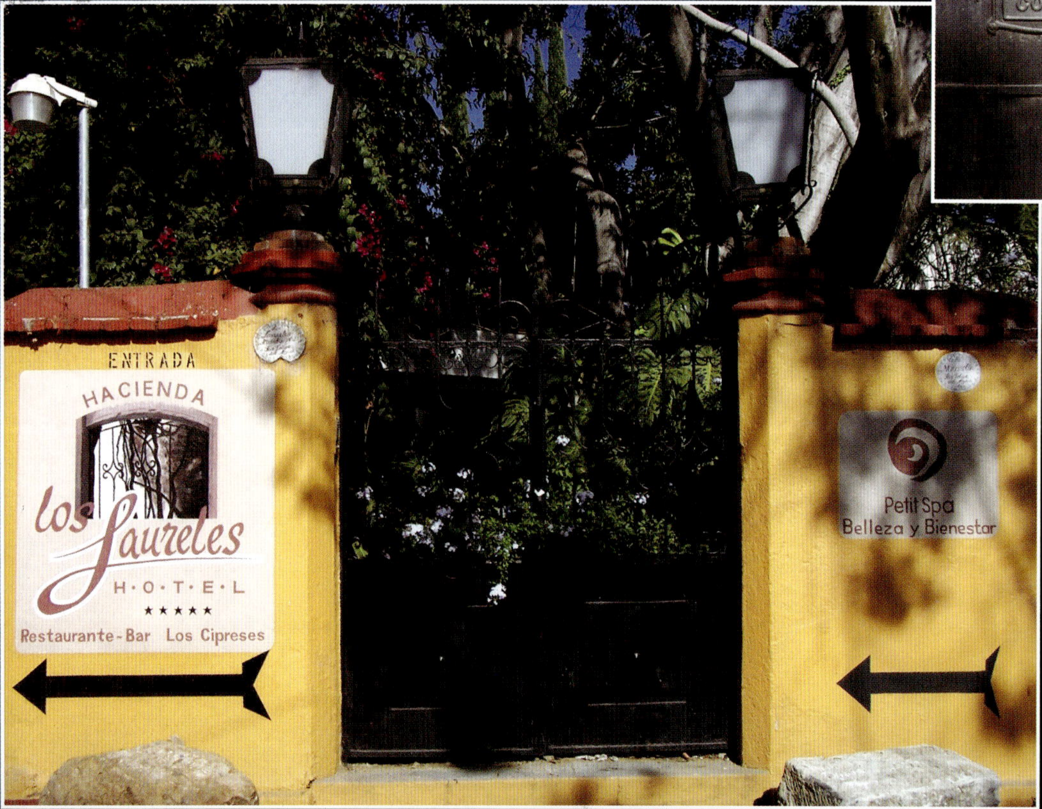

The Hotel Hacienda Los Laureles.

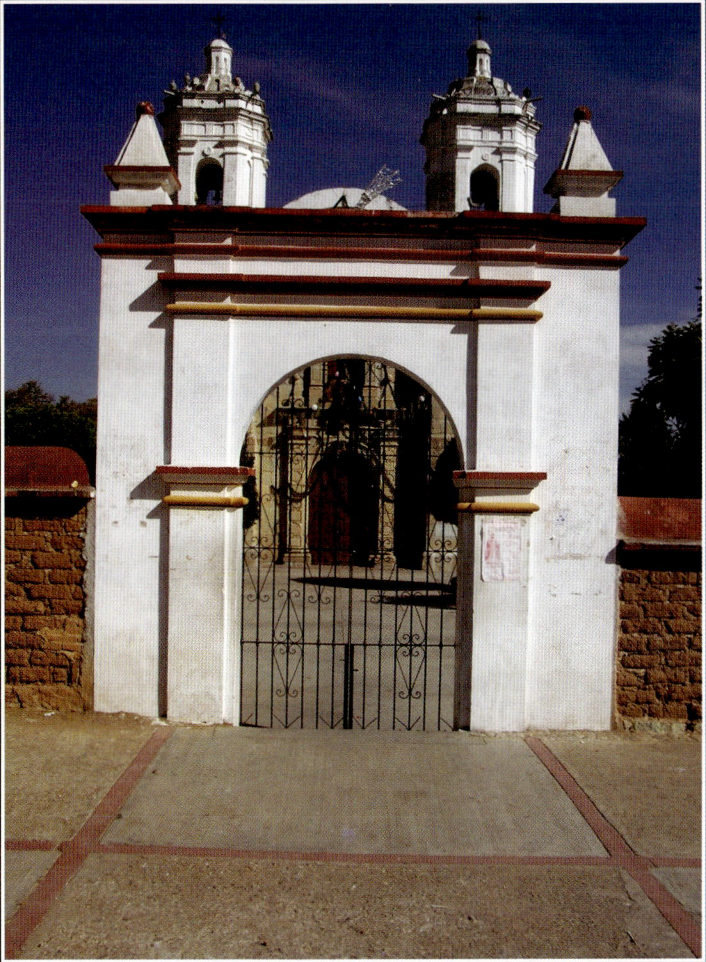

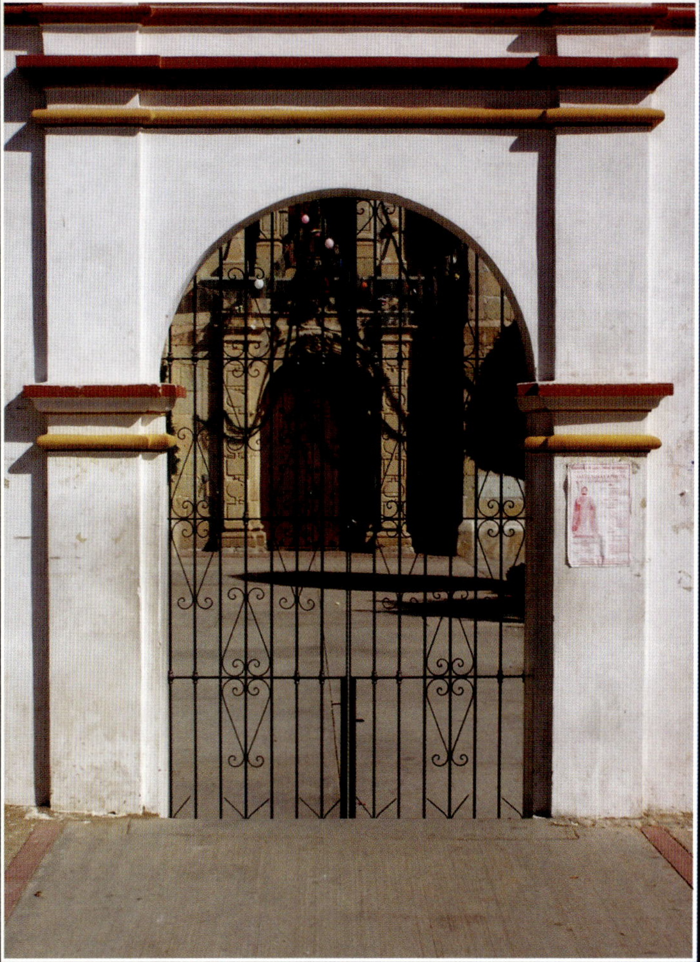

The Church of San Felipe del Agua.

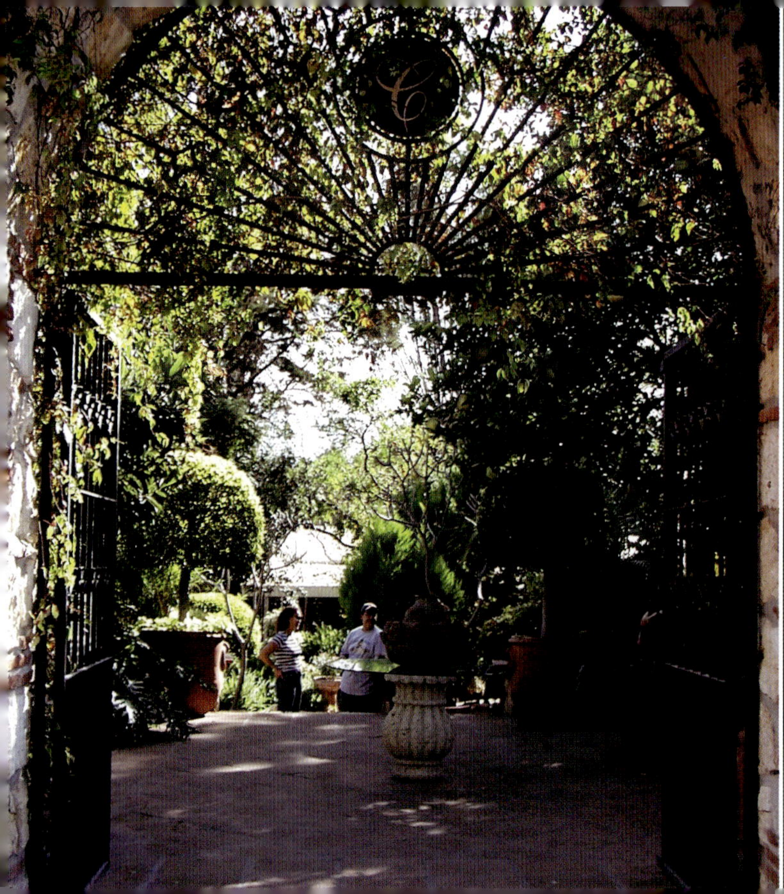

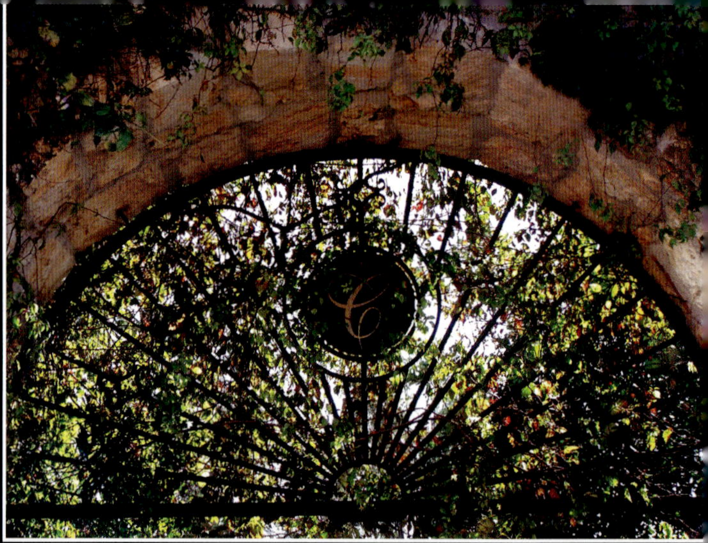

The "C" on this door stands for Las Campanas (The Bells). It is a large outdoor restaurant and banquet hall. There are several cute bungalows for rent on the grounds as well. Las Campanas is a great small town getaway.

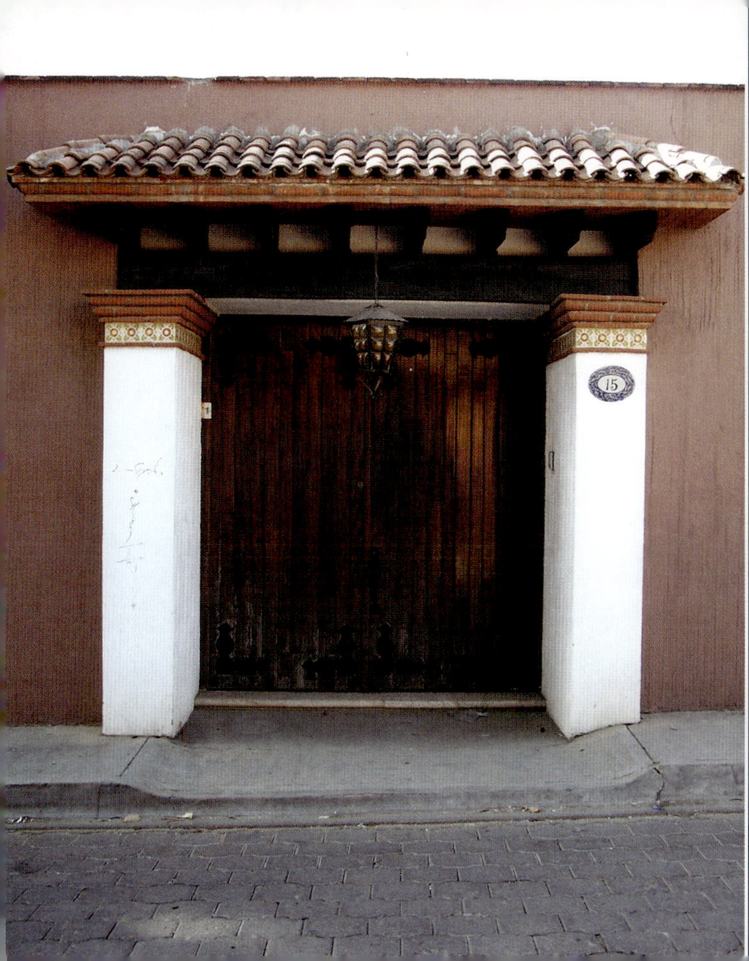
15

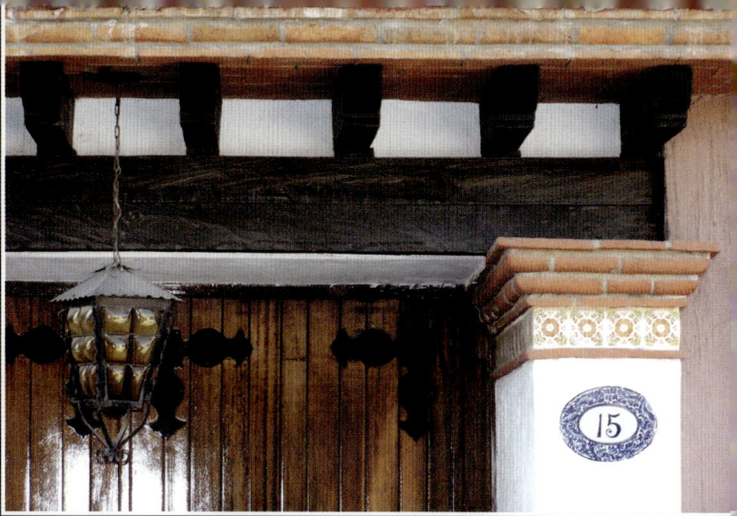
15

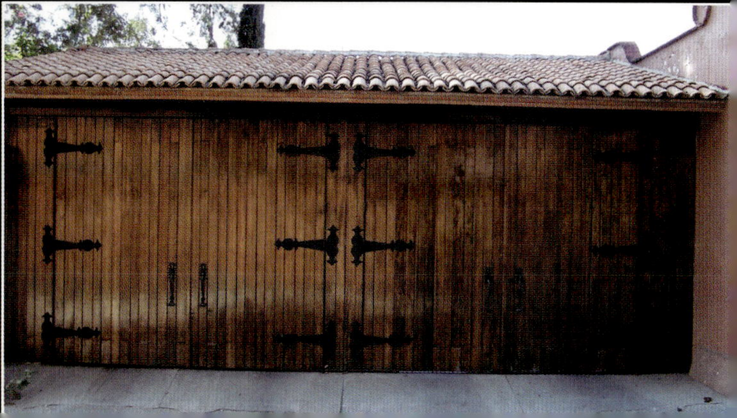

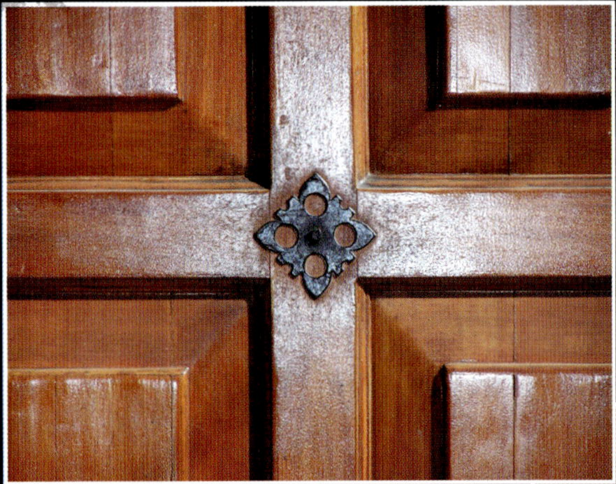

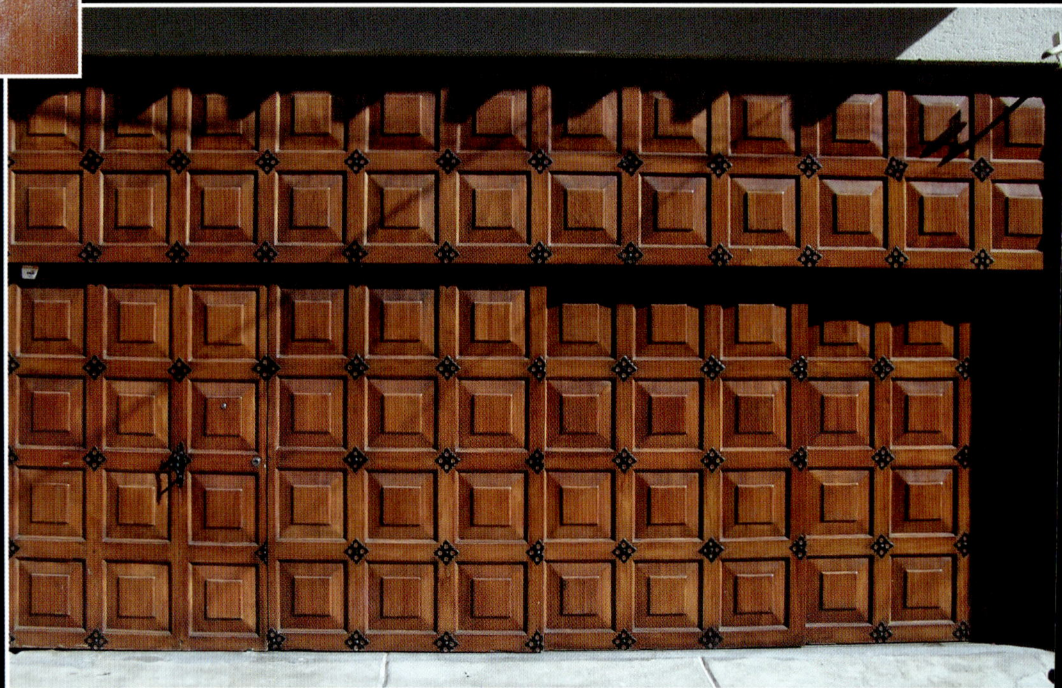

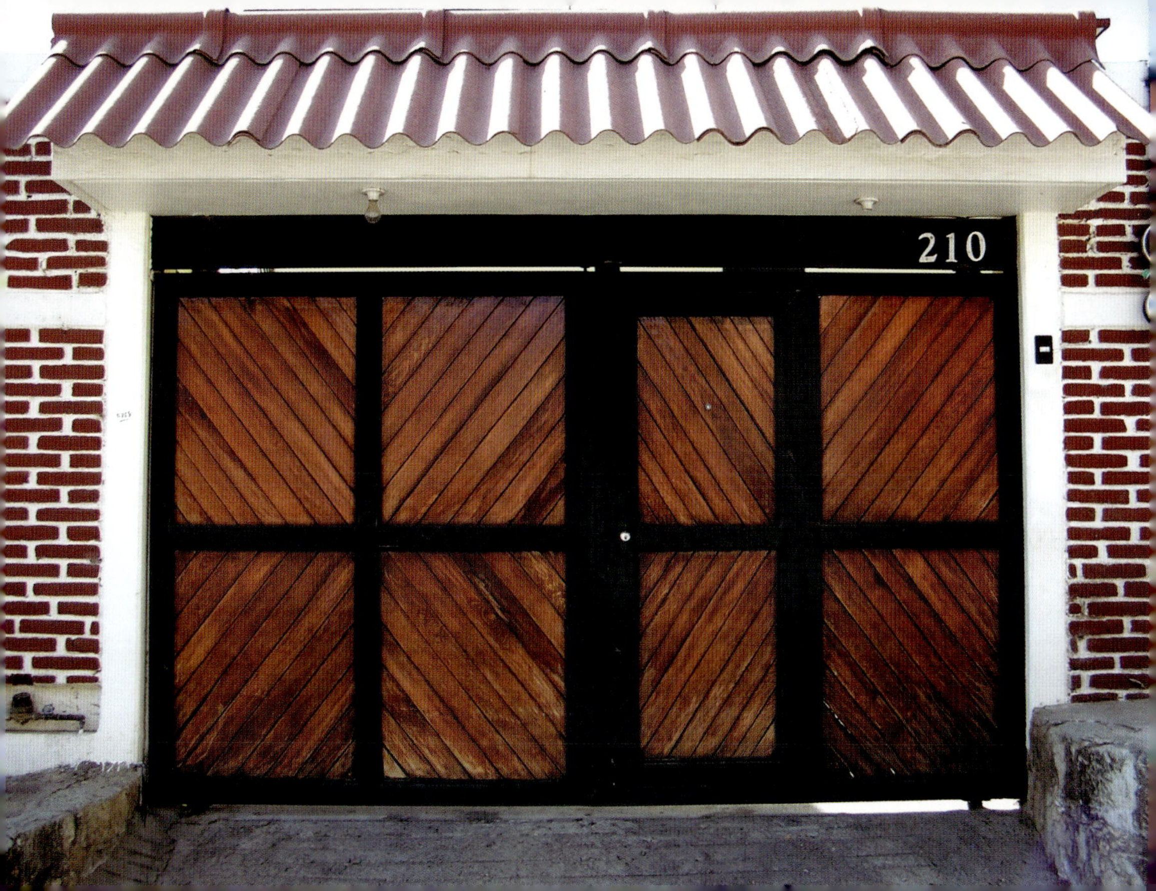
210

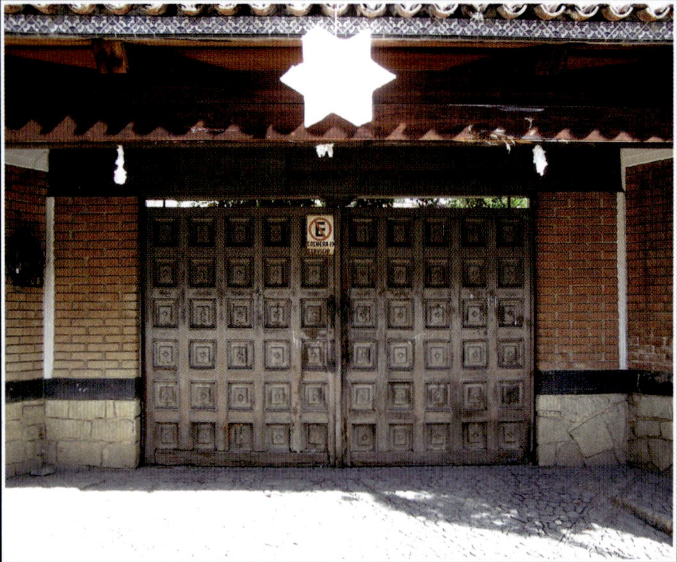

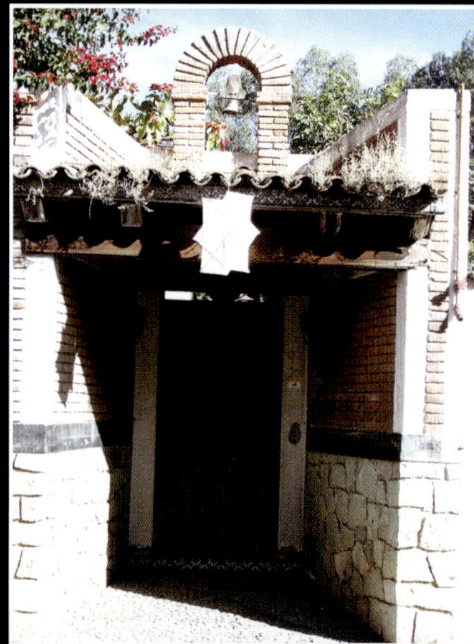

Hidalgo Street
in San Felipe del
Agua.

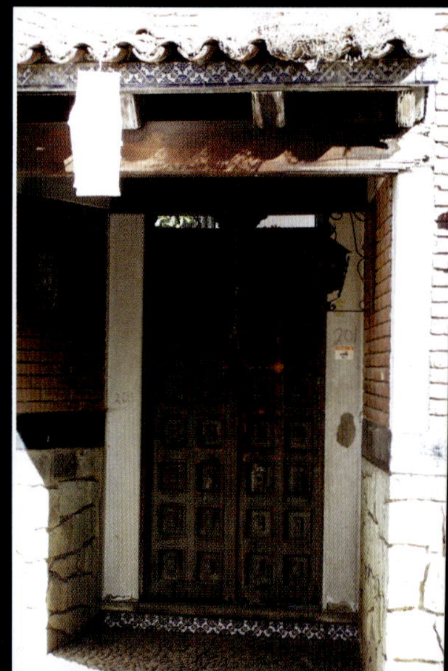

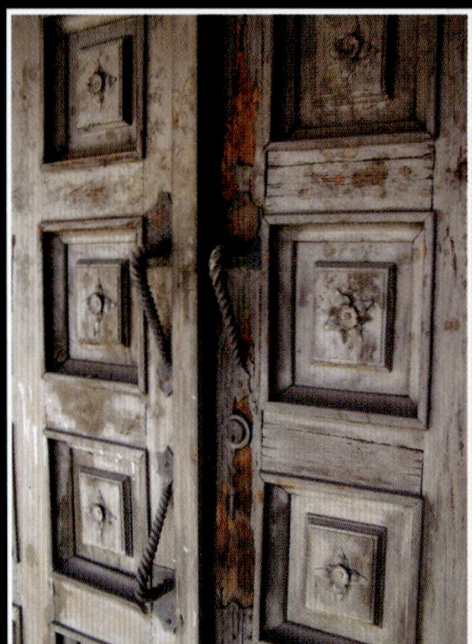

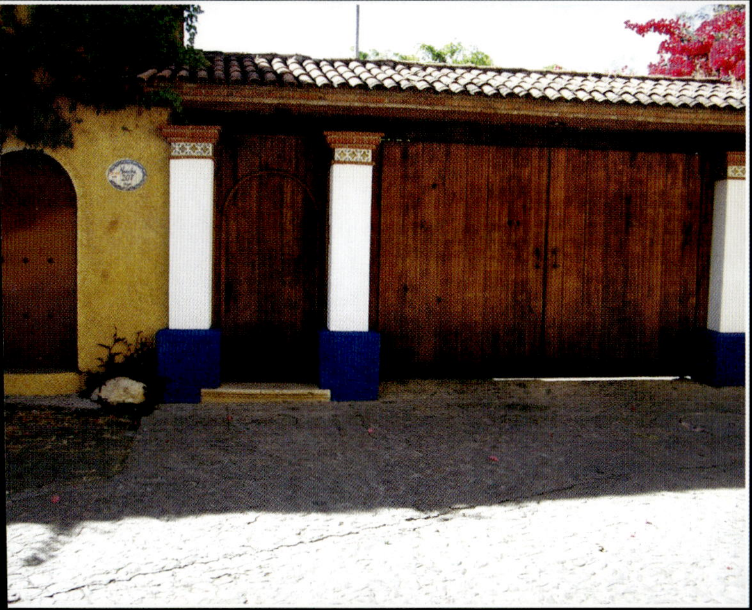

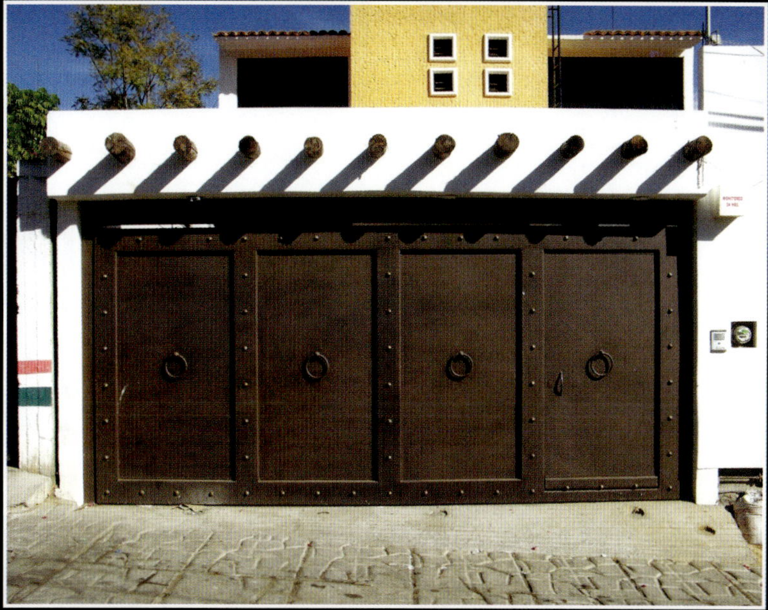

Morelos Street in San Felipe del Agua.

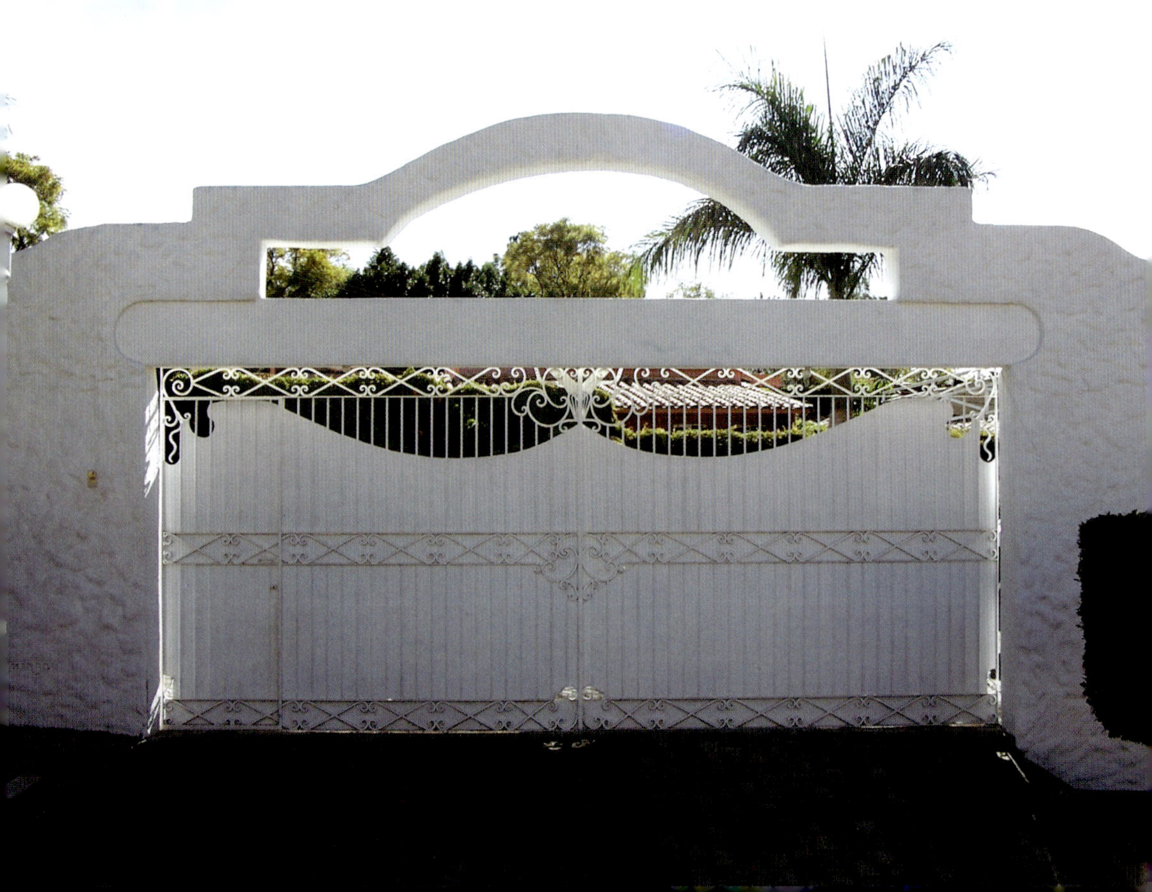

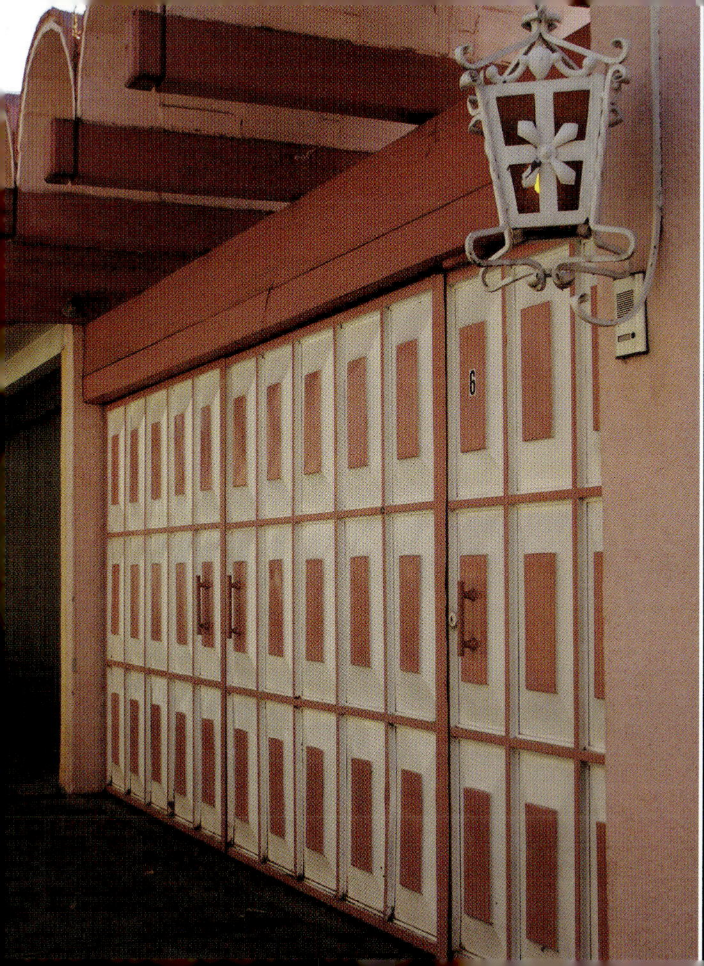
6

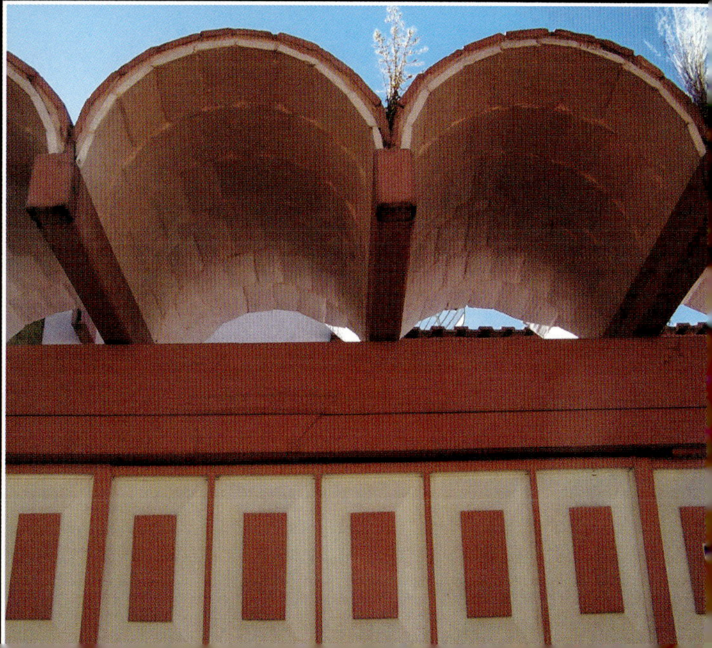

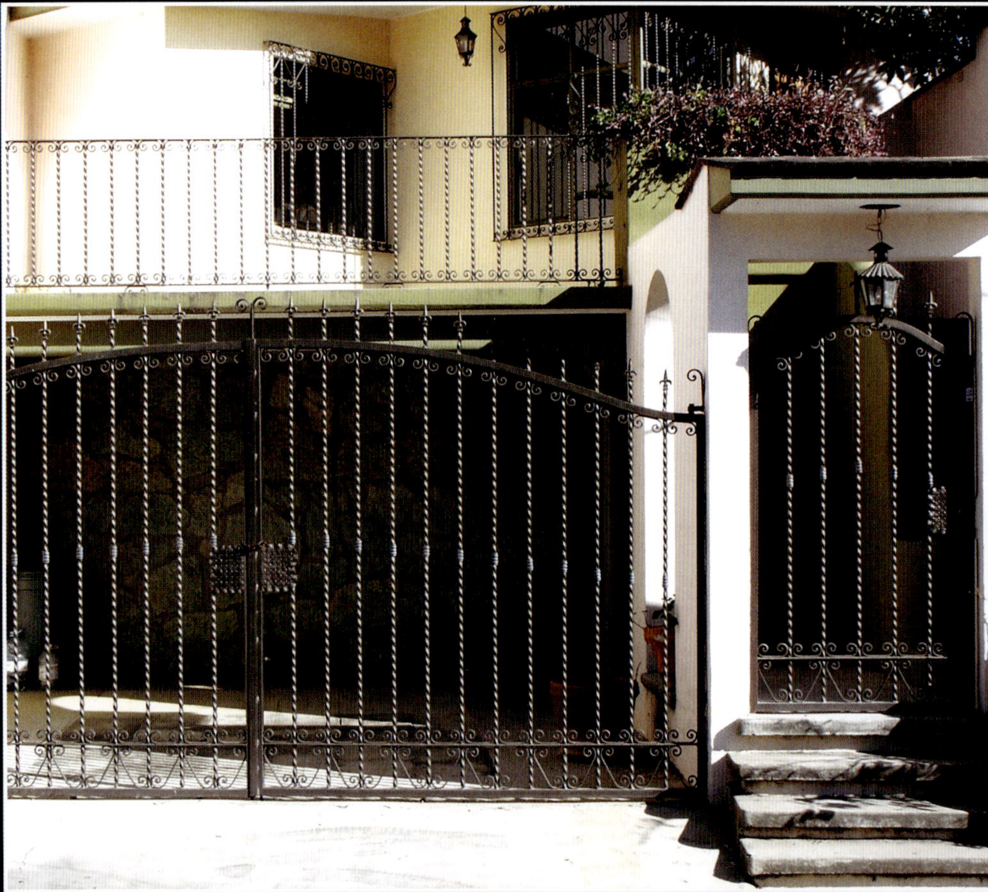
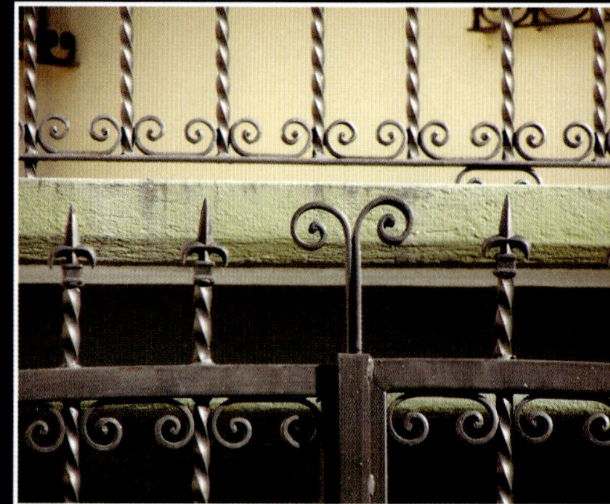
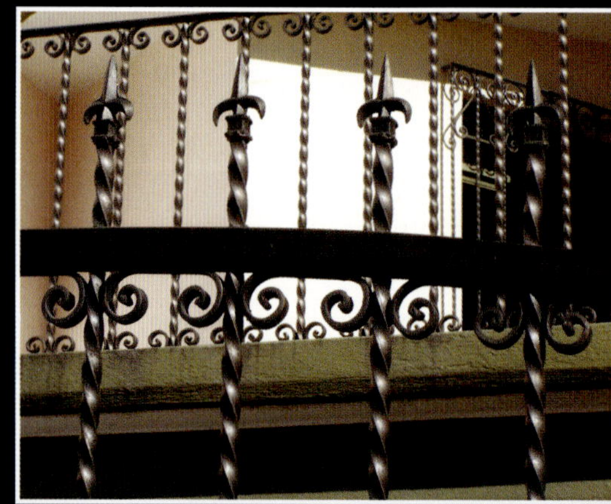

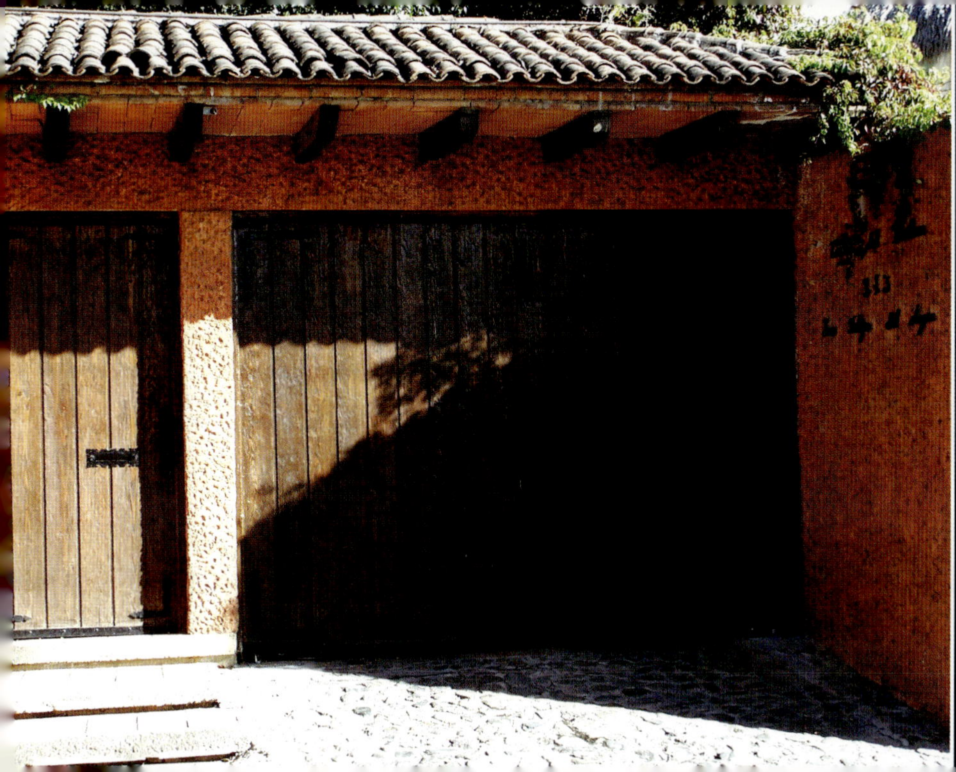
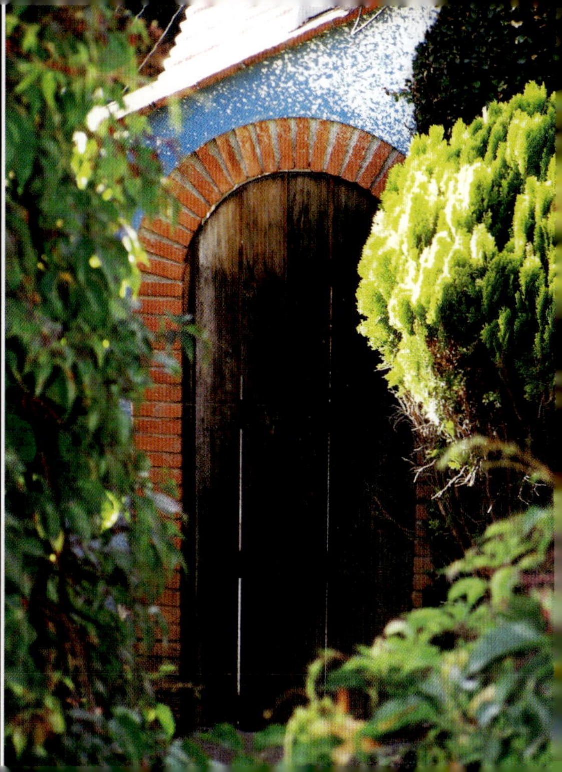

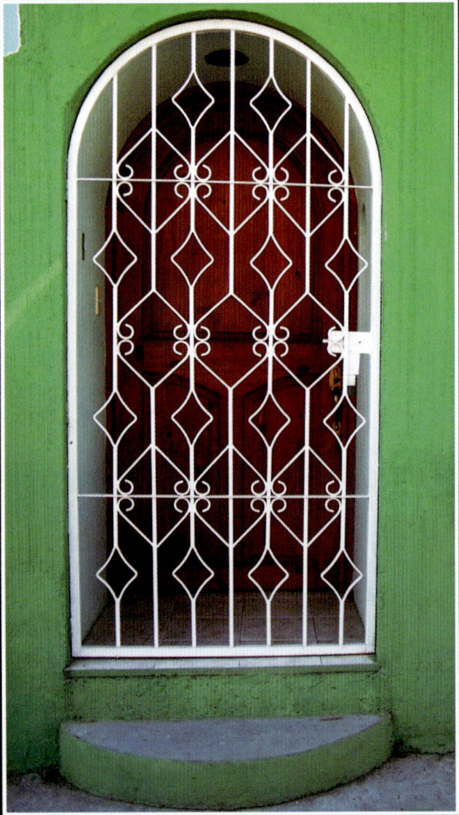

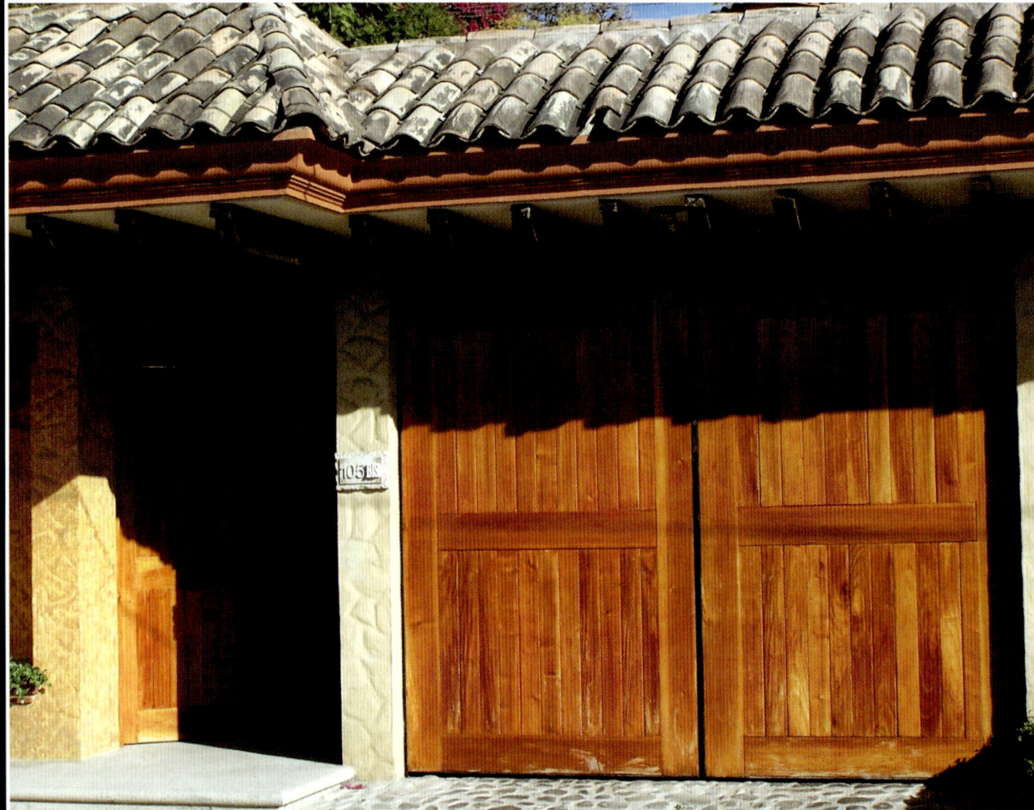
105 BIS

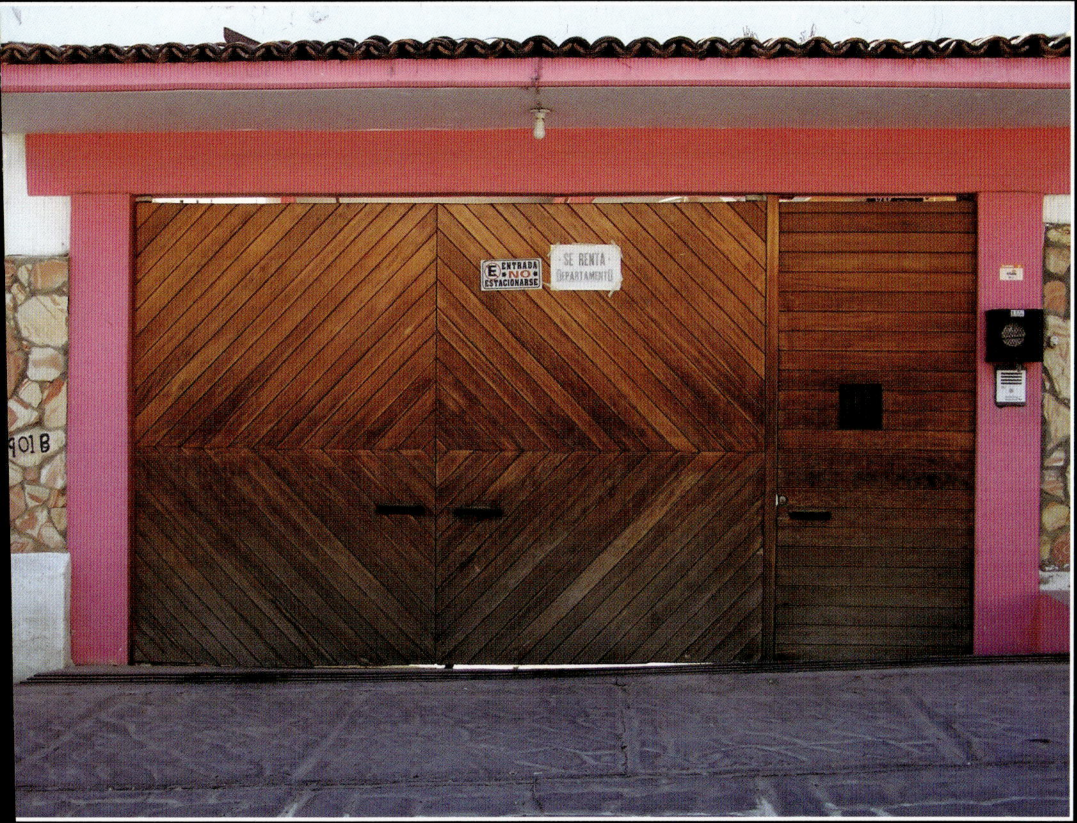
E ENTRADA NO ESTACIONARSE
SE RENTA DEPARTAMENTO
901B

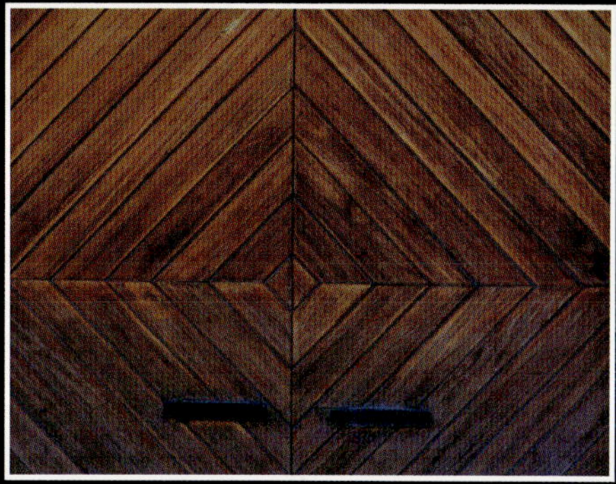

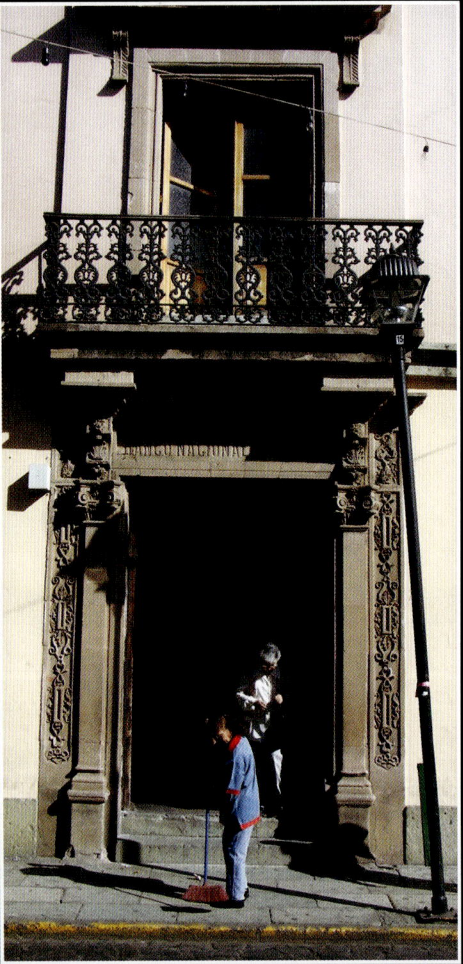

The National Bank of Mexico (BANAMEX) located on the corner of Hidalgo Street and Armenta y López Street.

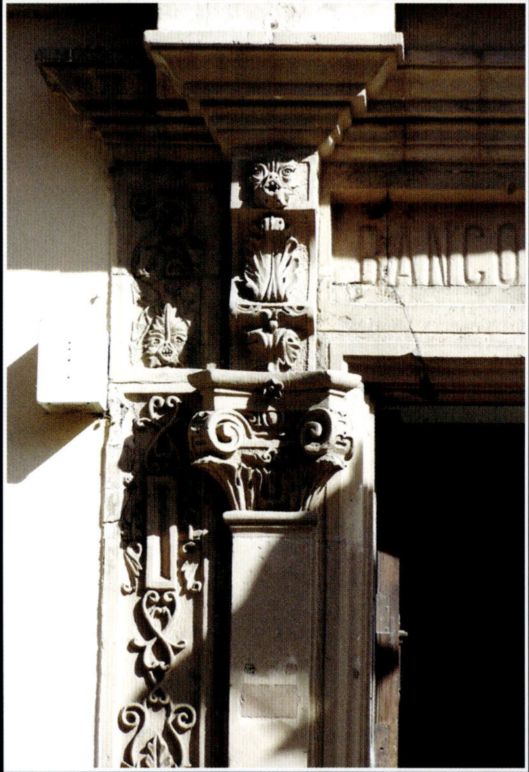

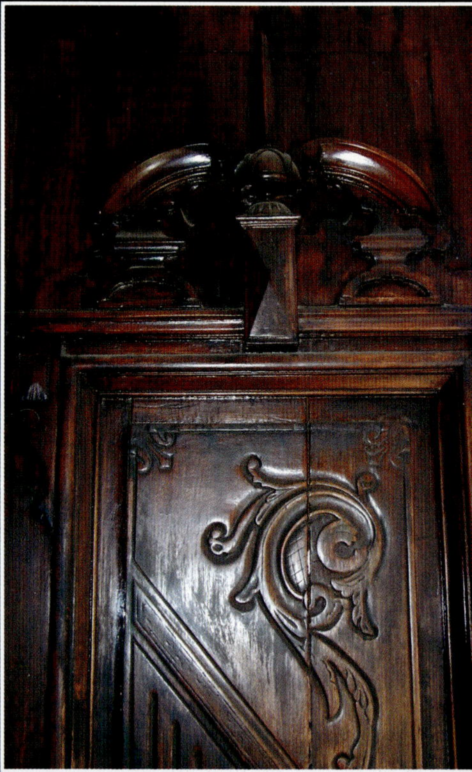

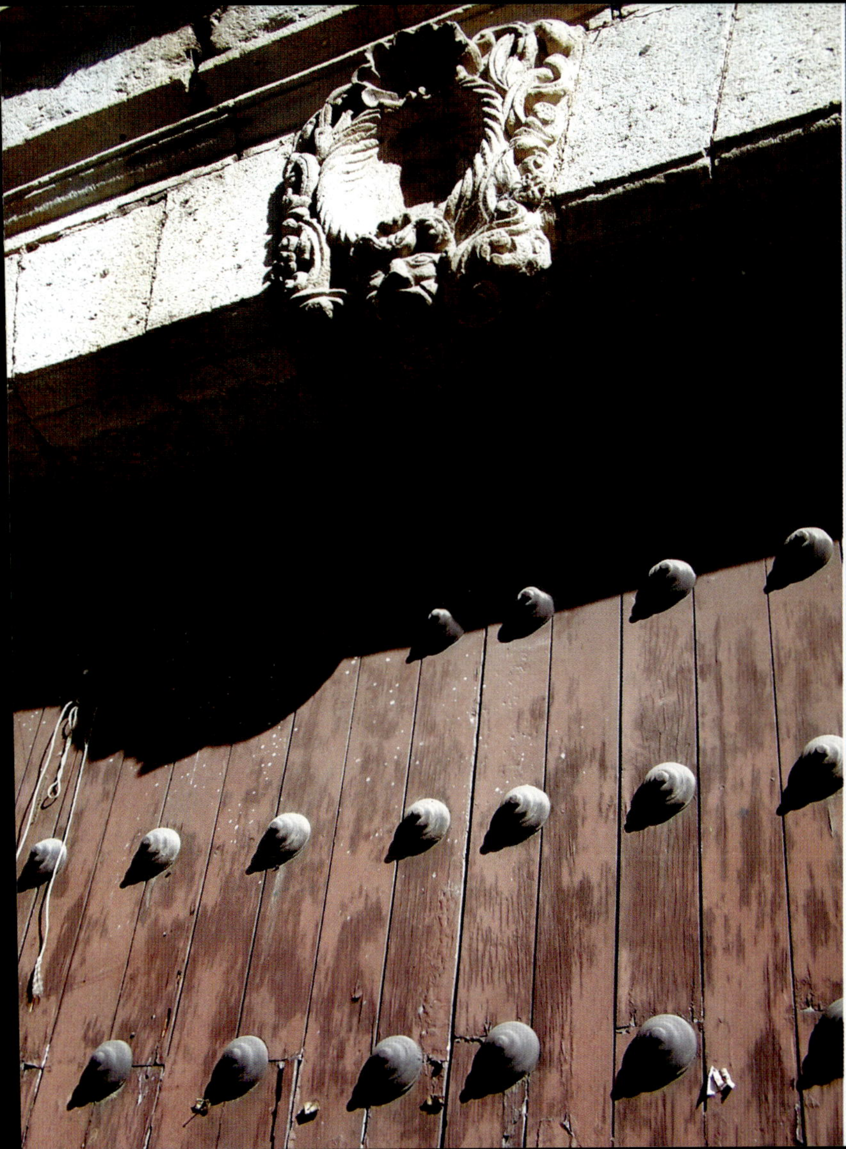

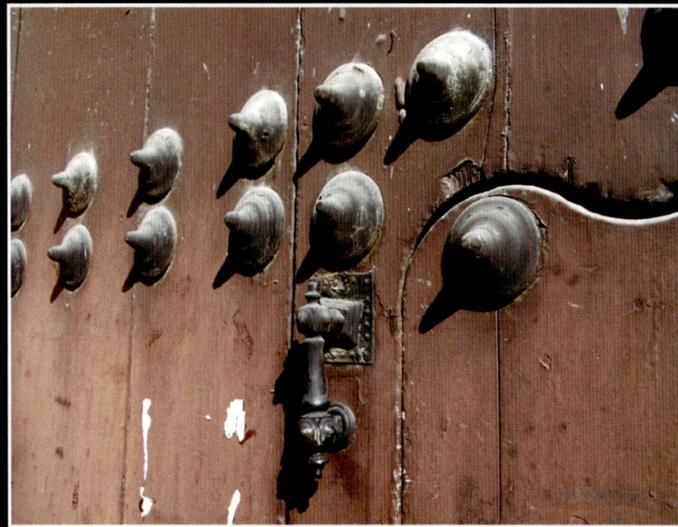

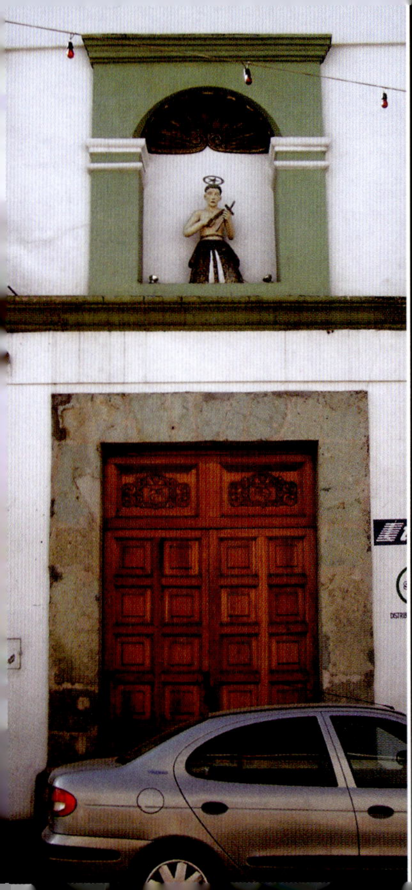

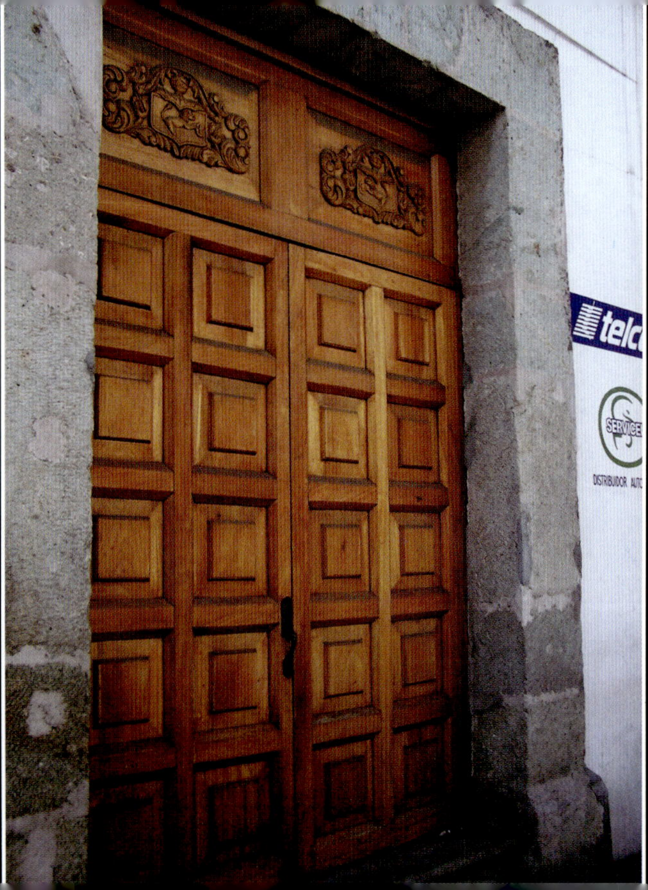

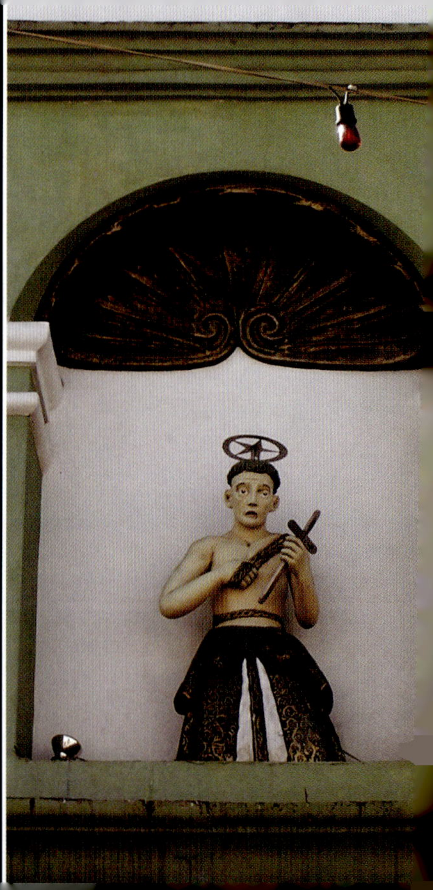

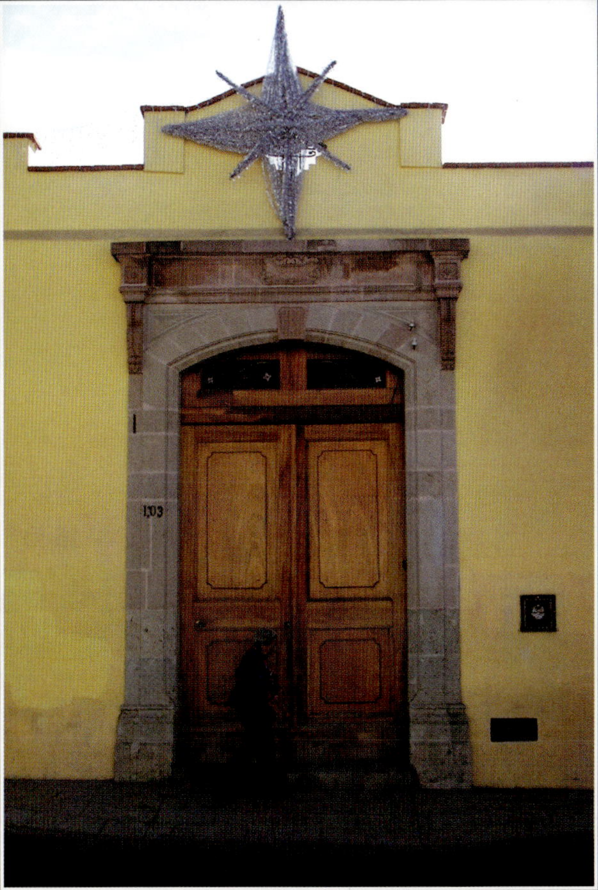

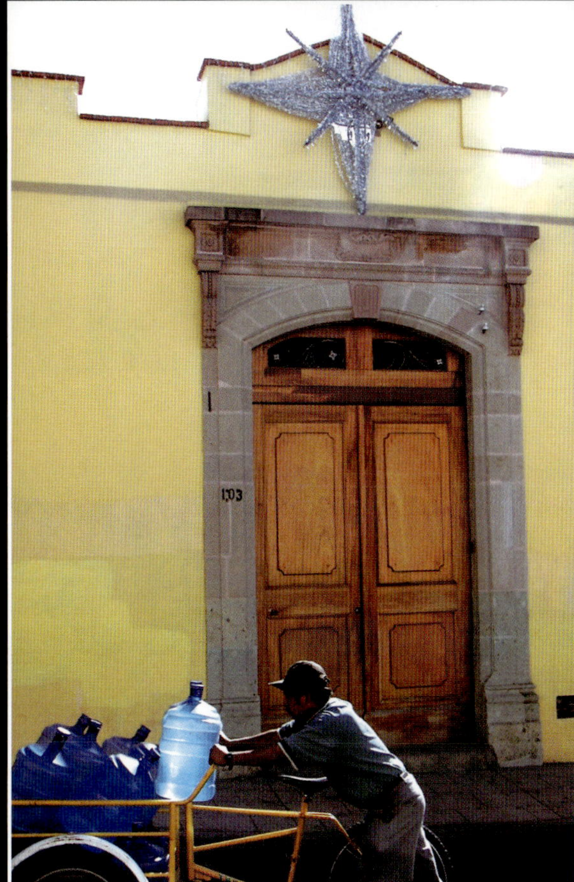

An evangelical church located Fiallo Street.

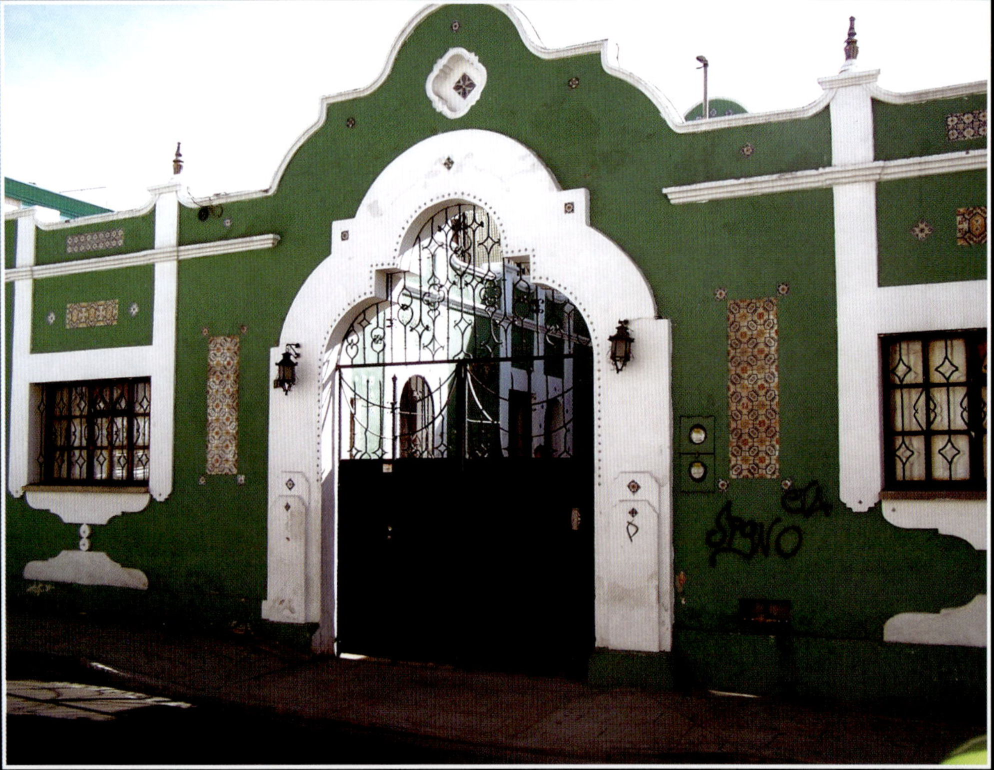

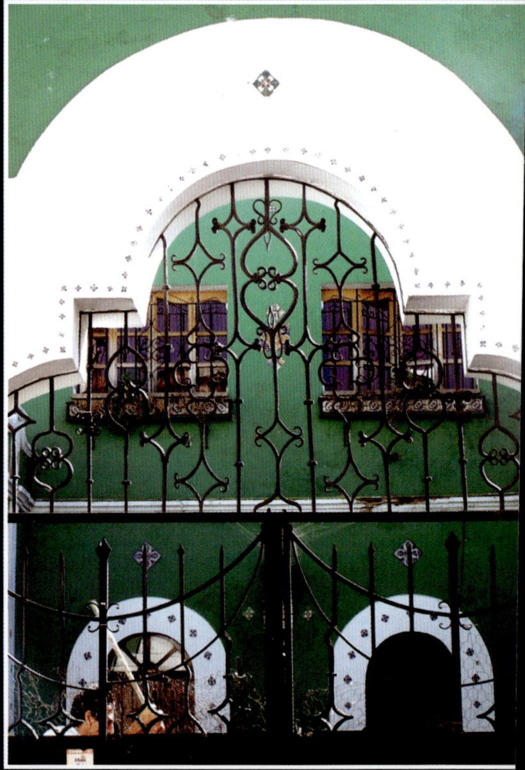

103 Fiallo Street.

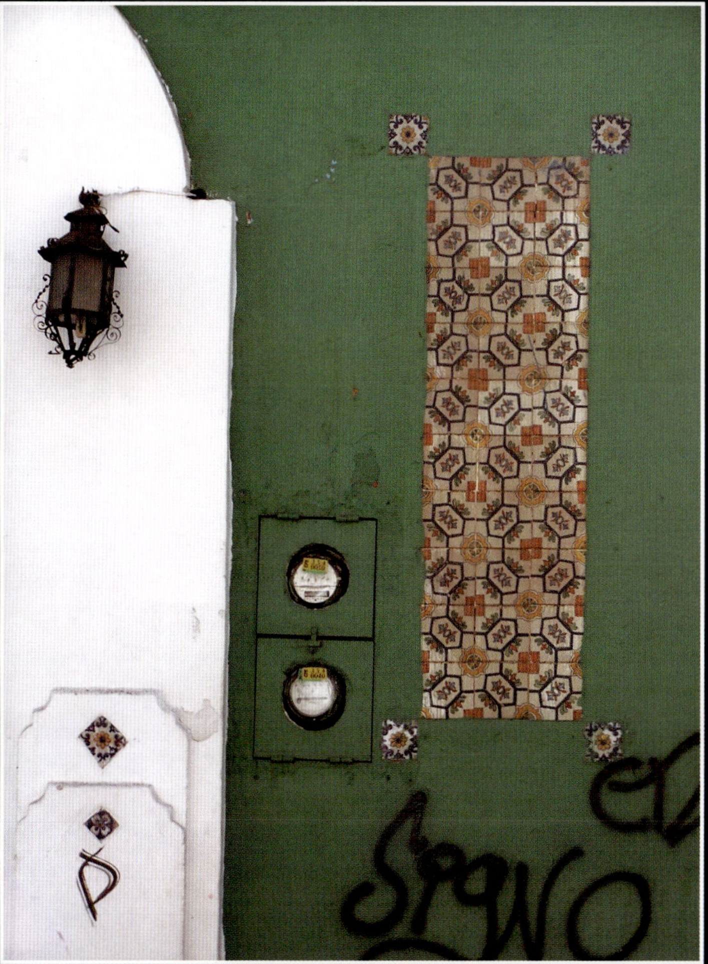

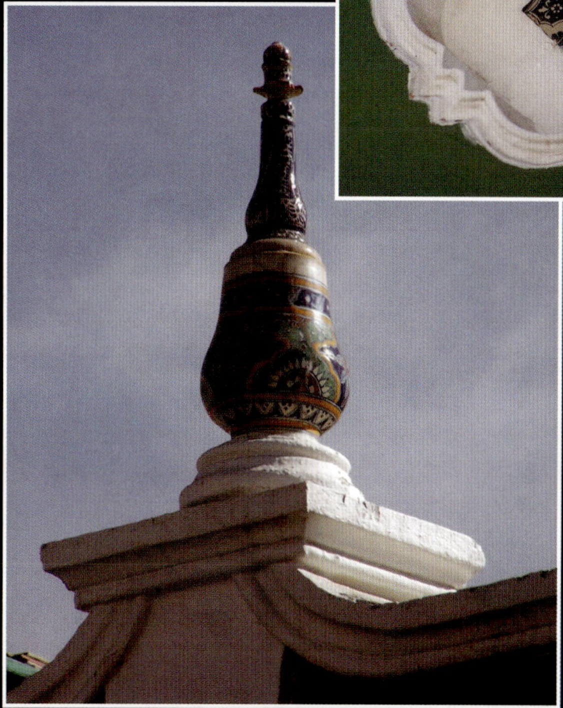

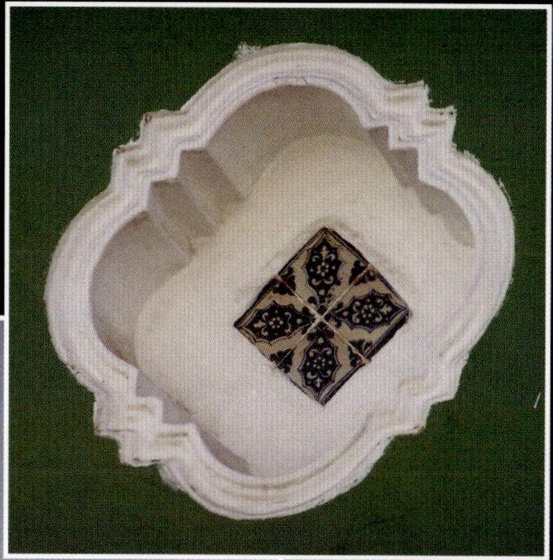

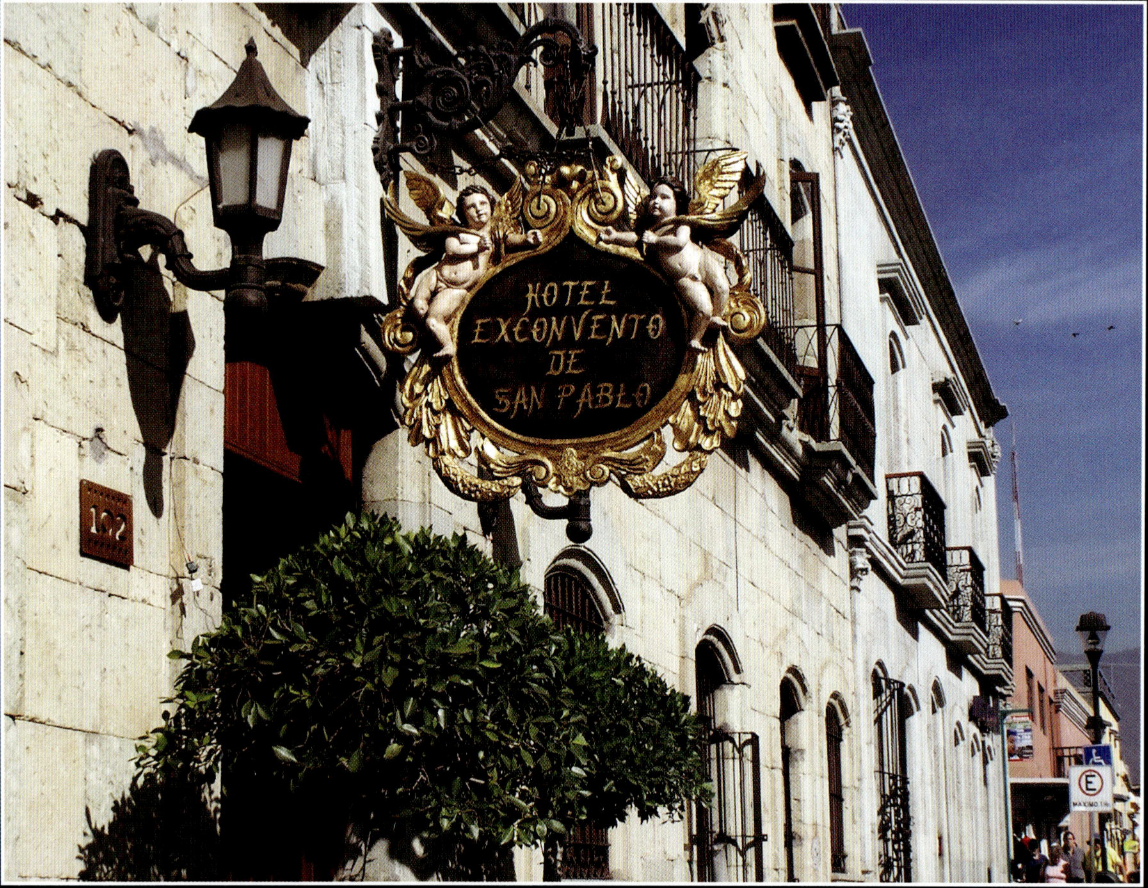

A charming and rustic hotel that was once the San Pablo convent.

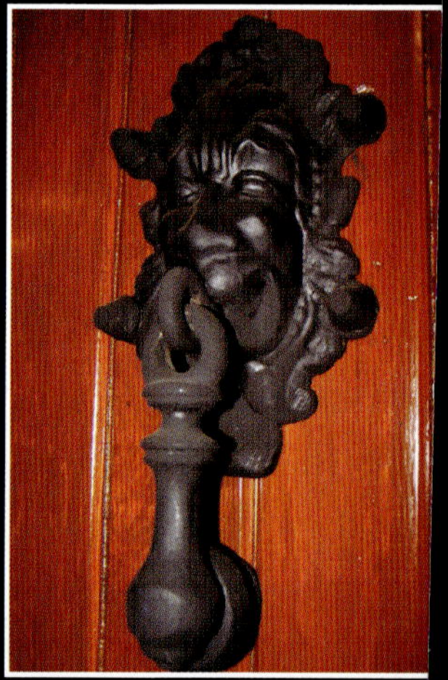

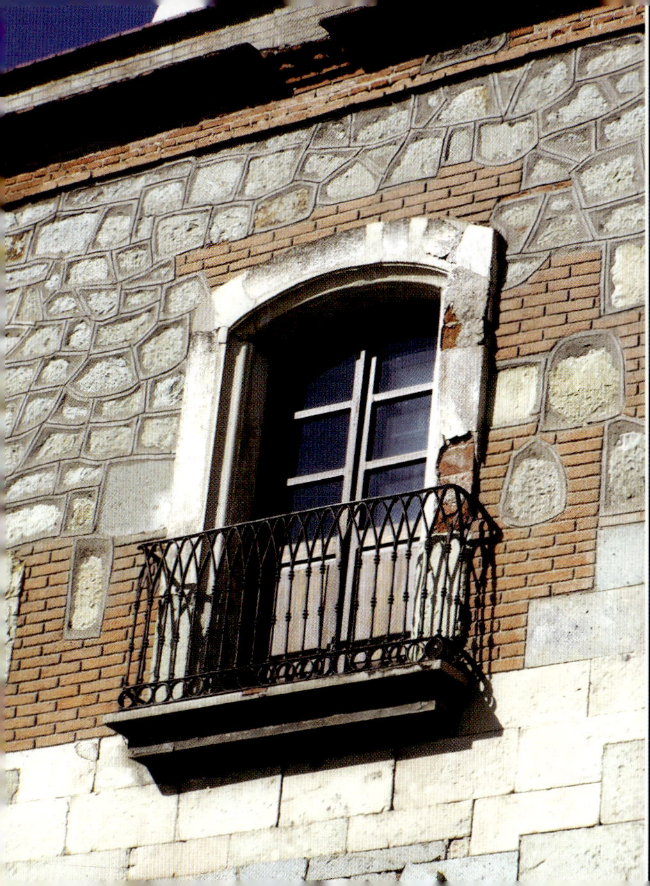
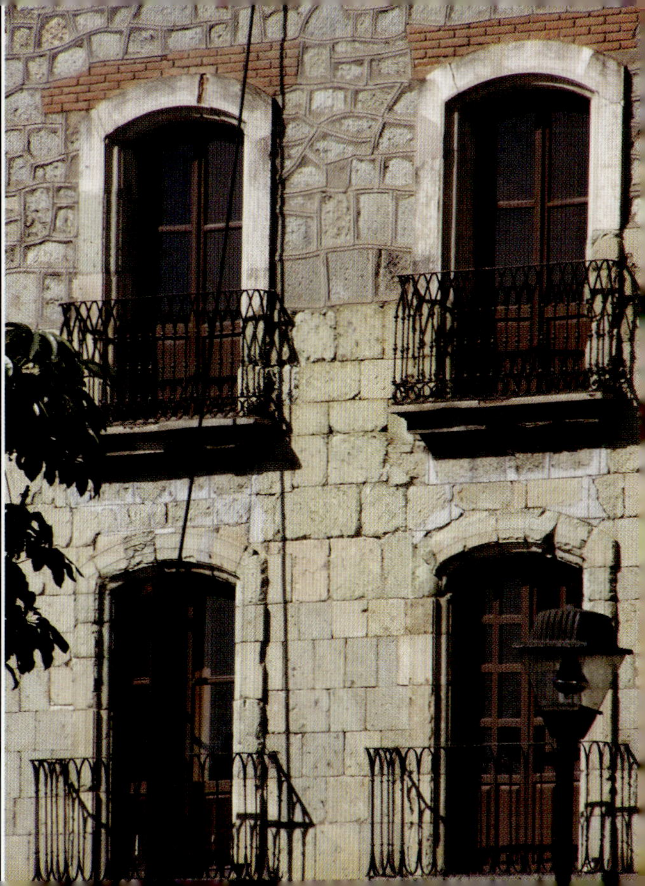

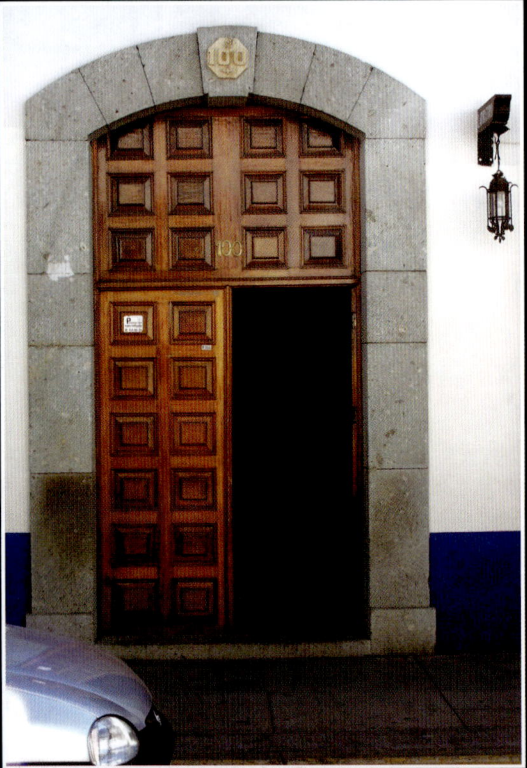

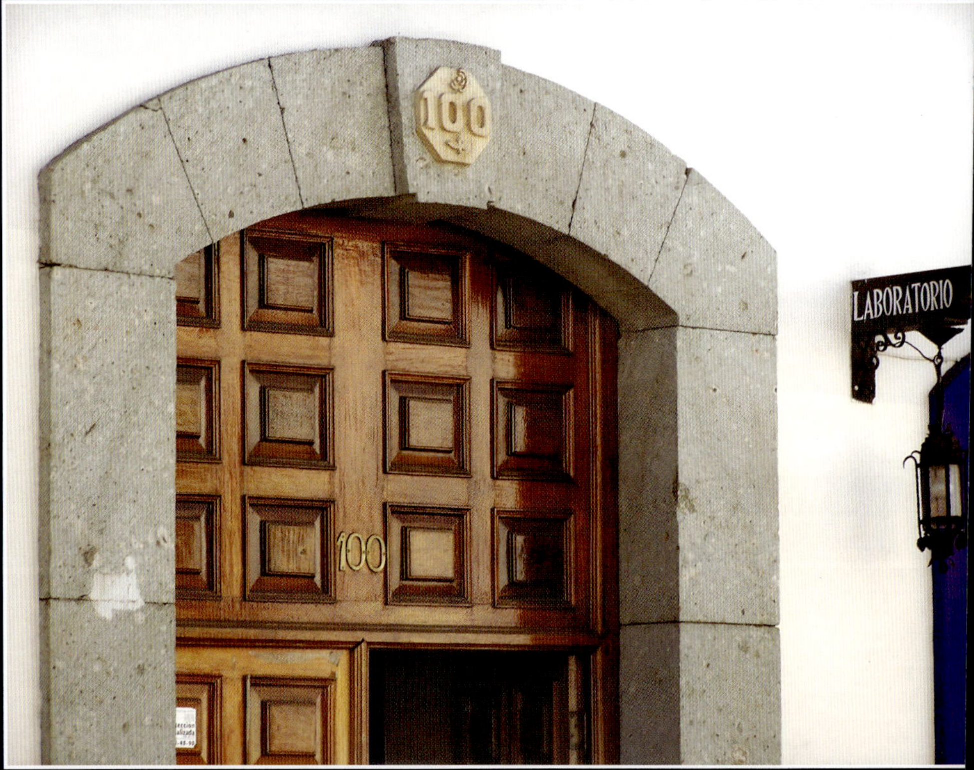

The corner of Hidalgo Street and Melchor Ocampo Street.

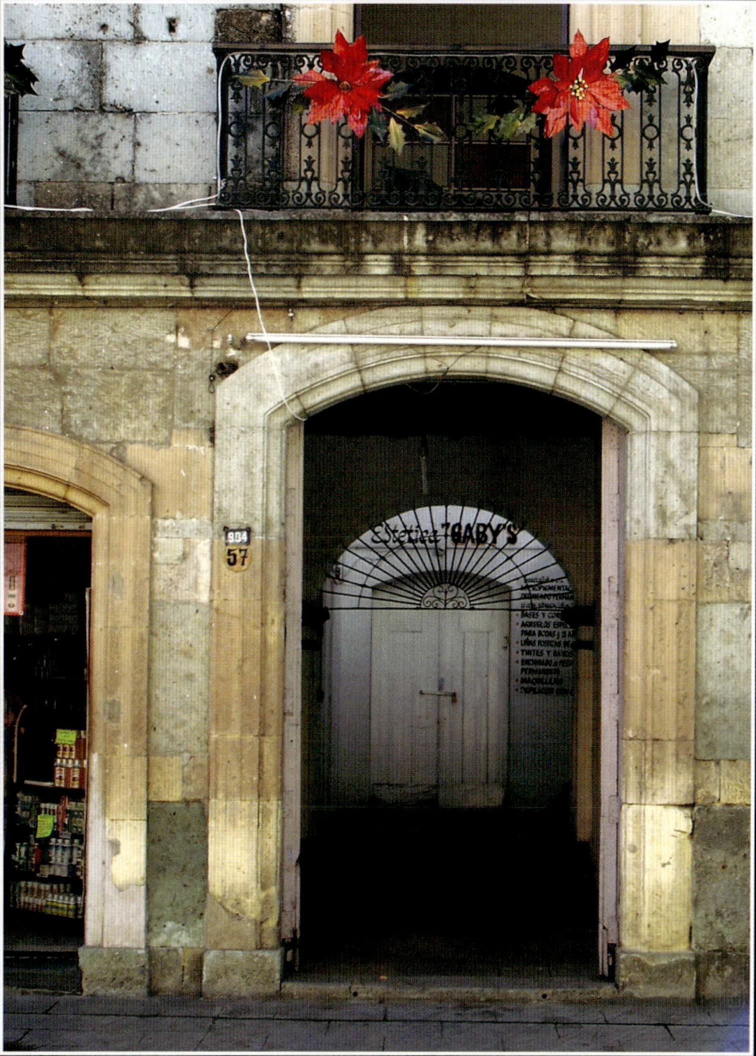

The white double door is a unisex hair salon, called Estetica "Gabys."

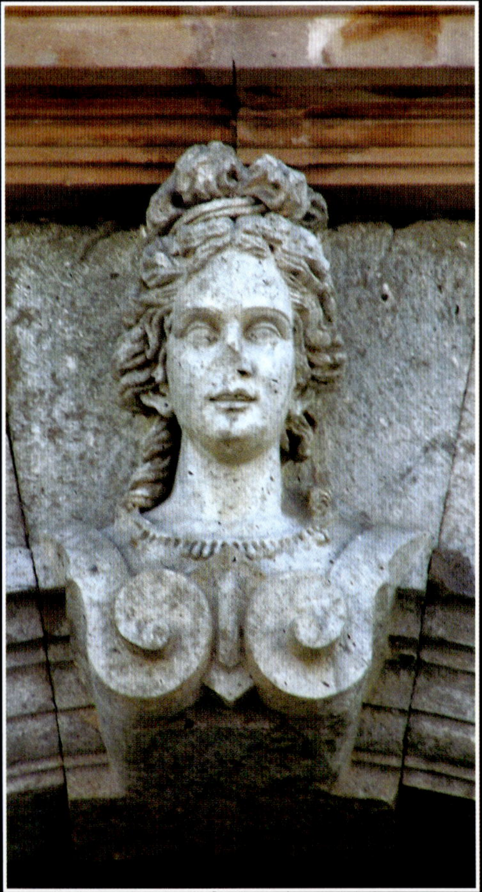
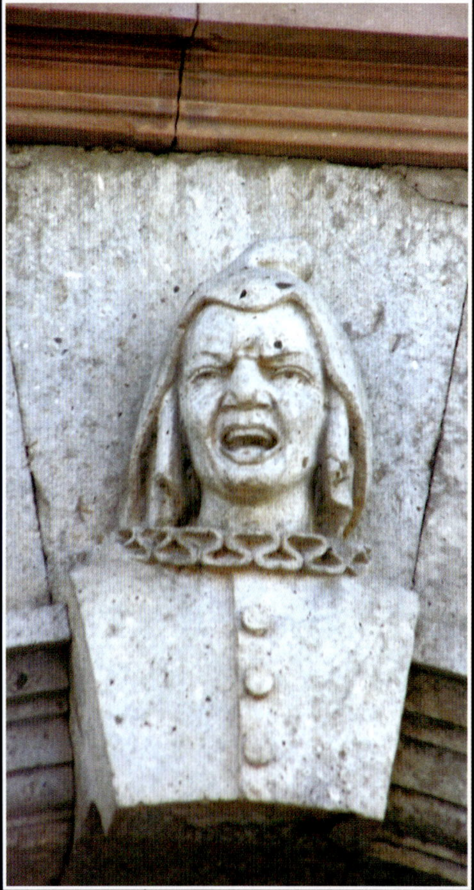
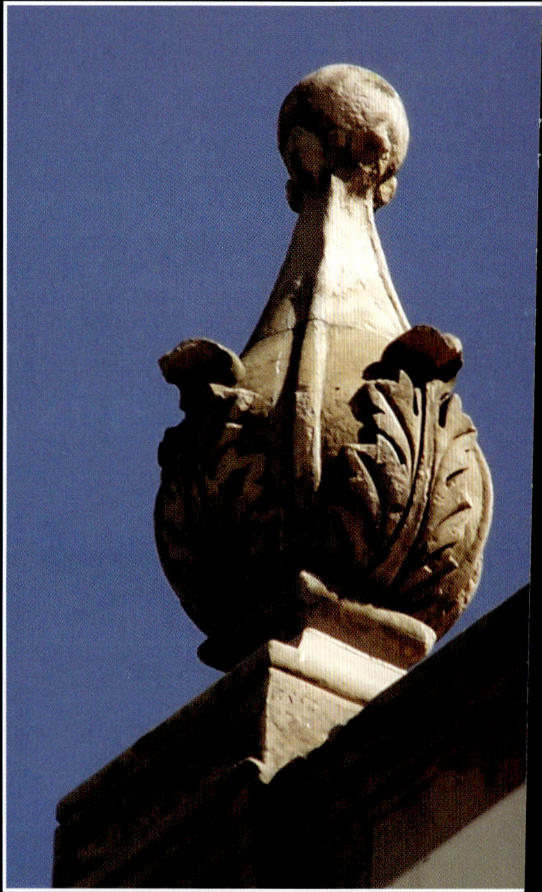

Once the state library, it is now an architectural school.

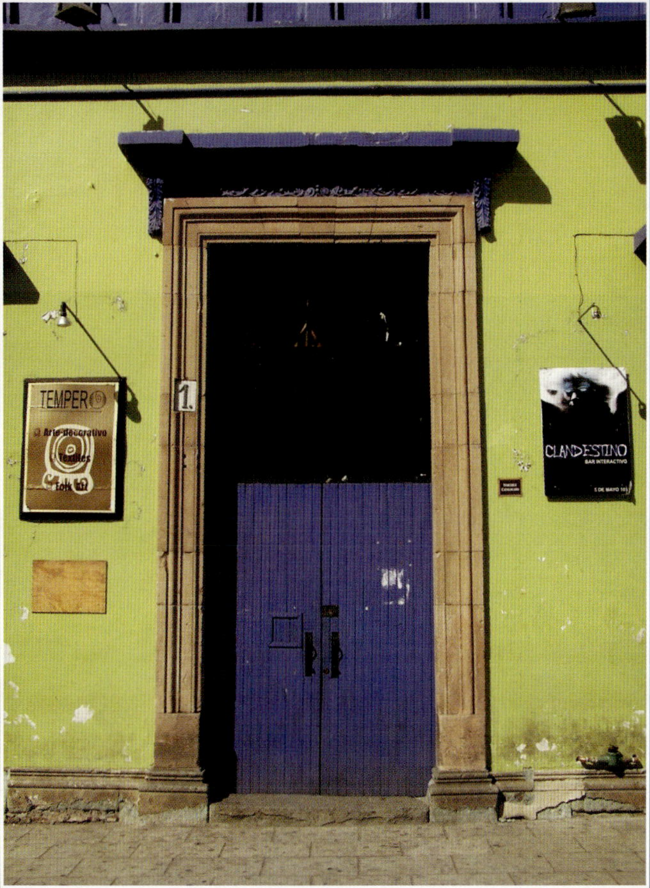
TEMPERO
Arte decorativo
Textiles
Folk Art
1.
CLANDESTINO
BAR INTERACTIVO

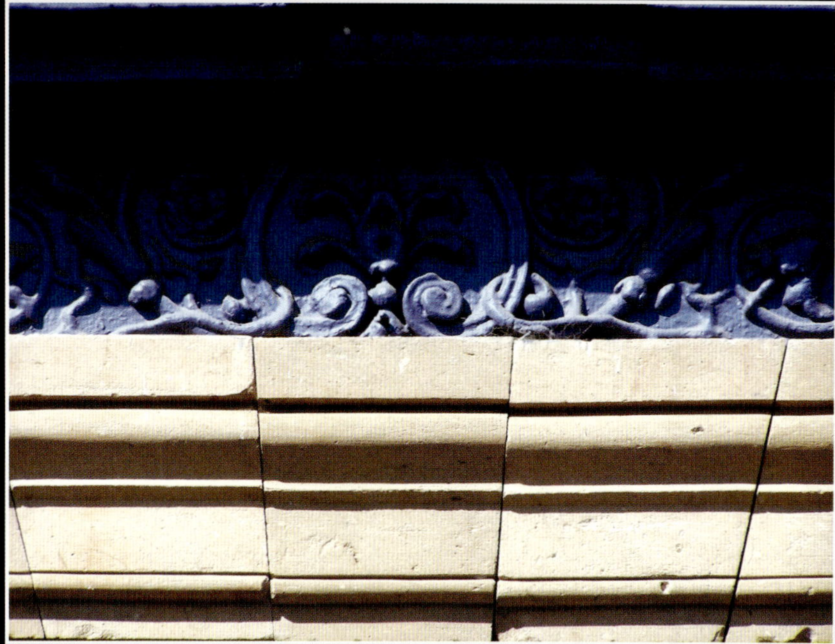

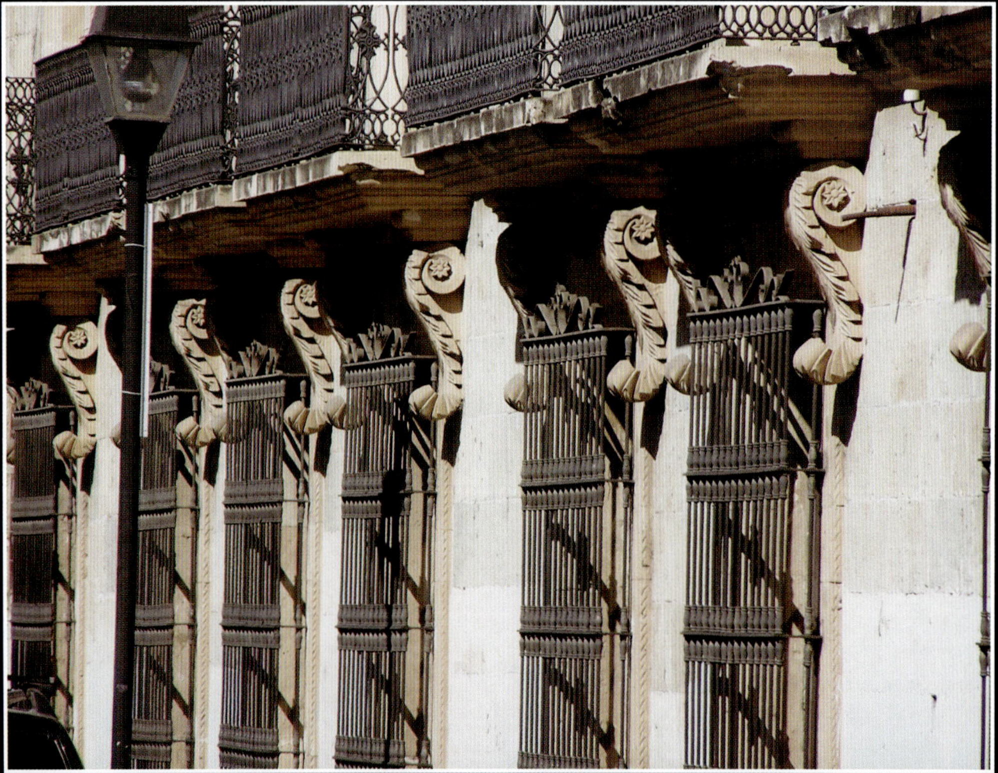

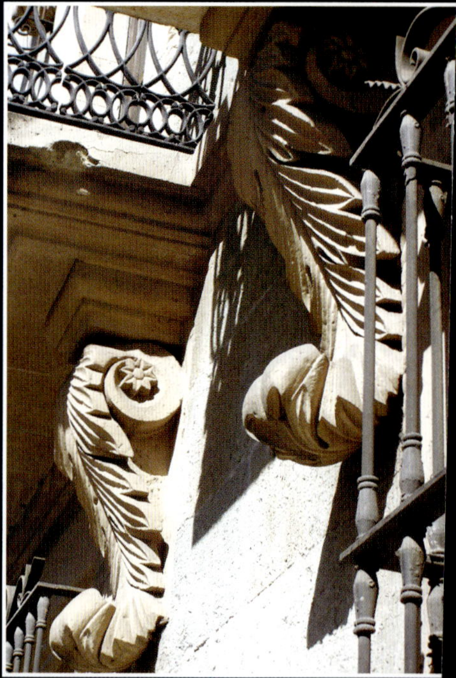

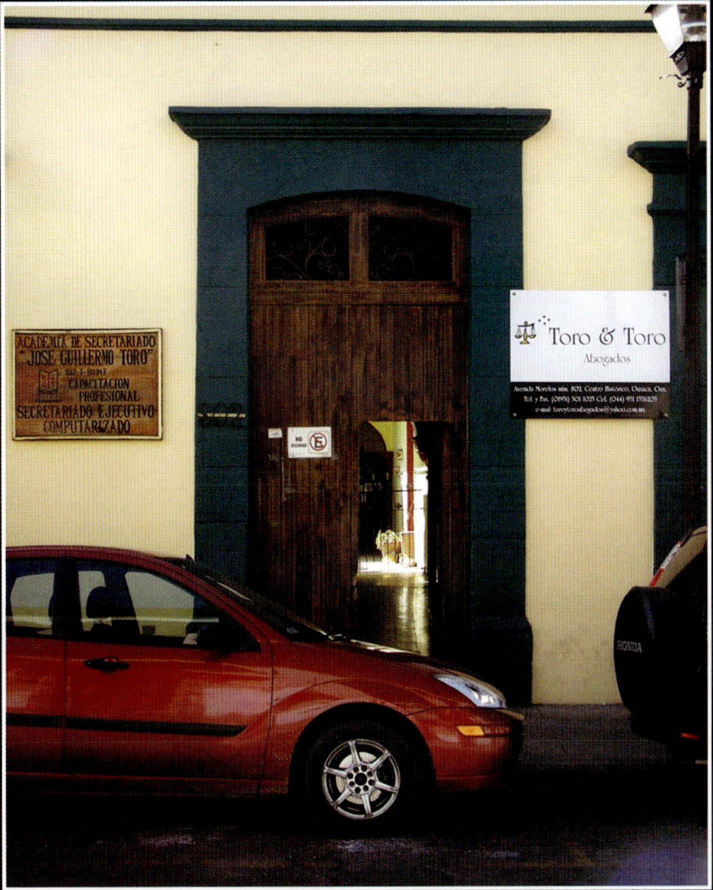

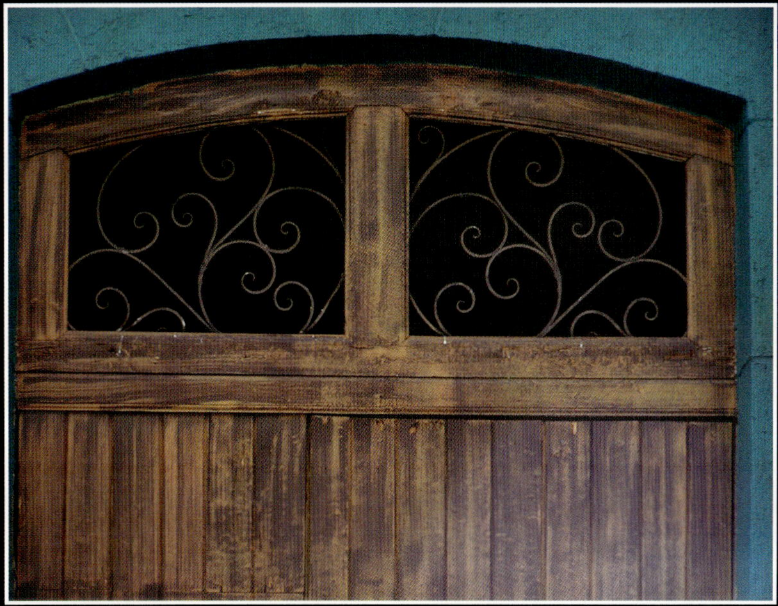

A school that trains secretaries, located at 802 Morelos Street.

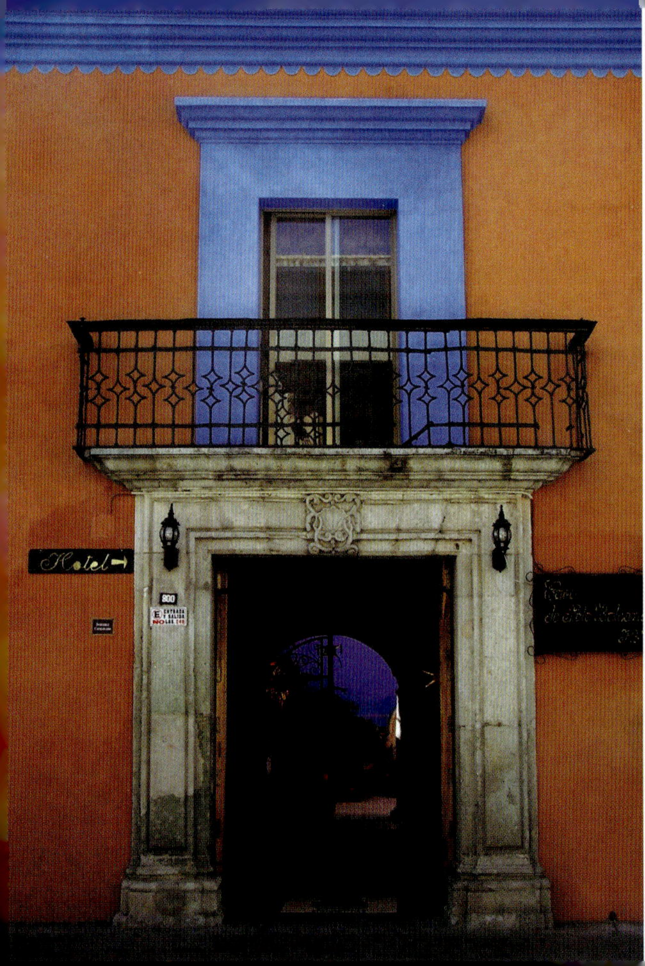

A hotel called, Casa do Roto Balcones, which is Portuguese for "House of the Ragged Balconies."

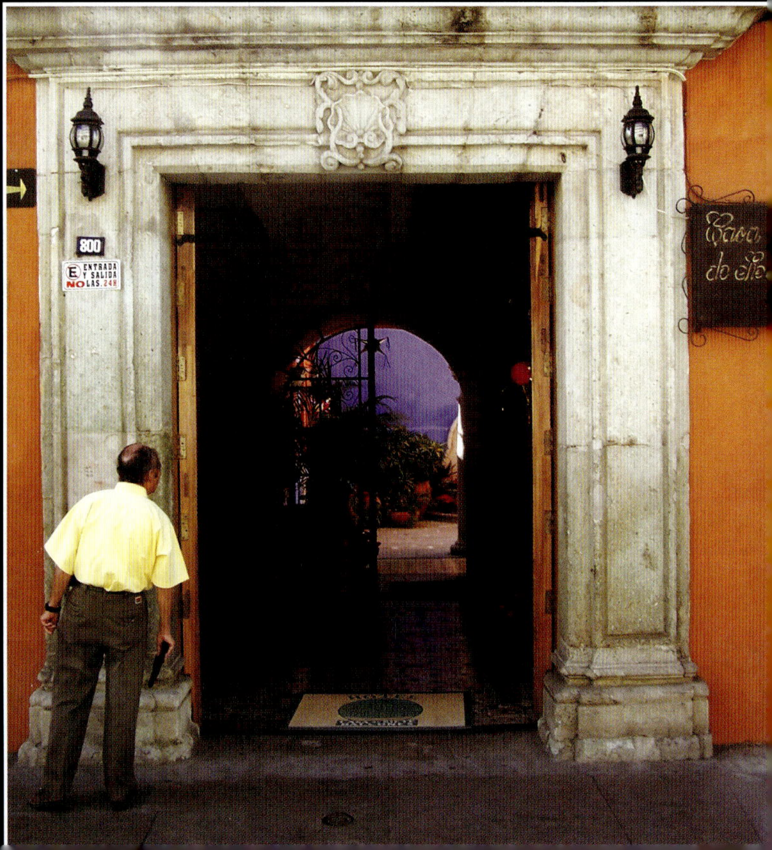

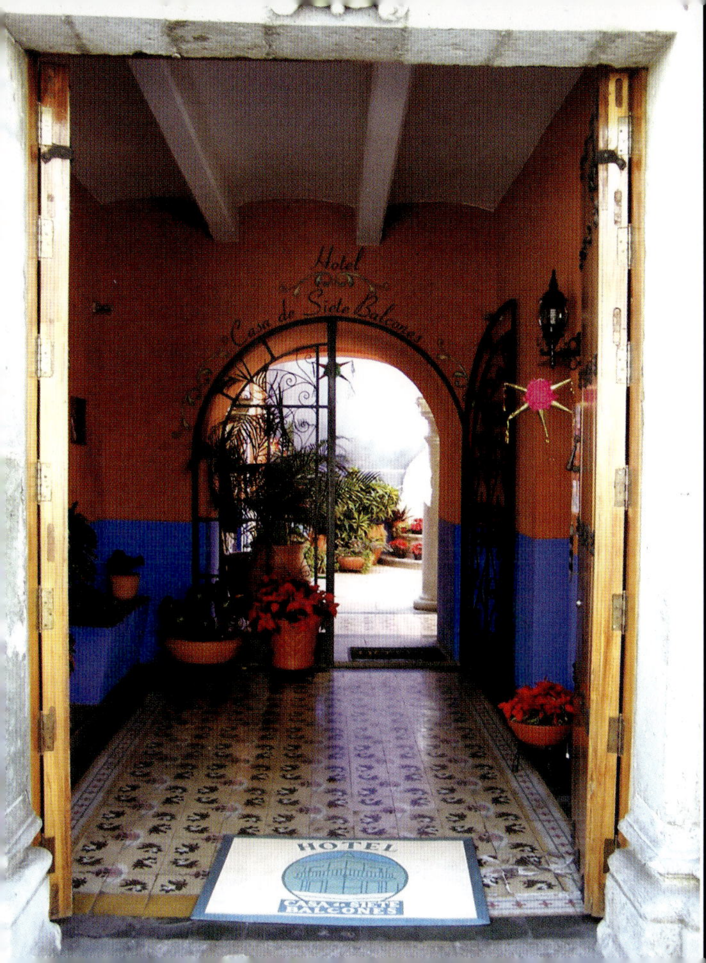
Hotel
Casa de Siete Balcones
HOTEL
CASA de SIETE
BALCONES

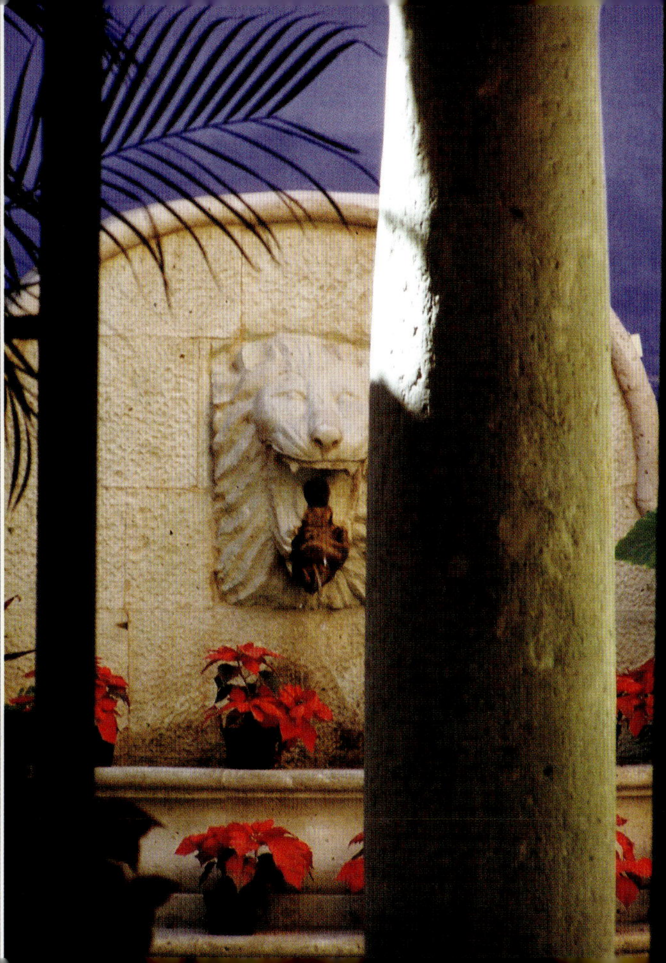

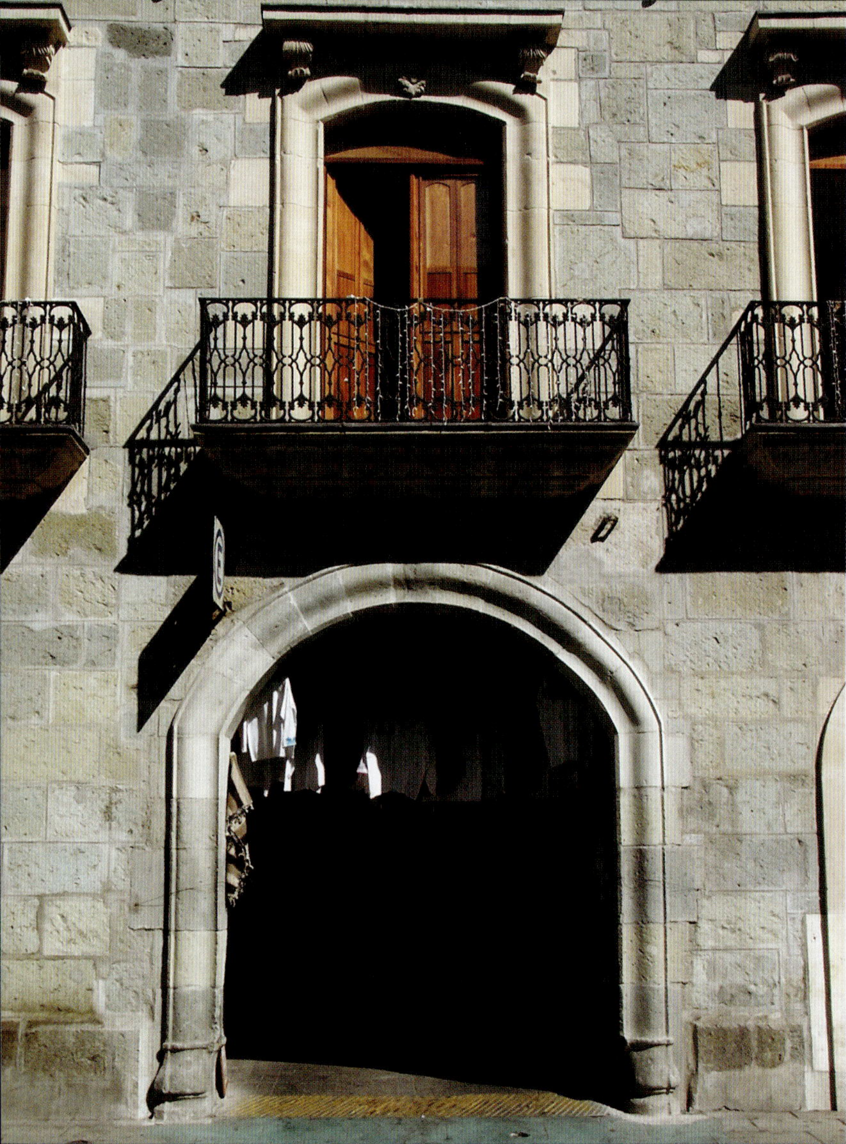

Once the Oaxacan Movie Theatre and now a public parking lot, with some offices for rent on the second level.

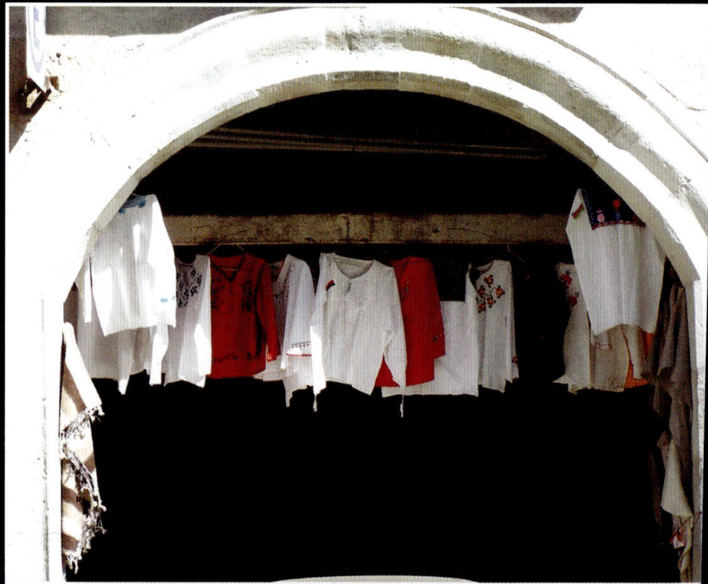

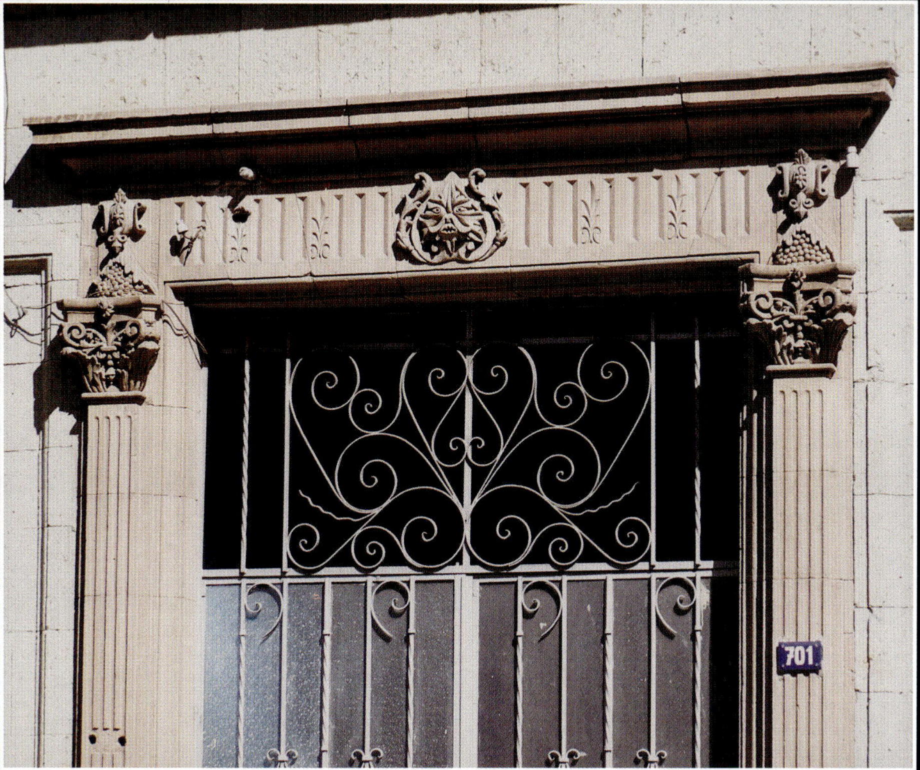
701

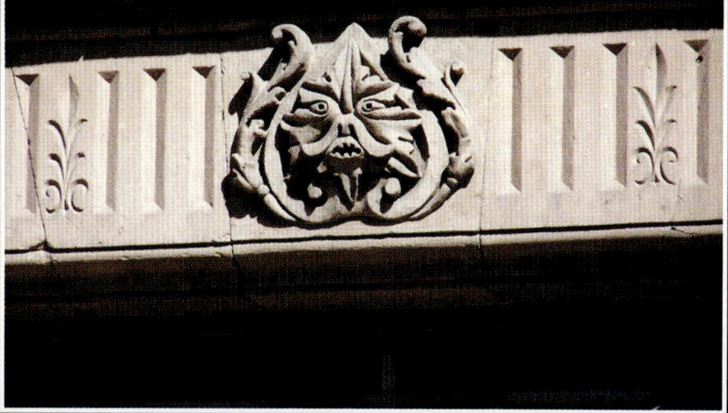

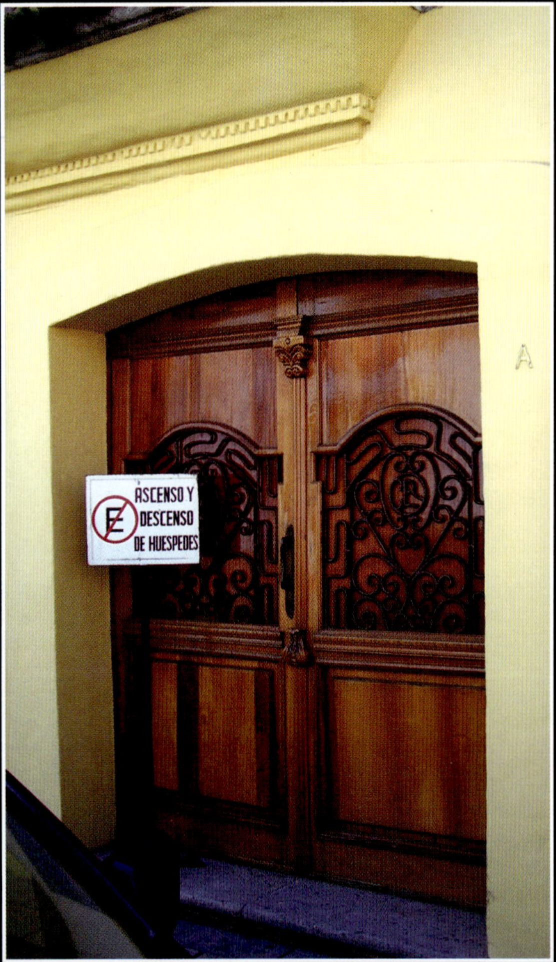
E
ASCENSO Y
DESCENSO
DE HUESPEDES

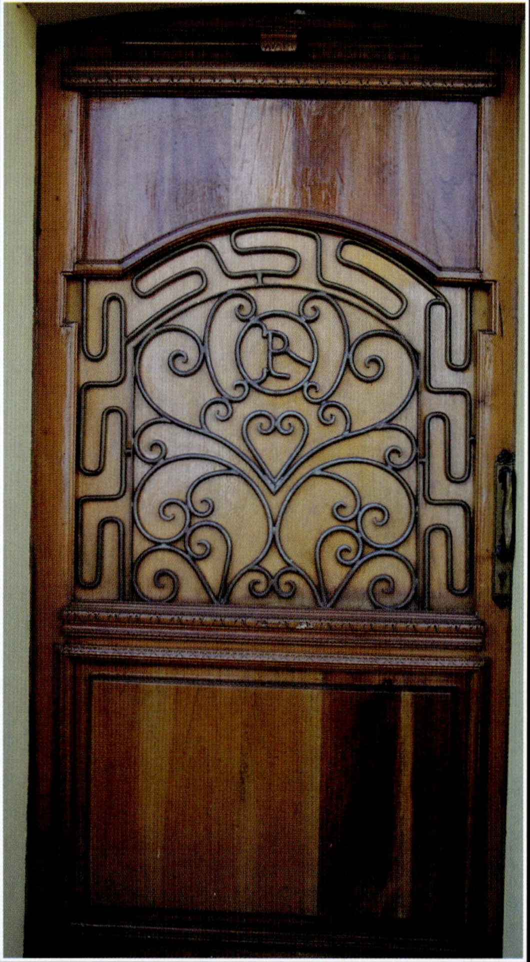

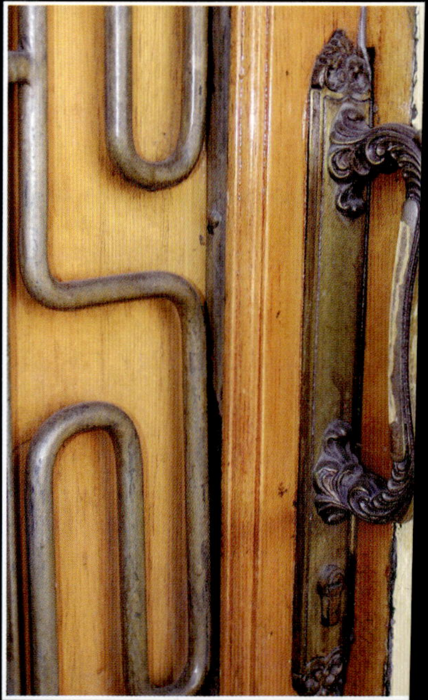

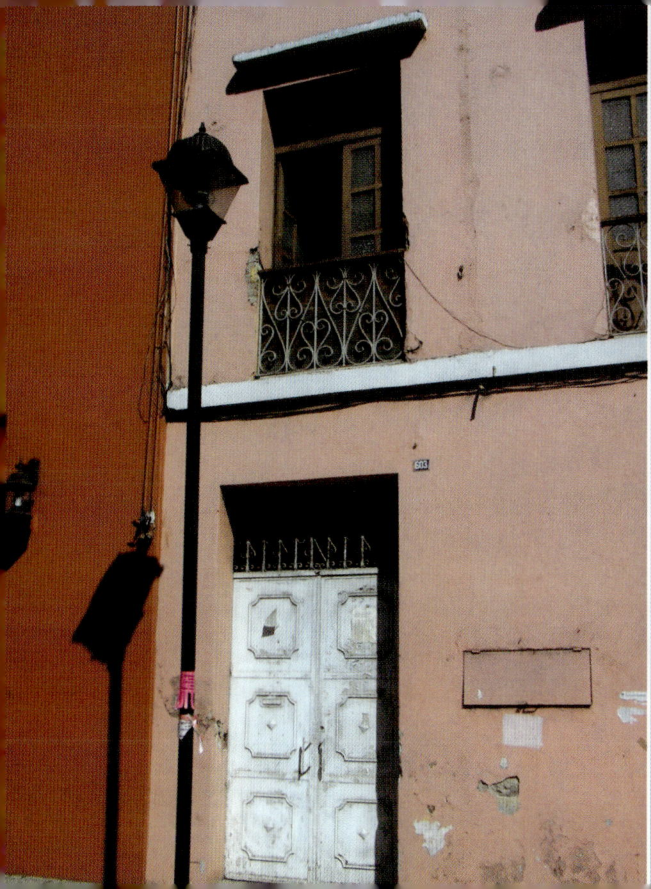
603

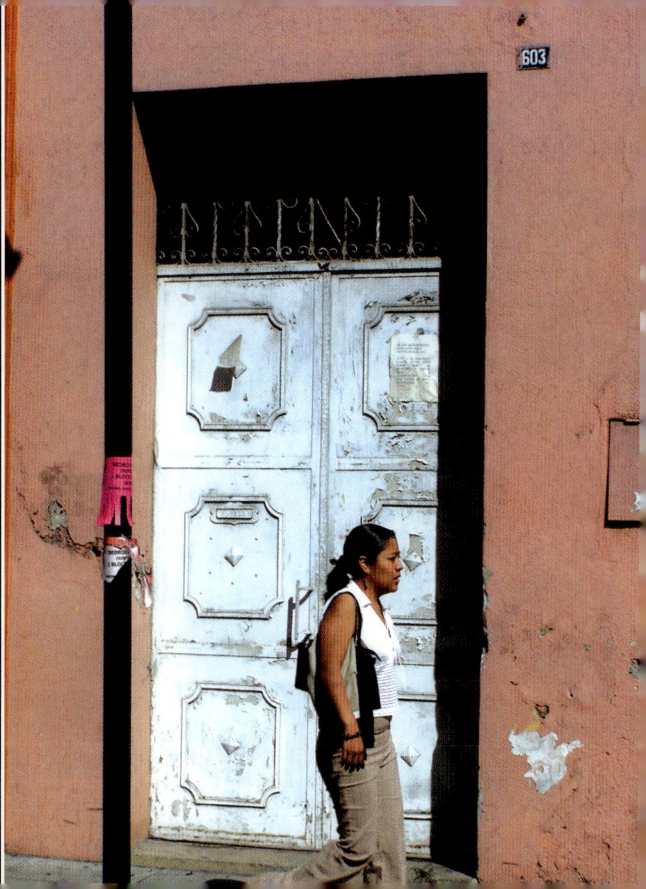
603

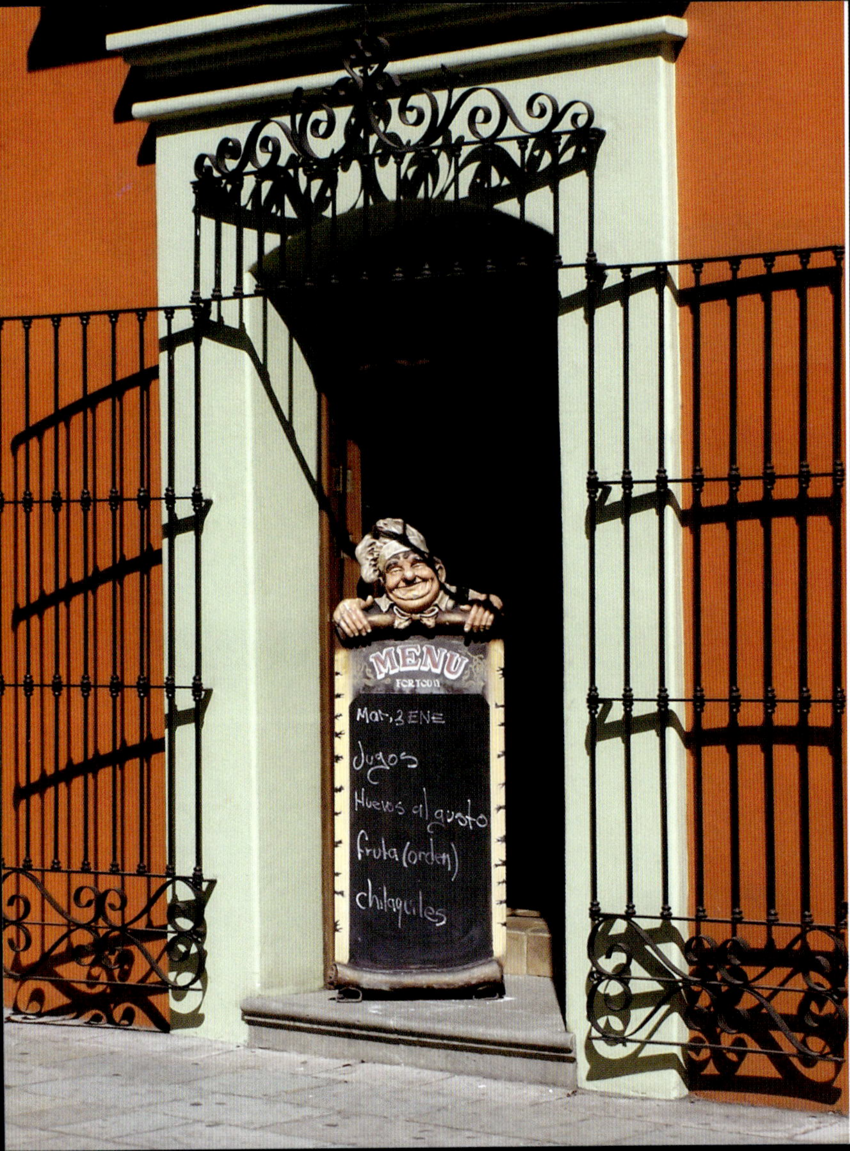

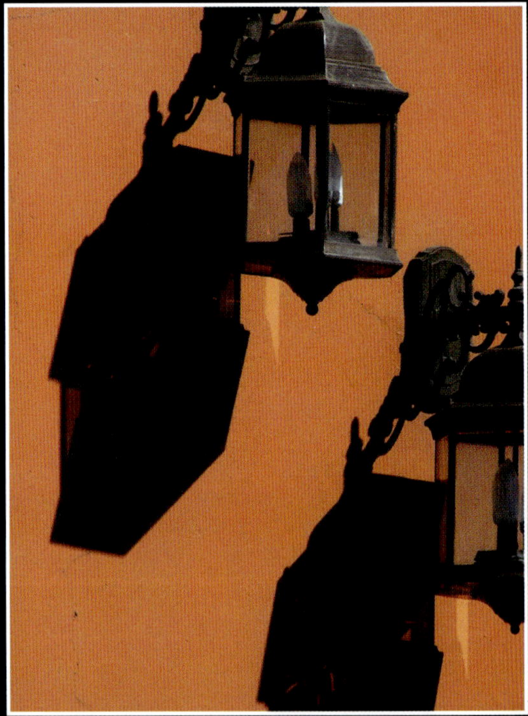

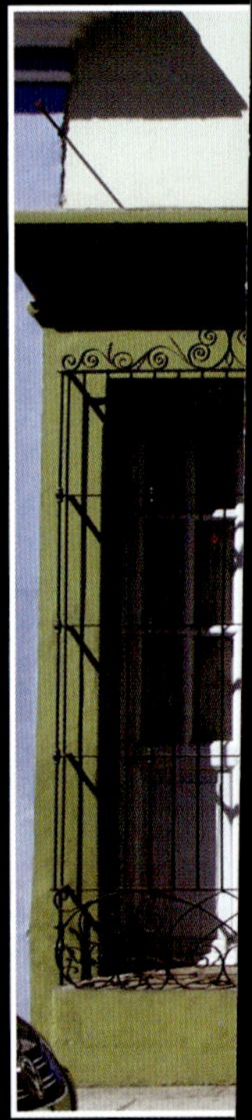

A family restaurant with a breakfast menu that reads, "Tuesday, January 3, 2006, Juices, Eggs to order, fruit plate, and Chilaquiles (a tasty plate of fried shredded tortillas swimming in a salsa broth)."

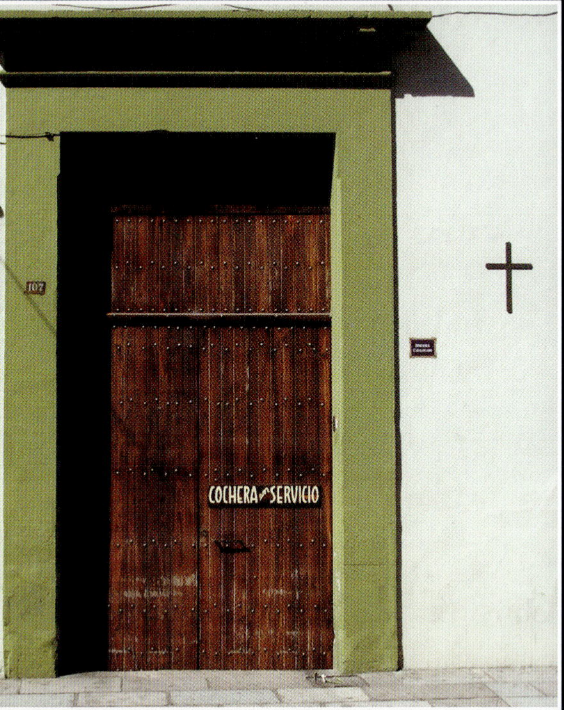
COCHERA SERVICIO

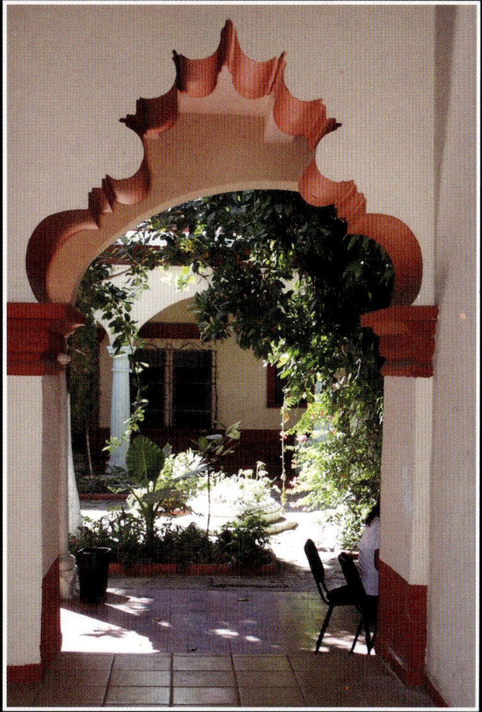

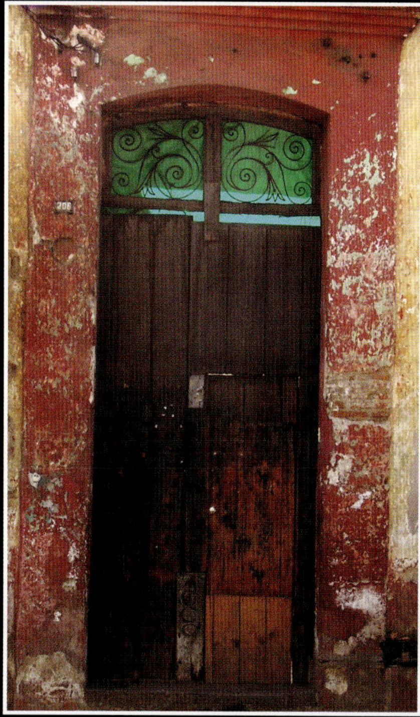

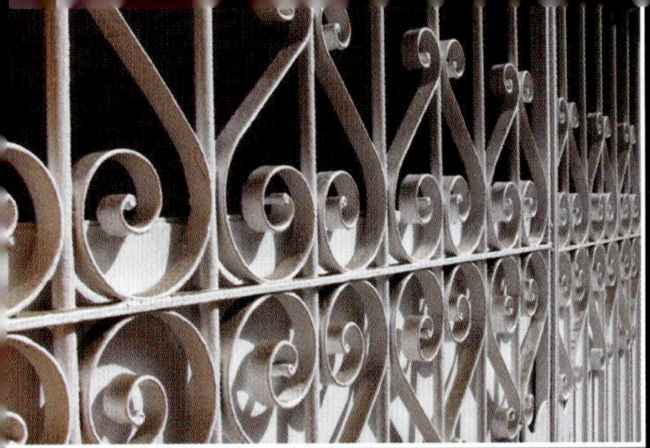

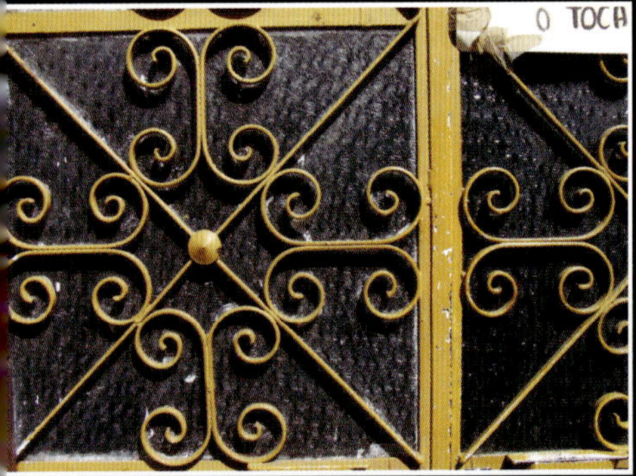
O TOCA

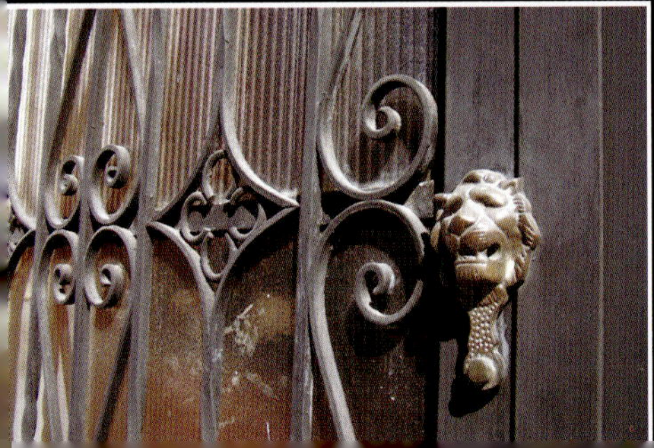

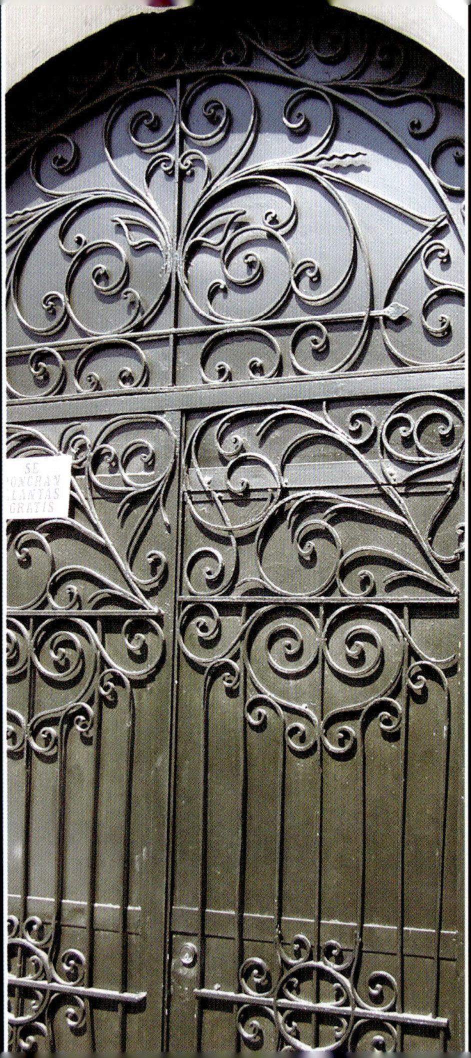
SE
ONCHAN
LANTAS
GRATIS

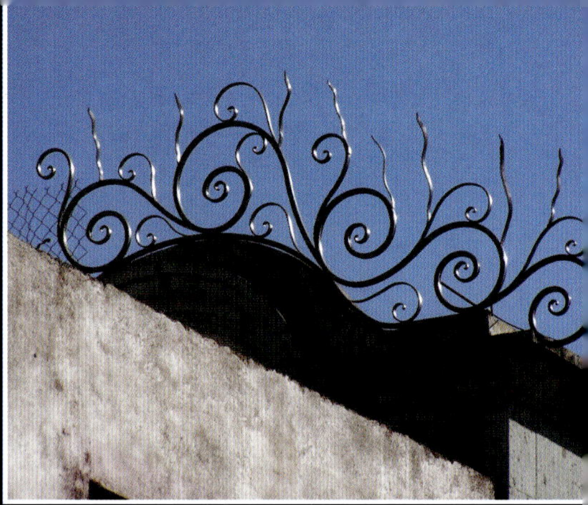

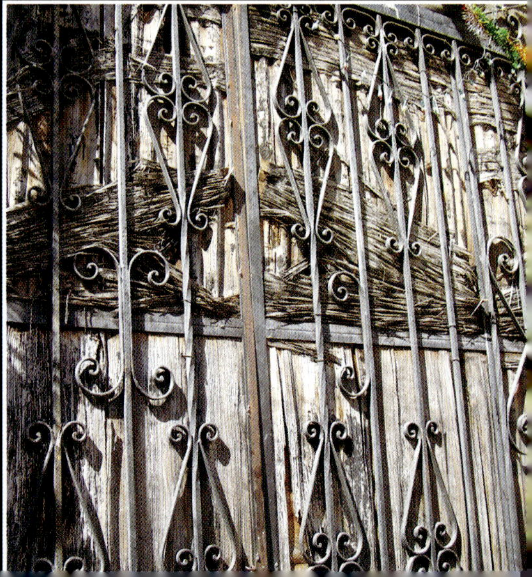

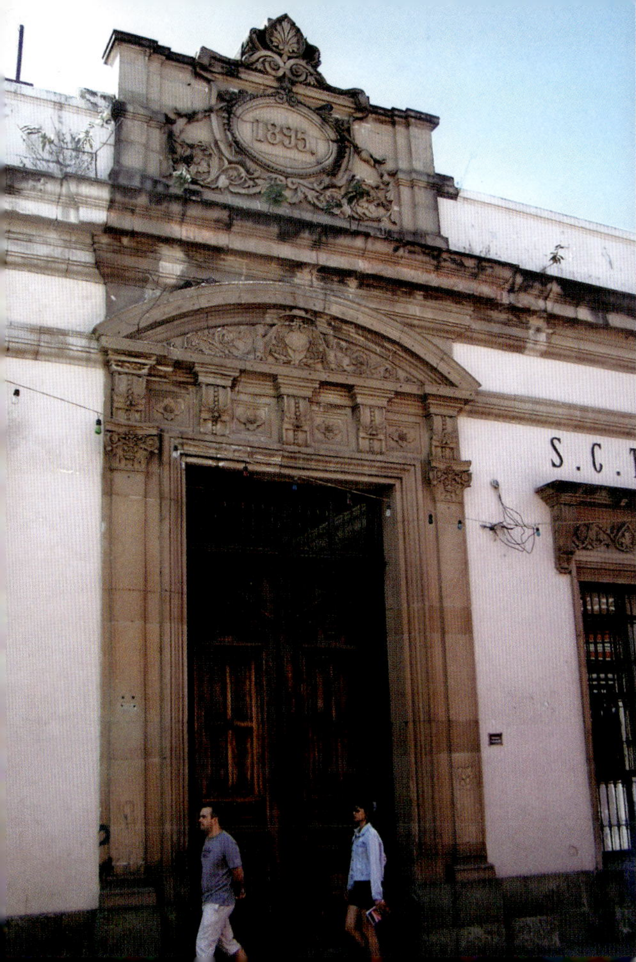

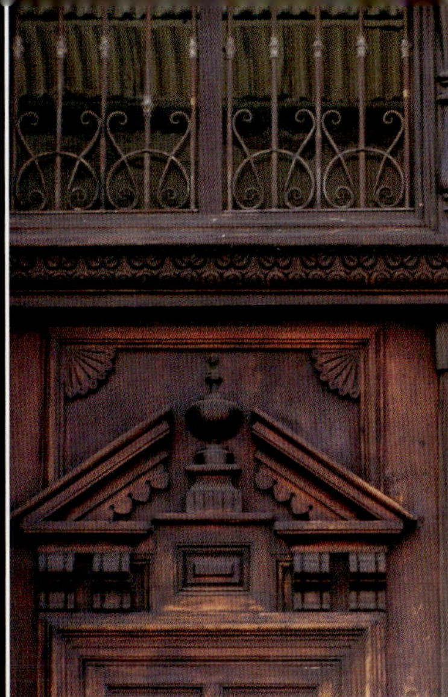

This is the Post Office building that displays beautiful paintings and authentic dresses from each Oaxacan region.

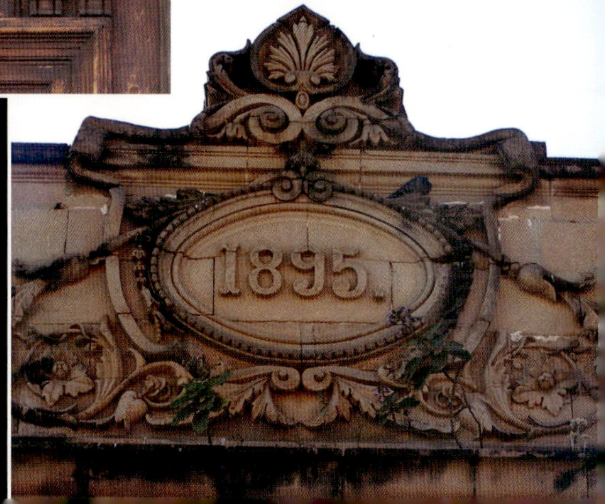

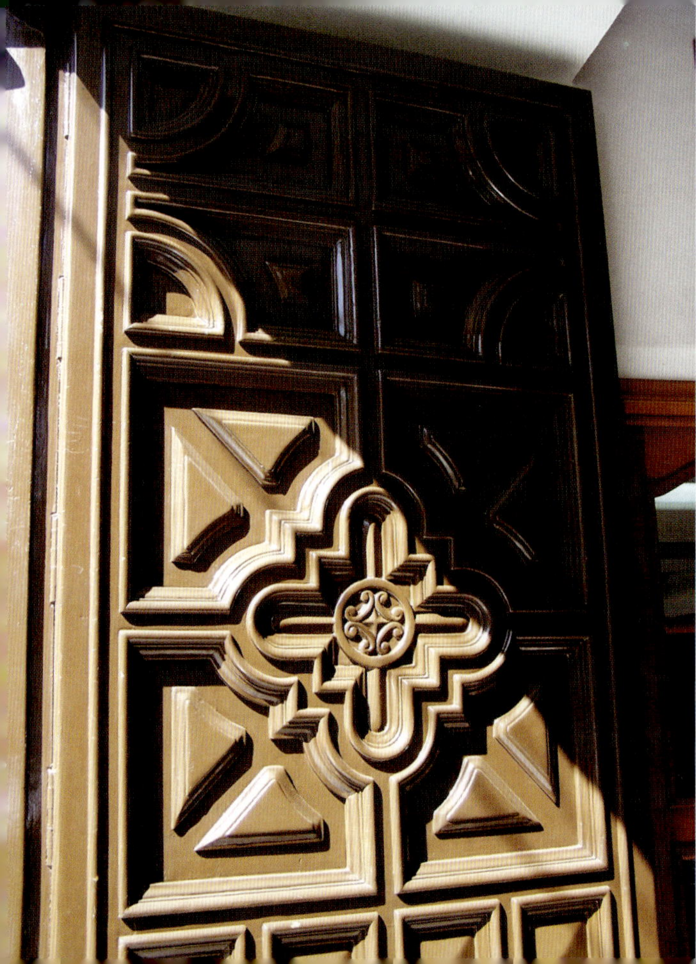

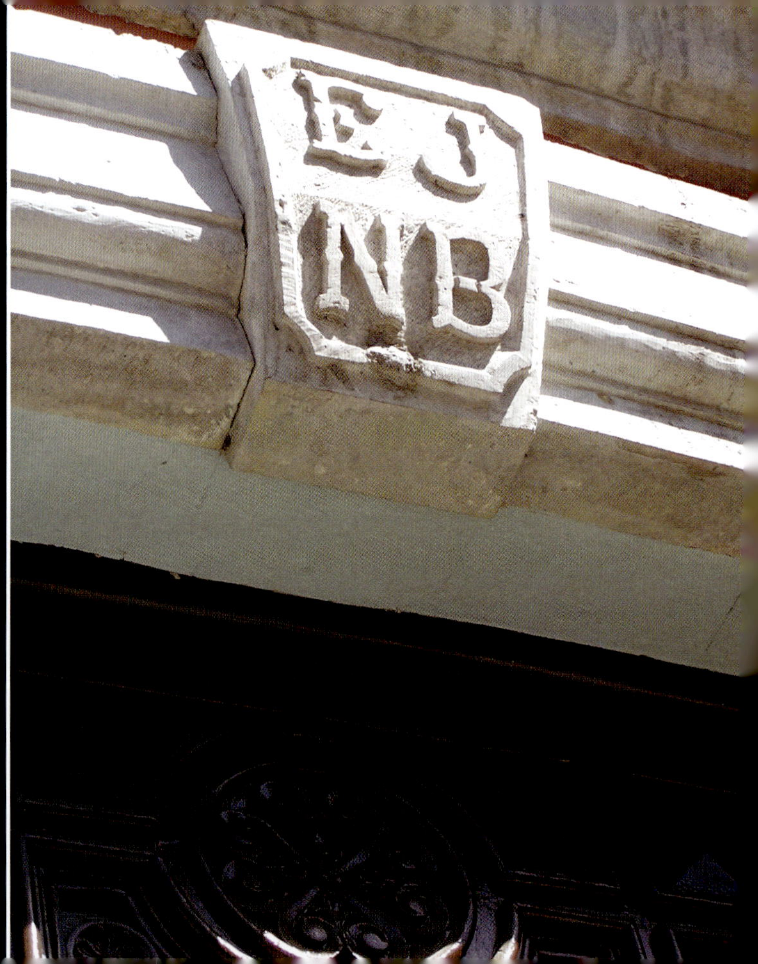
E J
NB

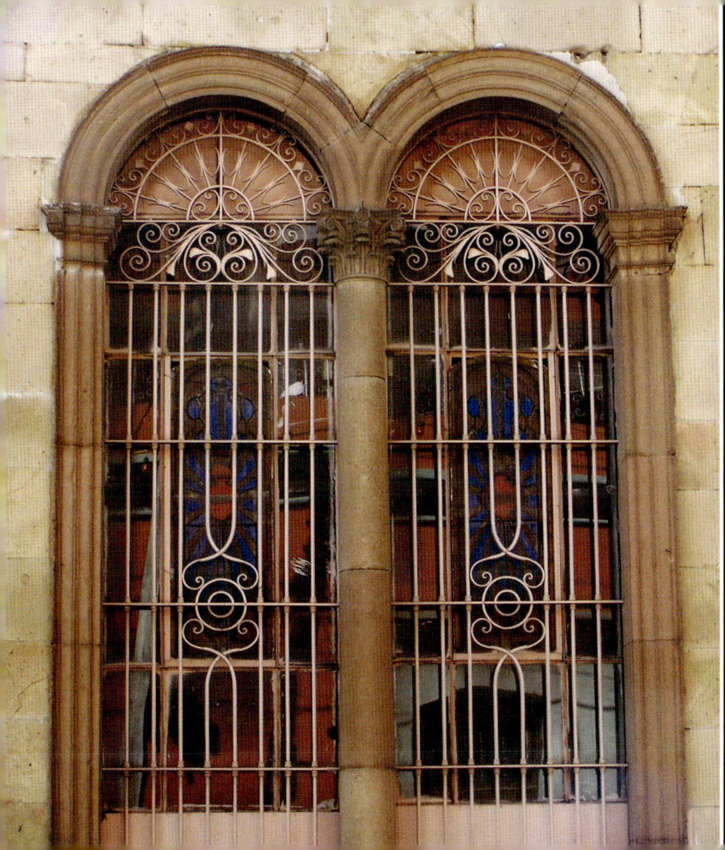

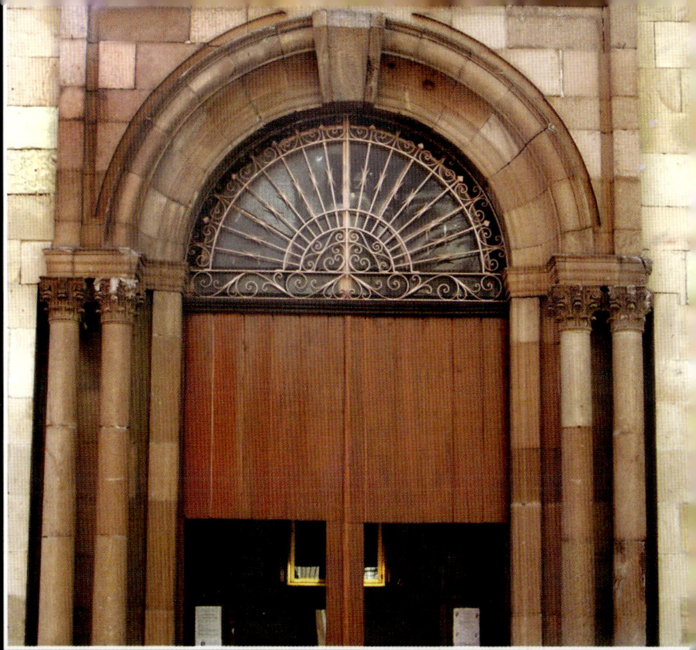

The San Cosme Church, located on the corner of Independencia and J.P. García Street.

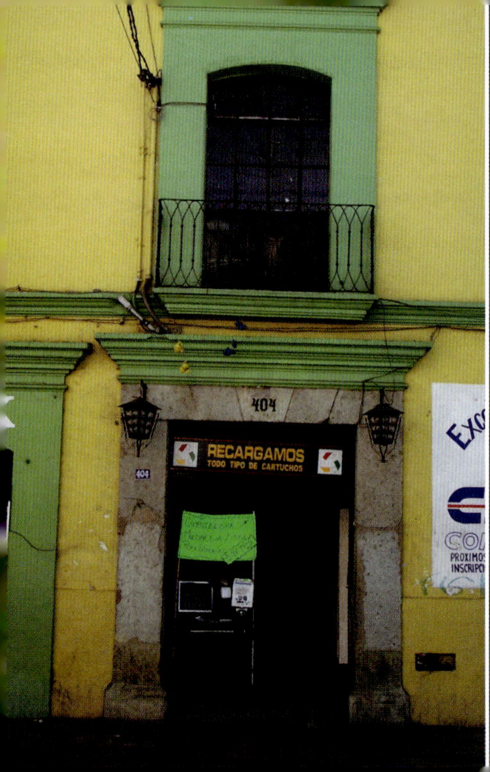
404
RECARGAMOS
TODO TIPO DE CARTUCHOS
404

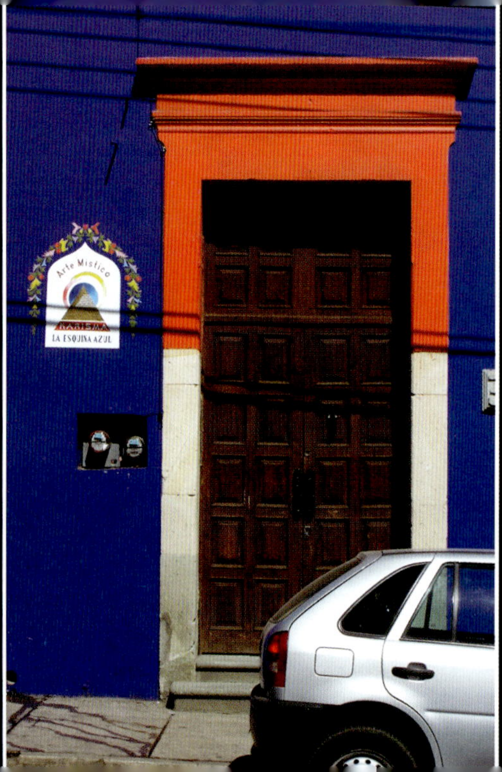
Arte Místico
LA ESQUINA AZUL

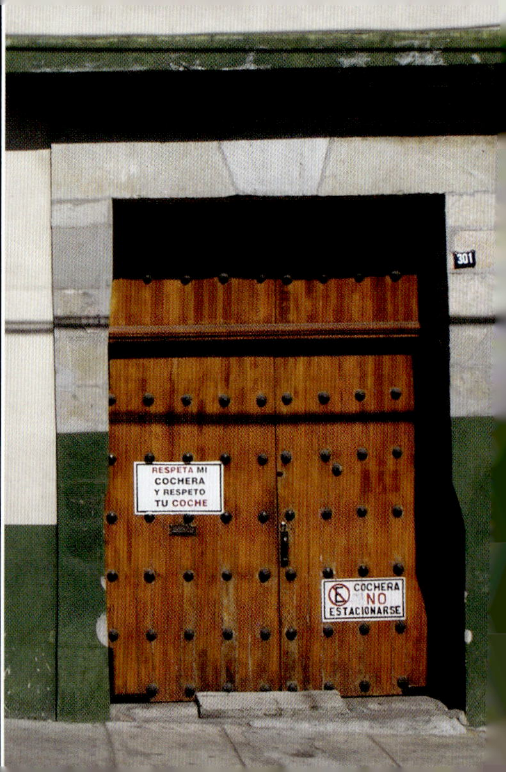
301
RESPETA MI
COCHERA
Y RESPETO
TU COCHE
COCHERA
NO
ESTACIONARSE

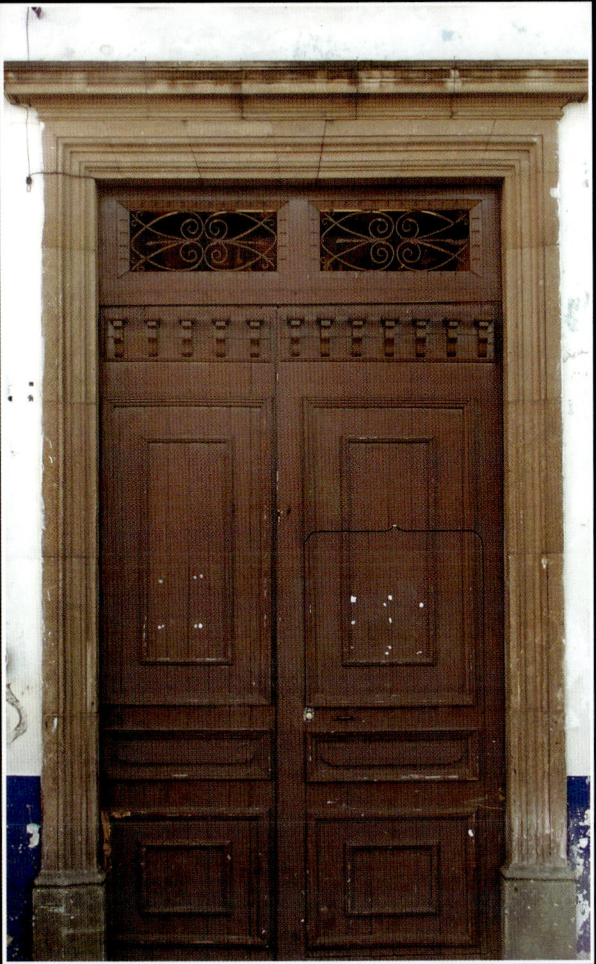

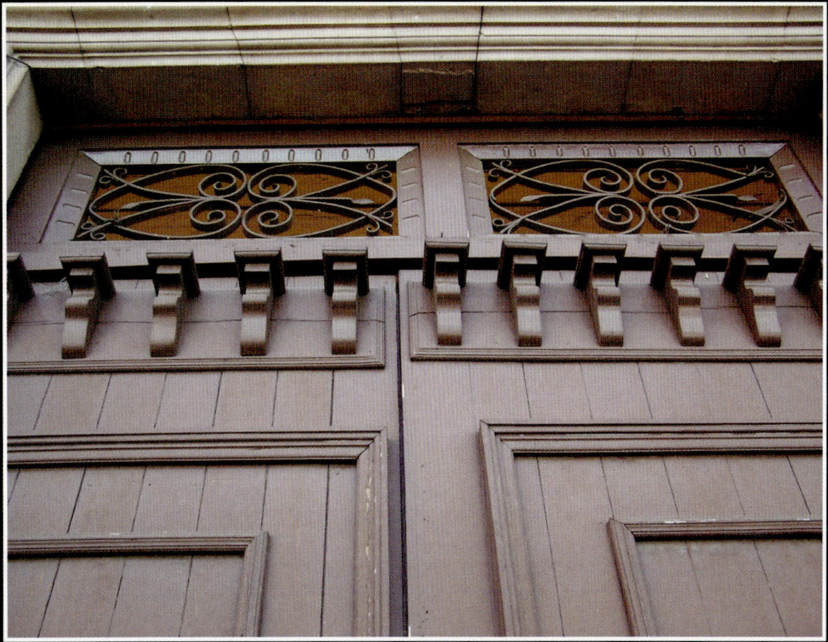

Independencia Street.

Independencia Street.

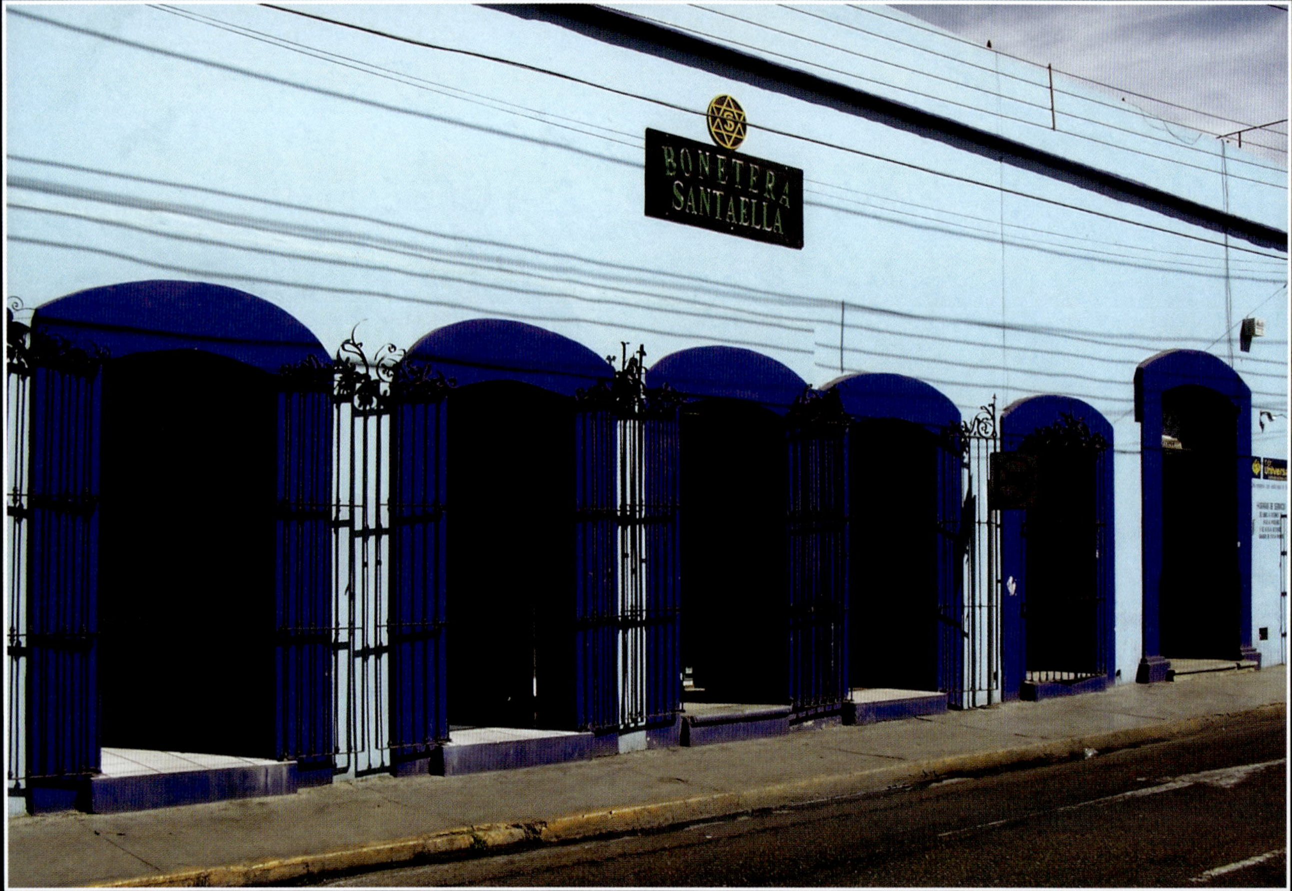

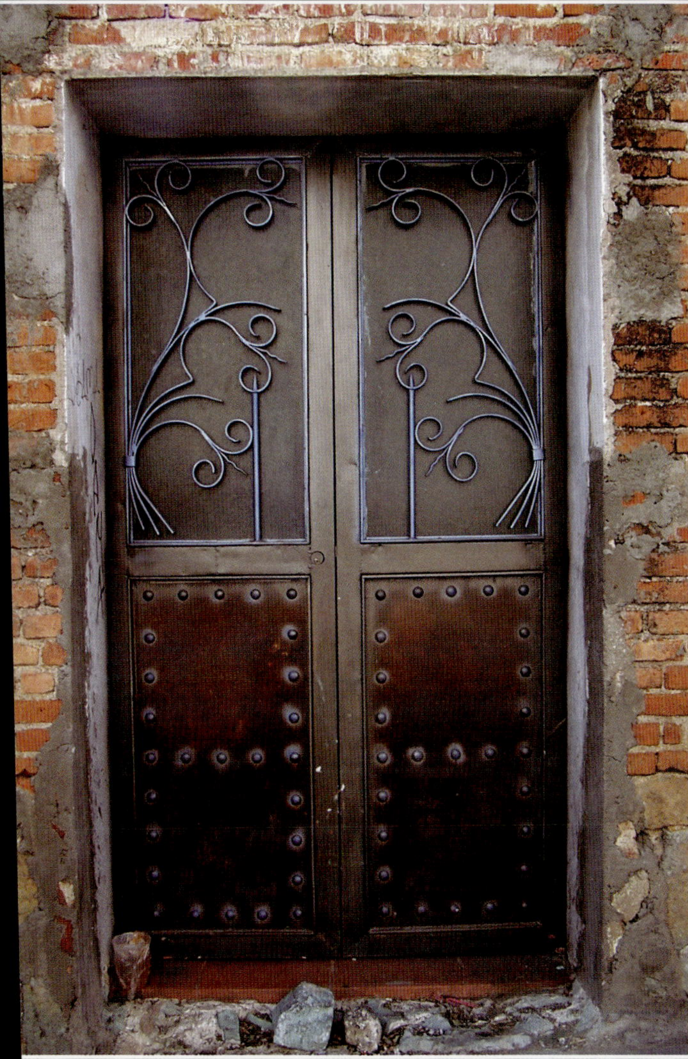

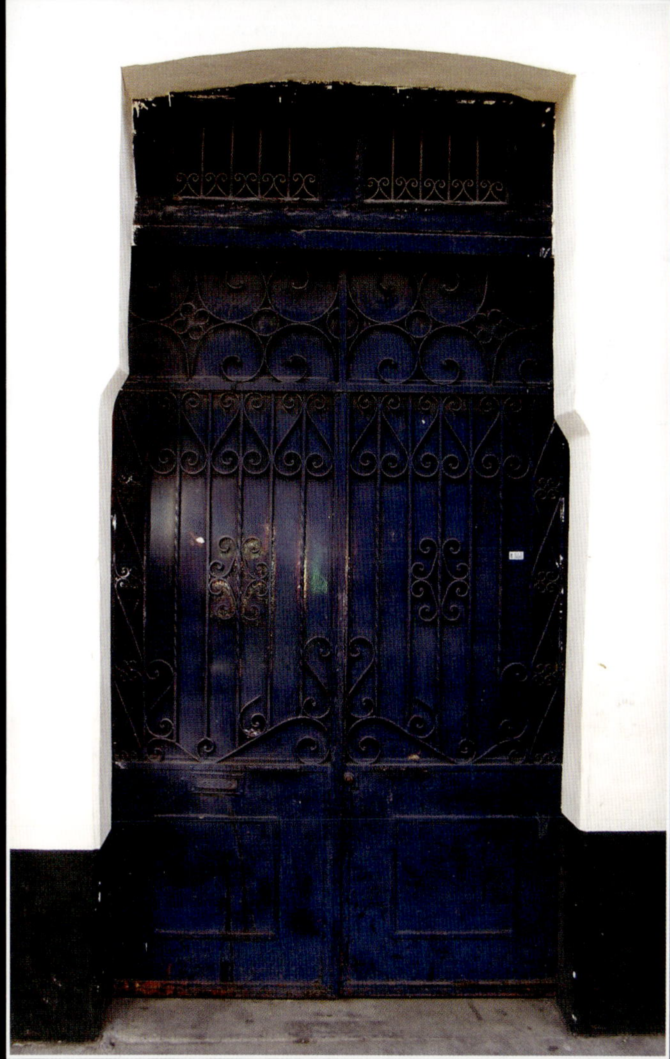

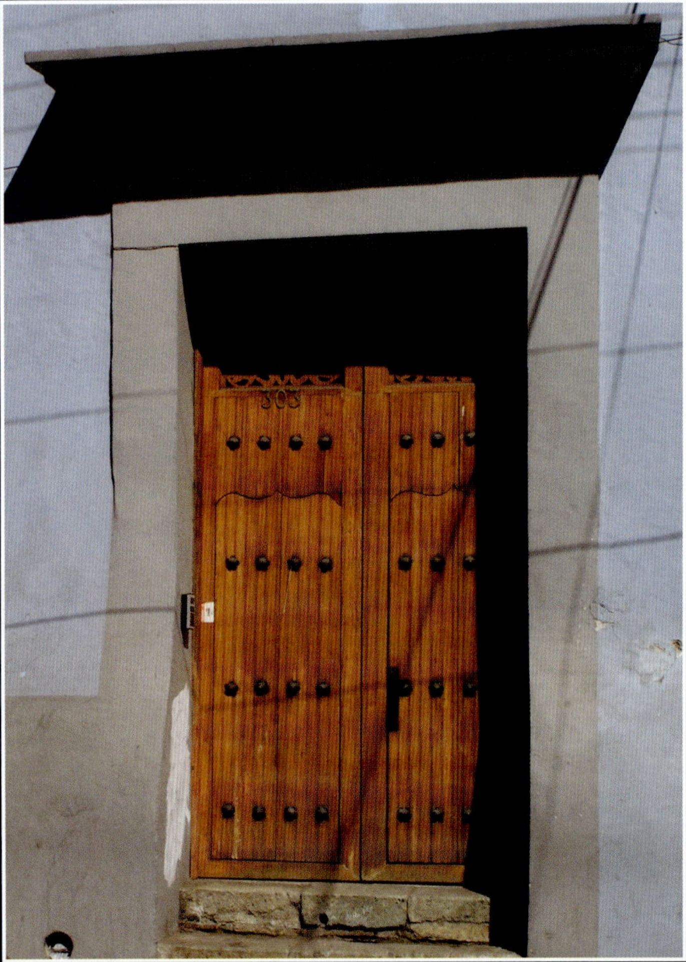
303

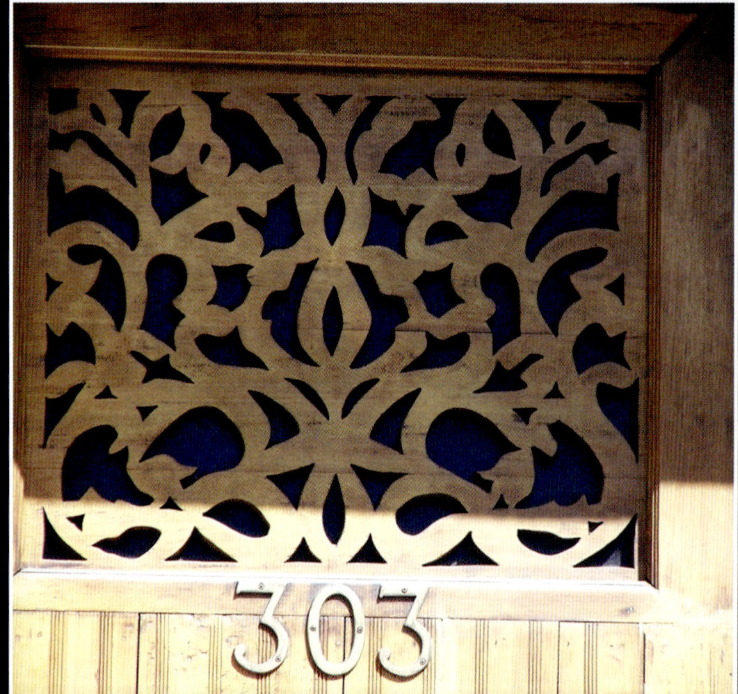
303

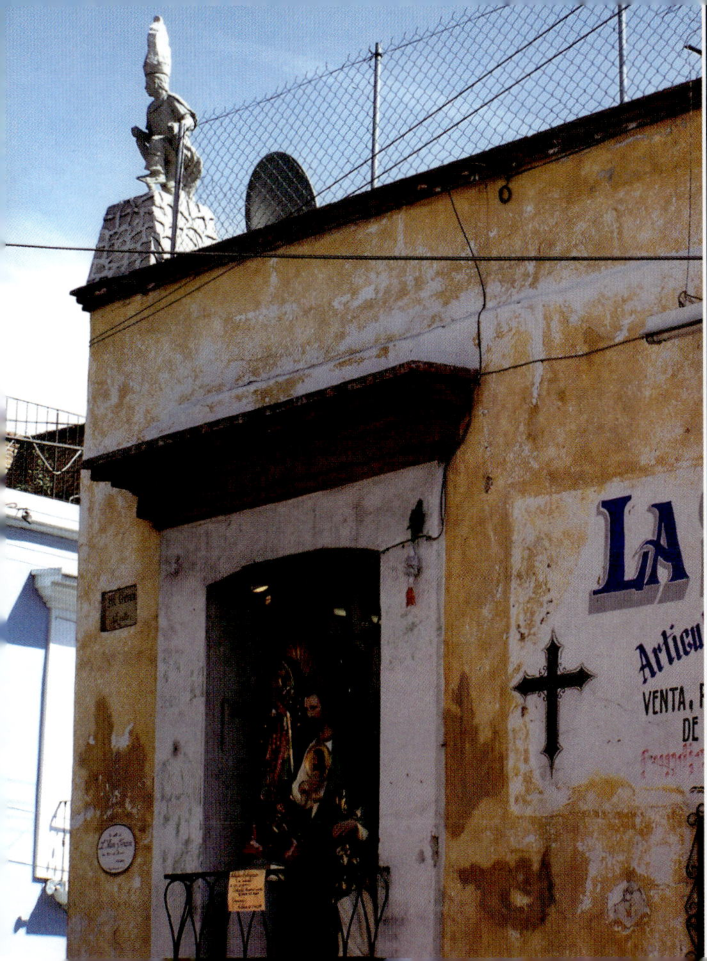

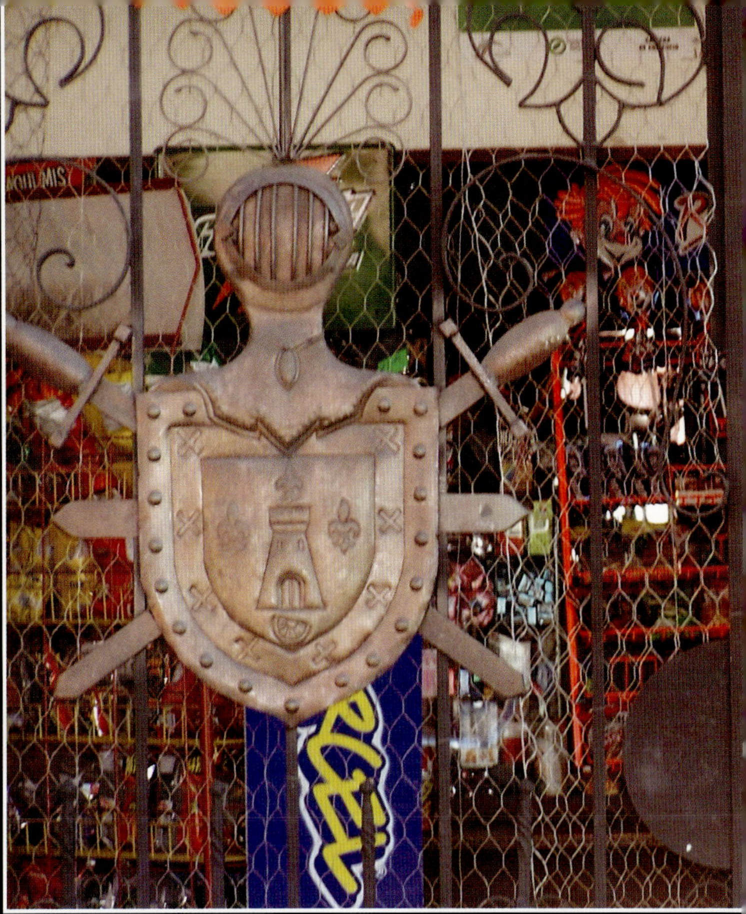

A store that sells religious articles, located on Mier Street and Ter

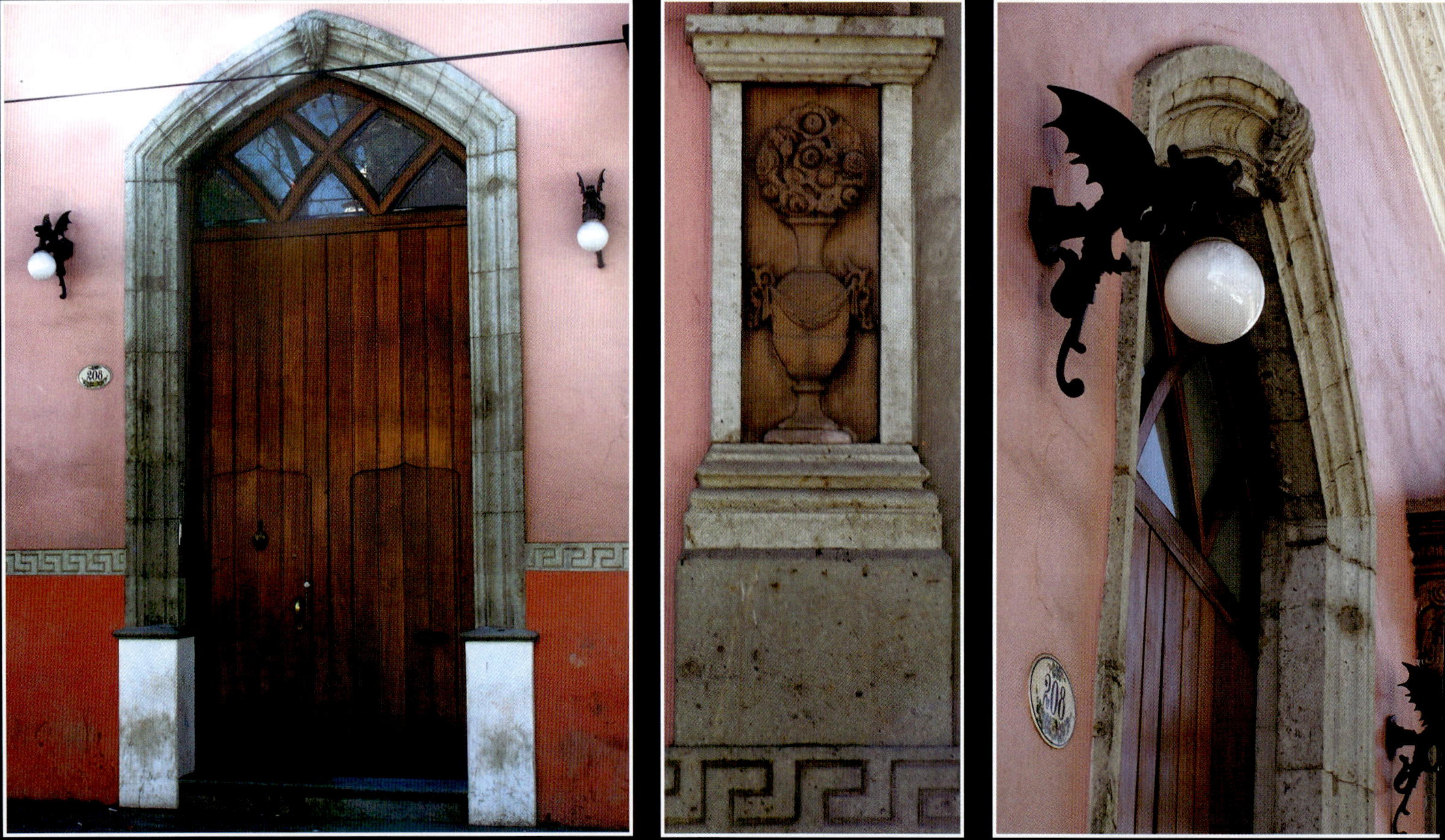

208 Independencia Street.

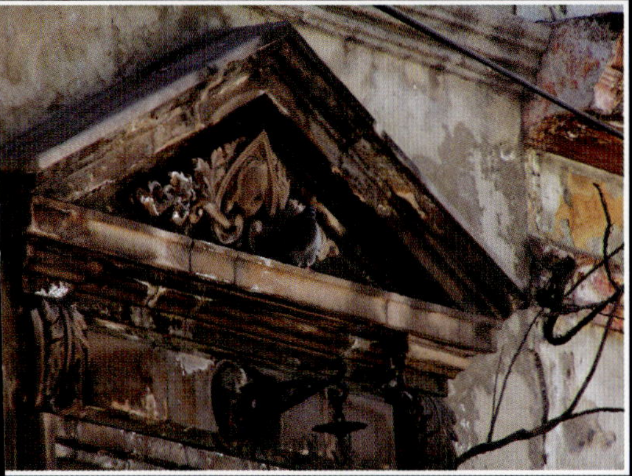
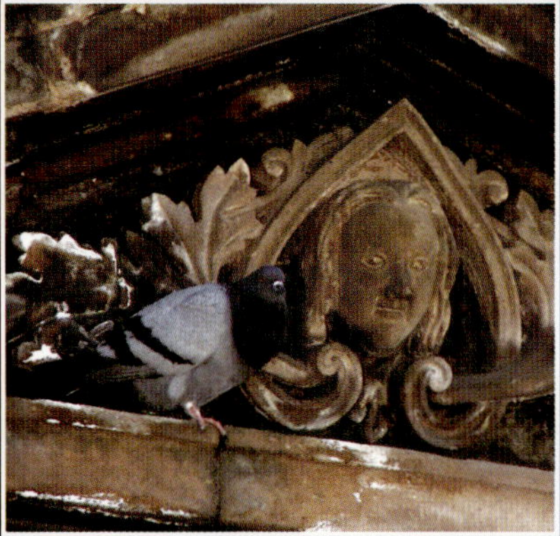
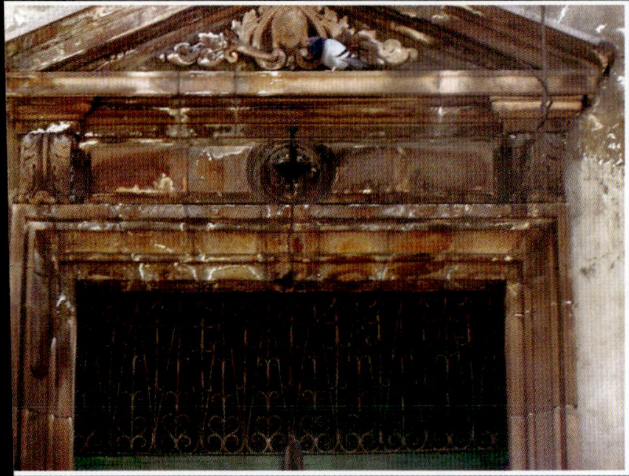
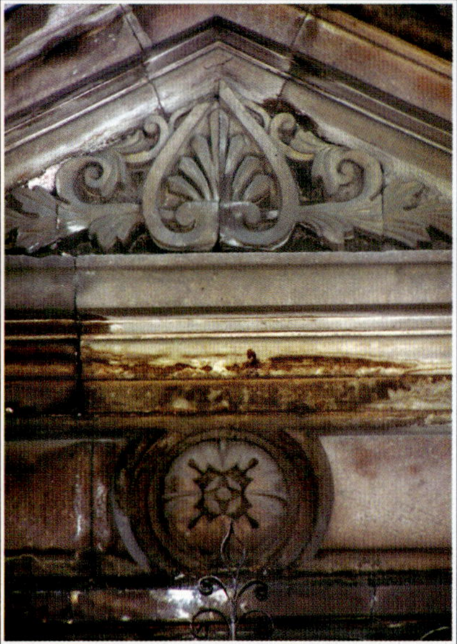
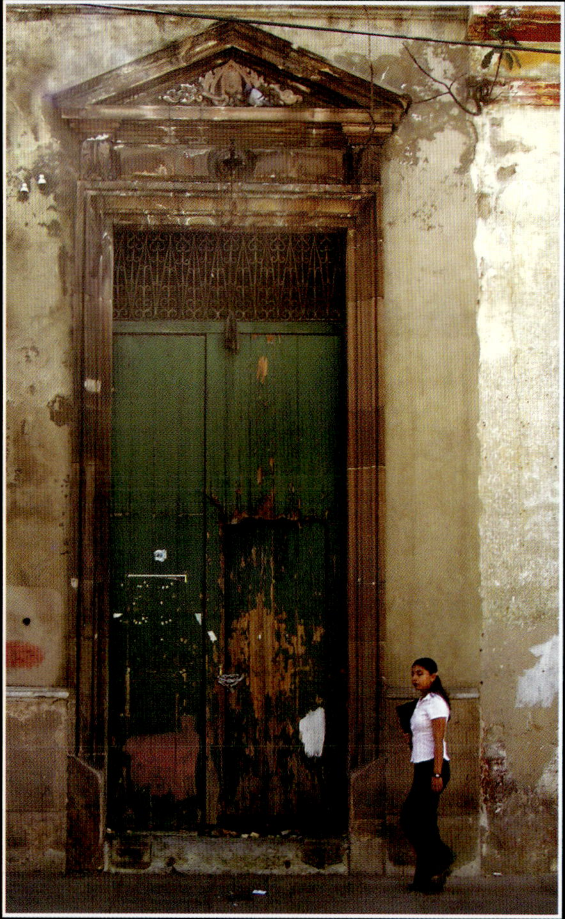

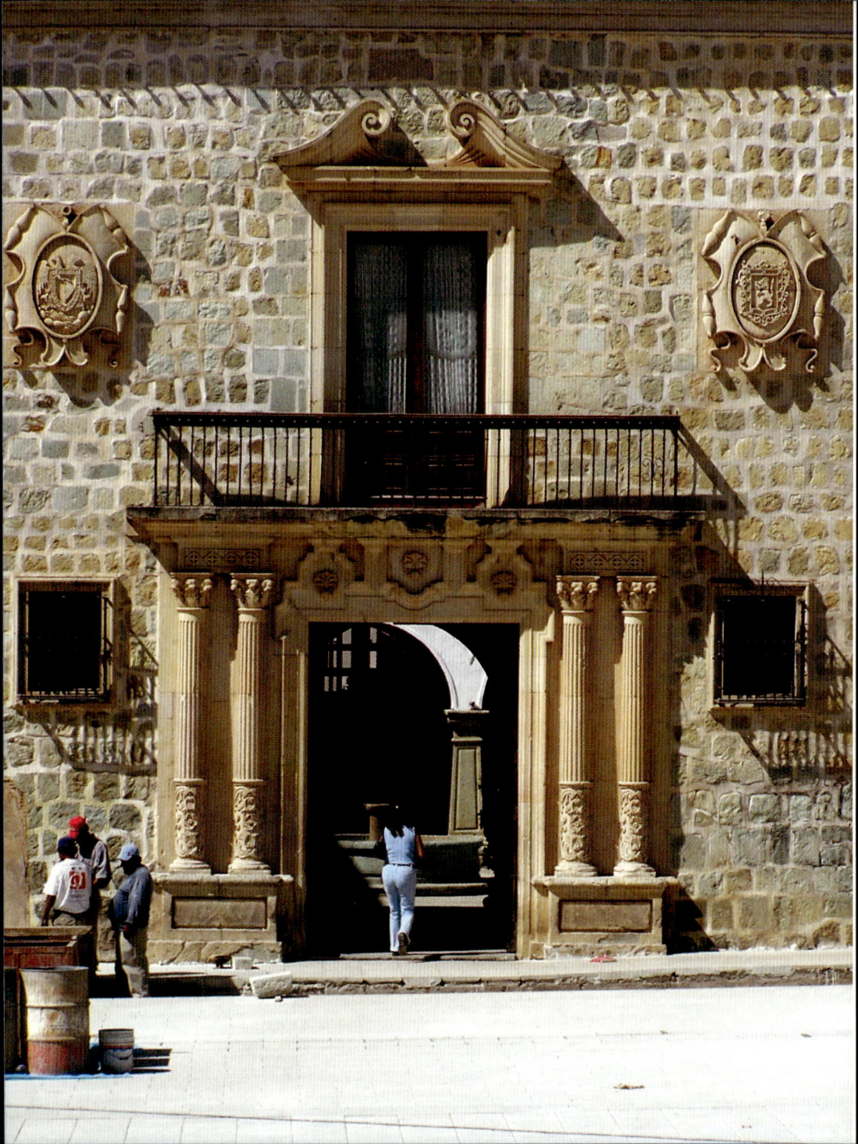

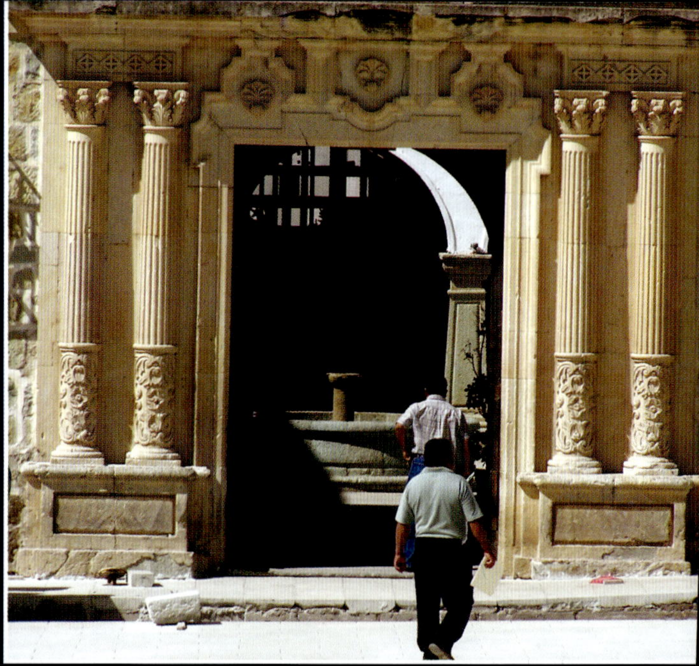

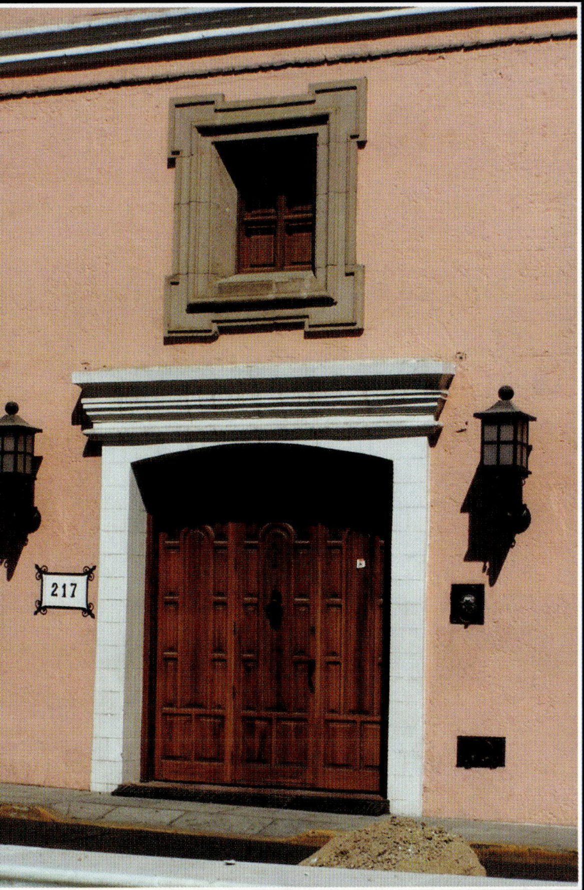

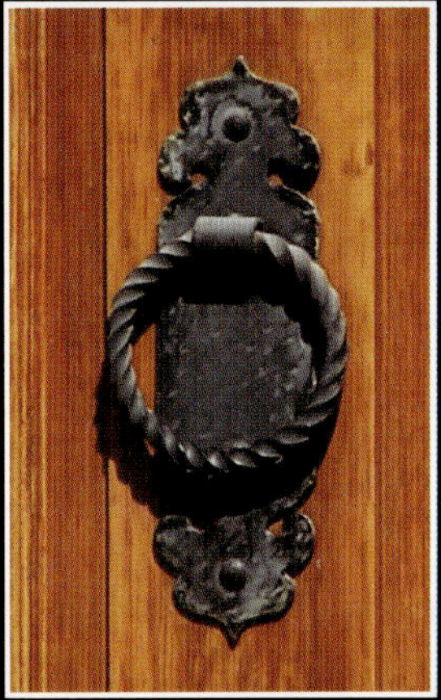

Morelos Street, in front of the public dance plaza, called Plaza de la Danza.

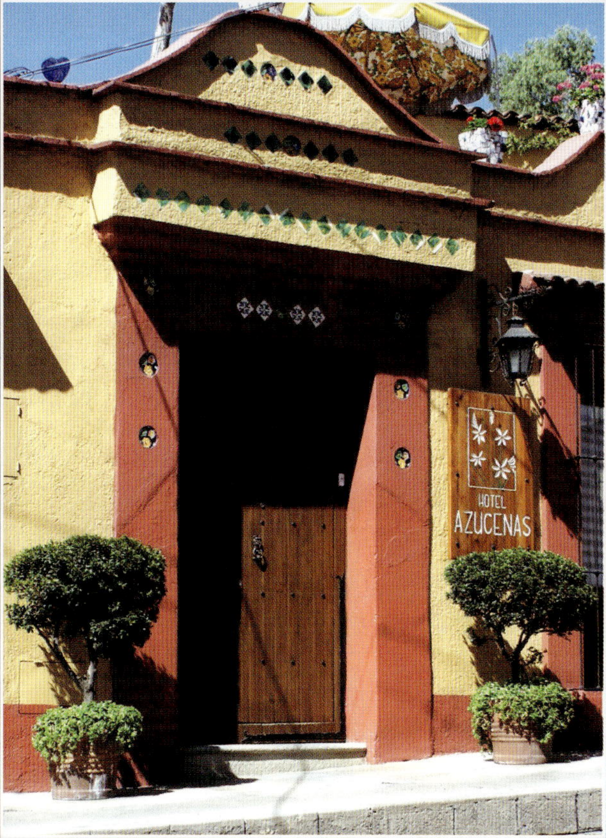

Hotel Azucenas located at 203 Profesor M. Aranda Steet

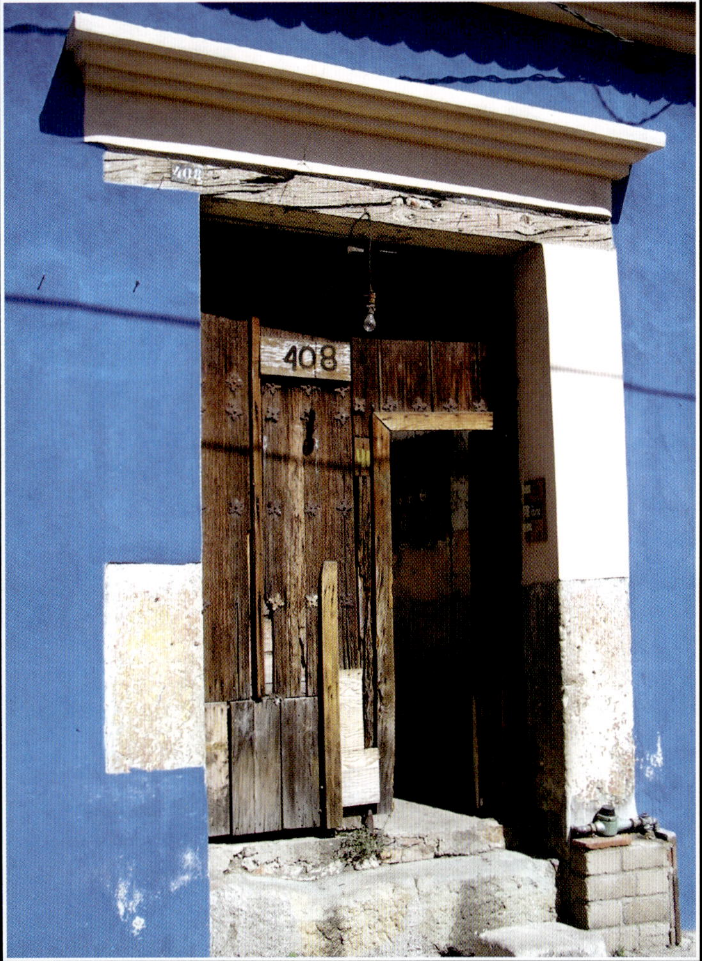

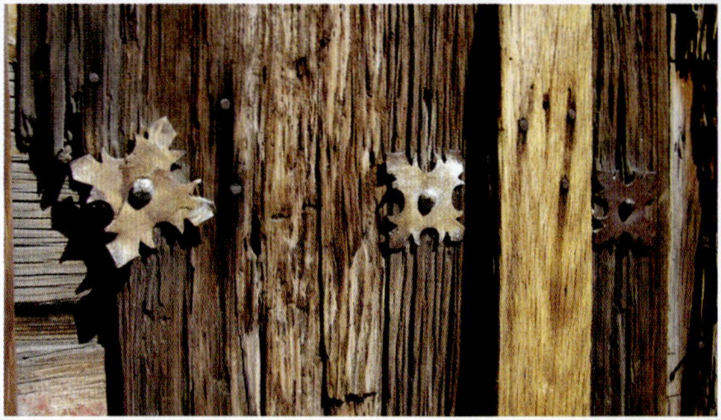

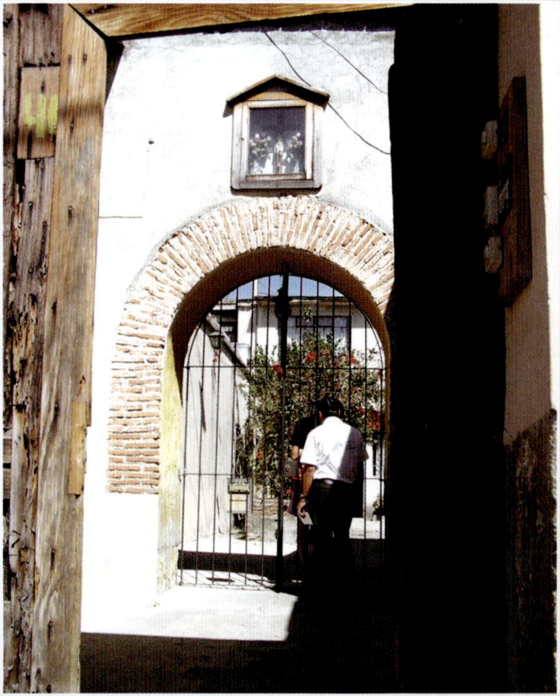

Postman delivering the mail.

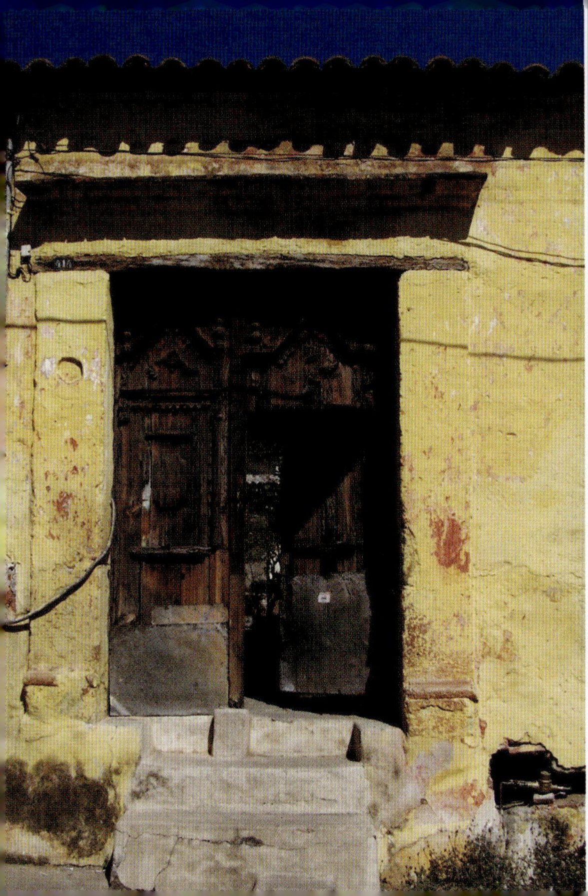

414 M. Bravo Street.

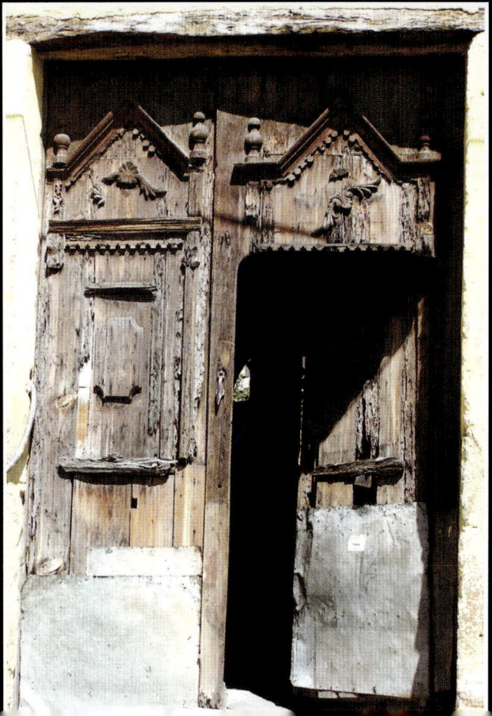

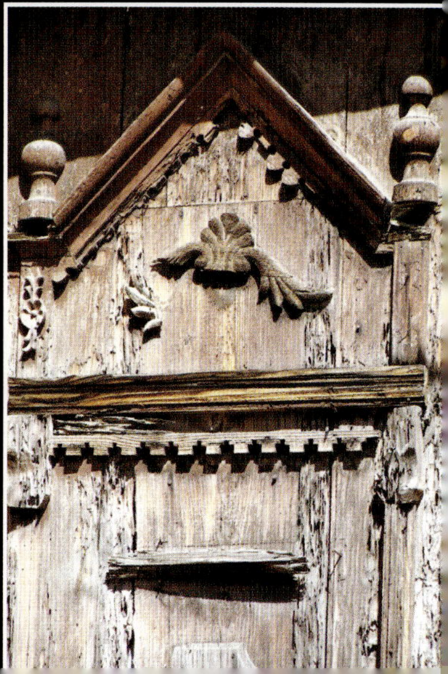

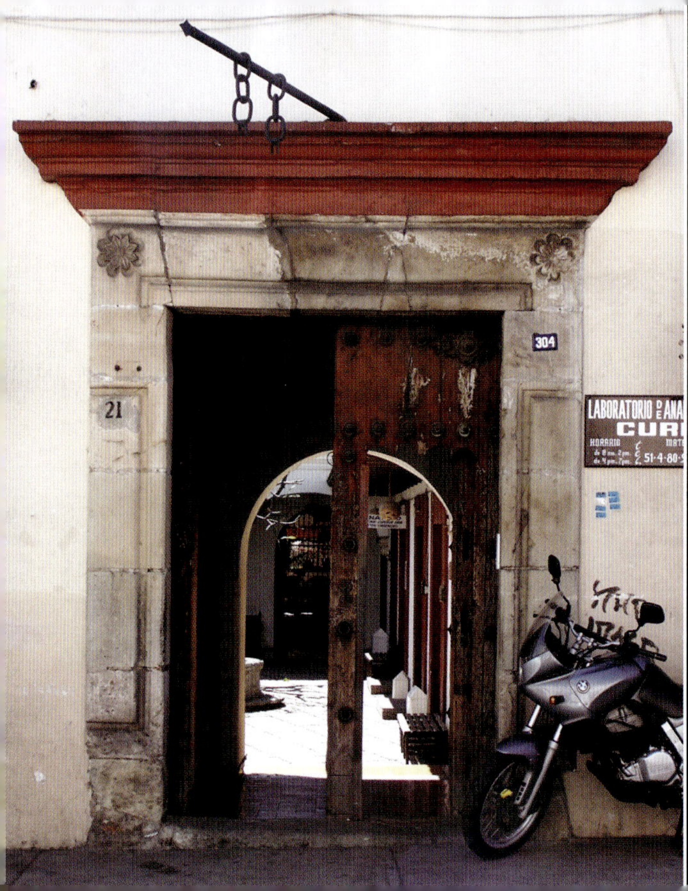

A medical laboratory located at 304 Matamoros Street.

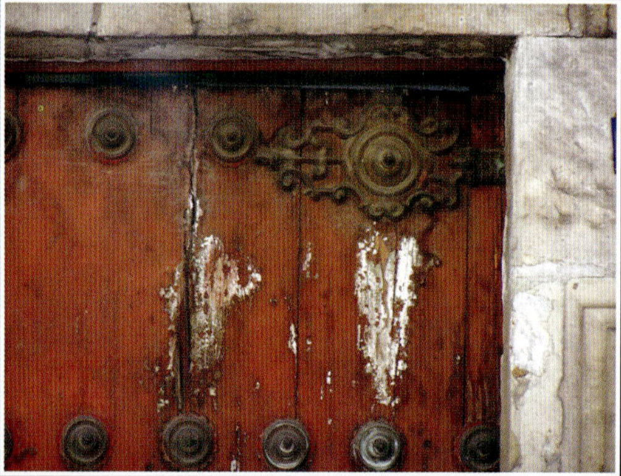

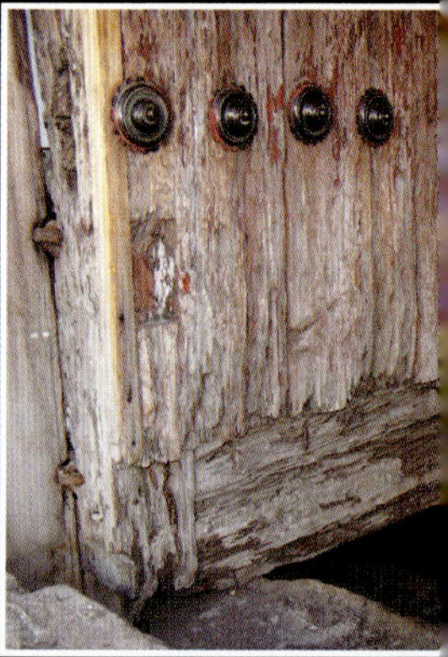

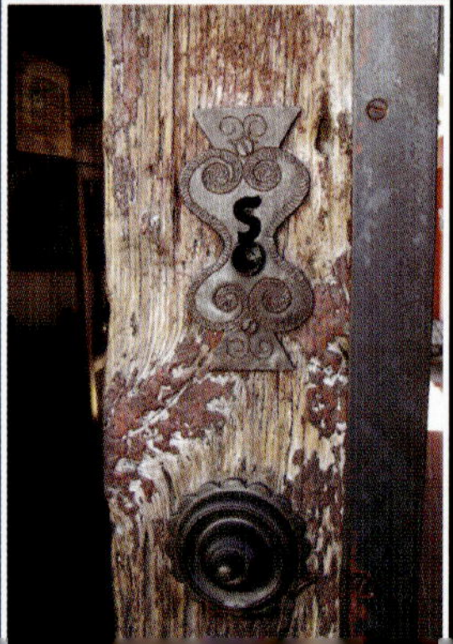

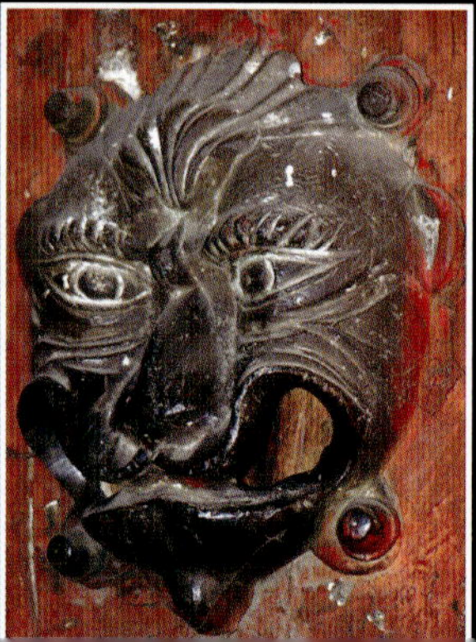

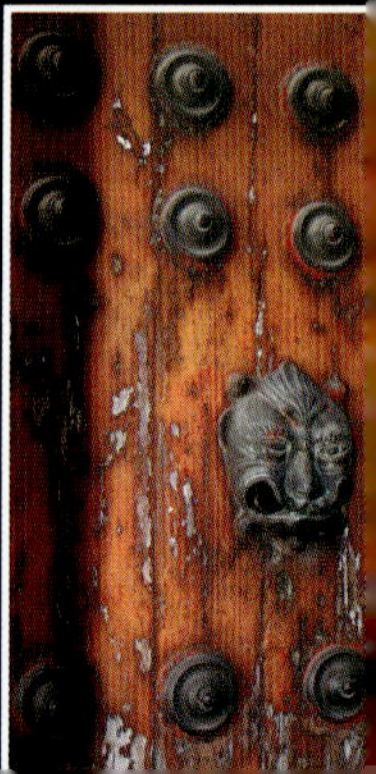

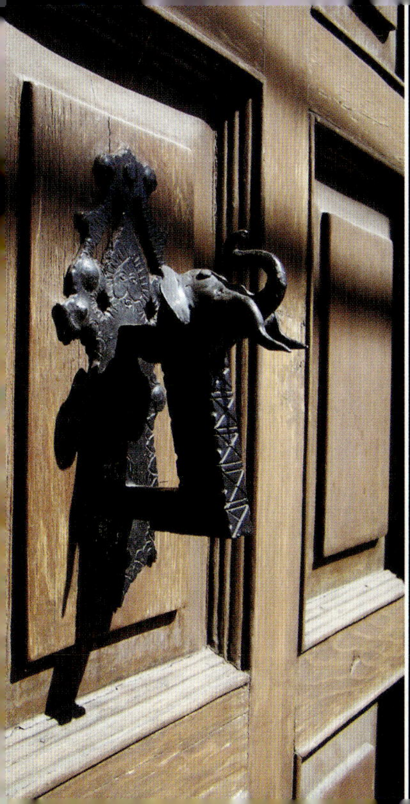
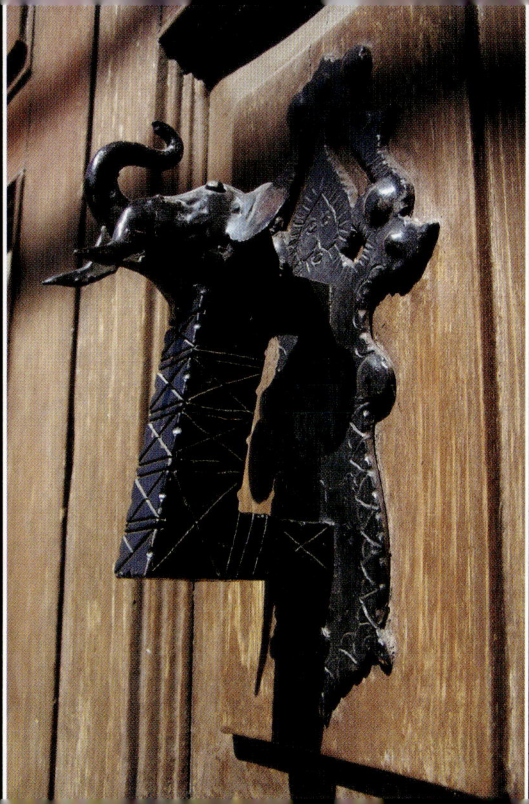
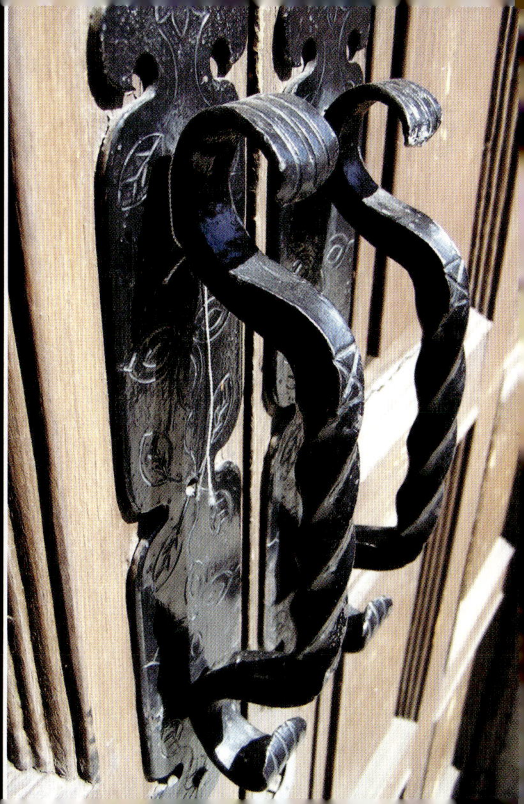

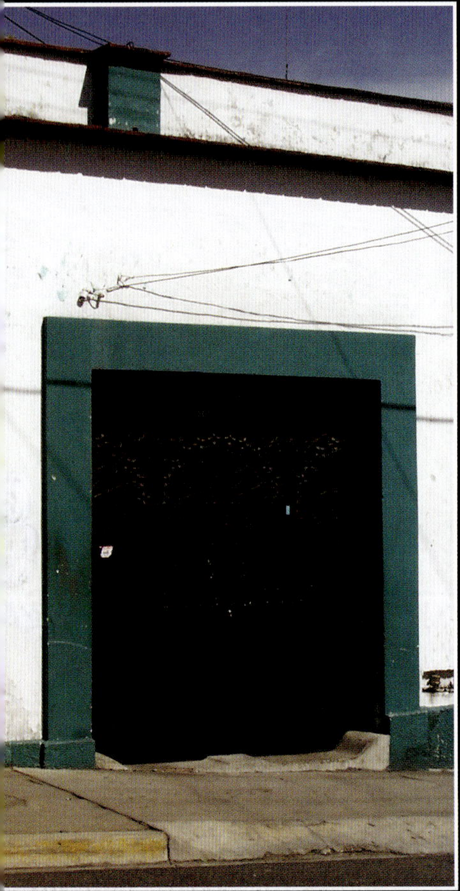

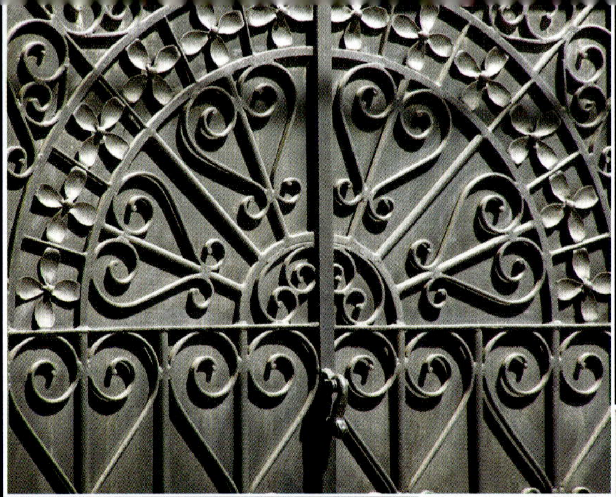

304 M. Bravo Street.

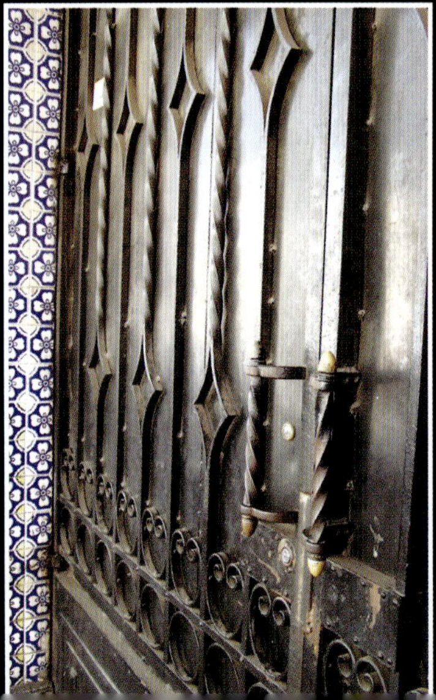

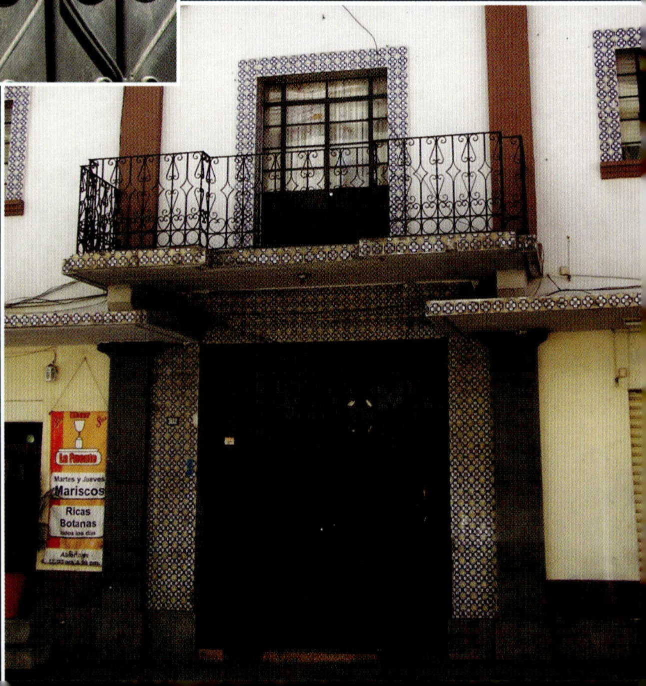

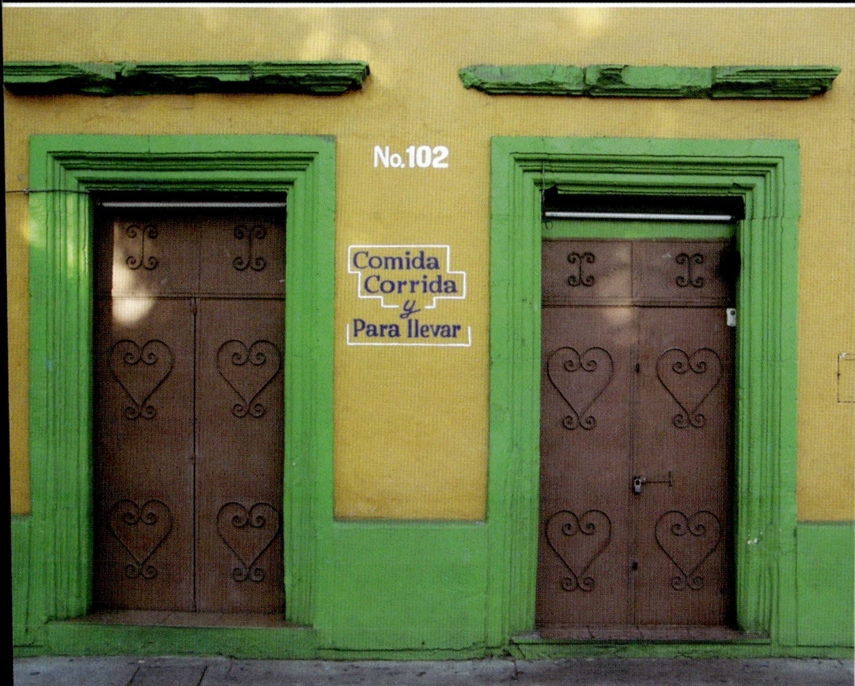

102 Fiallo Street.

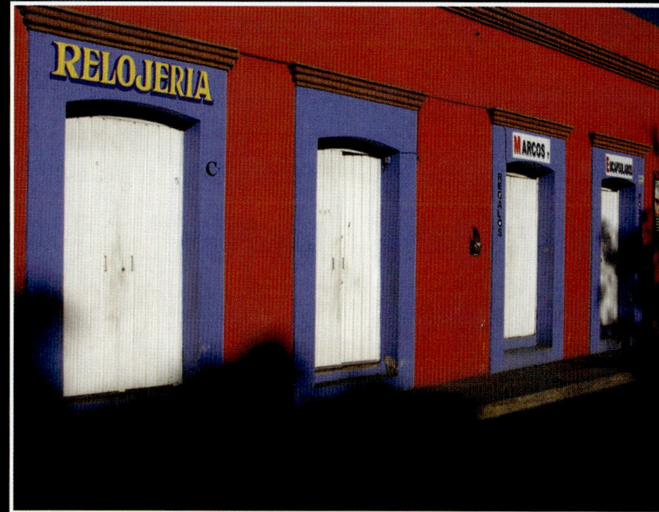

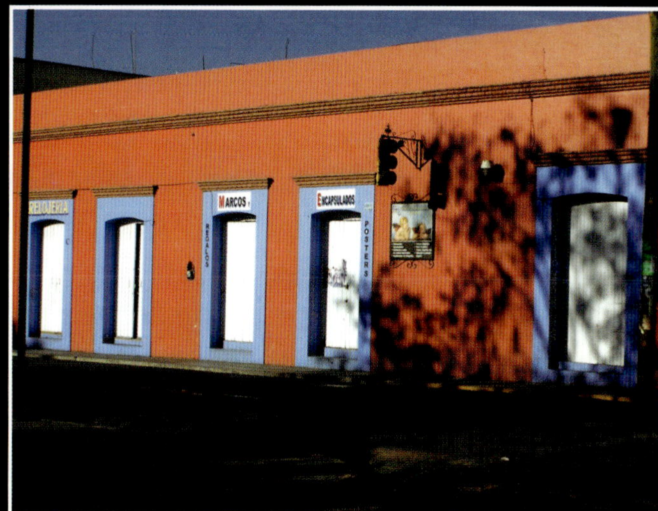

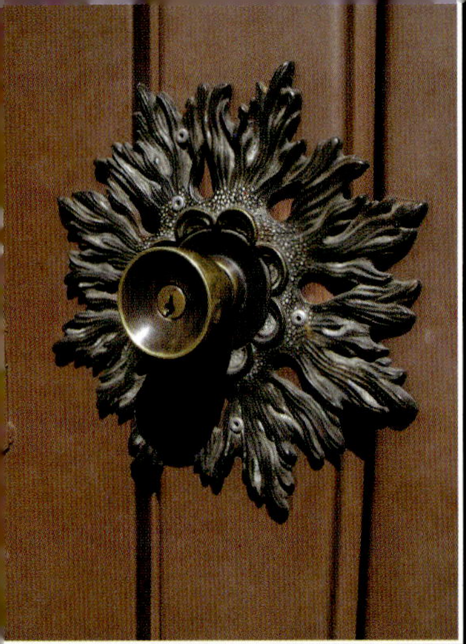
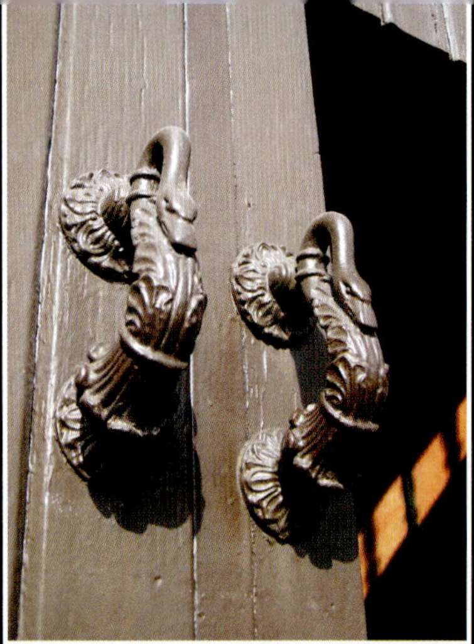
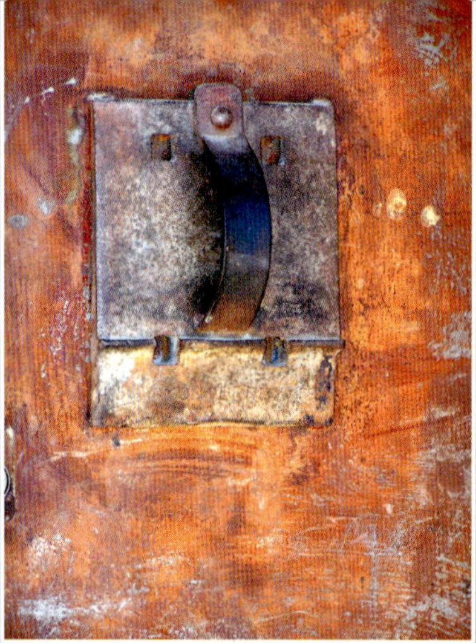
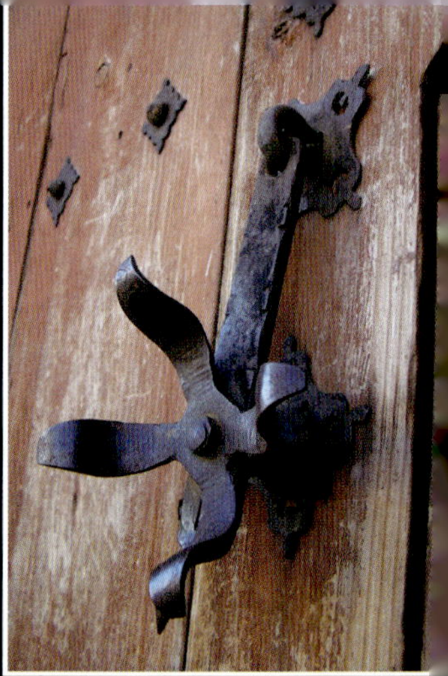
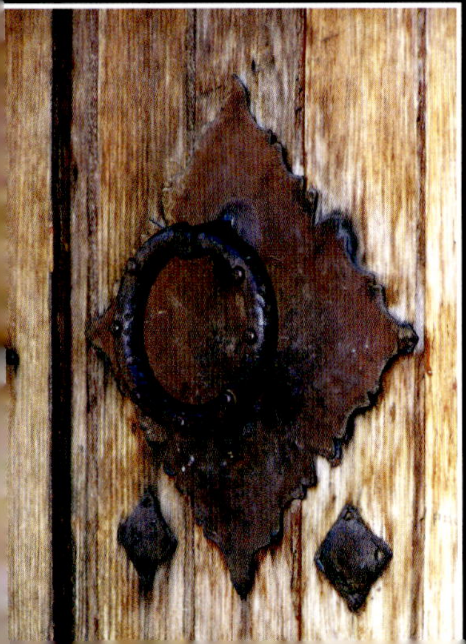
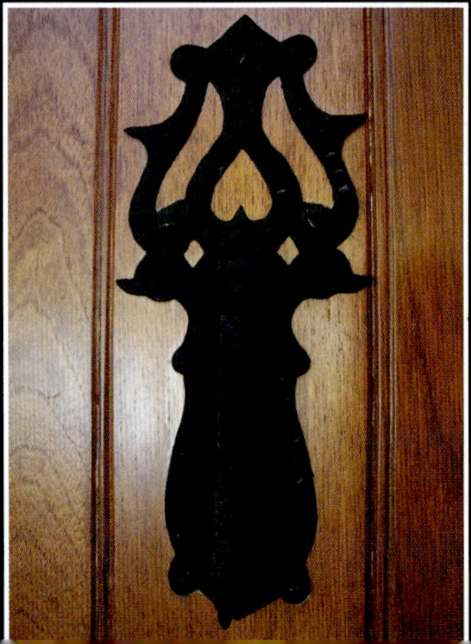
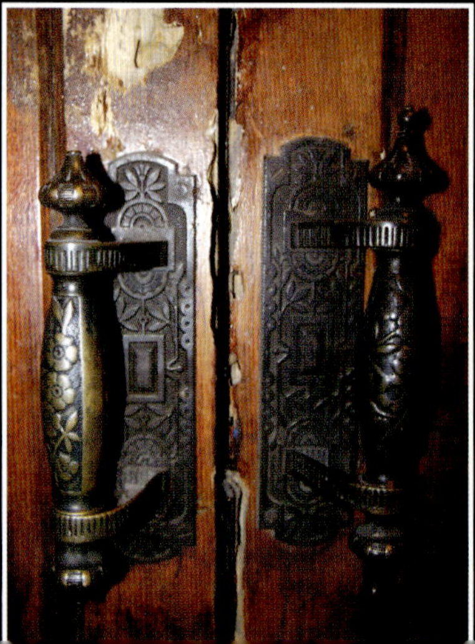
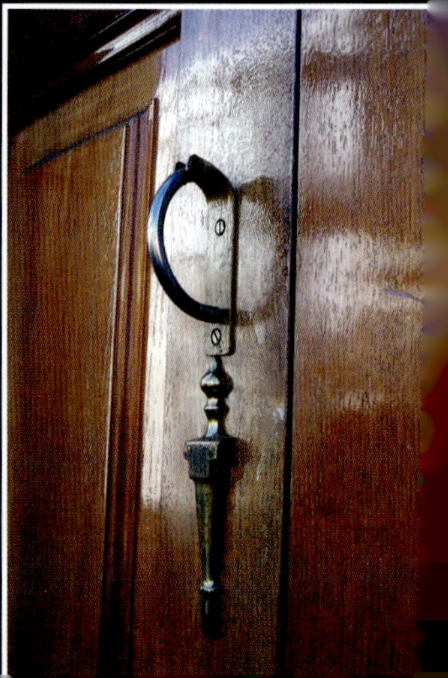

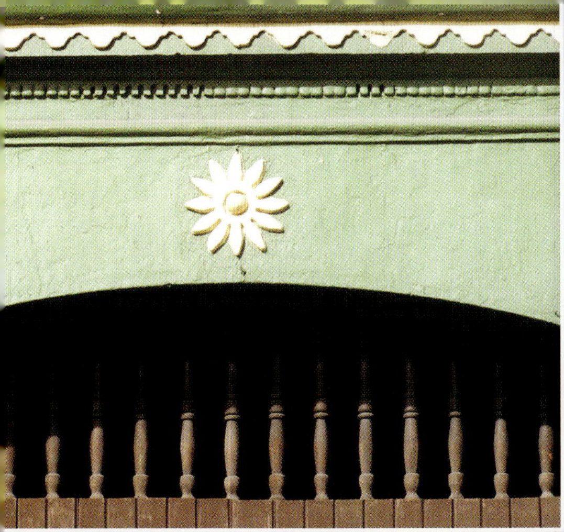
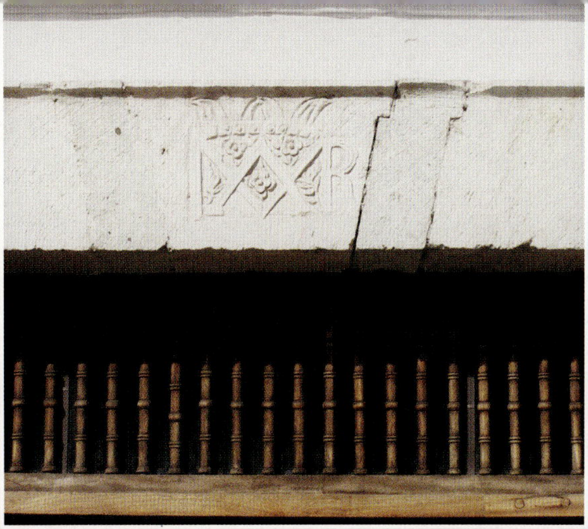
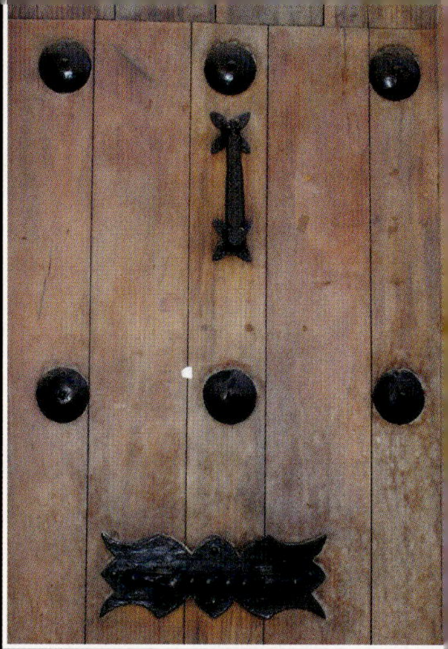
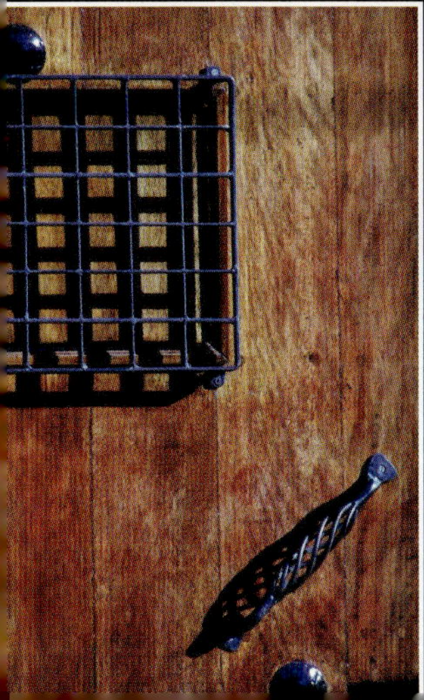
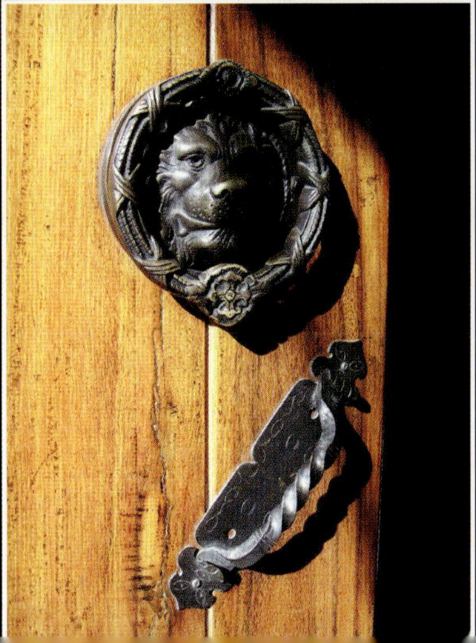
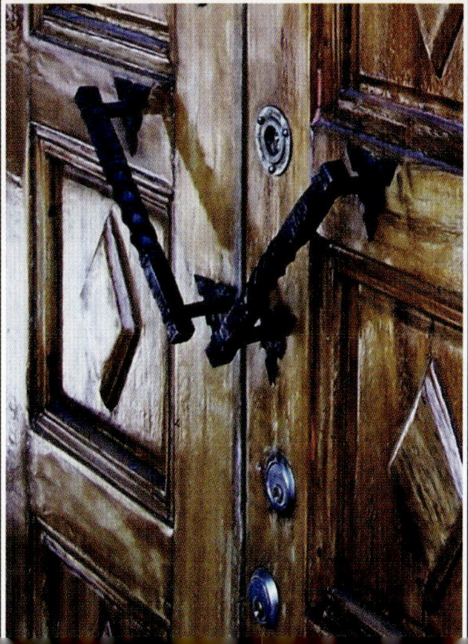
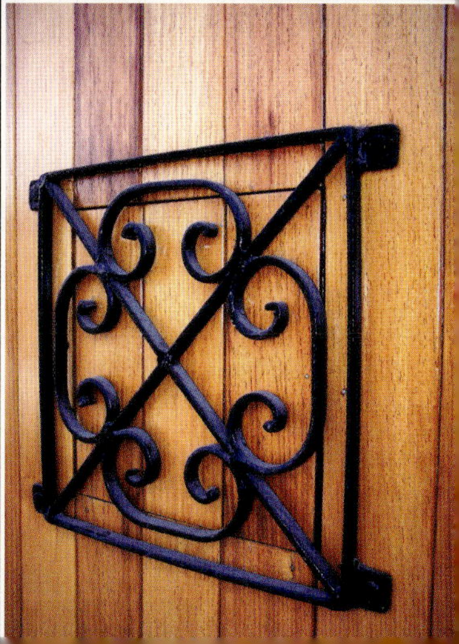

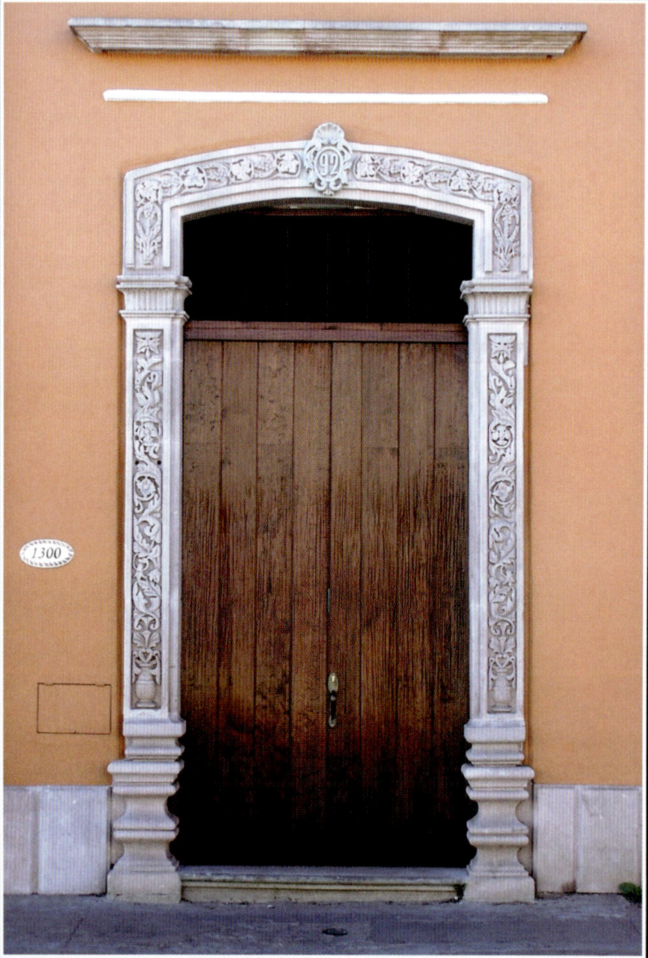
1300
92

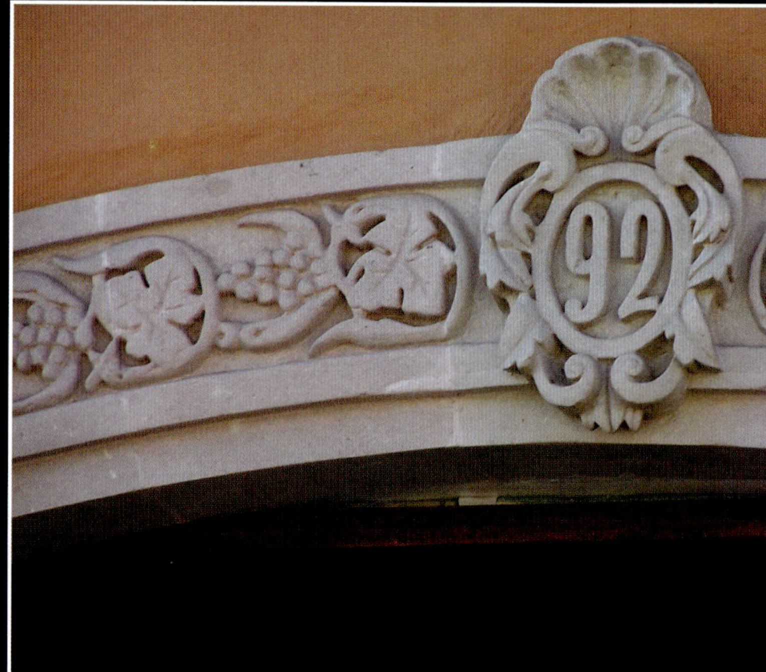
92

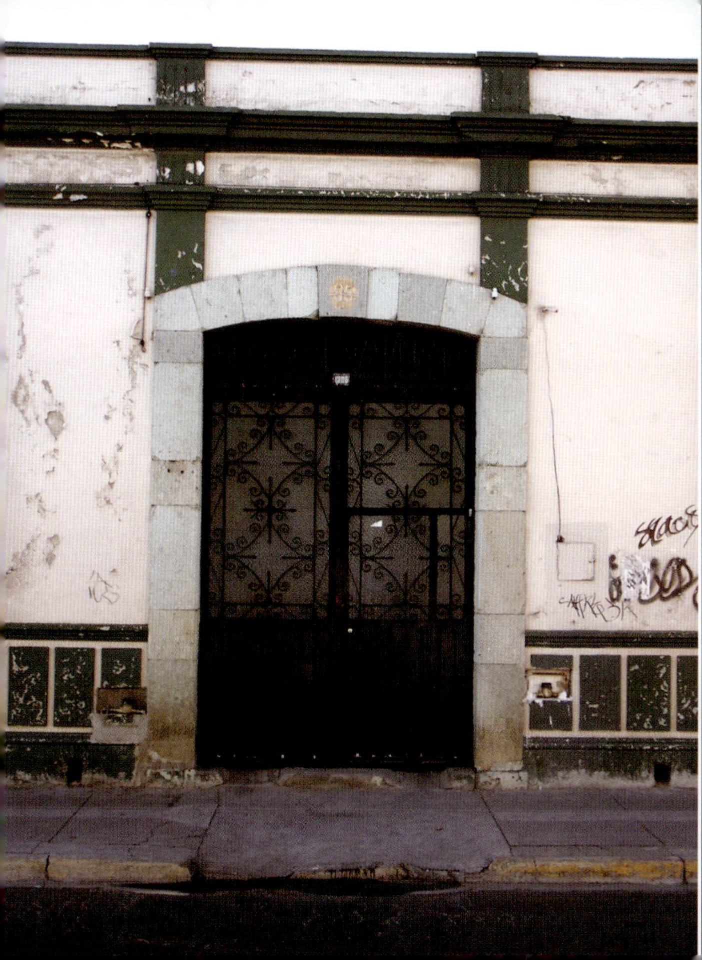
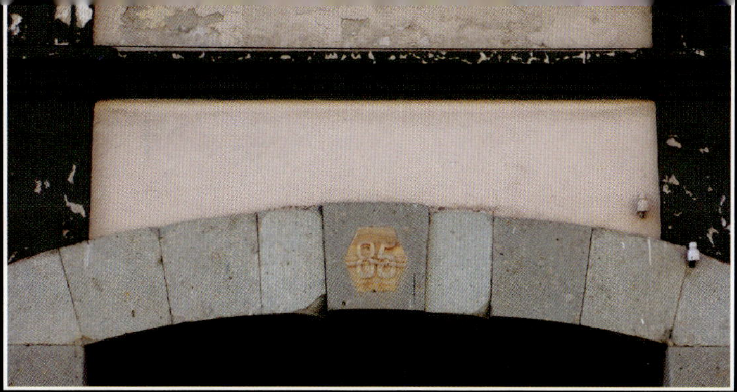
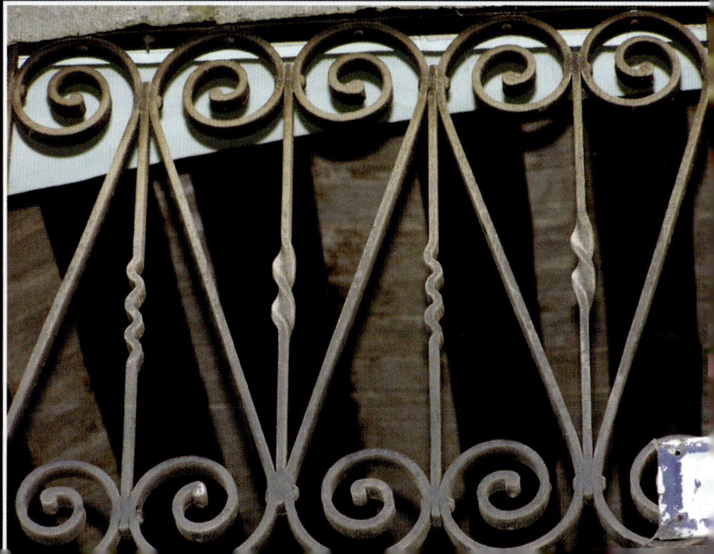

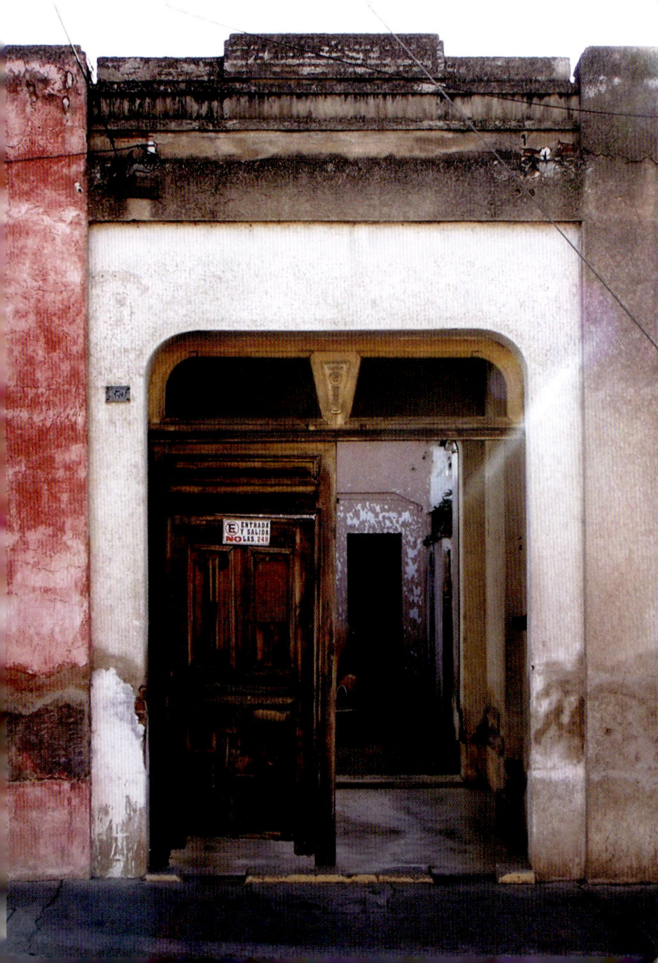
1

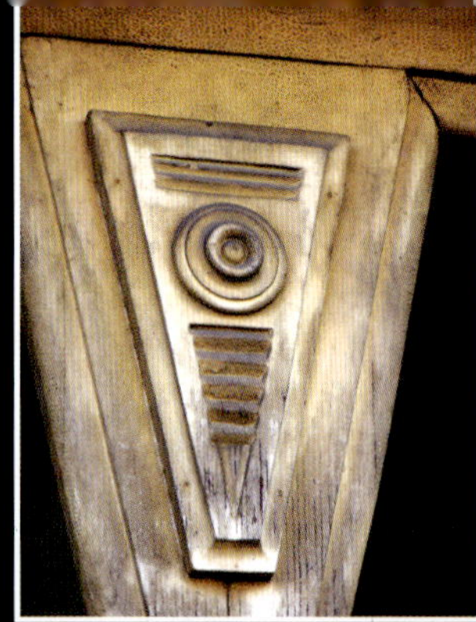

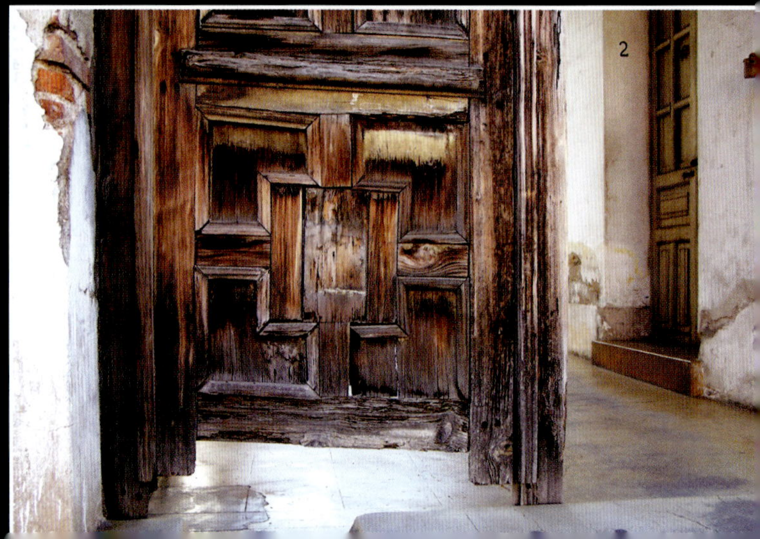
2

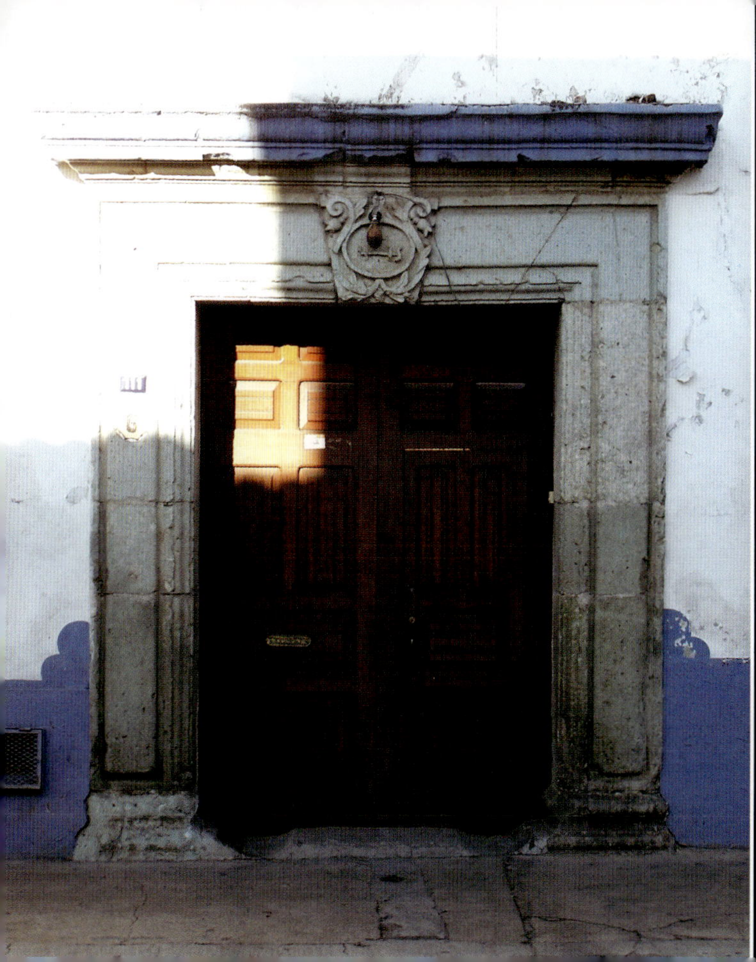

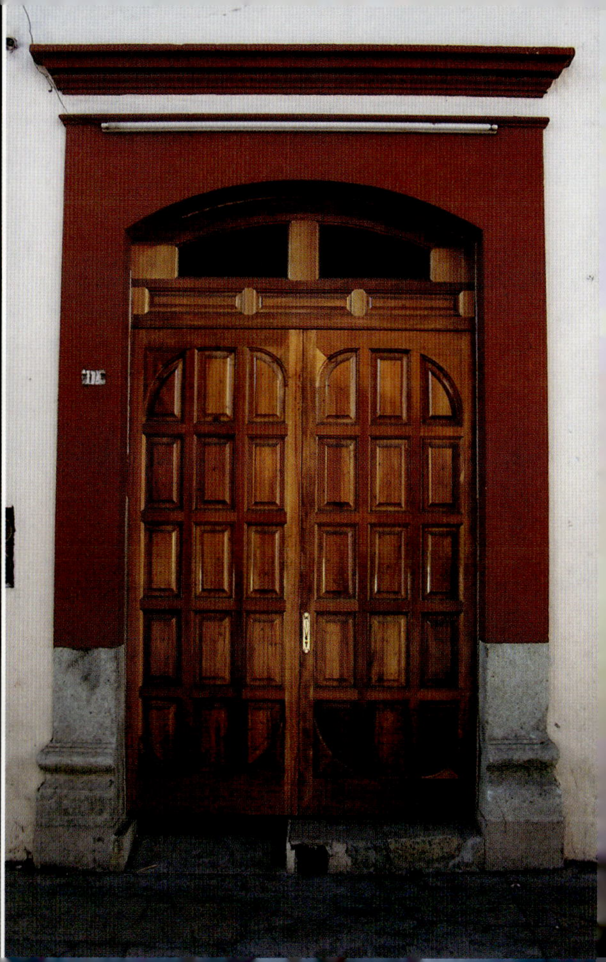

A bed and Breakfast called, The Casa de la Tía Tere (The House of Aunt Terry).

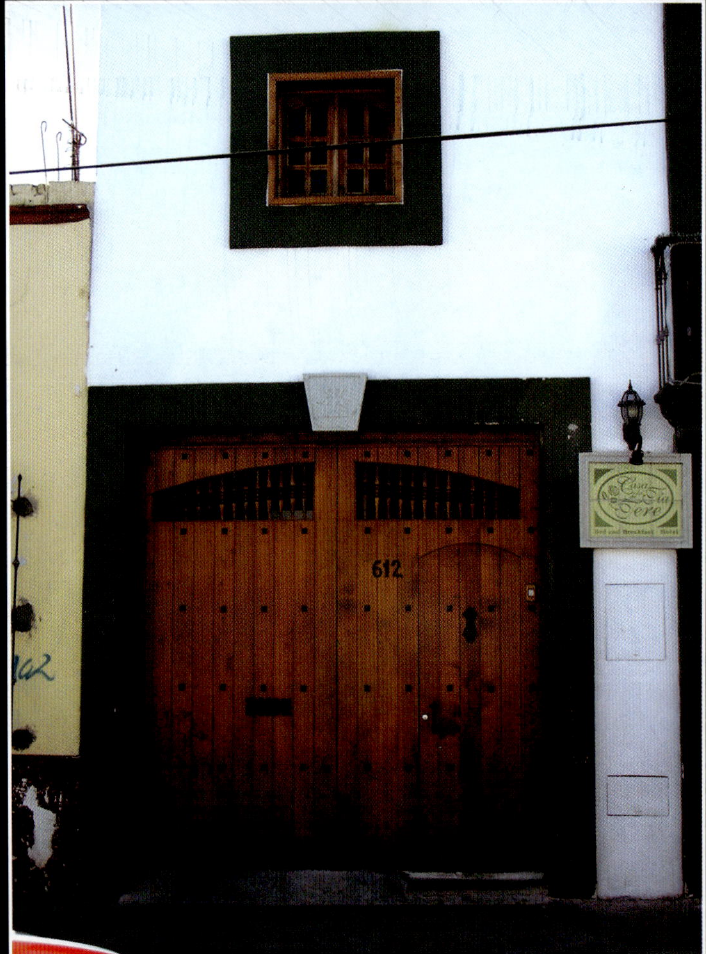

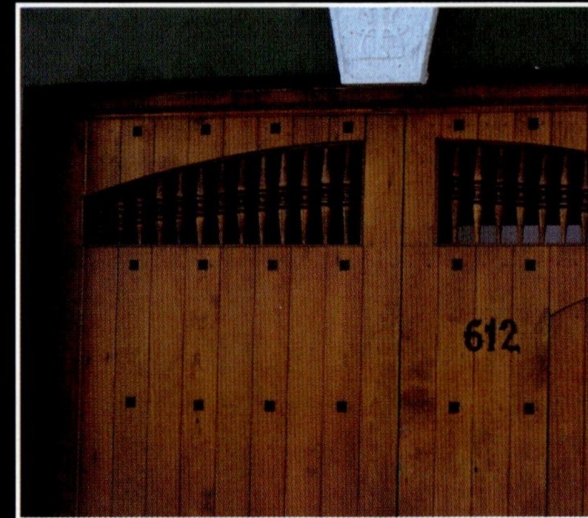

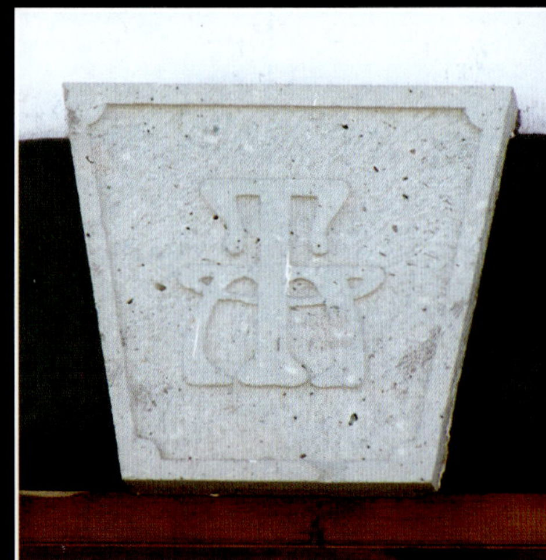

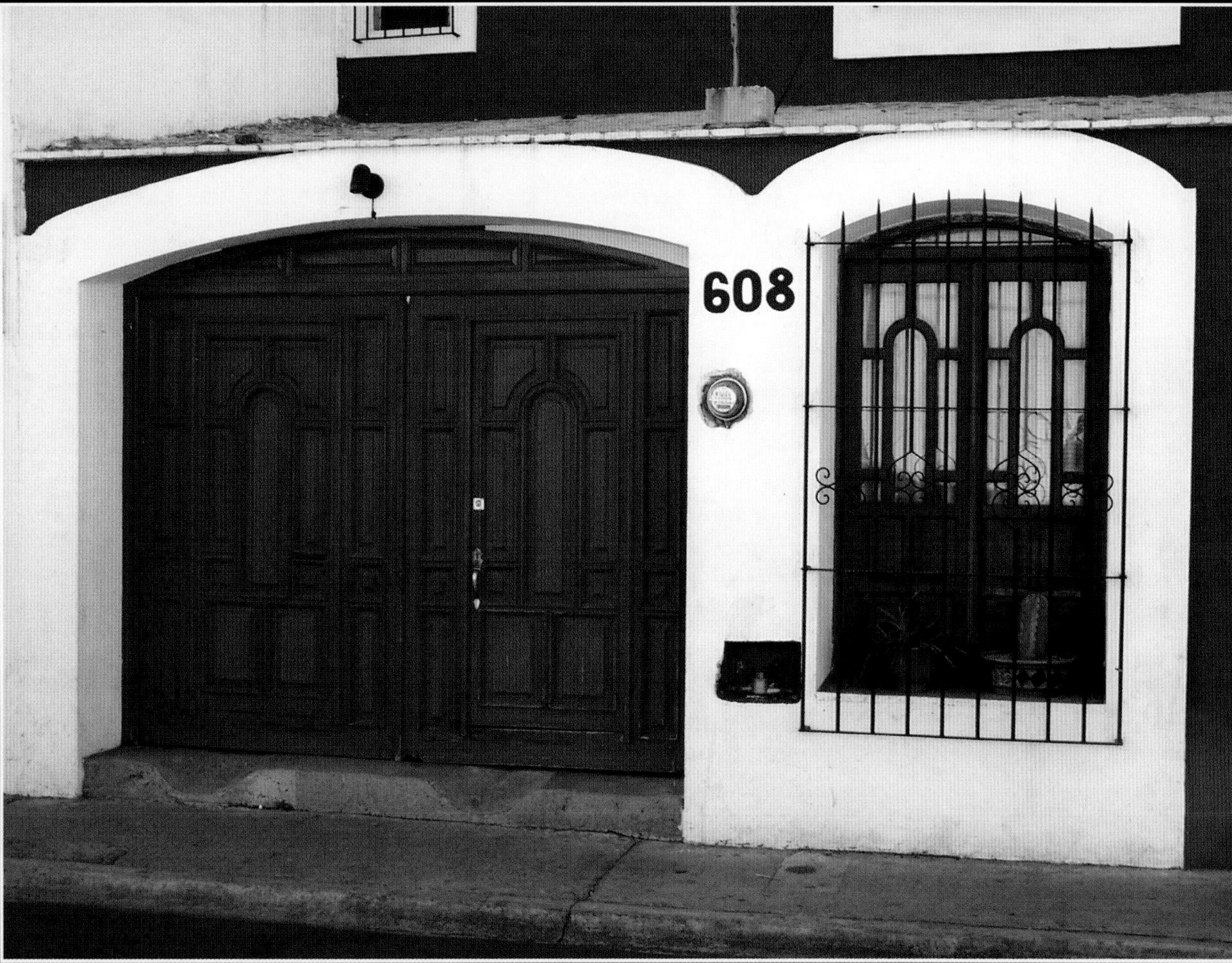

608 Murgía Street.

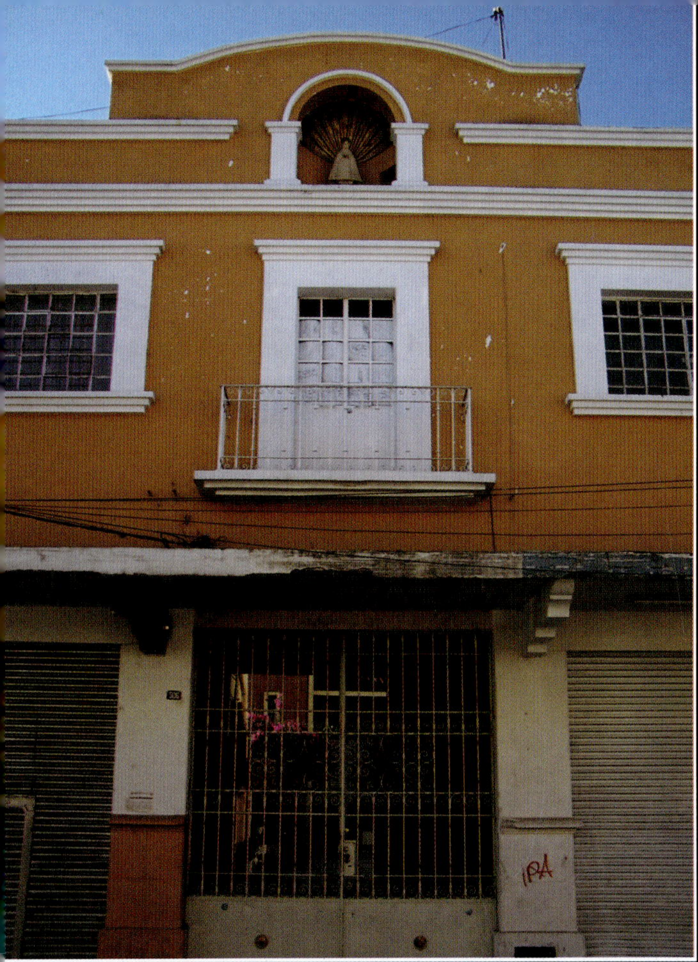

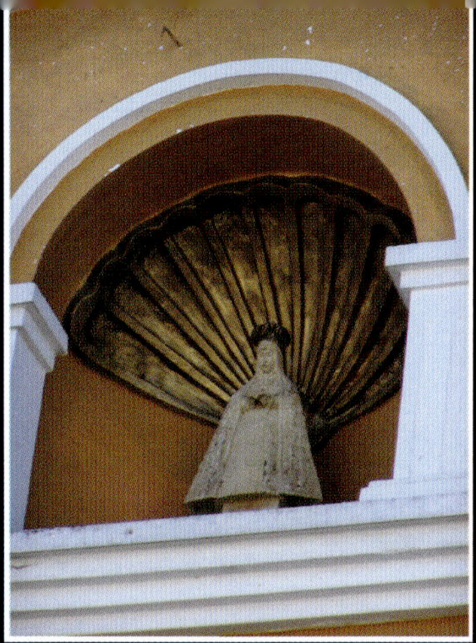

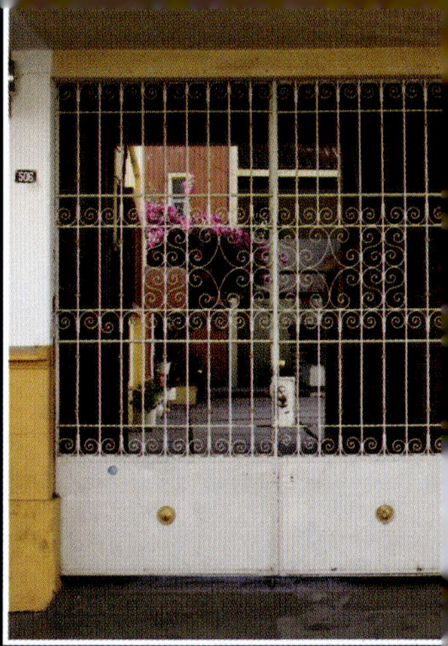

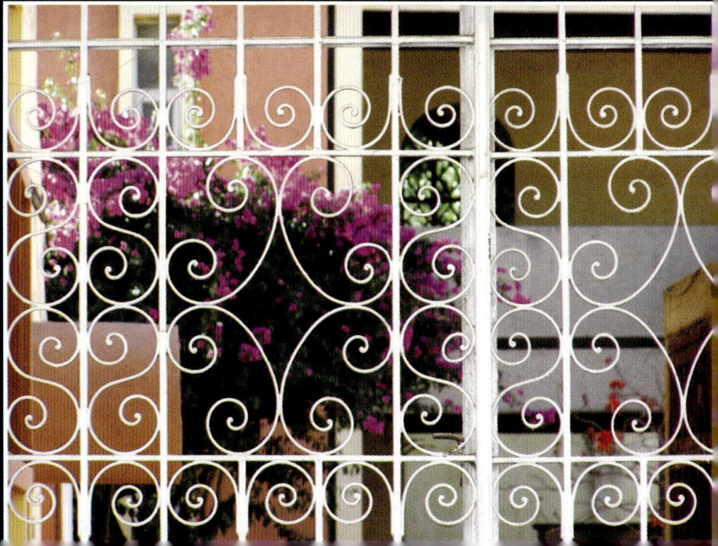

506 Murgía Street.

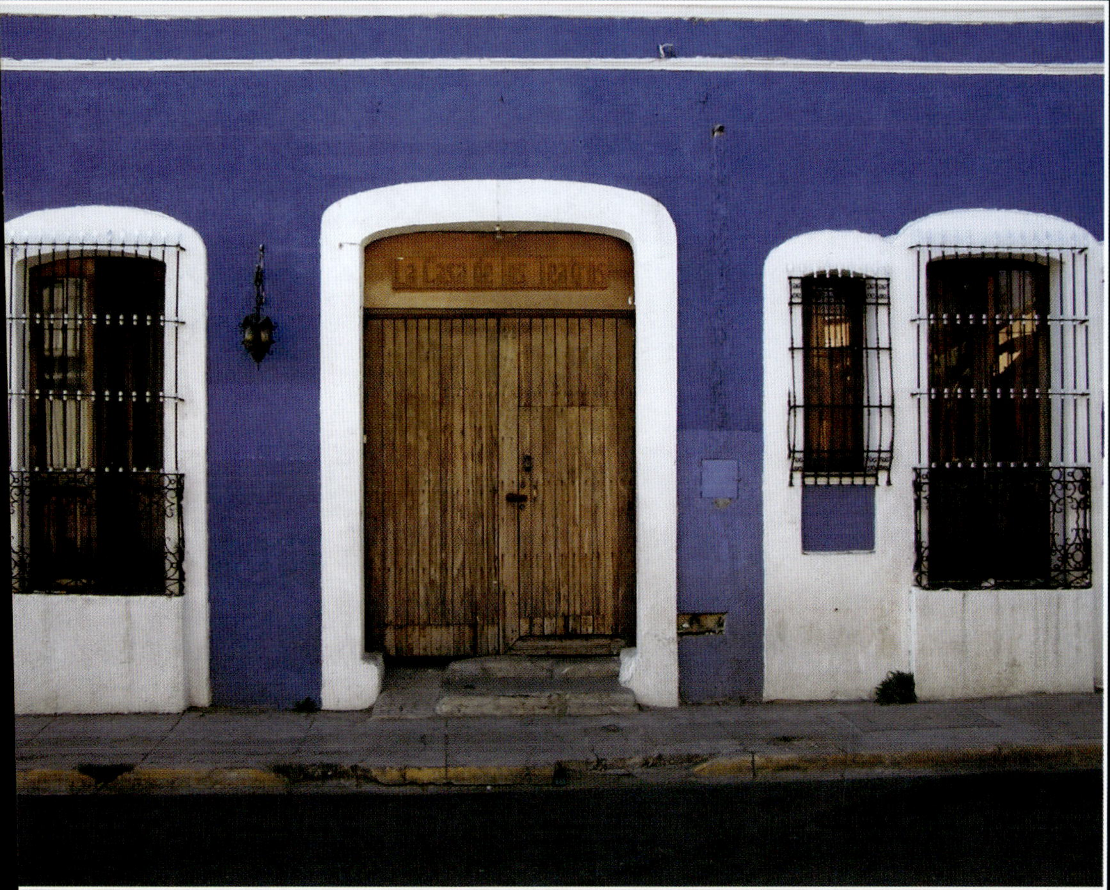

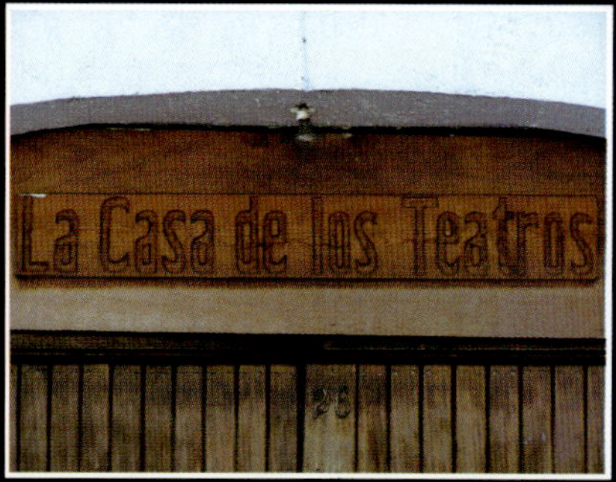

Las Casa de los Teatros (The house of Theatres).

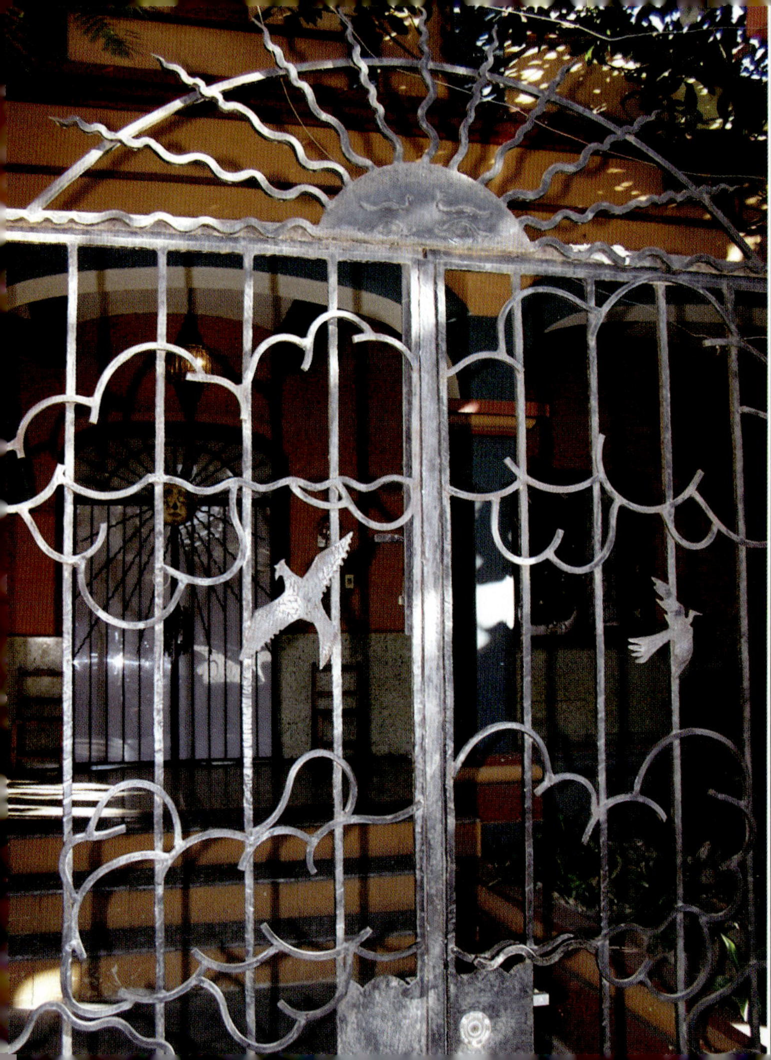
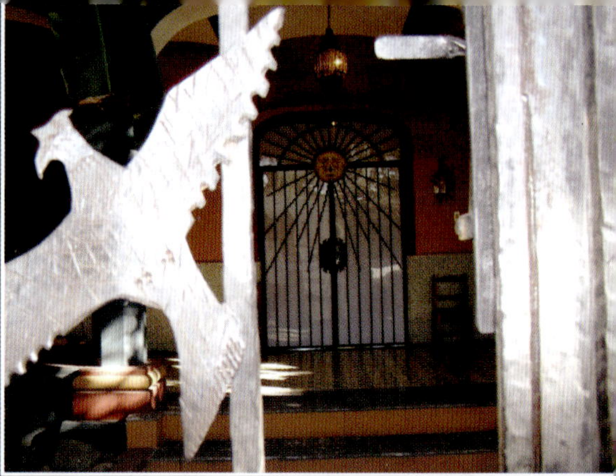
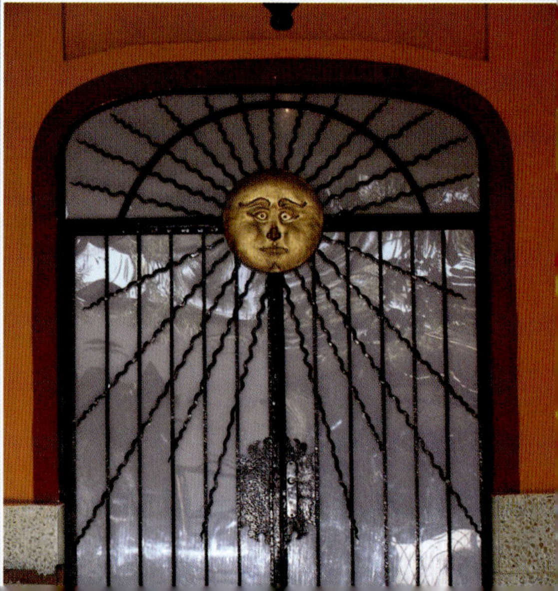

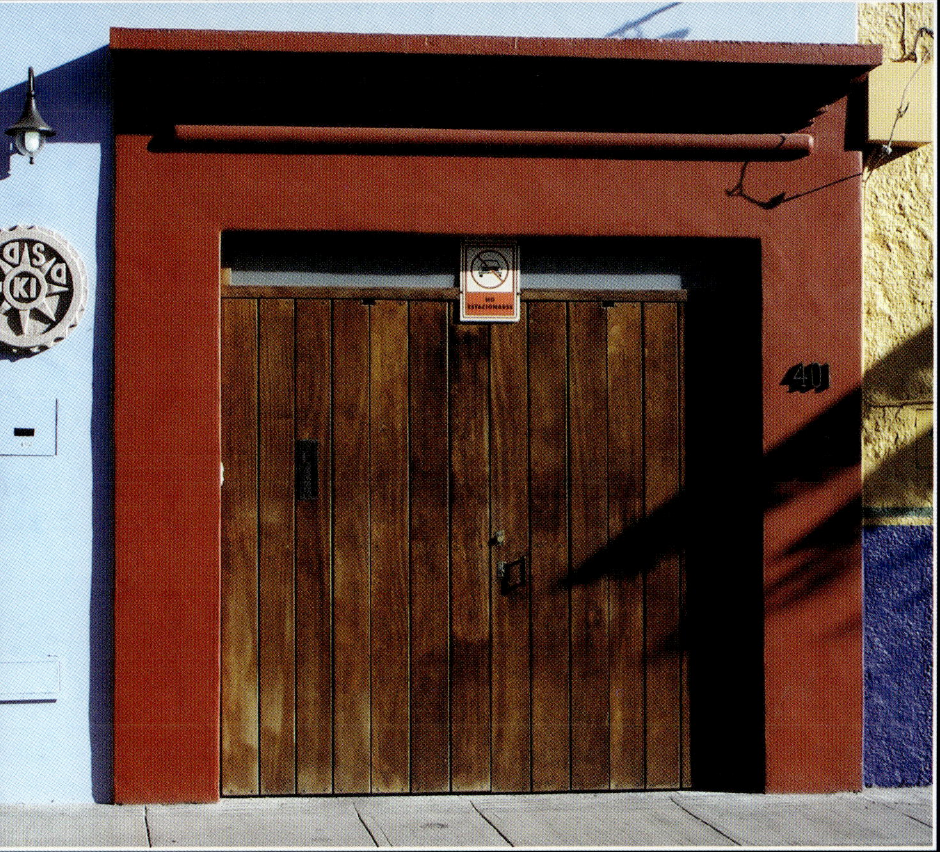
NO ESTACIONARSE
401

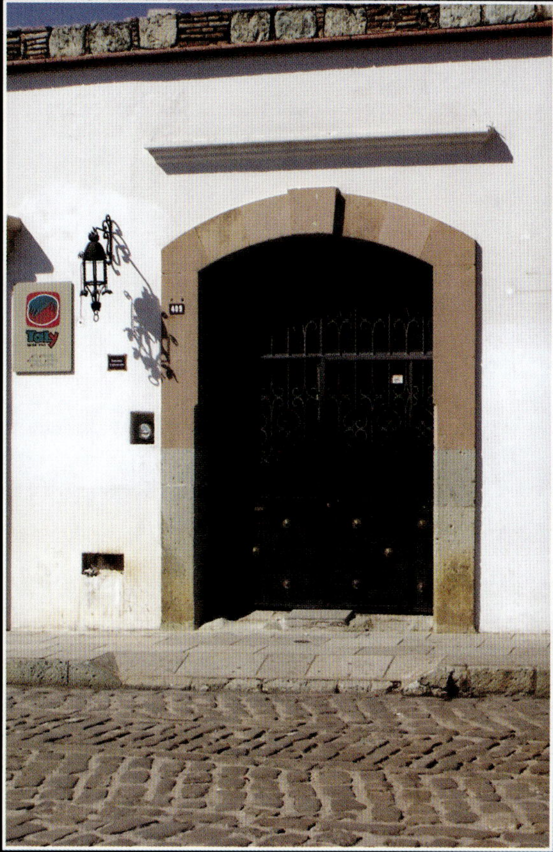

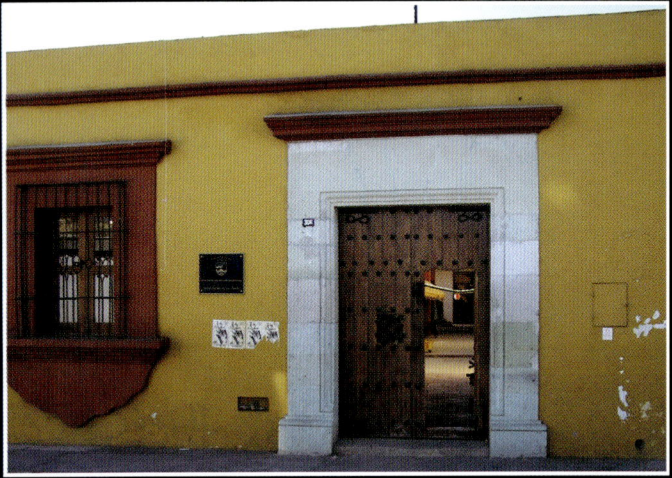

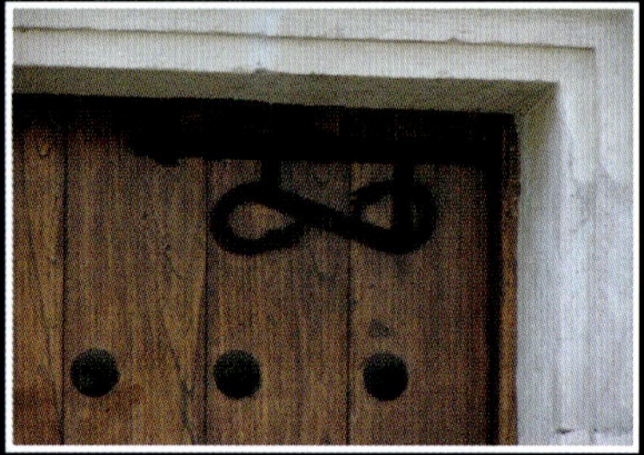

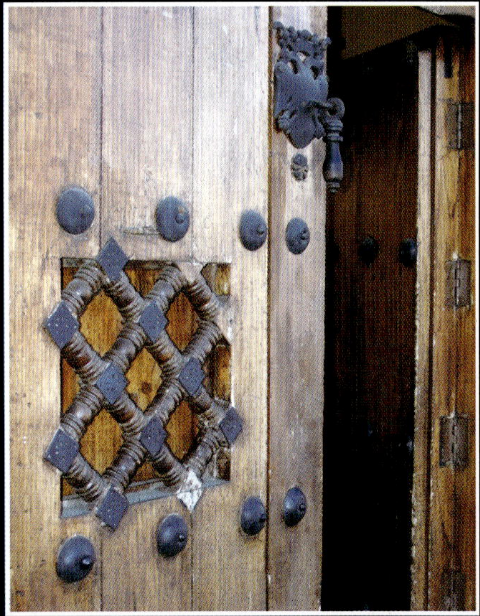

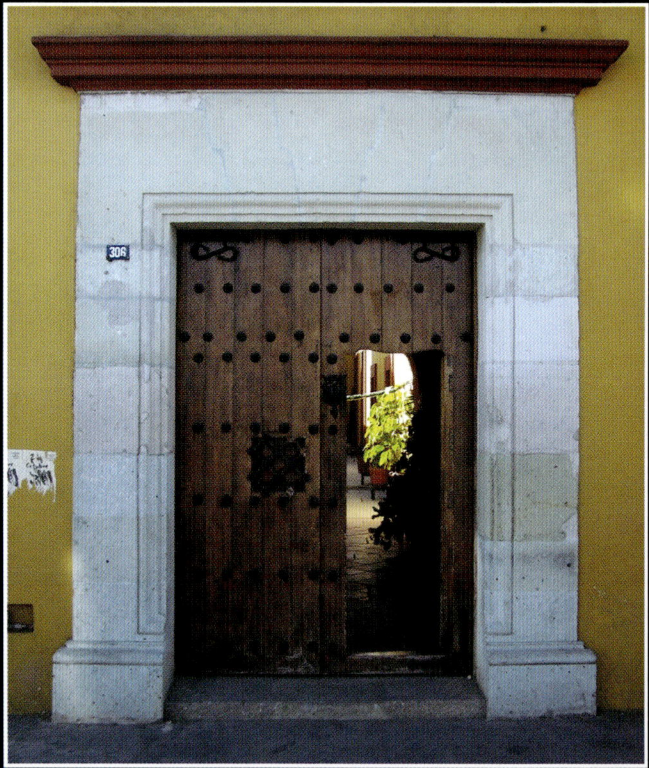

The Institute of Sociological Research.

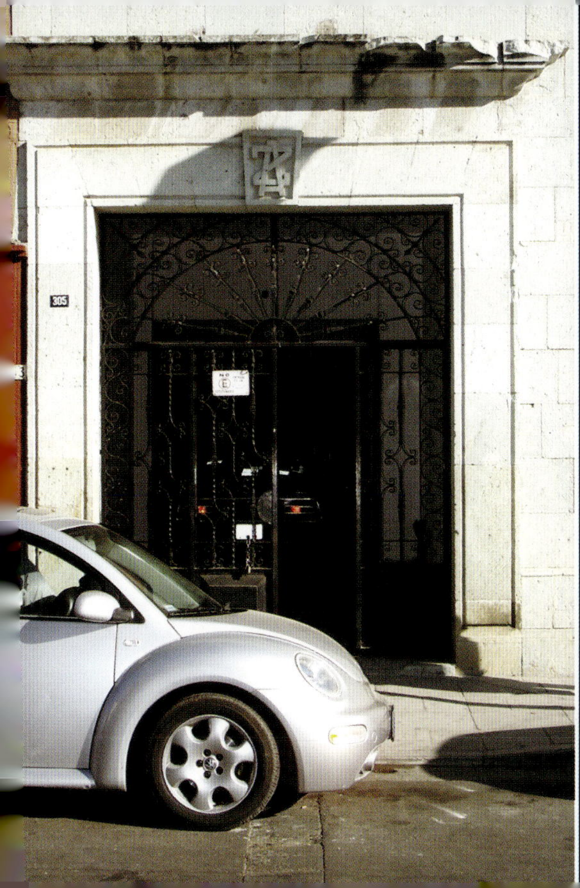

The house is located at 305 Murgía, and was the home of a former governor, Manuel Zárate Aquino, who died in 1994. His initials are above the door.

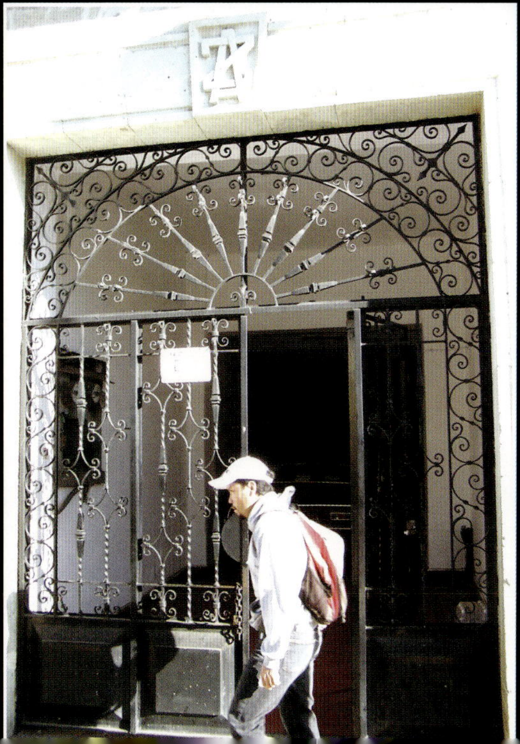

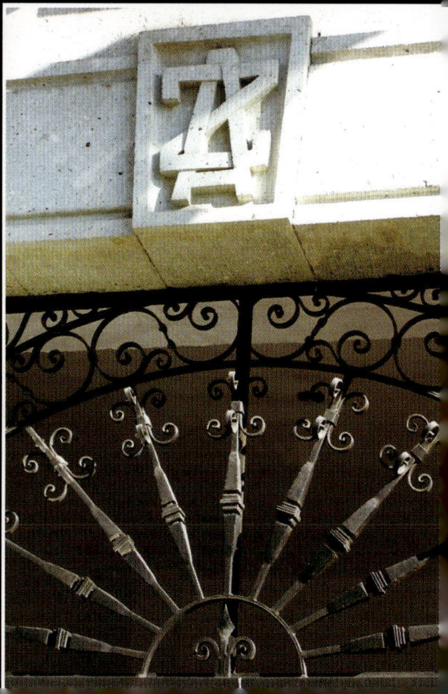

Murguía Street.

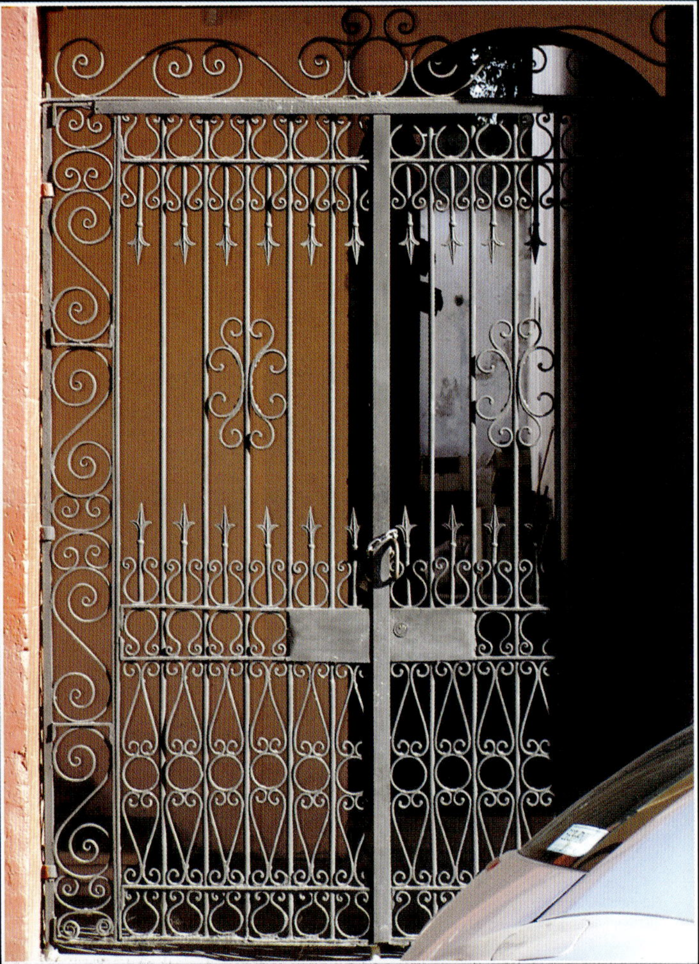

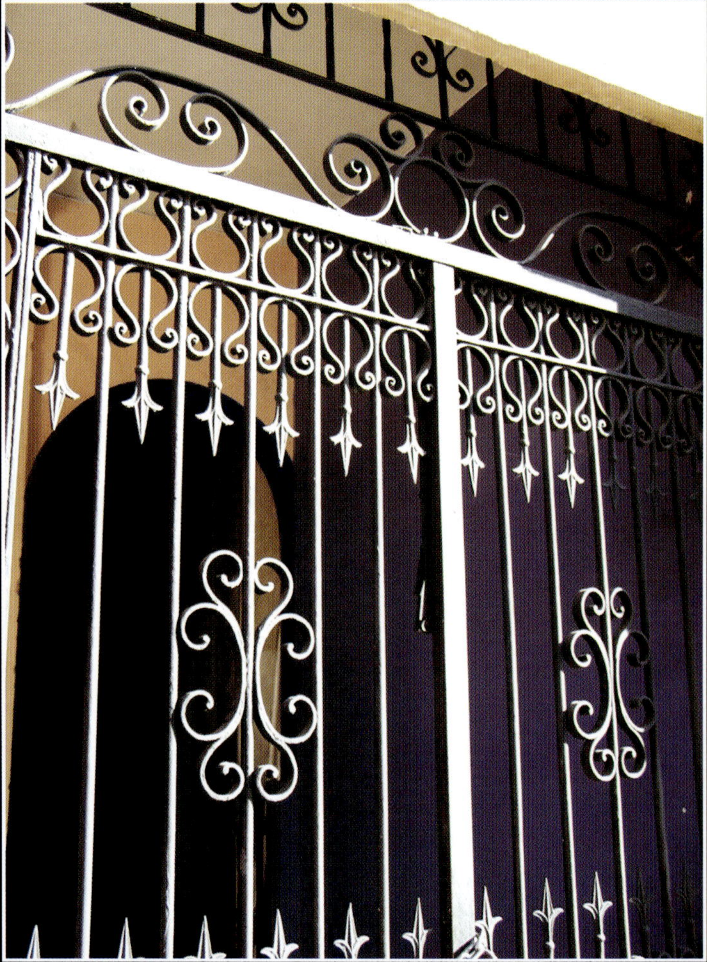

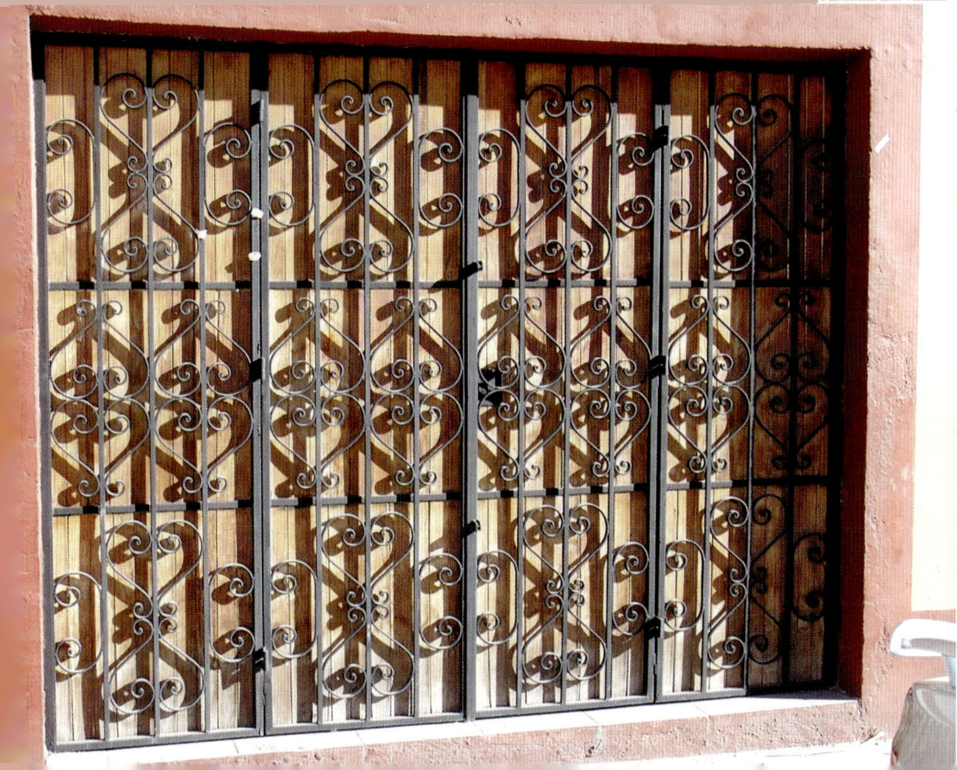

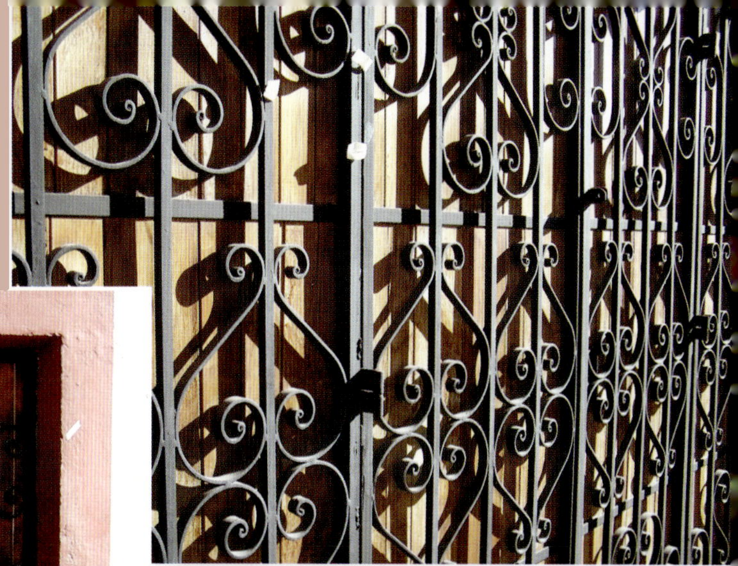

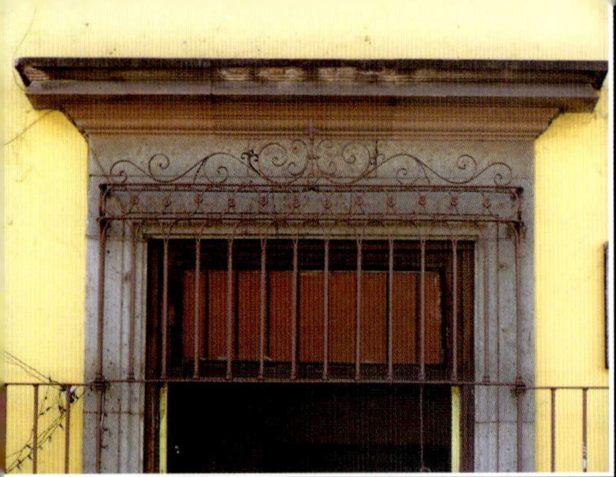
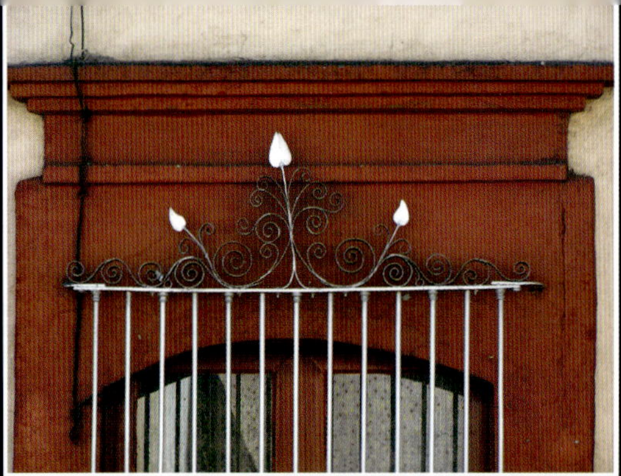
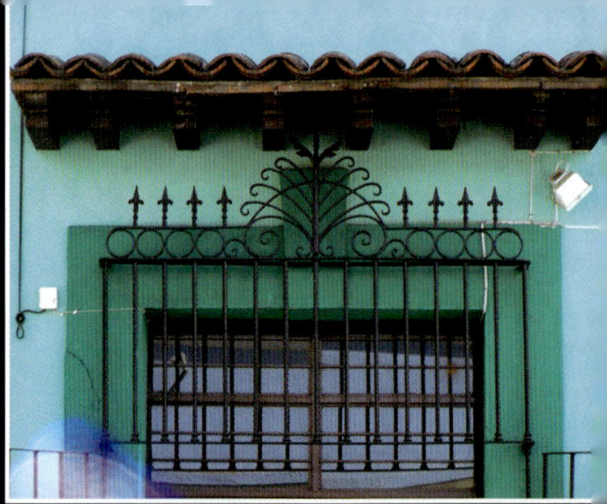
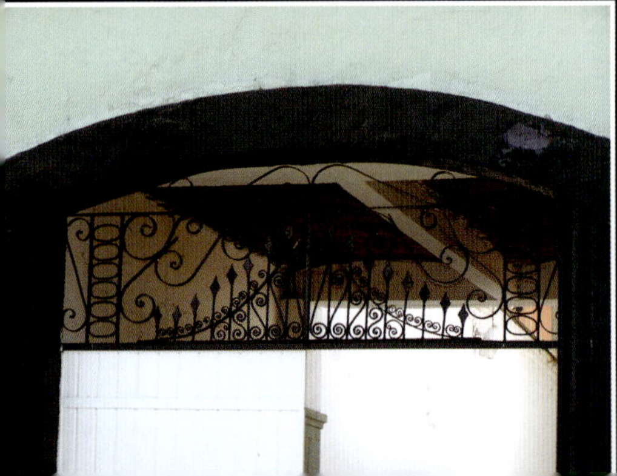
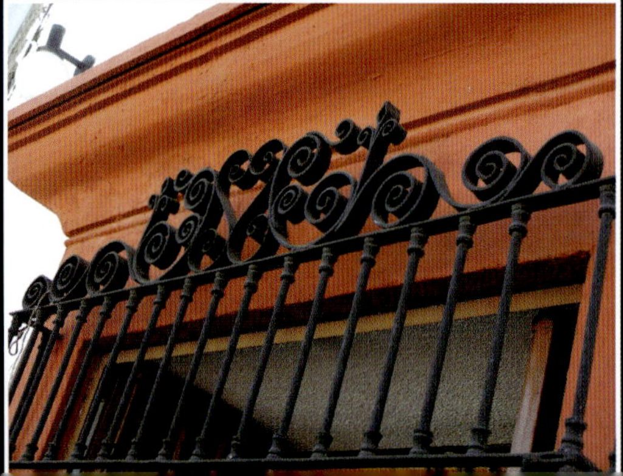
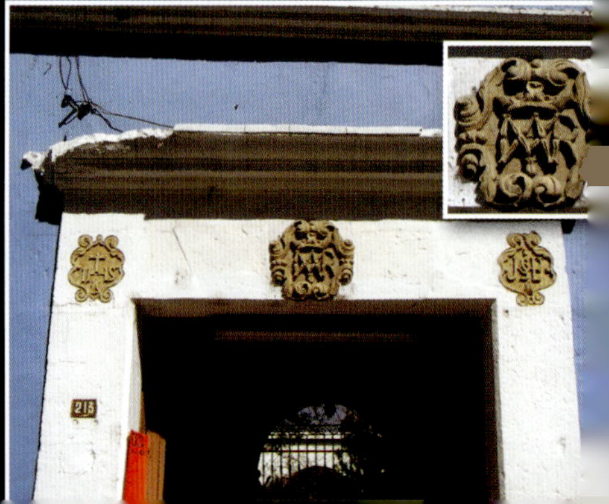

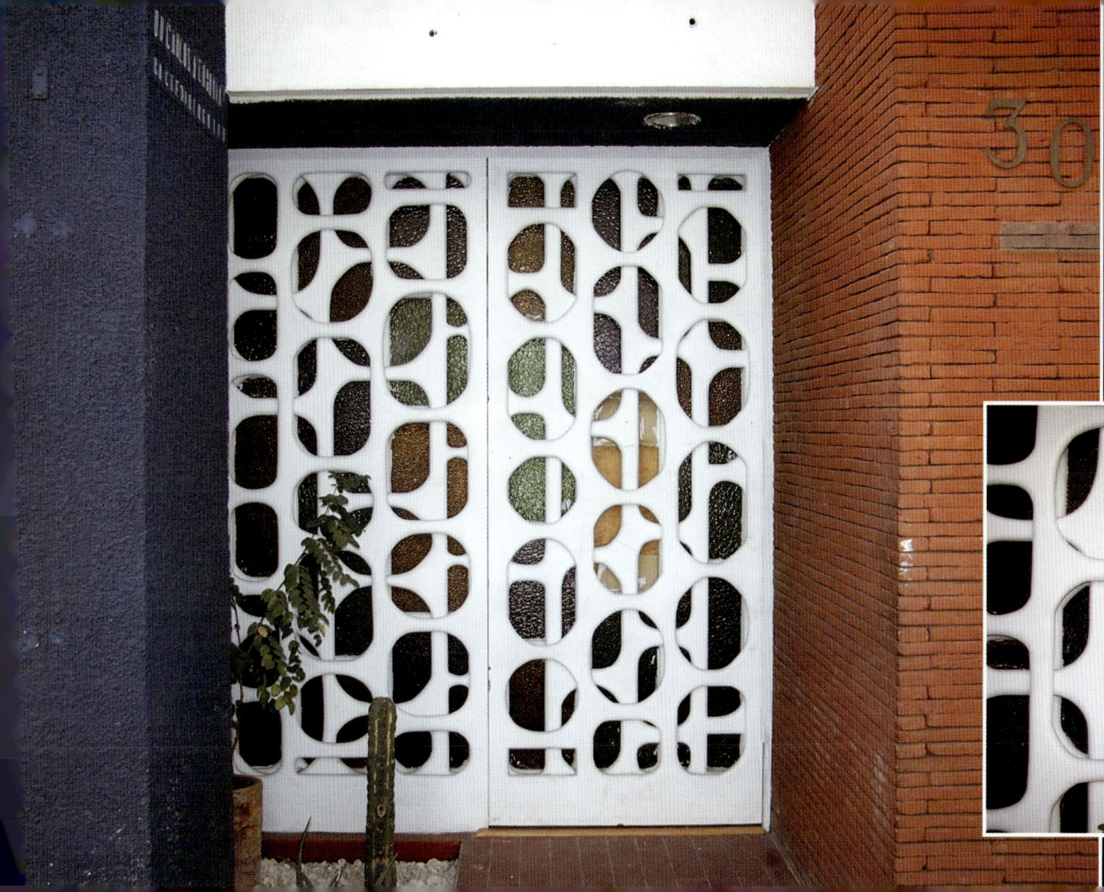

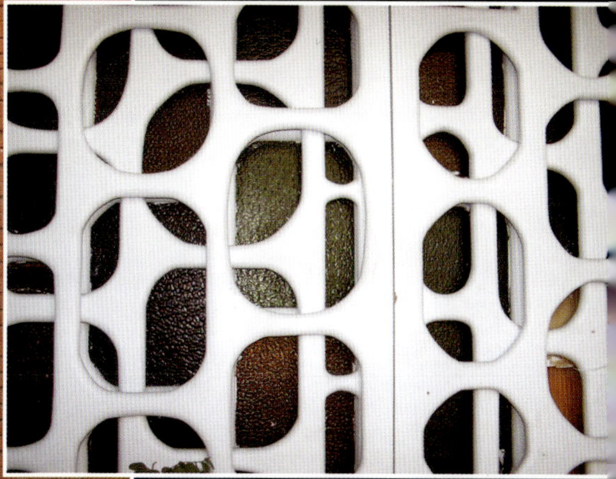

Murguía Street.

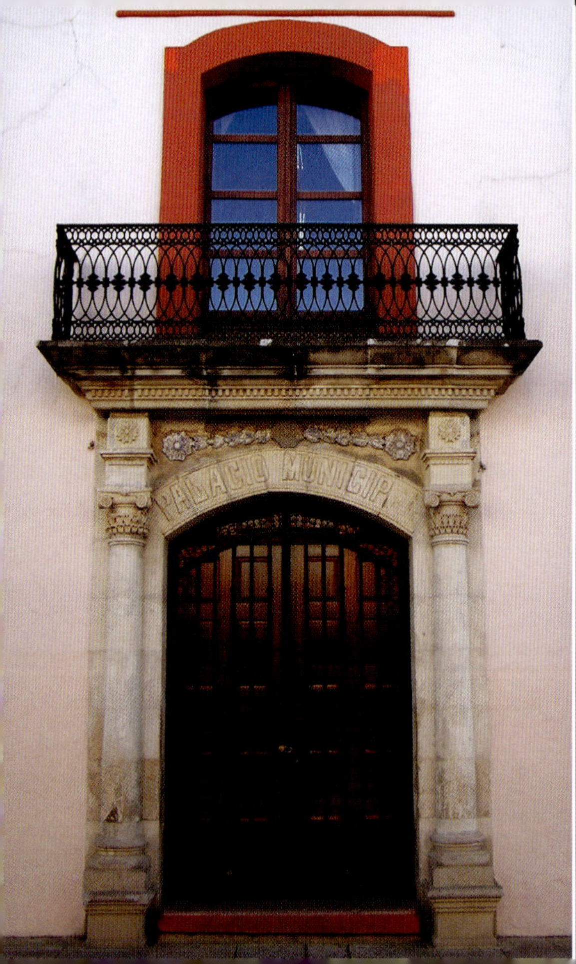

El Camino Real Hotel. Located on Cinco de Mayo Street, this door is part of the famous, ex-convent of Santa Catalina, now a luxury hotel, El Camino Real (formerly known as the Hotel Presidente). This particular door is the entrance to a tucked-away bar called Las Novicias, wh means "nuns in training."

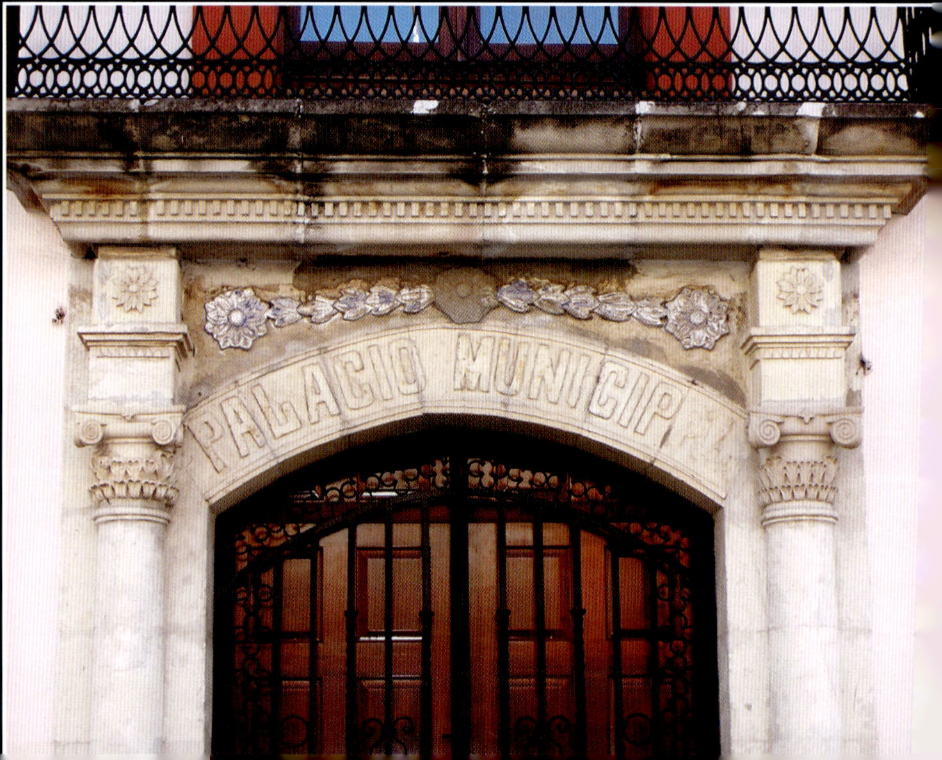

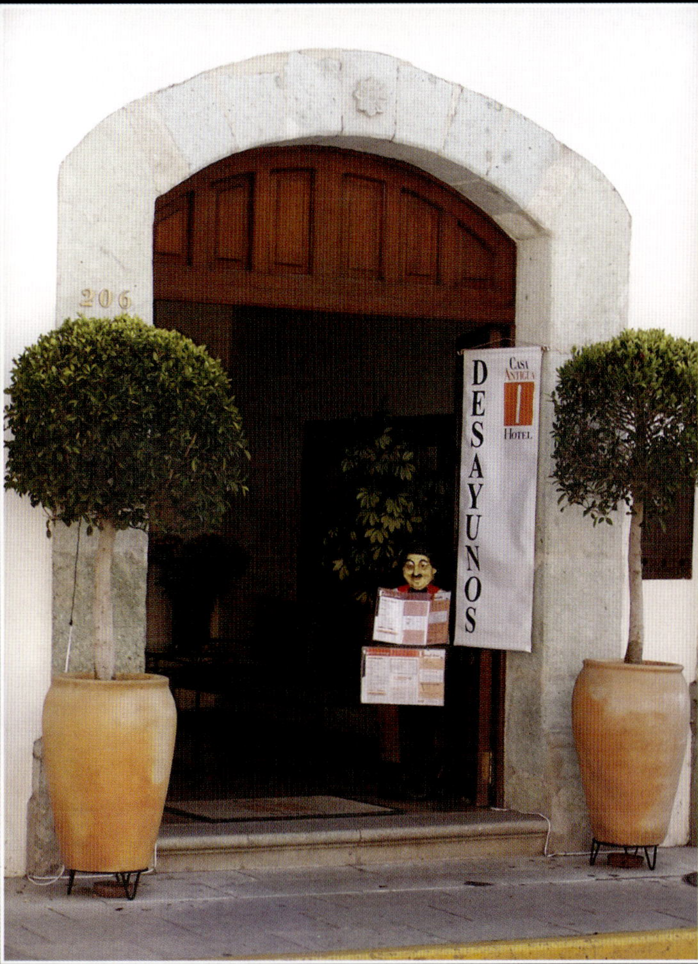

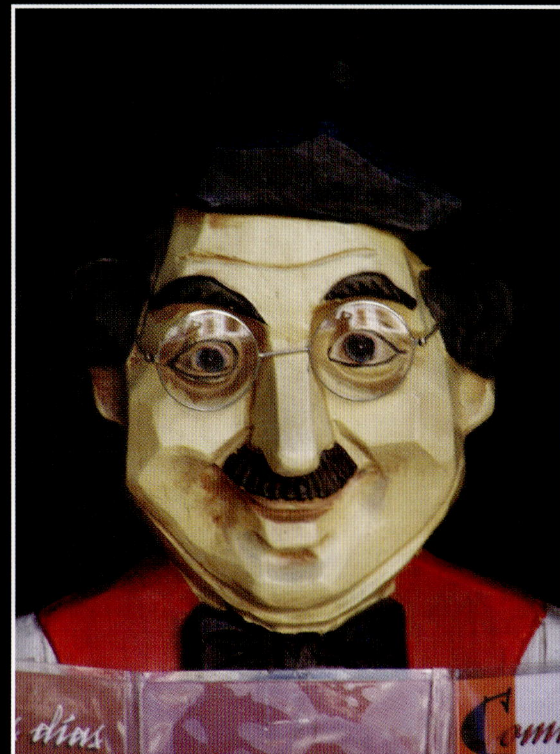

The main lobby doors to the hotel Camino Real.

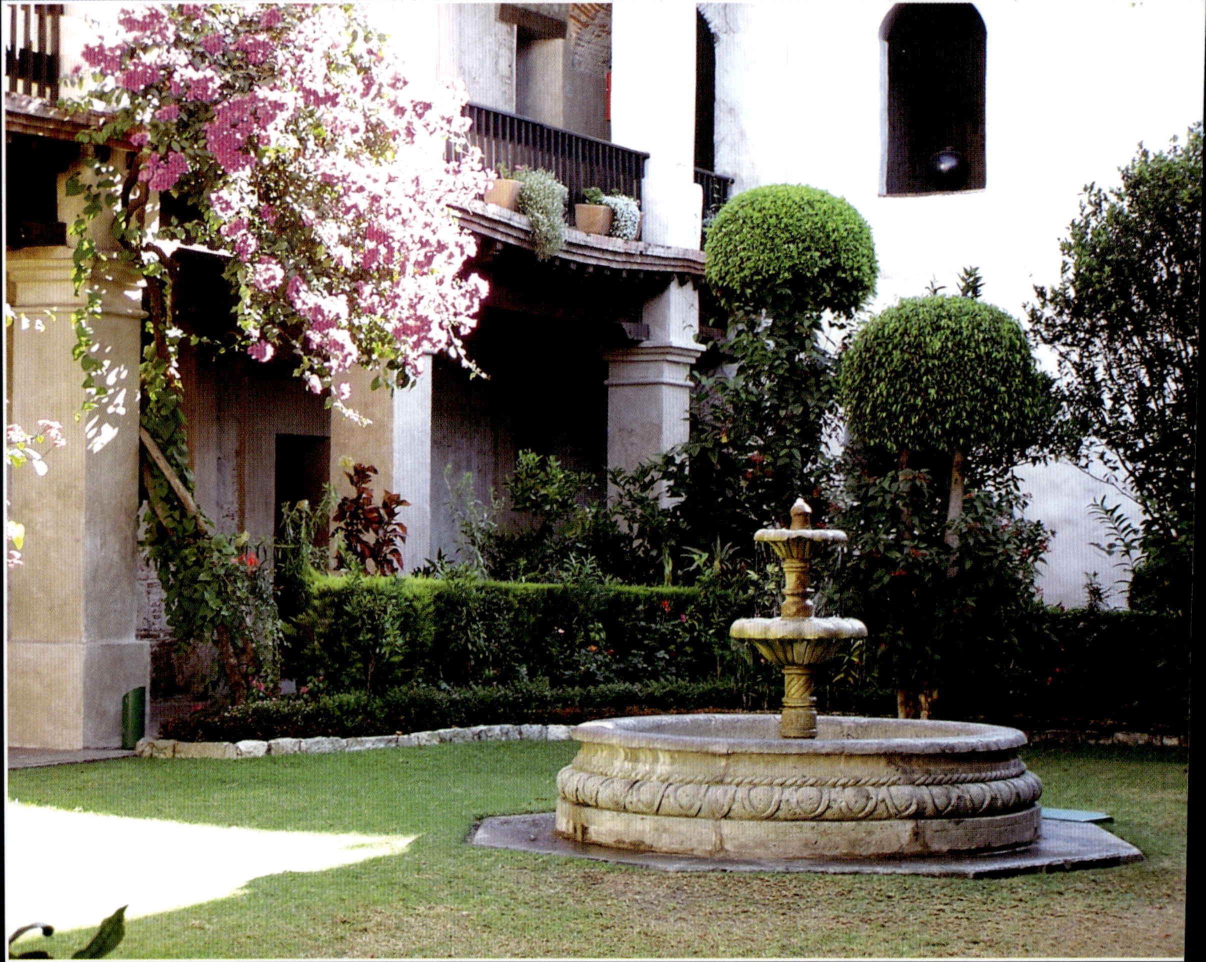

Under an archway of the main garden in the Hotel Camino Real.

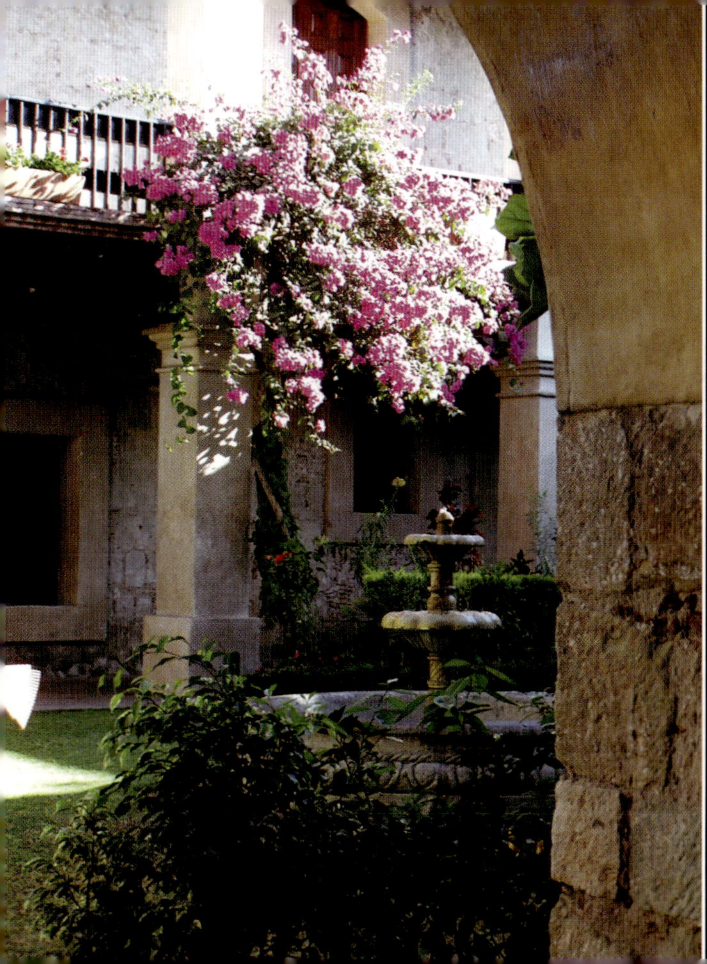

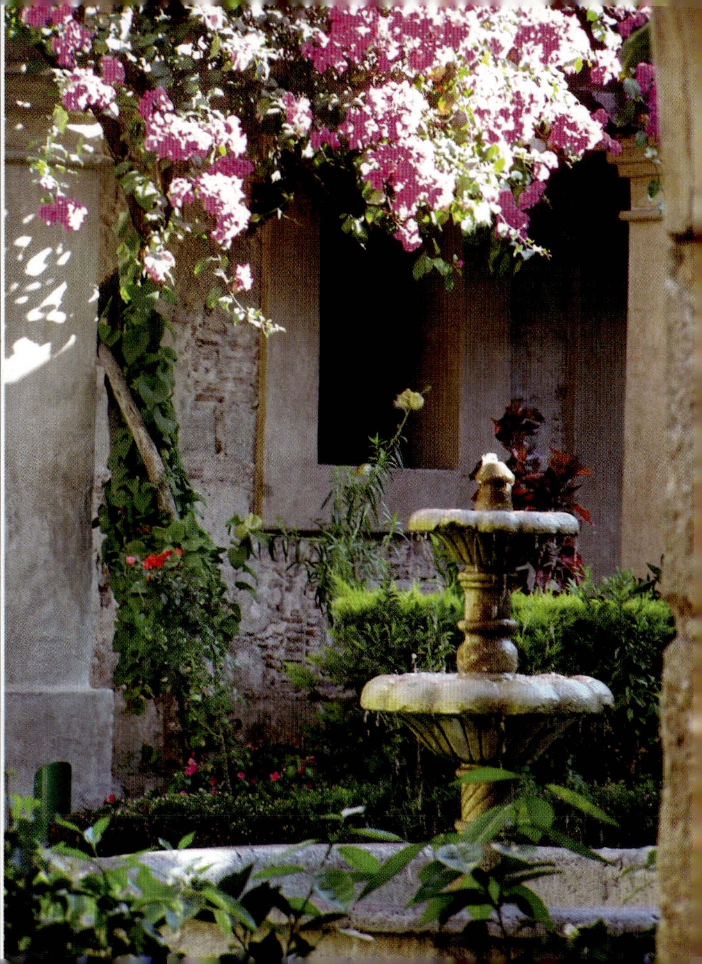

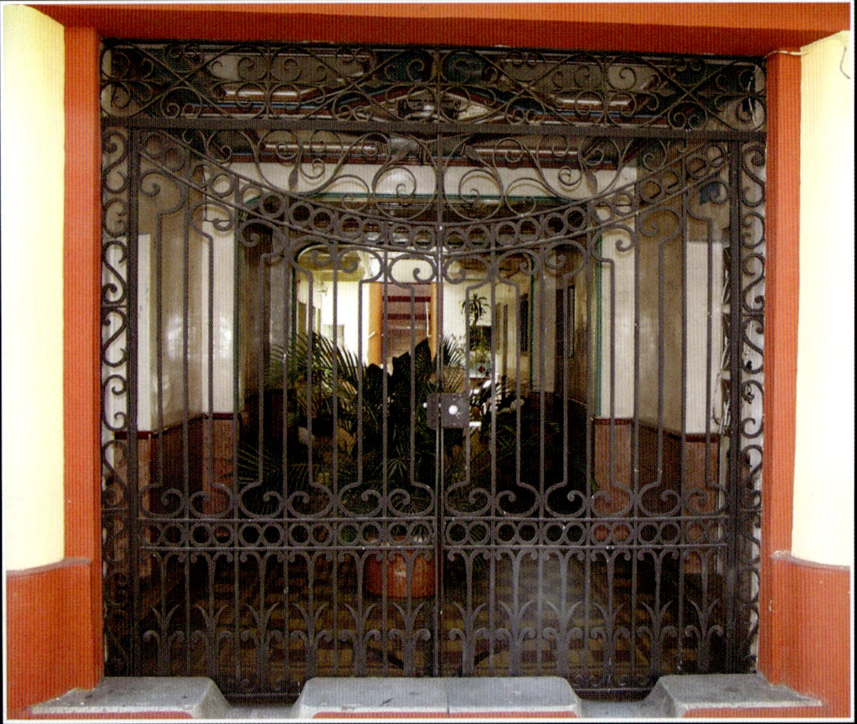

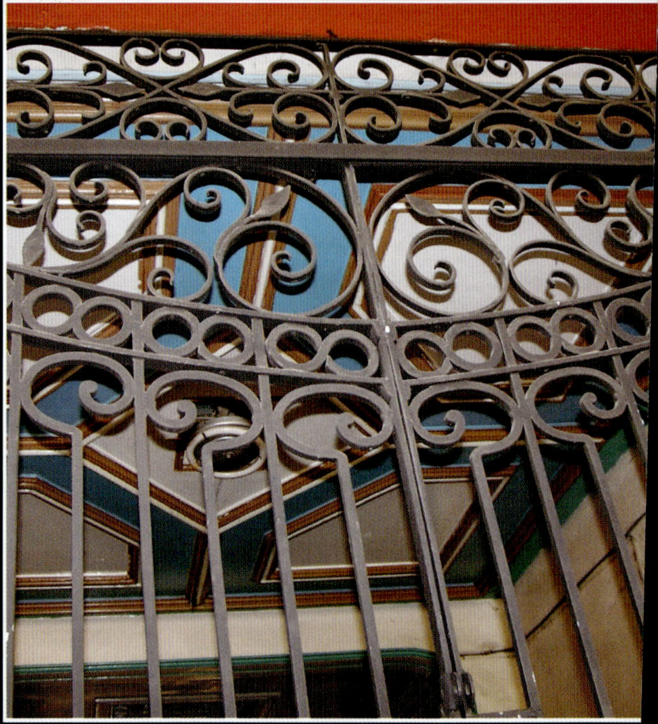

The corner of Murguía Street and Reforma Street.

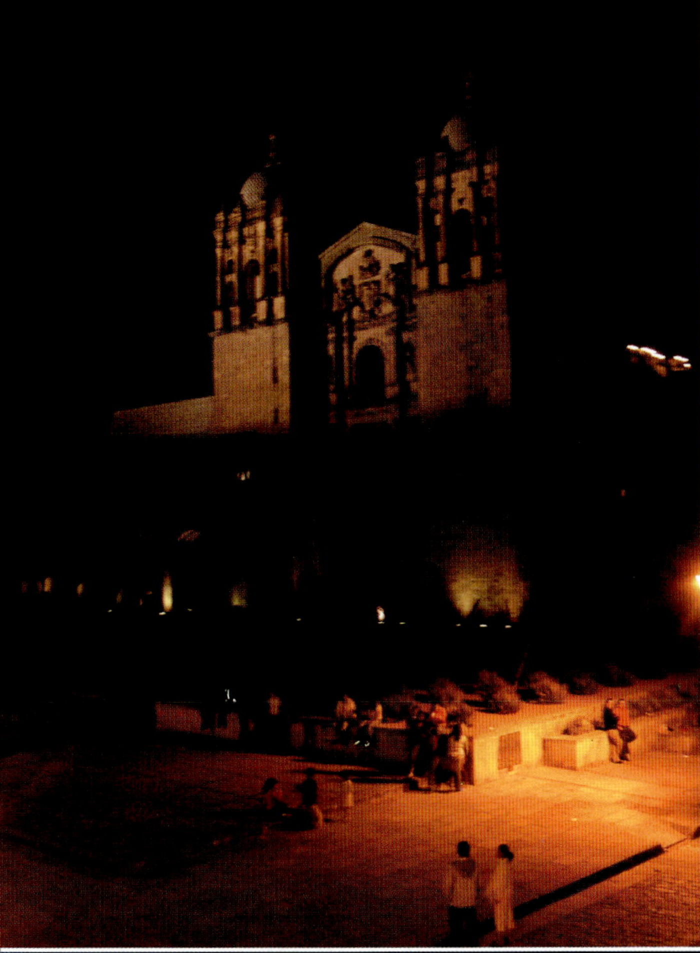

Santo Domingo Church de Guzmán.

This door is a side entrance to the ex-convent (referred to at left).

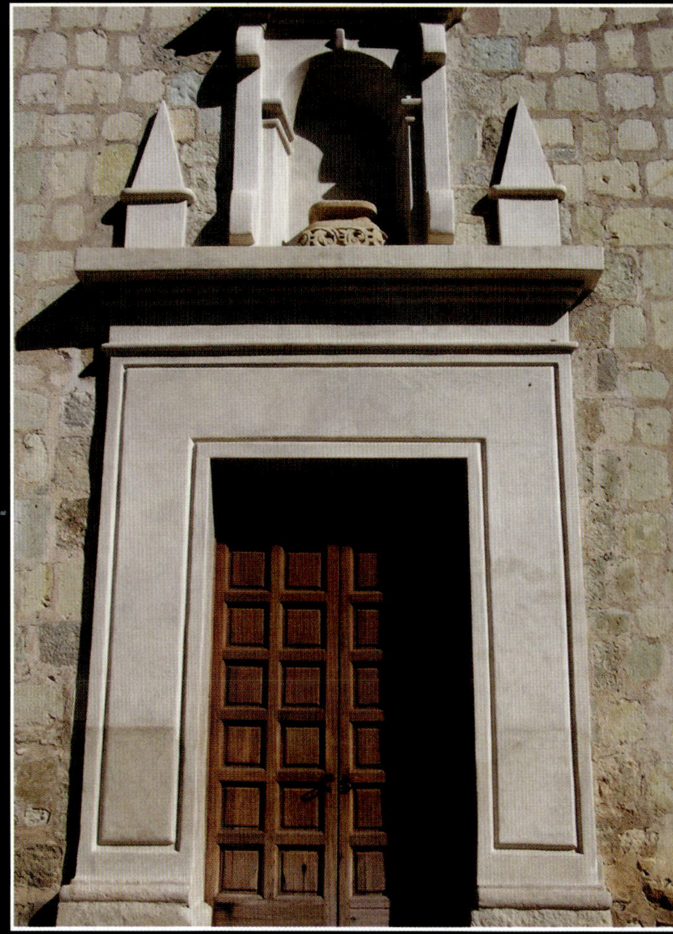

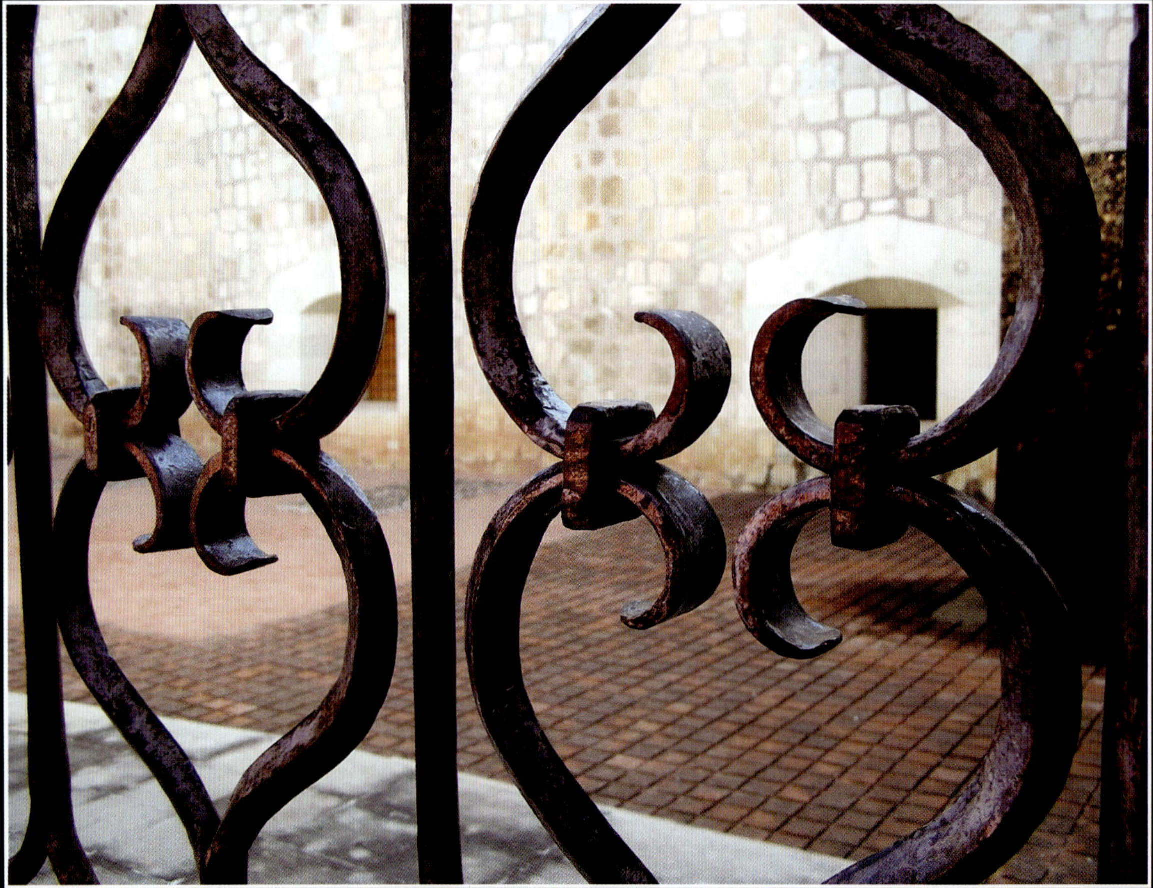

The Santo Domingo de Guzmán. View into one of the many patios in the ex-convent of Santo Domingo de Guzmán, now the largest museum in Oaxaca, and one of the most famous in Mexico. It is attached to the Santo Domingo Church, one of the oldest and most famous churches in Mexico.

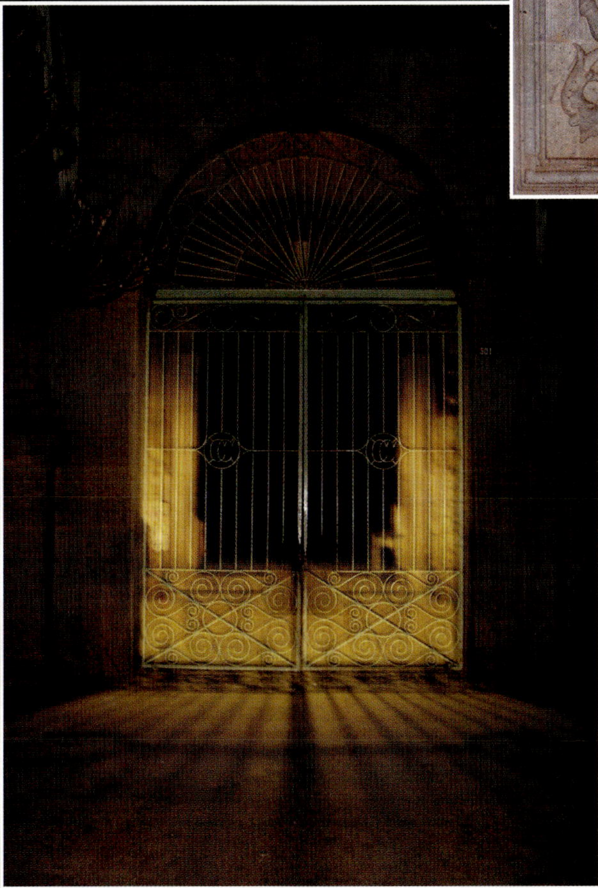

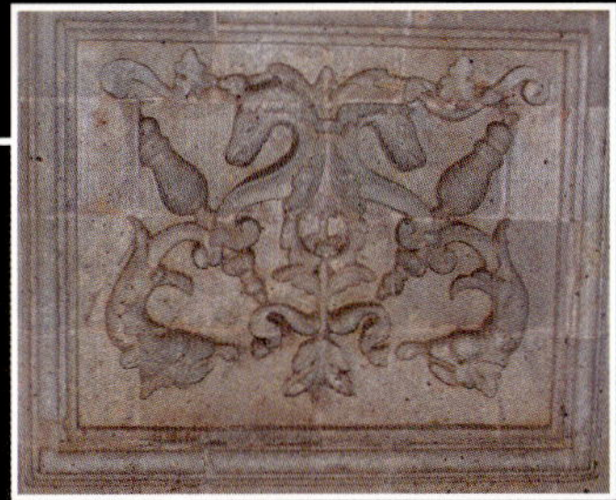

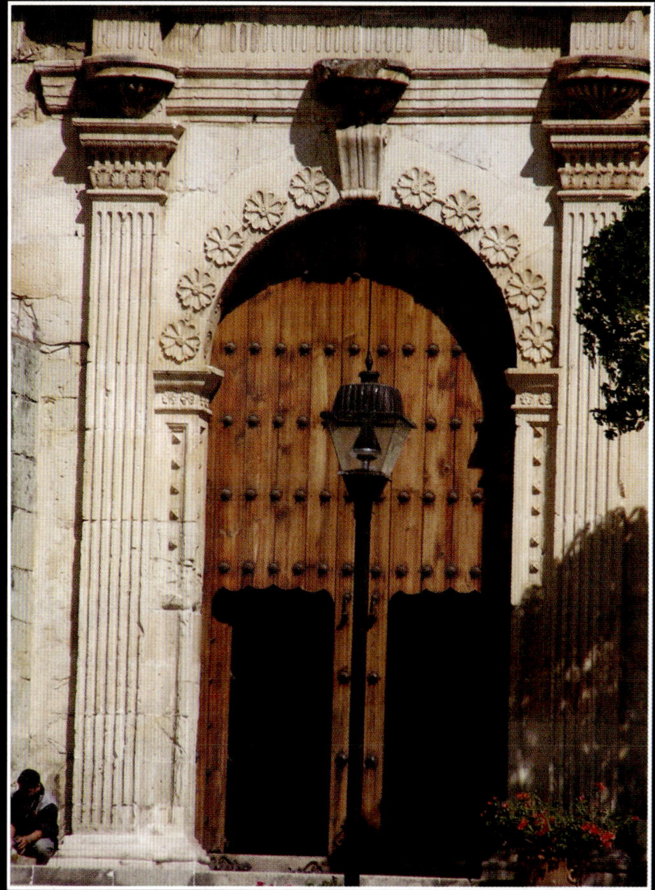

The South entrance to the church Santo Domingo de Guzmán.

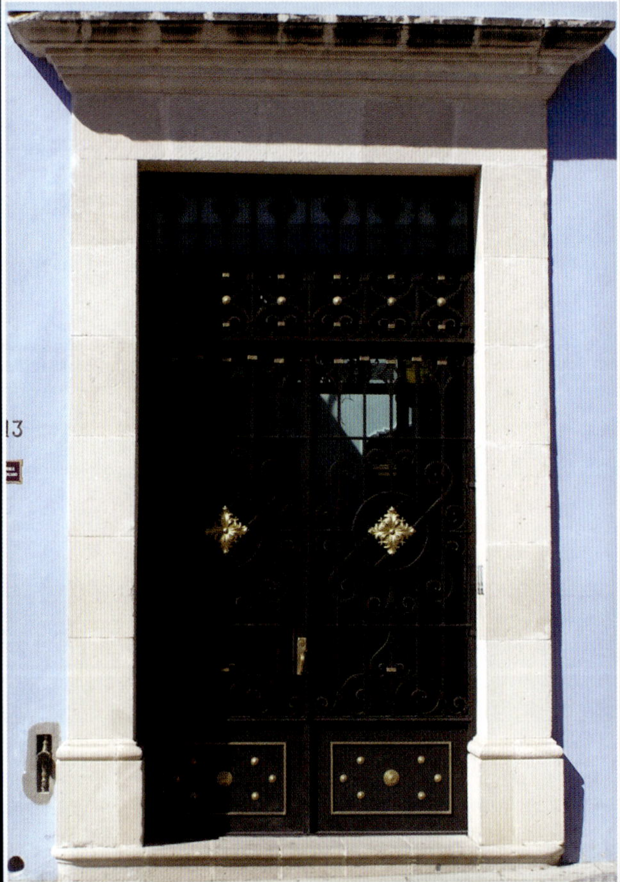

A restaurant called, El Ché, located on Cinco de Mayo Street directly South of the Santo Domingo Church.

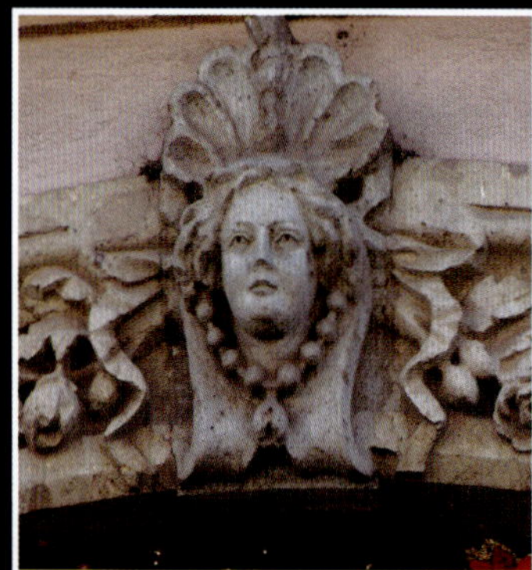

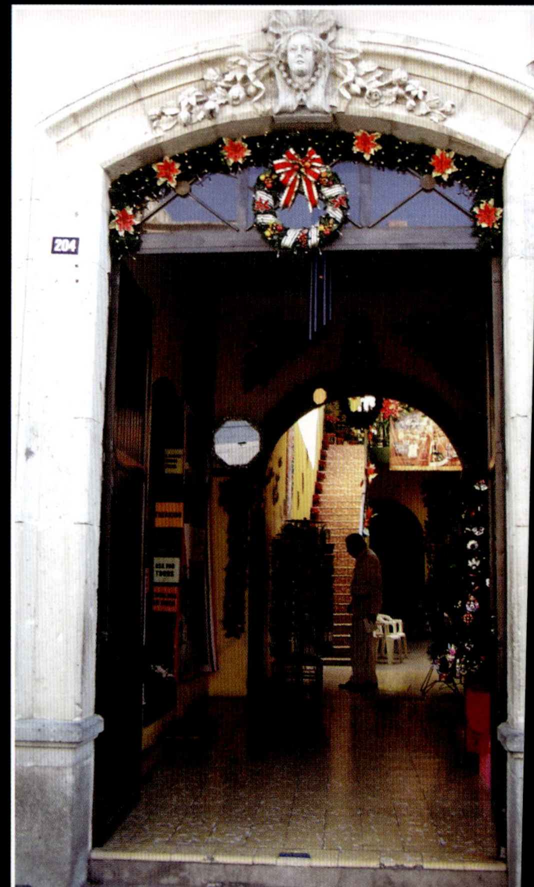

One of many small shopping malls located on García Vigil Street.

411 Cinco de Mayo Street.

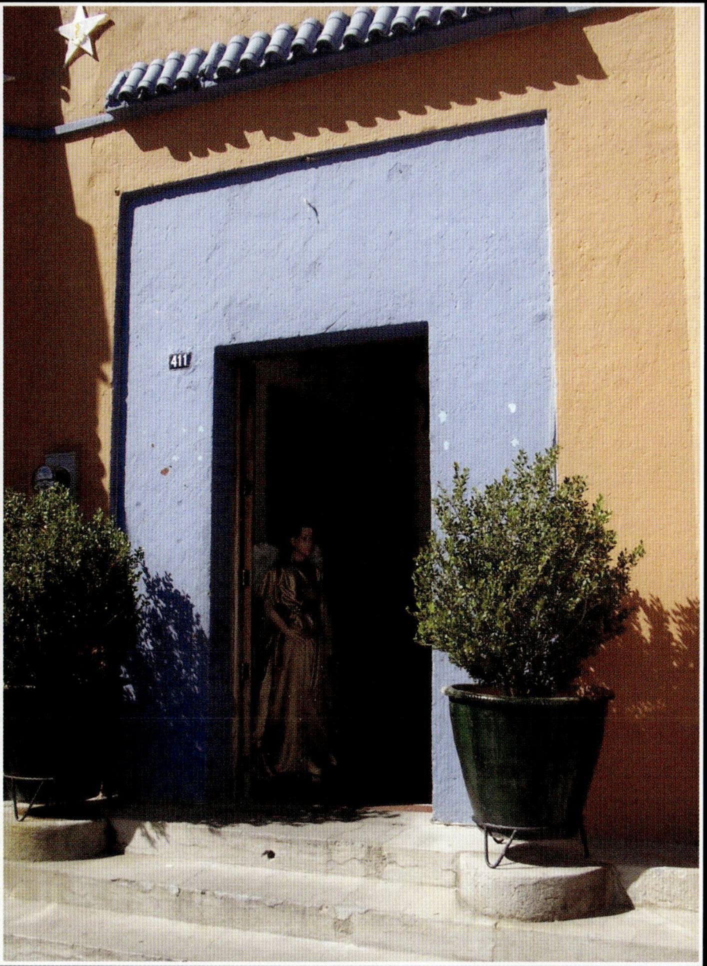

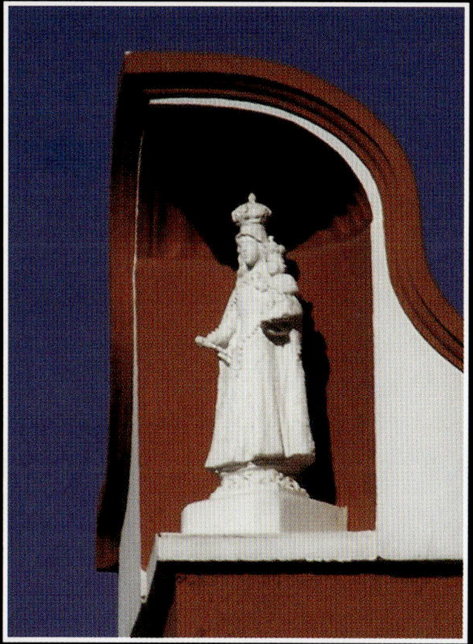

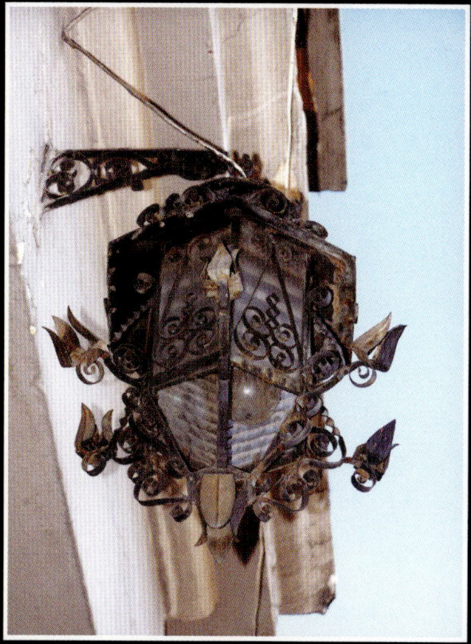

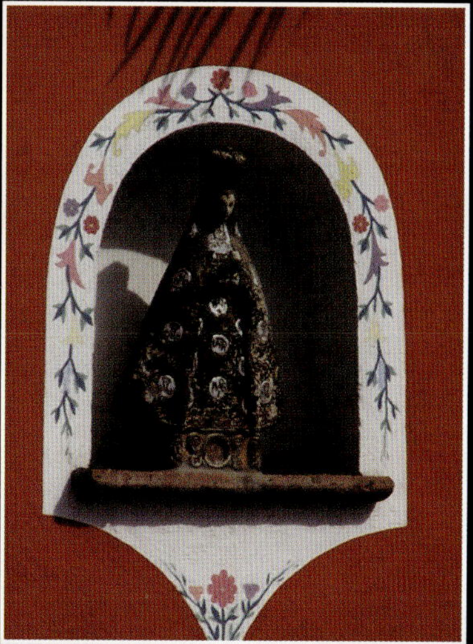

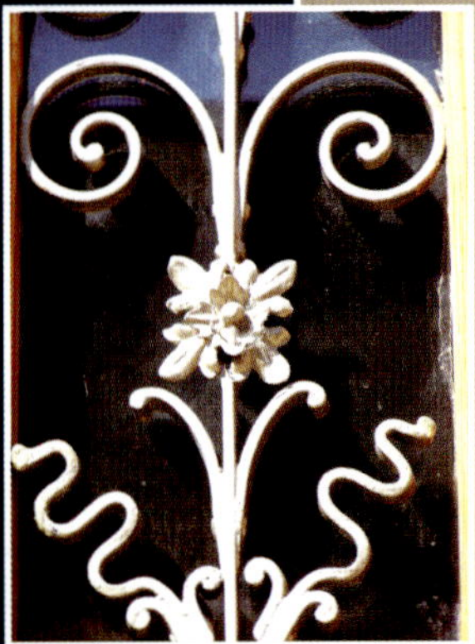

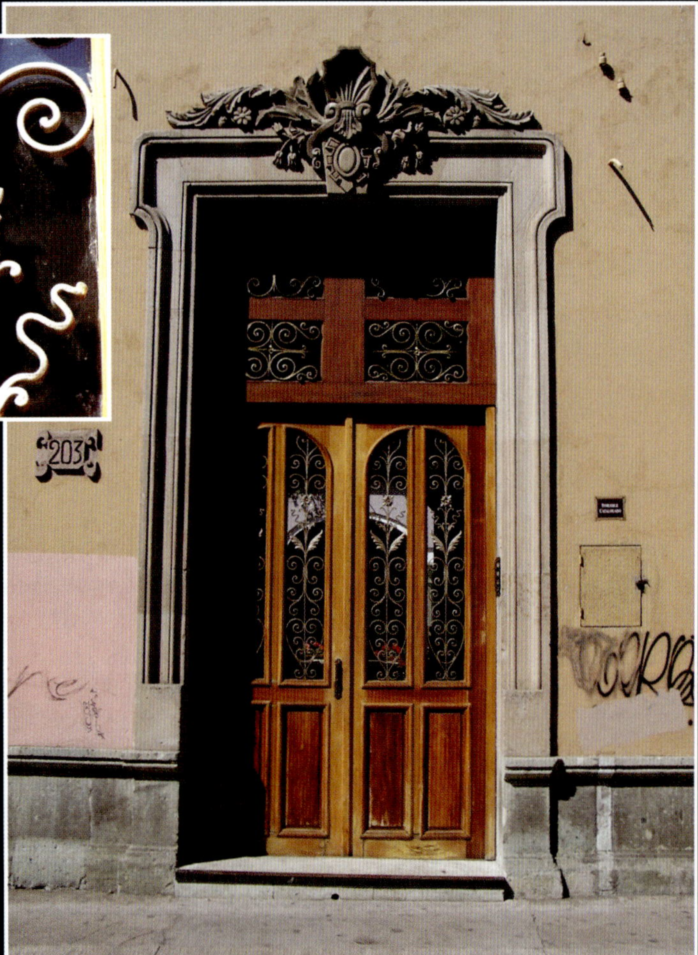
203

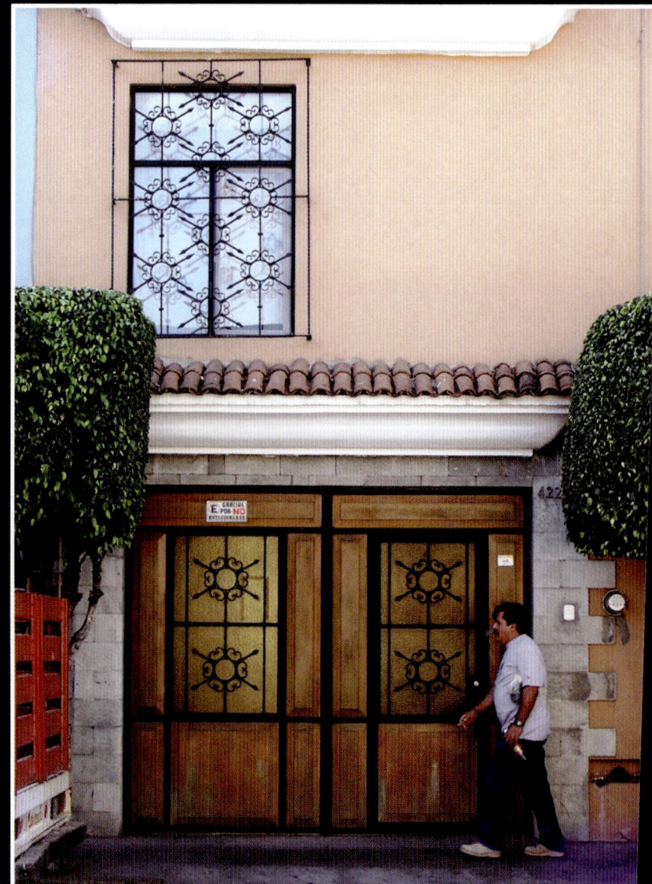

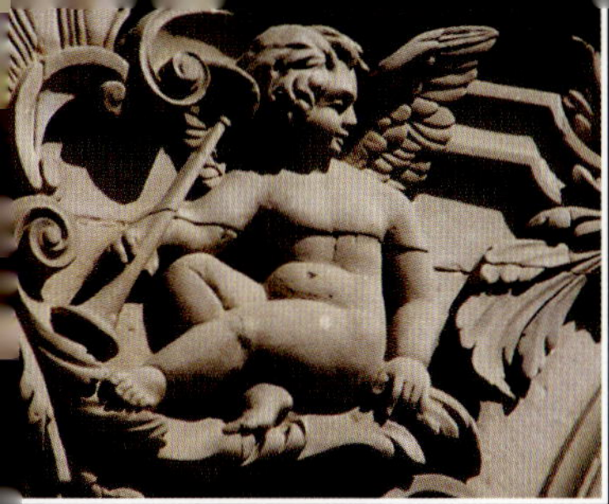

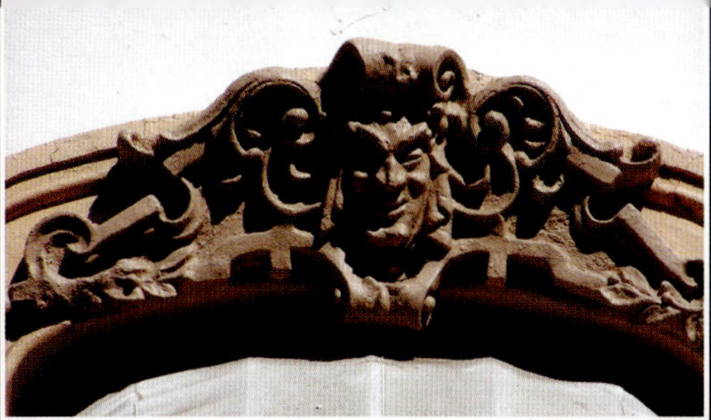

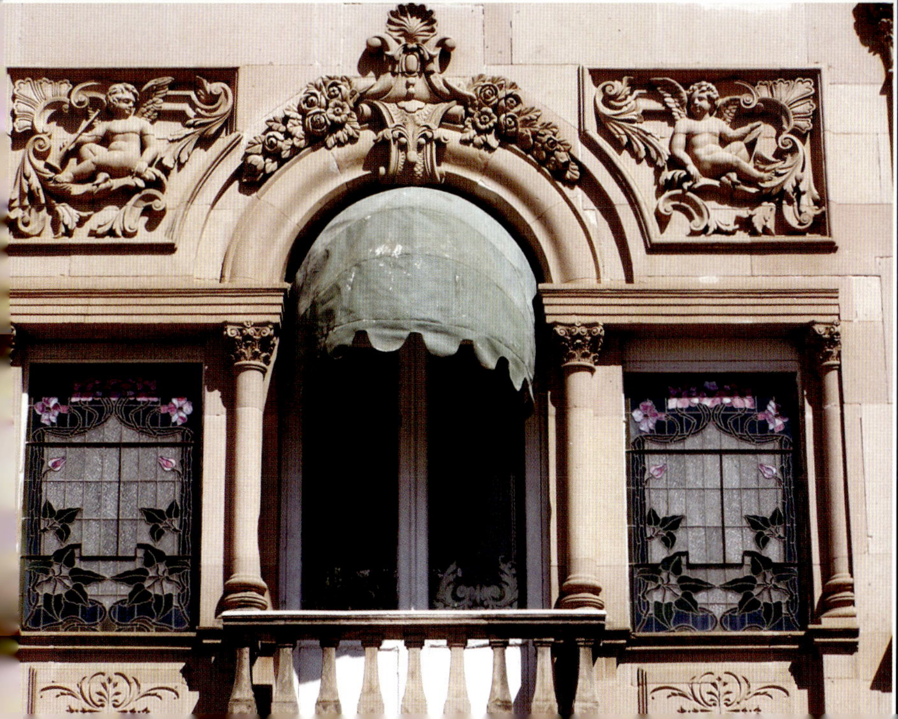

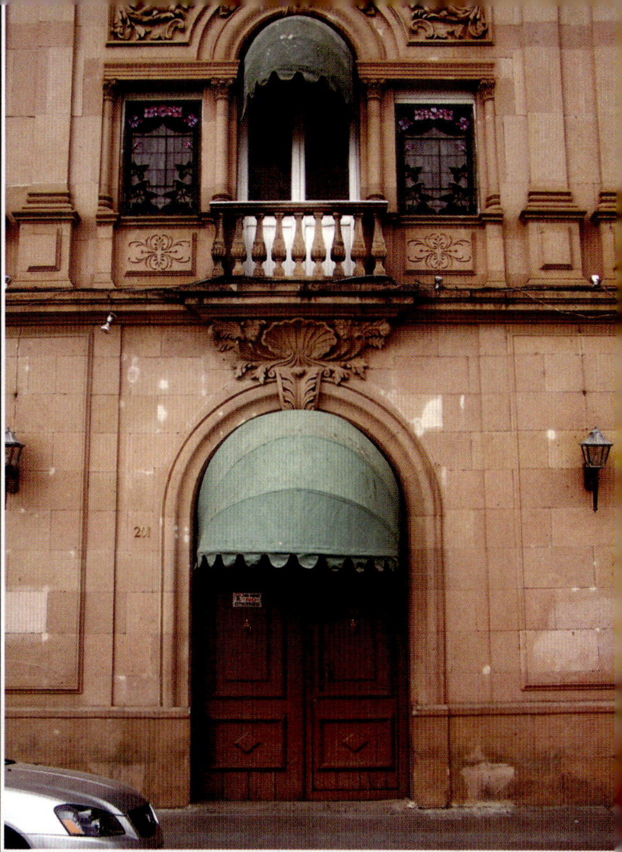

A local landmark located on the corner of Guerrero Street and Armenta y López Street.

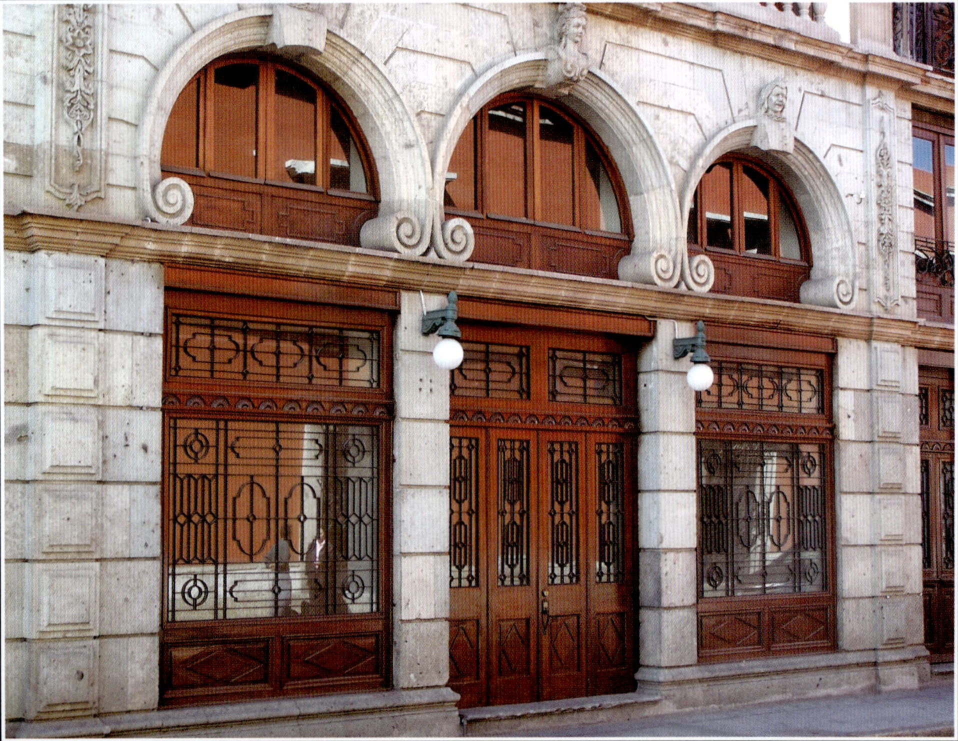

Macedonio Alcalá Theatre, located on the corner of Independencia Street and Armenta y López Street. Construction began in 1903 and was completed in 1909. Over its one hundred years, it has been a boxing and wrestling arena, circus tent, government inauguration hall, and movie theatre, among other things.

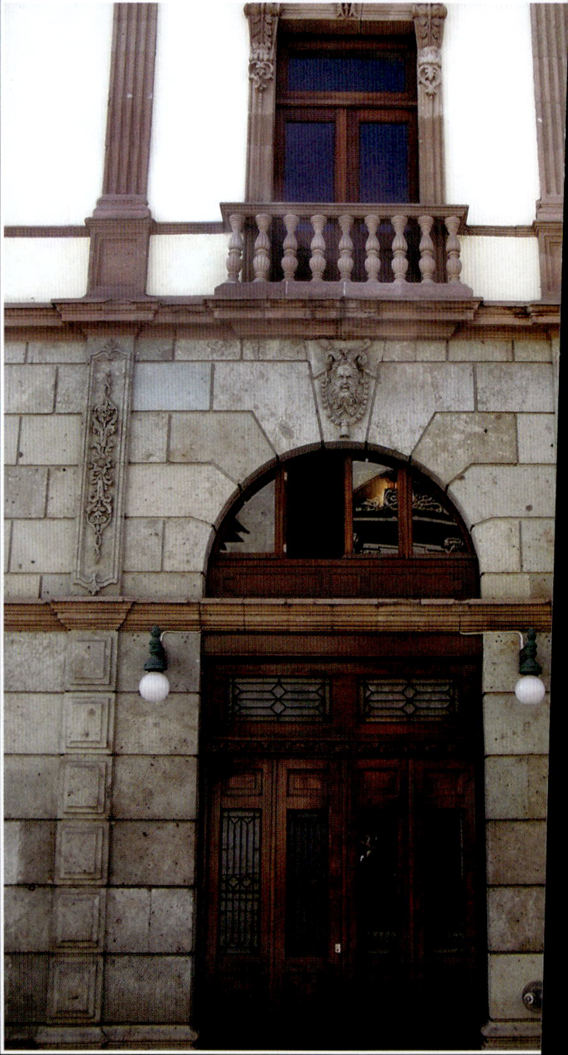

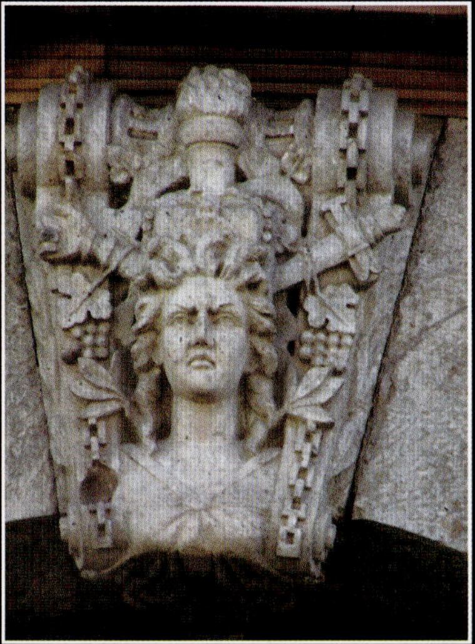
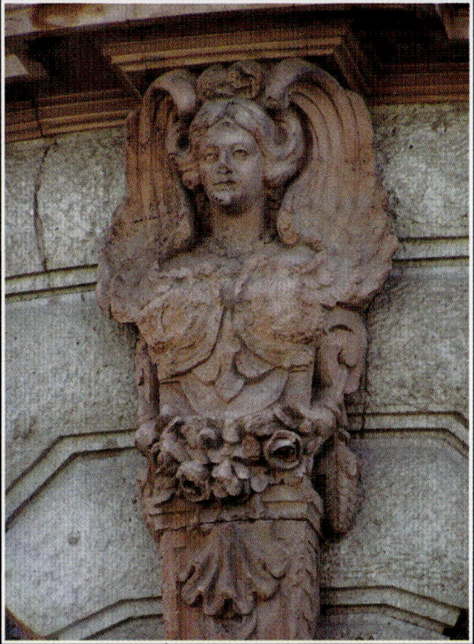
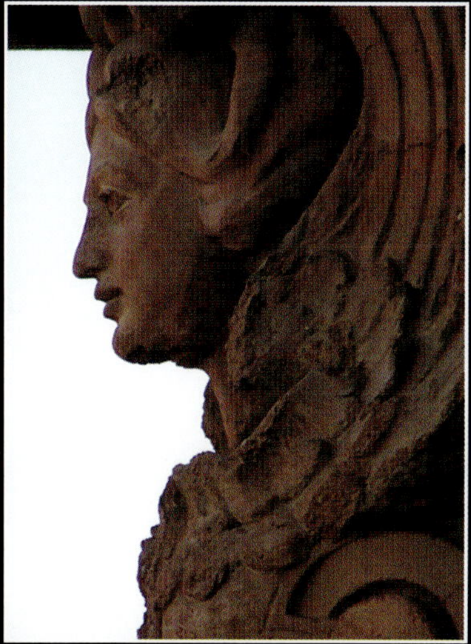
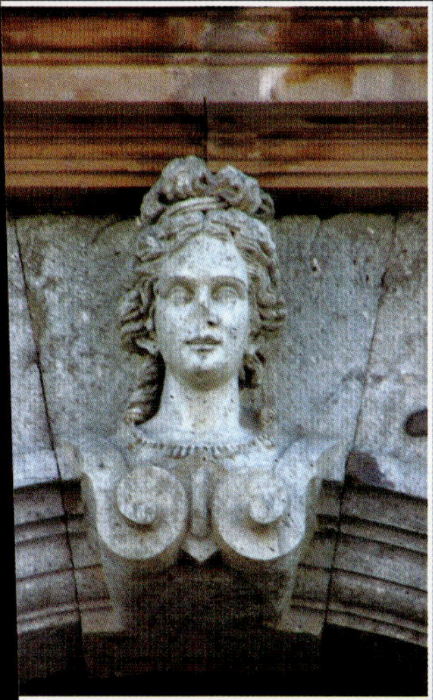
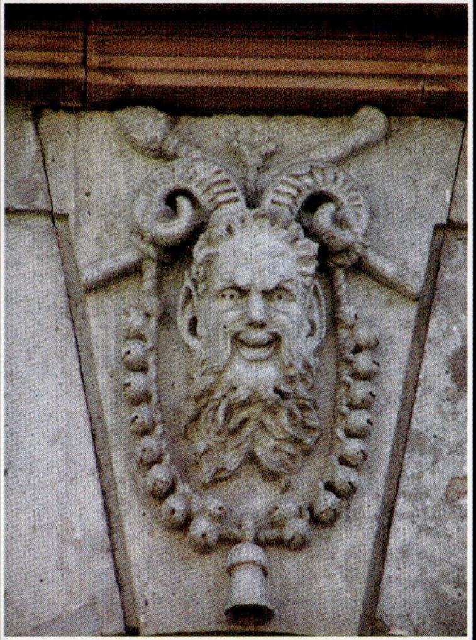
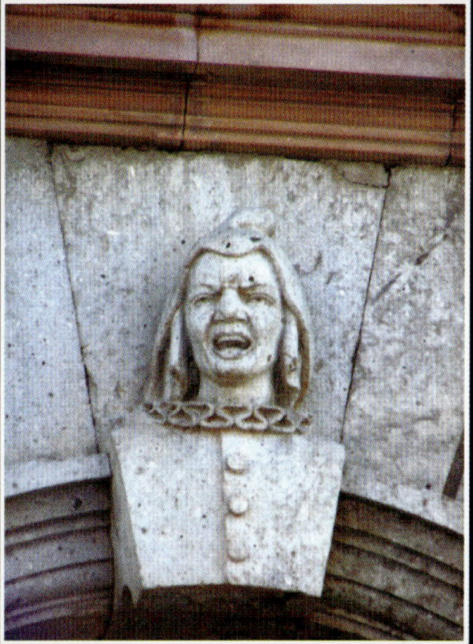
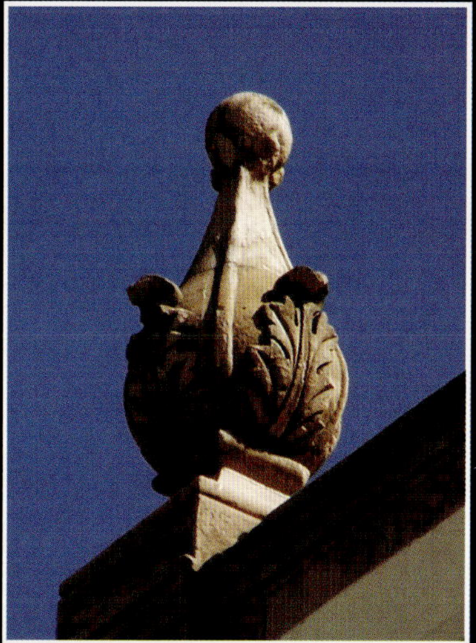

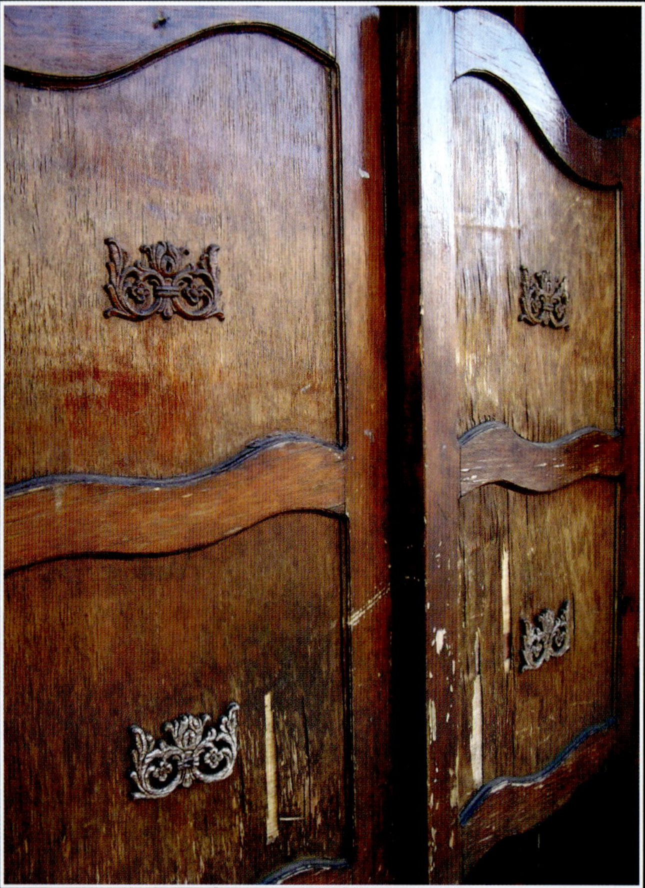

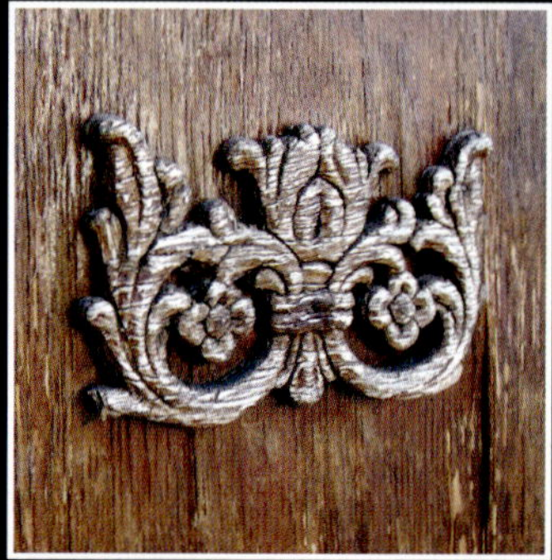

One of many local "men only" cantinas called, La Barca de Oro (The Gold Boat).

The window to a local barber shop.

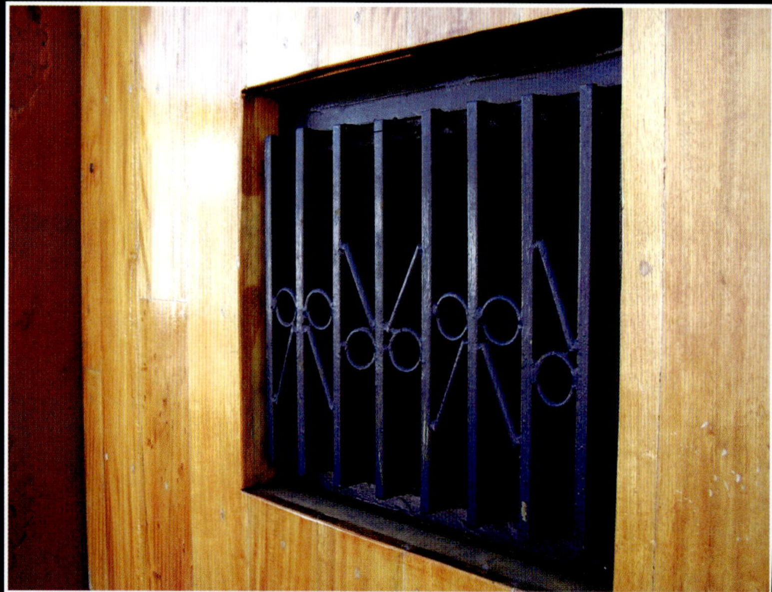

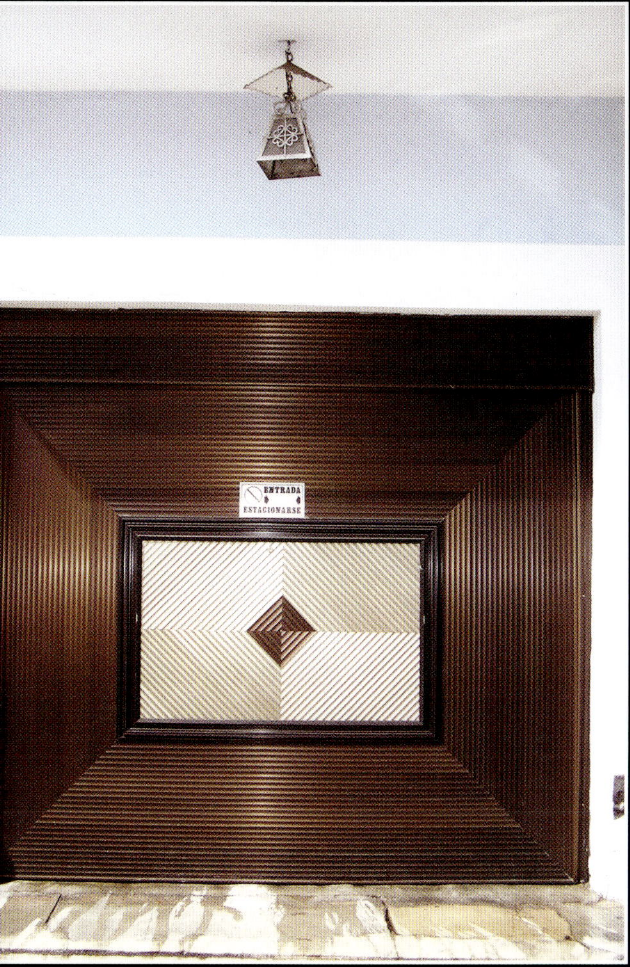
ENTRADA
ESTACIONARSE

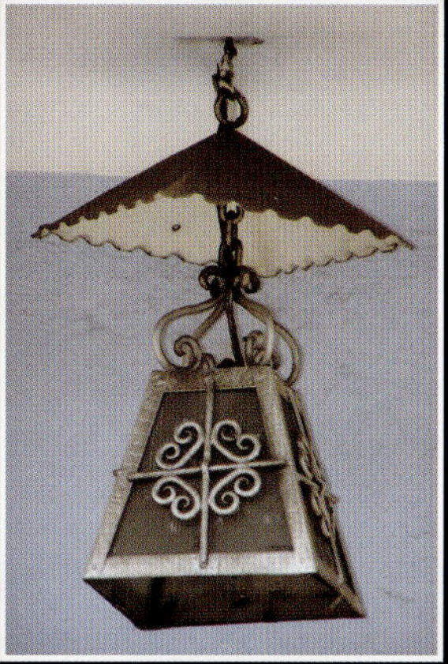

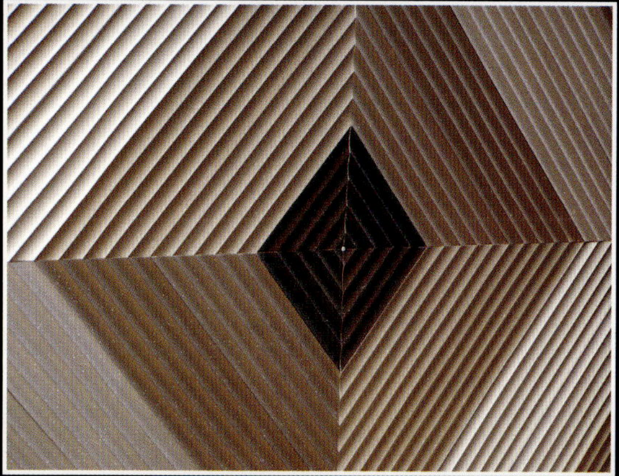

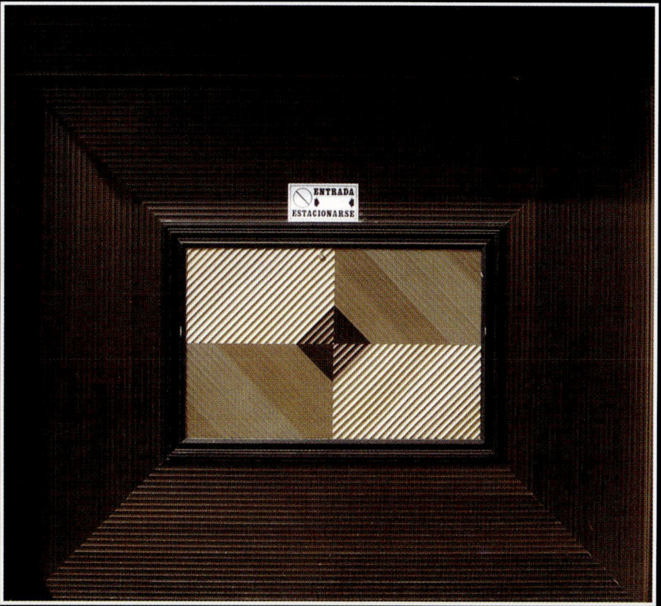
ENTRADA
ESTACIONARSE

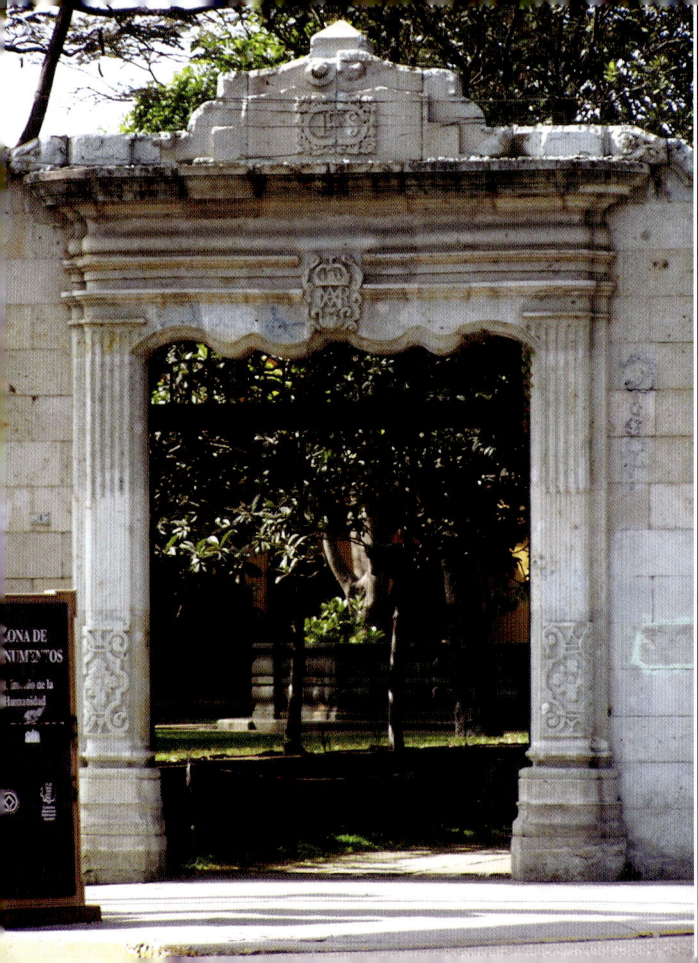

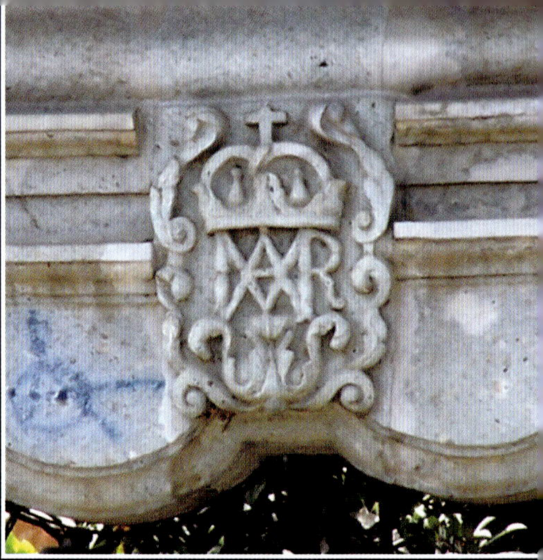

This building is a language school located on the corner of International Highway and Avenida Juárez Street. Avenida Juárez was named after Benito Juárez, an Oaxacan who became the most famous President in Mexican history.

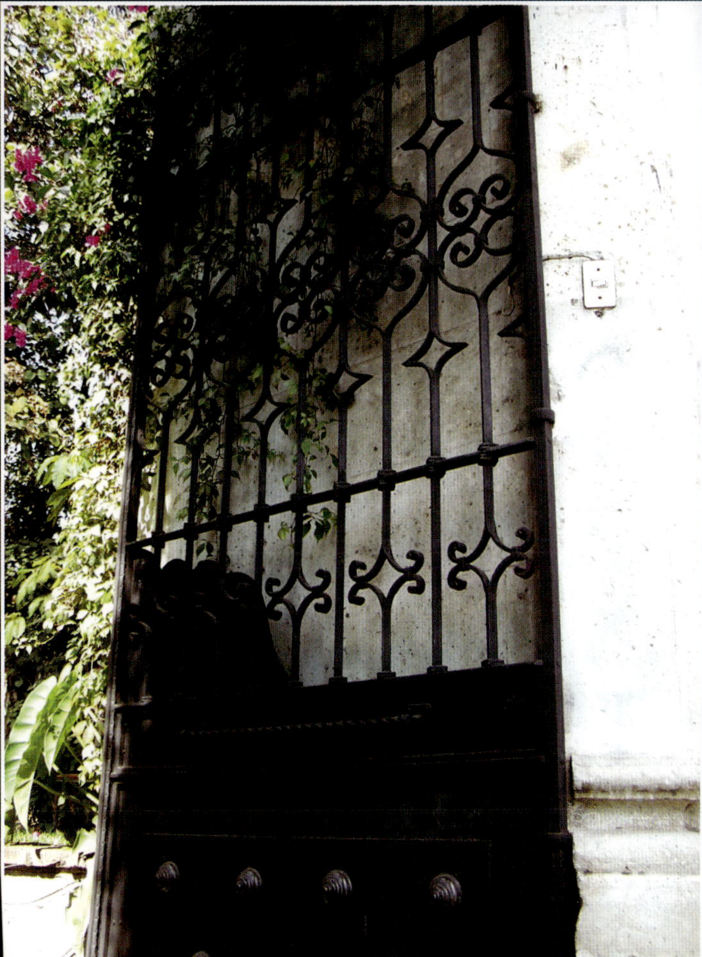

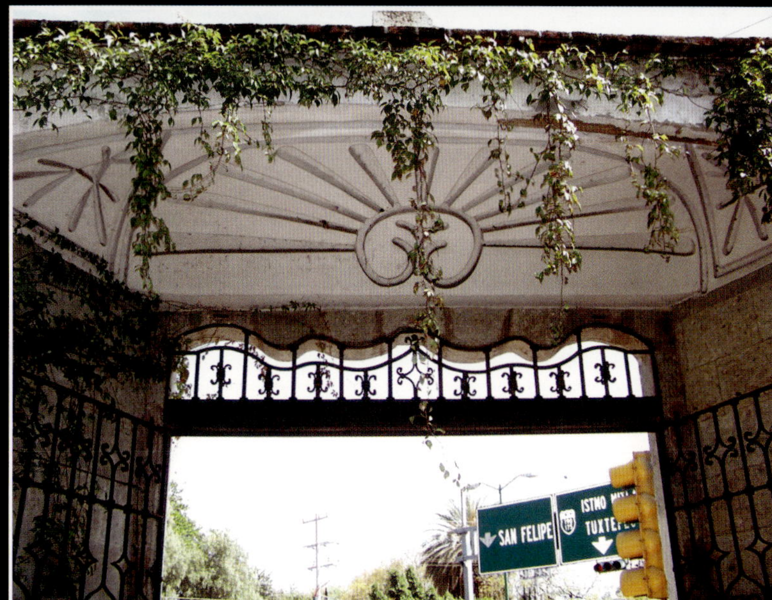

SAN FELIPE
ISTMO

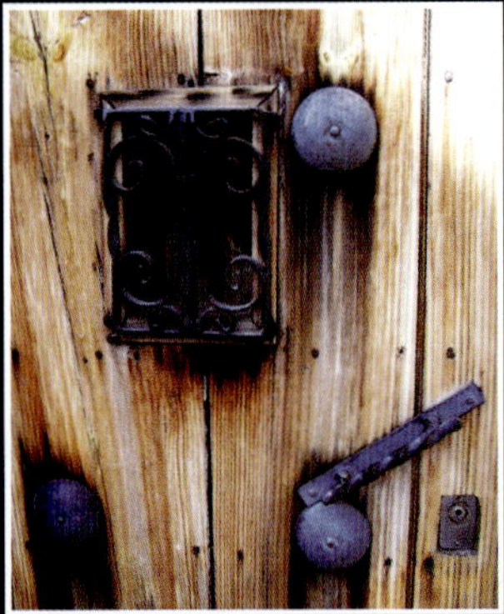

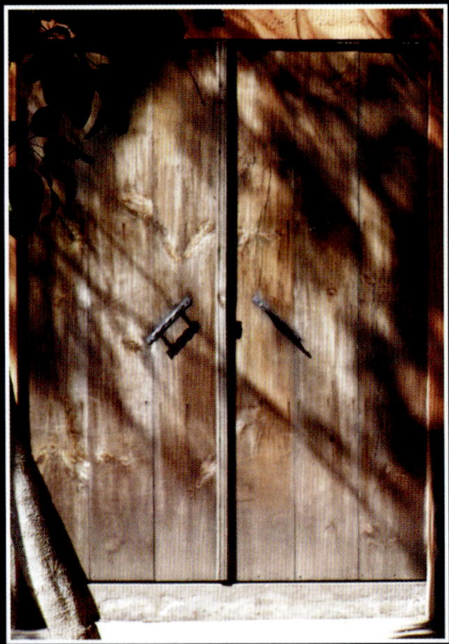

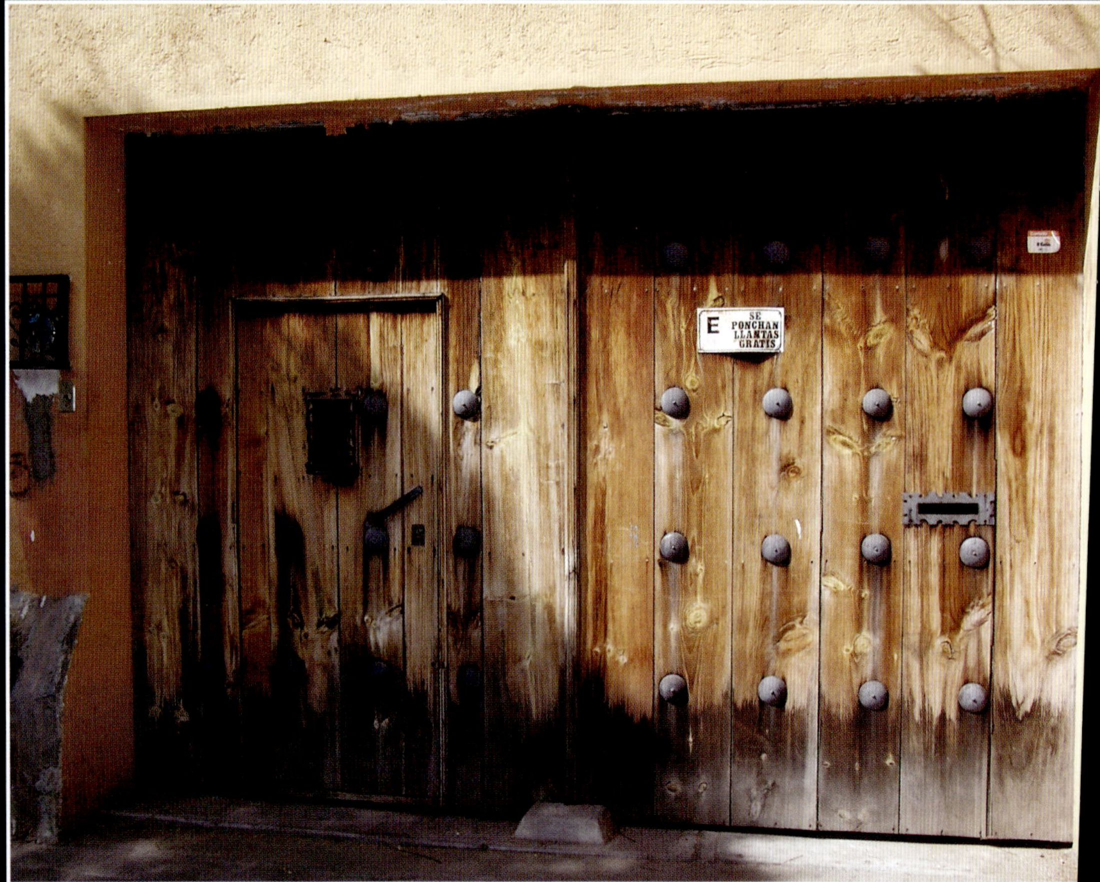
E
SE
PONCHAN
LLANTAS
GRATIS

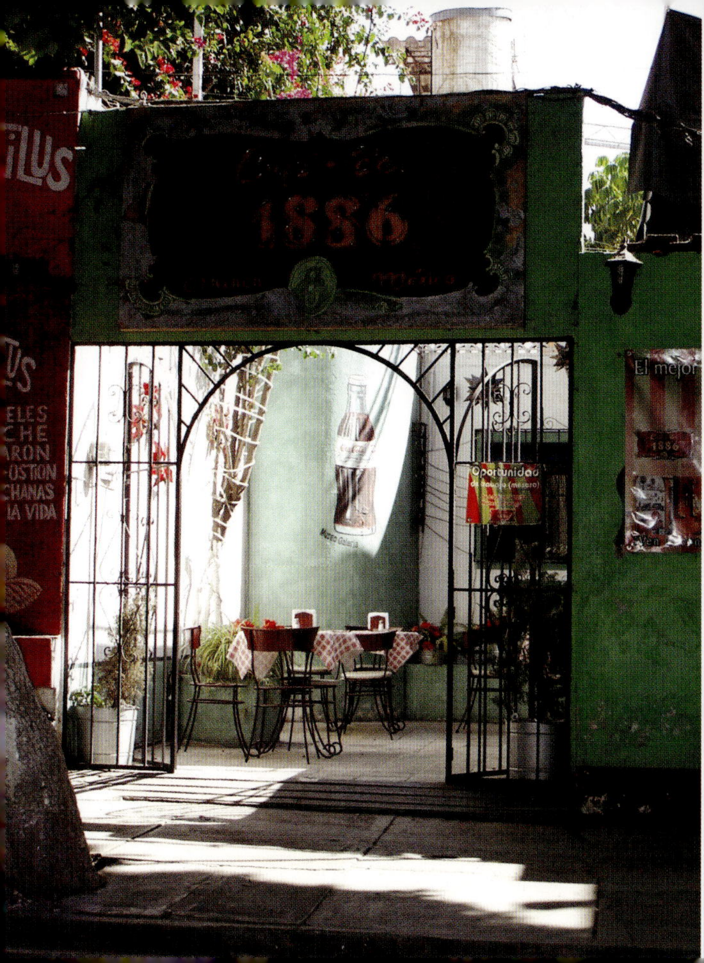

A small outdoor café on Reforma Street in front of the Conzzati Garden.

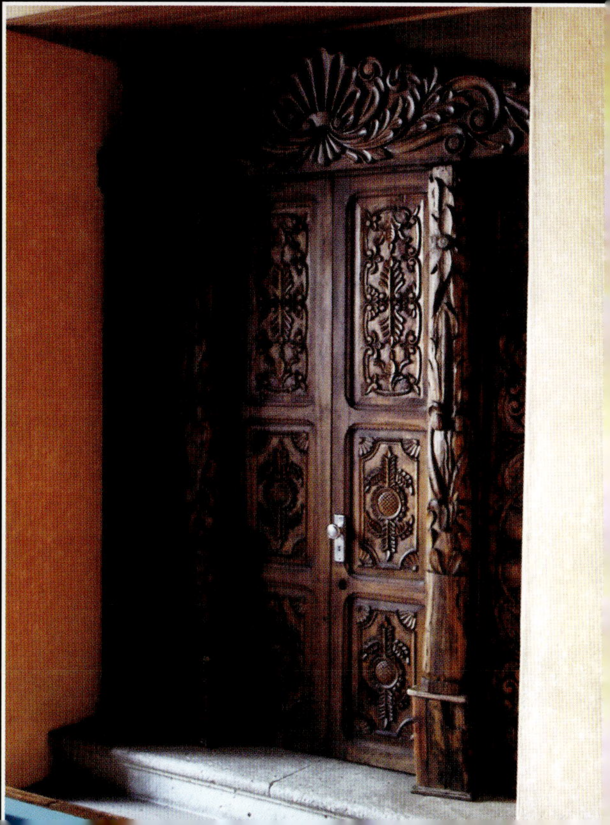

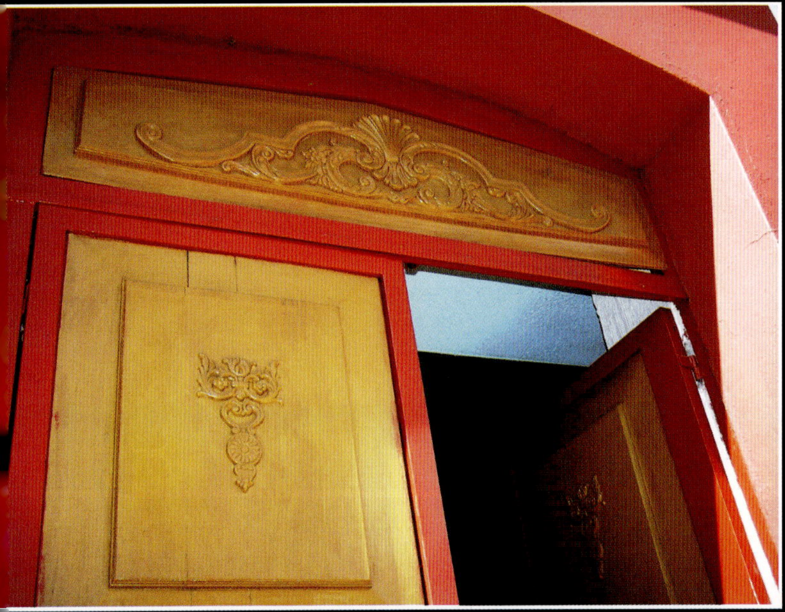

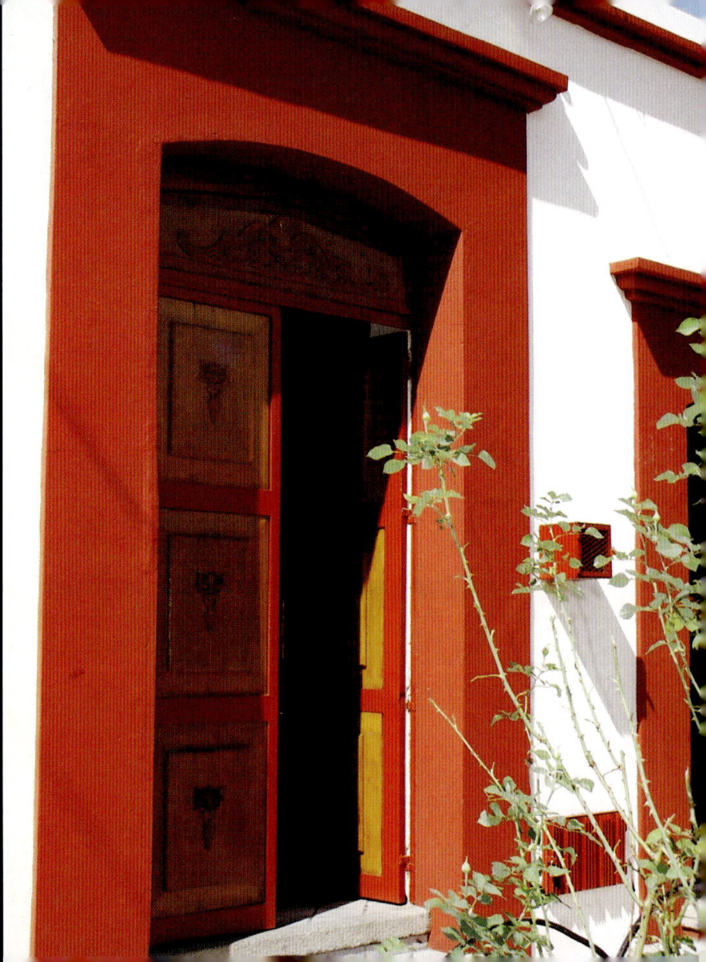

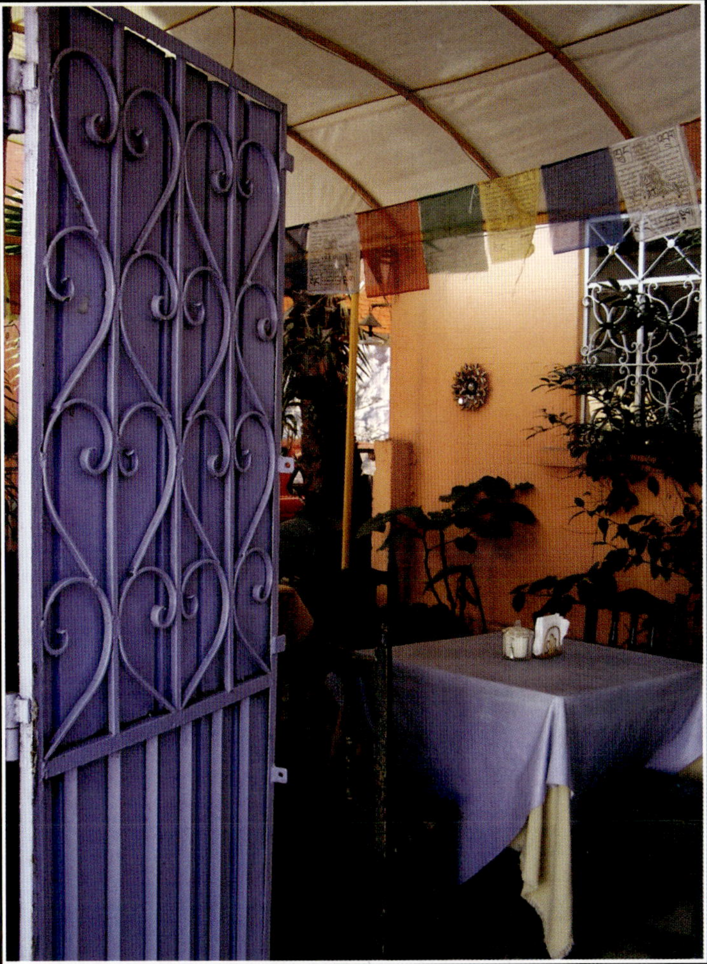

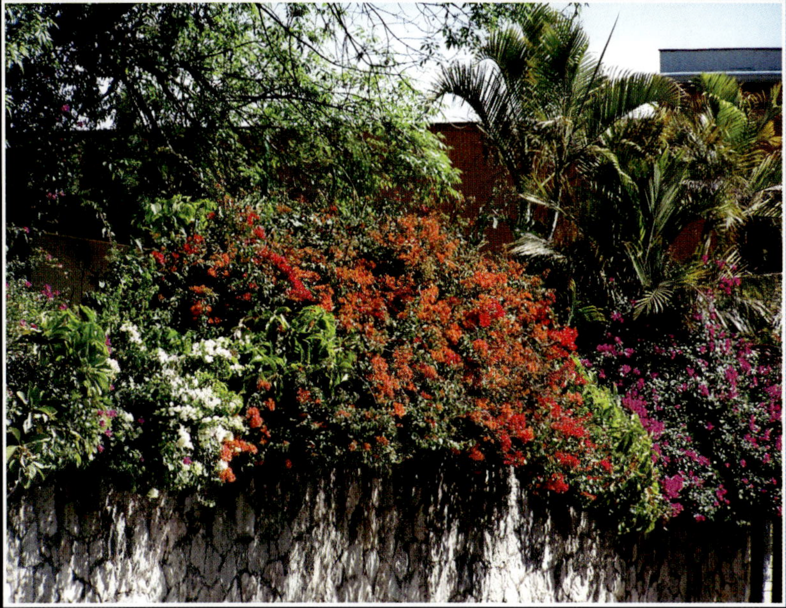

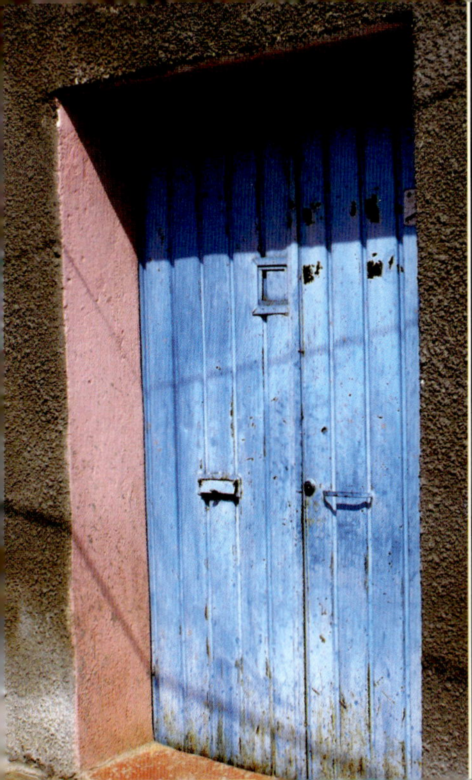

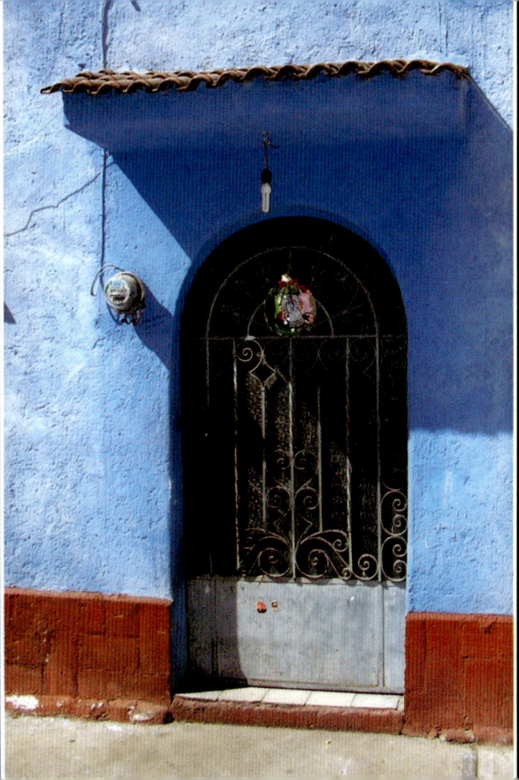

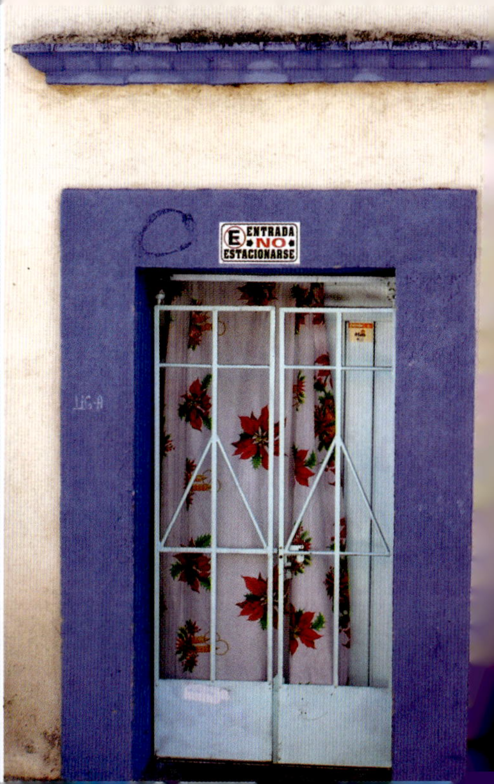
E
ENTRADA
NO
ESTACIONARSE

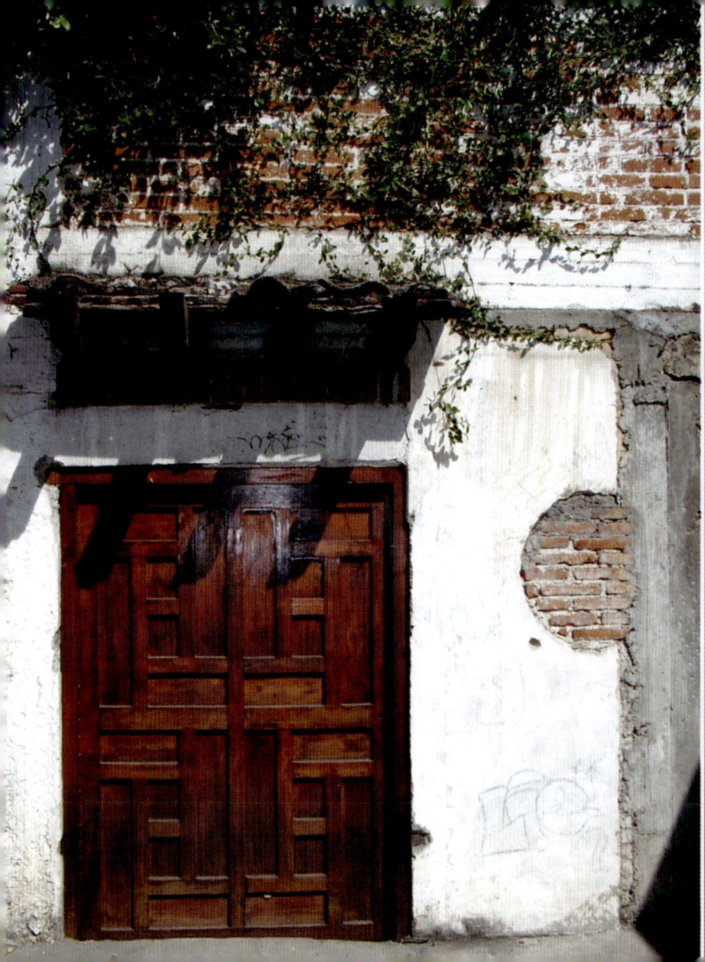
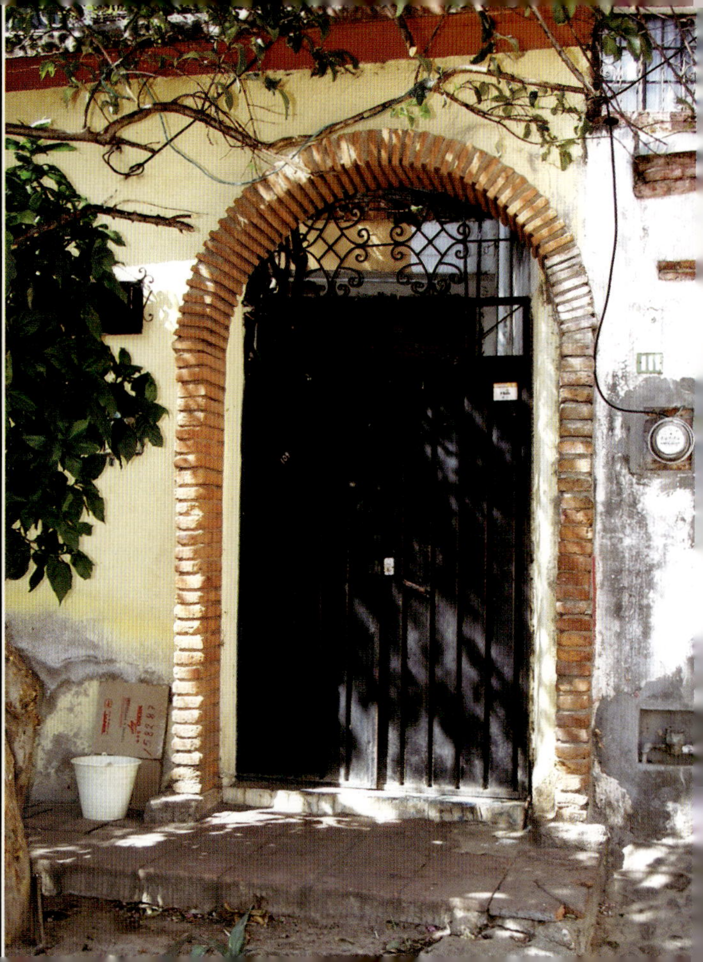

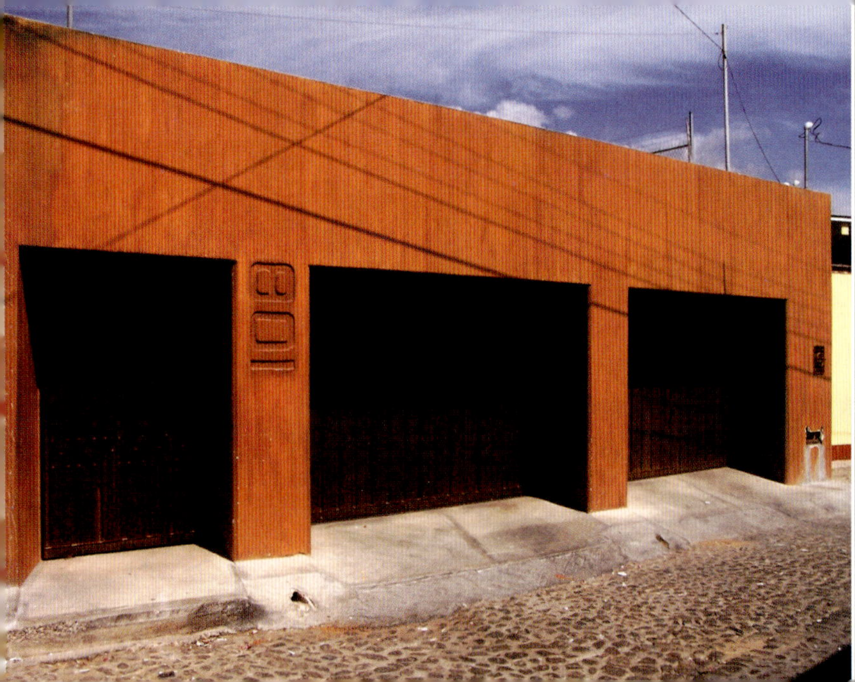

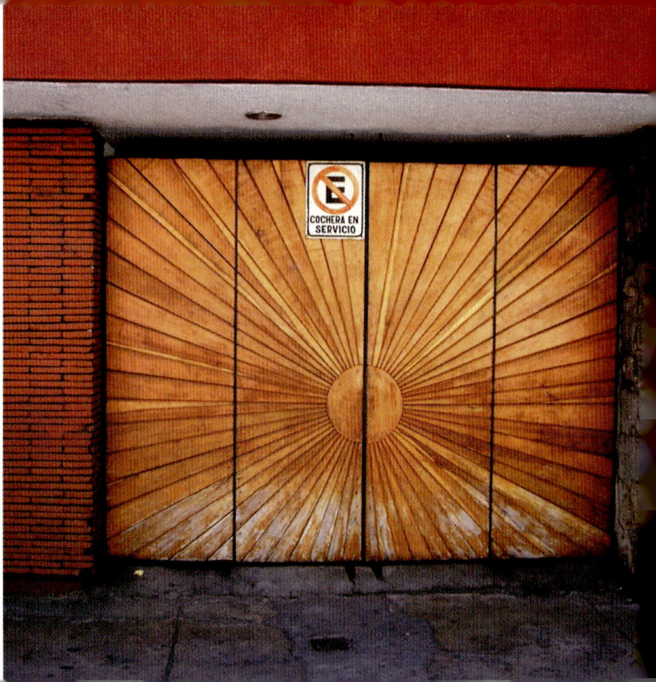
COCHERA EN
SERVICIO

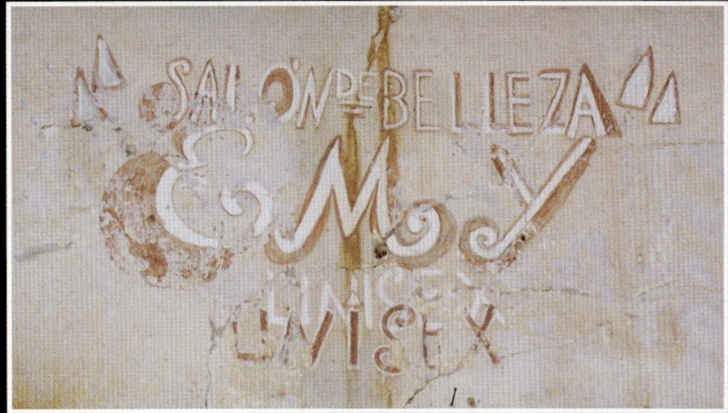
SALÓN DE BELLEZA
UNISEX

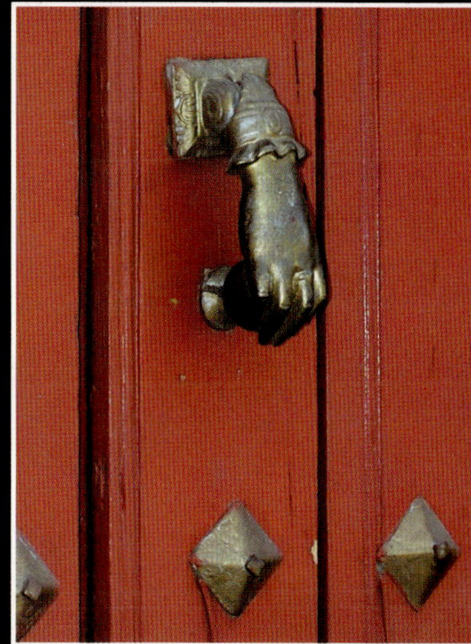

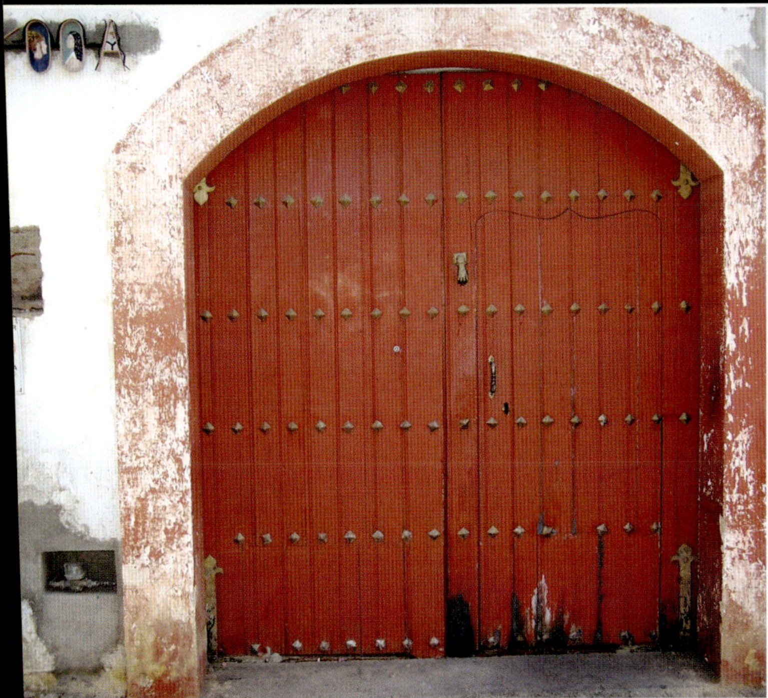

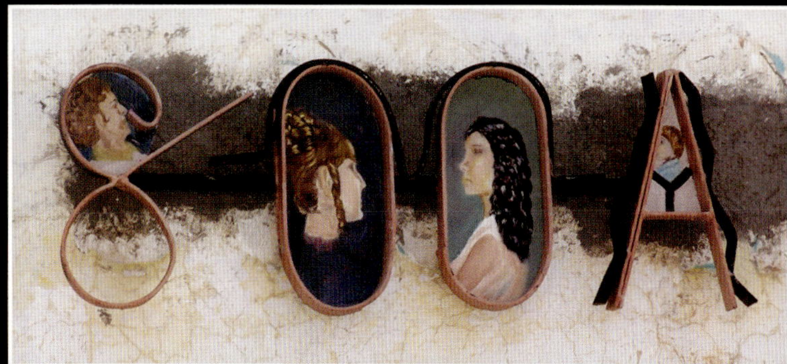

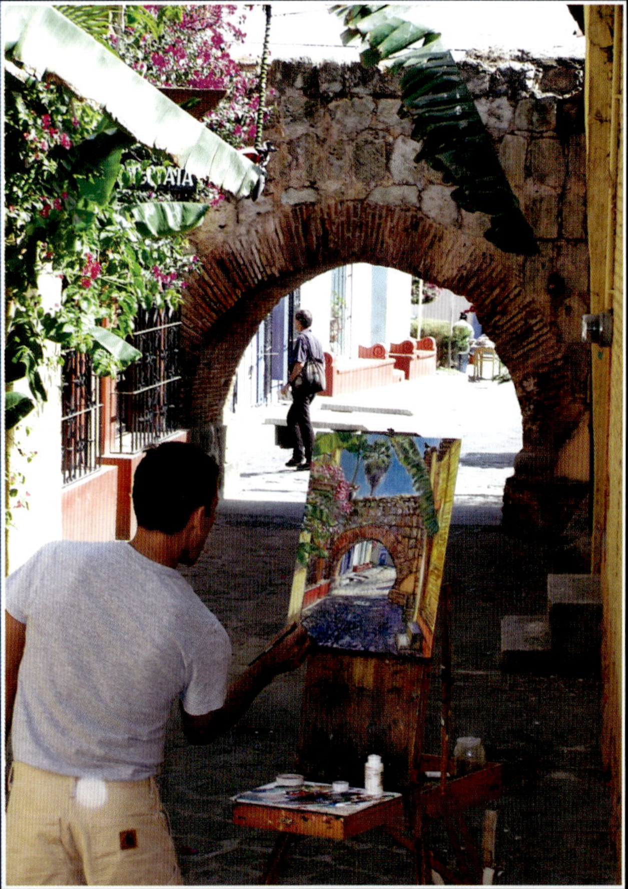

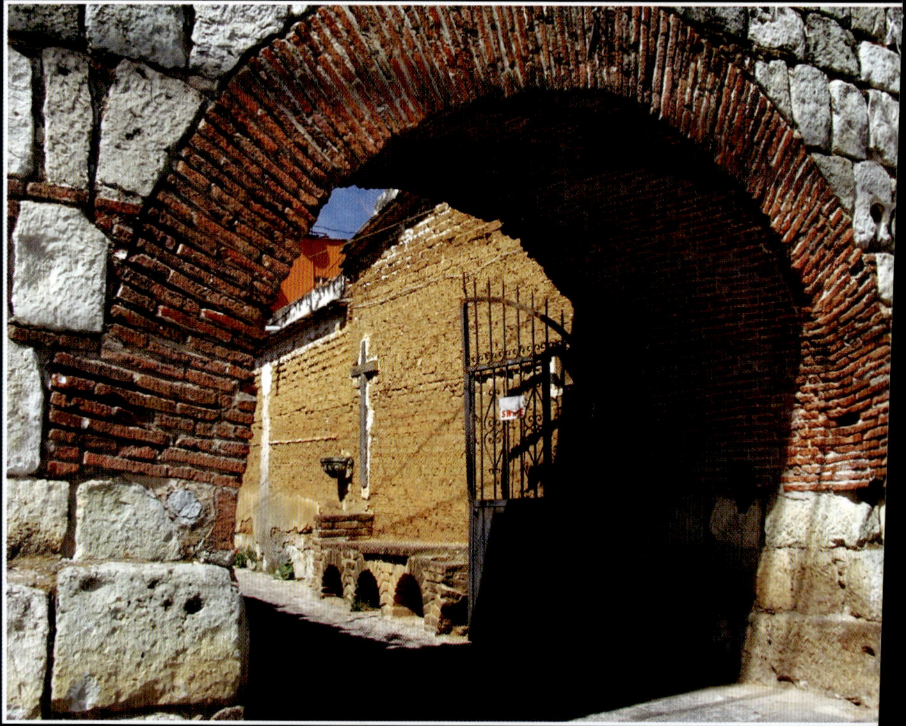

The ancient aqueduct that used to feed water to Oaxaca.

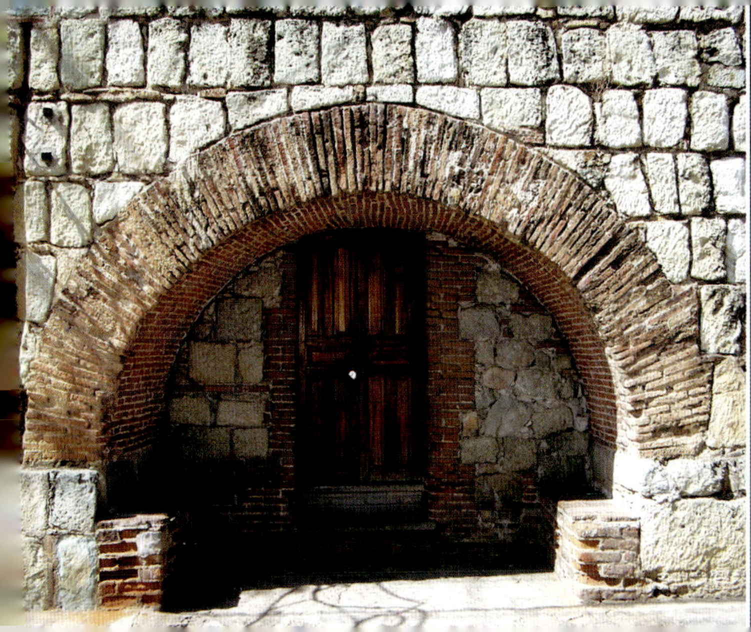

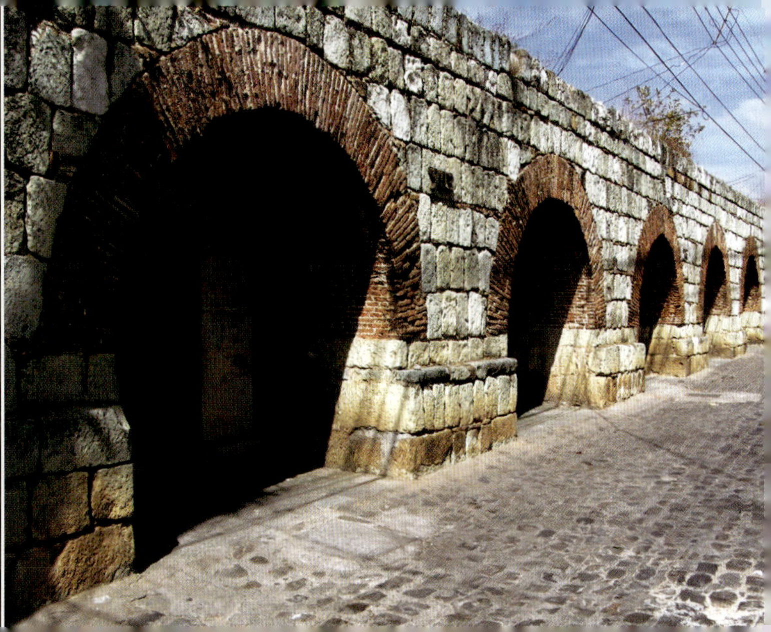

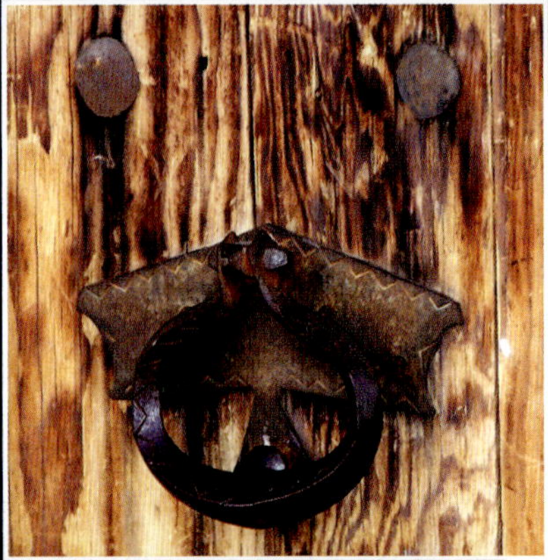

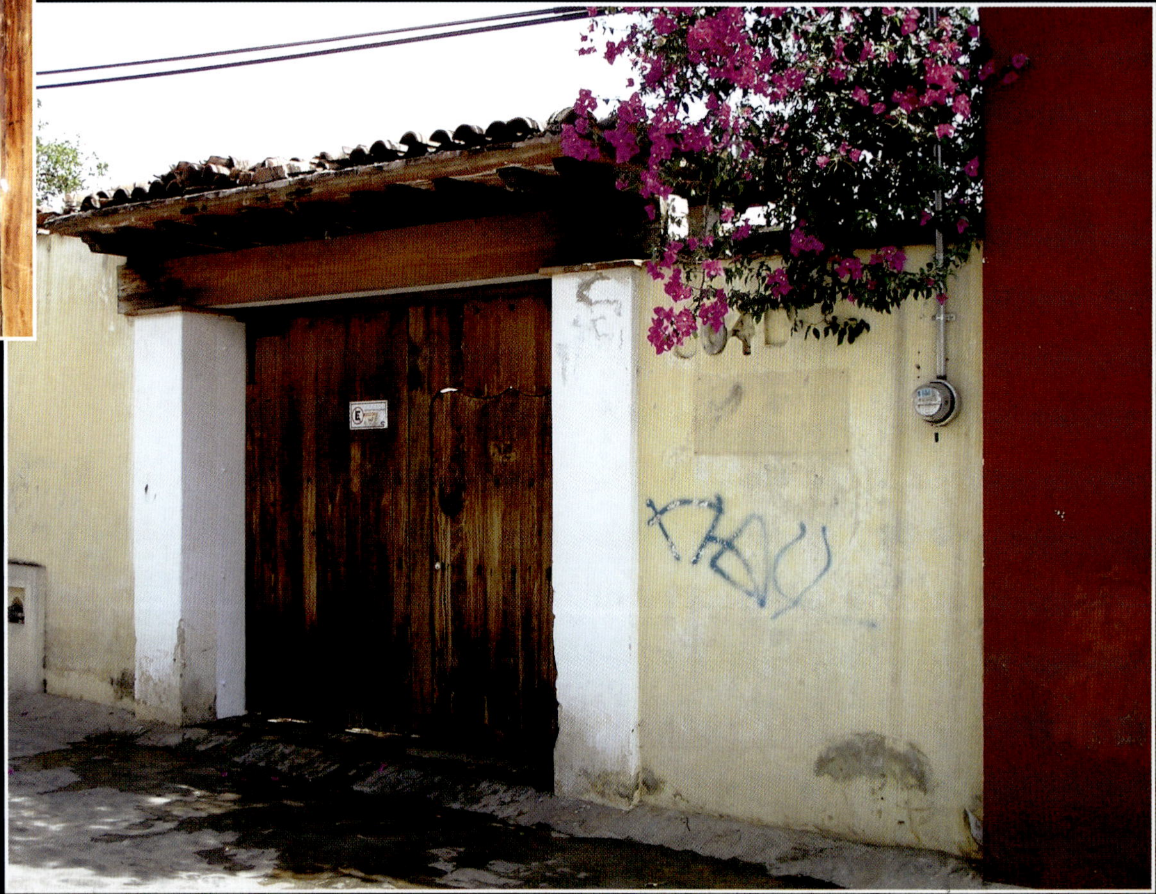

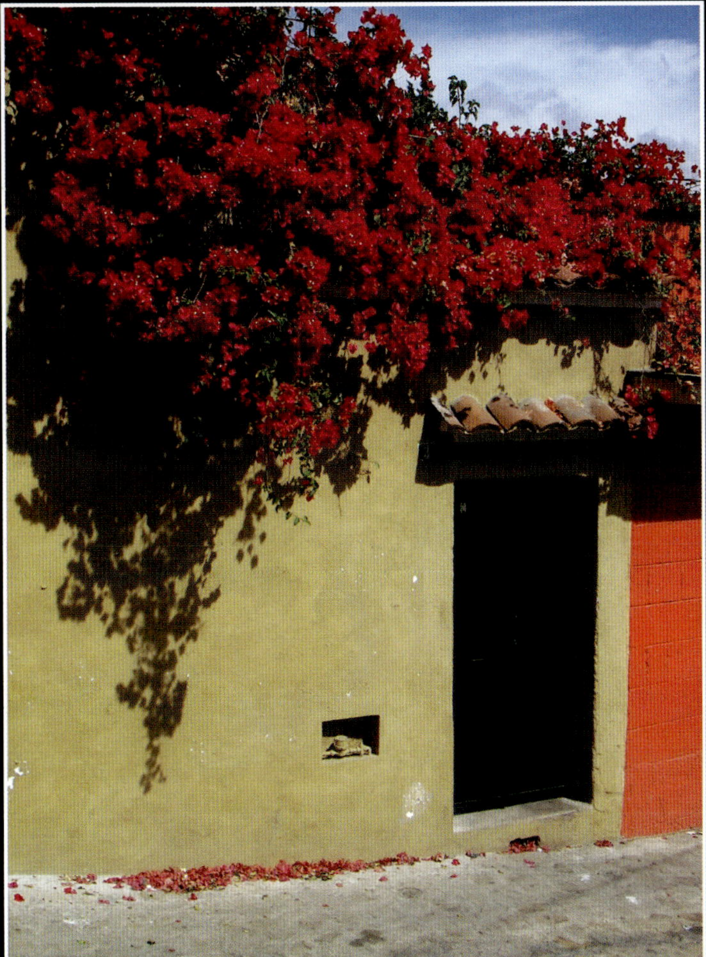

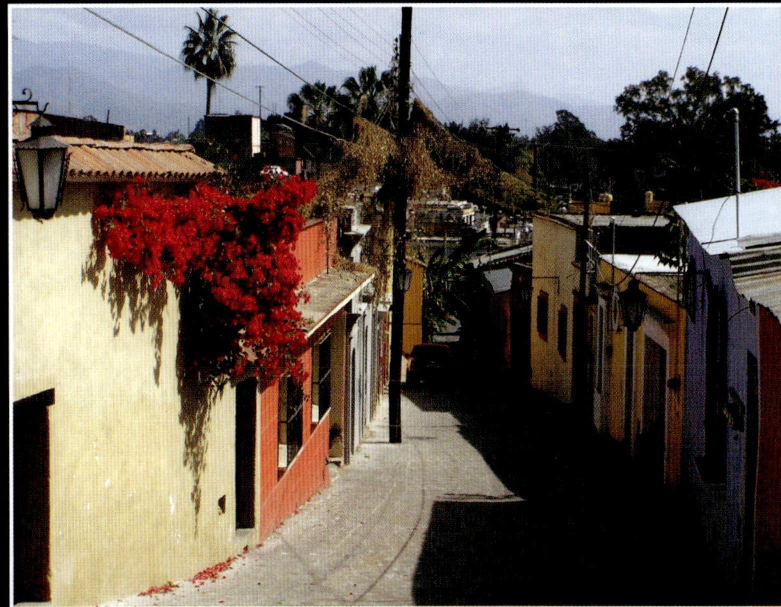

Marcos Pérez Street.

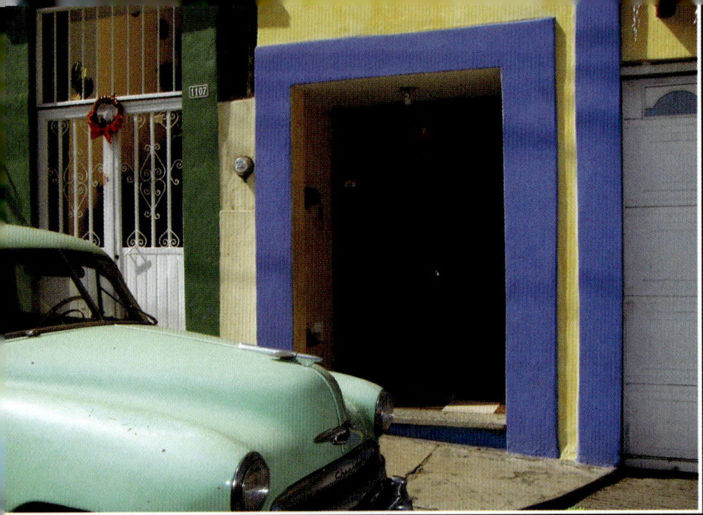
1107

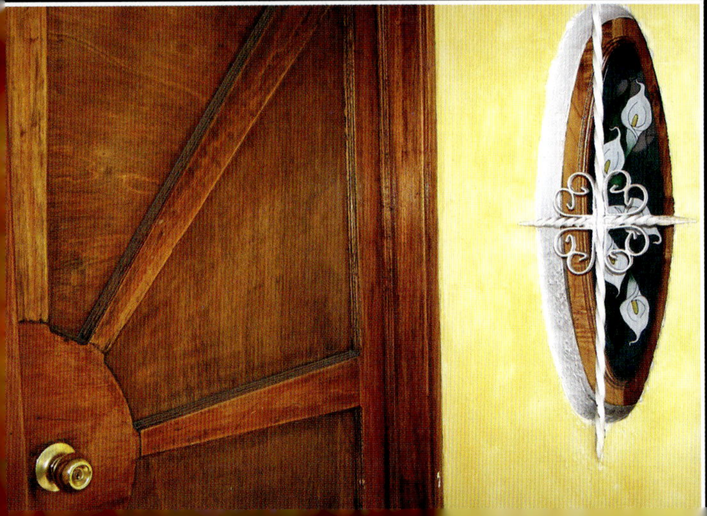

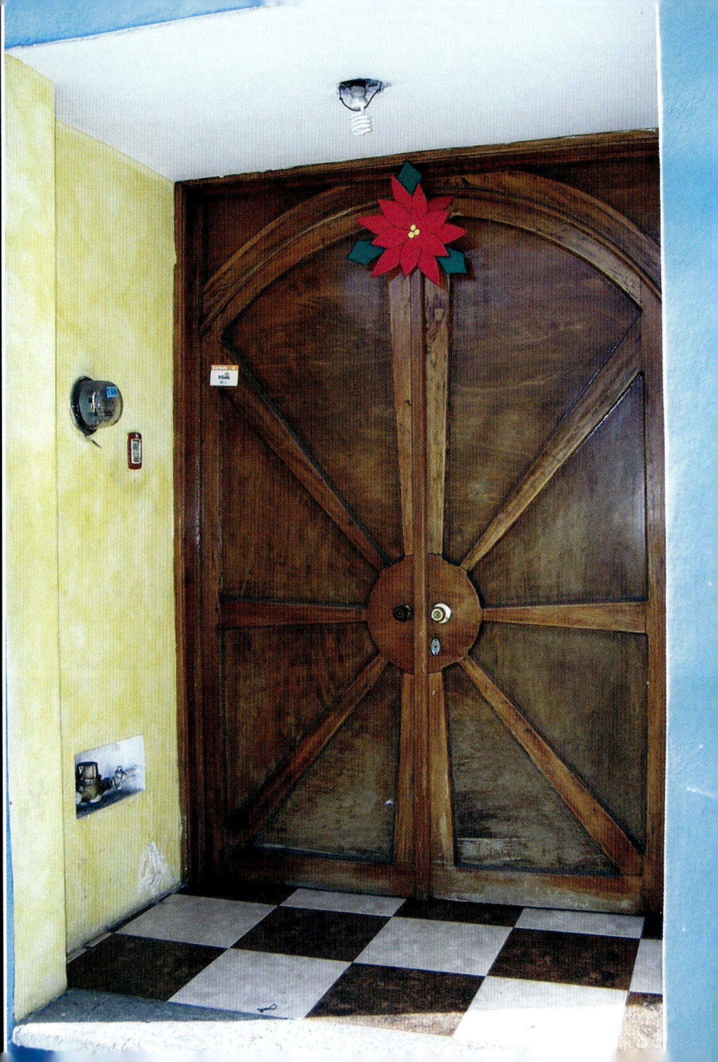

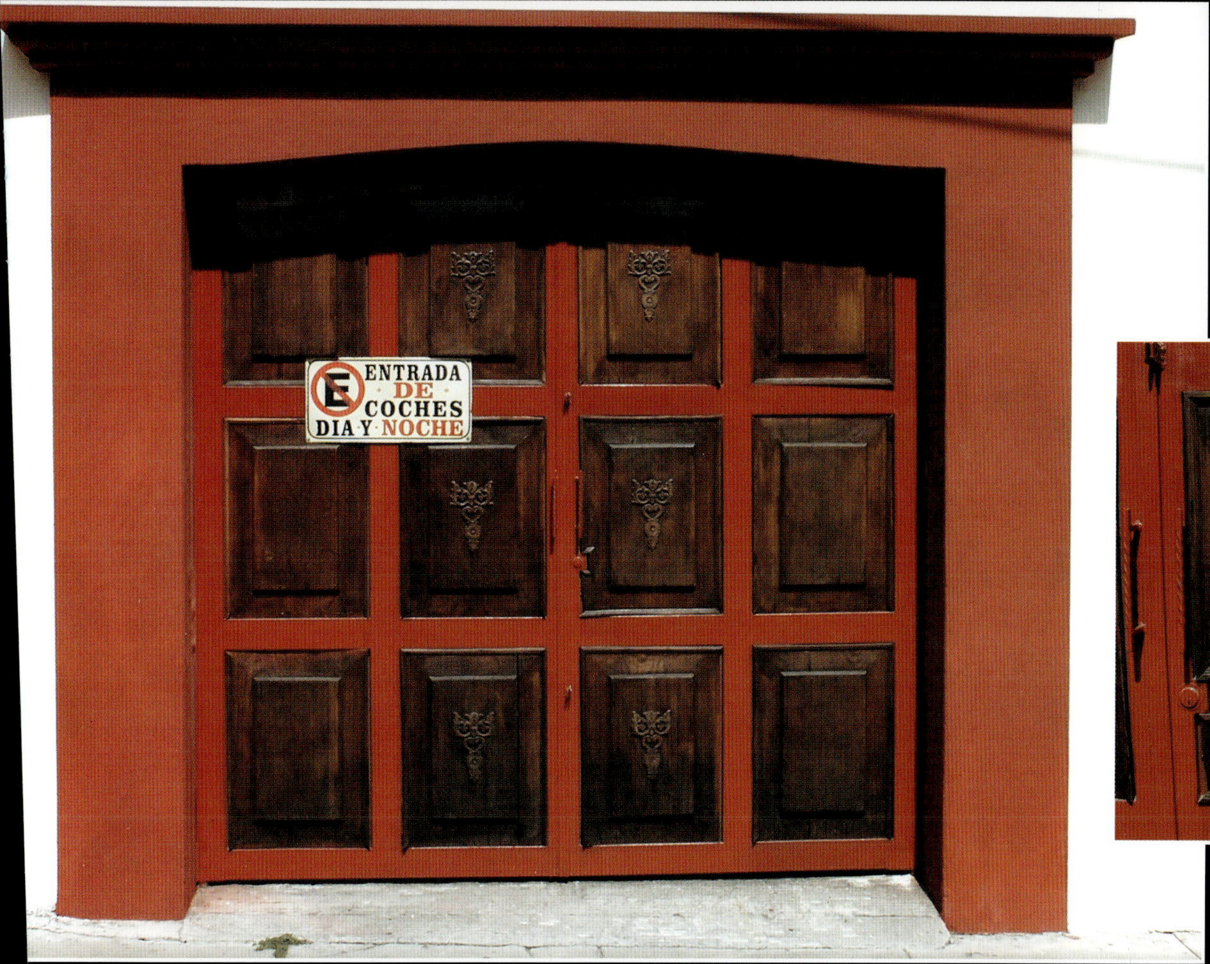
ENTRADA
DE
COCHES
DIA Y NOCHE

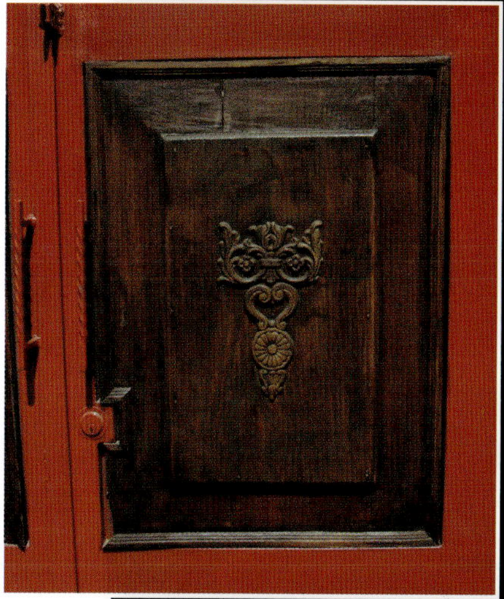

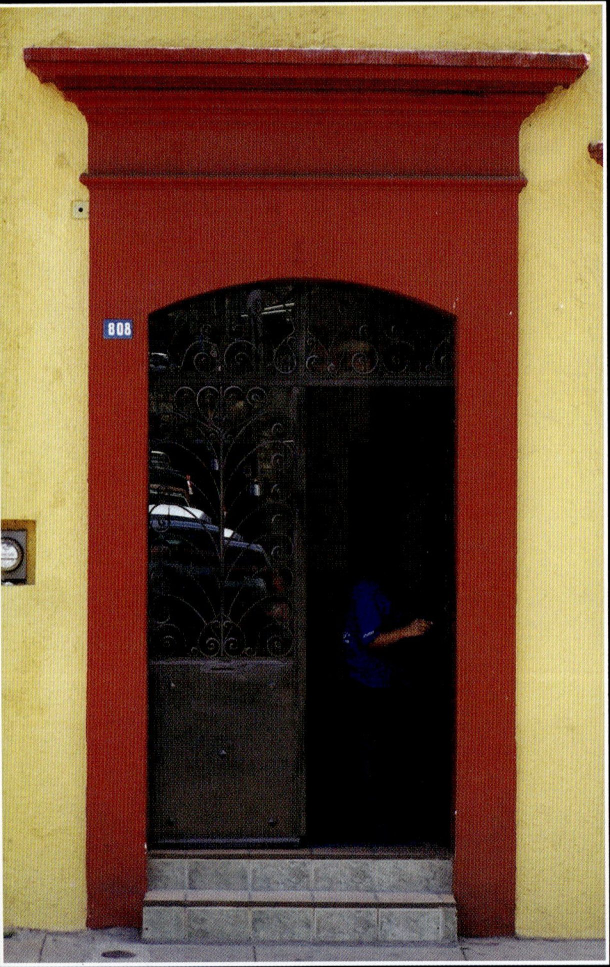

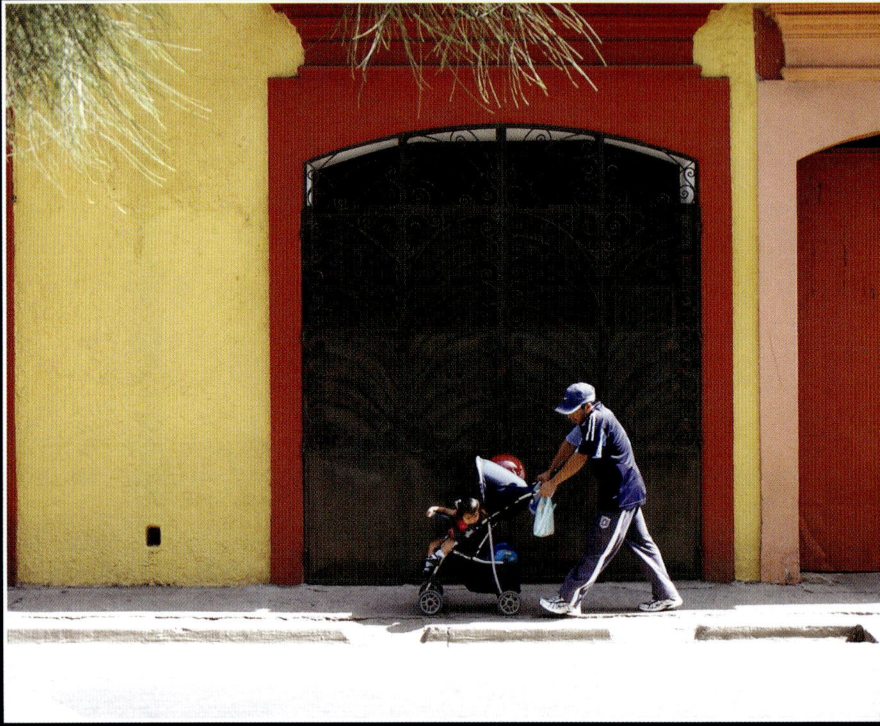

A medical center located on Macedonio Alcalá Street.

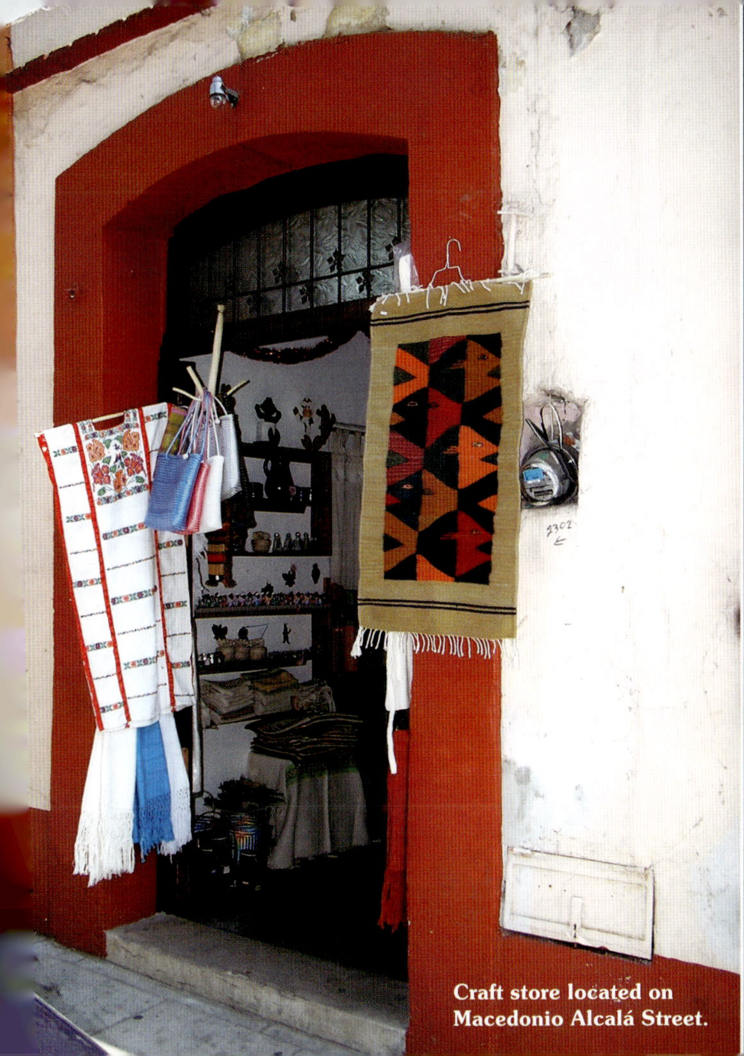
Craft store located on Macedonio Alcalá Street.

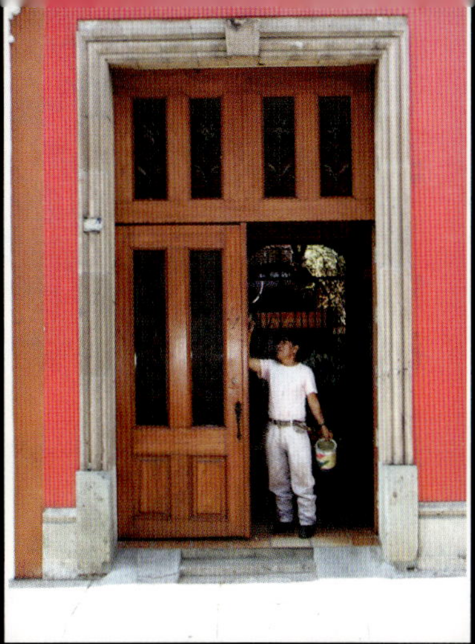

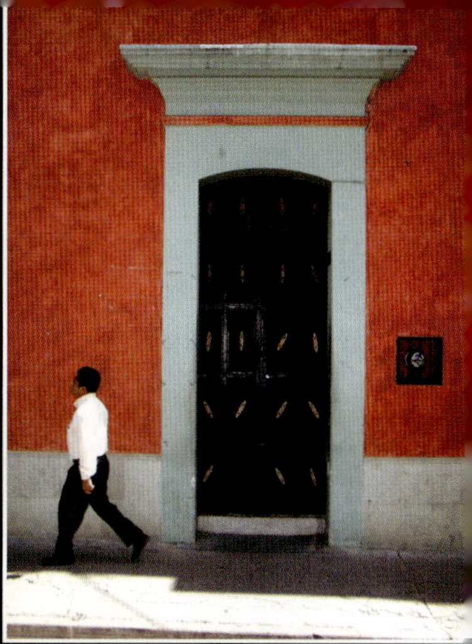

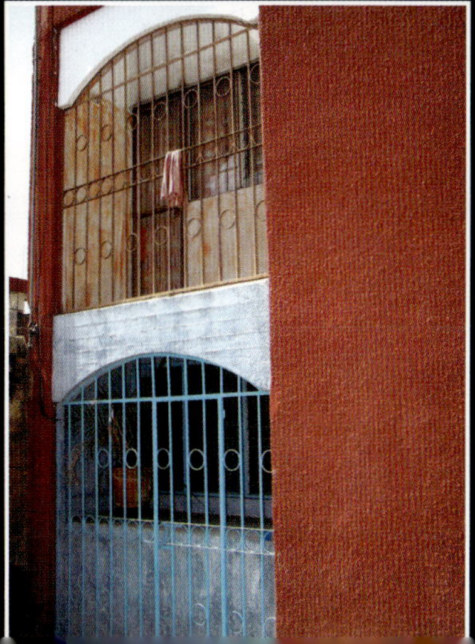

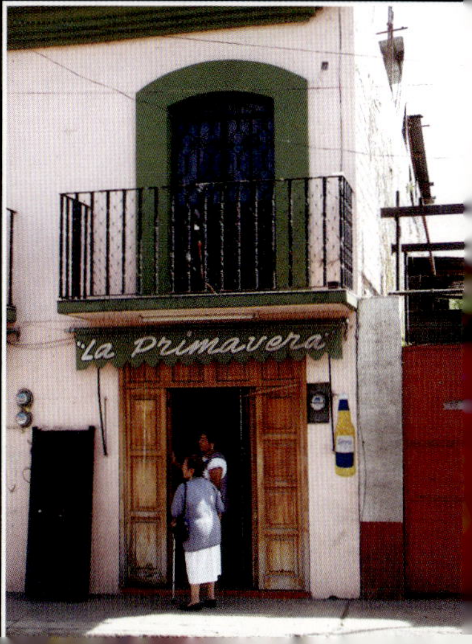

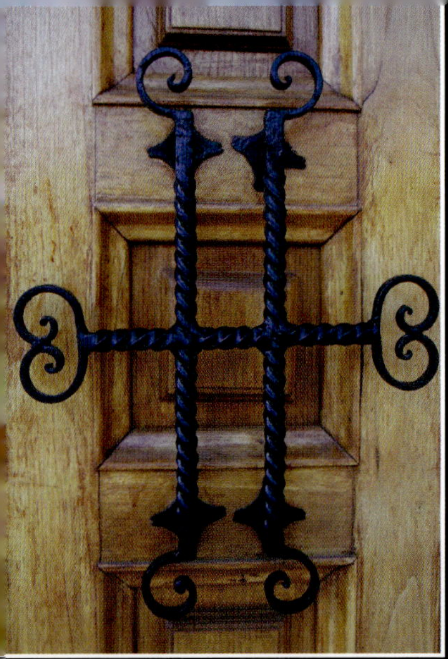
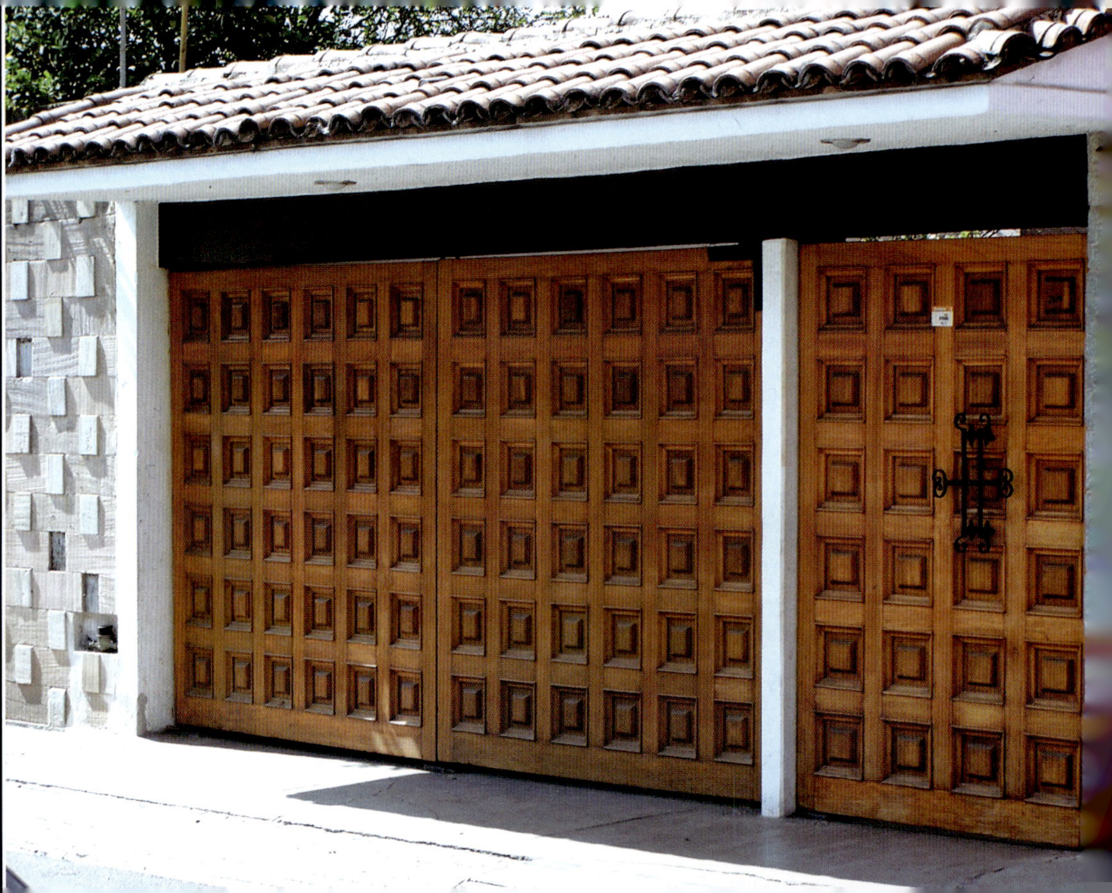

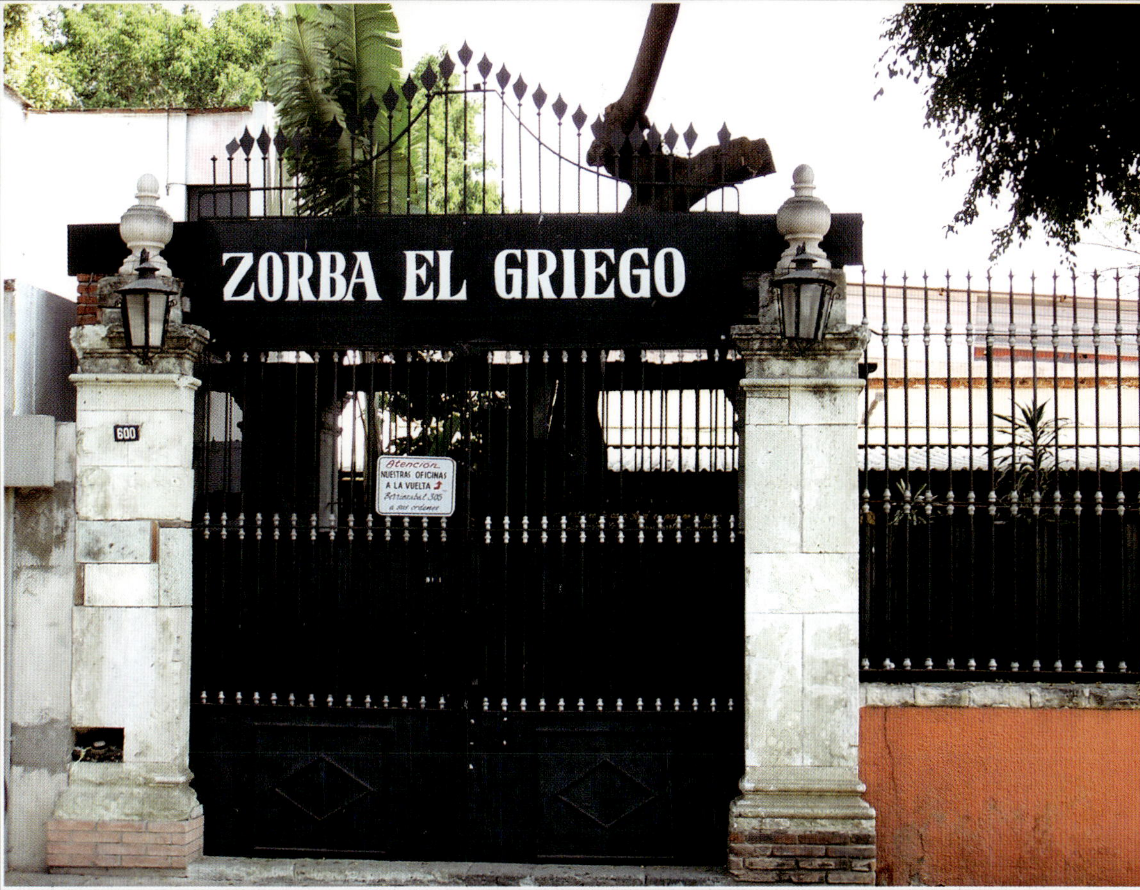

A banquet hall called "Zorba the Greek," located on the corner of Berriozábal Street and Reforma Street.

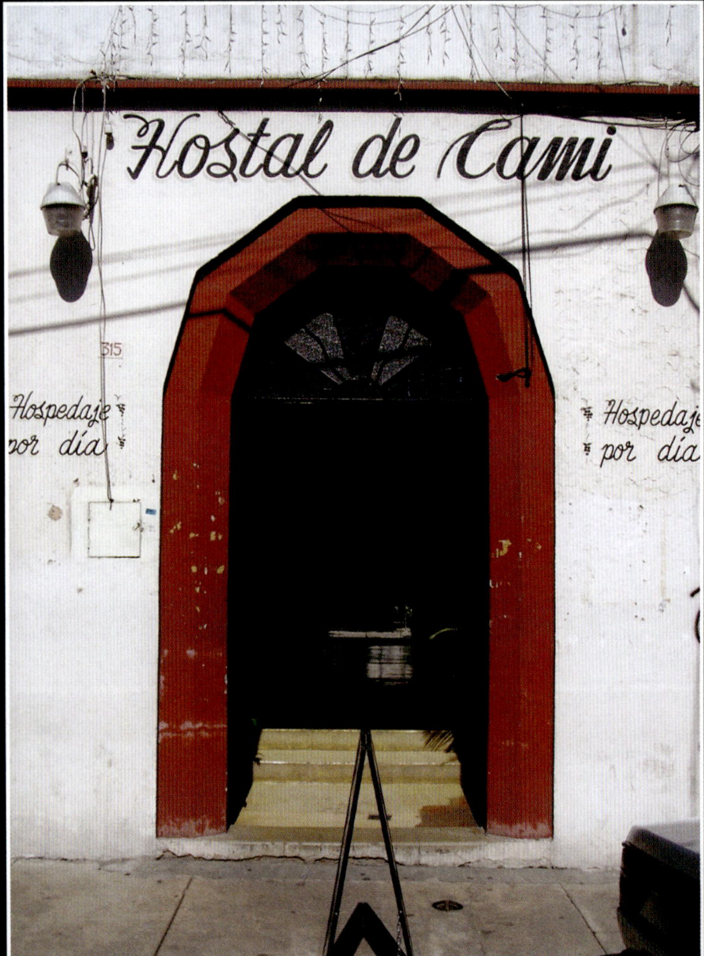
Hostal de Cami
315
Hospedaje
por día
Hospedaje
por día
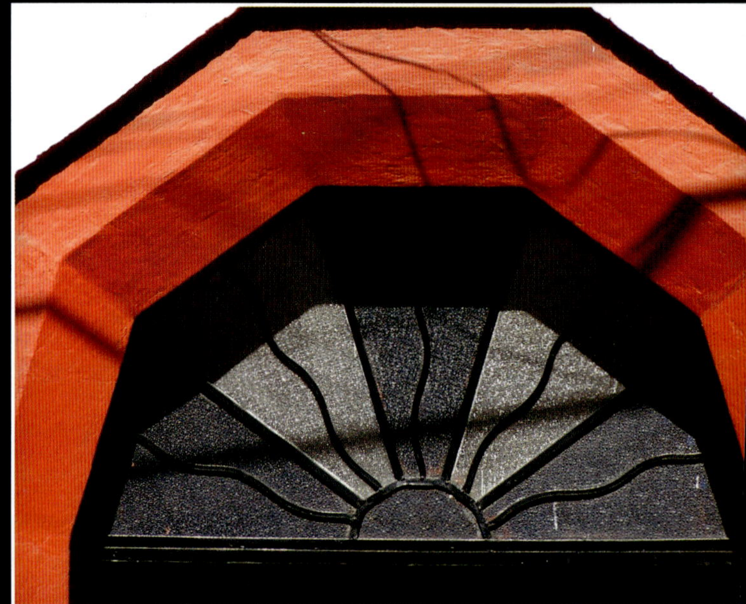

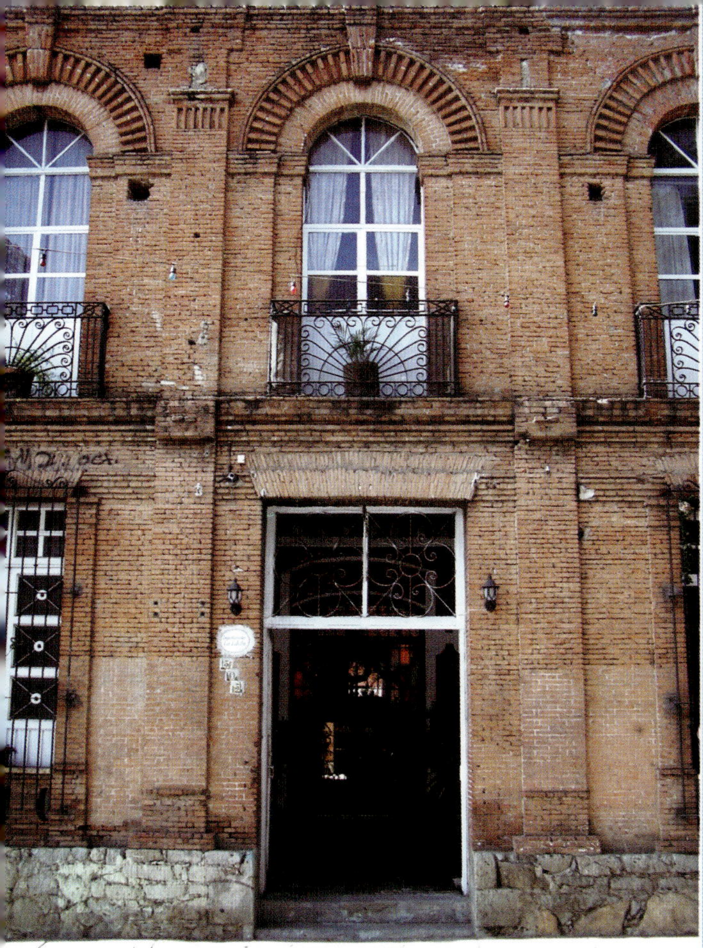

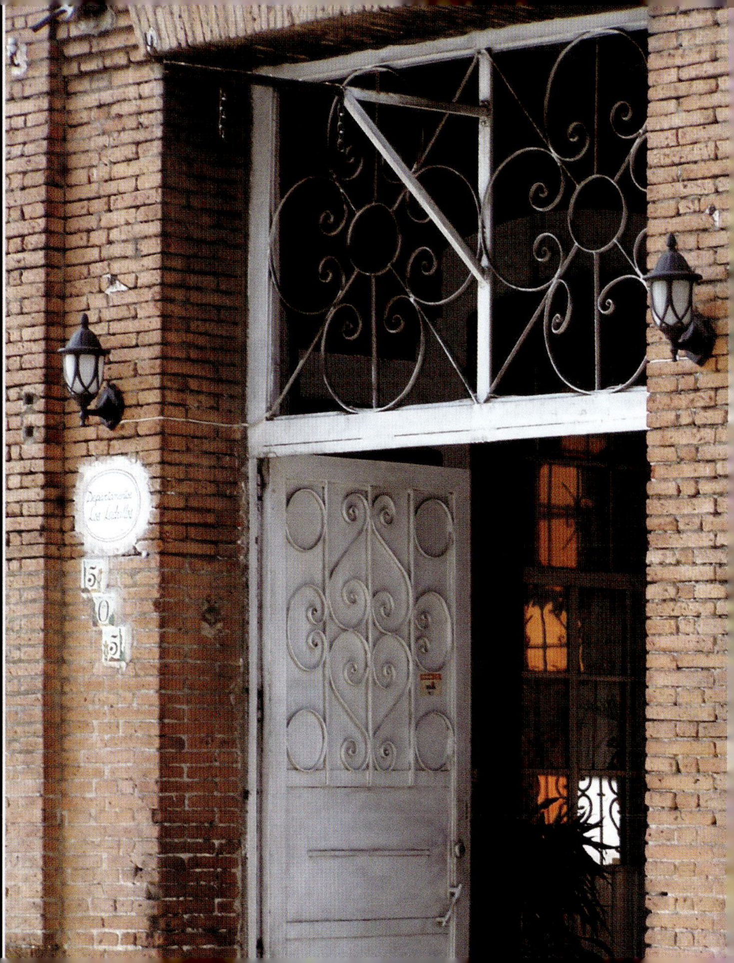

5
0
5

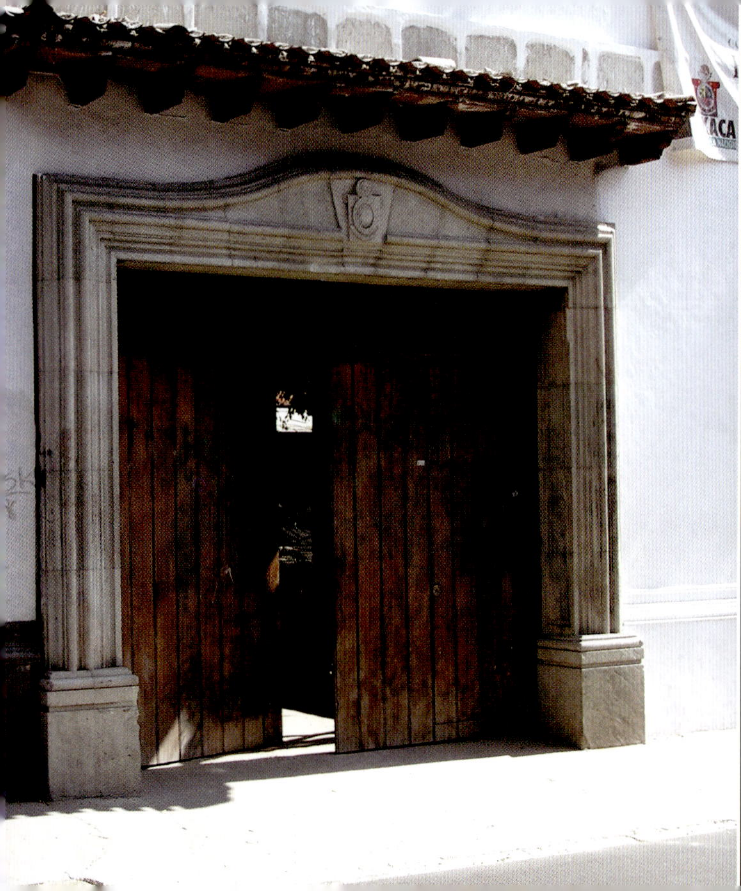

The former official House of the Governor.

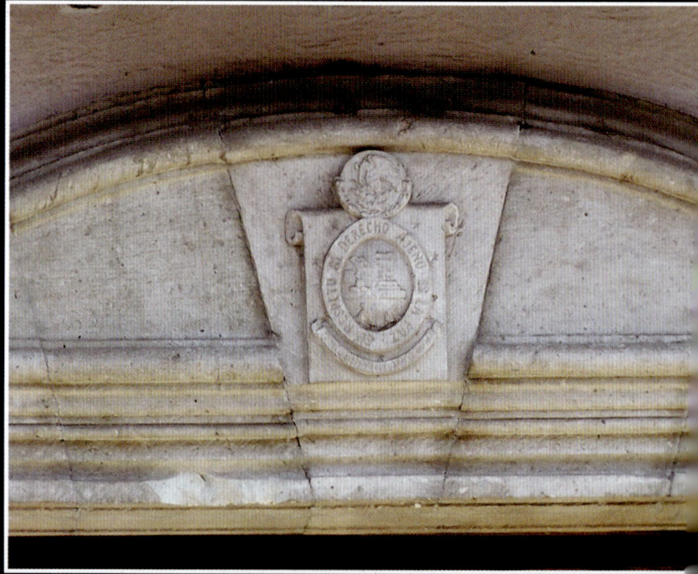

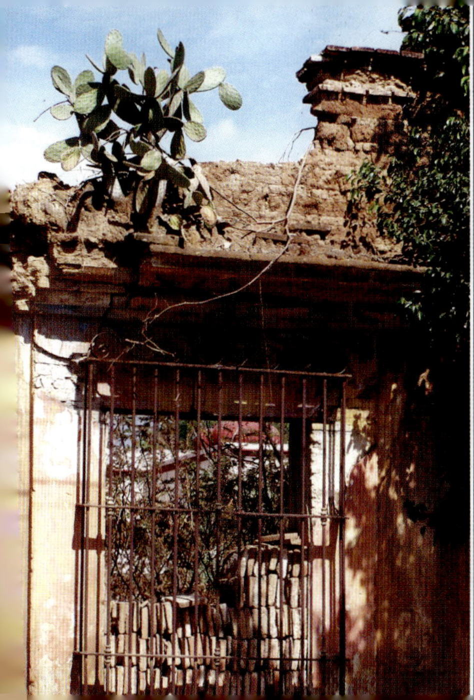

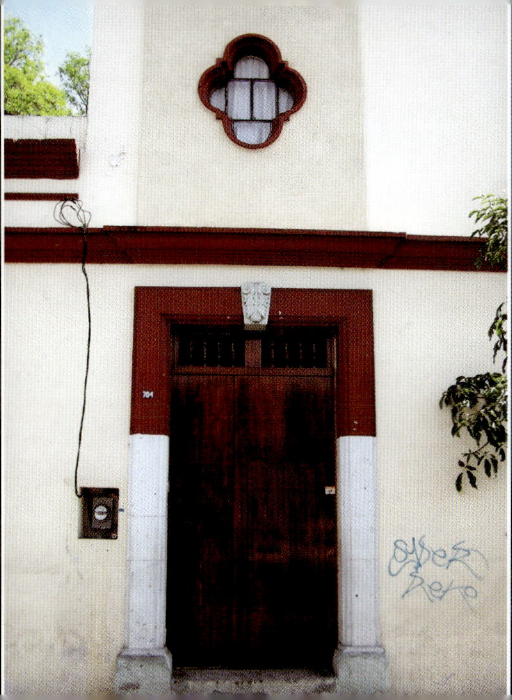

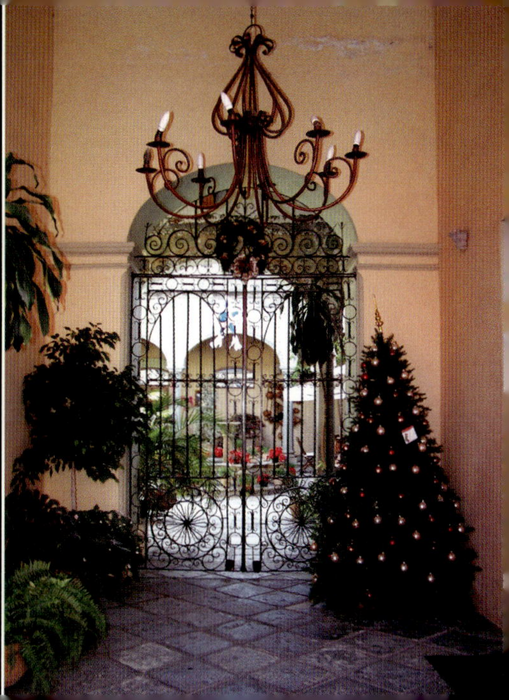

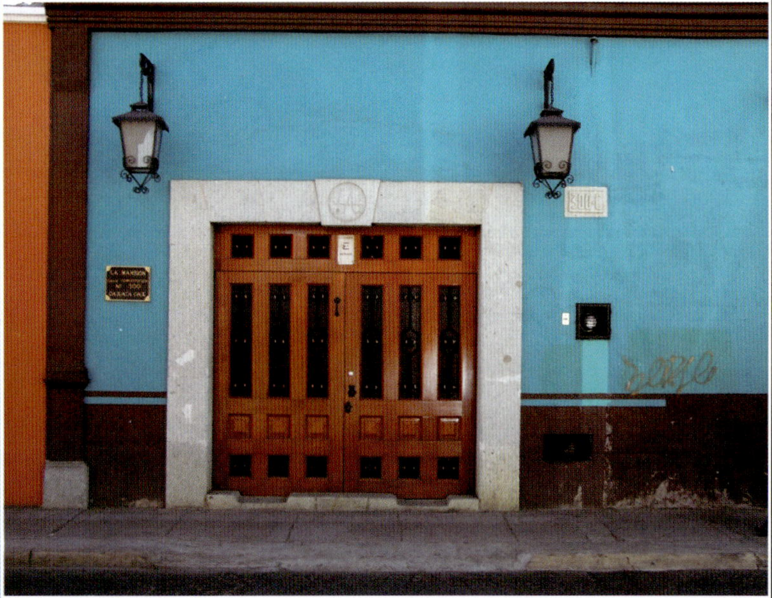

300 Constitución Street.

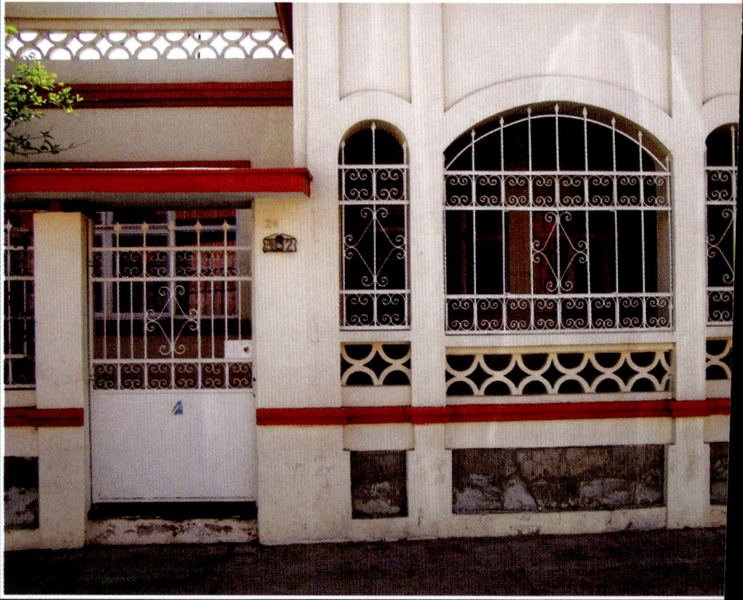

Constitución Street.

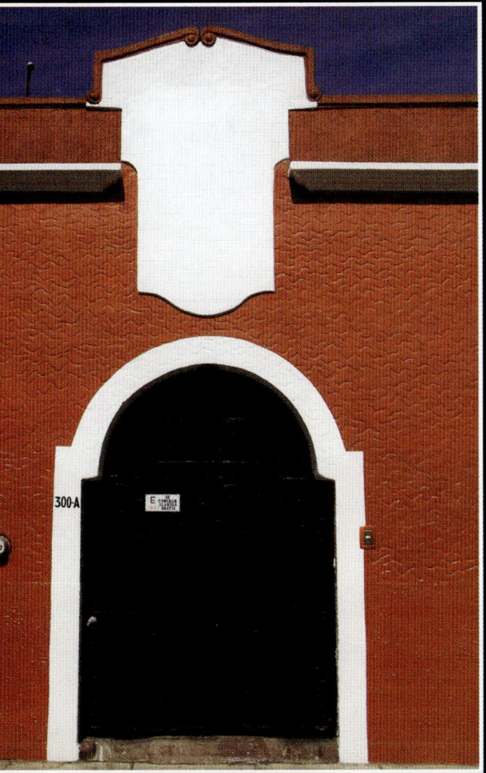
300-A

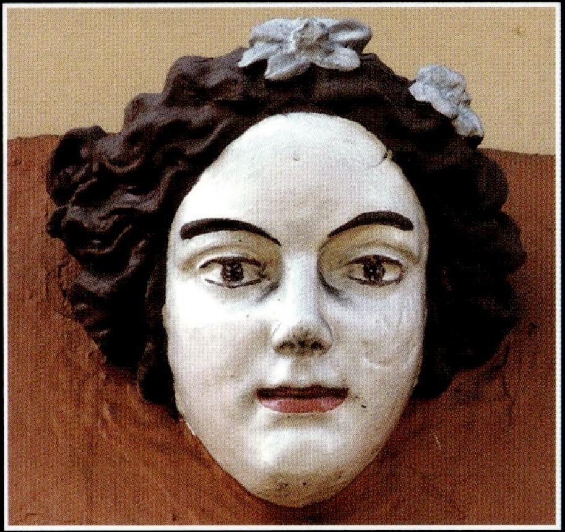

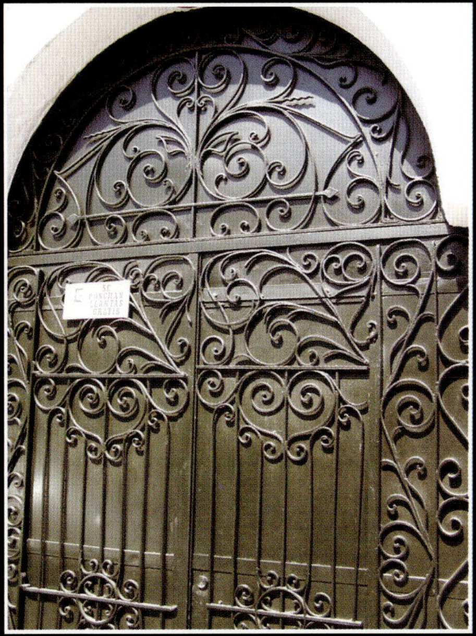

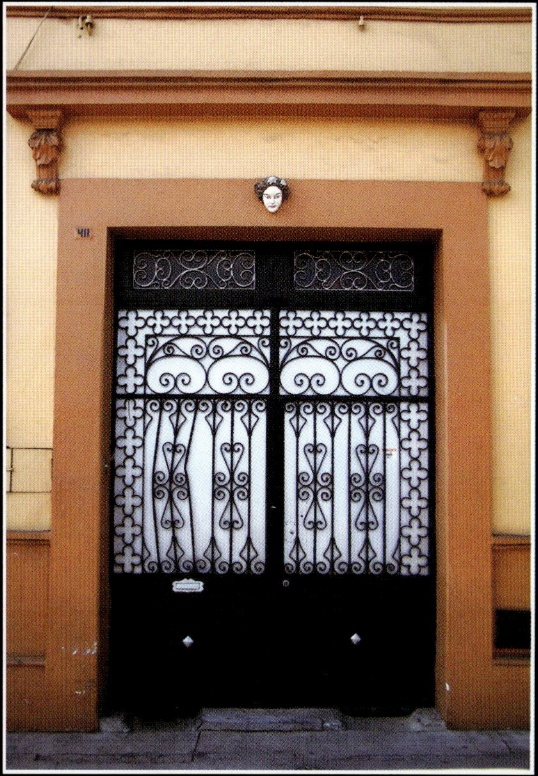

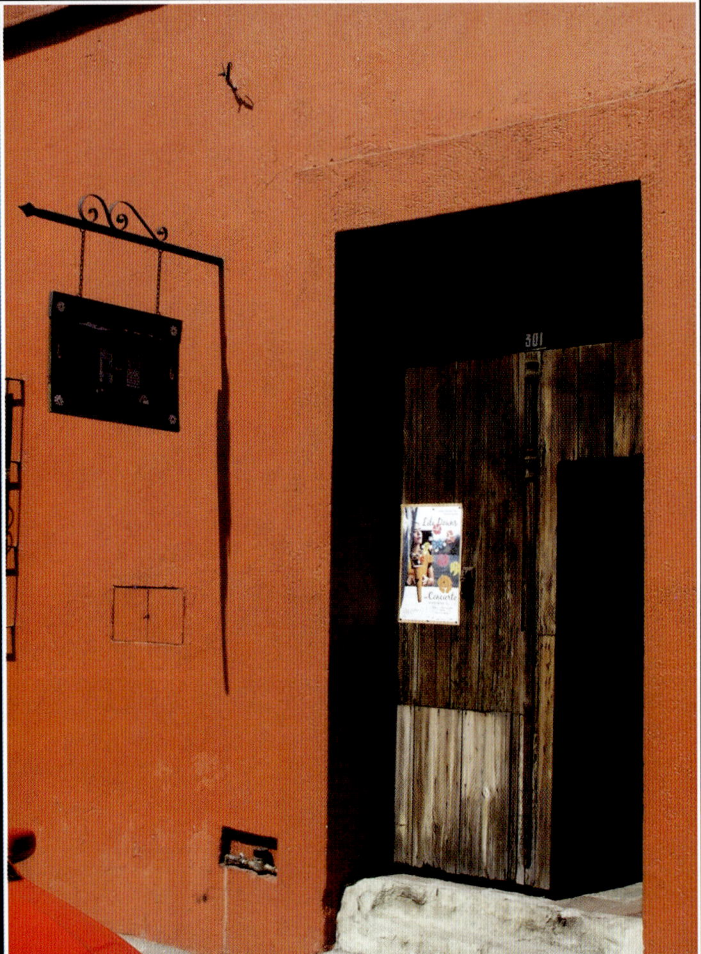

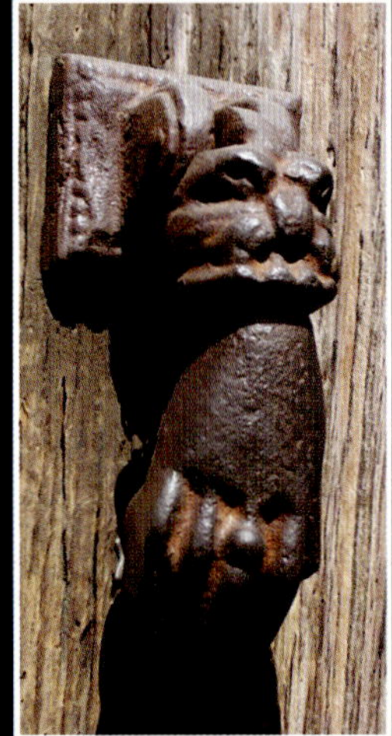

This house is called La Casa de La Mujer Rosario Castellanos (House of the Woman), which is an institution that provides women with legal services, psychological counseling, and sexual health and reproductive counseling.

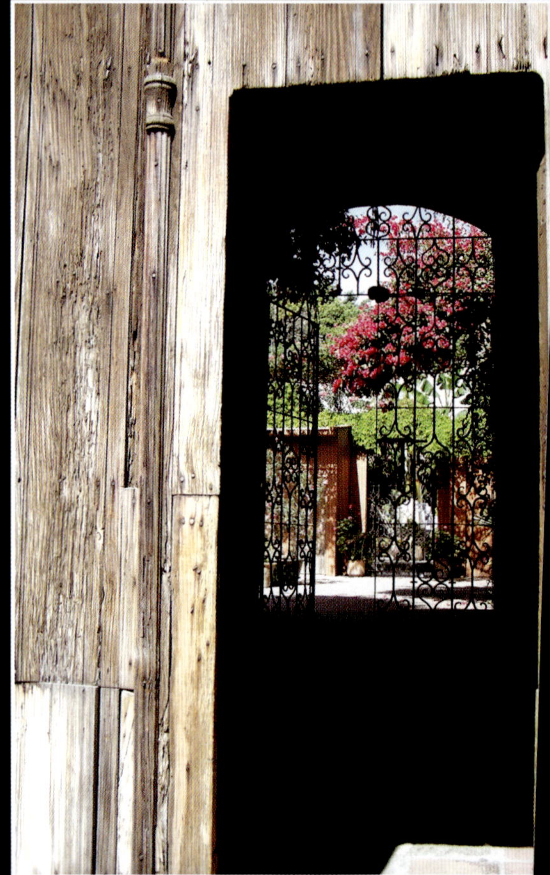

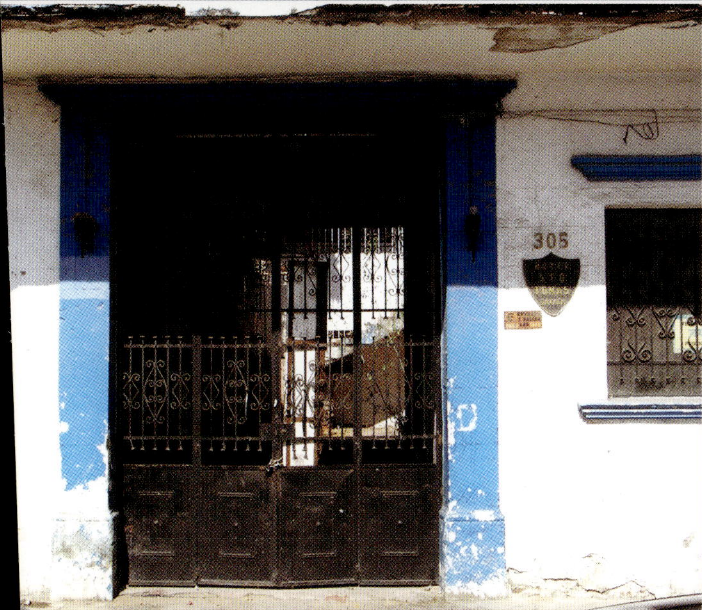

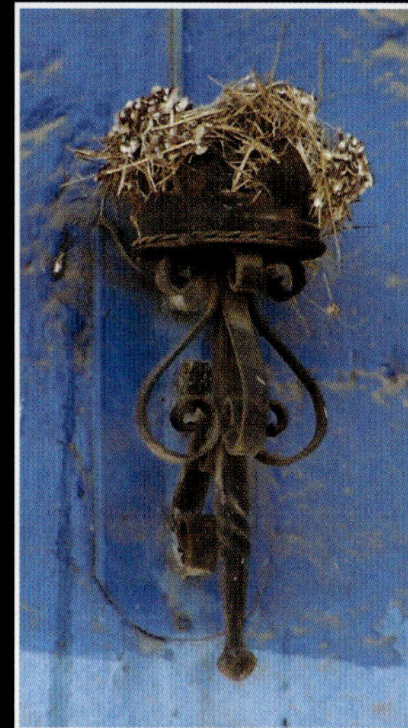

Now in ruins, this building used to be the Santo Tomás Hotel.

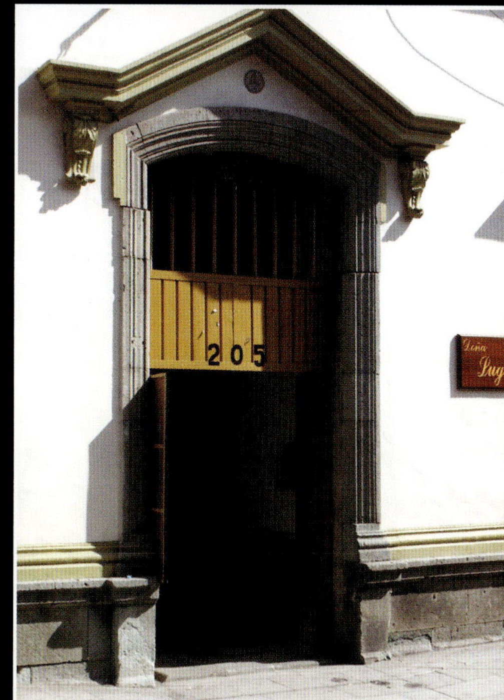

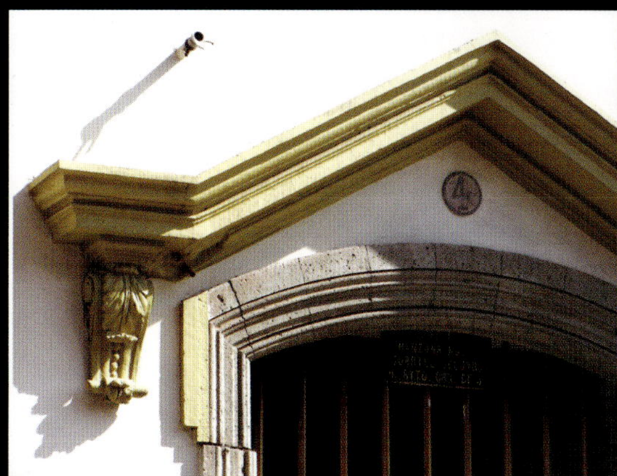

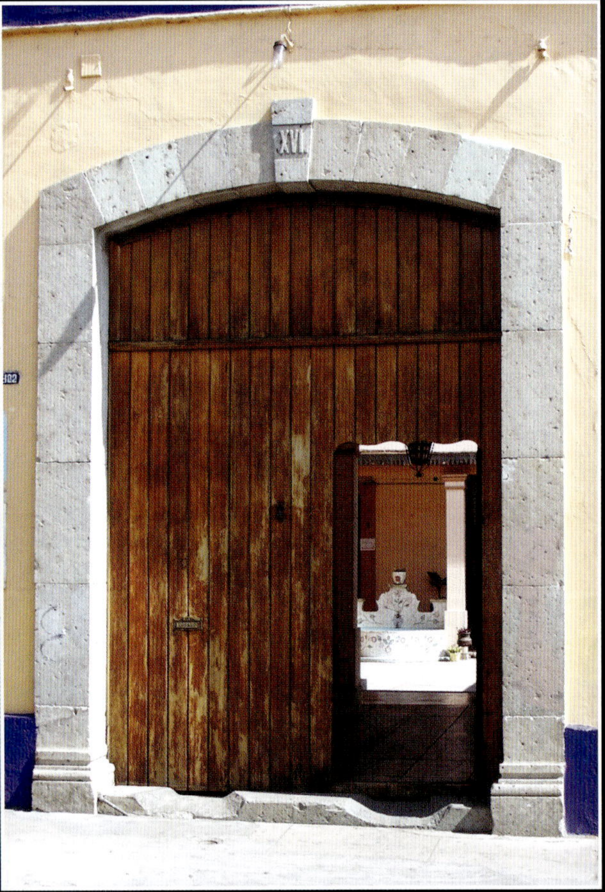

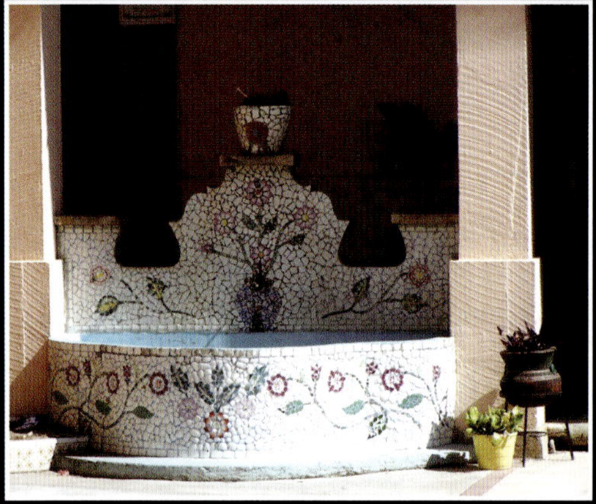

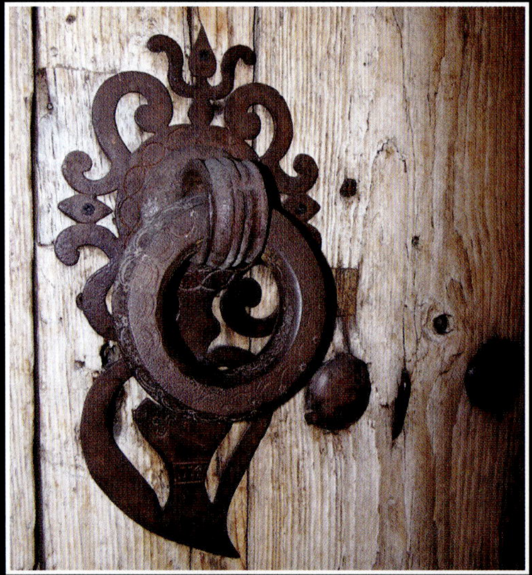

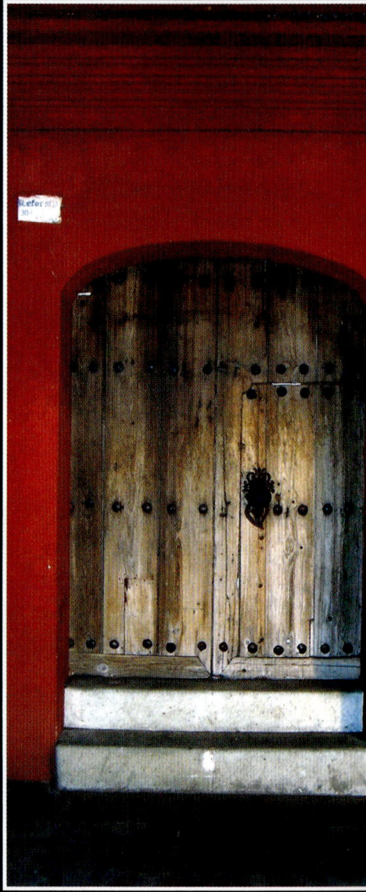

The door knocker on this door was made in 1774.

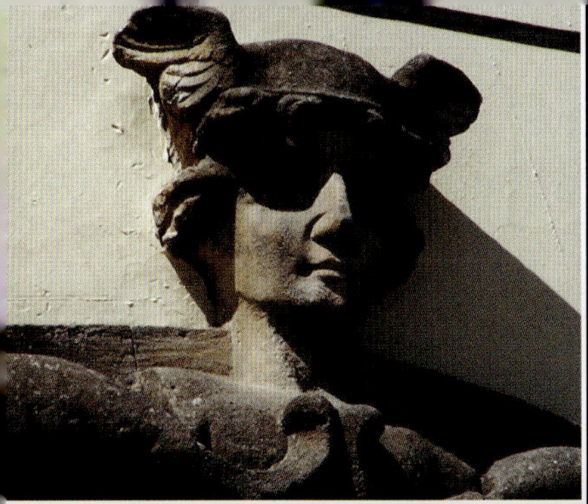
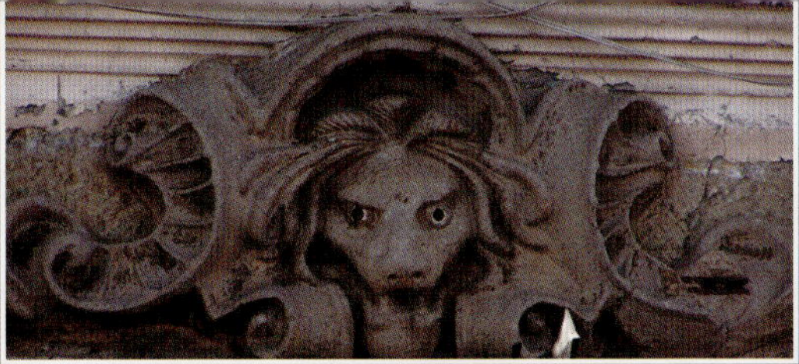
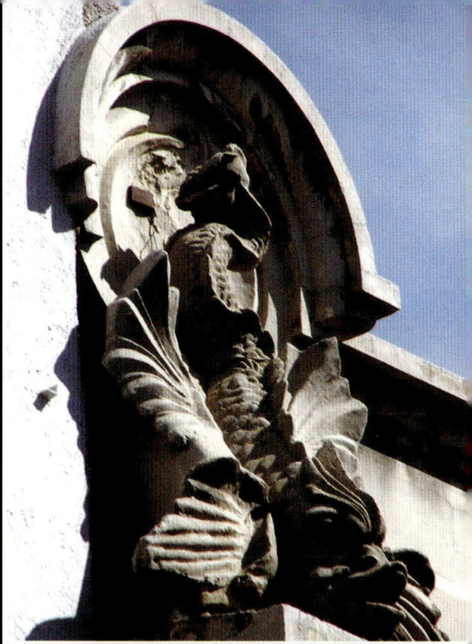
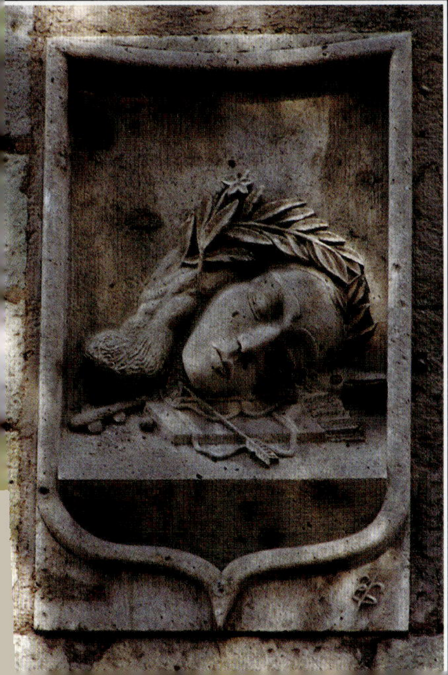
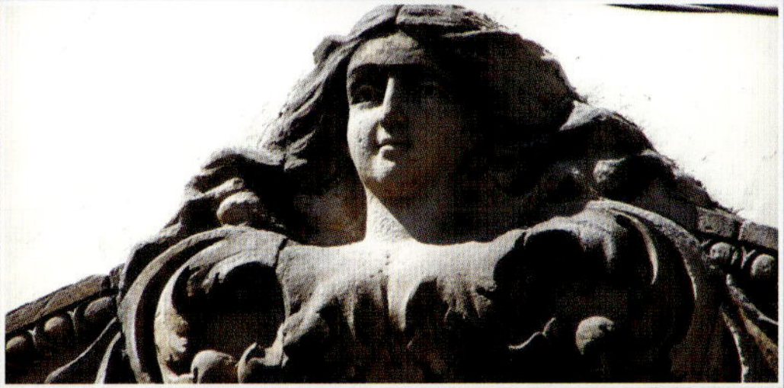
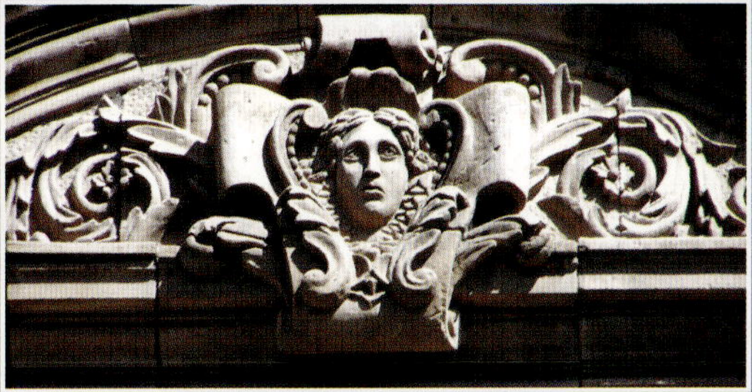
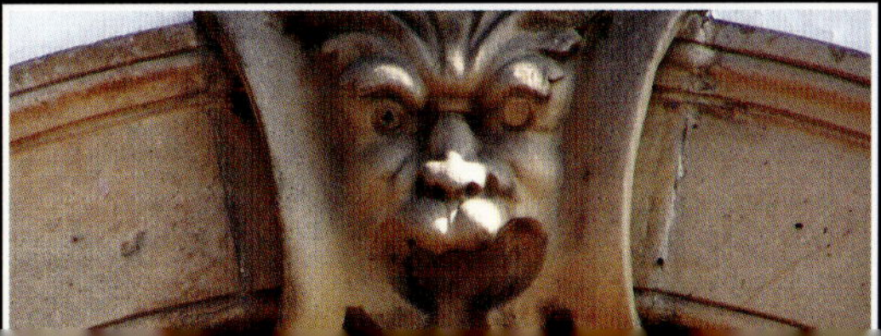
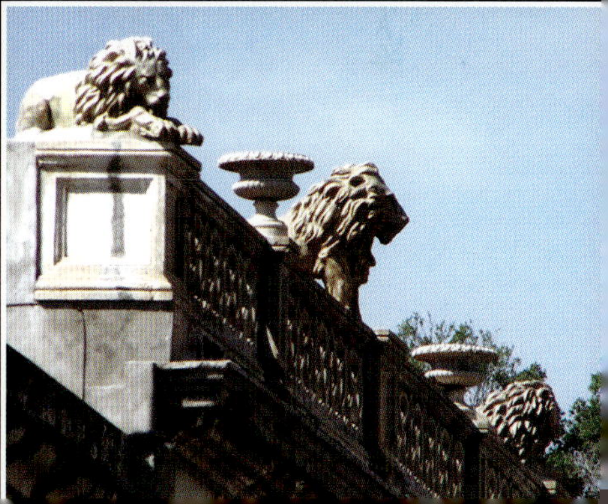

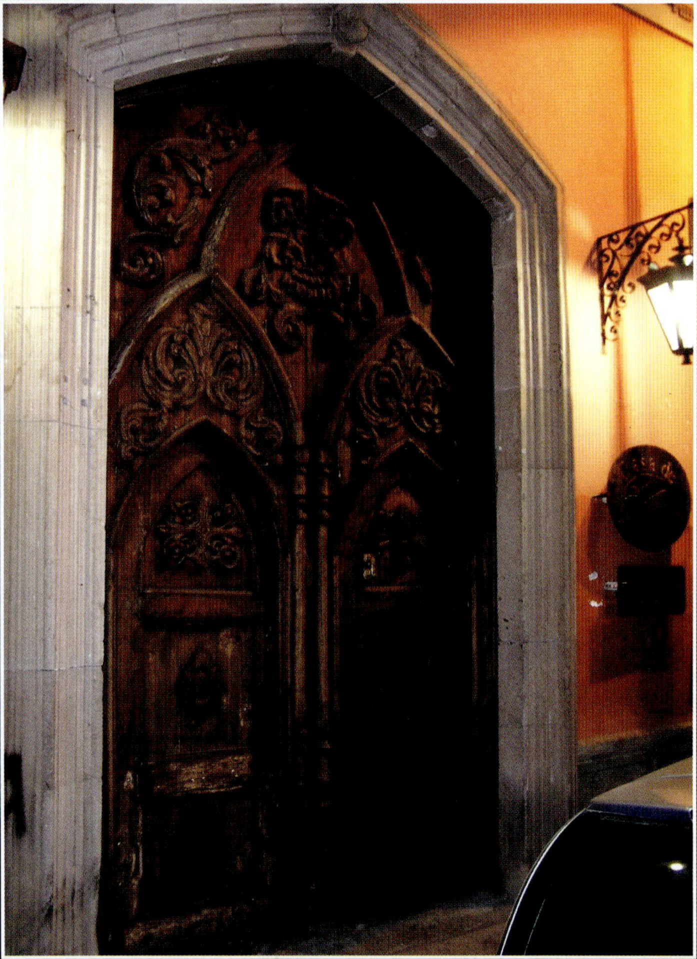

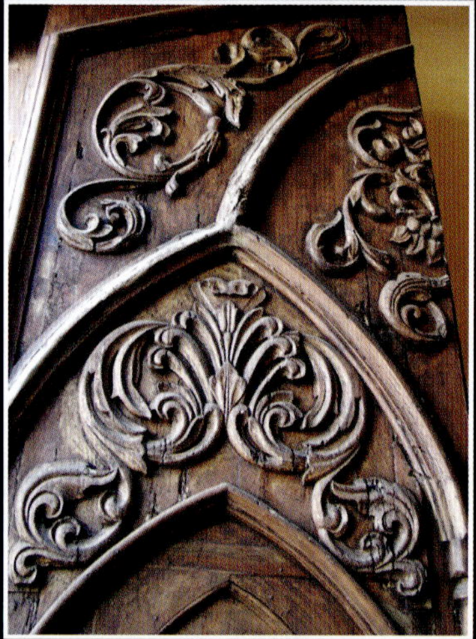

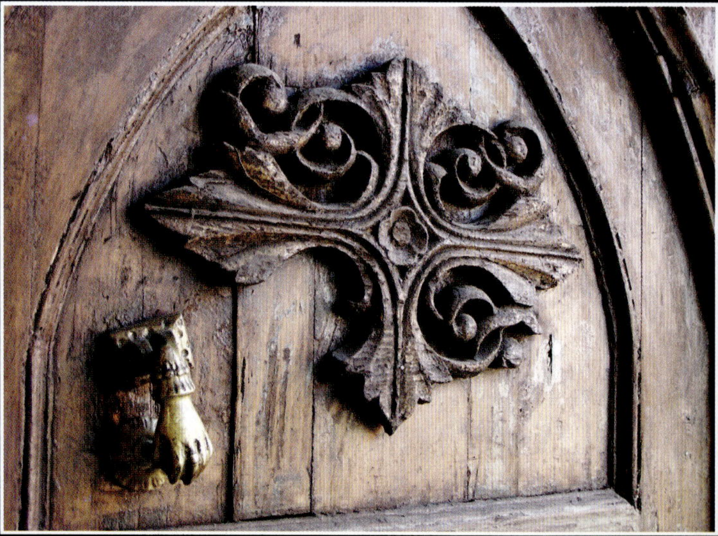

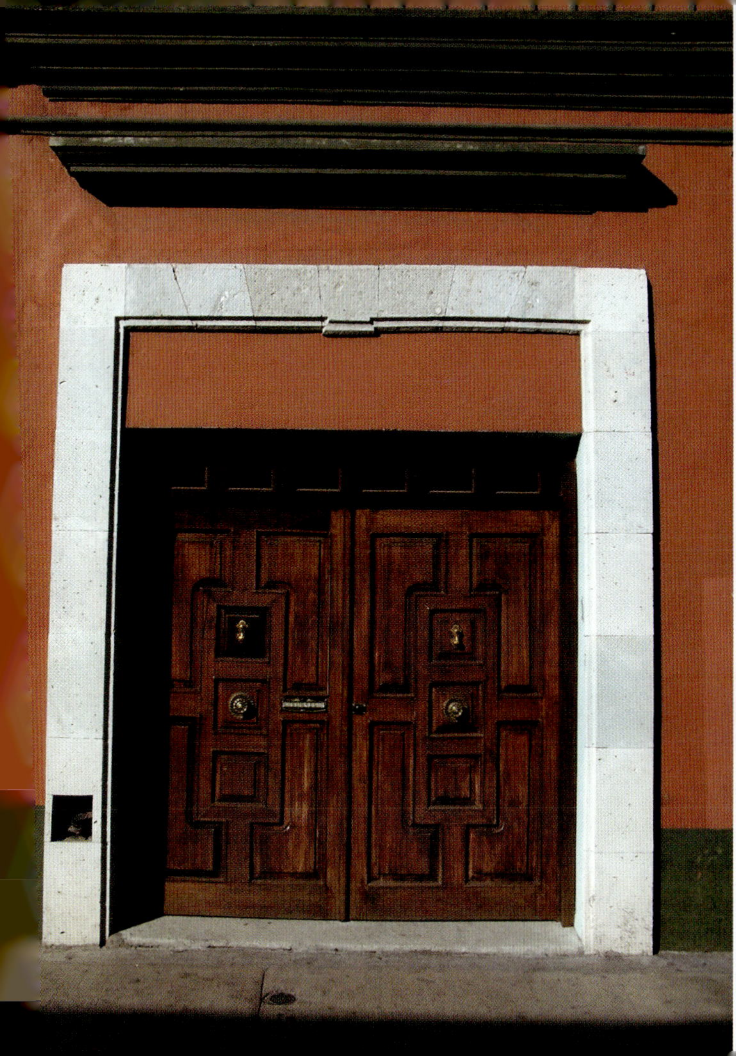
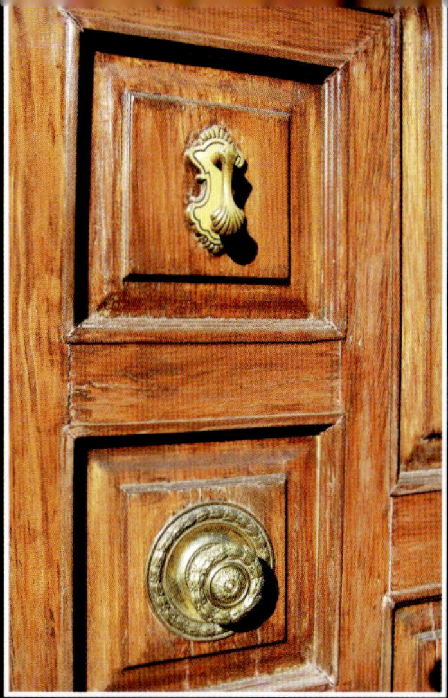
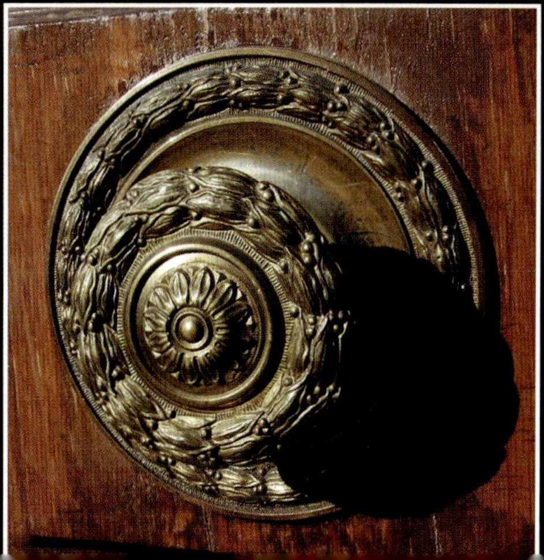
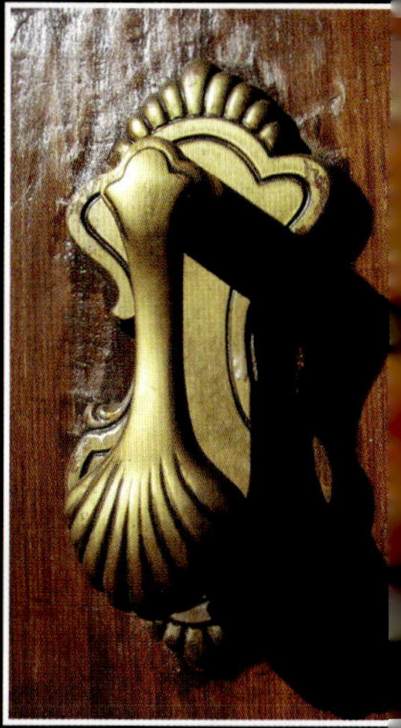

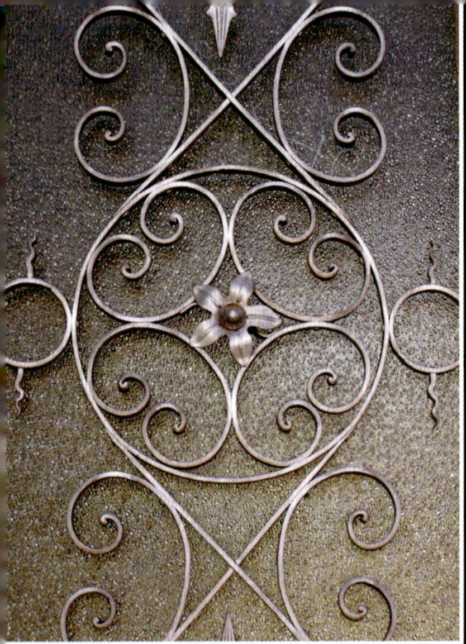
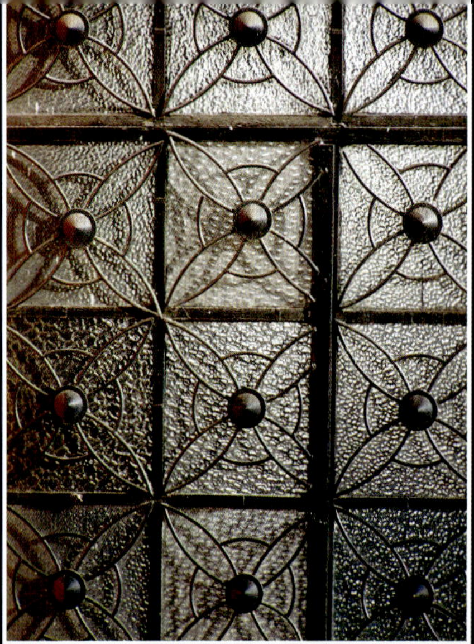
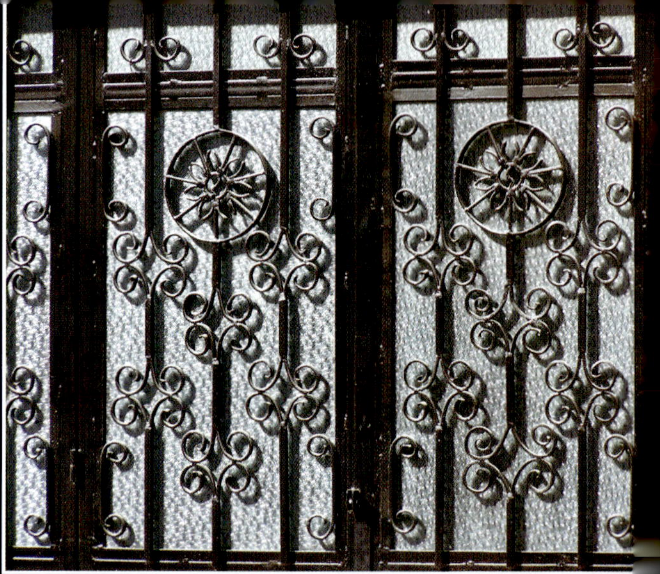
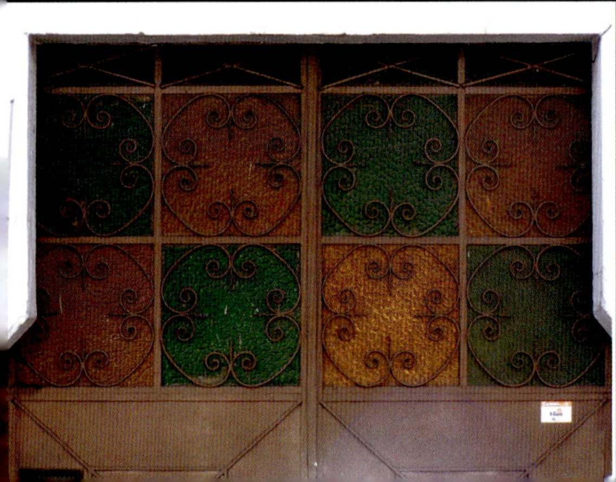
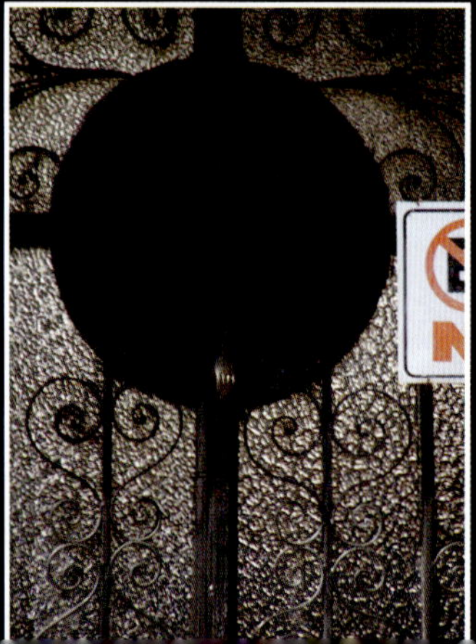
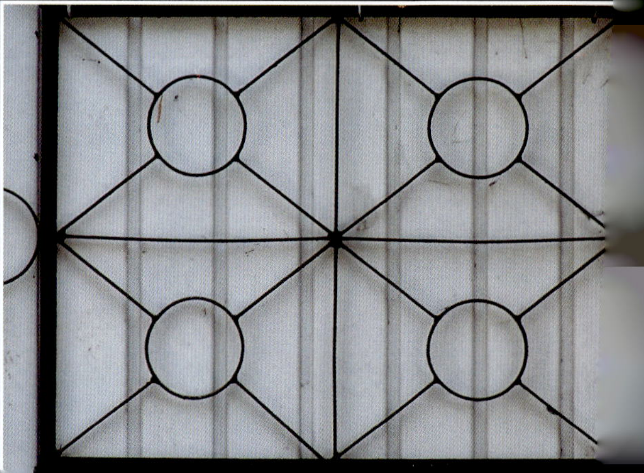

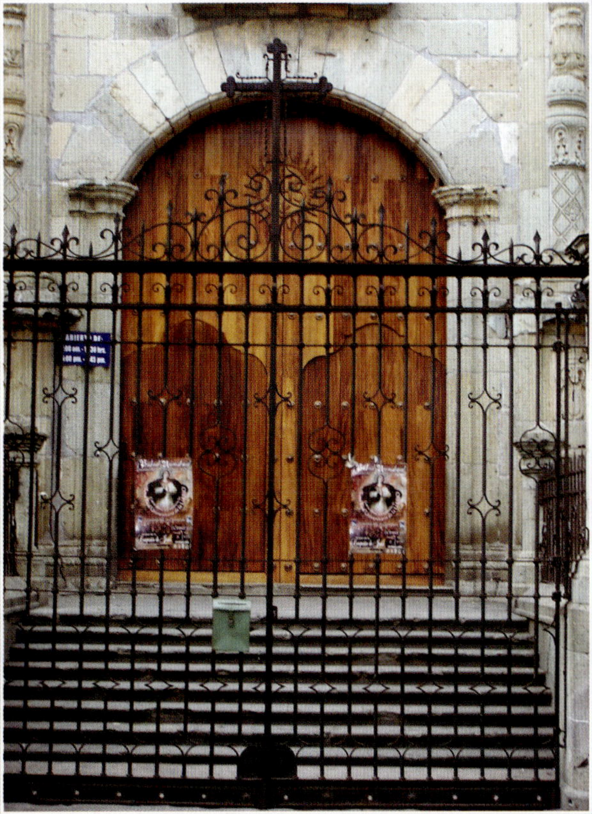

The corner of Flores Magón Street and Trujano Street. This church is called the Compañía de Jesús (the Company of Jesús).

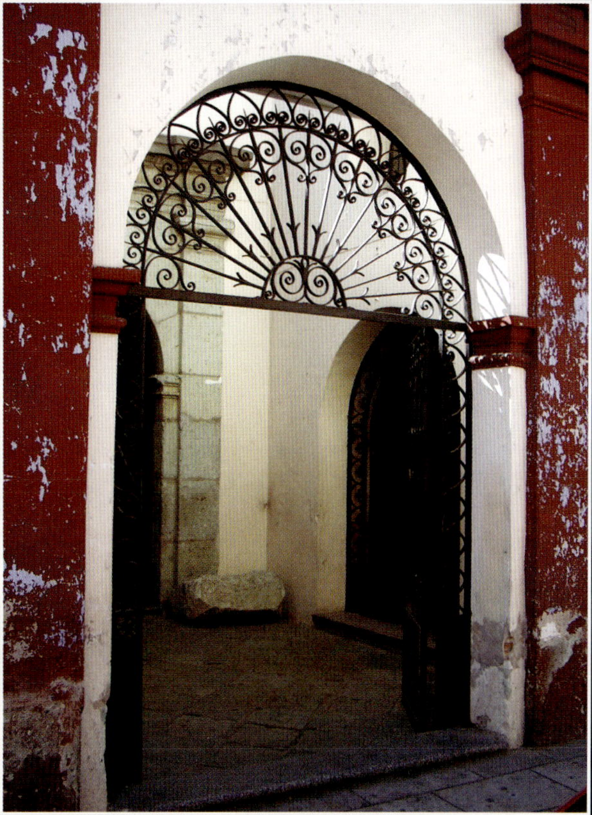

The Carmen Bajo Church, located at the corner of Porfirio Díaz and Morelos Street. It was built in the sixteenth century and revised in the nineteenth century.

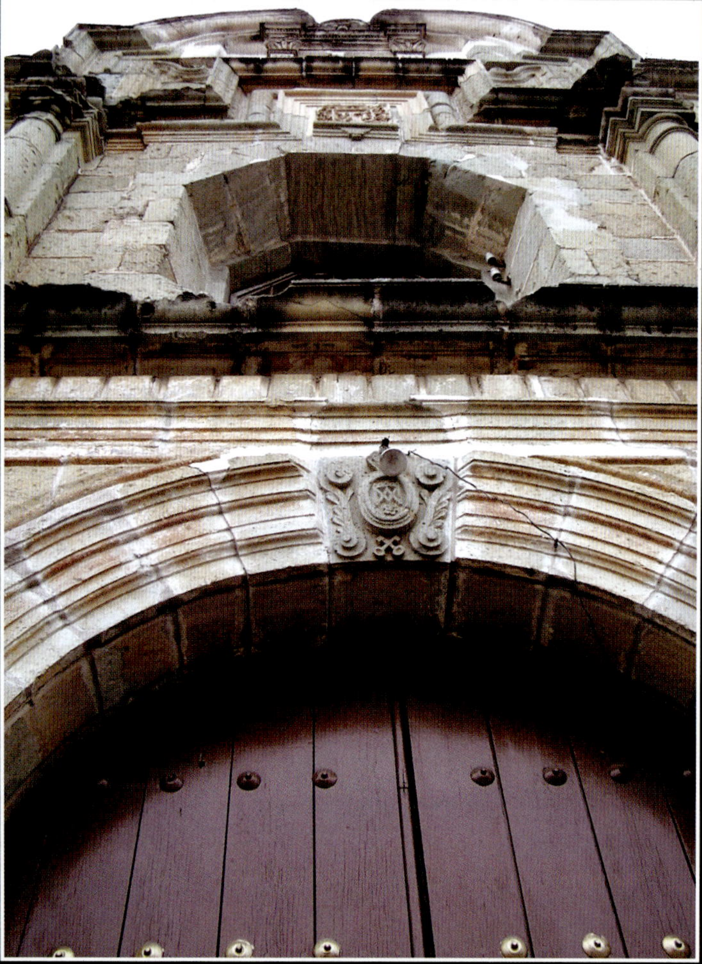

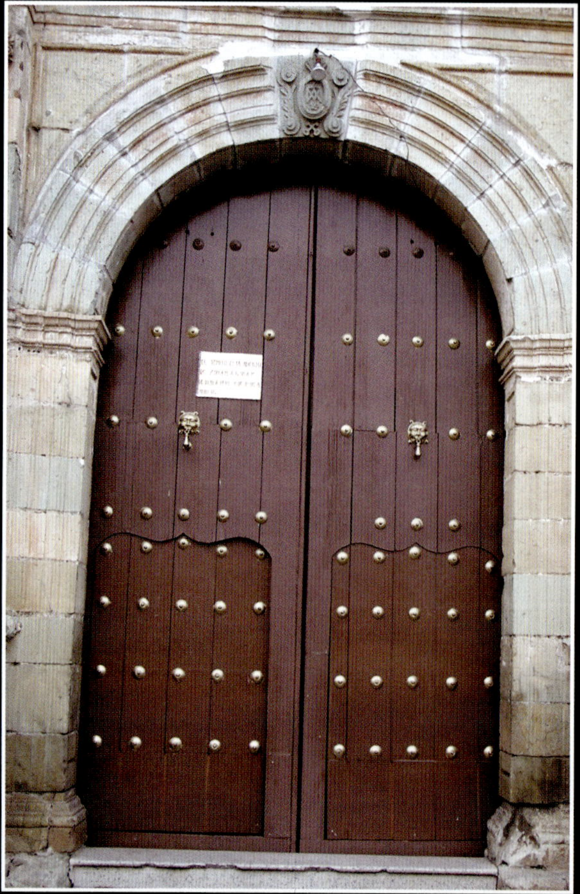

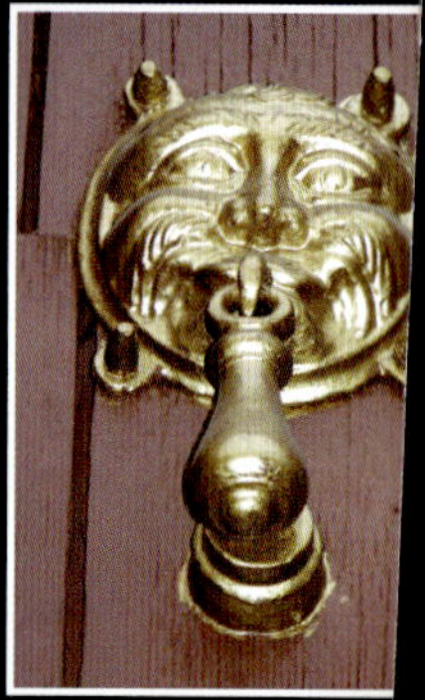

This Church is call
La Iglesia de las
Nieves (the Church
the Snow).

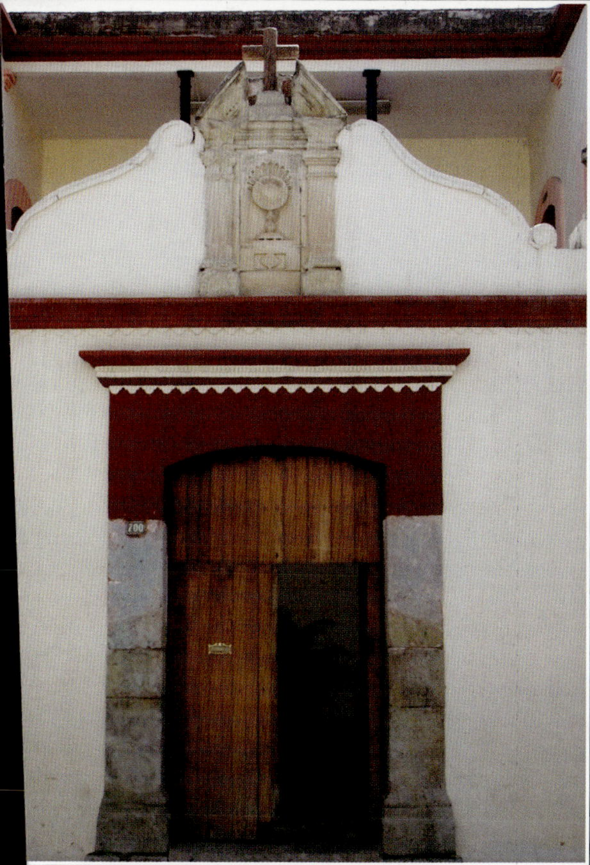

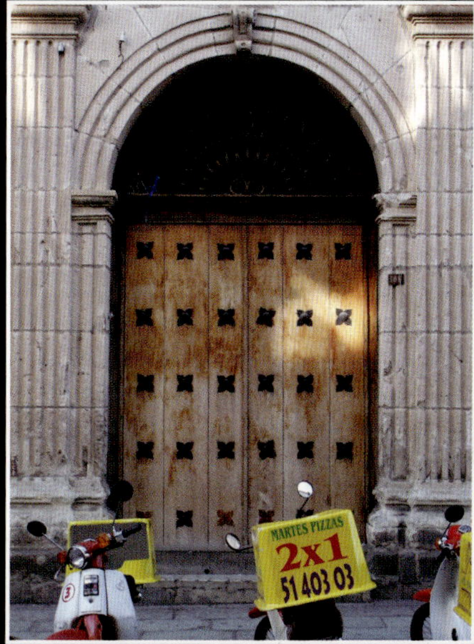

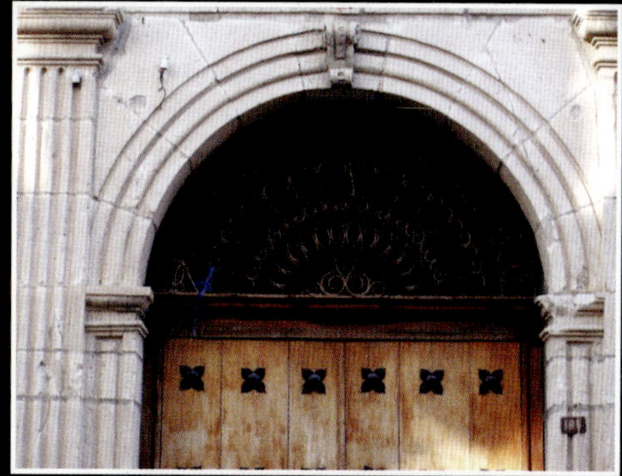

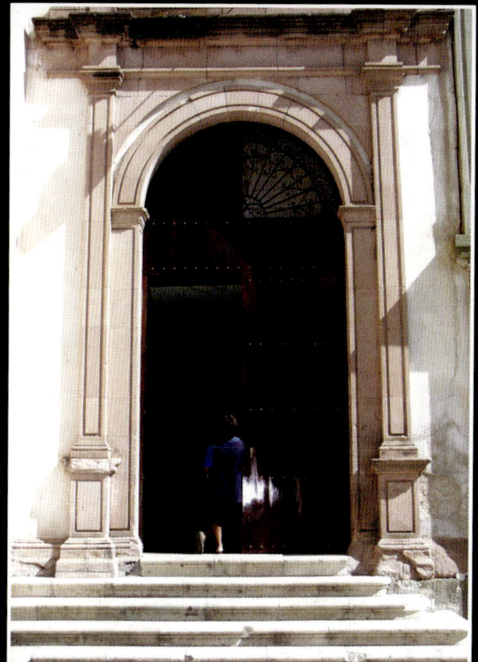

Several doors of the famous Cathedral Church.

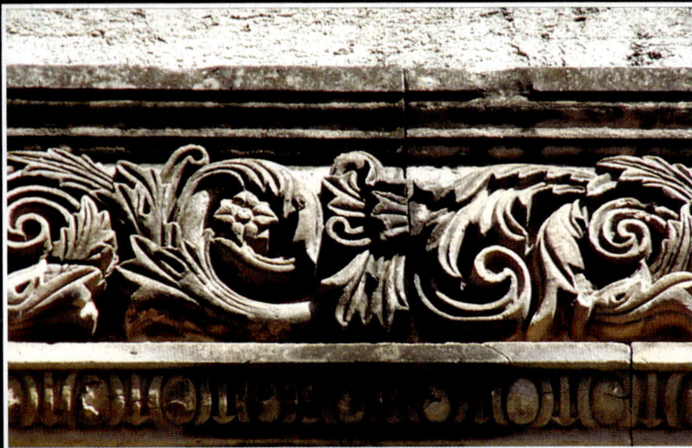
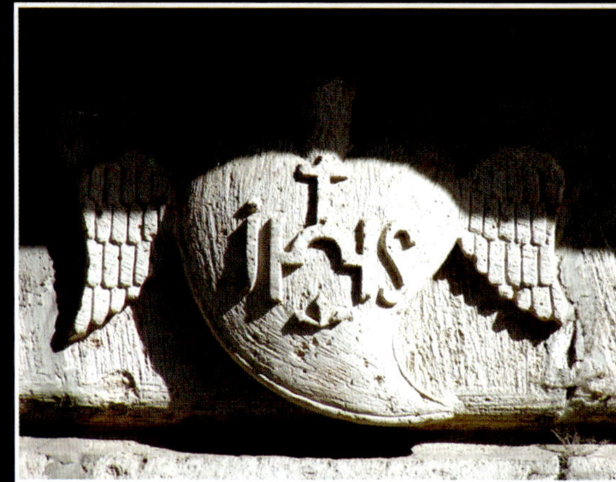
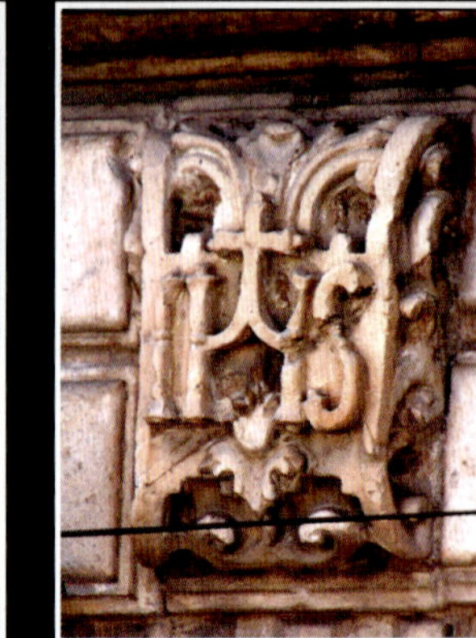
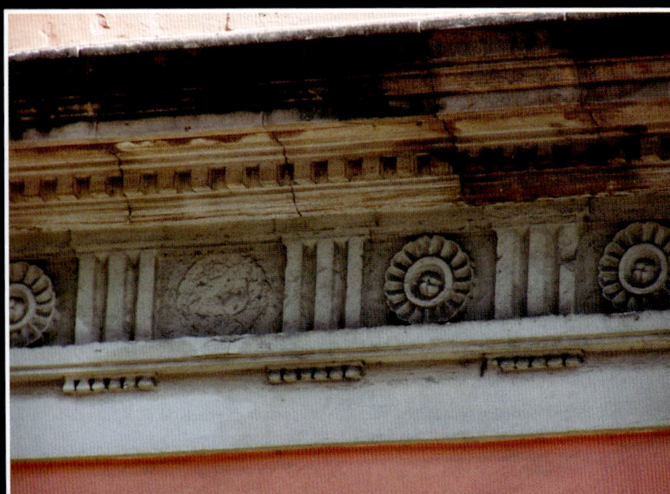
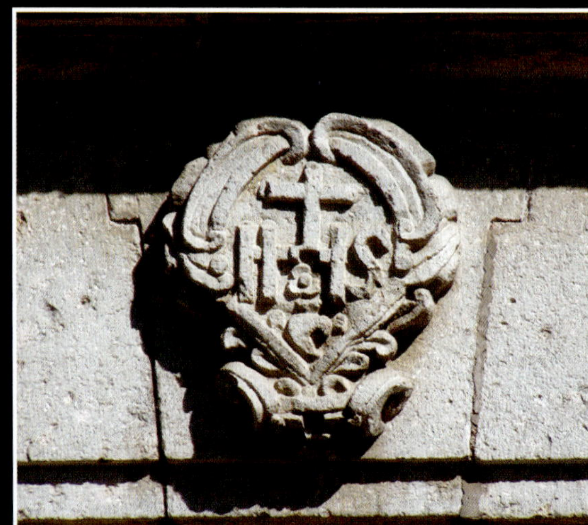
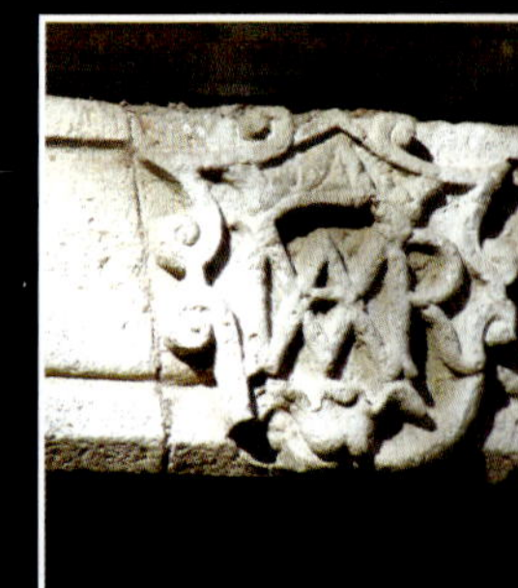
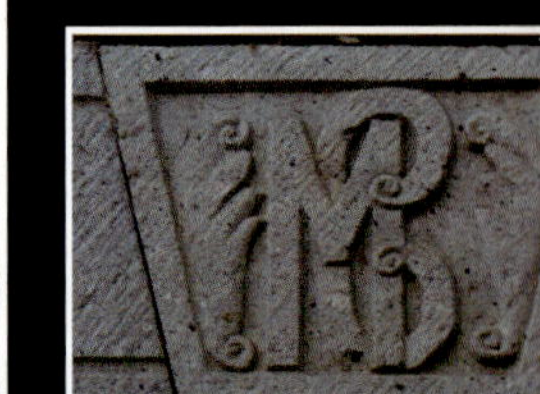